Legal and Psychological Perspectives on Prostitution and Human Trafficking

Aradhya Singh
Banaras Hindu University, India

Sara Balkh
https://orcid.org/0009-0004-4317-7954
United Nations Association of Orange County, USA

Amit Anand
https://orcid.org/0000-0002-9219-5858
REVA University, India

IGI Global
Scientific Publishing
Publishing Tomorrow's Research Today

Published in the United States of America by
IGI Global Scientific Publishing
701 East Chocolate Avenue
Hershey, PA, 17033, USA
Tel: 717-533-8845 | Fax: 717-533-7115
Website: https://www.igi-global.com E-mail: cust@igi-global.com

Library of Congress Cataloging-in-Publication Data

Names: Singh, Aradhya, 1992- editor | Balkh, Sārā, 1986 or 1987- editor | Anand, Amit, 1989- editor
Title: Legal and psychological perspectives on prostitution and human trafficking / Aradhya Singh, Sara Balkh, Amit Anand.
Description: Hershey : IGI Global Scientific Publishing, 2026. | Includes bibliographical references and index. | Summary: "This volume offers a global, interdisciplinary examination of sex work and human trafficking, analyzing legal frameworks, psychological impacts, and socio-political dynamics. It distinguishes consensual labor from coercion, highlights state control and silence, and applies intersectional, comparative perspectives to inform policy, human rights, and survivor-centered interventions"-- Provided by publisher.
Identifiers: LCCN 2025054464 (print) | LCCN 2025054465 (ebook) | ISBN 9798337358413 hardcover | ISBN 9798337358420 paperback | ISBN 9798337358437 ebook
Subjects: LCSH: Human rights | Prostitution--Law and legislation | Human trafficking--Law and legislation | Sex work--Legal status, laws, etc. | Consent (Law) | Sex crimes--Law and legislation
Classification: LCC K3240 .L439 2026 (print) | LCC K3240 (ebook)
LC record available at https://lccn.loc.gov/2025054464
LC ebook record available at https://lccn.loc.gov/2025054465

British Cataloguing in Publication Data
A Cataloguing in Publication record for this book is available from the British Library.

Table of Contents

Detailed Table of Contents

and ideological foundations of sex work to a comparative analysis of different legal frameworks through a global case study, and to proposing recommendations for addressing human rights and public health issues.

This chapter is a critique of definitional shortcomings of voluntary prostitution in international and domestic law, and more specifically, the conflation of coercion and consent. The terminology used in law and policy is too broad or moral, labelling all types of prostitution as exploitative or equivalent to trafficking. Such conflation, and ignoring the heterogeneity of the sex workers' experience, also obliterates the fact of consensual, voluntary entry into the profession. As a result, voluntary sex work—particularly those in vulnerable groups—are rendered outside of legal status, social protection, and labor rights. The chapter analyzes important documents like the 1949 UN Convention, CEDAW, the Palermo Protocol, and India's Immoral Traffic (Prevention) Act, utilizing feminist legal theory, intersectionality, and comparative legal analysis. It reveals how these documents' ambiguous or moralistic language allows states to regulate sex work without sufficiently protecting their rights.The chapter argues that prostitution should be reimagined in law.

This chapter interrogates Scotland's Equally Safe strategy, arguing that its conflation of consensual sex work with human trafficking reproduces epistemic violence and exclusion within feminist statecraft. Framed as a progressive, gender-based violence policy, Equally Safe instead enacts carceral feminist logics that criminalise, surveil, and silence sex workers under the guise of protection. Through analysis of legal frameworks, NGO–state relations, and lived experiences, the chapter reveals how moral governance displaces rights-based and harm-reduction approaches. Drawing on feminist theory, intersectionality, and comparative insights from Ireland and New Zealand, it demonstrates that Scotland's end-demand trajectory undermines autonomy, safety, and justice for marginalised women. The chapter concludes by calling for a shift toward participatory, decriminalised, and plural feminist policymaking that centres sex workers' expertise and dismantles punitive state practices.

Sex work in India occupies a paradoxical position tolerated in practice yet criminalized and morally condemned in law and society. However, this paradox is not merely a product of legal ambiguity; it is deeply entrenched in India's historical caste hierarchies, gender norms, and systems of informal governance. This article critically interrogates the intersection of caste and sex work in India, focusing on how marginalized caste communities engaged in traditional and contemporary forms of sexual labor are governed not only by a punitive legal framework but, more insidiously, through caste-based informal regulation and entrenched social surveillance. The state's neglect, combined with a moralized legal discourse, contributes to what this article terms "legal apathy"- a systemic failure to extend legal rights, protections, or recognition to sex workers, particularly those from oppressed caste locations.

India's moral imagination has combined prostitution and trafficking into a single vice that has miserably failed to distinguish the tragic realities of gender vulnerabilities. Colonial notions of morality attempted to control women's sexuality and viewed their bodies as sites of moral decay. The impact of these colonial obsessions can still be seen in legislative policies as well. Inefficient laws fail to protect the fundamental right guaranteed by the Constitution under Article 15(3), leading to constitutional infirmity. The right to life with dignity guaranteed under the Grundnorm feels like a vision deferred to eternity. Presently, the Immoral Traffic (Prevention) Act, 1956 (ITPA) aims to adhere to international commitments under the UN Convention for the Suppression of the Traffic in Persons, but it embodies inconsistencies in India.

In many rural areas of India, women find that legal protections exist mostly in theory, not practice. This study examines the situation in Sagar and Damoh districts of Madhya Pradesh, revealing how the inability of police, courts, and legal aid to enforce women's rights forces reliance on patriarchal, informal systems. Through interviews with women, legal aid workers, and officials, it documents how this legal vacuum increases economic hardship, worsens health outcomes, and allows cycles of vulnerability to continue across generations. The research calls for urgent reforms to strengthen the justice system and ensure women's rights are honored not just in law but in daily life.

Child labor remains a critical issue, particularly in developing nations like India, where millions of children are deprived of their right to education and safe childhood due to poverty, marginalization, and inadequate policy implementation. This study explores the underlying causes, occupational patterns, and harmful consequences of child labor in Dehradun, Uttarakhand. It highlights that children are primarily engaged in agriculture, domestic work, and small industries, often facing physical and mental exploitation. Despite existing legal frameworks and initiatives like the Child Labor (Prohibition and Regulation) Act and National Child Labor Projects, enforcement challenges persist. The study uses cross-sectional and triangulation methods to analyze data from 42 child laborers and suggests a holistic approach, including poverty alleviation, quality education, community empowerment, and rehabilitation services, as key to combating child labor. It emphasizes the need for multi-stakeholder participation to ensure child rights and reduce labor dependency among vulnerable families.

Foreword

Few subjects in the realm of international human rights, law, and public policy evoke as profound and polarized a discourse as the exchange of sexual services. For decades, the global community has grappled with the profound legal, moral, and psychological questions surrounding commercial sex. Today, we stand at a critical jurisdictional and ethical crossroads where the lived reality of those at the center of this storm exists in the messy, often violent intersections of state power and bodily autonomy. It is within this vital gap that *Legal and Psychological Perspectives on Prostitution and Human Trafficking* emerges. Edited with scholarly precision by Aradhya Singh, Sara Balkh, and Amit Anand, this volume is not merely a collection of essays; it is a rigorous, interdisciplinary intervention into one of the most enduring human rights dilemmas of our time.

The most striking feature of this work is its refusal to simplify what is inherently complex. At its core lies a fundamental recognition that law without psychology is blind, and psychology without law is toothless. Legal systems worldwide have long struggled to balance the scales of criminal justice with the protection of the vulnerable, often failing because they overlook the profound psychological impacts of coercion, stigma, and state-sanctioned trauma. By weaving together these two threads, the contributors to this volume challenge us to move beyond the reductive "victim vs. agent" binary. They demand that we confront the "contested bodies" of sex workers and trafficking survivors not as abstract legal subjects, but as individuals navigating complex socio-political landscapes.

A central pillar of this work is the rigorous interrogation of prostitution as a form of "structural violence". As articulated in the opening sections by Sara Balkh and Amit Anand, there is a compelling mandate within international human rights law grounded in binding instruments like CEDAW, the ICCPR, and the Palermo Protocol to view the commodification of the human body as an inherent affront to dignity. This perspective posits that inequality is not an accidental byproduct of the sex trade but its foundational requirement. By analysing how cultural norms normalize coercion and "demand," the book establishes that prostitution systematically violates rights to equality, health, and freedom from ill-treatment. From this vantage point, an abolitionist legal framework is presented as a requirement for states committed to genuine gender equality. It is a perspective grounded in the undeniable reality that for far too many, entry into the sex trade is dictated by poverty, coercion, and a profound lack of viable alternatives.

However, the genius of this collection is its refusal to remain within the safety of a single ideological camp. The editors have curated a dialogue that bravely explores the "conflation" of consensual sex work and human trafficking. In several chapters, we see how broad, moralistic legal definitions such as those historically found in India's Immoral Traffic (Prevention) Act can inadvertently strip individuals of their legal status, pushing them further into the shadows. As Amit Anand astutely demonstrates, when the law operates in absolutes, it risks erasing the heterogeneity of lived experiences. This "epistemic violence" is a recurring theme: the way in which the law often silences the voices of those it purports to save, replacing their lived expertise with paternalistic statecraft.

The geographical and legislative breadth of this volume provides a global laboratory for the reader. From the "carceral feminism" critiques of Scotland's *Equally Safe* strategy, as interrogated by Hannah Jane Simpson, to the analysis of regulated markets in Nevada and Germany by Angelo Kevin Brown, the book offers an evidence-based roadmap of how different legislative choices impact human lives. We are compelled to look closely at policies framed under the progressive guise of protection that may instead enact carceral logics of surveillance and exclusion. The exploration of New Zealand's decriminalized model provides a stark contrast, prompting us to ask whether the law should serve to punish a moral transgression or to protect the safety and labour rights of the marginalized.

Furthermore, this volume excels in its application of an "intersectional lens." The authors remind us that vulnerability to trafficking and the choice to enter the sex trade are never divorced from caste, race, disability, and economic displacement. The psychological toll of navigating these layered identities is profound. For the practitioner, this book offers essential insights into how trauma manifests in environments of "forced criminality" or "survival sex." For the policymaker, it provides a stern warning: legislation that ignores the social determinants of vulnerability such as poverty and gender-based discrimination is destined to fail. It is not enough to change the laws; we must change the social conditions that make the exchange of sex a survival strategy rather than a choice.

The psychological perspectives offered here are particularly groundbreaking. The contributors move beyond traditional trauma narratives to explore the concept of "agency under duress." They ask: How does an individual maintain autonomy when their legal and social environment is designed to erase it? By centring "participatory, decriminalised, and plural feminist policymaking," the book advocates for a shift where sex workers and survivors are seen as architects of policy rather than mere subjects of it. This is a call for a more "humane law" one that recognizes that when moral governance displaces rights-based and harm-reduction approaches, autonomy is undermined and safety is severely compromised.

In assembling this volume, Singh, Balkh, and Anand have created a vital crucible for intellectual and practical advancement. They have brought together international scholars and legal experts to tackle a subject that remains, in many parts of the world, a taboo. Their work reflects a deep commitment to the principle that human rights must be universal, but their application must be nuanced. The result is a text that is as theoretically rigorous as it is practically relevant.

As we look toward the future of international law and clinical practice, *Legal and Psychological Perspectives on Prostitution and Human Trafficking* will undoubtedly serve as a foundational text. It is a mandatory resource for anyone be they a student of law, a clinical psychologist, or a government official who seeks to understand the complex entanglements of sexual labour, exploitation, and the law. It challenges us to look into the "grey zones" and to find there not just problems to be solved, but human lives to be respected and rights to be upheld.

In conclusion, this book reminds us that true justice and equality cannot be achieved through the silencing of contested bodies, but only through a rigorous, inclusive, and unflinching pursuit of truth. It is a work of great courage and even greater necessity.

Sehrosh Mustajab
Helping Hand, USA

Preface

INTRODUCTION

Legal and Psychological Perspectives on Prostitution and Human Trafficking emerges from a shared conviction that contemporary debates on sexual labor and exploitation demand greater conceptual precision, interdisciplinary dialogue, and global attentiveness. Across jurisdictions and ideological positions, prostitution and human trafficking continue to occupy contested terrain—legally, politically, and morally. Yet the urgency of these debates has too often been accompanied by analytical conflation, rhetorical polarization, and the marginalization of lived experience. This volume seeks to intervene in that space.

A foundational premise guiding our editorial vision is the conceptual differentiation between consensual sex work and human trafficking. While these phenomena are frequently collapsed in legal and policy discourse, they are neither sociologically identical nor normatively interchangeable. To conflate them risks obscuring both the agency of sex workers and the coercive violence that characterizes trafficking. Accordingly, we have invited contributors to adopt analytically rigorous frameworks that acknowledge complexity without sacrificing clarity. The volume does not prescribe a singular ideological position. Rather, it offers a scholarly forum in which divergent perspectives can coexist, provided they are grounded in careful legal reasoning, empirical engagement, and theoretical transparency.

States produce silence—through legislative gaps, selective enforcement, evidentiary burdens, and systemic neglect. At the same time, they exercise control through criminalization, surveillance, moral regulation, and border governance. This dual dynamic is neither geographically confined nor historically static. It manifests across diverse legal regimes and political contexts, often in ways that reproduce social hierarchies while claiming protective intent. By examining these dynamics comparatively, this volume situates national legal frameworks within broader currents of international human rights law and psychological scholarship.

An explicit commitment to intersectionality underpins the volume's theoretical orientation. Systems of power—gender, caste, race, class, sexuality, migration status, and other axes of marginalization—do not operate in isolation. They converge to structure vulnerability, shape access to justice, and influence both stigma and resistance. Contributors engage these layered dynamics to illuminate how individuals encounter law not as an abstract norm, but as a lived and embodied reality. Intersectional analysis is not treated here as a rhetorical gesture; it is an essential methodological tool for understanding the structural production of harm and the possibilities for resilience.

The global orientation of the volume is reflected in its comparative architecture. Chapters engage jurisdictional clusters across South Asia, Sub-Saharan Africa, Latin America, Western Europe and North America, Southeast Asia, and the MENA region. This structure enables both regional specificity and cross-jurisdictional dialogue. By placing diverse legal models in conversation—criminalization, partial criminalization, legalization, decriminalization, and hybrid regimes—the volume underscores that regulatory choices are shaped by historical trajectories, cultural narratives, economic inequalities, and international obligations.

We anticipate that this collection will contribute meaningfully to feminist legal theory, international human rights law, transnational feminism, global public policy, and trauma psychology. Among its central contributions are: clarifying conceptual ambiguities that cloud legal discourse; examining the interpretive and normative force of key international instruments, including the Palermo Protocol, CEDAW General Recommendation No. 38 (2020), and ICCPR/ICESCR protections; foregrounding the psychological dimensions of exploitation, trauma, recovery, and resilience; and articulating intersectional frameworks capable of addressing compounded vulnerabilities. The volume also provides grounded, regionally informed analyses of state practice, civil society interventions, and reform efforts, thereby bridging theory and policy.

This work is particularly timely. Renewed global attention to gender-based violence, the commitments embodied in the Sustainable Development Goals—especially Targets 5.2 and 8.7—and ongoing debates over carceral versus rights-based approaches to prostitution and trafficking have intensified the need for careful, interdisciplinary scholarship. In polarized policy environments, clarity is often mistaken for advocacy and nuance for ambivalence. We hope this volume demonstrates that intellectual rigor and normative engagement need not be mutually exclusive.

Finally, we acknowledge that scholarship on prostitution and trafficking cannot be disentangled from the lived realities of those whose lives are shaped by law, stigma, and state power. While this volume is academic in orientation and intended for scholars, students, legal professionals, policy-makers, and practitioners, it is animated by an ethical commitment: to treat its subjects neither as abstractions nor as symbols, but as persons situated within complex social worlds.

It is our hope that *Legal and Psychological Perspectives on Prostitution and Human Trafficking* will serve not only as a reference text, but as an invitation—to rethink entrenched categories, to engage across disciplinary divides, and to confront silence with sustained and critical inquiry.

ORGANIZATION OF THE BOOK

In assembling this volume, we were attentive not only to thematic coherence but also to the intellectual tensions that animate contemporary debates. The chapters that follow reflect a spectrum of jurisprudential, feminist, psychological, and policy-oriented engagements—often in productive disagreement—yet united by a shared commitment to analytical rigor and human dignity.

Chapter 1 advances a forceful abolitionist thesis, conceptualizing prostitution as structural violence incompatible with binding international human rights norms. Drawing on instruments such as the International Covenant on Civil and Political Rights, International Covenant on Economic, Social and Cultural Rights, Convention on the Elimination of All Forms of Discrimination against Women, Convention against Torture, Convention on the Rights of the Child, and the Palermo Protocol, the author contends that prostitution inherently violates rights to equality, dignity, health, and freedom from ill-treatment. Through intersectional analysis and survivor testimony, the chapter situates prostitution within structures of subordination and argues for demand-focused, survivor-centered abolition as a legal imperative grounded in States' international obligations.

Chapter 2 broadens the inquiry by mapping the moral, linguistic, and regulatory terrain of sex work globally. Attentive to the politics of terminology and the fraught distinction between consent and coercion, the chapter situates contemporary debates within longer ideological histories. Through comparative case studies, it evaluates divergent legal frameworks and proposes evidence-based recommendations attentive to public health, labor rights, and human rights considerations, underscoring the necessity of conceptual clarity in shaping sound policy.

Chapter 3 offers a sustained critique of definitional ambiguities in international and domestic law, particularly the conflation of voluntary prostitution with trafficking. Engaging instruments such as the Convention for the Suppression of the Traffic in Persons, Convention on the Elimination of All Forms of Discrimination against Women, the Palermo Protocol, and India's Immoral Traffic (Prevention) Act, the author demonstrates how moralized or expansive language permits regulatory control while denying sex workers labor protections and legal recognition. The chapter calls for a reimagining of prostitution in law—one that distinguishes coercion from consent and acknowledges the heterogeneity of lived experience.

Chapter 4 turns to Scotland's Equally Safe strategy, interrogating how progressive gender-based violence frameworks may nonetheless silence sex worker voices. Through feminist and intersectional analysis, and with comparative reference to Ireland and New Zealand, the chapter critiques carceral feminist logics embedded in end-demand approaches. It argues that conflation of trafficking and consensual sex work produces epistemic exclusion and advocates instead for participatory, decriminalized, and plural feminist policymaking that centers the expertise of those directly affected.

Chapter 5 examines the expanding deployment of artificial intelligence and facial recognition technologies in anti-trafficking and prostitution enforcement in India. The authors probe whether such tools enhance victim protection or intensify surveillance and stigma. By highlighting algorithmic bias, risks of wrongful identification, and psychological harms, and by comparing Indian initiatives with global practices, the chapter calls for robust legal safeguards, transparency, and rights-centered technological governance.

Chapter 6 introduces digital legal aid platforms as a transformative response to the access-to-justice crisis produced by prohibitionist, abolitionist, and regulatory regimes alike. By offering anonymous, encrypted, and immediately accessible support, digital legal aid mitigates financial, geographic, and psychological barriers. The chapter argues that thoughtfully designed platforms—emphasizing data security and user safety—can function as a de facto rights-enhancing mechanism, empowering sex workers to document abuse and access know-your-rights resources.

Chapter 7 situates sex work within India's caste hierarchies, exposing how informal regulation and social surveillance intersect with punitive law. The author develops the concept of "legal apathy" to describe the state's systemic failure to extend meaningful protection or recognition to marginalized caste communities engaged in sexual labor. By foregrounding caste governance, the chapter deepens our understanding of how structural inequality shapes both vulnerability and resistance.

Chapter 8 combines legal and psychological analysis to examine the plight of migrant women prosecuted under the Immoral Traffic (Prevention) Act. Tracing colonial moral legacies and constitutional tensions, the chapter argues that India's framework collapses prostitution and trafficking, thereby criminalizing vulnerability. It highlights the disjunction between statutory promises, constitutional guarantees of dignity, and lived realities of enforcement.

Chapter 9 documents the "legal vacuum" experienced by women in rural districts of Madhya Pradesh. Through empirical research in Sagar and Damoh, the chapter reveals how ineffective policing, inaccessible courts, and fragile legal aid systems compel reliance on patriarchal customary practices. The resulting cycles of economic hardship and intergenerational vulnerability illuminate the gulf between formal rights and substantive justice.

Chapter 10 expands the lens to child labor in Dehradun, offering a multidimensional account of poverty, marginalization, and policy failure. Despite statutory safeguards and national initiatives, enforcement gaps persist. Through cross-sectional and triangulated research, the chapter advocates holistic strategies—combining education, poverty alleviation, community empowerment, and rehabilitation—to break cycles of exploitation and safeguard children's rights.

Chapter 11 examines how armed conflict and displacement create fertile conditions for trafficking. Through case studies of Syria, Haiti, and Gaza, the chapter demonstrates how weakened institutions, fragmented law enforcement, and humanitarian breakdowns enable exploitation. It calls for integrating anti-trafficking norms into peacebuilding and humanitarian frameworks, emphasizing survivor-centered accountability in crisis contexts.

Chapter 12 interrogates trafficking along the India–Bangladesh border through the lenses of securitization and fragmented governance. The author argues that framing trafficking primarily as a national security threat diffuses accountability and privileges performative enforcement over substantive protection. By exposing bureaucratic fragmentation, the chapter invites a reorientation toward human rights–centered governance.

Chapter 13 synthesizes intersectional and comparative approaches to sex work and trafficking law. It explores how gender, race, migration status, and class mediate experiences of stigma and criminalization across jurisdictions. By centering lived experience alongside doctrinal analysis, the chapter underscores the unintended consequences of ostensibly protective legislation and advocates context-sensitive, participatory reform.

Chapter 14 offers a comparative evaluation of criminalization, legalization, decriminalization, and neo-abolitionist models, with particular attention to implications for India. Critiquing the conflation embedded in the Immoral Traffic (Prevention) Act, the author contends that India's framework falls short of constitutional and human rights commitments. The chapter ultimately endorses a rights-oriented neo-abolitionist approach that shifts legal responsibility to purchasers while emphasizing rehabilitation and social support.

Chapter 15, by contrast, advances a feminist case for regulated or decriminalized models, arguing that conflation of consensual sex work with trafficking perpetuates stigma and exclusion. Through doctrinal and comparative analysis, the chapter concludes that India must move beyond moralistic criminalization toward a rights-based framework recognizing sex work as labor and ensuring dignity, safety, and equality.

Finally, Chapter 16 confronts the paradox at the heart of anti-trafficking enforcement: individuals framed as victims are frequently treated as offenders. Through legal and psychological analysis, and with comparative reference to the United Kingdom, the chapter reveals how immigration control and prosecutorial priorities eclipse the non-punishment principle. It calls for decoupling trafficking enforcement from immigration policing and embedding rights-based remedies within judicial practice.

Taken together, these chapters do not speak in a single voice. Rather, they reflect the intellectual and normative diversity that defines this field. Our aim as editors has been to curate a dialogue—sometimes convergent, sometimes sharply contested—grounded in scholarship, attentive to lived realities, and animated by an unwavering concern for justice.

CONCLUSION

As we bring this volume to a close, we return to the animating questions that shaped its conception: How should law distinguish between consensual sex work and human trafficking without erasing lived complexity? When does state intervention protect, and when does it punish? How do legal categories, psychological narratives, and political ideologies converge to produce both visibility and silence?

Across the chapters, several themes emerge with clarity. First, conceptual precision is not a mere academic exercise; it is a precondition for justice. The conflation of prostitution and trafficking—whether advanced in the name of morality, protection, or security—carries profound consequences for those whose lives are regulated under these frameworks. The contributors demonstrate that definitional ambiguity often licenses overreach, diffuses accountability, and obscures the distinct realities of coercion and consent.

Second, the state's role is deeply ambivalent. Legal regimes may promise dignity and protection while simultaneously enacting surveillance, criminalization, or neglect. Whether through carceral approaches, securitized border governance, technological enforcement, or legal apathy, state power can reproduce structural inequalities even when framed as benevolent. Yet the state also remains a necessary site of reform. International human rights instruments—including the International Covenant on Civil and Political Rights, the Convention on the Elimination of All Forms of Discrimination against Women, and the Palermo Protocol—continue to offer normative anchors for accountability, even as their interpretation and implementation remain contested.

Third, intersectionality is indispensable. Gender, caste, race, migration status, class, age, and geography intersect to structure vulnerability, resilience, and access to justice. The experiences documented in this volume—from rural India to conflict zones, from digital spaces to borderlands—underscore that exploitation does not occur in a vacuum. It is produced within layered systems of inequality that law must confront if it is to be transformative rather than merely regulatory.

Fourth, the psychological dimensions of exploitation and governance demand sustained attention. Trauma, stigma, institutional mistrust, and epistemic silencing shape how individuals encounter legal systems. Survivor-centered approaches, trauma-informed policy design, and participatory reform are not optional supplements; they are essential components of any framework that claims to prioritize dignity and rights.

We have deliberately curated chapters that do not converge on a single prescriptive model. Some contributors advocate abolitionist approaches grounded in structural critiques of commodification and demand. Others argue for decriminalization or regulated frameworks that foreground labor rights and autonomy. Still others expose the harms embedded in securitized and punitive enforcement regimes. This diversity is not a weakness of the volume; it is its strength. It reflects the intellectual honesty required to grapple with one of the most polarizing and morally charged areas of contemporary law and policy.

Our hope is that this book serves as both reference and provocation: a resource for scholars, practitioners, and policy-makers seeking comparative and interdisciplinary insight, and an invitation to question entrenched assumptions. If there is a unifying commitment across these pages, it is to human dignity—understood not as abstraction, but as lived reality shaped by law, power, and social context.

Silence, as our title suggests, is never neutral. It is produced—by stigma, by fear, by moralism, by bureaucratic fragmentation, and at times by well-intentioned policy that fails to listen. To confront silence requires more than denunciation; it requires sustained inquiry, conceptual clarity, and engagement across difference. As editors, we offer this volume in that spirit: not as the final word on prostitution and human trafficking, but as a carefully assembled forum for critical dialogue, principled disagreement, and renewed commitment to justice.

Aradhya Singh
Banaras Hindu University, India

Sara Balkh
United Nations Association of Orange County, USA

Amit Anand
REVA University, Bengaluru, India

Acknowledgement

We extend our sincere gratitude to all the contributing authors whose rigorous scholarship and critical engagement made this volume possible. Their willingness to engage with complex, and often contested, questions surrounding prostitution and human trafficking has enriched this collection both intellectually and normatively.

We are equally thankful to the reviewers for their careful evaluations and constructive feedback, which strengthened the analytical clarity and coherence of the chapters. The editors are especially thankful to Dr.Farid Azadbakht, Mohammad Bagher Balkh,Davina Haggar, Sara Hosseini, Sima Hosseini, Azadeh Janghorban, Zahra Mirabian, Sara Rosi, Osia Varghese (REVA University), Razina Ahmed (Presidency University) and Priya Pallavi Sahu (REVA University) for their rigorous peer review and constructive recommendations, which helped refine the conceptual and methodological foundations of the contributions in this volume. Our appreciation also goes to the editorial and production team at IGI Global for their guidance and professionalism throughout the publication process.

Finally, we acknowledge the broader academic and practitioner communities whose ongoing research, dialogue, and advocacy continue to shape meaningful conversations in this field. It is through such collective effort that interdisciplinary inquiry and principled reform become possible.

Aradhya Singh
Banaras Hindu University, India

Sara Balkh
United Nations Association of Orange County, USA

Amit Anand
REVA University, Bengaluru, India

Chapter 1
Prostitution as Structural Violence: A Human Rights Law Mandate for Abolition

Sara Balkh
http://orcid.org/0009-0004-4317-7954
United Nations Association of Orange County, USA

Amit Anand
http://orcid.org/0000-0002-9219-5858
REVA University, India

ABSTRACT

This chapter argues that prostitution must be legally recognized not as labor but as structural violence irreconcilable with international human rights law. Grounded in binding instruments including the ICCPR, ICESCR, CEDAW, CAT, CRC, and the Palermo Protocol, as well as treaty-body interpretations, jurisprudence, and survivor testimony, it demonstrates that prostitution systematically violates rights to equality, dignity, health, and freedom from torture and ill-treatment. The analysis establishes prostitution's foundations as structural subordination, documents its inherent human rights violations, examines the cultural normalization of coercion through pornography and demand, and evaluates competing legal models. It further applies an intersectional lens to groups facing heightened vulnerability. The chapter concludes by articulating survivor-centered, demand-focused pathways toward abolition consistent with States' obligations under international law, arguing that human dignity cannot be commodified and that equality and justice require an abolitionist legal framework.

DOI: 10.4018/979-8-3373-5841-3.ch001

INTRODUCTION: PROSTITUTION AS STRUCTURAL VIOLENCE

Prostitution sits at the fault line between the rhetoric of human rights and the tolerated commodification of human beings. Where some frame it as "sex work," international law and feminist jurisprudence have consistently identified it as structural violence rooted in inequality, coercion, and patriarchal demand. Consent in this context is rarely free; it is extracted under conditions of poverty, displacement, and systemic exclusion. To rename such exploitation as labor is not a neutral choice but a normative distortion that masks violence as contract.

International law has never been silent on this contradiction. The 1949 Convention for the Suppression of the Traffic in Persons and of the Exploitation of the Prostitution of Others (1949 Traffic Convention) declared prostitution "incompatible with the dignity and worth of the human person" (United Nations, 1949, preamble). That principle has since been reinforced: the Convention on the Elimination of All Forms of Discrimination Against Women (CEDAW) Committee has clarified—in General Recommendation No. 38—that the exploitation of prostitution is a manifestation of structural sex-based discrimination amounting to gender-based violence (CEDAW Committee, 2020, para. 10). Most recently, the United Nations (UN) Special Rapporteur on violence against women and girls affirmed that prostitution cannot be reconciled with States' obligations under international human rights law (Alsalem, 2024).

The paradox is clear. States that prohibit slavery, torture, and trafficking under binding treaties simultaneously tolerate prostitution regimes that normalize the sale of sexual access. This inconsistency is not marginal—it strikes at the coherence of the international legal order itself. Just as slavery could not be legitimated by contract, prostitution cannot be insulated from scrutiny by appeals to individual choice. Its very existence presupposes entrenched structural inequality, rendering it irreconcilable with the guarantees of equality, dignity, and freedom from torture enshrined in the International Covenant on Civil and Political Rights (ICCPR), the International Covenant on Economic, Social and Cultural Rights (ICESCR), CEDAW, the Convention against Torture and Other Cruel, Inhuman or Degrading Treatment or Punishment (CAT), the Convention on the Rights of the Child (CRC), and the Protocol to Prevent, Suppress and Punish Trafficking in Persons, Especially Women and Children (Palermo Protocol) (United Nations, 1966a, 1966b, 1979, 1984, 1989, 2000).

This chapter advances a single claim: measured against the standards of international human rights law, prostitution must be recognized as a system of structural violence that States are legally obligated to abolish. The analysis proceeds in stages. It first examines the conceptual and theoretical foundations of prostitution as structural subordination. It then documents how prostitution violates core rights, analyzes the cultural infrastructures that normalize coercion through pornography and demand, and evaluates competing legal models. Finally, it maps States' positive duties grounded in the principle of due diligence, including obligations to prevent, protect, prosecute, and provide reparations for harms committed by private actors. It further examines victim/survivor-centered reparations anchored in the binding legal framework of victims' rights and feminist commitments to survivor agency and dignity, alongside demand-side accountability and the dismantling of structural conditions that sustain exploitation.

The stakes are not merely theoretical. The question is whether human rights law will tolerate the commodification of human dignity under the language of choice, or whether it will affirm equality as indivisible and non-derogable, meaning that such rights may not be suspended even in times of the most serious public emergency. On the record of doctrine, jurisprudence, and empirical evidence, only one conclusion follows: prostitution must be confronted and abolished as a system of violence.

This chapter proceeds in seven parts. Following this Introduction, Part I establishes the conceptual foundations for understanding prostitution as structural violence. Part II examines the specific human rights violations inherent in prostitution under binding international law. Part III analyzes the cultural infrastructures—particularly pornography and demand—that normalize coercion. Part IV evaluates competing legal models. Part V articulates States' due diligence obligations under international law. Part VI applies an intersectional lens to groups facing heightened vulnerability. Part VII outlines concrete pathways toward abolition consistent with treaty obligations.

I. CONCEPTUAL AND THEORETICAL FOUNDATIONS

A human rights law perspective on prostitution requires more than cataloguing harms; it requires exposing the structures that make it possible. Prostitution is not reducible to private choice or isolated conduct but is sustained by systemic patterns of power, inequality, and global exploitation. How prostitution is named, how it is situated in relation to patriarchy, and how it intersects with poverty and racialized inequality all determine whether law treats it as labor or as violence. This chapter builds on international law and feminist legal theory, which UN treaty bodies have echoed in their articulation of States' gender-equality obligations, to demonstrate that prostitution must be understood as structural violence.

1.1 The Politics of Language: "Sex Work" vs. Prostitution

Language is law's first battleground. To call prostitution "sex work" is not descriptive but normative: it reframes a system of exploitation as labor, smuggling coercion into the vocabulary of consent. As affirmed in the preamble of the 1949 Traffic Convention, prostitution is incompatible with human dignity — a principle later reinforced by feminist legal theorists and UN doctrine (United Nations, 1949, preamble).

Seventy-five years later, the UN Special Rapporteur on violence against women and girls warned that the term "sex work" conceals the reality of coercion and normalizes violence. In her 2024 report, Reem Alsalem described prostitution as a system of violence against women and girls, not an occupation, and cautioned that no legal regime can legitimize prostitution without violating human rights obligations (Alsalem, 2024).

Feminist legal theorists anticipated this danger — a critique that later resonated in UN women's rights discourse. MacKinnon (2011) argues that prostitution exists only because entrenched gender and power inequalities sustain it, and that framing it as "work" legitimizes subordination rather than dismantling it (pp. 271–309). Dworkin (1993) argued that prostitution is intrinsically abusive — a form of sexual violation that money cannot legitimize. She compared it to gang rape punctuated by a financial transaction, stressing that no woman can remain whole under such conditions (pp. 4–6). Together, these analyses show that prostitution is not merely an issue of "choice" or terminology but a structural practice of violence — a conclusion that directly supports the obligations states carry under CEDAW, ICCPR, and CAT to abolish such exploitation.

1.2 Patriarchy, Power, and Poverty

If language conceals the reality of exploitation, the material drivers that sustain it are equally decisive. Prostitution does not exist outside power relations; it is their expression. Male demand drives the market, patriarchal norms legitimize it, and systemic poverty supplies it. The Special Rapporteur underscored that prostitution is rooted in patriarchal norms, economic inequality, and intersecting forms of discrimination, which together drive women and girls into sexual exploitation (Alsalem, 2024).

Empirical research underscores these structural drivers. Farley et al. (2003), in a nine-country study, found that 71% of prostituted women reported physical assaults, 63–75% reported rape, 68% met clinical criteria for PTSD, 75% had experienced homelessness, and 89% wanted to leave prostitution but lacked alternatives (pp. 34, 40–44, 51). Survivor testimony likewise confirms that what is often framed as "choice" is overwhelmingly conditioned by socio-economic deprivation, gendered subordination, and systemic violence.

International law echoes these insights. The CEDAW Committee, in General Recommendation No. 38, affirmed that trafficking and the exploitation of prostitution of women and girls are rooted in structural, sex-based discrimination constituting gender-based violence. It further emphasized that States must address the structural drivers — including economic injustice, patriarchal norms, and discriminatory migration and asylum regimes — rather than treating prostitution as an individual lifestyle choice (CEDAW Committee, 2020, paras. 10, 13–15).

Taken together, this doctrinal and empirical record demonstrates that prostitution is not the exercise of free will but the predictable outcome of entrenched structural inequality. A human rights law framework therefore imposes on States not only the duty to alleviate poverty or reduce violence in the abstract but the specific obligation to dismantle the patriarchal and economic systems that sustain prostitution itself.

1.3 Globalization and Racialized Exploitation

Prostitution is embedded in global hierarchies of race, class, and migration. The Global Report on Trafficking in Persons 2024 shows that women and girls from the Global South are disproportionately trafficked for sexual exploitation into wealthier regions, reinforcing global inequalities. For example, African women are trafficked at significant rates into Europe, the Middle East, East Asia, and North America, often through organized transnational networks that exploit poverty and displacement (United Nations Office on Drugs and Crime, 2024, p. 71). Women and girls from South and East Asia are also detected as victims trafficked into the Middle East, alongside flows from South America, confirming that cross-regional trafficking is a broader global pattern and not confined to Africa (United Nations Office on Drugs and Crime, 2024, pp. 116–117).

These patterns reveal prostitution and sexual exploitation as an international system of stratified exploitation, mapping directly onto structural inequalities of wealth and power. Victims from low-income and marginalized regions are funneled into sex markets in more affluent countries, demonstrating how globalization reproduces racialized and gendered vulnerabilities in the international sex trade.

Feminist critiques of international law — now echoed in UN gender-equality frameworks — help explain this pattern. Charlesworth, Chinkin, and Wright (1991) demonstrated that international law has historically erased women's lived experiences and reinforced male-centred structures (pp. 614–616). Later feminist and postcolonial scholars have extended this critique, showing how these gendered structures intersect with and reproduce colonial hierarchies, a theme now reflected in contemporary UN gender-equality frameworks. That critique remains urgent: prostitution disproportionately targets racialized and migrant women, embedding colonial legacies of dispossession into contemporary sexual markets.

Indigenous women's scholarship reinforces this. Bourgeois (2015), in colonial exploitation: The Canadian state and the trafficking of Indigenous women and girls in Canada, highlights how Indigenous women are vastly overrepresented in prostitution and trafficking due to colonial dispossession, systemic racism, and gendered poverty (pp. 1426–1463). This shows prostitution is not an abstract phenomenon but a continuation of colonial and racialized violence. Seen through a human rights lens, prostitution cannot be abstracted into isolated transactions. It is a globalized system that reproduces patriarchal power, racial subordination, and economic deprivation.

Recognizing prostitution as structural violence is therefore not rhetorical but descriptive of its material and legal reality. The next step is to trace how this violence concretely manifests in binding human rights law.

2. HUMAN RIGHTS VIOLATIONS INHERENT IN PROSTITUTION

Having established prostitution as a structurally coerced system, the analysis now turns to how this system violates specific, binding human rights norms under international law. When assessed through the lens of binding treaties and authoritative UN interpretation, prostitution emerges not as a neutral market activity but as a continuum of human rights violations that engage the prohibitions against gender-based violence, torture, and ill-treatment, as well as the rights to health, privacy, dignity, family life, and protection from sexual exploitation.

2.1 Violence Against Women

Prostitution operates within a continuum of gender-based violence. The CEDAW Committee, in General Recommendation No. 19, clarified that gender-based violence constitutes discrimination under Article 1 of the Convention and triggers States' due diligence duties to prevent, investigate, and punish such acts (CEDAW Committee, 1992, para. 6). As noted in General Recommendation No. 38 (CEDAW Committee, 2020, paras. 10–13) — discussed in Section 1 — trafficking and the exploitation of prostitution are rooted in structural, sex-based discrimination constituting gender-based violence.

Empirical data confirms the scale of harm. *The* Global Report on Trafficking in Persons 2024 found that women and girls constitute 61% of all detected trafficking victims worldwide, with sexual exploitation the predominant form (United Nations Office on Drugs and Crime, 2024, p. 3). This pattern reflects what Kelly (1988) conceptualized as a "continuum of sexual violence," where coercion operates not as isolated incidents but as an ongoing system of gendered domination — a framework that has informed subsequent UN analyses of violence against women. This evidence places prostitution squarely within the architecture of gender-based violence and demonstrates that treating it as labor would normalize gendered harm, undermining the guarantees of equality and non-discrimination in international law.

2.2 Torture and Ill-Treatment

The prohibition of torture and cruel, inhuman, or degrading treatment is absolute under Article 7 of the ICCPR (1966) and Article 2 of the CAT (1984). The Human Rights Committee, in General Comment No. 20, confirmed that Article 7 applies to all acts of sexual violence, including those committed by non-State actors (Human Rights Committee, 1992, para. 2).

Alsalem's (2024) report documents that prostitution routinely involves rape, gang rape, severe beatings, burning, mutilation, forced unprotected sex, and insertion of foreign objects, leaving many with lasting physical disabilities or death (paras. 10–11). Survivors testify that repeated unwanted sexual penetration under economic coercion produces the kind of severe physical and psychological pain recognized in international jurisprudence as torture or ill-treatment. Alsalem further highlighted how digital platforms now facilitate and normalize this abuse, with 75% of sex trafficking victims advertised online.

International criminal jurisprudence affirms this classification: the ICTY in Prosecutor v. Furundžija (1998, para. 295) and the Inter-American Court in Miguel Castro-Castro Prison v. Peru (2006, pp 106-107) held that rape constitutes torture because of the severe physical and psychological pain inflicted. These practices meet the threshold of intentional infliction of severe pain or suffering for purposes of coercion, punishment, or discrimination and are incompatible with the non-derogable protections of ICCPR Article 7 and CAT Article 2.

2.3 Violations of Health, Privacy, Dignity, and Family Life

Prostitution also erodes multiple substantive rights protected by international law. The ICESCR guarantees "the right of everyone to the enjoyment of the highest attainable standard of physical and mental health" (International Covenant on Economic, Social and Cultural Rights, 1966, art. 12). United Nations Office on Drugs and Crime (2024, pp. 12–14) reports that prostituted women and girls disproportionately suffer overlapping harms — sexual violence, forced labor, and coercion into criminality — driving high rates of sexually transmitted infections, depression, and trauma disorders.

The right to privacy and dignity, protected under ICCPR Article 17, has been interpreted by the Human Rights Committee in General Comment No. 16 as encompassing personal autonomy, bodily integrity, and freedom from surveillance (Human Rights Committee, 1988, paras. 1, 7–8, 10). By commodifying sexual access, prostitution erodes sexual autonomy itself, transforming intimate relations into acts of surveillance and coercion, violating the essence of human dignity.

The right to family life, safeguarded by ICCPR Article 23, is also disrupted. Alsalem (2024) reports that many women in prostitution lose custody of their children after being labelled "bad mothers," and that their children often experience neurodevelopmental delays, maltreatment, and heightened risk of trafficking and sexual violence. Prostitution thus corrodes not only individual dignity but also the collective institution of the family, undermining the protective guarantees of ICCPR Articles 17 and 23.

These violations rarely occur in isolation. Human rights bodies have increasingly recognized that overlapping infringements on health, dignity, privacy, and family life produce cumulative harms that intensify trauma and entrench social exclusion (CESCR, 2000, General Comment No. 14, paras. 3, 8).

2.4 Child Rights and Sexual Exploitation

Prostitution also constitutes a grave violation of children's rights. The CRC affirms the child's right to be free from all forms of sexual exploitation and sexual abuse (CRC, 1989, art. 34). According to United Nations Office on Drugs and Crime (2024), children now account for a growing share of detected trafficking victims worldwide, with girls increasingly trafficked for sexual exploitation, while boys are more often trafficked for forced labor or forced criminality. Between recent reporting periods, the share of girls among detected victims has sharply increased, especially in Europe, North America, and parts of Africa (United Nations Office on Drugs and Crime, 2024, pp. 42–43).

Alsalem warns (2024) that pornography fuels the sexual exploitation and prostitution of children, with girls being recruited at increasingly younger ages — some as young as eight — and that regular exposure to pornography is linked to a fourfold increase in child sexual offences, predominantly against girls. UNICEF underscores that sexual exploitation and abuse inflict severe social, emotional, psychological, economic, physical, and security-related harms on victims, and that responses must be victim-centered, safe, culturally relevant, and age- and gender-appropriate (United Nations Children's Fund, 2021, p. 6). Such practices cause profound and often irreversible harm, including developmental trauma, chronic mental health disorders, and disruption of education and family life.

From a human rights perspective, the sexual commodification of children collapses the foundational guarantees of the CRC: the right to development (art. 6), the right to protection from economic exploitation (art. 32), and the right to be free from sexual exploitation (art. 34). No notion of "consent" can legally attach to children in this context. Their involvement in prostitution is *per se* exploitative and incompatible with the core principles of dignity, best interests, and special protection that underpin international child rights law.

3. STRUCTURAL NORMALIZATION OF VIOLENCE

Having established that prostitution violates core human rights—including the rights to equality, freedom from violence and torture, health, privacy, dignity, and family life—this section analyzes how cultural infrastructures—most notably pornography, stereotypes, and male demand—function to naturalize subordination and mask exploitation as "consent." International law requires States not only to respond to individual violations but also to dismantle the cultural and systemic conditions that enable them.

Rather than treating sexual access as a neutral market commodity, international human rights law recognizes that sexual exploitation is sustained by cultural infrastructures that manufacture inequality. States must therefore address not only isolated acts of abuse but also the systemic and cultural patterns that perpetuate gendered harm.

Doctrinally, Article 5(a) CEDAW requires States to transform stereotyped roles that naturalize subordination; Article 7 ICCPR prohibits cruel, inhuman, or degrading treatment; and Article 34 CRC obliges States to protect children from all forms of sexual exploitation and abuse. Read together, these provisions create positive duties to disrupt the cultural mechanisms that make exploitation appear normal, tolerable, and repeatable. Prostitution and its cultural accelerants—most notably the industrialized pornography ecosystem—operate as such mechanisms: they script sexual expectations, habituate consumers to inequality, and normalize coercive practices under the guise of "consent."

3.1 Male Demand and the Manufacture of Sexual Expectations

At the level of political economy, prostitution is demand-led. The buyer's willingness to pay for sexual access creates the price signal to which criminal networks, pimps, and exploiters respond. At the level of social meaning, that same demand manufactures expectations about what sex is—transactional, male-directed, and premised on female submission. Human rights law requires States to interrupt these dynamics: Article 5(a) CEDAW imposes a duty of cultural transformation, not merely punitive regulation, dismantling stereotypes that normalize the purchase of women's bodies.

Contemporary pornography markets intensify these demand dynamics. High-velocity, high-novelty online pornography conditions arousal to commodified, asymmetric sexual scripts and is empirically associated with cue-reactivity, craving, escalation to more extreme content, and tendencies toward problematic use. A peer-reviewed study by Kamaruddin et al. (2025, pp. 117–120) demonstrates that sexual arousal during pornography consumption is the single strongest predictor of compulsive use, establishing a reinforcement loop between demand and expectation. This aligns with addiction-model mechanisms (cue reactivity, craving, tolerance) and shows how cultural exposure trains consumers toward coercive scripts in the marketplace of sexual access.

From a human rights standpoint, this matters because what buyers expect in commercial sex environments migrates into non-commercial contexts, eroding the boundary between consent and compliance. When States tolerate such dynamics, they fail their due-diligence duties under the ICCPR and CEDAW. The "choice" presented at the point of sale is already pre-structured by conditioning that reduces women's sexual autonomy to purchasable acts. The legal consequence is clear: demand-side accountability (criminal liability for buyers and exploiters), coupled with stereotype-disrupting measures under Article 5(a) CEDAW, is not ideological but treaty-mandated.

3.2 Pornification of Culture and the Erosion of Consent

The "pornification" of culture—ubiquitous, always-on exposure to commodified sexual content—does more than reflect inequality; it produces it. Empirical research documents desensitization effects (users requiring higher-intensity content to achieve arousal), cue-induced cravings, and escalation to aggressive scripts. Kamaruddin et al. (2025, pp. 117–120) show that pornography motivation, sexual arousal, and gratification jointly predict problematic pornography use, with sexual arousal emerging as the strongest predictor. These findings demonstrate that reinforcement cycles are embedded in consumption itself, consistent with cue-reactivity, craving, and tolerance mechanisms identified in behavioral addiction models. The result is a cultural environment that normalizes entitlement and aggression-coded scripts as "ordinary" sex.

This cultural normalization carries direct legal implications. Under Article 5(a) of the CEDAW, States must take "all appropriate measures" to eradicate sex-role stereotyping—not as cultural preference but as a structural condition of violence. Under Article 34 of the CRC, States must prevent children's exposure to sexual exploitation and abuse; where pornified environments drive earlier exposure, escalate risk, and blur consent norms, prevention becomes a structural—not merely individual—obligation. Under Articles 7 and 17 of the ICCPR, tolerating cultural markets that routinize degradation undermines both the prohibition of ill-treatment and the protection of privacy, honor and dignity.

3.3 Normative Payoff

Calling prostitution "work" while disregarding the cultural machinery that manufactures buyer demand is a categorical error in human rights law. The doctrinal center of gravity—Article 5(a) CEDAW, Articles 7 and 17 ICCPR, and Article 34 CRC—requires de-normalizing commodified sexual access through:

1. demand-side criminalization and accountability;
2. decriminalization of the prostituted person; and
3. stereotype-disrupting measures targeting pornified scripts.

Where evidence shows reinforcement loops between pornography consumption and entitlement-coded expectations, States' due-diligence duties attach ex ante: they must regulate markets, invest in public education that centers consent and equality, and fund victim/survivor-led exit services. In short, the pathway from screen to street is legally cognizable; the response must be structural. This doctrinal baseline clarifies why regulatory and decriminalization models—which leave demand intact—cannot meet States' human rights obligations, as the next section demonstrates.

4. COMPARATIVE LEGAL MODELS: PROHIBITION, LEGALIZATION, DECRIMINALIZATION, AND ABOLITION

This section evaluates regulatory approaches not as policy preferences, but through the lens of States' binding obligations under international human rights law.

Having established that prostitution constitutes structural violence and engages States' binding obligations under multiple human rights instruments, it becomes necessary to evaluate the regulatory models through which States seek to govern it. The international human rights system is not neutral in this regard: each model either aligns with or contradicts these treaty obligations. Contemporary law and policy reveal four principal approaches — prohibition, legalization, full decriminalization, and abolition (often called the Equality or Nordic model). This section argues that, of these, only the abolitionist model — which criminalizes demand, decriminalizes the prostituted person, and provides exit and support services — can be reconciled with international human rights law.

4.1 Prohibition: Criminalizing Both Sides

Under the prohibition model, both the sale and purchase of sex are criminalized. This approach continues to predominate in the United States (outside the licensed counties of Nevada) and in parts of Asia and Africa. Although framed as deterrence, prohibition entrenches structural discrimination: it criminalizes those who are coerced into prostitution while leaving the structures that generate demand intact. This contradicts States' obligations of non-discrimination under Articles 2 and 5(a) of CEDAW, which require dismantling discriminatory structures rather than punishing their victims. Empirical evidence confirms that prohibition drives prostitution underground, heightens exposure to violence, and deters victims from seeking police or health assistance. Treaty bodies, including the CEDAW Committee, have repeatedly criticized regimes that criminalize prostituted women and girls while failing to address male demand, emphasizing that States must decriminalize victims and adopt measures to discourage the demand that fosters exploitation and trafficking (CEDAW Committee, 2020, paras. 6, 38, 42; Alsalem, 2024).

4.2 Legalization and Regulatory Models: Structural Incompatibility

Legalization and regulatory approaches proceed from the premise that prostitution can be rendered safe through licensing regimes, health regulations, or zoning restrictions. Jurisdictions such as Germany, the Netherlands, and the Australian Capital Territory have adopted this approach. Empirical evidence shows that legalization has significantly increased trafficking inflows, expanding the overall market for prostitution and thereby intensifying the demand that sustains exploitation (Cho et al., 2013, pp. 67–68). Instead of eliminating harm, these regimes have created dual markets: a small, regulated sector and a much larger illicit one that thrives on impunity.

Doctrinally, this model is irreconcilable with States' treaty obligations. Article 6 of CEDAW requires States to "suppress all forms of traffic in women and exploitation of prostitution." The travaux préparatoires (preparatory works) confirm that "exploitation of prostitution" is incompatible with gender equality, irrespective of its regulatory form. Treaty bodies have reinforced this view: in General Recommendation No. 38, the CEDAW Committee emphasized that trafficking and the exploitation of prostitution are rooted in structural sex-based discrimination constituting gender-based violence, and that States must adopt measures to discourage demand and dismantle the systems that sustain it (CEDAW Committee, 2020, paras. 10–13). The paradox is striking: States that prohibit slavery under Article 8 of the ICCPR and define trafficking to include "the exploitation of the prostitution of others" under Article 3 of the Palermo Protocol simultaneously construct domestic markets that normalize sexual access to women's bodies. The promise of "safe" regulation collapses under this evidence, confirming that legalization violates States' due-diligence duties.

4.3 Full Decriminalization: A Partial Advance, But Normatively Incomplete

Full decriminalization, exemplified by New Zealand's Prostitution Reform Act (2003), removes criminal penalties from both buyers and prostituted persons. Often presented as a harm-reduction approach aimed at destigmatization, it has been celebrated for improving access to health services. Yet this model fails the treaty test because it leaves demand intact and thereby normalizes male entitlement to sexual access. It thus conflicts with Article 5(a) of CEDAW, which obliges States to dismantle sex-role stereotypes that subordinate women.

Evaluations of the New Zealand model reveal that decriminalization has expanded the size of the prostitution market, increased demand, emboldened buyers, and heightened risks of trafficking and violence, while failing to deliver the promised protections (Alsalem, 2024). Survivors consistently report that "choice" remained conditioned by poverty, abuse, and the absence of viable alternatives. From a human rights standpoint, decriminalization reduces stigma but not structural coercion. It leaves intact the demand dynamics that sustain exploitation and therefore fails to meet States' obligations under Article 7 of the ICCPR and Article 12 of the ICESCR. This model treats male violence as a private hazard rather than a systemic rights violation, offering only the illusion of safety.

4.4 The Abolitionist or Equality Model (the so-called Nordic Model): Treaty-Consistent

By contrast, the abolitionist — or equality — model, first adopted in Sweden (1999) and now implemented in Norway, France, Ireland, Canada, and Israel, criminalizes the purchase of sex while decriminalizing those who are prostituted. This approach explicitly grounds itself in human rights law: it frames prostitution as structural violence that cannot be rendered safe and therefore targets demand rather than supply.

Empirical evaluations support its effectiveness. Sweden's official evaluation—summarized in a government follow-up report—found that, after the 1999 law, street prostitution was reduced by about half, the ban exerted a clear normative and deterrent effect on buyers, and there was no evidence of displacement to indoor or online markets or of increased buyer violence (Government Offices of Sweden, 2014, paras. 28–30). While some underground activity persists, the normative shift is unmistakable: male demand is delegitimized, and women exiting prostitution gain access to state-funded support services. Crucially, this model aligns with the obligations articulated in CEDAW General Recommendation No. 38, which call on States to address the structural and systemic factors sustaining the exploitation of prostitution (paras. 10–13), and with Article 7 of the ICCPR prohibiting cruel, inhuman, or degrading treatment. It also advances the protective aims of Article 34 of the CRC by disrupting the market dynamics that drive child sexual exploitation.

This approach is gaining international recognition. The European Parliament has recognized the Nordic model as an effective means of combating the trafficking of women and girls for sexual exploitation and promoting gender equality, noting evidence of its deterrent effect on trafficking inflows and its positive shift in public attitudes (European Parliament, 2014/0420, paras. 29–31). UN treaty bodies have increasingly referenced this model as a good practice in fulfilling States' due diligence obligations to reduce demand rather than regulate exploitation (see e.g., CEDAW Committee, General Recommendation No. 38, 2020, paras. 10–13). By reframing prostitution as a system of inequality rather than a neutral market, the Equality Model uniquely aligns domestic policy with States' binding obligations under international human rights law.

4.5 Normative Synthesis

The comparative evidence points to a single conclusion: prohibition re-criminalizes victims, legalization expands exploitation, decriminalization reduces stigma but leaves demand intact, and only abolition aligns domestic law with international human rights obligations. The Equality Model operationalizes the indivisibility of rights by affirming women's dignity (ICCPR arts. 7, 17), equality (CEDAW arts. 1, 5, 6), health (ICESCR art. 12), and protection from sexual exploitation (CRC art. 34; Palermo Protocol art. 9).

Where States normalize prostitution, they institutionalize discrimination. Where they adopt abolition, they fulfill their duty of due diligence to protect against violence and exploitation. The record is clear: the path consistent with international human rights law is not regulatory compromise or full decriminalization, but structural transformation through the abolitionist model.

5. STATE OBLIGATIONS UNDER INTERNATIONAL HUMAN RIGHTS LAW

The preceding analysis established that prostitution is a system of structural violence that engages multiple non-derogable and affirmative human rights norms. Under international law, States bear binding positive obligations to prevent exploitation, protect victims, prosecute perpetrators, and provide reparations. These duties are codified across the core human rights treaties (Convention on the Elimination of All Forms of Discrimination against Women, 1979; International Covenant on

Civil and Political Rights, 1966; International Covenant on Economic, Social and Cultural Rights, 1966; CAT, 1984; CRC, 1989) and further reinforced by the Palermo Protocol (2000). Complementary policy commitments in the Beijing Declaration and Platform for Action direct States to suppress trafficking, address the root factors that encourage trafficking "for prostitution and other forms of commercialized sex," and assist victims of violence due to prostitution and trafficking (United Nations General Assembly, 1995, paras. 113(b), 122, 130(b), 145(e), 230(n)).

Neutrality is not permissible: treating prostitution as "work" while leaving demand intact is incompatible with States' due diligence duties. These obligations fall into four interdependent pillars — prevention, protection, prosecution, and reparations — which together give effect to States' human rights commitments. Accordingly, this section examines each pillar in turn — prevention, protection, prosecution, and reparations — to demonstrate how these obligations operationalize States' human rights commitments.

5.1 Prevention: Due Diligence Before Harm

Prevention is the cornerstone of State responsibility. Article 2 of CAT requires States to take "effective legislative, administrative, judicial or other measures" to prevent torture and ill-treatment, while Article 5(a) of CEDAW obliges them to transform discriminatory social and cultural patterns that sustain women's subordination. In line with the UN Guiding Principles on Business and Human Rights, human rights due diligence (HRDD) is defined as an ongoing process of identifying, preventing, mitigating, and accounting for adverse human rights impacts (Office of the High Commissioner for Human Rights, 2011, Guiding Principle 17; Office of the High Commissioner for Human Rights, 2012/2021, pp. 31–36). Although elaborated in the corporate context, HRDD equally clarifies the scope of States' preventive obligations: prevention is not passive but requires proactive assessment and action before harm occurs.

CEDAW General Recommendation No. 19 (1992, paras. 11–12) underscores that gender-based violence stems from traditional attitudes that propagate pornography and the commercial sexual objectification of women. Building on this, General Recommendation No. 38 (CEDAW Committee, 2020)—as discussed in Sections 1 and 2—clarifies that States must dismantle the structural discrimination sustaining trafficking and the exploitation of prostitution.

The Beijing Platform similarly directs States to address "the root factors... that encourage trafficking in women and girls for prostitution and other forms of commercialized sex" (United Nations General Assembly, 1995, para. 130(b)), while the Palermo Protocol requires educational, social, and cultural measures to discourage demand (Palermo Protocol, 2000, art. 9(5)).

Applied to prostitution, due diligence requires that States suppress demand, regulate and reduce pornography markets that normalize commodified sexual access, and deliver public education to dismantle stereotypes of female sexual availability. Allowing prostitution markets to flourish, even under regulatory or decriminalization regimes, entrenches the very structural inequality that international law obliges States to eliminate.

5.2 Protection: Safeguarding Victims, Not Criminalizing Them

Article 34 of the CRC obliges States to protect children from "all forms of sexual exploitation and sexual abuse" (CRC, 1989, art. 34). The Human Rights Committee has clarified that Article 7 of the ICCPR protects individuals from torture and ill-treatment inflicted by public officials or private actors alike, and that States must ensure effective legal protection, prompt investigation, and remedies for such violations (Human Rights Committee, 1992, paras. 2, 14).

Building on these core protections, CEDAW General Recommendation No. 38 establishes the most detailed framework on victim support and non-criminalization. It requires States to ensure that trafficked and sexually exploited women and girls—especially migrants—receive comprehensive, trauma-informed support and are shielded from re-victimization (CEDAW Committee, 2020, paras. 89–97). This includes protection from forcible return where there is risk of re-trafficking, persecution, or stigma; safe and accessible shelters with specially trained staff; psychosocial care; legal aid; access to education, healthcare, employment, and housing; family reunification; and child-sensitive case management grounded in the best interests of the child.

General Recommendation 38 further establishes the principles of non-criminalization and non-conditionality: victims must never be detained in "rehabilitation" centred, and no woman or girl may be arrested, prosecuted, or penalized for acts that are a direct consequence of being trafficked or prostituted (paras. 92, 94, 98). States must also grant reflection periods, residence permits, and access to support without requiring cooperation in prosecutions.

Abolitionist regimes align with this framework by treating prostituted persons as rights-holders rather than offenders. Prohibitionist models violate it by criminalizing victims, while full decriminalization without demand-side accountability leaves structural coercion intact, failing to discharge the treaty-based duty to protect, support, and reintegrate victims while dismantling the systems of exploitation.

5.3 Prosecution: Accountability for Exploiters and Buyers

Building on the prevention and protection duties outlined in Sections 5.1–5.2, States also bear an affirmative obligation to prosecute those who sustain and profit from the prostitution system. While prevention addresses structural drivers and protection centers survivors, prosecution targets the demand side of the market—pimps, traffickers, brothel owners, and buyers—whose actions perpetuate the system of exploitation.

This obligation flows from the same due diligence framework: having undertaken to prevent and protect, States must also enforce. Under international human rights law, the duty to ensure effective remedies requires not only compensating victims but also investigating and prosecuting perpetrators (International Covenant on Civil and Political Rights, 1966, art. 2(3); Human Rights Committee, 2004, paras. 15–18). A failure to prosecute constitutes a breach of due diligence where serious human rights violations are foreseeable yet tolerated.

As noted earlier, States' due-diligence obligations under CEDAW Article 6 and Palermo Protocol Article 5 require prosecuting those who sustain the prostitution system. Consistent with this framework, the UN Special Rapporteur on violence against women and girls rejects framing prostitution as legitimate work and identifies buyers as "the main perpetrators of violence, including femicide" (Alsalem, 2024, paras. 6, 26). On this view, States breach their obligations when they penalize prostituted persons while leaving exploiters untouched.

International criminal law reinforces this duty to prosecute serious sexual exploitation. The Rome Statute of the International Criminal Court explicitly classifies enforced prostitution, sexual slavery, and other forms of sexual violence as crimes against humanity when committed as part of a widespread or systematic attack (ICC, 1998, art. 7(1)(g)). While earlier international tribunals primarily addressed rape and sexual slavery in conflict settings, the inclusion of enforced prostitution in Article 7 reflects an emerging opinio juris —the belief among States that a practice is legally obligatory under international law— that such exploitation warrants the highest level of individual criminal responsibility. Translating this principle into domestic law requires States to ensure that pimps, traffickers, and buyers face prosecution as rights violators, while prostituted persons are decriminalized and provided exit support.

Abolitionist regimes operationalize this duty by decriminalizing prostituted persons while prosecuting buyers and profiteers. By contrast, regulatory and full decriminalization regimes leave demand intact and effectively immunize buyers, perpetuating structural impunity. Such impunity is incompatible with States' due diligence obligations, which require not only suppressing trafficking but prosecuting those who sustain the system of exploitation.

5.4 Reparations: Restoring Dignity

While protection obligations focus on shielding victims from further harm, international human rights law also requires that States provide reparations as part of the right to an effective remedy. Building on the remedial duty set out in Article 2(3) of the ICCPR (see 5.3), this obligation extends beyond compensation to include measures that restore rights and dignity. The UN Basic Principles and Guidelines on the Right to a Remedy and Reparation detail five forms of reparation: restitution, compensation, rehabilitation, satisfaction, and guarantees of non-repetition (United Nations General Assembly, 2005, paras. 19–23).

Unlike protection measures, which aim to halt ongoing violations, reparations address structural harm and restore the enjoyment of rights. Yet no binding treaty instrument has codified a right to reparations specifically for women and girls exploited in prostitution, leaving survivors dependent on fragmented welfare schemes that do not recognize their legal status as rights-holders.

As discussed in Section 5.2, CEDAW General Recommendation No. 38 requires States to provide long-term reintegration and social inclusion supports—such as safe housing, education, healthcare, psychosocial services, and access to livelihoods—for trafficked and sexually exploited women and girls (CEDAW Committee, 2020, paras. 89–97). However, GR 38 frames these primarily as preventive and rehabilitative measures, not as reparations owed for past violations. This distinction has left a doctrinal gap: survivors receive assistance, but not recognition as victims entitled to redress.

Reconceptualizing these measures as forms of restitution and rehabilitation would align them with established categories of reparation under international human rights law. A human rights–based approach to prostitution therefore requires treating these measures not as welfare but as legally mandated reparations, restoring dignity and autonomy under ICESCR Article 12 and ICCPR Article 17. States that normalize prostitution obstruct this reparative duty by reframing structural harm as "work," erasing victims' entitlement to redress.

5.5 Normative Conclusion

Read together, prevention, protection, prosecution, and reparations form a unified due diligence framework under international human rights law. The Beijing Platform reinforces that States must not only suppress trafficking but also assist victims of violence linked to prostitution and trafficking as part of their substantive equality obligations (United Nations General Assembly, 1995, para. 130(b)). As elaborated further in Section 6.1, the principle of substantive equality requires

States to address structural and intersectional inequalities that funnel marginalized groups into prostitution.

This framework leaves no legal space for regulatory or full decriminalization models that preserve demand and perpetuate inequality. Only the abolitionist model fulfils States' obligations: it dismantles the structural conditions of exploitation, provides exit and support to victims, and enforces accountability against buyers and profiteers.

In doing so, it reorients the legal order from one that normalizes sexual inequality to one that affirms human dignity and substantive gender equality.

6. MARGINALIZED GROUPS AND INTERSECTIONAL VULNERABILITIES

Building on section 4's articulation of States' due diligence duties, this section examines how those obligations must be applied with heightened rigor where intersecting forms of discrimination intensify vulnerability to prostitution.

Prostitution does not affect all women and girls equally. International human rights law recognizes that structural violence is concentrated at the margins: migrants, refugees, racial and ethnic minorities, Indigenous women, persons with disabilities, LGBTQ+ individuals, and those living in poverty or conflict-affected settings. For these groups, prostitution is rarely a discrete event; it is the endpoint of cumulative inequalities that restrict access to education, housing, labor markets, justice systems, and political participation.

This intersectional lens shifts the analytical frame. It requires moving beyond formal declarations of equality to interrogate how entrenched hierarchies of race, class, gender, disability, and citizenship channel specific groups into prostitution while shielding others from its harms. Under international law, the principle of substantive equality—embedded across the CEDAW, ICCPR, ICESCR, CRC, and The Convention on the Rights of Persons with Disabilities (CRPD) frameworks—demands that States dismantle these overlapping structures of exclusion, not treat them as neutral background conditions. Only by addressing these structural drivers can States meaningfully fulfil their obligations to prevent exploitation, protect victims, and provide redress.

6.1 Treaty Framework: Substantive Equality and Intersectionality

International human rights law requires States to address not only individual acts of discrimination but also the structural patterns that systematically marginalize women facing overlapping inequalities. This obligation is grounded in the principle of substantive equality, which goes beyond formal equal treatment to require transforming discriminatory social, economic, and institutional systems so that women and girls can enjoy their rights equally in practice (, 1979, art. 1; International Covenant on Civil and Political Rights, 1966, art. 26; International Covenant on Economic, Social and Cultural Rights, 1966, art. 2(2)).

The CEDAW Committee has emphasized that achieving *substantive equality* entails "equality of results" through concrete and effective measures that redress entrenched disadvantage (CEDAW Committee, 2004, para. 8; 2010, para. 20). The Human Rights Committee has likewise affirmed that the guarantee of equality before the law and equal protection under ICCPR Article 26 obliges States to secure effective, not merely formal, equality for all persons irrespective of sex, race, or other status (Human Rights Committee, 1989, paras. 6–7). Similarly, the Committee on Economic, Social and Cultural Rights underscores that the right to non-discrimination is immediate and cross-cutting across all ICESCR rights, requiring States to dismantle legal and structural barriers to equal enjoyment (CESCR, 2009, paras. 7–9).

Together, these instruments establish that achieving substantive equality demands a differentiated and intersectional approach: States must recognize groups facing multiple and overlapping forms of oppression, address the structural barriers that funnel them into prostitution, and ensure their equal access to protection, justice, and redress. This framework provides the legal foundation for understanding prostitution not as an individual choice but as a system of targeted harm concentrated on marginalized groups.

6.2 Migrants, Refugees, and Displaced Women

Migrant and refugee women are disproportionately represented among prostituted populations across Europe, the Middle East, and North America. Trafficking networks exploit their precarious legal status, language barriers, and social exclusion, while restrictive border and asylum regimes often deny them access to justice. UNODC confirms that Sub-Saharan African, North African, and increasingly East and South Asian women are heavily overrepresented among cross-border trafficking flows into Western and Southern Europe, where sexual exploitation—particularly forced prostitution and sexual slavery—remains the predominant form of exploitation (United Nations Office on Drugs and Crime, 2024, pp. 53, 87–90).

This overrepresentation is not the product of individual risk but of systemic exclusion. Migration and asylum systems often entrench precarity by denying secure status, work authorization, or social protections, thereby pushing marginalized women into informal economies where sexual exploitation flourishes. Such structural precarity functions as a conduit into prostitution.

This dynamic directly undermines the obligation to secure substantive equality as set out in Section 6.1. Legalized prostitution regimes intensify the pattern: evidence shows that migrant women often form the backbone of the commercial sex market while simultaneously facing deportation, detention, and exclusion from labor protections (Vuolajärvi, 2019, p. 8). Regulatory models thus exploit migrant precarity to sustain prostitution markets, entrenching racialized hierarchies of gender and citizenship instead of dismantling them.

6.3 Racial and Indigenous Women

Racialized and Indigenous women are disproportionately impacted by prostitution. In North America, First Nations and Native American women are vastly overrepresented among prostituted populations, reflecting the enduring legacies of colonial dispossession, systemic racism, and gendered violence. The Inter-American Commission on Human Rights documents that these vulnerabilities stem from a history of discrimination beginning with colonization and continuing through laws and policies such as the Indian Act and residential schools (Inter-American Commission on Human Rights, 2019, paras. 7–8). The Commission further observes that long-standing social and economic marginalization contributes to Indigenous women's disproportionate engagement in high-risk activities, including prostitution, which perpetuate exposure to violence (Inter-American Commission on Human Rights, 2019, para. 78).

Legally, this pattern engages the substantive-equality duties set out in the core treaties (see Part 7.1): States must dismantle intersecting structures—racism, colonial expropriation, exclusion from land, education, housing, health, and labor markets—that funnel Indigenous and other racialized women into prostitution. Meeting those obligations requires structural remedies (not merely individual services): culturally safe access to justice and social supports; removal of discriminatory barriers to land, housing, education, and decent work; and targeted measures that break the pipeline from structural deprivation to sexual exploitation.

6.4 Persons with Disabilities

Women and girls with disabilities face a disproportionately high risk of coercion into prostitution, driven by intersecting structures of guardianship abuse, institutionalization, poverty, and denial of legal capacity. These systemic barriers isolate them from education, employment, healthcare, and justice systems, creating structural vulnerability that traffickers and exploiters readily target.

International human rights law prohibits exploitation and violence against persons with disabilities, but it has not explicitly addressed their disproportionate exposure to prostitution—revealing a significant normative gap. The CRPD obliges States to adopt targeted measures to combat gender- and disability-based discrimination (art. 6) and to protect against all forms of exploitation, violence, and abuse (art. 16) (Convention on the Rights of Persons with Disabilities, 2006). Recent UN reporting confirms that women and girls with disabilities are up to ten times more likely to experience gender-based violence while simultaneously facing higher barriers to sexual and reproductive health services (United Nations Population Fund, 2024, pp. 4–5).

Read in light of the principle of substantive equality, these obligations require States to treat disability-based vulnerability not as a private misfortune but as a structural human rights concern. Protection systems must be redesigned to include disability-specific safeguards within anti-trafficking and exit programs, ensuring that services do not replicate the segregation, neglect, and institutional violence that enable sexual exploitation.

6.5 LGBTQ+ Communities

LGBTQ+ persons—particularly transgender women—face disproportionate vulnerability to prostitution as a result of entrenched exclusion from education, housing, employment, and health systems. UNFPA reports that LGBTQIA+ persons experience persistent discrimination and stigma that translate into serious disparities in access to essential services (United Nations Population Fund, 2024, pp. 4–5). These structural exclusions are not incidental; they operate as mechanisms of systemic marginalization that channel LGBTQ+ persons into economic precarity, where exposure to sexual exploitation becomes heightened.

International human rights law recognizes this exclusion as a violation of equality norms. The Human Rights Committee has held that discrimination on the basis of sexual orientation falls within the scope of ICCPR Articles 2(1) and 26 (Toonen v. Australia, HRC, 1994, paras. 7.3–7.5). Likewise, the Committee on Economic, Social and Cultural Rights has clarified that Article 2(2) of the ICESCR prohibits discrimination based on sexual orientation and gender identity (CESCR, 2009, para. 32).

Addressing these barriers is integral to fulfilling the obligation of substantive equality. Unless States dismantle the structural exclusions that deny LGBTQ+ persons equal access to livelihoods and protections, they will remain systemically channeled into prostitution under conditions of discrimination and violence.

6.6 Normative Synthesis

Intersectional vulnerability is thus not an ancillary concern but a core legal determinant of State responsibility, requiring differentiated and targeted measures to dismantle the pathways that funnel marginalized groups into prostitution.

The analysis of migrants, Indigenous and racialized women, persons with disabilities, and LGBTQ+ communities confirms that prostitution is not evenly distributed harm but a structurally targeted one. It functions as the endpoint of layered exclusions—legal, social, and economic—that international law obliges States to dismantle.

Read through the lens of substantive equality, the implication is clear: States cannot discharge their human rights duties by adopting neutral or one-size-fits-all policies. Intersectional vulnerability requires differentiated responses that confront the specific structures—migration regimes, colonial legacies, institutional neglect, or systemic stigma—that funnel marginalized groups into prostitution.

In this light, intersectional justice becomes a legal condition of compliance. Failure to address these compounded inequalities does not merely weaken protection but constitutes a breach of States' treaty obligations to secure equality in fact, not only in law.

VII. CONCLUSIONS AND PATHWAYS FORWARD

The preceding analysis has shown that prostitution is structurally sustained by inequality, normalized by culture, and perpetuated by failed legal models. International law does not permit neutrality in the face of such systemic violence. The task, therefore, is not only to recognize prostitution as irreconcilable with human rights but to articulate concrete pathways for abolition that are victim/survivor-centered, demand-focused, and structurally transformative. This section sets out those pathways in four parts: centering victims and survivors through reparations and exit systems; enforcing demand-side accountability; transforming cultural infrastructures that normalize exploitation; and strengthening international legal harmonization.

7.1 Victim/Survivor-Centered Reparations and Exit Systems

Prostituted persons must be recognized not as offenders but as victims of structural harm entitled to reparations under international law. States should institutionalize long-term, trauma-informed exit systems that include housing, psychosocial care, education, and sustainable livelihoods. Crucially, these supports must be framed not as charity or conditional welfare, but as reparations—restoring dignity and equality under the ICCPR, ICESCR, and CEDAW. Survivor-led organizations should be central to design and implementation, ensuring policies are not paternalistic but rooted in lived expertise.

7.2 Demand-Side Criminal Liability and Structural Accountability

The persistence of prostitution is driven by demand. Human rights law, read in light of CEDAW Article 6 and the Palermo Protocol, requires that responsibility be shifted to those who buy and profit—pimps, traffickers, brothel owners, and increasingly, digital platforms. Criminal liability must attach to these actors, alongside measures that dismantle the financial and technological infrastructures sustaining prostitution markets. This reallocation of responsibility from the prostituted to the exploiters is not ideological but legally mandated.

7.3 Transforming Cultural Norms and Pornified Economies

Abolition requires dismantling the cultural scripts that normalize commodified sexual access. Under Article 5(a) CEDAW, States are obligated to transform discriminatory stereotypes, which includes addressing the pornography industry and wider "pornified" culture that manufactures male entitlement. Legal reform must therefore be paired with structural interventions: education on equality and consent, campaigns de-normalizing buyer behavior, and strict regulation of digital platforms that facilitate exploitation. This is not cultural engineering but compliance with treaty obligations.

7.4 Intersectional Justice and Substantive Equality

Prostitution disproportionately targets those at the margins—migrant and refugee women, racialized and Indigenous women, persons with disabilities, LGBTQ+ communities, and women in poverty. A human rights–based abolitionist framework must therefore be intersectional, dismantling the layered exclusions that funnel these groups into prostitution. This requires secure migration pathways, anti-racist reforms, disability-specific safeguards, and targeted socio-economic measures. Neutral or one-size-fits-all policies cannot satisfy States' obligations; substantive equality requires differentiated responses that reach those most exposed to systemic harm.

7.5 Harmonizing Law and Strengthening International Cooperation

The core human rights treaties already provide a normative blueprint: ICCPR Articles 7 and 17, ICESCR Article 12, CEDAW Articles 5 and 6, CRC Article 34, CAT Article 2, and the Palermo Protocol collectively prohibit States from normalizing prostitution. Domestic laws that legalize or regulate prostitution contradict these instruments and must be repealed. At the international level, cooperation is essential: cross-border trafficking, cyber-facilitated exploitation, and demand-driven migration vulnerabilities require harmonized legal frameworks and shared enforcement mechanisms. The path forward is not fragmented national experiments but alignment with the international system's binding obligations.

CLOSING REFLECTION

The prostitution system exposes the unresolved tension at the very core of international human rights law: the gulf between the promise of equality and the tolerated commodification of human bodies. Nowhere else do States proclaim dignity as inalienable while simultaneously licensing markets that turn human beings into consumable objects. This contradiction is not accidental; it reflects the endurance of patriarchal demand, economic coercion, and systemic exclusion within legal orders that have yet to fully confront them.

The analysis advanced in this chapter demonstrates that abolition is not an ideological project but a legal necessity. States cannot credibly uphold non-derogable protections against torture, discrimination, and exploitation while legitimizing a market that normalizes coercion as "consent." To tolerate prostitution is to hollow out the very treaties that bind the international community and to concede that human dignity can, in practice, be bought and sold.

The conclusion is compelling: prostitution is structurally irreconcilable with human rights. Abolition—anchored in survivor-centered, demand-side accountability, cultural transformation, intersectional justice, and international legal harmonization—is the only framework consistent with the indivisibility of rights and the non-commodifiability of human dignity. These are not aspirational ideals, but binding duties already embedded in CEDAW, ICCPR, ICESCR, CAT, CRC, and the Palermo Protocol.

Yet the stakes reach beyond doctrine. At issue is whether international law will become an instrument of emancipation or a mask for inequality. If prostitution can be normalized under the language of "work," then the foundational principles of human rights collapse into rhetoric. If abolition is pursued, international law fulfills its promise: to protect the most vulnerable, to dismantle structures of exploitation, and to affirm that human worth is never contingent on market demand.

To persist in normalization is to entrench inequality, reproduce colonial and patriarchal legacies, and betray the very foundations of the human rights system. To pursue abolition is to enact its deepest claim: that dignity is indivisible, equality is non-negotiable, and justice requires more than words—it requires the courage to dismantle systems of violence.

REFERENCES

Alsalem, R. (2024). Report of the Special Rapporteur on violence against women and girls, its causes and consequences: Prostitution and violence against women and girls (Vol. A). United Nations Human Rights Council., HRC/56/48.

Bourgeois, R. (2015). Colonial exploitation: The Canadian state and the trafficking of Indigenous women and girls in Canada. *UCLA Law Review. University of California, Los Angeles. School of Law*, *62*, 1426–1463.

CEDAW Committee. (1992). *General recommendation No. 19: Violence against women* (CEDAW/C/GC/19). United Nations.

CEDAW Committee. (2004). *General recommendation No. 25 on the core obligations of States parties under article 2 of the Convention* (CEDAW/C/GC/25). United Nations.

CEDAW Committee. (2020). *General recommendation No. 38 on trafficking in women and girls in the context of global migration* (CEDAW/C/GC/38). United Nations.

Charlesworth, H., Chinkin, C., & Wright, S. (1991). Feminist approaches to international law. *The American Journal of International Law*, *85*(4), 613–645. DOI: 10.2307/2203269

Cho, S.-Y., Dreher, A., & Neumayer, E. (2013). Does legalized prostitution increase human trafficking? *World Development*, *41*, 67–82. DOI: 10.1016/j.worlddev.2012.05.023

Committee on Economic. Social and Cultural Rights. (2000). *General comment No. 14: The right to the highest attainable standard of health (Art. 12)* (E/C.12/2000/4). United Nations.

Committee on Economic. Social and Cultural Rights. (2009). *General comment No. 20: Non-discrimination in economic, social and cultural rights (Art. 2(2))* (E/C.12/GC/20). United Nations.

Convention on the Elimination of All Forms of Discrimination against Women. (1979). Dec. 18, 1979, 1249 U.N.T.S. 13.

Convention on the Rights of Persons with Disabilities. (2006). Dec. 13, 2006, 2515 U.N.T.S. 3.

Convention on the Rights of the Child (CRC). (1989). Nov. 20, 1989, 1577 U.N.T.S. 3.

Dworkin, A. (1993). Prostitution and male supremacy. *Michigan Journal of Gender & Law, 1*(1), 1–12.

European Parliament. (2014, February 26). *Resolution on sexual exploitation and prostitution and its impact on gender equality* (2013/2103(INI)) (P7_TA(2014)0162).

Farley, M., Cotton, A., Lynne, J., Zumbeck, S., Spiwak, F., Reyes, M. E., Alvarez, D., & Sezgin, U. (2003). Prostitution and trafficking in nine countries: An update on violence and post-traumatic stress disorder. *Journal of Trauma Practice, 2*(3–4), 33–74. DOI: 10.1300/J189v02n03_03

Government Offices of Sweden. (2014). *Sweden's follow-up of the Platform for Action from the UN's Fourth World Conference on Women in Beijing 1995—covering the period between 2009–2014.* Government Offices of Sweden.

Human Rights Committee. (1988). *General comment No. 16: Article 17 (Right to privacy)* (HRI/GEN/1/Rev.1). United Nations.

Human Rights Committee. (1989). *General comment No. 18: Non-discrimination* (HRI/GEN/1/Rev.1). United Nations.

Human Rights Committee. (1992). *General comment No. 20: Article 7 (Prohibition of torture or other cruel, inhuman or degrading treatment or punishment)* (HRI/GEN/1/Rev.1). United Nations.

Human Rights Committee. (2004). *General comment No. 31: The nature of the general legal obligation imposed on States parties to the Covenant* (CCPR/C/21/Rev.1/Add.13). United Nations.

Human Rights Committee. (1994). *Toonen v. Australia* (Communication No. 488/1992) (CCPR/C/50/D/488/1992). United Nations Human Rights Committee.

Inter-American Commission on Human Rights. (2019). *Missing and murdered Indigenous women in British Columbia, Canada* (OEA/Ser.L/V/II. Doc. 30/14).

Inter-American Court of Human Rights. (2006). *Miguel Castro-Castro Prison v. Peru* (Merits, Reparations and Costs), Series C No. 160.

International Covenant on Civil and Political Rights (ICCPR). (1966). Dec. 16, 1966, 999 U.N.T.S. 171.

International Covenant on Economic, Social and Cultural Rights. (1966). Dec. 16, 1966, 993 U.N.T.S. 3.

International Criminal Tribunal for the former Yugoslavia (ICTY). (1998). *Prosecutor v. Furundžija* (Trial Chamber Judgment), IT-95-17/1-T.

Kamaruddin, M. S., Chong, S. K., Mohamad Taha, M., Murad, F. A., & Ma'rof, A. A. (2025). Online pornography consumption: Examining its role in sexual motivation, arousal, gratification, and problematic use. *Journal of Cognitive Sciences and Human Development, 11*(1), 110–126. DOI: 10.33736/jcshd.8829.2025

Kelly, L. (1988). *Surviving sexual violence*. University of Minnesota Press.

MacKinnon, C. A. (2011). Trafficking, prostitution, and inequality. *Harvard Civil Rights-Civil Liberties Law Review, 46*(2), 271–309.

Office of the High Commissioner for Human Rights. (2011). Guiding principles on business and human rights: Implementing the United Nations "Protect, Respect and Remedy" framework. United Nations., HR/PUB/11/04.

Office of the High Commissioner for Human Rights. (2012/2021). *The corporate responsibility to respect human rights: An interpretive guide.* United Nations. New Zealand Parliament. (2003). *Prostitution Reform Act 2003,* Public Act 2003 No 28.

Palermo Protocol. (2000). *Protocol to Prevent, Suppress and Punish Trafficking in Persons, Especially Women and Children, supplementing the United Nations Convention against Transnational Organized Crime,* Nov. 15, 2000, 2237 U.N.T.S. 319.

United Nations. (1949). *Convention for the suppression of the traffic in persons and of the exploitation of the prostitution of others,* Dec. 2, 1949, 96 U.N.T.S. 271.

United Nations Children's Fund. (2021). *Technical note on the implementation of the United Nations protocol on the provision of assistance to victims of sexual exploitation and abuse*. UNICEF.

United Nations General Assembly. (1995). *Beijing Declaration and Platform for Action* (A/CONF.177/20/Rev.1). United Nations.

United Nations General Assembly. (2005). Basic principles and guidelines on the right to a remedy and reparation for victims of gross violations of international human rights law and serious violations of international humanitarian law (Vol. A). United Nations., RES/60/147.

United Nations Office on Drugs and Crime. (2024). *Global report on trafficking in persons 2024*. United Nations.

United Nations Population Fund. (2024). *State of world population 2024: Interwoven lives, threads of hope*. UNFPA.

Vuolajärvi, N. (2019). Governing in the name of caring—The Nordic model of prostitution and its punitive consequences for migrants who sell sex. *Sexuality Research & Social Policy, 16*(2), 151–165. DOI: 10.1007/s13178-018-0338-9

Chapter 2
A Global Analysis of Sex Work, Morality, and Regulation

Angelo Kevin Brown
http://orcid.org/0000-0001-8167-5090
Arkansas State University, USA

ABSTRACT

Exchange of sexual services for payment has been a morally and legally difficult issue today that relates to issues of labor, sexuality, gender, public health, and criminal justice. The language used to describe this field is itself a moral, legal, and political issue. To understand this problem, it is necessary to understand core concepts of the debate, including the politics of terminology, the distinction between consensual work and criminal exploitation, and the relationship between agency and consent. The chapter will provide an evidence-based analysis of these issues, from the historical and ideological foundations of sex work to a comparative analysis of different legal frameworks through a global case study, and to proposing recommendations for addressing human rights and public health issues.

INTRODUCTION

It is important to define the Common words used to discuss the commercial sex industry, as they often have a serious political and cultural impact. The choice of words used can impact the framing of the discussion, determining policy goals and

DOI: 10.4018/979-8-3373-5841-3.ch002

public perception (Wagenaar & Altink, 2012). The main terms used are 'prostitution' and 'sex work', which give a framing of how this issue is viewed.

The term 'prostitution' is the historically established of the two terms and is derived from the Latin *prostituta*. Its use has been, for centuries, for moral condemnation and legal punishment. The act is often categorized under statutes on public morality and decency, making it a moral and criminal issue rather than a commercial transaction. For abolitionists and other groups, this term is often preferred because it carries this meaning of harm, objectification, and victimhood as it frames the practice as a form of violence against women that should be eradicated (Weatherall & Priestley, 2001). For those who engage in it, the word 'prostitute' is often seen as demeaning and stigmatizing, which reduces sex workers' agency, treating them as criminals (Verez, 2023).

The term 'sex work' was becoming more commonly used, especially starting in the late 1970s, with the support of activists like Carol Leigh, to reframe the selling of sexual services as a form of labor. Sex work is used for a wide range of activities, from prostitution to erotic dancing and pornography production. This use of language helped shift the conversation from morality to labor rights, enabling a focus on occupational health, safety, and economic self-determination (Tiefenbrun, 2002).

A global movement of sex worker-led organizations, were arguing that the term 'sex work' reinforces the idea that sexual labor is work and should receive labor protections as other types of work do (Yale Global Health Justice Partnership, 2020), and has since been used by the various international organizations like the World Health Organization (WHO), UNAIDS, and Amnesty International, with their evidence-based rights-focused approach to reducing harm and protecting vulnerable populations (Amnesty International, 2016; UNAIDS, 2024).

Another term used, 'intimate labor', provides a broader term that describes a range of historically feminized services, including health aides, housekeepers, and sex workers. This concept is used to place sex workers within a larger history of labor, challenging the hierarchy between "skilled" and "unskilled" or "legitimate" and "illegitimate" work.

The debate over these terms has created a definitional conflict for policy. Using the term 'prostitution' that is attached to a negative perception often leads to the policy goal of abolition, while accepting 'sex work' as a form of labor can lead to policies focused on rights, safety, and self-determination, such as decriminalization policies.

Sex work vs. Human trafficking

The conflation of consensual sex work with the crime of human trafficking has created more misunderstanding and misinformation about this issue. There is an important overlap between the two, but they should also be considered separate issues. Understanding the important differences is essential to creating effective policy.

Human trafficking is a crime under international laws such as the United Nations' Palermo Protocol and national laws such as the United States' Trafficking Victims Protection Act (TVPA) (United Nations, 2000). The definition of the crime often includes acts, such as recruitment and transportation, carried out by means of force, fraud, or coercion, for the purpose of exploitation (United Nations, 2000). Current data indicate that more people are trafficked into non-sex work, like agriculture and domestic labor (Yale Global Health Justice Partnership, 2020), and any recruitment of a minor into sex work can be considered illegal trafficking (Amnesty International, 2016).

Sex worker rights groups have generally defined sex work as the consensual financial exchange of sexual services between adults (Amnesty International, 2016). Consent and the absence of force are what separate it from sex trafficking. Human rights organizations such as Amnesty International have observed that the blurring of the two is a political strategy used by abolitionists and others to undermine other policy options (Amnesty International, 2016).

Framework Of Analysis

Consent, which is ongoing and can be rescinded at any time, requires legal frameworks for trafficking to rely on a clear definition of coercion that is not always clearly defined in national laws and policies (Amnesty International, 2016; Yale Global Health Justice Partnership, 2020). This definition does not account for the broader socioeconomic pressures that constrain choices, especially for those facing significant structural vulnerabilities that can shape a person's position in society, reducing their agency and increasing their risk. Factors such as poverty, systemic discrimination, the lack of healthcare, and past trauma are structural conditions that can greatly limit a person's practical choices (Ramirez, 2023). Criminalization, for example, is a structural factor that creates more risk for those in sex work, in which exploitation is often increased (Rhodes et al., 2011).

It is important to understand that people make a choice to engage in sex work as their best available option (Levitt & Venkatesh, 2007), and it recognizes that this choice is made in a context created by societal forces beyond their control (Moore et al., 2014). They can help change the focus from judging an individual's choice to addressing the structural conditions that enable policies to reduce the causes of exploitation by providing housing, healthcare, and economic opportunities.

HISTORICAL FOUNDATIONS

The debate about sex work has been impacted by social, moral, and ideological factors that have shaped the regulation of sexuality for hundreds of years, if not more. To understand current policy, it is important to understand how we got here. The response to prostitution has changed throughout history from practical management to moralistic prohibition. Legal frameworks have been a way for societies to address concerns about gender, religion, and social order through law.

In our knowledge of ancient cultures, prostitution was a recognized profession, such as in Greece, where both women and men engaged in prostitution as a line of work, and one of the Seven Sages of Greece, Solon, established categories of the workers that led to the establishment of regulated brothels in the sixth century BC. The state taxed prostitutes, treating the practice like any other job that made a profit as a taxable part of life. This continued throughout the Middle Ages, when prostitution was often regulated by law until around the 16th century, with the Protestant and the Catholic Counter-Reformation, and an increase in sexually transmitted diseases, led to a change in public policy.

The sexual morality that came as a part of these religious movements led to stricter controls to try to control sex work, leading to moral prohibition that did not actually stop the profession, just pushed it into the black market, especially in the 19th century in Protestant countries like the United States and the UK. The rise of the temperance movement helped create a powerful anti-prostitution lobby (Connelly, 2018). The reformers saw women in prostitution as "fallen women", and victims of social decay who should be rescued (Connelly, 2018), leading to placing these women into asylums, placing them in isolated households, and assigning them to forced labor.

Reformers conflated prostitution with slavery, often ignoring the activism of the women themselves, who were trying to define the value of their own labor through collective employment agencies by and for women. The abolitionist feminist stance that all sex workers should be treated as victims who need to be rescued is based on the rhetoric of the Magdalen Asylum reformers, who helped create the moral panic of the 19th century, leading to giving more government's control over women.

In the United States, the Mann Act of 1910, which outlawed the interstate transportation of women for "immoral purposes," is an example of the increase in the government's power, a law that was recently used to prosecute R. Kelly, Ghislaine Maxwell (partner of Jefery Epstein), and Diddy (Bouché et al., 2025). By 1915, states passed laws banning brothels and criminalizing the profits of prostitution, based on the prohibitionist model that is still common today throughout the country. Prostitution laws have changed to address issues of public order, to disease in the

16th century, to moral decay in the 19th century, and to public health fears like AIDS in the 1980s, and human trafficking is the focus in recent times (Connelly, 2018).

Feminist Views

This debate has been split within feminism, as feminists condemn forced prostitution and human trafficking, and that authentic consent is the foundation of legitimate sex, but the disagreement is often based on the issues around consensual sex work (Shrage, 2004). This has created two main issues, which are the solution and the moral justification. These two perspectives generally form the abolitionist feminist and the rights-based feminist perspectives, which help give the foundations for and against the differing legal models.

The abolitionist view is closely related to the radical feminism perspective (Shrage, 2004). This perspective sees prostitution and the sex industry as a base of patriarchy and an example of violence against women (Tiefenbrun, 2002). The sex industry is about male sexual entitlement and reduces women to being objects for men, which allows for the perpetuation of the sexual subservience of women (MacKinnon, 2007).

The idea of "consensual" sex work can be an issue for those who argue that, within the environment of systemic gender inequality and in patriarchal society, a woman's "choice" to be involved in prostitution is not really free (Lux, 2009). The power imbalances that are at play in the transaction, where a man with social and economic power is able to purchase sexual access to a woman's body, can be viewed as highly coercive, reducing the free choice of a woman (Shrage, 2004). The reasons given that women get involved in prostitution are closely connected to reasons women may feel pressured to stay in abusive relationships, such as economic dependence, psychological or even physical manipulation and control, and lack of realistic alternatives (Tiefenbrun, 2002). These various reasons can make the act of engaging in sex work not a normal commercial transaction but an act of sexual violence.

The policy conclusion taken from this understanding often leads to the abolition of the sex industry. This can lead to supporting the justification for various outcomes, including the Nordic Model, which attempts to abolish sex work by ending the demand through criminalizing the act of buying sex but decriminalizing the person selling it. The law is attempting to hold men accountable for the harms that are caused by sex work and send a moral message that women's bodies should not be purchased.

Rights-Based Policy

The rights-based perspective is an opposing view to that of the abolitionist. This perspective is generally associated with liberal or sex-positive feminism and asserts the importance of distinguishing between forced prostitution, such as in sex trafficking, and consensual sex work (Shrage, 2004). They claim that to deny this important distinction can weaken fundamental feminist values of bodily autonomy, self-determination, and sexual liberation (Tiefenbrun, 2002).

To understand this perspective and policy recommendations associated with it, it is important to view the work in the sex trade as a form of labor deserving the same rights and protections as any other legitimate and legal job (Shrage, 2004). Many of those who support this view have argued that the stigma, danger, and exploitation of sex workers are not intrinsic to the act of selling sex, but are the results of its criminalization and the social bias against female sexual expression. The problems that are often common in sex work, such as low pay, unsafe and unhealthy working conditions, and lack of medical and other benefits, are also common in other low-wage service industry jobs, which are often mostly done by women and marginalized groups of people (Shrage, 2004).

Criminalization is one of the main causes of harm according to this viewpoint, as it places the workers into dangerous environments by restricting their access to law enforcement and other types of legal protection, creating an environment where they can be easily abused, and exploitation can happen with a lack of legal consequence (Joulaei et al., 2021). The policy goal is to decrease the harm caused to the workers through the decriminalization of consensual adult sex work. This will take away the criminal penalties, allowing sex workers to work in the open, be able to unionize for safety, screen clients, report crimes to the police without being afraid of being arrested, creating significantly better working conditions, ensuring that they have standard labor laws (Brents & Hausbeck, 2005).

The prohibitionist model, which leads to complete criminalization, is the most restrictive approach to sex work. It makes all aspects of the occupation illegal, putting criminal penalties on the sex workers who sell their services, the buyers or pay for the services, and any third parties that are involved in the trade, such as advocates, solicitors, brothel owners, etc. (Joulaei et al., 2021). This policy framework is the prevalent framework in the US, except in a few counties in Nevada that allow sex work in a highly regulated format (Brents & Hausbeck, 2005; Yale Global Health Justice Partnership, 2020).

A justification for this model is based on morality, in which the advocates argue that prostitution is incompatible with human dignity, and that the state has a responsibility to stop it, no matter the cost (Joulaei et al., 2021). By criminalizing all parts of sex work, the law sends a message of public disapproval, with stated goals to discourage people from the sex trade in any way, hoping to reduce the overall demand, and to limit the ability for human sex trafficking (Joulaei et al., 2021).

This model has criticized by public health experts, criminologists, public policy researchers, sociologists, human rights organizations, and sex worker advocates, who reason and provide empirical evidence that it can lead to the most harmful outcomes. There is significant evidence that has shown that it does not usually lead to eliminating prostitution, but it just forces the industry to go underground, creating an environment where people are susceptible to violence and exploitation. Fear of arrest from law enforcement prevents sex workers from screening clients, working in safer indoor locations, or even reporting crime, including violence, to the police, which can provide perpetrators with freedom from legal punishment and increase the likelihood of people taking the law into their own hands (Joulaei et al., 2021). This negative relationship with law enforcement can even lead to police harassment and abuse (Yale Global Health Justice Partnership, 2020).

Criminalization can significantly undermine public health by creating barriers to accessing services and causing a huge tax cost through enforcement and the spread of disease. This can have even led to the possession of condoms being used by police as evidence of conspiracy, as it can show intent to commit a crime, discouraging their use and increasing the risk of HIV and other deadly sexually transmitted infections (STIs) (Joulaei et al., 2021). The threat of fines, arrests, trials, jail and prison sentences, and a criminal record creates a negative sequence creating potently lifelong difficulties for sex works to accessing housing, education, and legitimate employment, which can lead people to feel that the sex trade is their only viable option due to survival and economic necessity (Brents & Hausbeck, 2005; Yale Global Health Justice Partnership, 2020).

Legalization

The legalization model often involves a serious transformation from legal prohibition to state control and regulation, where the government permits sex work but creates a specific set of regulations and policies. These regulations usually include the licensing of brothels and individual workers, mandatory registration, health examinations, and the restriction of sex work to designated areas often called "tolerance zones" (Brents & Hausbeck, 2005; Joulaei et al., 2021). If sex work occurs outside of these state-sanctioned parameters, it remains criminalized. This model is implemented in Germany and in rural Nevada's legal brothels.

Supporters of legalization state that this practical approach recognizes the sex industry will continue to exist and that it is important to manage it to improve public health and order (Joulaei et al., 2021). Opening the industry could improve workers' health and safety by mandating STI testing and implementing regulated workplace standards. It offers the potential for sex workers to be recognized as formal employees with access to social security, health insurance, and legal recourse against non-paying clients, while generating tax revenue for the state (Joulaei et al., 2021).

The legalization model is criticized by sex worker rights organizations and human rights advocates. The major critique is that it creates an unequal system of small, privileged sex workers who are able to meet the licensing requirements, while the majority, especially marginalized groups like migrants, people of color, and others, are excluded from the illegal market that endangers them (Yale Global Health Justice Partnership, 2020). The regulations can be stigmatizing, such as requirements for workers to have a "prostitute" identification card, singling them out from others. This model can lead to state surveillance and policing, reducing their autonomy (NSWP, 2024). There are examples that legalized prostitution can lead to an increase in human trafficking, due to the open market creating more opportunities for traffickers to operate under the cover of a legal business (Joulaei et al., 2021). An important difference between decriminalization and legalization is the mode of control, as legalization is top-down and decriminalization is more bottom-up.

Neo-Abolitionism

The neo-abolitionist approach, such as the Nordic Model, is a progressive, gender-equality-focused alternative. This began in Sweden in 1999 and has been followed and modified by countries like Norway, Iceland, Canada, and France.

The Nordic Model has uneven criminalization as it decriminalizes the selling of sex, viewing the seller as a victim who should not be punished, but uses the criminal law on the demand side. The act of buying sex is illegal, and any third-party involvement, such as promoting or organizing prostitution (Joulaei et al., 2021). The goal is to abolish the sex industry by eliminating the demand side· The argument is that this approach holds the buyers accountable for the harm that is caused and thereby reduces the overall size of the sex trade and acts as a deterrent to human traffickers.

Despite its success, the Nordic Model is opposed by various human rights organizations, such as Amnesty International, which believe it is very harmful in practice (Vuolajärvi, 2022). Critics contend that by criminalizing clients, the model does not eliminate demand but simply drives it further underground (Vuolajärvi, 2022). This forces sex workers to take greater risks to protect their clients from arrest, such as rushing negotiations, forgoing screening practices, and moving to more isolated and dangerous locations (Vuolajärvi, 2022). This helps move the power to the consumer disproportionality, leaving the worker more subject to violence, abuse, and exploitation (NSWP, 2015). A broad law against "promoting" prostitution can be used to penalize sex workers for working together in the same apartment for safety, having a driver, or advertising online, thus in effect criminalizing the strategies they use to stay safe (NSWP, 2015). Critics argue that the Nordic Model does not remove the harms of criminalization; it simply relocates them onto the clients and the working environment, with terrible consequences for the safety and autonomy of sex workers.

Full Decriminalization

Full decriminalization is very different from the other policies that are common around the world. These models involve the complete removal of criminal penalties and laws for consensual adult sex work (Joulaei et al., 2021). In these countries, sex work is treated like any other form of labor, so the workers and companies that they operate under have to follow the general laws governing commerce, health and safety, and employment. It is important to understand that decriminalization is not the absence of all laws related to the sex industry because serious crimes such as sex trafficking, violence, rape, and the inclusion of minors remain illegal and should continue to be investigated and prosecuted (Brents & Hausbeck, 2005).

This policy has been supported by various international public health and human rights groups, including UNAIDS, Amnesty International, Human Rights Watch, and the Global Network of Sex Work Projects, among others (Amnesty International, 2016; UNAIDS, 2024; Yale Global Health Justice Partnership, 2020). This has been based on the empirical evaluations showing that decriminalization can be one of the most effective models for protecting the health, safety, and rights of sex workers.

Supporters of this have argued that if you remove the threat of arrest, decriminalization can greatly change the relationship between sex workers and the government, especially law enforcement, from hostile and fearful to trusting and cooperative (Brents & Hausbeck, 2005). It allows the sex workers to report violence and exploitation to the police with reduced fear of being accused of crimes and self-incriminating against themselves, which can result in their increased safety, while also leading to holding those who commit crimes accountable (Abel, 2014). This has the potential to create safer working practices, such as working collaboratively inside a secure building, screening clients thoroughly with background checks, and requiring condom use without the fear that condoms will be used as evidence of a crime and confiscated by the police (Joulaei et al., 2021). This has been shown to have significant public health benefits, where a study had estimated that decriminalizing sex work could potentially prevent between 33% and 46% of any new HIV infections among sex workers and their clients over a ten year time (Shannon et al., 2015). Decriminalization enables labor organizing and advocacy, helping workers fight for their rights and better working conditions (UNAIDS, 2024).

The primary arguments against decriminalization come from abolitionists, who make the argument that it can "normalize" an exploitative and harmful practice, especially for young women (Joulaei et al., 2021). They argue that it legitimizes and benefits third-party exploiters like pimps and could lead to an increase in the sex trade and an increase in human trafficking (Joulaei et al., 2021). As the case study of New Zealand has shown, the fully decriminalized jurisdiction contradicts these claims. This model, shows a significant disconnect between evidence-based policy and the political ideology driving most national laws on this issue.

GLOBAL CASE STUDIES

Moving from legal theory to real-world examples, the outcomes of different regulatory models in specific jurisdictions will be discussed. The political factors shape the real-world impact of any law. By examining countries that have applied the Nordic Model, decriminalization, and legalization, we can see why some have succeeded and others have failed, giving a detailed understanding of effective policy.

Nordic Model

The Nordic Model, which criminalizes the purchase of sex, is seen by its supporters as the most ethical and effective way to achieve gender equality. The evidence from countries that have implemented it shows mixed results.

The Swedish government, around the year 1999, began its policy change and became an important case for testing this model. The government and supporters of the law have seen it generally as a success. They utilize the data showing that street prostitution was significantly reduced in the years following the law's start, even when data showed that it was increasing in other Scandinavian areas like Denmark and Norway. A change in public attitudes, with the majority of Swedish people seeming to be in support of the ban, and fewer people have been reported purchasing sex. The data and reports published have found that the law has had a significant effect on reducing human sex trafficking as well.

This narrative has been somewhat debated by other research and qualitative data from sex workers themselves. Some have stated that the government's claims of success are based on incomplete data that focus on visible street-based sex work, which was only a small part of the industry (NSWP, 2015). They state that the law did not reduce the overall amount of sex work but moved it to less visible but also more dangerous locations (NSWP, 2015). Research based on interviews with sex workers in the region shows the law's negative and unintended consequences. A report published by the London School of Economics found that about 96% of sex workers surveyed stated the law made them feel less safe. They had reported that because clients often fear being arrested, negotiations are rushed, leading to screening being often abandoned, and workers are pressured into more secretive locations chosen by the client, giving the customer much more control over sex workers (Vuolajärvi, 2022; NSWP, 2015). The law has also shown to have increased stigma and led to increased police harassment, creating an environment of fear that prevents workers from seeking help (Vuolajärvi, 2022). A connection has been shown between the suppression of the sex market and an increase in reported domestic violence suggests a possible displacement of violence and aggression.

The examples and studies that came out in Norway and France show similar issues, such as the law in Norway had a measurable reduction in prostitution. The reports show that police may use the law as a pretext to have landlords evict sex workers, and trafficking victim numbers have fluctuated over the years (NSWP, 2015).

In France, the outcome of the 2016 law was used to help reduce the demand by criminalizing the people who made the purchase, but not the sex workers (Giametta & BAIL, 2023). The law was believed to make the French sex workers more exposed to violence and less able to control which customers used protection. The supporters of the policy often dismissed these claims, blaming it on the poor implementation rather than a flaw in the model itself, which there was a lack of data on the violence due to many of them not filing official reports. The evidence for the Nordic Model's success is still being debated and understood. The difference between the official government data reports that claim success based on systems of measurements, such as street prostitution levels and qualitative research from the communities involved, shows signs of a significant increase in harm.

New Zealand Experiment

New Zealand began a policy change as well in 2003, becoming the first country to decriminalize sex work completely (Abel, 2014). The Prostitution Reform Act (PRA) was a law that was created with the help of the New Zealand Prostitutes' Collective (NZPC), a sex worker-led organization. The Act's purpose was to decriminalize prostitution, leading to the protection of the human rights of sex workers, by protecting and supporting their health and safety.

The outcomes have been generally positive from various reports and data measurements, and the model is now used as a case example by various support and advocacy groups. The 2008 Prostitution Law Review Committee (PLRC) report found that the fearful predictions of skeptics did not come true (Prostitution Law Review Committee, 2008), as the majority of the studies found that decriminalization did not lead to a larger sex work market (Abel, 2014).

The result of decriminalization has led to examples of improved sex workers' relationships with the police and other government agencies (Abel, 2014), as they could work without the fear of arrest. Workers were more willing and able to report cases of crime and violence, leading to the arrest and prosecution of more of the offenders (Prostitution Law Review Committee, 2008). Many sex workers felt the law had reinforced their rights and allowed them to refuse problematic clients and not have to go to unsafe locations (Abel, 2014). The data has shown a lack of an increase in human trafficking after the years following the law's implementation, doing the opposite of what many critics had thought would happen.

The New Zealand model has various limitations to point out. There might be various adverse side effects due to the government's reliance on the NZPC for information, according to some critics (Family First New Zealand, 2023). They have stated that the official data on the industry's size is inaccurate, and that violence continues to remain widespread but just unreported, and the exploitation by those who manage the workers is infrequently investigated, reported, and prosecuted, due to issues like the mandated brothel inspections being rarely done (Family First New Zealand, 2023).

Another problem that has been highlighted in the research was the government's treatment of migrant workers. The PRA's protections do not have the same impact on individuals on visas, who were limited from engaging in sex work. This has led to a criminalized group of migrant sex workers who are not able to access the law's protections and continue to face the threat of deportation if they report any crimes committed against them as sex workers. This progressive legal policy, without reform, has led to the benefits not being distributed equally. The effectiveness of the New Zealand policy also seems to be closely supported by various local factors, especially due to the country's strong social safety net, including universal healthcare, education, and the NZPC's role in providing various services, advocating, and their ability to build trust with the right authorities. This suggests that you cannot just export the laws and policies of the PRA to a different nation; if that nation does not have similar social support, it may not produce the same positive outcomes.

Legalization: Germany and Nevada

The legalization policies, which allow sex work within a country's policy of licensing does not always create the positive outcomes like New Zealand. The case studies of Germany and Nevada show how this approach can fail to have the same positive results as its promises of safety, often creating unintended issues and problems.

After Germany legalized prostitution in 2002 with the Prostitution Act, attempting to destigmatize the trade and improve the work conditions of sex workers by giving them access to be able to have legal contracts, health insurance, and social security benefits. There have been many who report the German experiment as a failure, using it to show that legalization in a nation with open borders can create an increase in sex trafficking (Kraus, 2018). Many have reported that the law created an expansion of the sex market, causing a significant price war leading to brothels using exploitative flat-rate deals, where the clients were able to pay a single fee for unrestricted access to women (Trauma and Prostitution, 2018), which reports show this was degrading to the sex workers and have led to a drop in the quality of working conditions and health outcomes (Trauma and Prostitution, 2018). There was also some evidence that many of the sex workers had not actually registered for social security or health benefits, this was especially reported for migrant women, remain in an unregulated state similar to before the law was implemented. Another complaint was that the law has reduced the power of police to enforce and stop sex trafficking within the legal brothel system due to not knowing which people were forced and which were there voluntarily (Trauma and Prostitution, 2018).

Supporters of legalization believe that the adverse outcomes are not a direct result of legalization itself, but of poor implementation, external market factors, and corruption. When the state failed to properly follow through with the essential social outreach to help workers access benefits, the problems were made even worse by the significant amount of migration of poor women from countries from various areas, but especially Eastern Europe (Kraus, 2018). Later in 2017, the German government passed the Prostitute Protection Act, which required sex workers have mandatory registration and health counseling. There was evidence that this reform just gave more government control and increased the stigma without fixing the underlying economic issues that were leading to the abuses.

Nevada offers a different style of legalization, where sex work is permitted only in licensed brothels within a few counties and is still illegal everywhere else, most notably in the major urban areas of the largest cities, Las Vegas and Reno. The legal system primarily serves cisgender women and has been shown to discriminate against male and transgender workers. Other issues that have been reported include the regulations being inconsistently applied across counties, and workers face exploitative contracts and high fees charged by brothel owners. Some have even reported that Nevada's reputation as a sex tourism area leads to increased human trafficking throughout the state, and the brothels create a cover of legitimacy for the illegal operations (Awaken, 2019). Recent lawsuits filed on behalf of women who worked in legal brothels have shown that some of the brothels have conditions of debt bondage, illegally restricted movement, and financial exploitation within these brothels. While the system is intended to be highly regulated, with mandatory STI testing on a regular basis and mandatory condom use. This system has been shown to create a much safer, more controlled environment compared to the black-market workers. A few measurable outcomes for workers in legal brothels experience significantly less violence and have much lower STI rates than those in the illegal black markets (Brents & Hausbeck, 2005).

In Germany and Nevada, legalization has led to an unequal class system where only a small section of the sex industry functions legally, but the most marginalized workers, such as migrants, remain working in the black market, still at high risk for exploitation and abuse. This is an example that others should learn from that just changing the legal status of sex work within a jurisdiction without addressing the underlying issues of the workers can be an ineffective policy.

Structural Vulnerability

Sex work in the developing world is often handled very differently from in developed nations, but is also connected in many ways. Tourists from the developing world are known to travel to places in the developing world, like Thailand, Colombia, Costa Rica, the Philippines, and many other regions, to engage in the sex industry. While the main driver for those to become involved in sex work in many of the poorer nations is financial incentives, scholars have described that differences between sex work and slavery are often very hard to differentiate for many in the "Third World" (Kempadoo, 1999). Poverty in regions like the favelas of Brazil, being improved, can often lead you to no legal representation, and you can be arrested by law enforcement for just about any reason, and lose your freedom, which is especially true for sex workers.

The gangs and organized criminal groups here and in many other nations with high levels of government corruption are able to control many of the streets and areas where sex work is prevalent (Stahlberg, 2022). These gangs offer young girls "protection," which they often use to control them and pressure them into sex work.

The laws themselves can be arguably less important than the socioeconomic factors that influence the sex industry. A structural vulnerability perspective provides an outsider a way to understand the paths into sex work and the conditions that can control those within it, by moving the focus from individual choice to the systemic inequalities, such as poverty, discrimination, trauma, and lack of opportunity, that create the circumstances where people are more likely to consider selling sexual services for a living. This is why there are many examples to show that criminalization does not solve these problems but often exacerbates them.

The decision to enter sex work is based on economic factors, structural disadvantages, and personal histories of trauma that influence it. A common reason for entering sex work is economic need. It can be a response to poverty, debt, unemployment, or the inability to earn a living wage in other available low-wage sectors (Levitt & Venkatesh, 2007). Sex work can pay four times what an individual might earn in a comparable legal job, making it an option for financial survival (Levitt & Venkatesh, 2007). The lack of economic alternatives is a considerable factor leading to entry in the industry (Levitt & Venkatesh, 2007).

These economic factors are made worse by overlapping structural disadvantages. There is an overrepresentation of people from marginalized communities within the sex industry. In the United States and Canada, this includes Black and Indigenous people, Latinx individuals, and Lesbian, Gay, Bisexual, Transgender, and Queer (LGBTQ+) people, especially transgender women in various nations (Yale Global Health Justice Partnership, 2020; Vuolajärvi, 2022). These groups face systemic discrimination in housing, employment, and education, which limits their legitimate options and increases their risk. Sex work can become a way of survival when threatened by hate, such as racism, transphobia, and homophobia that limit them from the formal economy (Yale Global Health Justice Partnership, 2020).

A link has been found between a history of trauma, especially abuse, and entry into sex work. Data on sex workers has found high rates of adverse childhood experiences, most notably childhood sexual abuse (Footer et al., 2020). For a significant portion of the population, entry into the sex trade is often part of a history of vulnerability and victimization, especially for minors. Data on women who first became involved in sex work before the age of 18 were significantly more likely to report having been coerced or forced into it, often physically or by the threat of physical violence. Those who enter before the age of 18 also experience increased risk of long-term homelessness, food insecurity, and HIV infection compared to those who enter later in life (Footer et al., 2020).

This challenges the belief that all these people have a real choice to enter the industry. But a list of factors severely limits the realistic decisions they can make. An effective policy response should address the root causes that make people consider entering the industry. An effective policy would generally include housing policy, anti-poverty programs, anti-discrimination law, and accessible mental and physical healthcare.

Laws Exacerbating the Issue

Punitive legal frameworks can create structural factors that increase the vulnerabilities that lead many to become involved in sex work. Criminalization can cause harm that disproportionately affects the most marginalized and makes it harder for people to survive, creating a negative cycle of criminalization. An arrest for sex work can result in a criminal record and become a lifelong obstacle to getting legal employment, housing, financial aid for education, and even child custody (Brents & Hausbeck, 2005). This exclusion from the legal economy can make it even more difficult for someone to leave the sex trade.

Policing under these punitive models can create a form of structural violence and fear among sex workers (Rhodes et al., 2011). The threat of police harassment or arrest causes workers to become even more isolated, often in dangerous environments where they are at increased likelihood of victimization, such as assault, rape, and robbery, and limits their social support, for example, a sex worker who is robbed or beaten by a client will be unlikely to report the crime due to risking their own arrest (Yale Global Health Justice Partnership, 2020). This creates conditions where violent perpetrators are not punished due to a hostile relationship with law enforcement, which in some cases includes abuse of sex workers by police officers themselves (Joulaei et al., 2021). One sex scandal out of the Oakland Police Department led to a million-dollar settlement after officers were having sex and abusing a teenage sex worker, where the police would tip her off about prostitution stings.

This legal vulnerability also has a serious impact on internet sex workers. The Fight Online Sex Trafficking Act (FOSTA) and Stop Enabling Sex Traffickers Act (SESTA) in the United States have been reported to have negative impacts on sex workers and their safety (Ramirez, 2023). These policies hold those companies and people involved liable for user-generated content that could be seen as "promoting or facilitating" prostitution, leading to major platforms shutting down websites that sex workers had used to advertise, screen clients for safety risks, and share information with each other about clients and areas that might be dangerous. This led to a displacement of workers from the safety of the online environment back to the streets, reducing their ability to control their clients and environments. This was especially damaging to those sex workers who were in the lower economic classes, where they do not have access to their own secure rooms, but often were reliant on their clients' locations.

Regulation of Sexuality

The legal regulations governing sex work are often not positively impactful on public safety. The history and language of these laws show that they are more for controlling forms of sexual expression that challenge traditional social norms. The moral basis of anti-prostitution law is often explicit in the language of the law, for example, in North Carolina, prostitution statutes are codified under the "Offenses Against Public Morality and Decency". This shows the reason for the law is based on a moral judgment, showing sex work as a threat to society's view of public decency, family values, and traditional sexual understanding.

The roots of these laws are important to consider and are generally religiously based. The 1919 North Carolina statute, for example, criminalized "sexual intercourse for hire" but also "indiscriminate sexual intercourse *without* hire" (Verez, 2023). The second part shows a broader legislative goal of criminalizing sexuality itself when it is not for procreative norms, especially against gay couples. The stigma of sex work is a consequence of the legislation as moral views toward nonprocreative sex (Verez, 2023).

This has helped create arbitrary and inconsistent legal distinctions for sex workers, and the various ways the government can try to control society from what they consider immoral, while protecting other multi-billion-dollar forms of commercial sex work, such as pornography. This is an example showing that the law is based on a limited perspective of intimacy issues that sanctions activities outside of state-sanctioned relationships, such as marriage. This framework to view criminal law is used for enforcing moral beliefs of sexual expression, punishing those who engage in acts of sexuality that are commercial, as it is a threat to the norm of sex within a marital partnership. The use of criminal law to enforce a particular sexual morality has been highly debated, even with libertarian and some conservative arguments overlapping with those of sex worker rights, because they both criticize the government's interference in the private lives of consenting adults.

The libertarian perspective is often concerned that the criminalization of prostitution is a case of the government overstepping its reach. From this perspective, if an activity is consensual between adults and causes no direct harm to others, it should, in general, be outside the government's control. This view of government is based on individual freedom and choice. For advocates who want less government intervention in areas like gun ownership and the economy, while supporting the use of state power to regulate private sexual choices, many have argued that there is a lack of logical consistency.

The legal conflict lies between those who believe the state's interest is in upholding an ever-changing idea of 'public morality' and those who believe that laws should increase public safety and reduce harm, because the two cannot go together. The criminalization of sex work contributes to increased violence, higher rates of disease, police abuse, and economic disadvantage. Arguments for decriminalization are usually based on causing less harm and using a harm-reduction approach. The history of morality-based laws, such as the prohibition of alcohol and cannabis, has shown that laws can have significant negative consequences and still be supported by people's moral and religious values.

RECOMMENDATIONS FOR AN EFFECTIVE RIGHTS-BASED POLICY

The global regulation of sex work shows the impact of ideology on law, even if it is causing significant levels of measurable harm, despite having policies that can reduce harm and support human rights and public health. A comparative analysis of legal frameworks for sex work shows which can help reduce the harms. The failures of prohibition provide lots of data that criminalization can be a damaging model due to creating an intimidating relationship with the government, pressuring sex workers into the black market, encouraging violence, blocking access to healthcare, enabling police abuse, and creating a cycle of poverty and incarceration, which significant impact on marginalized communities (Joulaei et al., 2021).

The issue that has come out of partial criminalization, such as with the Nordic Model, which has been seen as a progressive alternative, continues many of the main harms of complete criminalization due to the law enforcement focus on the sex trade, targeting clients and third parties, it has been shown that this continues to push the workers underground, increasing risks for them and their clients. It reduces their ability to use safety strategies (Vuolajärvi, 2022), and does not remove many of the harms of criminalization; it just transfers them to other areas, with the workers having to deal with the cost in their safety and freedom. The effectiveness this has on reducing the sex trade has not been successfully found in many current forms that have been evaluated.

It is important to understand the negative risks and examples of legalization, as well as this has, its own issues, depending on how it is carried out. Legalization has produced negative findings in places like Germany and in areas of Nevada, USA. While it led to improved conditions and legal protections for those sex workers who have been able to follow its strict requirements, it has also seemed to create a two-tiered system (NSWP, 2024). This caused an underclass of workers (often marginalized and migrant) in an illegal market, who continue to be a target of law enforcement, and lack the benefits that the other sex workers get. Legalization has also been shown to lead to other forms of state-sanctioned control and exploitation, as critics have argued that these top-down regulation strategies are not a perfect solution for everyone either, but might have better outcomes than criminalization.

Full decriminalization, as groups like UNAIDS and Amnesty International have supported, for its success in improving many aspects of public safety, including the health, safety, and rights of sex workers (Amnesty International, 2016; UNAIDS, 2024). The New Zealand case study has shown the great benefits that this approach may offer. It has led to improved police relations, increased reporting of violence from victims within the industry, and improved worker rights. It has not resulted in a serious increase in the industry or human trafficking, as many had worried about, and has been able to also improved the health of clients since less disease is spread (Abel, 2014). The New Zealand experience shows the key requirements for its success, including a social safety net that the nation has had for its citizens for many years, strong anti-discrimination laws, and the establishment of a well-funded, independent, sex worker-led organization to provide services for their workers and be an advocate for them with the government (Prostitution Law Review Committee, 2008).

POLICY RECOMMENDATIONS FOR A HARM-REDUCTION

An effective policy for future governments considering a harm reduction strategy should move away from practices of moral judgment and criminal punishment toward a framework that considers the importance of labor rights and public health of sex workers. It is clear through recorded history that the sex industry will exist at similar levels whether you criminalize it or not. It is important that our governments help lead to a society with less harm, even if people disagree morally with the act of selling sex, as many of us do because of our religious or ideological beliefs, and would prefer that not be an option people decide to choose for their livelihood. The following policy recommendations offer an evidence-based approach to creating a safer society and provide more treatment for people by their governments.

Governments should consider modifying their laws and penalties that criminalize the consensual exchange of sexual services between consenting adults, including the sellers, buyers, and even the third parties, such as businesses that ensure the workers' safety, such as renting locations, acting as security, facilitating online systems, and more. Sex work should be regulated by the same laws as other forms of labor through effective health and safety regulations. This also aligns with many of the general recommendations of international human rights and public health organizations that have studied the issue (Amnesty International, 2016; UNAIDS, 2024).

The decriminalization of consensual activities should be implemented with a focus on resources for fighting sexual exploitation of minors and others who are trafficked against their free will. Law enforcement resources should be redirected from policing consensual sex work to investigating and prosecuting forms of violence, abuse, fraud, and human trafficking. Laws against commercial sex work involving minors and others who cannot consent must be strictly enforced. A decriminalized environment, where workers can safely and easily report crimes to the police, is an effective strategy for identifying and combating these abuses.

For this to be effective, there must be a recognition that sex work is connected to broader social and economic policy that provides resources to those in need. The most effective way to reduce exploitation and ensure that entry into sex work is a free choice is to fix the root causes that allow people to be exploited. The public investment in access to healthcare, including non-judgmental mental health services and substance use treatment are essential for this. Affordable housing programs and policies to support food security have also been shown to be very important. Increasing access to higher education and job training that allows more people to have economic opportunities that pay a living wage can also address the root causes of human trafficking and exploitation (Levitt & Venkatesh, 2007).

To have an effective policy, governments should include experts from organizations that study or advocate for sex workers, as they will have insider perspectives on how laws might have adverse effects, and ongoing policy evaluations should be supported. Funding also needs to be given to support independent organizations that can provide services to sex workers, such as the successful model of the New Zealand Prostitutes' Collective (Prostitution Law Review Committee, 2008).

Legal reform should also consider migrant workers. Immigration laws should consider migrants as well, so that they are not afraid that their participation would lead to deportation, and that migrant workers have labor rights similar to those of citizens. This is important to prevent the issues that others have caused, like the creation of an unequal class system where the migrants, who often are disproportionately involved in the sex industry, remain criminalized and exploitable.

The evidence-based strategy is a potentially practical approach to sex work that requires many governments to move away from criminalization. Using this framework that decriminalizes the activity while still prosecuting and enforcing exploitation, and that reduces the inequality that limits choices and endangers the lives of those in the industry.

REFERENCES

Abel, G. M. (2014). A decade of decriminalization: Sex work 'down under'but not underground. *Criminology & Criminal Justice, 14*(5), 580–592. DOI: 10.1177/1748895814523024

Amnesty International. (2016). *Policy on State Obligations to Respect.* Protect and Fulfil the Human Rights of Sex Workers.

Awaken. (2019). *Here's why Nevada is not safe for women.*

Bouché, V., Robichau, R. W., Tipton, T., Metcalf, M., & Clark, T. A. (2025). Human Trafficking Policy Evolution: Analyzing Punctuated Diffusion Across Two Decades. *Journal of Human Trafficking*, 1–16. DOI: 10.1080/23322705.2025.2529713

Brents, B. G., & Hausbeck, K. (2005). Violence and legalized brothel prostitution in Nevada: Examining safety, risk, and prostitution policy. *Journal of Interpersonal Violence, 20*(3), 270–295. DOI: 10.1177/0886260504270333 PMID: 15684138

Connelly, M. T. (2018). *The response to prostitution in the progressive era.* UNC Press Books.

Family First New Zealand. (2023). *Prostitution law review: Benefits exaggerated, shortcomings ignored, denied or hidden.*

Footer, K. H., White, R. H., Park, J. N., Decker, M. R., Lutnick, A., & Sherman, S. G. (2020). Entry to sex trade and long-term vulnerabilities of female sex workers who enter the sex trade before the age of eighteen. *Journal of Urban Health, 97*(3), 406–417. DOI: 10.1007/s11524-019-00410-z PMID: 32034655

Giametta, C., & Bail, H. L. (2023). The national and moral borders of the 2016 French law on sex work: An analysis of the 'prostitution exit programme'. *Critical Social Policy, 43*(2), 214–233. DOI: 10.1177/02610183221101167

Joulaei, H., Zarei, N., Khorsandian, M., & Keshavarzian, A. (2021). Legalization, Decriminalization or Criminalization; Could We Introduce a Global Prescription for Prostitution (Sex Work). *International Journal of High Risk Behaviors & Addiction, 10*(3), e106741. DOI: 10.5812/ijhrba.106741

Kempadoo, K. (1999). Slavery or work? Reconceptualizing third world prostitution. *Positions, 7*(1), 225–237. DOI: 10.1215/10679847-7-1-225

Kraus, I. (2018). The German Model, 17 years after the liberalization of prostitution. *Speech by Dr. Ingeborg Kraus at the Italian parliament in Rom, 28*, 2018.

Levitt, S. D., & Venkatesh, S. A. (2007). *An empirical analysis of street-level prostitution* (pp. 1-29). University of Chicago working paper–B.

Lux, K. (2009). Work, violence, or both? Framing the sex trade and setting an agenda for justice. In *Advocates' Forum, 2009.*

MacKinnon, C. A. (2007). *Women's lives, men's laws.* Harvard University Press.

Moore, L., Chersich, M. F., Steen, R., Reza-Paul, S., Dhana, A., Vuylsteke, B., Lafort, Y., & Scorgie, F. (2014). Community empowerment and involvement of female sex workers in targeted sexual and reproductive health interventions in Africa: A systematic review. *Globalization and Health, 10*(1), 47. DOI: 10.1186/1744-8603-10-47 PMID: 24916108

NSWP. (2015). *Community Guide.* The Real Impact of the Swedish Model on Sex Workers.

NSWP. (2024). *Decriminalisation vs. legalization: Understanding Key Differences in Sex Work Legislation.*

Prostitution Law Review Committee. (2008). *Report of the Prostitution Law Review Committee on the operation of the Prostitution Reform Act 2003* (Vol. 121). New Zealand Ministry of Justice.

Ramirez, T. (2023). *Sex worker criminalization in the United States: A landscape analysis of the criminalization health effects on the sex worker population in the United States.* AIDS United.

Rhodes, T., Wagner, K., Strathdee, S. A., Shannon, K., Davidson, P., & Bourgois, P. (2011). Structural violence and structural vulnerability within the risk environment: theoretical and methodological perspectives for a social epidemiology of HIV risk among injection drug users and sex workers. In *Rethinking social epidemiology: Towards a science of change* (pp. 205–230). Springer Netherlands.

Shannon, K., Strathdee, S. A., Goldenberg, S. M., Duff, P., Mwangi, P., Rusakova, M., Reza-Paul, S., Lau, J., Deering, K., Pickles, M. R., & Boily, M. C. (2015). Global epidemiology of HIV among female sex workers: Influence of structural determinants. *Lancet, 385*(9962), 55–71. DOI: 10.1016/S0140-6736(14)60931-4 PMID: 25059947

Shrage, L. (2004). Feminist perspectives on sex markets.

Stahlberg, S. G. (2022). From prison gangs to transnational mafia: The expansion of organized crime in Brazil. *Trends in Organized Crime, 25*(4), 443–465. DOI: 10.1007/s12117-022-09453-2

Tiefenbrun, S. (2002). The saga of Susannah-A US remedy for sex trafficking in women: The Victims of Trafficking and Violence Protection Act of 2000. *Utah L. Rev.*, 107.

Trauma and Prostitution. (2018). *The German Model: 17 years after the legalization of prostitution.*

UNAIDS. (2024). *HIV and sex work—Human rights fact sheet series 2024.*

United Nations. (2000). Protocol to prevent, suppress and punish trafficking in persons, especially women and children, supplementing the United Nations convention against transnational organized crime. In Vienna: United Nations Office on Drugs and Crime, United Nations Convention against Transnational Organized Crime and the Protocols Thereto.

Verez, M. (2023). An Ever-Narrowing Divide: Morality and Decriminalizing Sex Work in North Carolina. *NCCRL Rev.*, *4*, 455.

Vuolajärvi, N. (2022). Criminalising the sex buyer: experiences from the Nordic region.

Wagenaar, H., & Altink, S. (2012). Prostitution as morality politics or why it is exceedingly difficult to design and sustain effective prostitution policy. *Sexuality Research & Social Policy*, *9*(3), 279–292. DOI: 10.1007/s13178-012-0095-0

Weatherall, A., & Priestley, A. (2001). A feminist discourse analysis of sexwork'. *Feminism & Psychology*, *11*(3), 323–340. DOI: 10.1177/0959353501011003005

Yale Global Health Justice Partnership. (2020). *Sex work vs. trafficking: How They are different and why it matters.* Yale Law School.

Chapter 3
Contested Bodies, Contested Definitions:
Voluntary Prostitution and the Limits of Legal Catergorization

Razina Ahmed
http://orcid.org/0000-0003-4839-1445
Presidency University, Bengaluru, India

ABSTRACT

This chapter is a critique of definitional shortcomings of voluntary prostitution in international and domestic law, and more specifically, the conflation of coercion and consent. The terminology used in law and policy is too broad or moral, labelling all types of prostitution as exploitative or equivalent to trafficking. Such conflation, and ignoring the heterogeneity of the sex workers' experience, also obliterates the fact of consensual, voluntary entry into the profession. As a result, voluntary sex work—particularly those in vulnerable groups—are rendered outside of legal status, social protection, and labor rights. The chapter analyzes important documents like the 1949 UN Convention, CEDAW, the Palermo Protocol, and India's Immoral Traffic (Prevention) Act, utilizing feminist legal theory, intersectionality, and comparative legal analysis. It reveals how these documents' ambiguous or moralistic language allows states to regulate sex work without sufficiently protecting their rights.The chapter argues that prostitution should be reimagined in law.

INTRODUCTION

Legal and policy systems have long grappled with how to define prostitution. Norms clash between countries, too; the 1949 U.N. Trafficking Convention treated

DOI: 10.4018/979-8-3373-5841-3.ch003

all acts of prostitution as trafficking; but the 2000 U.N. Palermo Protocol defined trafficking in terms that focus on "abuse, violence and exploitation," including explicitly "the prostitution of others" as one form of exploitation. As La Strada International has observed, this phrasing was a diplomatic attempt between an abolitionist and a labor-rights approach. In practice, the Protocol's ambiguous language – linking trafficking to prostitution – has allowed widely divergent interpretations, leaving countries free to treat prostitution either as inherently exploitative or as a form of work. And these high-altitude definitions have concrete implications when it comes to how and whether consensual sex work is viewed as criminal, tolerated or protected by the domestic law.

There are also perverse legal effects to the definitional conundrum of prostitution at a national level. For instance, in India, the legislation, simultaneously tolerates prostitution under certain circumstances and bans its manifestations. An analysis. observes, "Sex work is not illegal in India. However, various related activities, such as operating brothels, soliciting in public and living on earnings from prostitution are criminalized and penalized under [the Immoral Trafficking (Prevention) Act]". This dual approach — of legalizing individual sex work while banning almost all ways of organizing it — is confusing and complicated. In reality it translates into the routine criminalization of hundreds, even thousands, of voluntary sex workers. In fact, an estimated 14,000 Indian female sex workers are arrested each year under the ITPA even though sex work itself is legal. Because the vague law is such a sweeping threat, these prosecutions often rest on flimsy "evidence" (such as possessing condoms or providing money to colleagues), punishing vital health-and safety practices. he result is that consensual adult prostitution becomes a de facto crime in many situations, even though the statutes ostensibly target only trafficking and exploitation.

Recent jurisprudence has started to challenge this ambiguity. In Budhadev Karmaskar v. West Bengal, the Indian Supreme Court has explicitly stated that sex workers have a constitutional "right to a life of dignity" within the meaning of Article 21. A three-Judge bench pronounced sex work to be a profession like any other and prostitutes entitled "to equal protection of the law" if they are adults, operating with consent. The Court cautioned police that if consent is present, officials "should not interfere or take any criminal action". And importantly, it clarified that "sex worker or prostitution is not illegal in India though its associated activities are offences". This ruling represents a significant departure: It positions sex workers' agency and dignity as the fulcrum, around which legal reasoning must revolve. Simultaneously, the Court ordered that normal protections (e.g., carrying condoms or practicing self-defense) should not be used as evidence of criminal behavior. As a whole, the new judgment of the apex court does not amount to automatic criminalisation of consensual sex work and it protects voluntary workers against police harassment (Chowdhury, 2022).

These are the developments that echo key feminist critiques. A number of scholars have challenged the simplistic and damaging nature of the sharp "voluntary vs. forced" dichotomy central to such laws. Peng (2009), for instance, shows how campaigns that insist on proving sex workers' lack of agency can end up "reinforc[ing] the stigma on 'voluntary' prostitutes". Peng introduces the notion of contingent consent: that a woman's agreement to sell sex may be conditioned on poverty, gender inequality or deception, in which case consent can never be anything other than "vague, contingent and relative". She maintains that feminist and sex-worker movements should reject the inflexible victim/agent dichotomy. She argues that feminist and sex-worker movements should abandon the rigid victim/agent binary. Instead of debating whether women "truly" consent, activists should focus on the working conditions of sex workers (health, safety, rights, wages) to protect against abuse. This iteration paints a picture of the labor of those who resist being treated as an object ("the modified whore stigma") and suggests that all sex workers – regardless if they are coerced or not – would be better off with job protections and social safety nets. Peng's account shows how doubling down on a clean voluntary forced dichotomy is dehumanizing to women who freely choose sex work and obfuscating, and not just polishing or stabilizing, the actual, pressing harm at issue.

The impact of these binary legal categories is far-reaching. Sex workers disappear between the cracks when law and policy require that they be one thing or another. Meanwhile, those who assert on their agency (voluntary sex workers) may be dismissed as complicit or even criminal and left with minimal access to health services and legal rights. In India, for instance, hundreds of consenting members of the work force are regularly rounded up by the police — their condom possession taken as a sign of criminal activity. Victims can also be picked up rescued, arrested or moved. Research on anti-trafficking interventions indicates that in fact most "rescues" ensnare women in abusive state custody. One survey finds that an alarming 8 in 10 women taken into custody as presumed victims were detained "against [their] will" and many experienced trauma and isolation rather than favors. Victims themselves inform researchers that they are afraid to accept the category "trafficking victim," partly because it robs them of autonomy and dignity. As one advocate put it plainly, "The real problem here is not trafficking, but anti-trafficking" (Najar, 2021). The rigid binaries also mean that sex workers can be punished when they claim agency and then re-victimized again when they are saved.

This chapter explores these issues in depth. Law's conflicting portraits of the sex worker — as incapable victim or empowered professional — influencing policy results is explored. By genealogically tracing critical cases (such as Budhadev Karmaskar), global standards (the Palermo Protocol), and feminist criticisms (Peng's contingent consent), it is established how the voluntary/forced victim/agent frameworks push aside the lived experience of sex work. It is contended that these binaries fail at both — they deny agency and dignity to many sex workers, while blinding the law to new forms of exploitation. A more nuanced legal regime would acknowledge the range of contexts in which people sell sex while affirming everyone's rights to safety, health and autonomy and criminalizing only bona fide exploitation.

FEMINIST JURISPRUDENCE: PARADIGMS AND CRITIQUES

Feminist legal scholars have long been at odds when it comes to prostitution and sex work. On one side are radical feminists who see prostitution as inherently exploitative and a recalcitrant form of male violence against women. For instance, Serughetti (2013) claims that "radical feminist perspectives represent prostitution as the cornerstone of women's sexual exploitation, implying a strong call to eradicate sexual commerce in any form". These writers (MacKinnon, 1989; Barry, 1997) contend that sex industry participation amounts to a form of economic and social violence against women as polities whereby they are forced into the sex trade by social and economic inequalities (poverty, racism, patriarchy). Liberal (or "sex-positive") feminists, by contrast, highlight women's autonomy and choice. They advocate for the idea that consensual adult sex work can be a valid form of labor, and that women ought to have control over how they want to use their own bodies. In this way of thinking, prostitution is not inherently violent but work that can be regulated or decriminalized. That is why liberals call for policies that respect the rights and agency of sex workers, not punish or imprison them. In short, for the radical camp prostitution is a system of domination to be ended; liberal camp it's one of personal agency and labor rights to be protected.

These countervailing paradigms also conceptualize consent and agency in profoundly different ways. Radical feminists usually see the concept of "free consent" in prostitution as a chimera. If a woman exchanges sex for survival, radicals argue, then her "consent" is effectively coerced by the circumstances. Catherine MacKinnon, for example, has argued that when sex is performed under conditions of survival or economic compulsion it is "sex… compelled by the need to survive" and as such constitutes a transaction equivalent in law to sex discrimination or harassment. In this model, the women in prostitution are considered "victims" of sexual abuse regardless of their apparent consent. Liberal feminists, in contrast, emphasize consent as key. Consenting adults, they say, have a moral and legal right to engage in sex work the way they do any other consensual employment. Serughetti (2013) brings into focus this symbolic divide: "the notion of 'women's consent' is crucial in both perspectives, being rejected as impossible or inexistent by [radical feminists] who reduce all sexual commerce to forced prostitution, and emphasized as a key discriminant by [liberal feminists] distinguishing voluntary sex work from trafficking and forced prostitution". In practice, the liberal position is that it makes sense to prosecute only non-consensual or exploitative transactions, while between consenting adults sex work should be decriminalized and regulated. Hence, whereas radicals frequently call for Nordic or abolitionist models that frame consent sceptically, liberals demand decriminalization models that presuppose agency and defend the labour rights of workers.

There's also been harsher scrutiny of the obsessive emphasis on consent by feminist scholars, who consider a "free versus forced" binary as too simplistic. Peng (2009) maintains that framing the issue in terms of whether prostitutes do or can truly consent serves only to maintain stigma, not save women. It is the focus on a need, she writes, which marginalizes "voluntary" sex workers and leaves them vulnerable to having their moral characters or characterological faculties called into question. Peng coins the phrase "modified whore stigma" to explain how demands for evidence of "real" consent can rebound on sex workers, stigmatizing them as deviant or not credible. Instead, Peng encourages feminist activists to reject the strict binary of voluntary or forced. She insists that consent is "vague, contingent, and relative" — determined by context, inequality and circumstance— and accordingly too weak a basis for the primary legal marker. Instead of policing women's subjective consent, Peng argues focus should be on the structural conditions of sex work. She contends that it's more practical to fight for better material and legal conditions (wages, health care, workplace safety, green cards) on behalf of sex workers if the concern is about preventing abuse — rather than denying the matter of consent at play at large. For Peng placing consent within a broader political and economic environment serves to "de-specialize and de-stigmatize" sex work.

Inspired by the kinds of critiques like Peng's, many feminists are working toward a new middle ground that transcends the old binary. This is a view that respects women's autonomy and the constraints of economic necessity. The 'middle ground' position of feminisms, in Prabha Kotiswaran's (2011) words, consists of a "position that is sympathetic to the empirical variation of sex trades and ...the self-advocacy of women who work within them"—acts as an example. Middle-ground feminists understand that sex workers sometimes mobilize in defense of their rights, civil and economic, and they engage critically with sex-worker advocacy for decriminalization and unionization. They may acknowledge that the sex industry is *gendered* – often reflecting men's demand – yet they also acknowledge that many women exercise agency within it and seek better labor conditions rather than abolition. This view does not consider all prostitution to be identical or naturally violent, but rather identifies different contexts and conditions of work. As Kotiswaran suggests, consenting sex workers see paid erotic labour like other low-status service or caregiving work (nannies, eldercare, hospitality) and should not be seen as inherently degrading. From a labor-rights standpoint, middle-ground feminists therefore argue against criminal penalties for sellers of sex and for recognizing sex work as work. They frequently support things like decriminalization plus strong workplace protections — health standards, anti-discrimination laws, union rights and access to social services. This is in line with the upswell of international rights-based demands for bodily integrity and gender justice: as Amnesty International has recently put it, decriminalisation is "key to ensuring that women retain control over their sexual and reproductive health" (2024).

To sum up, contemporary feminist analysis seeks to move beyond simplistic pro/anti dichotomies. Sex workers' labor rights, agency and dignity are now regarded by scholars as core. Rather than viewing sex workers as passive victims or exceptional outsiders, middle-ground approaches seek to "find common cause" with sex-worker unions and rights movements. This entails recognizing intersectional factors — race, class and migration, disability — that shape women's options, and designing law and policy to reduce harm while preserving agency. A significant number of feminist legal theorists are coalescing around the idea that disagreements over nomenclature (voluntary vs. forced) should not obscure the focus on safeguarding women's health, safety, and choice. By focusing on concrete *working conditions* and empowering workers, this jurisprudence aims to secure justice for sex workers while also challenging the structural inequalities that limit all women's consent.

INTERNATIONAL LEGAL FRAMEWORKS

First-generation international law on prostitution was directed against what were then known as "white-slave" traffic networks. Beginning with the League of Nations conventions (1904, 1910, 1921, and 1933), the UN Convention for the Suppression of the Traffic in Persons and the Exploitation of the Prostitution of Others was adopted in 1949 as a first legal instrument establishing this area. This treaty amalgamated previous treaties and stated that trafficking and prostitution were "incompatible with the dignity and worth of human person". It embraced what academicians call an "abolitionist approach" to prostitution: the preamble presents both prostitution and trafficking as moral detritus, and the operative provisions oblige States to penalise traffickers, pimps or clients while shielding prostitutes themselves from criminal liability. For instance, *Article 6* directed parties "not [to] regard the prostitute as committing a punishable offence". But the language of the Convention itself was broad: it urges states to "abolish" prostitution and deter women from entering any part of the sex industry, even on their own accord. *CEDAW (1979)* also reflects this abolitionist frame, requiring States to "take all appropriate measures to suppress traffic in women and exploitation of prostitution of women".

The 1949 Convention therefore contains a moral position: it is prostitution in itself that is considered contrary to both human dignity and the social order. This was reinforced by Council of Europe institutions, who bracketed trafficking with the "exploitation of prostitution "with or without consent" because it is so degrading. As De Sena notes, the Convention employs the rhetoric of human dignity to "fuel a moral condemnation of prostitution" (Scarpa, 2019). The Convention contains no formal definition of "prostitution" or "exploitation," but it incriminates any person who procures, abducts or otherwise facilitates another into prostitution. Member states were also required to work internationally to stamp out "the traffic in persons for the purpose of prostitution." In practice, this frequently entailed criminalizing traffickers and clients, but not prostitutes.

The first significant development was the *2000 Palermo Protocol of the UN (Protocol to Prevent, Suppress and Punish Trafficking in Persons, especially Women and Children)* which actually provided a legal definition to "trafficking in persons" for the first time on an international level. The Protocol describes trafficking as the "recruitment, transportation, transfer, harbouring or receipt of persons by means of threat or use of force, fraud, coercion etc., for the purpose of exploitation". The language of the Protocol is crucial in so far as it clarifies that "exploitation shall include, at a minimum, 'the exploitation of the prostitution of others or other forms of sexual exploitation'". By listing sexual exploitation (including prostitution) alongside forced labour and slavery, the Protocol embeds the moral view from 1949 that prostitution by others is an exploitative end. But by stipulating an act and means of trafficking (e.g. force, or deception) in theory the Protocol differentiates it from purely consensual sex work. Pursuant to Article 3, it is considered legally irrelevant if an adult has consented to prostitution where force or coercion has been employed. No evidence of coercion is required in case of child victims.

Notwithstanding this definition, the Protocol's approach is unclear with regards to prostitution. It neither employs "voluntary prostitution" nor "sex work", but rather subsumes sexual exploitation (including prostitution) into trafficking. In other words, voluntary sex work is beyond the scope of the Protocol unless it contains the proscribed "means." The broad language of the Protocol fails to specifically define "exploitation", which has resulted in certain states or readers seeking to conflate all prostitution with exploitation. In fact, Human Rights Watch raises the concern that the Protocol "does not specifically define exploitation [...] which may mean different things to different people". Feminist academic discussions have been about whether the focus of the Protocol on exploitation is able to accommodate sex work choice. Some argue that in listing prostitution as one form of "exploitation" under the protocol, although subject to (formal) consent, the protocol embeds an abolitionist logic. Others point to an evolution: Amnesty International's (2016) subsequent position advised decriminalizing consensual sex work while targeting exploitation through states' laws.

In sum, neither the 1949 Convention nor the Palermo Protocol are morally neutral towards prostitution. They do not enshrine any notion of sex work as a legitimate form of labor. Instead, they look at prostitution mostly under the lens of human rights abuses. This has led to heated discussions in the world of gender and law. From the side of abolitionist feminism these instruments are celebrated as tools to shield women from exploitation, while sex workers rights activists and some human rights bodies denounce them for not taking agency and choice seriously. For instance, the Commissioner for Human Rights of the Council of Europe (2023) cautions that: [m]ixing all sex work with trafficking "can make sex workers…more vulnerable to violence and harm". The same Commissioner quotes the UN Working Group, who conclude that laws prohibiting consensual sex work by women lead to "injustice [and] vulnerability". Amnesty International similarly stressed that laws should protect sex workers' rights rather than attempting to abolish the trade. In brief, opponents contend that the international framework's ambiguous treatment of "voluntary" sex work undermines rights for those who do choose to engage in sex work and is harmful.

At the regional level, legal perspectives on these issues are broadly consistent with the international model. In Europe, the EU's 2011 Trafficking Directive (2011/36/EU) and the Council of Europe's Trafficking Convention (2005) echo those in the Palermo Protocol, and they are designed to standardize anti-trafficking legislation. Both instruments do not legalize or define prostitution per se, but concentrate on the offences related to trafficking and protection of victims. The EU Directive was "created with the aim of harmonising national anti-trafficking legislation" and requires states to outlaw trafficking (as defined above) and help victims but it does not touch prostitution law which is left up to individual member states. Notably, recent debates in the Council of Europe highlight diverging views on prostitution: a 2024 Parliamentary Assembly resolution (ref. 2668) recommended decriminalizing sex workers and refocusing on abuse by others, reflecting growing concern about the impact of criminalization on sex workers' rights. (The resolution was later postponed amid controversy.) Therefore, in Europe some bodies have moved to separate out trafficking from consensual sex work and to promote the human rights of sex workers.

In Africa, the African Union as well as sub-regional organisations have started to develop anti-trafficking frameworks. The 2003 Maputo Protocol or the AU Protocol on Women's Rights leads states to criminalise sex trafficking and the exploitation of women in prostitution. A 2008 resolution, from the African Commission, specifically said that the 1949 Convention will "abolish prostitution by preventing … the movement of women even voluntarily into this sector". Acknowledging these gaps, the AU in 2014 endorsed a Continental Plan of Action on Trafficking in Persons to which members states pledged to collaborate on prevention, prosecution and protection of victims. This policy notes that trafficking is a violation of human rights and requires multi-faceted response (laws, victim assistance, reduction of demand). In real terms, most African jurisdictions make sex work overwhelmingly illegal and the regional framework is also concerned primarily with cross-border trafficking as opposed to decriminalising voluntary prostitution. Critics note that continuing to frame things as "exploitation" leaves voluntary sex workers almost entirely out of these laws.

The Association of Southeast Asian Nations (ASEAN), meanwhile, promulgated the 2015 ASEAN Convention Against Trafficking in Persons (ACTIP) for Southeast Asia. The definition of trafficking in ACTIP is almost identical to Palermo's: it covers sexual exploitation, and expressly says that "exploitation shall include ... the exploitation of the prostitution of others or other forms of sexual exploitation". Like UN Protocol, ACTIP considers adult consent irrelevant if coercion is involved and treats such matters as a global crime. So the Convention is not an instrument that legalizes prostitution; but it addresses it as a possible form of trafficking exploitation. ASEAN's Plan of Action and subsequent national laws therefore target trafficking networks and exploitation, however they fail to enact legislative recognition of voluntary sex work. Civil society in the region has raised concerns that anti-trafficking enforcement sometimes ensnares sex workers, whether as victims or perpetrators, much like "conflation" elsewhere around the world.

At the global level, international frameworks have been shaped by abolitionist moral narratives: they conceptualize trafficking as an umbrella category and connect prostitution with exploitation implicitly. The Palermo Protocol's monumental silence over consensual adult sex work is theoretically significant, though in practice many states apply it in manners that leave the voluntarist sex worker exposed to loss of protection or criminalisation. Feminist and human rights critiques have been influential in recent years, calling for clearer distinction between trafficking and consensual sex work and for decriminalization policies that prioritize agency and safety. The result is a pervasive contestation: while trafficking law emphasizes victimization and condemns third-party exploiters, it also all too often does so at the price of sex workers' autonomy. Contemporary debates continue to revolve around these definitional ambiguities and moral questions, as feminist scholars and rights bodies press for legal approaches that recognize consensual sex work as work, within or alongside existing anti-trafficking instruments.

COMPARATIVE LEGAL DEFINITIONS AND APPROACHES TO PROSTITUTION

India (Prohibition model)

Definition: Prostitution is not a crime in India – however, soliciting sex is against the law as are brothels, pimps and organised solicitation of paid-for sex – but there is no legal definition. It does so in language that exactly assumes that all paid sex is exploitative.

Voluntary vs Forced: The ITPA and related laws, however, do not distinguish voluntarily willing sex workers from forced prostitutes but criminalize any common exploitative context. Consensual sex work by adults is not exactly criminal, but those things associated with it (brothel-keeping, pimping, solicitation) are. But being trafficked, or forced into prostitution, is classified as a serious criminal offense under India's anti-trafficking laws.

Criminalisation/Regulation: The Indian approach to the sex industry is criminalised: while sex workers are not by and large punished for selling their bodies, those who exploit or profit from them – brothel keepers, pimps and clients of minors face jail. Prostitution as a job is not recognized under law, and sex work is widely permitted in the grey area of the law. The police approach is usually focused on solicitation and third party involvement. So India's model is generally "prohibitionist": while consensual adult prostitution isn't flatly illegal, almost every aspect of it is criminalized.

Case Law/Reform: During recent decades, Indian courts have become more protective of sex workers' rights. For instance, in *Budhadev Karmaskar* v. *State of West Bengal* (2011), the Supreme Court justified police in raids providing condoms and protected sex work on grounds that "these women have a right to protect themselves from the sexually transmitted diseases (STD)". In 2022, a three-judge bench said that "sex work is just like any other" occupation, ordering that adults engaging in consensual sex work should not be subjected to harassment by the police. State high courts (for instance, the Bombay HC in 2020) have ruled that sex workers have the right to choose their profession and that consensual adult sex work is not a crime. Meanwhile, India has formulated more stringent laws on trafficking (e.g. Trafficking of Persons Bill 2022) to prevent forced prostitution.

United States (Prohibition model)

Definition: In the United States, prostitution is regulated by the individual state (there is no procedure for the federal control of voluntary prostitution). Some state codes define prostitution as simply the exchange of sexual services for money (for example, Florida's law — which calls it "the giving or receiving of the body for sexual activity for hire"). Usually these are laws that both prohibit the sale and purchase of sex for money. A notable exception is Nevada, where licensed brothels operate legally in some rural counties; elsewhere prostitution is criminalized.

Voluntary vs. Forced: The dominant U.S. approach is criminalization. In most states prostitution is a misdemeanor or felony for sellers and often for buyers (as in Florida, which penalizes offers to commit prostitution and purchasing sex). Trafficking and pimping are felonies. Only in Nevada (outside Las Vegas and Reno) is prostitution licensed as regulated labor. Otherwise, consensual adult sex work has no legal labor protections. The U.S. therefore embodies a prohibitionist model: sex work is generally illegal, while forced prostitution is combated through anti-trafficking laws.

Criminalization/Regulation: U.S. mainstream thinking is that education works against sex work and leads to criminalization. Prostitution is a misdemeanor for sellers and often for buyers (as in Florida, which criminalizes offers to commit prostitution, as well as the purchase of sex) in most states. Trafficking and pimping are felonies. Prostitution is accepted as one of only seven forms of legal, regulated labor in Nevada (excluding Las Vegas and Reno). Consensual adult sex work lacks most labor protections outside of contracts, as well. Instead, the U.S. represents this prohibitionist regime: While sex work is generally illegal, forced prostitution is attacked by way of anti-trafficking legislation.

Case Law/Reform: Prostitution law is almost never confronted at the federal US level. The Supreme Court has held (in *Murdock v. Pennsylvania*, 1943) that a city can't prevent all distribution of religious literature, even by donation — a principle sometimes analogized to sex work — but it hasn't squarely addressed the constitutionality of prostitution. More recent efforts have also sought to make a legislative distinction between trafficking and voluntary sex work. For instance, many states have adopted statutes mandating social-service diversion when minors or trafficking victims are arrested for prostitution. In 2018, the Congress enacted the "FOSTA-SESTA" amendments, which increased liability for online platforms that purportedly promoted prostitution, amid continuing debates over decriminalization and trafficking.

Germany (Legalization model)

Definition: According to German law, prostitution is considered a legal profession. According to the German Prostitutes Protection Act (ProstSchG 2017) "sexual services" refers to any sexual act executed in front of another person against payment, and a “prostitute” is someone who offers this type of sexual services. These definitions view prostitution as a job like any other.

Voluntary vs. Forced: The 2002 Prostitution Act (Prostitutionsgesetz (ProstG)) decriminalized consensual professional sex work by adults, but made forced or coerced prostitution a crime in Germany. The forced prostitution is punished as human trafficking according to §232a StGB. Being a pimp (pimping, §180a StGB) or profiting by a prostitute’s employment in sex business forced labor is illegal. Voluntary sex work is in practice legal, but any use of force, fraud or exploitation makes the transaction illegal.

Criminalization/Regulation: Germany uses a method of legalization/regulation. Sex work is acknowledged as regulated labor: brothels and escorts have business licenses, sex workers are eligible to apply for work and residence permits, and they’re technically required to pay taxes like other professionals. Health and safety regulations are in place (operators are required to advise on safer sex). In 2017, Germany unveiled the Prostitutes Protection Act which made sex workers register with local officials and undergo mandatory health counselling. The goal of this was to further regulate the industry (although registration remains a bitterly controversial topic among workers). On the other hand, non-consensual trade in the sex form is a matter that the government rigorously crack down on. Germany therefore regards sex work as an ordinary occupation with legal protections, and it prosecutes trafficking and forced prostitution vigorously.

Case Law/Reform: Key reform campaigns include the Prostitution Act for 2002 (decriminalizing brothels, legalising contracts for sex) and the Prostitutes Protection Actof 2017. Sex workers now have labor rights as well in Germany; for example, the federal Labor Court has ruled that prostitutes may be classified as “employees” based on contract (making them entitled to compensation and benefits) if the relationship had some employer-employee characteristics. Supporters frequently point to these rulings as proof that sex work is work. German law continues to add to the anti-trafficking legislation: in 2016, new laws were further implemented that enforced heavier penalties for pimping and trafficking under article 232.

Netherlands (Legalization model)

Definition: Dutch law allows and regulates private adult prostitution. Since October 2000, the Netherlands has been known for its policy on sex work.; Dutch penal law is no longer applicable to consensual adult prostitution (or “voluntary” prostitution); involving adults aged 18 and over who agree with contracting prostitutes. While there is no one “definition” of prostitution on the books, in practice prostitution often refers to consensual sexual services exchanged for payment among consenting adults.

Voluntary vs. Forced: In Dutch regulation there is an explicit exception for exploitation and child prostitution. Under Penal Code article 273f it is a crime to involve minors in sex work, or to coerce, threaten or deceive someone into commercial sex. Therefore, for adults prostitution is legal, but any type of child prostitution or trafficking is illegal and a punishable offense. In other words, consenting adults can take up prostitution but anyone employing children below 18 years of age or using the services of one is a criminal. The law operates on the assumption that force or fraud negates consent and treats "trafficking" acts as distinct crimes regardless of the formal, legal "consent" given by a purported victim.

Criminalization/Regulation: The Netherlands has a legal/regulatory model. After 2000, sex work was treated as an ordinary occupation: brothels operate under municipal licenses, sex workers pay taxes, and labor laws apply. They include regulations of workplace conditions, health and safety, zoning. The industry is regulated in an attempt to curb abuses, but consensual sex work is legal and subject to official discretion. Recent discussions of reform have been characterized by 'law and order' concerns to make rules in the sex industry: for example, create a permit system for sex workers or require national registration, and regulate home-based prostitution. Those plans have been controversial. Today, the Netherlands still officially labels sex work as a legitimate and regulated trade, subject to public-health and labor laws that explicitly forbid coercion or under-age participation.

Case Law/Reforms: Significant reforms include the removal of brothel ban in 2000 and subsequent amendments targeting trafficking. Between 2015 and 2020, the Dutch government suggested a new licensing regime (including interviews and age checks) for those who plan to have sex work from home or via internet-based platforms with control as its main rationale. Critics (including sex-worker groups) caution that re-criminalizing unlicensed work would hurt safety. In practice, enforcement distinguishes clearly between voluntary sex work (unpunished) and forced prostitution (always prosecuted). Recent evaluations by non-governmental organizations note that while legalization gave sex workers rights, migrant and illicit labor in the industry remain challenges.

New Zealand (Decriminalization model)

Definition: New Zealand does not refer to "prostitution" in its law but makes commercial sex services legal under Prostitution Reform Act, 2003. Also, under the Act any agreement for commercial sex between consenting adults is definitively non-void. The law thus recognizes sexual services for payment as valid work. "Commercial sexual services" are like any other service contract under New Zealand law.

Voluntary vs. Forced: The Act legalises voluntary adult sex work but makes an explicit difference between consensual versus forced activities. It creates offences for inducing or compelling anyone to provide sexual services for payment (Section 16). It also safeguards people who don't want to work, and allows workers to reject clients without repercussions. Basically, all voluntary prostitution is legal and all involuntary prostitution (pimping or living off the avails of another through by force or fraud) is a crime. Importantly, the onus is put on clients and others not to encourage sex workers.

Criminalization/Regulation: New Zealand has decriminalized sex work. Adults may work individually or within a business (such as a brothel, escort agency). There are health-and-safety regulations (brothel operators must, by law, provide safe-sex practices – though this doesn't necessarily protect sex workers from the less-than-reputable types). Local councils can also apply zoning restrictions to brothels. Workers have the rights to reject work, and enjoy legal protection (labor law, insurance). There is no licensing scheme for workers. Thus, sex work is treated similarly to other occupations, with a focus on occupational health (e.g. requiring condom use) rather than criminal penalties.

Case Law/Reforms: A separate Prostitution Law Review Committee (PLRC) reviewed the Act in 2008 and 2015. Its reports (and subsequent studies) generally found that decriminalization improved sex workers' safety and health, with no evidence of increased trafficking or abuse attributable to the law. The PLRC found that the reform was largely successful in achieving its aim to protect human rights and inhibit children. There have been no significant court cases undermining the Act, with the focus being on regulation (eg Health and Safety at Work Act 2015 which applies to brothels) and enforcement of anti-exploitation provisions. New Zealand is frequently referred to as an example (including by Amnesty International) of a successful decriminalization having balanced the rights of sex-workers and anti-trafficking action.

Sweden (Nordic/"Equality" model):

Definition: Sweden was the first country to pass the so-called Nordic model. It is a crime, under Swedish law (Penal Code, Chapter 6, section 11, since 1999), to buy sexual services; the sale of sexual services by the self is decriminalized. There is no positive statutory definition regarding "prostitution" as such; the law merely renders it "illegal for someone to obtain a casual sexual relationship with another as consideration for payment". In practice this means that consensual pay-for-sex is unlawful.

Voluntary vs. Forced: Sweden's law supports the perception that any prostitution is potentially exploitative. Voluntary prostitution (the sale of sex by adult consenting adults) is technically legal, albeit only technically, as, since the purchase of sex is prohibited, consensual sex work lacks any legal market. Any sex work that's forced, fraudulent, or involving minors is also specifically criminalized as rape or human trafficking under Swedish criminal law. Buyers and third parties are then prosecuted no matter whether a prostitute alleges consent. Assessments have observed that the strategy presumes that prostitution damages women; the law would protect sex workers by aiming the customers and the pimp's offenses.

Criminalization/Regulation: Sweden's regime is a blend: sex workers themselves are technically decriminalized as sellers, yet the environment around the transaction remains very restrictive. Procuring, or buying sex, incurs fines or jail, as does benefiting financially from someone else's prostitution. Pimping, keeping a brothel, and loitering for purposes of prostitution are also crimes. There is no permitting or regulation of prostitution itself – instead, the emphasis is on demand-reduction. State services include exit programs and social services for sex workers, who are treated as (potential) victims who need assistance. In short, Sweden criminally punishes buyers and money-makers, while decriminalizing those who sell sex – although practice-wise, consensual sex work has no market framework.

Case Law/Reforms: The 1999 law ("Sex Purchase Act") was revised in 2018 to tighten definitions of exploitation. Swedish courts have generally upheld the law's intent to protect equality; for example, courts have penalized those who coerce or buy sex under threat, without requiring proof of violence. Globally, the Swedish approach impacted Norway and other nations. At domestic level, the model's effectiveness is questioned (by critics, including human-rights organizations), yet to date (2025) the law persists. Remarkably, Sweden's Equal Opportunities Ombudsman has come to the model's defense as promoting the equality of women, echoing the law's ideological intent to discourage all prostitution.

Norway (Nordic/"Equality" model)

Definition: Norway follows the Swedish model. Criminal law doesn't forbid the sale, only the purchase, of sexual services: through the amendment to the Criminal Code (adopted 2008, came into force 2009), "buying a sexual act" is outlawed, while the prostitution itself is left untouched by law. Soliciting clients and advertising sexual services are also prohibited (to further discourage the practice). Essentially, paid consensual sexual intercourse is no lawful transaction, as any payment is criminal.

Voluntary vs. Forced: There is no legally sanctioned "voluntary prostitution" market under Norwegian law; purchase is criminalized on the spot. As in Sweden, nonetheless, prostitution that comes with a minor or coercion is also prosecuted under child protection or trafficking laws. Prosecutors treat those engaged in prostitution as victims or potential victims, not as perpetrators. Notably, research after Norway criminalized the act in 2009 determined that demand reduction also decreased human traffickings: a review report by the government determined that a prohibition on purchase aided Norway in being a less desirable spot for prostitution-related traffickings as well as decreased street prostitution (without demonstrating increasing violence to workers).

Criminalization/Regulation: Like Sweden, Norway's approach punishes buyers, pimps, and brothel operators, but not the prostitutes themselves. Section 378 of the Criminal Code outlaws profiteering from another's prostitution, and Section 202 prohibits "benefiting" from a prostitute's income (aiming to catch pimps). In practice, sex work operates clandestinely if at all. Norway provides social services (through the Pro-Senteret and EXIT programs) to help sex workers exit the industry. The model is thus partially decriminalizing: sex work is not formally illegal for the provider, but the surrounding ecosystem is criminal.

Case Law/Reforms: Norway's buyers-only purchase-ban law was also approved as compatible with Norway's international commitments regarding trafficking by the Supreme Court. No significant legal challenge has reversed the policy. Norway, since enactment, has enhanced exploitation laws (e.g. permitting stiffer sentences for trafficking). Norwegian debate now concentrates on whether to fully decriminalize sex work (recommended by some advocates) or maintaining the buyers-only ban as leverage against exploitation. Up until now, the Nordic model remains Norway's approach, as research validates that after the 2009 reform, both trafficking as well as street prostitution diminished.

THE INDIAN REGIME

Statutory Framework:

India's Immoral Traffic (Prevention) Act, 1956 (ITPA) is the primary legislation on sex work. Crucially, however, the Act does not criminalize the act of selling sex itself. Instead, its Section 2(f) of the Act defines "prostitution" as "the sexual exploitation or abuse of persons for commercial purposes." In other words, the law presumes prostitution itself to be exploitative. As one analysis describes it, "selling sex is not expressly illegal, but many activities around it are criminalized." This creates a legal grey area: consensual private sex work is technically still legal, but the law presumes exploitation in every case of "commercial" sex. Thus, Sections 3–9 of the ITPA target the regulation and facilitation of sex work. For example,

Section 3 criminalizes keeping or managing a brothel;
Section 4 criminalizes anyone "knowingly living wholly or in part on the earnings of prostitution";
Section 5 criminalizes procuring or bringing a person into prostitution;
Section 6 criminalizes keeping a person for prostitution;
Section 7 forbids the continuation of prostitution near public places like schools or temples;
Section 8 forbids soliciting prostitution in public;
Section 9 also forbids leading or bringing a person to a brothel for prostitution.

These provisions are traditionally written on a protecting women and children premise, but have the de facto application of criminalizing brothel-keeping, pimping, solicitation, and even communal sex worker living arrangements.

The law's text is internally ambiguous and prescriptive. In equating prostitution with "exploitation or abuse", the ITPA assumes that all money-for-sex deals involve exploitation. It even embeds presumptions of exploitation in its penalties. Section 4, for instance, has a conclusive presumption that everyone found to be living with or "habitually in the company of" a sex worker is living off her earnings – de facto treating any co-residing partner like a pimp unless innocent. Similarly, the ITPA's brothel provision (Section 3) automatically presumes two or more sex workers co-residing are running a brothel, and hence "presum[ing] exploitation whenever two or more sex workers live together." Critics note that this punishes cooperative safety practices and blurs the line between consensual sex work and trafficking. Privately selling sex in general is not a crime, but the ITPA's definitions and presumptions are so sweeping that almost any aspect of sex work can trigger criminal liability.

Constitutional Rights:

In the recent decades, India's courts have begun to recognize sex work under the rubric of fundamental rights. The Constitution – Article 21 – that safeguards the right to life with dignity has been interpreted to encompass voluntary sex work. The Supreme Court itself specifically held that sex workers are entitled to "live with dignity" under Article 21.

Key Case Laws:

1. *Gaurav Jain v. Union of India* (1997) – In this PIL, the Supreme Court took a highly prohibitionist stance while being sympathetic to sex workers at the same time. The Court invoked Article 23 (banning trafficking) to say that "the evil of prostitution must be curbed." It told governments to establish programs aimed at eradicating prostitution and rehabilitating "fallen" women. It also acknowledged that "a prostitute is equally a human being" who is entitled to dignity. The court focused on welfare: prostitution children have to be taught and offered social services, and institutional care has to be short-term. Of importance, Gaurav Jain did not equate guilt with being present in a brothel; there had to be evidence before one would be termed a trafficker. The judgment, though, reaffirmed some ITPA assumptions (e.g., automatically treating minors in brothels as exploited) and reasserted strong controls over sex work as part of a "cancerous growth" that has to be cut out. On the whole, Gaurav Jain combined strong words about prostitution as a social ill with appeals for rehabilitation, reflecting the times' ambivalence: prostitution itself was condemned, but prostitutes were also seen as victims deserving of rights and alleviation.
2. *Vishal Jeet v. Union of India* (1990, PUCL) – In this case the Supreme Court addressed sex workers' rights under HIV/AIDS policy. It struck down state policies mandating the compulsory HIV testing of sex workers on the grounds that such measures interfered with their dignity and privacy. The Court invoked principles of sex workers as rights-holders of the Constitution: public health measures must be respectful of individual consent. (As an example, the Court ruled that coercive HIV testing or punitive segregation of sex workers were unlawful.) This was a landmark in determining that sex workers' health rights cannot be pre-empted by broad anti-trafficking legislation. (There were no textual references, but the case is infamously renowned for testing compulsory and requiring consent.)
3. *Budhadev Karmaskar v. West Bengal* (2011)- In this case, the Court went a step further, and termed sex work as a "profession" and gave a warning that consenting adult sex workers "should not be arrested, harassed, or penalized" for mere presence in brothels. The judgment was precipitated by the brutal murder of a sex worker from Kolkata, and the Court took suo motu cognizance to term sex work as labour in need of protection.It set up a committee to recommend welfare schemes (rehabilitation, health, vocational training) and even directed to enroll sex workers under Aadhaar (biometric identification) and other social schemes – steps which accord the same treatment to sex workers as any citizen. The Court again reaffirmed that the assurance of dignity and autonomy in Article 21 extends in entirety to sex workers and their children.

4. *Kajal Mukesh Singh v. State of Maharashtra* (2020) – The Bombay High Court heard a petition by sex workers who were "rescued" and taken to a shelter on remand. The court struck down their detention, claiming that adult women have the right to choose their vocation under Article 19(1)(g) and to move/reside under Article 19(1)(d). It observed that the ITPA "did not criminalize 'prostitution' per se" and categorically distinguished between involuntary trafficking and consenting sex work. The HC accordingly recognised that sex work in itself is an entrenched right. Paradoxically, however, the same judgment stated that Sections 3–9 of the ITPA only impose "reasonable restrictions" on this right. In practice this would encompass women who agree to have sex agreeing to work, while most ancillary activities (brothel-keeping, soliciting, etc.) are illegal – tension that the court could not deal with.

Analysis:

In practice, India's legal system contains a contradiction by design. On paper, technically, voluntary sex work is not criminalized, but most ways of exercising it are. It is said that the ITPA criminalizes "sexual exploitation/abuse" – not consenting sex and various judgments have held that voluntary adult sex work falls within constitutional rights. Yet the Act simultaneously outlaws brothel-keeping, pimping, solicitation, and even cohabitation of sex workers. The Supreme Court's latest ruling affirmed this point: "running a brothel is illegal and voluntary sex work is not". Therefore, despite the fact that the state de jure recognizes sex work as work, de facto law enforcement in practice treats sex workers like criminals. Brothel raids continue to occur, and rescued women are usually detained in shelter homes as suspected trafficking victims.

There has been a sighting of tension between rights and moralism in this regime. The ITPA and courts historically at one end of the spectrum focus on abolition and trafficking and reflect a moralistic understanding of prostitution as inherently harmful. Some analysts describe this as a continuum of consent: sex work can range from coercion to choice, and law must navigate that spectrum. In India the pendulum often swings: progressive judgements recognize consent and labor rights, but implementation still leans on old abolitionist presumptions. For example, countless women in Mumbai's red-light districts have reported being "rescued" into protective custody with no evidence of trafficking – a practice criticized by activists as encroaching on fundamental rights. The net effect is that adult sex workers are rhetorically acknowledged as rights-bearing citizens, but subjected to persistent harassment in practice.

Legislative Ambiguities:

The terminology of the ITPA remains ambiguously vague and gendered. It still explains prostitution in terms of "exploit[ation] or abus[e]". Assuming consent not to be universal. Though the enforcement is aimed at male and female exploitators, in practice almost only women are arrested under the Act. Critics point out that a formally sexually-neutral law has never been practiced equally by gender, often routing poor women into state custody. There are loopholes too: the ITPA confers enormous powers (even to arrest without warrant) upon the police which conflict with customary criminal procedure safeguards. Significantly, the law still does not reliably distinguish between a victim of trafficking and an independent sex worker. Ambedkar-era scandals suggest that the Act was originally meant to criminalize prostitution per se, but its latest draft criminalizes "sexual exploitation" – a distinction that the 2022 court repeatedly criticized. Reformers therefore demand that the law be changed so as to explicitly exclude consensual adult sex work and focus only on trafficking and coercion, in keeping with constitutional principles of dignity and equality.

Consent, Coercion, and Stigma in Law

Voluntariness vs. Exploitation

Legal regulation of prostitution frequently hinges on the line between voluntary sex work and exploitative trafficking. Indian legislation, specifically the Immoral Traffic (Prevention) Act (ITPA), is often based on the assumption that prostitution always carries some element of coercion, particularly through criminalizing ancillary activities such as brothel-keeping and solicitation. Such framing makes the assumption of exploitation, practically excluding the possibility of consent (CLPR, 2022). Section 4 of the ITPA, for instance, criminalizes surviving on the proceeds of prostitution, even if the prostitute is voluntarily involved in the occupation and financially sustaining another.

These sorts of statutory assumptions are most often rebuked by rights-based arguments that maintain a consenting adult has the legal and moral capacity to make sex work a choice. This is reflected in Supreme Court judgments such as *Budhadev Karmaskar v. State of West Bengal*, which recognize sex work as a "profession" under Article 19(1)(g) of the Constitution (JIER, 2021). And yet, even as these judgments move towards recognizing voluntary sex work, feminist legal thinkers caution that the dichotomous legal frameworks—"voluntary" and "forced"—could be defective by their very nature.

Peng (2009) and Serughetti (2013) posit that such binaries do not recognize that all human decisions, such as entry into sex work, take place in a continuum constituted by structural inequalities. As Serughetti points out, voluntariness is seldom absolute; consent might be there but highly conditioned by social, economic, and cultural forces. Therefore, what the law considers to be voluntary can actually be coerced by circumstances.

Contingent Consent: Between Choice and Necessity

Peng's (2009) model of "contingent consent" provides a strong critique of conventional legal definitions of autonomy in the context of sex work. Consent, she writes, must be recognized not as one isolated, definitive act but as a process conditioned by contingent circumstances—poverty, gender-based discrimination, illiteracy, and the lack of available employment alternatives. A woman may "choose" to become a sex worker not because she would prefer to do so, but because it is her sole economic survival option. In those situations, the law's obsession with establishing the existence of consent by individuals is blinkered.

Contingent consent unearths the flaws of binary legal categories that attempt to render sharp distinctions between the trafficked and the voluntary. When legal systems require an unambiguous display of "free will," they tend to obscure the social context on which such choices depend. Such legal tunnel vision threatens to make invisible the vast gray area in which structural coercion contours agency.

Legal systems, India's included, are prone to burdening sex workers with the task of proving that they were either coerced or willingly consenting. This does not take into consideration the interlayered realities of women whose choices, albeit technically "voluntary," result from extremely limited circumstances (Chatterjee, 2017). The contingent consent model, on the other hand, requires an expanded conception of agency—one that acknowledges autonomy while remaining critically sensitive to the power dynamics that influence decision-making.

Modified Whore Stigma and Despecialization

Even while the rights movement for sex workers aims to reconstitute them as respectable laborers, Peng (2018) cautions against a phenomenon she terms the "modified whore stigma." Trying to make sex work normal by representing sex workers as ordinary workers is likely to lead society to re-stigmatize them differently—particularly when they cannot neatly fit the victim script or engage in moral atonement.

This "despecialization" approach, designed to destigmatize, can frequently be counterproductive. Rather than lowering stigma, it can create new sources of judgment and exclusion, especially for those sex workers who claim their autonomy without apology. The world, Peng contends, prefers sex workers depicted as coercively victimized or as those who desire "rescue," not as self-sufficient actors making difficult decisions. This distinction is especially important in India, where sex workers are often cast in one of two roles: as helpless victims of trafficking or as criminals.

Peng thus not only calls for the legal recognition of sex work as work but also for its "normalization"—a cultural transformation that embraces sex work as a valid and ethically neutral occupation. Short of this transformation, even enlightened legislative changes are likely to be undercut by enduring institutional and social stigma.

Legal Focus and Its Consequences

The Indian legal system has started to recognize voluntary consent in the context of sex work, but the implications of such recognition are still uncertain. In *Sangita v. State of Maharashtra* (2015), the Bombay High Court ruled that adult sex workers were not to be detained in rehabilitation homes except on proof of trafficking. In like manner, in the Budhadev Karmaskar case, the Supreme Court ordered law enforcement not to raid the establishments of consenting adult sex workers or prosecute them (CLPR, 2022).

Nonetheless, in spite of such positive judicial pronouncements, ground reality is different. Accounts still come of police harassment, illegal raids, and social exclusion. The legal recognition of consent does not go very far in insulating sex workers from stigma, monitoring, and violence. The issue is the disparity between formal recognition and social attitudes—a disconnect which feminist legal scholars believe is inherent in the law's very structure.

The law's demand to put sex workers neatly into the category of "trafficked" or "free" is a convenience for administration but one that disregards the intersectional, fluid lives of people in the trade. Such categorical thinking, according to Serughetti (2013) and Chatterjee (2017), serves only to reinforce existing hierarchies and vulnerabilities, not break them down. Legal categories cannot address the stigma by themselves; they need to be supported by policy change, policing change, and change in public discourse.

DESTIGMATIZATION AND POLICY IMPLICATIONS

Sex Workers' Rights Movement

Over the past decades, there has been an emergent global movement among sex workers that changed the conversation around prostitution from deviancy or victimhood to labor. Activists have used the chant "Sex Work Is Work" as an effective statement affirming the legality of their work as they claim the same labor rights as other workers. This discourse attempts to eliminate moral consideration about the work itself and instead bring the attention to dignity, safety within the workspace, as well as legal protection. In India, there are organizations that have displayed this paradigm as they advocate for decriminalization as well as enhanced health outcomes and working conditions among sex workers (Kotiswaran, 2011).

Peng (2009) approves this line of work by advocating the "despecialization" of sex work. She warns that the persistence of exceptionalizing sex work fortifies stigmatizations as well as hinders incorporation into legal and welfare instruments. Rather than pursuing debates about whether or not sex work is morally justifiable, Peng proposes that legal and policy debate foreground working conditions, safety, as well as social protection. This labor-based vision allows the sex workers to be viewed as exercising agency rather than as anomalies, within the confines structured environments.

Legal Reform Debates

The question of how to legally govern prostitution remains one of the most contentious topics in the theory of feminist law. Current laws throughout the world fall into three categories: prohibition, legalization, as well as decriminalization. Prohibitionist systems, like those followed throughout the majority of the United States as well as once followed by India, criminalize all aspects of sex work, both purchase as well as sale. Legalization systems, as followed in the Netherlands as well as Germany, allow sex work yet within a very controlled environment, typically including licensure as well as zoning. Decriminalization, as followed significantly in New Zealand, removes criminal penalties entirely off the agenda regarding consensual adult sex work as well as treats it under common labor law (Shamir, 2012).

They all are flawed. Neo-abolitionist feminists, who borrow most often the Nordic model (e.g., Sweden), believe in criminalizing the clients while decriminalizing the sex workers themselves, to minimize demand without victimizing the individuals involved in prostitution. Critics, nevertheless, point out that this strategy still cements stigma as much as it exposes workers to risky working situations, as workers usually end up working covertly (Scoular, 2004).

On the other side, sex worker rights advocates argue for full decriminalization, viewing this as the only way to protect autonomy, labor rights, and dignity. Yet, as Shamir (2012) notes, pure models of either abolition or decriminalization fail to fully resolve the complexities of voluntary prostitution. She proposes a hybrid model—implemented partially in Israel—that combines regulation to protect health and safety with strong safeguards against coercion and trafficking.

In India, discussions regarding reform have to some degree come to a standstill due to cultural taboos as well as legal ambiguities. Despite post-Supreme Court recognition of the professional nature of the sex trade in *Budhadev Karmaskar,* India's legislative framework remains prohibitionist in practice. Policymaking must release itself from moral certainties rather than adopting a framework that contrasts voluntary as opposed to forced participation, with the lived experiences of the sex workers themselves remaining the ultimate priority.

Health and Safety

Health and safety concerns have been the common platforms on which the states govern prostitution. States tend to favor closure of sex work on grounds of public health concerns, most being the prevention of sexually transmitted infections (STIs), as well as safety against violence. Empirical studies, including those commissioned by the International Labour Organization (ILO) and World Health Organization (WHO), conclude that criminal laws make health outcomes worse because they push the practice of the profession into the underworld, where access to care is lower.

A feminist legal approach claims that destigmatization rather than criminalization is more efficacious in the promotion of health as well as safety. Peng (2009) observes that the attainment of labour rights, police accountability, as well as the delivery of non-judgmental health services, are more effective than prohibition laws. Following the same, the Supreme Court of India, in its directions issued in the year 2022, held that the states must ensure medical care to the sex workers, more so, where there is physical assault, and cannot withhold services based on moral grounds (CLPR, 2022). These guidelines reflect judicial recognition of the imperative to place welfare above punishment as the focus of legal reactions to prostitution.

Final Reflections

This chapter underscores the persistent inadequacy of legal definitions and frameworks in addressing the complexity of voluntary sex work. Binary division of the law—the dividing line between trafficking and freedom, coercion and consent—does no justice to the realities of the vast majority of the sex workers, whose realities are determined by a continuum of socio-economic pressures.

Peng (2009) suggests that the problem is to normalize, rather than exceptionalize, sex work. Stigma-removal hinges on the legitimation of sex work as work—that is, as work that is worthy of regulation, protection, and rights. Instead of be fixated on the moral admissibility of sex work or the voluntariness of each specific act, laws ought to shift their attention to the improvement of the working conditions, bodily integrity, and dignity of the workers in the profession.

A feminist response to law thus necessitates a reconfiguration of the debate. It necessitates recognition that the problem of consent is perhaps conditional, that coercion need be morally censurable, that the rights of the sex worker to dignity, labour protection, and social integration must be respected. It will necessitate a shift both legally and culturally—but a change that respects the very best values that underlie autonomy, justice, and equality.

CONCLUSION: REFRAMING LEGAL APPROACHES TO PROSTITUTION THROUGH DIGNITY AND RIGHTS

The legal and conceptual treatment of prostitution continues to be marked by contestation, contradiction, and moral ambiguity. This chapter has unpacked how statutory frameworks—both national and international—struggle to provide coherent definitions of prostitution, often conflating voluntary sex work with coercion and trafficking. As the case of India shows, laws, like the Immoral Traffic (Prevention) Act, 1956 (ITPA), don't criminalize the act of selling sex as such, but criminalize nearly every related circumstance—the act of soliciting, keeping a brothel, as well as gains procured through prostitution—leading to the effective criminalization of sex work. These inconsistencies see voluntary prostitution as a legal threshold entity: acknowledged as such, theoretically, yet criminalized, in practice.

This chapter utilized feminist jurisprudence to illuminate the defects of the binary between "forced" and "voluntary" prostitution. Authors such as Peng and Serughetti point to the ways that socio-economnic marginalisation, patriarchal order, as well as global economic inequality, blur the division between exploitation and agency. The "contingent consent" conception critiques the law's penchant to insist on categorical proof of coercion but ignore the everyday structural compulsions that act on the choices that the women make. Feminist theory insists that the law break free of formalised descriptives and address the realities of restricted autonomy, bringing to the centre the daily realities of the sex workers.

Comparative regimes also support the conclusion that there cannot be any universal legislative approach to the nuances of prostitution. Prohibitionist, decriminalization, and legalization-based jurisdictions all receive criticism either for depriving the agenic capacities of sex workers or subjecting them to additional regulation and monitoring. Shamir's middle-positioned hybrid structure presents a promising framework for building complex reforms. These observations emphasize that the legal categories need to be dynamic as well as reflexive, rather than moralizing or frozen.

India's progressive judicial discourse, especially in Budhadev Karmaskar v. State of West Bengal and subsequent judgments, has come a long way to affirm that sex working is a profession and protect the dignity of those who willingly practice their profession. Article 21 of the Constitution has been judicially interpreted to expand the right to life, as also the right to dignity, privacy, and bodily integrity. Article 19(1)(g) also assures the right to practice any profession, which has been cautiously carried over to consensual adult sex working, also. Statutory law, however, still has some catching up to do. Statutes still assume the exploitation inherent to this profession, empowering invasive policing authority, so the full protection of the rights of the sex workers remains partial.

Ultimately, the chapter recommends a recalibration of law and policy. It is imperative that the dignity of sex workers be protected through a transformation away from criminalization—a legal framework that values agency, understands the role of structural coercion without eroding the role of choice, and abolishes stigma. Definitions must move away from the criminal law's static moral binaries to complex social realities. Following Peng's plea to proceed with a notion of "despecialization," the future lies in transposing prostitution instead as an issue of labor, rights, and justice rather than as a moral issue. Legislative change must be brought into conformity with statutory architectures that advance the constitutional values of equality, liberty, and human dignity so that those who practice sex work are no longer regarded as criminal or victim rather than as rights-bearers within a democratic republic. As Melissa Gira Grant aptly reminds us,

"Sex workers are not problems to be solved, but people to be understood, respected, and protected under the law" (Grant, 2014, Playing the Whore).

REFERENCES

Barry, K. (1997). Prostitution of sexuality: A cause for new international human rights. *Journal of Personal and Interpersonal Loss*, *2*(1), 27–48. DOI: 10.1080/10811449708414404

Chatterjee, P. (2017). *Negotiating sex work in the global South.* Zubaan Books.

Chowdhury, M. (2022). MEASUREMENT OF HEALTH DIMENSION OF SEX-WORKERS'CHILDREN: A COMPARATIVE ANALYSIS ON THE BASIS OF NORTHERN AND SOUTHERN RED LIGHT AREAS OF WEST BENGAL.

CLPR. (2022). Voluntary sex work is legal: Supreme Court clarifies sex workers' rights. *Centre for Law and Policy Research.* https://clpr.org.in/blog/voluntary-sex-work-is-legal-supreme-court-clarifies/

Grant, M. G. (2014). *Playing the whore: The work of sex work.* Verso.

Kotiswaran, P. (2011). *Dangerous sex, invisible labor: Sex work and the law in India.* Princeton University Press.

MacKinnon, C. A. (1989). *Toward a feminist theory of the state.* Harvard University Press.

Najar, J. L. (2021). *Human trafficking in India: how the colonial legacy of the anti-human trafficking regime undermines migrant and worker agency. London School of Economics (LSE).* Human Rights.

Peng, I. (2009). Of course they claim they were coerced: On feminism, 'choice,' and the sex industry. *Bridgewater Review*, 28(2), 8–13. https://vc.bridgew.edu/br_rev/vol28/iss2/6/

Scoular, J. (2004). The 'subject' of prostitution: Interpreting the discursive, symbolic and material position of sex/work in feminist theory. *Feminist Theory*, *5*(3), 343–355. DOI: 10.1177/1464700104046983

Serughetti, G. (2013). Prostitution: A difficult choice. Between consent, coercion and recognition. *Revista de Bioetica y Derecho*, (29), 37–47. https://e-revistas.uc3m.es/index.php/EUNOM/article/view/1913

Shamir, H. (2012). A labor paradigm for human trafficking. *UCLA Law Review. University of California, Los Angeles. School of Law*, *60*(1), 76–136. https://papers.ssrn.com/sol3/papers.cfm?abstract_id=2047432

Weitzer, R. (2009). Sociology of sex work. *Annual Review of Sociology*, *35*(1), 213–234. DOI: 10.1146/annurev-soc-070308-120025

Chapter 4
Equally Safe or Equally Silenced?
The Scottish Anti-Trafficking Strategy and the Erasure of Sex Worker Voices

Hannah Jane Simpson
http://orcid.org/0009-0005-9375-7161
Independent Researcher, UK

ABSTRACT

This chapter interrogates Scotland's Equally Safe strategy, arguing that its conflation of consensual sex work with human trafficking reproduces epistemic violence and exclusion within feminist statecraft. Framed as a progressive, gender-based violence policy, Equally Safe instead enacts carceral feminist logics that criminalise, surveil, and silence sex workers under the guise of protection. Through analysis of legal frameworks, NGO–state relations, and lived experiences, the chapter reveals how moral governance displaces rights-based and harm-reduction approaches. Drawing on feminist theory, intersectionality, and comparative insights from Ireland and New Zealand, it demonstrates that Scotland's end-demand trajectory undermines autonomy, safety, and justice for marginalised women. The chapter concludes by calling for a shift toward participatory, decriminalised, and plural feminist policy-making that centres sex workers' expertise and dismantles punitive state practices.

DOI: 10.4018/979-8-3373-5841-3.ch004

1. INTRODUCTION: CONTEXT, FRAMING, AND ARGUMENT

Scotland is frequently praised for its progressive social welfare architecture, gender equality commitments, and inclusive approach to public policy. As a devolved jurisdiction within the United Kingdom, it holds significant autonomy in matters of criminal justice, health, and social services, allowing it to design and implement policies tailored to its national identity and social priorities. Among these is the *Equally Safe* strategy, a flagship national framework for preventing and eradicating violence against women and girls. Positioned as a feminist intervention into public policy, *Equally Safe* explicitly embraces a gendered analysis of violence and seeks to centre women's voices in state responses to harm (Scottish Government, 2018). On the surface, such a strategy may appear emblematic of a state deeply committed to feminist principles. However, this chapter contends that *Equally Safe* functions as a mechanism of exclusion, operating within a carceral and moralistic framework that conflates consensual sex work with human trafficking.

This seemingly unified feminist commitment has long been contested within the broader field of gender policy. Feminist approaches to sex work diverge sharply, with abolitionist, carceral, and decriminalisation-oriented camps articulating radically different visions of gender justice. Where abolitionist frameworks call for the eradication of the sex industry, rights-based and sex worker-led feminisms advocate for decriminalisation, bodily autonomy, and harm reduction (Levy, 2015). These tensions are not merely academic—they are embodied in the very design of legal strategies like Equally Safe. Moreover, global legal experimentation offers alternatives: from Germany's regulated but corporatised system, to New Zealand's rights-based decriminalisation model (Doezema, 2010). This chapter intervenes within these contested debates, arguing that Scotland's framework aligns closely with carceral feminisms that perpetuate, rather than dismantle, epistemic and material exclusions.

This chapter critically examines the Scottish Government's *Equally Safe* strategy, arguing that its conflation of consensual sex work with human trafficking leads to epistemic violence and the institutional silencing of sex workers. This policy architecture, rooted in a carceral feminist framework, undermines the agency of individuals engaged in sex work by framing them exclusively as victims, thereby justifying punitive and prohibitive policy measures (Davidson, 2023). Far from a neutral or protective framework, *Equally Safe* mobilises a specific understanding of morality, danger, and female vulnerability that excludes those who do not conform to dominant gendered scripts. As Patnaik (2023) notes, the state's alignment with "rescue-driven feminism" displaces lived experience in favour of ideology, and nowhere is this clearer than in the treatment of sex workers under Scotland's anti-trafficking regime.

The central claim advanced in this chapter is that *Equally Safe*, while seemingly feminist and protective, paradoxically reproduces conditions of marginalisation through mechanisms of legal exclusion and moral silencing. Feminist statecraft, when entwined with carceral logics, becomes a tool not only of protection but also of control; particularly when it refuses to recognise the autonomy and diverse subjectivities of sex workers. This analysis will further demonstrate how such statecraft, while framed as progressive, enacts a framework in which the voices and lived experiences of sex workers are systematically excluded from policy development (Patnaik, 2023).

At the heart of this discussion is the adoption and institutionalisation of the Nordic Model, or so-called "end-demand" approach, which criminalises the purchase of sexual services while ostensibly decriminalising the act of selling sex. In practice, however, this model imposes legal precarity and social stigma on sex workers by sustaining environments of surveillance, harassment, and restricted access to justice (Reilly et al., 2021). As Najar (2023) notes, the Nordic Model relies on the assumption that all sex work is exploitative and inherently violent - a logic that reinforces punitive measures under the guise of feminist solidarity. The Scottish policy environment reflects these international currents by targeting clients, increasing police powers, and actively marginalising sex worker-led organisations from policy consultations.

Moreover, this chapter interrogates the Scottish Government's deployment of carceral feminism, a term coined by Bernstein (2007) to describe the increasing reliance on criminal justice solutions to address gendered harm. In Scotland, carceral feminism emerges not simply through law enforcement practices but through a broader ideological configuration that casts the state as the sole legitimate protector of vulnerable women. Feminist groups and NGOs that endorse *Equally Safe* often frame sex workers as either coerced victims or criminal collaborators, erasing the nuanced realities of survival, labour, and consent. This results in what Spivak (1988) calls epistemic violence: the systemic erasure of subaltern knowledge, particularly that of women who speak from outside normative boundaries. While Bernstein (2007) theorised carceral feminism primarily within the context of U.S. penal expansion, this chapter extends that framework to a devolved governance setting, demonstrating how carceral logics operate not only through sentencing practices but through funding architectures, consultation regimes, and discursive boundary-making.

Through this lens, *Equally Safe* is revealed not as a gender-just framework but as a project of moral governance, one that simplifies complex socio-economic dynamics into a binary of victimhood and exploitation (Vollinger, 2020). The lived experiences of sex workers, especially those who are migrant, LGBTQ+, or working-class, are rendered invisible within the strategy's framework. Such erasures are not neutral - they have material and symbolic consequences, shaping how sex work is policed, discussed, and responded to within the public sphere.

Furthermore, the chapter will demonstrate that this approach frequently overlooks the diverse realities of sex work, reducing labour and economic survival to narratives of immorality and danger. By denying the possibility of informed consent and political agency among sex workers, the Scottish approach recapitulates colonial and patriarchal logics that define marginalised populations solely through their vulnerability and need for rescue (Das & Pande, 2021). This analysis also situates Scotland's policies within broader global patterns of criminalising clients and increasing state control over intimate and informal economies. Lamas (2016) highlights how client-focused criminalisation regimes, while nominally protective, often exacerbate harms for those engaged in sex work by pushing the industry underground and reducing access to legal redress and health services.

This chapter proceeds by critically analysing the *Equally Safe* strategy's legal, institutional, and ideological foundations. Drawing on feminist legal theory, intersectional analysis, and critical policy studies, it demonstrates that Scotland's anti-trafficking agenda, far from being an exemplar of progressive governance, reflects a broader international pattern in which carceral feminist logics produce exclusion and harm under the guise of protection. It ultimately calls for a reimagining of feminist policymaking that centres sex workers' voices, lived expertise, and demands for legal recognition, safety, and autonomy.

This chapter proceeds in seven parts. Part Two examines the legal and institutional architecture of the Equally Safe framework, with particular attention to trafficking law, devolved governance, and funding structures. Part Three analyses the operation of feminist statecraft and the consolidation of carceral logics within Scottish policy discourse. Part Four interrogates the institutional exclusion of sex worker-led organisations as a form of epistemic violence. Part Five centres lived experience, demonstrating how legal precarity manifests materially for marginalised sex workers. Part Six situates Scotland within a comparative international landscape, evaluating alternative regulatory models. Finally, Part Seven outlines policy recommendations grounded in decriminalisation, participatory governance, and rights-based reform.

2. EQUALLY SAFE AND THE SCOTTISH LEGAL LANDSCAPE

The *Equally Safe* strategy, introduced by the Scottish Government in 2014 and revised in 2018, is framed as Scotland's national strategy to prevent and eradicate violence against women and girls. Grounded in a gendered analysis of violence, the strategy aligns closely with international frameworks such as the UN's Convention on the Elimination of All Forms of Discrimination Against Women (CEDAW) and regional obligations under the Istanbul Convention. It conceptualises violence as a cause and consequence of gender inequality and commits to a "Scotland where women and girls live free from all forms of violence and abuse" (Scottish Government, 2018). Though initially broad in scope, the strategy has evolved into a highly targeted framework—particularly in its treatment of commercial sex, which it conflates with trafficking and gender-based exploitation.

Origins and Ideological Framework

The early foundations of *Equally Safe* were built through collaborations with third-sector organisations such as Rape Crisis Scotland and Scottish Women's Aid, reflecting a close relationship between state policy and feminist NGOs. These partnerships shaped the framework's ideological orientation: a model of protection rooted in moral abolitionism and underpinned by the assumption that all prostitution is inherently exploitative. While the original strategy focused on domestic violence and coercive control, by 2017 it had expanded to identify prostitution and human trafficking as forms of gender-based violence (Scottish Government, 2018).

This expansion was facilitated through public consultations, policy working groups, and parliamentary debates that heavily favoured anti-prostitution stakeholders. Notably absent were sex worker-led organisations such as SCOT-PEP and Umbrella Lane, whose submissions were either ignored or delegitimised as unrepresentative or complicit in harm (SCOT-PEP, 2020). The resulting policy landscape thus reflected the dominant ideology of carceral feminism, which frames state surveillance and criminal sanctions as necessary tools to achieve gender justice (Bernstein, 2007).

Devolved Legal Context and Human Trafficking

As a devolved nation, Scotland retains control over its criminal justice and civil law systems, allowing it to develop distinct legal frameworks around prostitution and trafficking. However, the legal treatment of human trafficking remains closely aligned with UK-wide legislation—particularly the Modern Slavery Act 2015. Scotland's equivalent, the Human Trafficking and Exploitation (Scotland) Act 2015, criminalises all forms of trafficking and includes specific provisions for support services. While this law was ostensibly designed to address serious organised crime, its implementation has blurred the line between trafficking and consensual sex work, reinforcing the *Equally Safe* strategy's ideological alignment.

Crucially, the Act provides law enforcement agencies broad discretionary powers to investigate suspected trafficking operations, often resulting in raids on brothels or private residences where sex workers operate collectively. These actions are often framed as victim-centred interventions, but they can lead to arrests, deportations, or evictions, particularly for undocumented or migrant sex workers (Ramberg, 2021). The legal ambiguity surrounding third-party management of sex work has made it difficult for workers to operate safely or collectively, despite the absence of laws criminalising the selling of sex itself.

A vivid example of this blurred boundary can be seen in the 2019 police raid on a flat in Leith, Edinburgh, where several migrant women were detained under trafficking suspicions despite clear indications of consensual sex work. The women, some of whom were members of SCOT-PEP, were not offered legal assistance or trauma-informed support but were instead issued deportation notices under UK immigration protocols (SCOT-PEP, 2020). The operation was publicised as a safeguarding success, yet testimonies later revealed that the women were evicted and criminalised despite their appeals for help. Armstrong (2024) argues that such incidents expose how anti-trafficking efforts can function as tools of immigration policing and moral enforcement, particularly when consent and labour are systematically excluded from policy definitions.

The "End-Demand" Shift and Legislative Evolution

Following increasing pressure from organisations such as the Women's Support Project and the End Prostitution Now campaign, Scotland has moved closer to adopting the Nordic Model, which criminalises buyers of sexual services while claiming to protect sellers. The policy rationale behind this model is the notion that reducing demand for sexual services will dismantle the commercial sex industry and prevent trafficking (Langford & Skilbrei, 2021).

However, in practice, this model has disproportionately harmed sex workers by driving the industry underground. Under Nordic Model regimes, sex workers report increased levels of isolation, reduced ability to screen clients, and heightened vulnerability to police harassment and coercion (Nield, 2024; Persson, 2022). In Scotland, proposals to formally adopt this model were brought forward through the Criminalisation of the Purchase of Sex (Scotland) Bill, first introduced as a consultation by members of Scottish Parliament in 2020. Although this specific bill did not pass, its principles have been embedded in policy discourse and supported by the Scottish Parliament's Cross-Party Group on Commercial Sexual Exploitation.

Government rhetoric in public consultations increasingly aligns with end-demand narratives, often invoking trafficking statistics to justify the need for client criminalisation—even when such statistics are vague or unsubstantiated (McConnell, 2019). The Scottish Government's repeated framing of all sex work as a form of violence reflects a policy drift away from harm reduction toward ideological moralism. As Kingston and Thomas (2019) argue, Scotland has sought to model its policy on Nordic frameworks despite their documented harms and lack of evidence for trafficking reduction.

Institutional Actors and Power Dynamics

The implementation of *Equally Safe* involves a wide network of institutional actors, including the Scottish Government, Police Scotland, the Crown Office and Procurator Fiscal Service (COPFS), and local authorities. The strategy's governance is coordinated through a multi-agency approach, yet decision-making power remains centralised within state bodies and selected NGOs that align ideologically with abolitionist feminism.

Police Scotland has played a particularly active role in enforcing anti-trafficking measures, conducting raids under the guise of victim safeguarding. However, these actions have faced criticism for endangering the very populations they claim to protect. Migrant sex workers, in particular, face dual threats of criminalisation and immigration enforcement, often being treated as perpetrators rather than rights-holders (Smith, 2024).

The Crown Office, through the use of statutory guidance and prosecutorial discretion, also shapes how laws are applied in practice. While the sale of sex is not illegal, surrounding activities - such as brothel-keeping, soliciting, and advertising - are policed aggressively. This results in what legal scholars describe as de facto criminalisation, where sex workers are pushed into precarious, unregulated environments despite official claims of legal tolerance (Nield, 2024).

At the NGO level, a handful of state-aligned feminist organisations have disproportionately influenced legal reform and public discourse. These include Rape Crisis Scotland, Scottish Women's Aid, and the Women's Support Project, all of which support end-demand policies and promote narratives of sex work as inherently harmful. In contrast, grassroots organisations such as SCOT-PEP, Umbrella Lane, and the Sex Worker Advocacy and Resistance Movement (SWARM) have been marginalised in official consultations, their expertise dismissed as anecdotal or ideologically suspect.

The Merging of Trafficking and Consensual Sex Work

One of the most significant concerns within Scotland's legal landscape is the rhetorical and legislative merging of trafficking and sex work. Though trafficking is defined in international law as involving force, fraud, or coercion, the Scottish policy framework increasingly treats all commercial sex as presumptively exploitative. This erasure of consent and agency serves to legitimise intrusive policing, reduce support options for undocumented workers, and silence critical voices within policymaking forums (Langford & Skilbrei, 2021; Reilly et al., 2021).

This blurring is not merely semantic—it has legal and material consequences. By conflating sex work with trafficking, Scotland's strategy enables the criminal justice system to extend punitive measures into consensual adult arrangements. It also curtails the ability of sex workers to access labour protections, organise collectively, or claim the legal status of workers. In effect, the moral authority of anti-trafficking discourse becomes a tool for normalising state violence under the banner of care.

State Feminism and Third Sector Funding

The entanglement of the Scottish state with feminist organisations through funding mechanisms reveals a deeper layer of structural co-optation that underpins the Equally Safe strategy. This phenomenon, sometimes described as NGO-isation or instrumentalised feminism, refers to the institutional incorporation of feminist goals into state-aligned third-sector bodies, often in exchange for financial stability and policy influence. While partnerships between government and feminist civil society are not inherently problematic, they become ethically and politically fraught when dissenting voices are excluded, and compliance becomes a condition of survival.

In the Scottish context, many third-sector organisations contributing to the Equally Safe delivery plan are directly funded by the government, including those that have publicly endorsed the Nordic Model. As Hill and Macleod (2023) argue, this creates a situation where the very NGOs tasked with challenging state power become enmeshed in its logic. Their report on gender-based violence services in Scotland found that organisations critical of carceral approaches — particularly those advocating for sex worker rights — faced funding exclusion, reputational risk, and marginalisation from official consultations. Such dynamics not only narrow the scope of feminist debate but also contribute to a climate of epistemic closure, where only certain 'respectable' forms of feminist knowledge are legitimised.

The funding architecture of Equally Safe thus performs a regulatory function: it disciplines the political field by rewarding ideological conformity. Organisations that adopt the state's moral framing of sex work as inherently exploitative are elevated as stakeholders, while those promoting decriminalisation are sidelined as radical or unrepresentative. This dynamic mirrors critiques advanced by Brown (2021), who contends that carceral feminist agendas increasingly rely on technocratic forms of legitimacy — impact metrics, safeguarding discourses, and partnership language — to suppress ideological dissent. Under the guise of neutrality and evidence-based policymaking, the state determines which feminisms count, and which are rendered irrelevant.

These dynamics are further intensified by the fragmentation of funding streams in the post-austerity context, which places additional pressure on feminist NGOs to demonstrate alignment with state-defined 'outcomes'. Organisations like SCOT-PEP and Umbrella Lane, despite offering peer-led and trauma-informed services, remain financially precarious precisely because they resist this framing. Their refusal to pathologise sex workers or position them as passive victims undermines the strategic narratives necessary for institutional recognition.

Moreover, this funding-based gatekeeping has epistemic consequences: it produces what Santos (2007) calls a "monoculture of knowledge", where only state-approved feminist perspectives are seen as valid, and alternative frameworks — such as anti-capitalist, queer, and migrant-led approaches — are erased. The implication is that feminist solidarity is not only conditional but contractual: a resource to be awarded based on ideological fit.

To understand Equally Safe's exclusions, then, we must interrogate not only its legal formulations but also the political economy of its feminist alliances. The state's preference for a sanitised, compliant feminism reinforces the broader carceral infrastructure and delegitimises the radical democratic potential of sex worker-led organising. In this light, any truly emancipatory policy future must confront the structural incentives that currently reward exclusion over pluralism, and narrative control over epistemic justice.

Judicial Interpretation, Statutory Ambiguity, and the Limits of Legal Protection

Despite the strategy's extensive reliance on statutory frameworks, relatively little attention has been paid to how Scottish courts interpret and apply the legal provisions underpinning anti-trafficking and prostitution enforcement. The Human Trafficking and Exploitation (Scotland) Act 2015 defines exploitation broadly, including sexual exploitation, slavery, servitude, and forced labour. However, the Act provides limited clarification regarding the role of consent in adult sex work contexts. While international law requires force, fraud, or coercion for trafficking to be established, domestic enforcement practices frequently treat commercial sex as presumptively exploitative, even in the absence of these elements (Scoular, 2015).

This ambiguity becomes particularly significant in relation to section 3 of the 2015 Act, which defines exploitation without clearly distinguishing coerced sexual exploitation from consensual adult sex work facilitated by third parties. As a result, police and prosecutorial discretion play a decisive role in determining when collective working arrangements are treated as trafficking indicators rather than safety strategies (Nield, 2024). The absence of sustained judicial clarification on these boundaries permits executive interpretation to harden into quasi-doctrine, enabling enforcement practices to operate as de facto law without meaningful appellate constraint.

UK Supreme Court jurisprudence demonstrates a more nuanced approach to vulnerability and consent in labour exploitation contexts. In *Hounga v Allen* [2014] UKSC 47, the Court recognised that exploitative working conditions can coexist with constrained but meaningful agency, rejecting a rigid application of the illegality doctrine. Although not a sex work case, the reasoning is instructive: vulnerability does not automatically negate consent, nor does illegality extinguish access to legal protection. Similarly, in *R v SK* [2011] EWCA Crim 1691, the Court of Appeal emphasised that trafficking requires proof of exploitation beyond mere participation in commercial sex, underscoring the necessity of evidential scrutiny rather than presumption.

Yet Scottish policy discourse increasingly collapses this evidential threshold. The rhetorical merging of trafficking and prostitution within Equally Safe effectively displaces the judicial insistence on coercion with a policy presumption of harm (Langford & Skilbrei, 2021). The limited volume of reported Scottish cases directly interrogating consensual adult sex work under trafficking provisions does not signal doctrinal clarity; rather, it reflects the informal resolution of many interventions through immigration enforcement, eviction, or prosecutorial discretion. This dynamic produces a form of shadow jurisprudence, where legal precarity is produced through enforcement practice rather than appellate adjudication.

Legal remedies theoretically available to sex workers remain structurally inaccessible in practice. Challenges under Article 8 of the European Convention on Human Rights (right to private life) or Article 14 (non-discrimination), incorporated domestically through the Human Rights Act 1998, could be advanced where disproportionate interference or discriminatory enforcement occurs. However, stigma, immigration precarity, financial barriers, and fear of exposure significantly constrain access to litigation (Benoit et al., 2018). Judicial review of police raids or exclusionary funding decisions is similarly improbable given resource asymmetries and reputational risk. Consequently, the formal availability of rights does not translate into meaningful legal protection.

The gap between statutory language, judicial reasoning, and enforcement practice underscores a central tension within the Equally Safe framework: while the law purports to target coercion and exploitation, its application frequently collapses the distinction between trafficking and consensual labour. With absent sustained doctrinal clarification regarding consent, proportionality, and evidential thresholds, the legal architecture underpinning Equally Safe remains susceptible to ideological expansion rather than principled limitation.

In sum, Scotland's legal landscape reveals not only ideological convergence between anti-trafficking and anti-prostitution agendas, but also significant doctrinal ambiguity. The absence of clear judicial boundaries permits expansive enforcement practices that exceed statutory intent, reinforcing a carceral orientation under the language of protection.

3. FEMINIST STATECRAFT AND THE ERASURE OF SEX WORKERS

Feminist engagement with the governance of sex work in Scotland is shaped by long-standing debates over autonomy, exploitation, and state power. Feminist statecraft - defined as the institutionalisation of feminist ideals into state mechanisms - has yielded both emancipatory policies and exclusionary practices. Nowhere is this tension more visible than in the treatment of sex work under the *Equally Safe* strategy, where feminist principles of protection and gender justice are operationalised through frameworks that pathologise and criminalise sex workers. This section argues that Scottish feminist policy-making is increasingly characterised by carceral logics that rely on a discourse of rescue, vulnerability, and punishment, marginalising those who resist this narrative.

The Framing of Sex Work as Inherently Violent

In the Scottish policy landscape, sex work is not understood as labour but as a form of violence. This perspective is reinforced by feminist NGOs such as Rape Crisis Scotland, Scottish Women's Aid, and the Women's Support Project, which advocate for an abolitionist stance. These organisations have been instrumental in shaping *Equally Safe*, and their influence has contributed to a narrative where all forms of commercial sex are regarded as inherently exploitative, irrespective of context, consent, or working conditions (Armstrong, 2024).

This ideological framing is based on the assumption that no woman can freely choose to engage in sex work and that structural coercion renders all transactions inherently violent. Such a framing denies the possibility of agency, particularly for marginalised women, and has been central to the push for Scotland to adopt the Nordic Model. While this perspective is presented as feminist, it overlooks diverse realities and reinforces state paternalism (Easton, 2023). Feminist organisations that advocate this line often draw upon individual survivor testimonies to generalise about the sex industry, framing women in the trade as passive victims needing rescue rather than autonomous actors navigating complex socio-economic terrain.

Rescue, Vulnerability, and the Rhetoric of Protection

A dominant feature of feminist statecraft in Scotland is the discourse of rescue and vulnerability. State and NGO actors frequently position sex workers as "at risk" populations in need of intervention. This rhetorical positioning justifies punitive state action, including criminalising clients, raiding premises, and forcibly "rehabilitating" women from sex work. As Ryan (2020) notes, these interventions are often couched in therapeutic language, framing exit from sex work as recovery, while concealing the structural violence enacted through surveillance, criminalisation, and exclusion from public policy processes.

This rescue narrative is aligned with what Bernstein (2007) terms carceral feminism: a mode of governance that advances gender justice through criminal law and state surveillance. Carceral feminism endorses the expansion of punitive power in the name of women's safety, yet often disregards the very women most affected by these interventions. In the Scottish case, this has meant that feminist organisations advocating client criminalisation have received state funding and policy influence, while sex worker-led organisations such as SCOT-PEP and Umbrella Lane are excluded from consultations and delegitimised in public debates. This transformation of feminist ideals into disciplinary governance reflects what Halley et al. (2006) describe as "governance feminism," whereby feminist agendas become institutionalised and repurposed through state power.

Protective Rhetoric, Punitive Outcomes

The contradictions between the rhetoric of protection and the outcomes of feminist policy are particularly stark in the Scottish context. Despite claiming to protect sex workers, the push for client criminalisation has contributed to increased surveillance, police violence, and housing insecurity for workers. The adoption of Nordic-style policies in other jurisdictions has produced well-documented harms: increased risk of violence, lack of access to justice, and reduced ability to negotiate working conditions (FitzGerald, O'Neill & Wylie, 2020). Scotland's trajectory suggests similar consequences, particularly given the use of anti-trafficking laws to justify brothel raids and immigration enforcement (Rowland, 2025). These punitive outcomes are frequently obscured by the moral authority of the feminist organisations promoting such policies.

While *Equally Safe* frames its approach as evidence-based and trauma-informed, its reliance on carceral strategies undermines its legitimacy. As Easton (2023) notes in her critique of UK-wide feminist prostitution discourse, protective laws often rest on contested definitions of harm and fail to engage with sex workers' own accounts of safety and agency. The exclusion of alternative feminist epistemologies results in a policymaking process that reproduces stigma while claiming to dismantle it.

Dominant Feminist Voices vs. Excluded Feminist Perspectives

The consolidation of abolitionist feminism within Scottish institutions has marginalised other feminist traditions - particularly those aligned with sex worker rights, intersectionality, and harm reduction. Sex worker-led feminist organisations articulate a feminist politics grounded in lived experience, bodily autonomy, and labour rights. However, these voices are routinely dismissed as "not real feminism" or as co-opted by the sex industry (Rowland, 2025).

This exclusion is not only discursive but institutional. In policy forums and government consultations, abolitionist NGOs are given privileged access, while sex worker organisations are tokenised, ignored, or completely excluded. This constitutes a form of epistemic violence, whereby the knowledge and experiences of sex workers are deemed illegitimate or irrelevant to public discourse (Spivak, 1988).

The dominance of rescue-oriented feminism also intersects with other axes of power - such as class, race, and citizenship. Migrant sex workers, for instance, face compounded exclusion due to immigration laws and cultural stigmas, yet are often rendered invisible in feminist policy proposals. As Armstrong (2024) notes in her cross-national study, the erasure of sex worker voices in Scotland reflects broader global patterns of moral governance dressed in feminist language.

What emerges here is not merely a contest over policy tools but a fundamental clash of feminist epistemologies. Abolitionist feminism, dominant in Scottish policymaking, frames sex work as inherently violent and incompatible with gender equality. In contrast, pro-decriminalisation feminists position sex work as a site of economic agency and bodily autonomy, embedded in systems of gendered and racialised labour (Scoular, 2015). Harding (2020) notes that governance feminists often wield state power to implement moral agendas, whereas sex worker rights activists draw on intersectional, queer, and postcolonial frameworks to demand legal pluralism and harm reduction. The failure of Equally Safe to accommodate such dissenting feminist voices is not incidental—it reflects a strategic narrowing of what counts as "legitimate" feminist politics within state institutions.

Towards Feminist Pluralism and Anti-Carceral Praxis

The current configuration of feminist statecraft in Scotland demands re-evaluation. Rather than reinforcing criminal justice as the solution to gendered harm, feminist policy must expand to include non-carceral, rights-based, and redistributive approaches. As Rowland (2025) argues, an anti-carceral feminism recognises the limits of punitive intervention and centres the voices of those at the margins of both feminist theory and state policy.

A pluralist feminist praxis would make room for the diverse realities of sex work, acknowledging both harm and agency. It would also involve the redistribution of resources and political capital to those historically excluded from the policymaking process. This entails a meaningful commitment to participatory governance, where sex worker organisations are not merely consulted but empowered to shape legal and social reforms.

In conclusion, feminist statecraft in Scotland, as exemplified by the *Equally Safe* strategy, illustrates the dangers of aligning feminist ideals with carceral logics. While well-intentioned, such strategies risk replicating the very power imbalances they seek to correct. A truly feminist approach to policy must embrace multiplicity, listen to those most affected, and refuse the seductions of punitive power.

In summary, Scottish feminist statecraft illustrates how protectionist rhetoric can crystallise into punitive governance. By narrowing feminist politics to a carceral register, Equally Safe marginalises alternative feminist epistemologies and consolidates institutional power around a singular moral vision of harm. While these ideological exclusions operate at the level of feminist governance, their consequences become most visible in the production of knowledge and the regulation of who is permitted to speak. It is to this epistemic dimension that the analysis now turns.

4. INSTITUTIONAL EXCLUSION AND EPISTEMIC VIOLENCE

Despite positioning itself as a feminist and inclusive policy framework, Scotland's *Equally Safe* strategy has systematically marginalised sex worker-led organisations and voices. This exclusion is neither incidental nor apolitical—it is a form of epistemic violence, a process through which certain knowledges are rendered invisible, illegitimate, or dangerous. Drawing on the work of Spivak (1988), epistemic violence in this context refers to the structural silencing of sex workers' experiential expertise, particularly when that expertise challenges dominant feminist or state logics. Within Scotland's anti-trafficking and violence against women policy environment, the erasure of sex workers' perspectives is not simply a discursive oversight; it is an embedded political strategy.

Sex Worker Exclusion in Policy Processes

Sex worker-led organisations such as SCOT-PEP and Umbrella Lane have routinely been excluded from policymaking forums, consultations, and legislative design processes. Despite repeated attempts to engage with the Scottish Government and share grounded insights into the lived realities of sex work, their contributions have often been dismissed or ignored. As Smith (2015) documents, the exclusion of these groups reflects a deeper discomfort among policymakers and mainstream feminist organisations with recognising sex work as labour, or sex workers as legitimate stakeholders.

The consultation processes leading up to legislative discussions about criminalising the purchase of sex and expanding anti-trafficking powers serve as illustrative examples. Submissions by sex worker-led organisations are frequently underrepresented in official reports, or selectively quoted to support pre-existing policy directions. As Christoffersen and McCabe (2025) argue, dominant white feminist organisations exert considerable "epistemic control" over the policy space, using their institutional authority to define the terms of debate and whose voices count as authentic.

This asymmetry is exacerbated by the tendency of state-aligned feminist NGOs to frame sex worker perspectives as either "captured" by industry interests or too compromised by trauma to be politically coherent. As FitzGerald, O'Neill and Wylie (2020) note in the Irish context, but with direct relevance to Scotland, this framing serves to delegitimise political claims made by current sex workers while elevating the testimony of those who have exited the industry and adopted abolitionist positions.

The Structural Mechanics of Epistemic Violence

The exclusion of sex worker knowledge is not limited to individual acts of silencing—it is a structural and institutional practice that spans government, academia, and feminist NGOs. Butler (2024) highlights that epistemic violence operates not only through exclusion from speech but through the structuring of intelligibility itself. In such frameworks, sex worker perspectives are rendered incoherent or deviant before they are even heard, foreclosing the possibility of recognition within policy discourse.

In the case of *Equally Safe*, epistemic violence is embedded in the strategy's foundational assumption that all prostitution is a form of violence against women. This precludes the possibility of alternative narratives - such as sex work as survival, labour, or even empowerment - from entering the conversation. As Armstrong (2011) notes, the radical feminist framing that dominates Scottish policy renders non-conforming standpoints unintelligible, often reducing diverse lived realities to a monolithic tale of harm and rescue.

The consequences of this are far-reaching. Without access to policymaking arenas, sex worker organisations cannot meaningfully shape the laws and policies that govern their lives. Nor can they counter the circulation of misleading or ideologically driven statistics that conflate trafficking with consensual sex work. This absence not only impacts policy outcomes but also reinforces stigma, isolation, and vulnerability among sex workers, particularly those at the intersection of multiple marginalised identities.

Intersectionality and Epistemic Silencing

The erasure of sex worker knowledge is especially acute for those whose identities intersect with other forms of structural oppression. Migrant sex workers, LGBTQ+ individuals, people of colour, and those with precarious immigration status often face compounded exclusion, both from feminist policy discussions and broader state protections. Christoffersen and McCabe (2025) point out that *Equally Safe* fails to operationalise intersectionality in any meaningful way, resulting in policies that are blind to the layered experiences of marginalised sex workers.

Hanscamp (2023) argues for a trauma-informed, intersectional feminist approach to working with sex workers—one that affirms rather than pathologises their lived experiences. However, such frameworks remain marginal in Scottish policymaking, where risk and rescue continue to dominate the narrative. Instead of being consulted as experts, sex workers are often treated as data points in public health studies or recipients of pre-designed interventions.

This structural silencing is part of a broader politics of knowledge in which certain feminist voices—those aligned with state-funded abolitionist NGOs—are granted epistemic authority, while others are systematically excluded. The feminist statecraft embodied in *Equally Safe* thus reproduces a hierarchy of speaking positions, where some women are allowed to speak on behalf of others, and some are perpetually spoken for.

Resistance, Visibility, and the Politics of Refusal

Despite these exclusions, sex worker-led organisations in Scotland have not remained silent. Groups like SCOT-PEP, Umbrella Lane, and the Sex Worker Advocacy and Resistance Movement (SWARM) have consistently challenged their exclusion through public advocacy, alternative data production, and coalition building. Their work illustrates what Grenfell et al. (2023) describe as a "politics of doing"—a mode of feminist resistance that does not wait for permission to speak but carves out alternative spaces for visibility, care, and mutual aid.

This resistance is also epistemological. By centring sex workers' experiences and producing their own research, sex worker collectives challenge dominant narratives about violence, harm, and justice. They expose the limitations of carceral frameworks and advocate for rights-based, decriminalised models grounded in harm reduction. However, these alternative epistemologies remain marginalised within official policy discourse, particularly where they contradict the state's preferred framing of sex work as violence.

As McKeown (2021) notes in her study of Scottish feminist anti-violence campaigns, the visibility of sex workers is often surveilled and contained rather than embraced. Sex worker resistance, when it does gain public traction, is frequently co-opted or reinterpreted to support mainstream narratives. Thus, even visibility does not guarantee epistemic justice—particularly in a policy environment where "listening" is often symbolic rather than substantive.

The institutional exclusion of sex worker voices from Scotland's *Equally Safe* framework exemplifies a broader pattern of epistemic violence within feminist statecraft. By privileging certain narratives of harm and marginalising those that do not conform, the state reproduces a politics of silence that undermines its claims to inclusivity and justice. This is not a failure of implementation but a reflection of the ideological architecture of *Equally Safe* itself. If feminist policymaking in Scotland is to move beyond symbolic inclusion, it must reckon with its own mechanisms of epistemic control. This requires not just inviting sex worker organisations to the table, but transforming the terms of engagement so that diverse forms of knowledge are genuinely valued. Until then, *Equally Safe* will remain, ironically, a strategy that protects some women by silencing others.

Yet resistance persists. Drawing on Foucault's (1980) notion of subjugated knowledges, sex worker communities actively produce alternative epistemologies grounded in lived experience and peer research. Lorde's (1984) famous warning that "the master's tools will never dismantle the master's house" underscores the need for structural transformation rather than symbolic inclusion. Sex worker-led organisations like Umbrella Lane are not simply advocacy groups—they are epistemic communities resisting erasure through care, storytelling, and horizontal governance.

In summary, epistemic exclusion within the Equally Safe framework is not a procedural oversight but a structural feature of governance. By privileging certain feminist narratives while marginalising sex worker-led knowledge, the policy consolidates moral authority at the expense of pluralism. The silencing of dissenting expertise stabilises carceral responses and forecloses alternative imaginaries of justice. If epistemic violence structures the terms of debate, its material consequences are borne in everyday life. The following section therefore centres lived experience to examine how legal precarity is experienced on the ground.

5. LIVED EXPERIENCES OF LEGAL PRECARITY

While the *Equally Safe* strategy is framed as a gender-just response to violence, its on-the-ground impact on sex workers in Scotland reveals a stark contradiction between policy intent and lived experience. The strategy's commitment to abolitionist and carceral responses has exacerbated legal precarity, especially among already marginalised sex workers—those who are migrant, LGBTQ+, working-class, or precariously housed. This section draws on qualitative studies, grey literature, and community-generated reports to highlight the systemic harms produced by Scotland's anti-prostitution policy environment, including intensified surveillance, housing and income insecurity, limited access to healthcare, and criminal justice exposure.

Criminalisation by Proxy: The Everyday Realities of Policing

Although the sale of sex is not itself illegal in Scotland, sex workers operate under a regime of criminalisation by proxy. Activities surrounding sex work—such as soliciting, brothel-keeping, and third-party advertising—remain criminal offences. These legal ambiguities allow for the persistent policing of sex workers' lives under the justification of public safety and anti-trafficking enforcement. According to Armstrong (2024), such policing is especially prevalent in the case of migrant sex workers, who frequently report being targeted in "rescue raids" that result not in support, but in arrest, detention, or deportation.

The pervasive threat of surveillance extends to digital platforms as well. Sex workers using online spaces to advertise services or screen clients have reported harassment and de-platforming, with no regulatory recourse (Rowland, 2025). As Brouwers (2022) highlights, the inability to work collectively or legally organise labour conditions contributes to profound insecurity, isolation, and heightened risk of exploitation.

Housing and Income Insecurity

The legal ambiguity surrounding shared working arrangements forces many sex workers to choose between safety and legality. Working in pairs or groups is often considered brothel-keeping, leading landlords to evict tenants under pressure from police or local authorities. As a result, sex workers frequently experience housing precarity or are forced into homelessness. Tweed (2022) documents the overlapping vulnerabilities of sex workers experiencing housing instability, mental health challenges, and criminal justice involvement. For many, the cycle of evictions, street-based work, and police contact creates a feedback loop of exclusion and risk.

Income insecurity further compounds these pressures. Many sex workers in Scotland are excluded from formal employment due to immigration status, criminal records, or stigma. With limited access to benefits or unionised work, sex work often becomes the only viable income source. Yet as Armstrong (2024) notes, Scottish policy discourse refuses to recognise sex work as labour, rendering these economic realities invisible in both welfare policy and anti-poverty interventions.

Health Access and Institutional Distrust

Stigma and fear of criminalisation significantly impact access to healthcare services. Sex workers - particularly trans and migrant individuals - report avoiding health facilities due to concerns about being outed, judged, or reported to authorities. The criminalisation of clients and the lack of formal workplace protections mean that health access is often mediated through third-sector providers, many of which operate with limited resources and within a rescue-oriented framework.

Community-led initiatives, such as those facilitated by Umbrella Lane, have attempted to fill these gaps through harm reduction, peer support, and outreach. However, as Rowland (2025) emphasises, these informal networks face constant pressure from institutional actors who question their legitimacy or co-opt their work without redistributing power or funding. This institutional distrust reinforces precarity by leaving sex workers reliant on underfunded and politically marginal support systems.

Intersectional Harms: Migrant and LGBTQ+ Sex Workers

The impact of Scotland's anti-prostitution framework is not evenly distributed. Migrant sex workers experience multiple, intersecting forms of precarity, including threats of immigration enforcement, language barriers, racial profiling, and exclusion from legal protections. Armstrong (2024) shows how the *Equally Safe* framework fails to address, or even acknowledge, these specific vulnerabilities, instead reproducing a universalised image of the sex worker as a white, cisgender Scottish woman in need of rescue.

Similarly, LGBTQ+ sex workers face compounded marginalisation. Stella and Binnie (2025) document the experiences of trans and queer migrants in Scotland, many of whom turn to sex work due to exclusion from formal employment or social services. These individuals are doubly marginalised by policies that criminalise their work and by LGBTQ+ organisations that are often silent or ambivalent about sex workers' rights. The invisibility of queer and trans sex workers in both feminist and LGBTQ+ policy spaces is a form of structural erasure, one that leaves individuals without institutional allies.

Community reports such as those cited by Vamvaka-Tatsi (2024) further highlight how queer migrants navigate a hostile policy landscape that treats their sexuality as both a basis for asylum and a reason for exclusion when linked to sex work. These overlapping forms of surveillance create what Stella et al. (2016) describe as a "matrix of vulnerability" that traps individuals in cycles of risk, dependence, and invisibility.

Precarity in the Pandemic

The COVID-19 pandemic exposed and exacerbated the structural vulnerabilities created by the criminalisation of sex work under Scotland's gender-based violence framework. While Equally Safe purports to prioritise the protection of vulnerable women, its exclusion of sex workers from formal recognition meant they were completely omitted from pandemic relief schemes. In the absence of legal recognition as workers, sex workers were ineligible for furlough, self-employment grants, or rent protection. This invisibility in emergency planning was not incidental but a direct consequence of the state's refusal to treat sex work as labour.

The crisis hit marginalised sex workers hardest — particularly undocumented migrants, trans women, and people of colour — many of whom rely on informal economies for survival. With physical distancing rules in place, these workers lost their income overnight, while others were forced into riskier or more hidden practices to survive. Reports from Umbrella Lane and SWARM documented cases of sex workers being evicted, losing custody of children, or taking on abusive clients due to economic desperation (SWARM, 2021; Umbrella Lane, 2022). Yet no funding under the Equally Safe delivery plan was redirected toward emergency support for this population.

Community-led responses, in contrast, were rapid and deeply effective. SCOT-PEP and Umbrella Lane coordinated crowdfunded emergency hardship grants, mutual aid networks, and health information distribution — filling the critical gaps left by state inaction. These grassroots strategies exemplify what Lorde (1984) would describe as "survival as resistance," where marginalised groups generate resilience through collective care. Yet their efforts also highlight the systemic absence of state accountability. As Armstrong (2024) argues, the Scottish Government's unwillingness to collaborate with these organisations — even in crisis — reveals a political choice to preserve a moralised policy stance at the cost of public health.

The pandemic also intensified policing and surveillance of sex workers under the guise of public health. In several cases, individuals reported being fined or threatened with arrest for breaching lockdown rules, while attempting to meet basic needs. This enforcement disproportionately targeted migrant and street-based workers, replicating existing patterns of over-policing. As Harding (2020) notes, crises often expand the reach of carceral governance, and COVID-19 provided the perfect pretext for further entrenching exclusionary legal norms under the cover of emergency.

In sum, the COVID-19 pandemic was not only a public health crisis but a litmus test for the inclusivity of Scotland's gender justice agenda — a test that exposed the structural limits of Equally Safe's inclusionary claims. By omitting sex workers from both support and consultation, the Scottish state reinforced the very precarity its strategy claims to eliminate.

Mutual Aid, Resilience, and Community Resistance

In response to these conditions, sex workers in Scotland have developed complex systems of mutual aid and informal resistance. From peer-run drop-ins to digital harm reduction tools and legal advocacy, these practices offer vital lifelines in the absence of state support. Umbrella Lane, SCOT-PEP, and SWARM are central actors in this landscape, offering non-judgmental services that prioritise autonomy and consent.

These initiatives reflect a broader feminist politics of refusal: a rejection of both victimhood narratives and carceral solutions. As Brouwers (2022) notes, sex workers often articulate safety not in relation to the law but in relation to one another. "I feel safe when I'm working with her," one interviewee stated, underscoring the collective dimensions of care that stand in contrast to individualised and punitive models of protection.

This resistance also takes epistemic form. Through community-led research and public advocacy, sex workers are challenging dominant narratives, producing knowledge grounded in lived experience, and demanding recognition not as victims but as rights-bearing workers. However, these efforts are frequently under-resourced and excluded from official platforms, revealing a persistent disjuncture between Scotland's rhetorical commitment to inclusion and the everyday realities of exclusion.

These patterns reveal not merely policy failure but governance design: precarity is not accidental but structurally produced by a legal regime that refuses recognition while sustaining regulation. The lived experiences of sex workers in Scotland under *Equally Safe* reveal a complex terrain of legal precarity, institutional abandonment, and collective resistance. Rather than delivering safety, the current framework institutionalises insecurity by criminalising survival strategies, denying access to services, and erasing the voices of those most affected. Migrant, LGBTQ+, and working-class sex workers face especially acute forms of vulnerability, exacerbated by intersecting regimes of surveillance, stigma, and structural violence. Until these lived experiences are centred in policy design, *Equally Safe* will remain a misnomer—providing safety only for some, while rendering others dangerously invisible.

Amid this dense policy and academic terrain, the voices of sex workers remain urgent and clarifying. "I don't need to be rescued—I need to be paid, housed, and safe," said a Scottish sex worker in a SCOT-PEP focus group, pushing back against the rescue rhetoric embedded in Equally Safe (SCOT-PEP, 2020). Another interviewee told Umbrella Lane: "They call it protection, but it feels like being hunted." These testimonies, often excluded from formal policy consultations, highlight how lived realities destabilise the clean moral binaries of violence, victimhood, and virtue. Rowland (2025) argues that these personal-political narratives form a counter-public archive, mobilising emotion, critique, and collective memory as tools of resistance. Including these voices is not symbolic inclusion but a requirement of epistemic justice. These lived experiences illuminate the material consequences of doctrinal ambiguity and carceral governance. Legal precarity is not merely theoretical but embodied in housing instability, health exclusion, policing, and economic vulnerability. The distance between protective rhetoric and lived reality underscores the urgent need for structural reform.

6. COMPARATIVE INSIGHTS AND ALTERNATIVE FUTURES

To understand the particularities of Scotland's *Equally Safe* framework, it is essential to situate it within a broader comparative context. Across the globe, jurisdictions have adopted markedly different legal approaches to sex work, ranging from full criminalisation to full decriminalisation. This section compares Scotland's increasingly Nordic-oriented policy trajectory with three contrasting models: England and Wales' limited legalisation, Ireland's adoption of the Nordic Model, and New Zealand's pioneering decriminalisation framework. Through this comparison, it becomes evident that harm-reduction and rights-based approaches produce far better outcomes for sex workers in terms of health, safety, and autonomy.

The Nordic Model in Ireland: Criminalising the Client

Ireland, like Scotland, has embraced the Nordic Model, which criminalises the purchase but not the sale of sex. Advocates claim that this "end-demand" approach protects those in prostitution while targeting exploiters. However, in practice, it reproduces many of the same harms associated with full criminalisation. Irish sex workers have reported increased violence, a reluctance to report crimes to the police, and deteriorating working conditions since the model's implementation in 2017 (Armstrong, 2024).

As Preston (2024) argues, these frameworks fail to dismantle stigma or facilitate access to justice. Instead, they intensify the risks faced by sex workers, pushing them into more clandestine and unsafe environments. The policy collapse of consensual sex work into anti-trafficking discourse is central to both Irish and Scottish discourses, and reinforces a moral panic that obscures the real voices and lived experiences of sex workers (Preston, 2024).

England and Wales: Legal but Fragmented

In contrast, England and Wales operate under a quasi-legalised regime where the exchange of sex for money is not illegal, but related activities, such as brothel-keeping and solicitation, remain criminalised. This partial tolerance results in a fragmented legal landscape where sex work is neither fully condemned nor protected. As Sequeira (2022) notes, this ambiguity contributes to a precarious status quo in which sex workers are tolerated but denied full labour rights and legal protections.

Legal inconsistencies across jurisdictions exacerbate this precarity. While some local authorities operate informal tolerance zones, others pursue punitive enforcement strategies. This creates confusion for workers, who may not know where they stand legally. Although this system avoids the overt carcerality of the Nordic Model, it fails to deliver the dignity, stability, and safety afforded by full legal recognition.

The German Model and Global South Critique

Germany offers another instructive contrast. Its legalisation model permits sex work under regulatory conditions, with licensing, taxation, and zoning controls imposed by the state. While this framework reduces overt criminalisation, it has been critiqued for fostering a two-tiered system: one for those able to comply with bureaucratic requirements, and another for precarious, often undocumented workers pushed into illegality (Wagenaar et al., 2017). Moreover, Global South feminists such as Kapur (2005) warn that even progressive regimes can reinscribe neocolonial logics by defining 'worthy' sex workers as those conforming to Western norms of productivity, hygiene, and visibility. The lesson for Scotland is not merely model selection, but interrogation of the normative assumptions that structure regulatory legitimacy. Without interrogating the moral and economic hierarchies embedded within regulatory design, legal reform risks reproducing stratified legitimacy rather than dismantling exclusion.

New Zealand: Decriminalisation and Human Rights

New Zealand's approach—established through the Prostitution Reform Act 2003—offers a compelling alternative to both criminalisation and partial legalisation. It removes criminal penalties for sex workers, clients, and third parties, while instituting workplace regulations that uphold labour rights, occupational safety, and public health. Critically, it reframes sex work as legitimate labour, and sex workers as citizens entitled to dignity and protection.

A growing body of research confirms the positive outcomes of this model. Armstrong (2021) reports that sex workers in New Zealand experience greater autonomy, reduced stigma, and improved relationships with law enforcement. The ability to refuse clients, negotiate safer working conditions, and report abuse without fear of criminalisation has enhanced both physical and psychological safety.

From a public health perspective, decriminalisation has significantly improved access to healthcare services. A scoping review by Macioti et al. (2023) found that decriminalised contexts like New Zealand exhibited higher rates of STI testing, reduced health disparities, and better communication between sex workers and clinicians. Armstrong, Phillips, and Ryan (2024) further show that sex workers in New Zealand report fewer instances of healthcare discrimination compared to those in Scotland or Ireland, underscoring the relationship between legal frameworks and stigma in medical settings.

The decriminalised model also excels in terms of participatory governance. As Zangger (2016) explains, the inclusion of sex workers in the design and implementation of policy has strengthened legitimacy and accountability, while simultaneously reducing state harassment and police overreach.

This rights-based, harm-reduction framework particularly benefits migrant, LGBTQ+, and working-class sex workers - groups disproportionately targeted under punitive regimes. By eliminating the fear of arrest, deportation, or outing, decriminalisation creates conditions in which the most marginalised can access justice, health, and mutual support networks.

Rethinking Futures: From Carcerality to Rights-Based Governance

Comparative research consistently indicates that decriminalisation outperforms criminalisation and end-demand approaches across the domains of public health, worker safety, legal equity, and human rights. Scotland's current policy trajectory, shaped by *Equally Safe*'s abolitionist logic, mirrors the failures observed in Ireland. It centres criminal justice solutions rather than addressing the structural conditions that underpin exploitation: poverty, stigma, migration precarity, and gender-based violence.

Future policy must move beyond punitive governance frameworks and embrace rights-based, harm-reduction governance. This means recognising sex work as legitimate labour, centring the knowledge and leadership of sex workers in policymaking, and dismantling the racial, moral, and class-based logics that currently drive Scottish law. New Zealand's model provides not just a vision, but a roadmap for how to achieve this. As Armstrong (2024) aptly concludes: "In an ideal world, it would be fully decriminalised." The evidence affirms that this ideal is both necessary and attainable. Comparative analysis therefore clarifies what domestic debate often obscures: criminalisation, whether direct or indirect, consistently amplifies harm, while decriminalisation enhances safety, autonomy, and access to justice. Scotland's current trajectory reflects ideological preference rather than empirical necessity.

7. CONCLUSION AND POLICY RECOMMENDATIONS

What Equally Safe Misrecognises

Scotland's *Equally Safe* strategy, while presented as a progressive intervention into gender-based violence, ultimately entrenches a punitive, carceral framework that conflates consensual sex work with trafficking. This ideological framing has institutionalised exclusion within policy design and implementation. As demonstrated across the chapter, this model not only fails to prevent exploitation but actively reinforces conditions of harm, surveillance, and legal precarity—particularly for migrant, LGBTQ+, and working-class sex workers (Armstrong, 2024; Patnaik, 2023).

A meaningful transition toward decriminalisation requires more than legislative change—it necessitates a robust framework for policy evaluation, accountability, and participatory governance. Drawing on Zangger's (2016) work in New Zealand, Scottish reform must include mechanisms to monitor health outcomes, legal rights access, police abuse, and stigma reduction. Policy success should be defined by improvements in sex worker safety and autonomy, not merely by prosecution rates or trafficking narratives. Abel (2010) also emphasises the role of sex worker leadership in shaping such frameworks, ensuring that legal transitions are both grounded in community needs and adaptable to changing socio-economic contexts.

What Comparative Evidence Demonstrates

By examining comparative legal frameworks, it becomes clear that Scotland's current trajectory mirrors the failures of Ireland's end-demand approach rather than the successes of more inclusive, rights-based models. The decriminalisation model in New Zealand, codified through the Prostitution Reform Act 2003, offers a compelling and well-documented alternative. It has led to improved occupational health, reduced violence, greater access to justice, and a significant decline in stigma, particularly where sex workers have been involved in policymaking processes (Armstrong, 2021; Macioti et al., 2023; Abel, 2010; Zangger, 2016).

What Reform Requires

Policy reform in Scotland would require the full decriminalisation of sex work. This means repealing laws that criminalise the purchase of sex, brothel-keeping, and third-party involvement, and replacing them with regulations that treat sex work as labour. In doing so, Scotland would not only reduce the harms associated with criminalisation but also lay the groundwork for a legal framework grounded in dignity, autonomy, and safety. A decriminalised framework should also institutionalise the inclusion of sex worker-led organisations in all areas of policy design, implementation, and review. Their absence in the current *Equally Safe* framework has led to deeply flawed laws and consultations that ignore the realities of those most affected.

Equally important is the rejection of end-demand approaches that criminalise clients while ostensibly "protecting" workers. As shown in the Irish case, these models force sex workers into more precarious and isolated conditions, where access to justice is diminished, and violence is more likely (Preston, 2024; Armstrong, 2024). Rather than reducing harm, such models reconfigure it—displacing responsibility while expanding the reach of the criminal justice system.

In place of criminalisation, Scotland must adopt a public health and labour rights framework that prioritises harm reduction. This entails recognising sex work as legitimate employment and guaranteeing protections such as workplace safety, anti-discrimination legislation, and access to healthcare. Training for law enforcement, social services, and healthcare providers should be grounded in rights-based engagement and informed by sex worker expertise. Without this shift, stigma and abuse will persist within the very institutions charged with offering support.

Finally, any strategy aimed at preventing exploitation must address the broader socio-economic conditions that shape vulnerability. Housing insecurity, precarious migration status, poverty, and gender-based violence all intersect with sex work in complex ways. Criminalising sex work does not alleviate these conditions—it exacerbates them. A meaningful commitment to equality and safety must therefore engage with these root causes through holistic, redistributive, and inclusive social policy.

In conclusion, Scotland stands at a critical policy juncture. It can continue to uphold a punitive model that excludes, endangers, and silences sex workers, or it can chart a new path—one that recognises sex work as labour, centres lived experience in policy, and dismantles the structures of epistemic and material violence. The evidence from decriminalised jurisdictions like New Zealand suggests that this alternative is not only possible but urgently necessary.

REFERENCES

Abel, G. (2010) *Decriminalisation: A harm minimisation and human rights approach to regulating sex work.* PhD thesis. University of Otago. Available at: https://ourarchive.otago.ac.nz/handle/10523/475

Armstrong, L. (2011) *Managing Risks of Violence in Decriminalised Street-Based Sex Work: A Feminist (Sex Worker Rights) Perspective.* Victoria University of Wellington. PDF

Armstrong, L. (2021) '"I can lead the life that I want to lead": Social harm, human needs and the decriminalisation of sex work in Aotearoa/New Zealand', *Sexuality Research and Social Policy.* Available at: https://link.springer.com/article/10.1007/s13178-021-00605-7

Armstrong, L. (2024) *"In an ideal world, it would be fully decriminalised": Stigma, Discrimination, and Sex Work Laws in Scotland, Aotearoa New Zealand, and the Republic of Ireland.* Victoria University of Wellington. Available at: https://openaccess.wgtn.ac.nz/articles/report/Stigma_Discrimination_and_Sex_Work_Laws_Insights_from_Aotearoa_New_Zealand_Scotland_the_Republic_of_Ireland/26778190

Armstrong, L., Phillips, J., & Ryan, B. (2024) '"I've just schooled you, so you can't shame me": Stigma, discrimination, and healthcare access among sex workers in Scotland, the Republic of Ireland, and Aotearoa/New Zealand', *Open Access Victoria University of Wellington.* Available at: https://openaccess.wgtn.ac.nz/articles/journal_contribution/_I_ve_just_schooled_you_so_you_can_t_shame_me_Stigma_Discrimination_and_Healthcare_Access_among_Sex_Workers_in_Scotland_the_Republic_of_Ireland_and_Aotearoa_New_Zealand/28138067

Benoit, C., Jansson, M., Smith, M., & Flagg, J. (2018). Prostitution Stigma and Its Effect on the Working Conditions, Personal Lives, and Health of Sex Workers. *Journal of Sex Research, 55*(4–5), 457–471. DOI: 10.1080/00224499.2017.1393652 PMID: 29148837

Bernstein, E. (2007). The Sexual Politics of the "New Abolitionism". *Differences: A Journal of Feminist Cultural Studies, 18*(3), 128–151. DOI: 10.1215/10407391-2007-013

Brouwers, L.H.E. (2022) *"I feel safe when I'm working with her": Sex Workers' Experiences of Management and Wider Work Relations.* University of Leeds. PDF

Brown, W. (2021). *In the Ruins of Neoliberalism: The Rise of Anti-Democratic Politics in the West.* Columbia University Press.

Butler, Y. (2024). Silencing the Sex Worker [PDF]. *UCLA Law Review. University of California, Los Angeles. School of Law*, *71*(2), 501–542.

Christoffersen, A., & McCabe, L. (2025). Operationalising Intersectionality in Equality and Domestic Abuse Policy in Scotland: Contradictions, Contestations and Erasure. *Critical Social Policy*, *45*(2), 234–258. Advance online publication. DOI: 10.1177/02610183241249696

Das, S., & Pande, A. (2021). Agency and Consent in the Global Sex Trade: Beyond Victim Narratives. *Global Gender Studies*, *9*(1), 15–34.

Davidson, C. (2023). *Feminism, Statecraft and Sex Work: Legal Narratives and Marginalised Voices*. Policy Praxis Press.

Doezema, J. (2010). *Sex Slaves and Discourse Masters: The Construction of Trafficking*. Zed Books. DOI: 10.5040/9781350222502

Easton, H.J. (2023) *Contested Discourses: A Feminist Socio-Legal Examination of Legal Responses to Prostitution in the UK*. Macquarie University. PDF

FitzGerald, S., O'Neill, M., & Wylie, G. (2020). Social justice for sex workers as a "politics of doing": Research, policy and practice. *Irish Journal of Sociology*, *28*(1), 44–60. DOI: 10.1177/0791603520911344

Foucault, M. (1980). *Power/Knowledge: Selected Interviews and Other Writings 1972–1977*. Pantheon.

Grenfell, P., Stuart, R., Eastham, J., Gallagher, A., Elmes, J., Platt, L., & O'Neill, M. (2023). 'Policing and Public Health Interventions into Sex Workers' Lives: Necropolitical Assemblages and Alternative Visions of Social Justice'. *Critical Public Health*, *33*(1), 97–112. DOI: 10.1080/09581596.2022.2096428

Halley, J., Kotiswaran, P., Shamir, H., & Thomas, C. (2006). From the International to the Local in Feminist Legal Responses to Rape, Prostitution/Sex Work, and Sex Trafficking: Four Studies in Contemporary Governance Feminism. *Harvard Journal of Law & Gender*, *29*(2), 335–423.

Hanscamp, E. (2023) *Developing an Intersectional Feminist Trauma- and Violence-Informed Practice Framework for Mental Health Services for Women in Sex Work*. RMIT University. PDF

Harding, R. (2020). Regulating Sex Work in the Neoliberal City. *Urban Studies (Edinburgh, Scotland)*, *57*(4), 845–861. DOI: 10.1177/0042098019857953

Hill, A. and Macleod, J. (2023). *Beyond Consent: Carceral Feminism and Gender-Based Violence Services in Scotland*. Policy Report.

Hounga v Allen [2014] UKSC 47.

Kapur, R. (2005) 'Travel Plans: Border Crossings and the New World Order of Feminism', *Harvard Journal of Gender & Law*, 28(2), pp. 321–354. https://harvardjlg.com/print/volume-28/

Kingston, S., & Thomas, T. (2019). No model in practice: A "Nordic model" to respond to prostitution? [Link]. *Crime, Law, and Social Change*, *72*(2), 139–157. DOI: 10.1007/s10611-018-9795-6

Lamas, M. (2016). Client Criminalization and the Limits of Feminist Governance. *Social Politics*, *23*(2), 240–265.

Langford, M., & Skilbrei, M. L. (2021). *Branding the Nordic Model of Prostitution Policy*. Routledge. PDF. DOI: 10.4324/9781003156925-11

Levy, J. (2015). *Criminalising the Purchase of Sex: Lessons from Sweden*. Routledge.

Lorde, A. (1984). *Sister Outsider: Essays and Speeches*. Crossing Press.

Macioti, P. G., Power, J., & Bourne, A. (2023) 'The health and well-being of sex workers in decriminalised contexts: A scoping review', *Sexuality Research and Social Policy*. Available at: https://link.springer.com/article/10.1007/s13178-022-00779-8

McConnell, O. (2019) *Assessing the Impact of the Nordic Model of Combating Prostitution*. Florida State University. PDF

McKeown, C. (2021) *Surveillance, In/visibility, Resistance: Searching for Beauty in Scottish Feminist Campaigns to End Men's Violence Against Women*. University of Stirling. PDF

Najar, K. (2023). Nordic Model in Practice: Criminalisation, Control, and the Politics of Rescue. *European Journal of Criminology*, *20*(1), 45–63.

Nield, L. (2024) 'UK Prostitution Legislation and the Implementation of the Nordic Model', *Student Law Journal*, 3, pp. 1–25. https://doi.org/DOI: 10.24377/LJMU.SLJ.vol3article2205

Patnaik, A. (2023). Sex Work, Knowledge, and the Carceral State: Epistemic Violence in Policy Making. *Feminist Review*.

Persson, H. (2022) 'Prostitution and trafficking: Does the Nordic Prostitution Model decrease the amount of sex trafficking?', *Working Paper Series, Uppsala University*. PDF

Preston, S. (2024) *Perspectives on Reform: A Cross-Border Analysis of Sex Work Policy in New Zealand.* MA thesis. University of Regina. Available at: https://ourspace.uregina.ca/bitstreams/e5dbfa43-ce1d-44ec-9a80-84ba93cfddef/download

R v SK (2011). EWCA Crim 1691.

Ramberg, M. S. (2021). *A Comparative Study of Norway and Scotland's Effort to Address and Counter the Threat of Organised Crime in a Globalised World.* PDF.

Reilly, J., Khan, A., & Mbatha, T. (2021). Criminalising Clients, Endangering Workers: An Evaluation of End-Demand Legislation. *Justice Quarterly*, *38*(5), 690–712.

Rowland, A. (2025) *Sex Worker Activism and the Regulatory Liminality of Rights.* University of California. PDF

Rowland, A. (2025). *Sex Workers, Work! Anticarceral Approaches to Decriminalisation.* Routledge. DOI: 10.4324/9781003401162-38

Ryan, A. (2020) 'Sex Work, Justice and Decriminalisation: Beyond a Politics of Recognition in Promoting a Social Justice Response to Women at the Margins', in *Women, Peace and Welfare*. Emerald Publishing. PDF DOI: 10.1108/978-1-83982-882-920200015

Santos, B. de S. (2007). *Cognitive Justice in a Global World: Prudent Knowledges for a Decent Life.* Lexington Books. DOI: 10.5771/9780739153130

SCOT-PEP. (2020) *Response to the Equally Safe Consultation.* Available at: https://www.scot-pep.org.uk/resources/response-to-the-equally-safe-consultation/ (Accessed: 18 August 2025).

Scottish Government. (2018). *Equally Safe: Scotland's Strategy to Prevent and Eradicate Violence Against Women and Girls.* Available at: https://www.gov.scot/publications/equally-safe/ (Accessed: 18 August 2025).

Scoular, J. (2015). *The Subject of Prostitution: Sex Work, Law and Social Theory.* Routledge. DOI: 10.4324/9781315778433

Sequeira, M. (2022) *Decriminalisation of Sex Work in England and Wales: A Step Towards Normalising Sex Work.* Available at: https://www.researchgate.net/publication/363383341_Decriminalisation_of_sex_work_in_England_and_Wales_A_step_towards_normalising_sex_work

Smith, E.J. (2015) *"Violence Can Mean a Lot of Things, Can't It?" An Exploration of Responses to Harm Associated with Indoor Sex Work in Scotland.* University of Stirling. PDF

Smith, J. (2024). Bending Reality to Match Ideology: A Critique of "Criminalising the Sex Buyer". *Review of Studies in State Policy*, *51*(2), 233–251. DOI: 10.1093/restud/rdx065

Spivak, G. C. (1988). Can the Subaltern Speak? In Nelson, C., & Grossberg, L. (Eds.), *Marxism and the Interpretation of Culture* (pp. 271–313). Macmillan.

Stella, F., & Binnie, J. (2025). Homing Desires: Transnational Queer Migrants Negotiating Homes and Homelands in Scotland. *Sociological Review*, *73*(1), 81–103. DOI: 10.1177/00380261241244654

Stella, F., Gawlewicz, A. and Flynn, M. (2016) *Intimate Migrations: Lesbian, Gay, Bisexual and Transgender Migrants in Scotland.* University of Glasgow. PDF

SWARM. (2021). *Sex Work During COVID-19: Impacts and Responses.* Sex Worker Advocacy and Resistance Movement. Available at: https://www.swarmcollective.org

Tweed, E.J. (2022) *Understanding the Health of People Experiencing Homelessness, Justice Involvement, Substance Use, Sex Work, and Severe Mental Illness.* University of Glasgow. PDF

Umbrella Lane. (2022). *Hardship and Health: A Community Response to the Pandemic.*

Vamvaka-Tatsi, O. (2024) *Examining the Strategic Response and Approach to Integration of Queer Forced Migrants in Wales.* Cardiff University. PDF

Vollinger, A. (2020). Victimhood and Visibility: The State's Role in Constructing Sex Work Discourse. *Feminist Legal Studies*, *28*(1), 67–89.

Wagenaar, H., Altink, S., & Amesberger, H. (2017). *Designing Prostitution Policy: Intention and Reality in Regulating the Sex Trade.* Policy Press.

Zangger, C. (2016) *For Better or Worse?: Decriminalisation, Work Conditions, and Indoor Sex Work in Auckland, New Zealand/Aotearoa.* PhD thesis. Available at: https://www.sexworklaw.co.nz/pdfs/Zangger_(2016)_PhD_Thesis.pdf

Chapter 5
AI and Facial Recognition in Trafficking and Prostitution:
Legal and Ethical Perspectives

Vaishali
http://orcid.org/0009-0003-4760-7918
University of Petroleum and Energy Studies, Dehradun, India

ABSTRACT

This chapter, per the authors, critically evaluates the use of Artificial Intelligence (AI) and facial recognition technologies (FRT) in addressing sex trafficking and prostitution in India. It explores whether these technologies enhance justice and victim protection or reinforce surveillance, stigma, and marginalization. The analysis highlights legal ambiguities and social biases, examining how AI and FRT can both aid law enforcement and introduce risks such as algorithmic bias and wrongful identification. The chapter compares Indian efforts with global practices, underscores the psychological and social impact on vulnerable groups, and calls for robust legal safeguards, transparency, and victim-centered reforms to ensure technology meaningfully serves justice without sacrificing rights or dignity.

1. INTRODUCTION

In an era where technology increasingly mediates the exercise of state power, Facial recognition In an era where technology increasingly mediates the exercise of state power, facial recognition technology (FRT) has emerged as one of the most

DOI: 10.4018/979-8-3373-5841-3.ch005

influential applications of artificial intelligence within contemporary biometric systems (Grubesic, Helderop, Sefair, & Roe-Sepowitz, 2025).

Facial Recognition Technology (FRT) is a biometric system that detects, analyzes, and matches distinctive facial features from digital images or video against stored databases to identify or verify individuals. It transforms a face into numerical data points and compares them for recognition, making it a powerful but controversial tool in policing, surveillance, and identity management (Monash University, 2025). By analysing and matching distinctive facial characteristics, the technology enables the identification and authentication of individuals with a degree of speed and efficiency that was previously unattainable (Li, Cui, Zhao, & Wu, 2023).

Key Concepts

To guide readers unfamiliar with technical terminology, several foundational concepts are clarified at the outset-

- Biometric data- Unique physical or behavioral traits such as facial features or fingerprints—that can be used to identify individuals. Unlike a password, these traits cannot be changed, which makes misuse especially risky (KPMG, 2025).
- Consent- A person's informed and voluntary agreement to the collection or use of their data. True consent requires that individuals understand what is being done with their information and have a genuine choice to say yes or no (Das, 2025).
- Privacy rights- Protections that allow individuals to control their personal information and safeguard their autonomy against unwanted intrusion (Dixit, 2025).
- Surveillance capitalism- An economic system where personal data is harvested and monetized, turning human experience into raw material for profit (Das, 2025).
- Profiling- The practice of analyzing personal data to make judgments or predictions about individuals such as their behavior, preferences, or risk level. In facial recognition, profiling can lead to unfair treatment if biased data is used (Dixit, 2025).
- Automated inference- Conclusions drawn by AI systems without human involvement, such as predicting identity or emotions. These inferences can be flawed or discriminatory if the system is biased (Das, 2025).

In the Indian context, FRT is no longer a theoretical innovation; it is increasingly embedded in practical governance and security frameworks, including policing, border management, e-governance initiatives, and broader public safety mechanisms. This rapid integration reflects the State's growing reliance on data-driven technologies to address complex administrative and security challenges. At the same time, the deployment of FRT raises profound legal and ethical concerns. Its capacity for constant and often invisible surveillance brings it into direct tension with constitutionally protected rights, particularly the right to privacy, dignity, and personal liberty. Following the Supreme Court's recognition of privacy as a fundamental right, the unchecked use of facial recognition systems invites closer judicial and legislative scrutiny.

From a functional perspective, FRT has become a central component of modern surveillance infrastructures due to its perceived utility in enhancing public safety. Its ability to identify individuals in real time by matching live camera feeds with existing databases offers significant operational advantages to law enforcement agencies, particularly in tracing suspects, locating missing persons, or responding swiftly to security threats (Vidhi Centre for Legal Policy, 2024). Yet, these benefits cannot be viewed in isolation. A balanced legal approach must assess whether such efficiency justifies the risks posed to civil liberties, and whether adequate safeguards exist to ensure that the technology serves public interest without eroding the foundational values of a constitutional democracy.

These tools promise unparalleled efficiency in identifying perpetrators, locating victims, and dismantling criminal networks. Yet, their deployment is far from neutral: when interfacing with highly marginalized populations particularly sex workers and survivors of human trafficking—AI-driven surveillance introduces complex legal, ethical, and social challenges that demand critical scrutiny.

Figure 1. Functional flow of a real-time facial recognition system

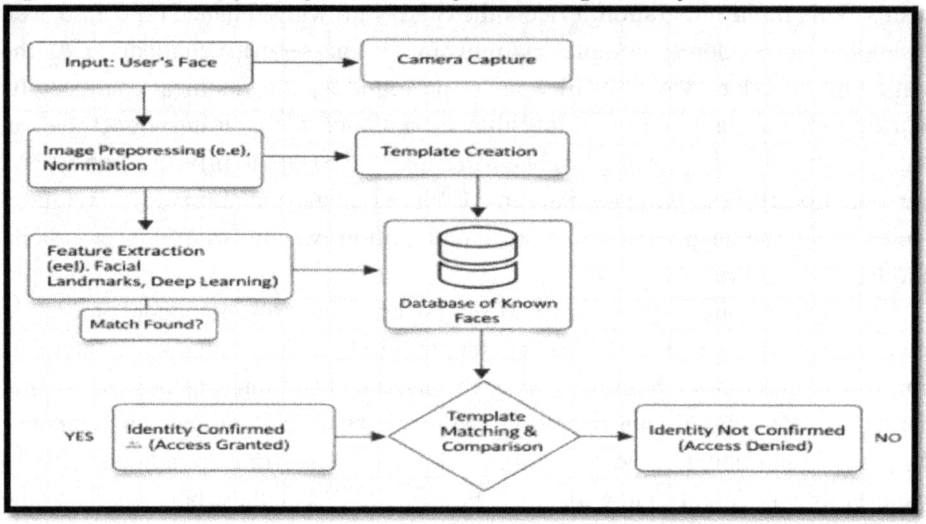

In India, facial recognition technology is no longer confined to experimental use and has steadily permeated both public administration and private enterprise. Its deployment spans diverse domains, including policing, crowd monitoring, and identity verification, alongside established digital identity frameworks such as Aadhaar. Despite this growing reliance on biometric technologies, the legal architecture governing their use remains fragmented and incomplete. This regulatory gap is particularly evident in the absence of clear statutory standards addressing the collection, storage, and secondary use of facial data.

While the Aadhaar (Targeted Delivery of Financial and Other Subsidies, Benefits and Services) Act, 2016 provides a legislative basis for biometric authentication within the Aadhaar ecosystem, its scope is narrowly tailored to that specific system. The statute does not meaningfully engage with facial recognition technologies, nor does it anticipate the broader risks associated with their deployment, including surveillance overreach and misuse beyond their original purpose. Consequently, the expansion of FRT operates within a legal grey area, underscoring the need for a more comprehensive and technology-sensitive regulatory framework (ET Online, 2024).

India's regulatory landscape adds further layers of complexity. The Immoral Traffic (Prevention) Act, 1956 simultaneously criminalizes certain practices associated with sex work while stopping short of fully prohibiting consensual adult engagement in the profession. Such partial criminalization leaves sex workers and trafficking survivors in a precarious position, where the promise of protection through technology can paradoxically translate into intensified scrutiny, profiling, and secondary victimization.

Against this backdrop, initiatives such as the National Automated Facial Recognition System reflect the state's ambition to leverage AI and FRT for targeted interventions and enhanced investigative capability. While these systems are framed as instruments of public safety and justice, their expansion raises pressing constitutional and ethical questions—touching upon the right to privacy, the presumption of innocence, and procedural due process. This chapter critically examines the intersection of AI-driven policing, legal frameworks, and the lived realities of those most affected, interrogating the tensions between technological promise and social justice in India's fight against sex trafficking and exploitation (Fussey & Murray, 2025).

1.1 The Rise of AI and Facial Recognition in Criminal Justice

Historical Evolution and Global Context

AI and its subdomains have moved from conceptual prototypes to sophisticated infrastructure in less than two decades. Early applications in criminal justice, such as crime mapping or forensic databases, have given way to more complex tasks real-time surveillance, predictive policing, risk assessments, and identification from digital traces. FRT represents a defining development within this trajectory, offering the ability to rapidly compare and match individual faces against large-scale criminal or civil databases.

While the most recent estimates from UNODC (United Nations Office on Drugs and Crime, 2024) indicate that trafficking for forced labor (~42%) is somewhat greater than that for sexual exploitation (~36%), much of the extant literature on human trafficking focuses on sex trafficking (Gozdziak & Bump, 2008). Women and girls continue to represent the majority of detected victims worldwide (61%), with adult women and teenage girls making up 39% and 22% of the total detected victims, as per UNODC. Globally, police forces in the United States, United Kingdom, China, and the European Union have adopted forms of FRT, encountering both operational successes and civil liberties challenges.

Notably, the London Metropolitan Police and certain U.S. city departments have faced public backlash and legal scrutiny leadings to suspensions or mandated audits of these systems. In China, mass surveillance using FRT is integrated into social credit regimes and public security apparatus, raising concerns about authoritarian overreach and social control.

Indian Context: Adoption and Applications

In India, FRT and AI have been piloted in several states and by major cities. The Delhi Police's use of facial recognition during public protests, the Hyderabad

Police's real-time surveillance systems, and the Mumbai Police's database-driven crime analysis reflect the broader adoption trend. Nationally, the NCRB's Automated Facial Recognition System (AFRS) aims to centralize police facial data and connect state crime records, missing persons databases, and CCTV footage under one surveillance framework (National Crime Records Bureau, 2021).

Key applications in India include-

i. Rescue Operations- FRT is used to identify and recover missing children and trafficking victims by matching their images with police and social media databases.
ii. Tracking Repeat Offenders- AI systems analyze behavioral and movement patterns to identify potential recidivists and monitor habitual offenders in prostitution-linked offenses.
iii. Border and Transit Surveillance- These technologies are used at airports, railway stations, and inter-state checkpoints to intercept suspected traffickers and victims.
iv. Crowd Monitoring- Police agencies use AI-powered cameras to screen individuals in public places, aiming to deter crime and quickly apprehend suspects.

Technical Strengths and Systemic Risks

The practical appeal of artificial intelligence and facial recognition technology in policing lies in their capacity to expand the speed, reach, and intensity of detection far beyond what is possible through conventional investigative methods. However, multiple studies underscore the existence of-

i. Algorithmic Bias- Incorrect matches and higher error rates for women, children, transgender persons, and individuals with darker skin—groups disproportionately targeted by anti-trafficking operations and suspected of sex work.
ii. Exclusion Errors- Victims, especially those lacking formal identification or from marginalized communities, may not be present in databases, leading to missed rescues or wrongful suspicion.
iii. Opaque Accountability- Lack of independent audits, public oversight, or judicial controls over the use and outcomes of these technologies creates systemic risks of misuse.
iv. Privacy and Consent Issues- Consent is rarely obtained for the use of individuals' biometric data, raising substantial questions under privacy jurisprudence and international human rights standards (Ashok et al., 2022).

1.2 Framing the Debate: Surveillance vs. Protection

Surveillance as Social Control

While intended to offer protection, surveillance tools historically serve as mechanisms of control, discipline, and exclusion. Michel Foucault's concept of "panopticism" remains instructive—the very awareness of being watched can alter behavior, foster compliance, and induce psychological stress, especially among vulnerable populations. In the Indian context, police surveillance of red-light areas and public spaces such as railway stations or bus terminals results in the constant monitoring of sex workers, many of whom may be present by compulsion, economic necessity, or, at times, by choice (Smyth, 2019).

Advocates warn that such surveillance often leads not to protection but to criminalization. Sex workers and trafficking survivors rather than gaining access to legal remedies or support may face arrest, harassment, data profiling, and outing to families or communities (Menéndez González & Mobilio, 2025). Documented cases reveal that police databases sometimes conflate sex workers and trafficking victims, further muddying legal distinctions and support pathways.

Protection Paradigm: Rhetoric and Reality

The narrative of "protection" is invoked to justify new surveillance powers. Law enforcement agencies argue that AI and FRT are essential to identifying exploiters, rescuing victims, and disrupting trafficking syndicates. There are indeed cases where such technologies have facilitated rescues or the dismantling of criminal networks, highlighting their positive potential.

However, the protection argument often presupposes a "victim" status for all those engaged in sex work, eliding distinctions between consensual sex work and trafficking. This framing can reinforce social stigma and medicalization, reduce agency, and justify intrusive interventions into lives and communities. Reports by organizations such as Amnesty International and Human Rights Watch point out that, without sufficient legal and social safeguards, surveillance technologies "protect" on terms defined by the surveillant state, not the supposed beneficiaries.

Legal and Psychological Implications

i. Constitutional Standards- Any technological intervention must satisfy tests of legality, necessity, proportionality, and procedural fairness as laid out by *Puttaswamy* and other Supreme Court judgments. Blanket surveillance or the collection of biometric data absent individualized suspicion fails these constitutional benchmarks.

ii. Psychological Impact- Surveillance-induced anxiety, trauma from past encounters with authorities, and social ostracism are well-documented among sex workers and trafficking survivors. The fear of being constantly watched, wrongfully profiled, or exposed has a chilling effect on accessing health care, legal support, and violence reporting mechanisms (Jain, 2023).

iii. Community-Led Responses- Successful interventions in trafficking and sex work globally have centered on community partnership, peer advocacy, and rights-based approaches—not coercive surveillance or punitive policing(Amnesty International, 2024).

2. LEGAL LANDSCAPE OF PROSTITUTION AND TRAFFICKING IN INDIA

India's regulatory framework for prostitution and trafficking has evolved to respond both to constitutional imperatives and ground realities, most recently through the Bharatiya Nyaya Sanhita, 2023 (BNS), which replaces the IPC as the central criminal statute.

2.1 Distinctions in Law and Policy

Historical and Policy Background

Prostitution in India is not expressly criminalized, but activities that facilitate or organize sex work such as brothel-keeping, solicitation, and trafficking—are prohibited under the Immoral Traffic (Prevention) Act (ITPA), 1956, and further regulated by the BNS, 2023. The policy aims to distinguish voluntary adult sex work from trafficking, the latter defined as recruitment, harboring, or movement for sexual or other forms of exploitation by force, fraud, or coercion (Nair, n.d.).

Recent Supreme Court directives reinforce the right to dignity for sex workers, directing authorities to ensure health, welfare, and safety without criminalizing consensual adult sex work. The government's "Ujjawala" scheme and NHRC's recognition of sex workers as informal workers reflect this evolving, victim-centric approach (Lok Sabha Secretariat, n.d.).

2.2 Overview of ITPA, BNS Provisions, and Court Interpretations

A. Immoral Traffic (Prevention) Act, 1956 (ITPA)

- Section 3: Punishes brothel management (1–3 years, up to 5 for repeat offenses).
- Section 4: Criminalizes living off the earnings of prostitution (2–10 years, depending if minor/child involved).
- Section 5: Penalizes procuring, inducing, or taking persons for prostitution; especially stringent for children/minors.
- Section 6: Covers detaining persons for prostitution (minimum 7 years).
- Section 7: Prohibits prostitution near public places.
- Section 8: Prohibits solicitation.
- Section 9: Seduction in custody, punishable by up to life imprisonment (Government of India, 1956).

B. Bhartiya Nyaya Sanhita, 2023 (BNS)

Table 1. Key sections from BNS, 2023 replacing IPC provisions relevant for trafficking and sexual exploitation

BNS Section	Offence	Punishment	Notes
143	Trafficking of person	7-10 years (min), extendable to life, plus fine	Defines trafficking broadly including physical and sexual exploitation, slavery, beggary, forced organ removal. Consent of victim immaterial. Enhanced punishment for child trafficking (10 years- life)
144	Exploitation of trafficked person	Strict punishment for sexual exploitation, esp. of children (min. 5 years to life + fine)	Sexual exploitation of trafficked children specifically penalized
141	Importation for illicit sexual exploitation	Not less than 10 years to life	Covers cross-border trafficking for sexual exploitation
99	Buying child for prostitution	7–14 years	Addresses child prostitution explicitly
111	Organized crime (including trafficking for prostitution)	5 years minimum, more for severe offences	Includes human trafficking as organized crime

continued on following page

Table 1. Continued

BNS Section	Offence	Punishment	Notes
69	Sexual intercourse on false promise/ concealment	Strict penalties	New in BNS—targets deceit in sexual exploitation
95	Employing/hiring child to commit offence	Severe penalties	
139	Kidnapping for begging	10 years to life	Also recognized as trafficking

Section 396 of the Bharatiya Nagarik Suraksha Sanhita, 2023 (BNSS) mandates state victim compensation schemes for rehabilitation.

C. Key Judicial Developments

i. K.P. Kirankumar v. State, 2025

In a significant 2025 ruling, the Supreme Court upheld the conviction in a child trafficking and commercial sexual exploitation case while articulating standards for judicial appreciation of minor victims' testimony. The Bench (Justices Manoj Misra and Joymalya Bagchi) held that the testimony of a trafficked minor, if credible, may by itself sustain a conviction and should be treated as that of an injured witness, not discarded owing to minor inconsistencies. The judgment stressed the sensitive and realistic appreciation of evidence in trafficking and sexual exploitation cases.

ii. Pragya Prasun & Ors. v. Union of India, 2025

The Court ruled that rigid FRT and biometric protocols in Aadhaar-linked digital KYC exclude vulnerable groups like those with facial injuries or disabilities violating Articles 14, 15, and 21 of the constitution. It mandated inclusive alternatives (e.g., offline options, thumb impressions) and accessibility audits by regulators like RBI, shifting blame from users to flawed system design.

iii. Budhadev Karmaskar v. State of West Bengal (2011, 2022)

In its landmark decisions in the original case (2011) and the subsequent Supreme Court orders (2022), the judiciary unequivocally recognized sex work as a legitimate profession for consenting adults. The Court affirmed that these individuals are entitled to equal protection under the law, emphasizing dignity and freedom from police harassment as core constitutional values under Article 21. It mandated that law enforcement must refrain from arbitrary raids, intimidation, or prosecution; instead, sex workers should be provided basic amenities, health care, education, and vocational training. These decisions also acknowledged that consent and adulthood are pivotal criteria, setting the groundwork for rights-based approaches in law enforcement and rehabilitation policies (Budhadev Karmaskar v. State of West Bengal, 2011).

iv. Supreme Court Directives (2022)

Building on Budhadev Karmaskar, the Supreme Court recently issued binding interim directives to all States and Union Territories. These include: mandatory non-disclosure of sex worker identities in judicial proceedings; guaranteed access to state support and rehabilitation services; prohibition of forcible separation of children from sex worker mothers; and targeted policing reforms to curb harassment, wrongful detention, and stigma. The Court also underscored the need for police sensitization and the right of sex workers to invoke protection under established criminal law. These instructions are operative until Parliament enacts comprehensive legislation.

v. Kerala High Court- Interpretation of ITPA Section 5 (2024)

The Kerala High Court delivered a significant judgment broadening the meaning of 'procurement' under Section 5 of the Immoral Traffic (Prevention) Act, 1956. It held that customers engaging in commercial sex acts and aiding in the facilitation of prostitution may be prosecuted under this Section, alongside pimps and brothel managers. The rationale given was that the Act's objective to suppress immoral trafficking and prevent exploitation justifies expanding criminal liability to customers who actively enable commercial sexual exploitation (Ahuja, 2024).

vi. Gaurav Jain v. Union of India (1997)

A public interest litigation brought urgent attention to the rights and rehabilitation needs of children of women in sex work. The Supreme Court held that these children are entitled to equality, dignity, care, and protection, and ordered the government to mainstream them into society without stigma. The court directed central and state governments to establish juvenile homes and formulate comprehensive schemes for the welfare of sex workers and their children. The justices grounded their decision in constitutional protections (Articles 14, 21, 23, etc.) as well as international conventions, emphasizing that women in the "flesh trade" are more often victims of adverse socio-economic circumstances than offenders, and stressed rehabilitation over punitive approaches. The resulting policy recommendations remain influential for government intervention and legislative reform.

vii. Fateh Chand v. State of Haryana (2009)

In this case, the Supreme Court dealt with the criminal liability for procuring and exploiting minors for prostitution. The accused was convicted of offenses under IPC Section 366 (kidnapping, abducting or inducing woman to compel her marriage, etc.) and Section 376 (rape). The prosecution established that the victim was a minor trafficked and assaulted under false pretenses, and the court affirmed the need for strict penal response against child trafficking and sexual exploitation, setting a precedent for lower courts in similar cases.

D. Contemporary Approach

The law now provides clear, distinct frameworks for punishment of trafficking (especially involving minors), protection and rehabilitation of victims, and regulation of support and compensation schemes. The shift to BNS, 2023 represents a historic overhaul, consolidating offences against women and children, increasing penalties, and emphasizing victim-centric justice.

3. TECHNOLOGY IN ACTION: USE OF AI AND FRT IN POLICING

The rapid adoption of artificial intelligence (AI) and facial recognition technology (FRT) has ushered in transformative changes in law enforcement operations worldwide. By enabling more rapid identification, advanced surveillance, and sophisticated pattern recognition, these technologies are being leveraged by police forces, border agencies, and international organizations to intercept trafficking, identify missing persons, and disrupt online sex trade networks.

Table 2. The role of technology in combating human trafficking

Aspect	Description	Technologies Involved	Benefits
Data Analysis	Utilizes deep learning to process vast amounts of data and identify patterns indicative of trafficking activities.	Deep learning algorithms, neural networks	Enhanced speed and accuracy in detecting trafficking patterns.
Pattern Recognition	Employs advanced algorithms to recognize complex patterns and relationships within large datasets.	Convolutional Neural Networks (CNNs), Recurrent Neural Networks (RNNs)	Improved identification of trafficking indicators such as unusual travel routes and financial transactions.
Real-Time Monitoring	Integrates AI to monitor social media and online platforms for suspicious activities.	Natural Language Processing (NLP), Machine Learning	Proactive identification and flagging of potential trafficking operations, enabling timely interventions.
Ethical and Legal Considerations	Ensures compliance with data privacy laws and ethical standards, balancing surveillance needs with individual privacy rights.	Data anonymization, Transparency protocols	Maintains public trust and protects personal freedoms while enhancing surveillance capabilities.

3.1 Use Cases in India and Globally

India

AI and FRT are now embedded in major policing initiatives addressing trafficking and sex crimes.

i. *Delhi Police* – Following *Sadhan Haldar v. State of NCT of Delhi* (2018), the Delhi High Court mandated Automated Facial Recognition Systems (AFRS) to trace missing children. Reports confirm over 3,200 children were reunited in the initial phase (Delhi Police, 2018). FRT was later expanded to crowd surveillance, including the 2020 North East Delhi riots, with integration into the ZIPNET database. Yet accuracy rates fell sharply—from 86% in controlled trials to below 1% in real-world conditions by 2019—prompting judicial skepticism and calls for safeguards (Ministry of Women and Child Development, Government of India, 2019).
ii. *Maharashtra's Operation Shakti* – Nagpur Police launched "Garuda Drishti," an AI system analyzing social media to detect trafficking patterns and fake job ads. Facial recognition cameras at transit hubs provide real-time alerts, enabling rapid intervention under the *Bharatiya Nyaya Sanhita* and ITPA. Official reports cite successful rescues and offender tracking (Nagpur Police, 2025).

iii. *National Initiatives* – The NCRB's centralized AFRS consolidates police databases, CCTV footage, and crime scene images to identify victims and suspects. Government reviews highlight its role in cross-jurisdictional investigations (Times of India, 2025). However, privacy advocates and judicial authorities stress proportionality and necessity, warning against unchecked mass surveillance (Ministry of Home Affairs, Government of India, 2022).

International

i. *INTERPOL*- The INTERPOL Facial Recognition System (IFRS), developed with IDEMIA, cross-references global biometric data (INTERPOL, 2025). Operations such as *Global Chain* (2025) involved 43 countries, checking over 924,000 persons and rescuing minors from online exploitation (INTERPOL, 2024).
ii. *United States*- Agencies including the FBI, DHS, and NCMEC use FRT to identify traffickers and reunite missing children. In 2024–25, the FBI Victim Service Division assisted in over 700 trafficking cases, while DHS provided relief to trafficked foreign nationals (U.S. Department of Justice, 2025; U.S. Department of State, 2025; U.S. Department of Transportation, 2024; White House Archives, 2024).
iii. *Europe*- Europol and national police employ FRT to analyze escort websites, raid evidence, and social media. In 2025, expanded Europol powers created the European Centre Against Migrant Smuggling (Privacy International, 2025). EU guidelines under GDPR and the AI Act permit FRT for victim searches with judicial approval and safeguards. Case studies show cross-border collaboration, such as Dutch and Venezuelan police matching images of trafficked women against Europol and INTERPOL databases (United Nations Office on Drugs and Crime, 2025).

3.2 Data-Driven Policing, Missing Persons Tracking, and Online Sex Trade Monitoring

Data-Driven Policing

AI and FRT have shifted policing from reactive to preventive strategies.

i. *Pattern Recognition and Hotspot Mapping*- Algorithms analyze surveillance feeds, geolocation data, and communications to detect trafficking patterns. In Nagpur, predictive mapping at transit hubs and markets identified 39 trafficking clusters in 2025, with 27 raids rescuing 77 victims (Government of India, Ministry of Home Affairs, 2023; Maharashtra Police, 2023; Times of India, 2025). Eurostat reported a 41% rise in trafficking detections in Europe in 2022 due to enhanced pattern recognition (Facia, 2024).

ii. *Behavior Analysis*- AI monitors social media for coercive language, fake job offers, and escort ads. NCRB's 2022 report noted a 13% increase in trafficking interceptions through optimized flagging of abnormal communication patterns (Ministry of Home Affairs, Government of India, n.d.).

Missing Persons Tracking

i. *Facial Recognition in Reuniting Families* – Delhi Police reunited over 2,800 missing children between 2020–25 using AFRS (Delhi Police: Best Practices, 2020). Nagpur's FRT cameras enabled raids recovering minors (Panoptic.in, 2020). Globally, INTERPOL rescued 240 trafficked minors in 2025, while DHS identified 311 abused children in one operation (Roeloffs, 2023).

ii. *Cross-Border Collaboration*- INTERPOL's biometric repository supports transnational rescues through "Blue Notices" and alerts. In 2024, its operations disrupted South America–Europe trafficking corridors and identified dozens of victims (Zarnowski, 2024; INTERPOL, n.d.).

Online Sex Trade Monitoring

i. *Crawling Digital Advertisements*- AI crawlers scan escort and classified sites, flagging age discrepancies and recruitment patterns. NCRB's 2022 report linked these tools to a 10% rise in convictions under ITPA and BNS. Europol and INTERPOL confirmed FRT's role in exposing hidden trafficking rings (Borak, 2025; Inspeq AI, 2025).

ii. *Image and Identity Verification*- FRT verifies identities in digital sex trade networks, detecting duplicates, underage victims, and trafficker links. Systems like NCRB's AFRS, INTERPOL's biometric database, and Europol's protocols strengthen prosecutorial evidence and rights-sensitive interventions.

4. LEGAL AND CONSTITUTIONAL CHALLENGES

The deployment of AI-driven surveillance and facial recognition technology (FRT) in criminal justice has generated widespread debate in India due to profound legal, constitutional, and ethical implications. While these technologies offer important advancements in combating trafficking and sexual exploitation, their unregulated use exposes serious risks related to privacy, due process, and regulatory accountability (Internet Freedom Foundation, 2023).

4.1 Right to Privacy and Data Protection

The right to privacy is a cornerstone of constitutional governance in India, articulated by the Supreme Court in *Justice K.S. Puttaswamy v. Union of India* (2017) as an intrinsic component of Article 21 (right to life and personal liberty). The use of FRT and large-scale biometric surveillance intrudes upon informational autonomy, bodily integrity, and decisional privacy, especially when conducted without informed consent or statutory basis (Akanksha, 2025).

India enacted the Digital Personal Data Protection Act, 2023, which introduces limited protections for individuals regarding the processing of personal data. However, this law provides broad exemptions for state surveillance and fails to include stringent safeguards for biometric data or transparency obligations for law enforcement agencies. This legislative gap, coupled with the lack of sector-specific FRT regulation, leaves individuals vulnerable to mass surveillance, function creep, and unauthorized profiling, disproportionately impacting marginalized communities including sex workers and trafficking survivors (Jyotish, 2025).

4.2 Due Process and Safeguards

For any technological intervention in law enforcement to be constitutionally valid, it must satisfy the principles of legality, necessity, and proportionality—established by the Supreme Court as tests for curbing fundamental rights. The deployment of AI and FRT, particularly for evidence gathering or suspect identification, has often bypassed these safeguards (Carnegie Endowment for International Peace, 2024):

- Cases illustrate reliance on FRT as primary evidence without independent corroboration, leading to wrong identification and acquittals.
- The absence of mandatory accuracy standards, audit trails, and mechanisms for individuals to challenge or correct algorithmic identification undermines both the presumption of innocence and fair trial rights (S.S. Rana & Co., 2025).
- Instances such as in Delhi, where FRT evidence was pivotal in hundreds of riot-related prosecutions with little judicial oversight, have spurred criticism regarding both procedural fairness and transparency (Rani, 2024).

Experts caution that FRT error rates are higher for darker-skinned individuals, women, and children, introducing algorithmic bias and compounding the risk of over-policing vulnerable populations (Pulitzer Center & The Wire, 2025).

4.3 Lack of Regulatory Oversight

Unlike the European Union's AI Act or GDPR, India does not have a dedicated oversight mechanism, independent regulatory authority, or statutory standards specifically governing the police use of AI or FRT. Key gaps include:

- No binding procedures for data minimization, security, or retention of biometric profiles (Freelaw, 2024).
- Absence of clear rules for the conditions and purposes for which FRT may be deployed in public spaces or criminal investigations.
- Lack of mandatory public consultation, impact assessment, or reporting on FRT deployment by police or government bodies (Zheng, 2021).

This regulatory void enables discretionary and potentially arbitrary surveillance, with high risk of function creep, data misuse, and unchecked state power over marginalized individuals and communities.

5. PSYCHOLOGICAL AND ETHICAL IMPLICATIONS

5.1 Trauma, Re-victimization, and Public Exposure

The use of AI and facial recognition in policing contexts involving sex trafficking and prostitution can amplify psychological harm for individuals already at risk. Survivors of trafficking and sex workers often suffer multiple forms of trauma, including physical, emotional, and social abuse. Technology-facilitated identification and monitoring can lead to public exposure, stigmatization, and repeated psychological distress—sometimes described as "re-victimization" (Bhatia, 2025).

Non-consensual data capture, such as using FRT in public spaces or scraping online profiles for identification, exposes individuals to new forms of sexual violence, such as image-based sexual abuse and "deepfake" pornography. Survivors report lasting emotional and social consequences resulting from such exposure including shame, fear, isolation, and ongoing vulnerability to exploitation. These impacts are compounded for marginalized groups, whose identities and circumstances are more likely to be misrepresented or disclosed without their consent (Dari et al., 2025).

5.2 Lack of Consent and Agency

Central to human rights-compliant policing is the principle of agency and informed consent. However, the deployment of AI-based surveillance systems in India routinely occurs without meaningful consultation or consent from those affected. Law enforcement use of facial recognition is often justified as a necessity for public safety, but this rationale rarely accounts for the lived experiences or wishes of sex workers and trafficking survivors. In Lucknow, for example, the police used automated emotion tracking and FRT to monitor women's "distress" at public hotspots without clear information, consent, or oversight.

Such approaches risk exacerbating feelings of powerlessness and erode individual control over one's image, data, and identity. Repeated encroachments on agency can worsen psychological outcomes for vulnerable populations, foster distrust of authorities, and create cycles of avoidance that impede access to care, justice, and rehabilitation (NITI Aayog, 2024).

5.3 Algorithmic Bias and Profiling

Algorithmic bias is a documented and urgent problem in AI-based criminal identification and monitoring. AI systems trained on non-representative datasets or flawed parameters disproportionately misidentify women, children, and people with darker skin tones categories highly overrepresented among victims and survivors of sex trafficking and prostitution. Such bias leads to increased risks of wrongful profiling, police harassment, and social condemnation (Mukherjee, 2025).

Research from India and other jurisdictions highlights the outsized psychological effects of being wrongly accused or surveilled by inaccurate or discriminatory technologies. Profiling based on flawed AI predictions can reinforce systemic inequalities in policing and justice, perpetuate historic injustices, and deepen public mistrust. Most critically, the lack of robust auditing, transparency, and accountability further entrenches these harms creating an environment where technological error becomes social destiny (Parkman & Stratton, 2025).

Algorithmic bias presents a major challenge to the effective, fair, and ethical deployment of artificial intelligence in the policing of trafficking and prostitution. In India and worldwide, AI-powered criminal identification tools especially facial recognition systems demonstrate marked variations in accuracy and error rates across demographic groups. This phenomenon results not merely from technical limitations, but from the historical and structural biases embedded in the datasets used to train these algorithms.

Disproportionate Impact on Marginalized Groups

Studies repeatedly demonstrate that AI systems are prone to higher rates of false positives and misidentifications among women, children, and individuals with darker skin tones. In 2022, the National Crime Records Bureau (NCRB) pilot of Automated Facial Recognition Systems recorded misidentification rates of up to 26% for women and over 32% for juveniles during citywide operations in Mumbai and Delhi compared to a general population error rate under 8%. This disparity was traced to a lack of representative imagery in the algorithm's training data and inconsistent lighting conditions for field-collected images (National Crime Records Bureau, 2022).

These limitations become especially dangerous in anti-trafficking contexts, as individuals from Dalit, Adivasi, and migrant backgrounds (who are systematically overrepresented among sex trafficking victims in India, per NCRB's "Crime in India 2022" report) are exposed to greater risk of harassment, arbitrary detention, and public stigma due to algorithmic misclassification.

Psychological and Social Harm

The psychological toll of wrongful profiling has been documented in governmental white papers and independent research. Field interviews with sex workers in metropolitan India, highlighted in a 2024 report by the Indian Council for Social Science Research, describe heightened anxiety, social isolation, and reluctance to access legal or health services due to repeated police questioning based solely on faulty AI matches. Such harms are magnified for those already facing intersectional discrimination along lines of caste, gender, or linguistic identity, reproducing cycles of fear and marginalization (Indian Council for Social Science Research, 2024).

Legal, Ethical, and Systemic Ramifications

Algorithmic profiling not only risks individual injustices but entrenches broader inequities in policing and judicial outcomes. Without mandatory, independent auditing and transparent oversight, biases can go uncorrected, leading to cumulative harms across thousands of policing encounters annually. The Supreme Court and Data Protection Committees in India have both flagged this issue, calling for explicit procedural safeguards, impact assessments, and public accountability mechanisms in the integration of AI into criminal justice processes (Ministry of Electronics and Information Technology, 2024; Supreme Court of India, 2022).

International evidence supports these concerns- studies in the US and UK have shown that AI misidentification rates for Black and minority ethnic individuals are up to two to three times those for White individuals. In India, similar trends are observable in states with high diversity in the population, underscoring the urgent need for localized algorithm training and ongoing bias monitoring.

Calls for Reform

In response, Indian parliamentarians, human rights groups, and judicial bodies have advocated for:

- Rigorous bias and error reporting in all AI policing technologies;
- Inclusion of civil society representation in technology oversight boards;
- Legal standards for consent, redress, and human review in automated decision-making.

The (Ministry of Electronics and Information Technology, 2024) and NCRB are piloting bias auditing protocols in select city deployments and are developing new guidelines promoting both technological accuracy and procedural fairness.

6. INTERNATIONAL COMPARATIVE ANALYSIS

Global regulatory and ethical responses to the use of artificial intelligence (AI) and facial recognition technology (FRT) in policing trafficking and prostitution illustrate the tension between innovation, rights protection, and social control. Europe and the United States offer distinct, instructive models combining broad data protection laws, targeted bans, and ongoing debates about responsible AI governance. For India, these models yield critical lessons on how to balance efficiency, human rights, and oversight in the unique context of technological intervention against trafficking and sex crimes.

6.1 Europe (GDPR, AI Act), U.S. Bans and Moratoriums

Europe

The European Union is a global leader in harmonizing privacy and technological governance through flagship legislation like the General Data Protection Regulation (GDPR) and the AI Act-

i. GDPR- The GDPR provides a robust framework protecting personal and biometric data, including strict controls on data processing, transparency, and individual rights to access, correction, and erasure. Facial recognition systems must satisfy purpose limitation, data minimization, and consent requirements, with sensitive data subject to even greater scrutiny (European Parliament, 2021).

ii. AI Act (2024–2025)- The AI Act is the world's first major AI-specific statute. Article 5 prohibits "real-time remote biometric identification" (including facial recognition) in public spaces for law enforcement, save targeted exceptions like searching for human trafficking victims or addressing imminent threats (MJIL Online, 2024; Holistic AI, 2024). It bans untargeted scraping of facial images from the internet or CCTVs for database expansion and mandates fundamental rights impact assessments for high-risk AI systems (European Union, 2025).

iii. Safeguards and Impact Assessments: Police must register facial recognition systems on the EU database and conduct ongoing rights audits. These requirements mitigate risks of mass surveillance, discrimination, and function creep, while enabling permissible use in crime investigation (European Union, 2025).

United States

The U.S. approach is marked by fragmented federal and local governance-

i. Bans and Moratoriums- Several major U.S. cities including San Francisco, Boston, and Portland have enacted outright bans or moratoriums on police use of facial recognition, citing its disproportionate impact on minorities, risks to civil liberties, and documented algorithmic bias. The proposed "Facial Recognition and Biometric Technology Moratorium Act" would restrict federal use and encourage broader state and local review.

ii. Exemptions for Trafficking- Even where bans exist, exceptions are often carved out for locating missing children, human trafficking victims, and serious violent crimes, provided systems meet transparency and audit requirements.

iii. Civil Society Oversight- Policy development is actively shaped by academic, activist, and community organizations. Key recommendations include establishing independent commissions, mandatory public impact reports, and frameworks for continuous monitoring and vetting of all AI surveillance tools (Security Industry Association, 2020).

6.2 Lessons for India

India's race to deploy AI and FRT against trafficking and prostitution has outpaced regulatory and human rights guardrails. Lessons from Europe and the U.S. include:-

i. Clear Statutory Frameworks- India must adopt comprehensive legal standards for AI and FRT, mandating usage restrictions, regular impact assessments, and transparent audit mechanisms to protect individuals from indiscriminate surveillance.
ii. Purpose Limitation and Consent- Systems should be designed for narrowly defined, legitimate policing purposes, with biometric data collection strictly limited and rights to consent, review, and deletion for affected individuals explicitly recognized.
iii. Safeguards for Marginalized Populations- Regulatory standards must include protections against algorithmic bias and profiling, alongside mandatory reporting on system performance and error rates—similar to requirements under the GDPR and AI Act (Two Birds, 2025).
iv. Independent Oversight- Establishment of independent data protection and AI authorities will facilitate responsible innovation, foster public trust, and encourage responsive regulation-countering risks identified in global experiences with FRT and predictive policing.
v. Policy Dialogue and Public Engagement: India should consult with civil society, technology experts, and affected communities (such as trafficking survivors and sex workers) to draft and review ethical codes, legal definitions, and regulatory priorities (TechGDPR, 2025).

7. RECOMMENDATIONS AND THE WAY FORWARD

The integration of AI and facial recognition technologies (FRT) into Indian criminal justice, particularly in contexts of trafficking and prostitution, presents both opportunities and risks. Responsible deployment requires clear regulation, victim-centric safeguards, and alignment with constitutional values.

7.1 Urgent Need for Regulatory Frameworks

Statutory and Policy Vacuums

India has rapidly adopted AI, FRT, and predictive analytics in policing without facial recognition–specific legislation. Unlike the EU or certain US jurisdictions, India lacks statutory principles of consent, proportionality, redress, and transparency. The Digital Personal Data Protection Act, 2023 offers general safeguards but broad government exemptions and no biometric-specific rules limit its effectiveness in criminal justice. As a result, arrests and surveillance often rest on discretionary power, disproportionately affecting sex workers and trafficking survivors.

Blueprint for Regulation

Reform must address five foundational areas:

i. *Purpose Limitation and Legislative Clarity* – Restrict FRT use to defined public purposes (e.g., trafficking prevention); prohibit untargeted scraping, indefinite database expansion, and secondary use without statutory mandate.
ii. *Judicial/Administrative Authorization* – Require prior judicial or independent approval, with necessity and proportionality assessments, public impact statements, and audits.
iii. *Rights to Review, Rectification, and Deletion* – Guarantee enforceable rights to access, challenge, correct, and delete biometric data, with simple grievance mechanisms for vulnerable groups.
iv. *Independent Oversight* – Establish a dedicated authority, modeled on EU Data Protection Supervisors, to license deployments, oversee audits, sanction misuse, and maintain a public registry.
v. *Algorithmic Transparency and Accountability* – Mandate explainability, bias and accuracy testing, and disclosure of error rates, training data, and model limitations to prevent "black box" policing.

International frameworks such as the GDPR and the EU AI Act's high-risk system registry provide pragmatic foundations for Indian reform, requiring contextual adaptation to national realities

7.2 Victim-Centric and Trauma-Informed Technology Deployment

Beyond Criminalization: From Victimization to Empowerment

India's use of AI and facial recognition in anti-trafficking and prostitution must move beyond punitive policing toward survivor empowerment. This requires-

- Informed Consent and Participation – Survivors, sex workers, and community representatives must be directly involved in system design and audits. Consent must be real, revocable, and transparent.
- Integrated Support Systems – FRT deployment should link identification to counselling, legal aid, shelter, and rehabilitation, ensuring care rather than punishment.
- Strict Confidentiality – Systems must protect survivor privacy, prevent exposure, and enforce penalties for breaches to avoid digital re-victimization.

- Trauma-Informed Policing – Law enforcement must be trained not only in technology but also in empathy, non-discrimination, and survivor-centered practices.

Protecting Agency and Choice

Survivors must retain real control over their data, identity, and outcomes. AI systems must guarantee opt-out options, easy withdrawal of consent, and clear remedies against misuse or misidentification. Special protections are essential for minors, LGBTQ+ persons, and other marginalized groups, ensuring their distinct vulnerabilities are prioritized at every stage.

7.3 Balancing Innovation with Human Rights

India's pursuit of "smart policing" and "AI for justice" must be disciplined by constitutional safeguards and ethical oversight.

i. Proportionality and Necessity- The Supreme Court in *K.S. Puttaswamy v. Union of India* (2017) affirmed that technological intrusions must be proportional and justified by compelling public interest. Ministry of Home Affairs guidelines (2024) require biometric collection for missing children only after manual methods fail. A 2023 review found 61% of police AI initiatives undergo proportionality analysis, though implementation varies across states (Takshashila Foundation, 2023).
ii. Transparency and Public Dialogue- Trust demands openness. Telangana Police's 2024 audit reported 85% accuracy and 124 bias complaints, prompting dataset retraining. National advisories now mandate annual impact reports, supported by 78% of agencies (NITI Aayog, 2024). Public forums such as Mumbai's "Data for Justice Forum" (Indian Express, 2023) have engaged NGOs and survivor groups in oversight.
iii. Audit and Continuous Review- Independent audits prevent misuse. The draft "Responsible AI for Policing" framework requires yearly audits with legal, technical, and survivor representation. Madhya Pradesh's 2023 pilot decommissioned a citywide FRT system after accuracy fell to 37% and complaints rose.
iv. Responsible Innovation Ecosystem- Government– academic partnerships now mandate impact monitoring. IIT Delhi–Delhi Police trials exemplify this, while 18 university–industry collaborations on ethical AI were active in 2024 (Europol, 2025). India's AI Task Force launched incubators emphasizing open data, bias testing, and explainability.

v. International Collaboration- India participates in OECD AI Principles, EU AI Act consultations, and INTERPOL forums. In 2024, the Data Security Council of India signed MoUs with the Netherlands and Singapore on privacy-by-design and bias auditing (DSCI, 2024).

The Path Forward

Embedding trauma-informed, rights-centric frameworks at every stage—from procurement to deployment and review is essential. NITI Aayog's 2024 survey found states with robust audits and dialogue programs saw a 28% drop in wrongful profiling. India's digital policing future will be judged not by technical sophistication but by its fidelity to dignity, rights, and constitutional accountability.

8. CONCLUSION

8.1 Reaffirming Dignity and Rights in the Age of Digital Policing

The increasing reliance on artificial intelligence and facial recognition technologies in contexts of trafficking, prostitution, and public order presents the Indian legal system with a profound constitutional challenge. While technological tools are often justified in the language of efficiency, prevention, and security, their deployment in socially sensitive and legally ambiguous domains exposes deep tensions between innovation and fundamental rights. This chapter has demonstrated that, in the absence of clear statutory limits and procedural safeguards, such technologies risk reinforcing existing vulnerabilities rather than alleviating them.

At the heart of this debate lies the constitutional commitment to dignity, privacy, and personal autonomy. The Supreme Court's recognition of privacy as a fundamental right in *Justice K.S. Puttaswamy (Retd.) v. Union of India* underscores that individuals cannot be reduced to data points or algorithmic risk profiles. When facial recognition systems are used to monitor, categorise, or predict behaviour particularly in relation to sex workers and trafficking survivors the line between protection and coercion becomes dangerously blurred. What is presented as a neutral technological intervention may, in practice, reproduce stigma, enable over-policing, and contribute to secondary victimisation.

The fragmented regulatory framework governing biometric technologies further compounds these concerns. Existing statutes, including the Aadhaar Act and the Immoral Traffic (Prevention) Act, operate within narrow silos and fail to meaningfully engage with the realities of contemporary surveillance technologies. This legal dissonance allows facial recognition systems to function within grey zones of authority, accountability, and oversight. Without explicit standards governing consent, purpose limitation, data retention, and remedies for misuse, the expansion of such technologies risks normalising invasive surveillance practices under the guise of welfare and law enforcement.

Ultimately, the question is not whether technology has a role to play in addressing trafficking or ensuring public safety, but whether its use is anchored in constitutional values and human rights principles. A rights-respecting approach demands transparent governance frameworks, legislative clarity, and a shift away from suspicion-based profiling toward victim-centred protection and rehabilitation. The future of AI-driven surveillance in India will be judged not by its technical sophistication, but by its ability to uphold dignity, prevent harm, and remain accountable to the rule of law. Whether facial recognition becomes a tool of empowerment or an instrument of control will depend on the legal choices made at this critical juncture.

8.2 Summary of Insights and Legal Implications

Key Insights

i. Legal Ambiguity and Statutory Gaps- India's rapid deployment of AI and FRT outpaces legal safeguards. The absence of facial recognition-specific legislation, sectoral privacy codes, and enforceable accountability mechanisms has created a vacuum where technology is often used with little oversight or recourse for affected individuals.

ii. Human Rights at Risk- Automated policing amplifies the risk of re-victimization, stigmatization, and misidentification, particularly for marginalized groups historically subject to over-policing. Algorithmic biases, lack of transparency, and public exposure can deepen psychological traumas and social exclusion.

iii. The Constitutional Imperative- The dignity, autonomy, and privacy of individuals—enshrined in Supreme Court jurisprudence must not be traded off for technological efficiency or "greater good" logic. Instead, technological innovation must be subject to legality, necessity, and proportionality; legal reforms must extend these principles to AI and biometric surveillance in policing.

iv. Victim-Centric and Trauma-Informed Responses- Future AI strategies should prioritize survivor consent, mental health support, confidential data governance, and embedded pathways for empowerment not mere detection or prosecution.

v. Regulatory and Institutional Reform- Independent oversight, algorithmic audits, and inclusive policy dialogue are essential to safeguarding democratic values, public trust, and accountability within digital policing ecosystems.

Legal Implications

Moving forward, several foundational reforms and practices are essential such as-

i. Standalone AI/FRT Regulation- India should enact facial recognition and biometric surveillance laws mandating purpose limitation, transparent system design, clear judicial authorization, and enforceable individual rights to challenge, rectify, or delete biometric data.
ii. Command Responsibility and Institutional Liability- Applying principles from international criminal law, "command responsibility" should extend to police supervisors and institutions deploying AI tools: All must be held accountable for rights violations, misuse, and algorithmic discrimination.
iii. Procedural Safeguards and Review Mechanisms- Every deployment should be subject to constitutional and statutory review with avenues for affected populations to contest misuse. Audit trails and remedies for wrongful identification must be established and enforced.
iv. Fostering Ethical Innovation- Government, academia, and industry must promote responsible research, participatory design, and practical technological solutions developed in consultation with survivors, civil society, and rights advocates.

AI and facial recognition technologies possess transformative potential in addressing human trafficking and supporting survivors, but cannot be divorced from the constitutional demand for dignity, rights, and justice. Ensuring these technologies serve as instruments of liberation rather than oppression depends on embracing regulatory clarity, institutional accountability, and sustained focus on the social and psychological needs of the most vulnerable. The path India chooses in the coming years will determine whether digital policing becomes a new horizon of hope or a deeper landscape of risk.

REFERENCES

Aayog, N. I. T. I. (2024). *Responsible AI: #AIForAll—Ethical principles in India.* https://www.niti.gov.in/sites/default/files/2024-06/document.pdf

. NITI Aayog. (2024). *The State of AI Governance in India*

Akanksha, S. (2025, April 18). *Facial recognition technology and the right to privacy in India.* Lawful Legal. https://lawfullegal.in/facial-recognition-technology-and-the-right-to-privacy-in-india/

Amnesty International. (2024). *Surveillance, discrimination and human rights: The dangers of unregulated AI.* Amnesty International.

Ashok, M., Madan, R., Joha, A., & Sivarajah, U. (2022). Ethical framework for artificial intelligence and digital technologies. *International Journal of Information Management, 62*, 102433. Advance online publication. DOI: 10.1016/j.ijinfomgt.2021.102433

Bhatia, S. (2025). AI-driven facial recognition: Human rights concerns and regulatory challenges. *MAGLAW, IV(1)*, 1–16. https://maglaw.puchd.ac.in/index.php/maglaw/article/download/345/74/1298

Borak, M. (2025, November 7). *EU lawmakers approve regulation to expand Europol's capabilities in biometric data processing*. BiometricUpdate. https://www.biometricupdate.com/202511/eu-lawmakers-approve-regulation-to-expand-europols-capabilities-in-biometric-data-processing

Budhadev Karmaskar v. State of West Bengal, (2011) 10 SCC 283 (India).

Carnegie Endowment for International Peace. (2024, November 20). *India's advance on AI regulation.* https://carnegieendowment.org/research/2024/11/indias-advance-on-ai-regulation?lang=en

. *Current Capabilities Future Prospects, and Governance*. The National Academies Press.

Dari, S. S., Ali, L., & Jadhav, B. (2025). AI-powered criminal identification in India: Evaluating human rights concerns in automated identification systems. *SGS - Humanities & Management*, 1(1). https://spast.org/index.php/sgshm/article/download/5302/479/10424

. Das, R. (2025). *Artificial intelligence, privacy, and the ethics of surveillance: A philosophical inquiry into autonomy and consent in the digital age*. The Academic Journal, 3(2).

Data Security Council of India. (2024). *Cross-border collaborations on privacy-by-design protocols and bias auditing tools.* https://www.dsci.in/

Delhi Police. (2018). *Facial recognition initiatives: Implementation of automated facial recognition systems for child protection.* Government of India.

Dixit, A. (2025). Digital surveillance and the right to privacy: Reassessing human rights in the age of technology. *Human Rights Law Review.*

European Parliament. (2021). *Regulating facial recognition in the EU: 2021/698021.* https://www.europarl.europa.eu/RegData/etudes/IDAN/2021/698021/EPRS_IDA(2021)698021_EN.pdf

European Union. (2025, February 1). *Article 5: Prohibited AI practices. EU Artificial Intelligence Act.* https://artificialintelligenceact.eu/article/5/.

European Union. (2025, March 31). *Understanding the EU AI Act: A security perspective. ASIS Online.* https://www.asisonline.org/security-management-magazine/monthly-issues/security-technology/archive/2024/april/Understanding-the-EU-AI-Act/

Europol. (2025, November 6). *EU lawmakers approve regulation to expand Europol's capabilities.* https://www.europol.europa.eu/newsroom/news/eu-lawmakers-approve-regulation-to-expand-europol%E2%80%99s-capabilities

Facia. (2024, May 17). *Human face recognition vs. human trafficking: Protecting human lives through real time liveness detection.* https://facia.ai/blog/human-face-recognition-vs-human-trafficking-protecting-human-lives-through-real-time-liveness-detection/

Fateh Chand v. State of Haryana, Crim. App. No. 1096 of 2004 (2009) (India).

Freelaw. (2024, October 31). The impact of AI and facial recognition on criminal investigations. https://www.freelaw.in/legalarticles/The-Impact-of-AI-and-Facial-Recognition-on-Criminal-Investigations

Fussey, P., & Murray, D. (2025). *Facial recognition surveillance: Policing and human rights in the age of artificial intelligence.* Oxford University Press. DOI: 10.1093/9780191979927.001.0001

Gaurav Jain v. Union of India, AIR 1997 SC 3021 (India).

Government of India. (1956). *The Immoral Traffic (Prevention) Act, 1956.* https://www.indiacode.nic.in/bitstream/123456789/15378/1/the_immoral_traffic_(prevention)_act,_1956.pdf

Government of India, Ministry of Home Affairs. (2023). *Crime analysis and predictive policing reports*. Government of India. https://www.mha.gov.in

Gozdziak, E. M., & Bump, M. N. (2008). *Data and research on human trafficking: Bibliography of research-based literature*. Georgetown University. https://t.ly/UUdYu

Holistic, A. I. (2024, August 5). *Navigating prohibited practices under the AI Act*. https://www.holisticai.com/blog/prohibitions-under-eu-ai-act

. *Indian Council for Social Science Research. (2024).* Tech and Surveillance in Marginalized Communities.

Indian Express. (2023, August 3). *SC directions on sex workers: History of the case and where it stands now*. https://indianexpress.com/article/explained/sc-directions-on-sex-workers-history-of-the-case-and-where-it-stands-now-7940364/

Inspeq, A. I. (2025, February 5). EU AI Act: Prohibited practices—European Commission guidelines (Article 5). https://inspeq.ai/blog/eu-ai-act-prohibited-practices-european-commission-guidelines-article-5

Internet Freedom Foundation. (2023). *AI, surveillance and privacy in India: Human rights in the age of technology*. Oxford Human Rights Hub. https://ohrh.law.ox.ac.uk/ai-surveillance-and-privacy-in-india-human-rights-in-the-age-of-technology/

INTERPOL. (2024, October 7). *Facial recognition system*. INTERPOL. https://www.interpol.int/en/operations/facial-recognition-system

INTERPOL. (2025, July 10). *Operation Global Chain*. INTERPOL. https://www.interpol.int/en/operations/global-chain

INTERPOL. (2025, March). *Statement to UNODC*. https://www.interpol.int/en

INTERPOL. (n.d.). *Facial recognition*. https://www.interpol.int/en/How-we-work/Forensics/Facial-Recognition

INTERPOL. *Facial recognition*. https://www.interpol.int/en/How-we-work/Forensics/Facial-Recognition

Jain, A. (2025, November 4). *NCRB's National Automated Facial Recognition System*. Panoptic. https://panoptic.in/case-study/ncrbs-national-automated-facial-recognition-system

Jain, S. (2023). Algorithmic bias and rights of marginalized populations. *Jindal Global Law Review, 14*(2), 145–168.

Jyotish, K. (2025, November 4). *The legal and ethical challenges of AI surveillance in India: Balancing national security and privacy*. International Journal of Legal and Law Research. https://www.ijllr.com/post/the-legal-and-ethical-challenges-of-ai-surveillance-in-india-balancing-national-security-and-privacy

Komal Ahuja. (2024, January 3). *The Kerala High Court's interpretation of the Immoral Traffic (Prevention) Act, 1956*. Bhatt & Joshi Associates. https://bhattandjoshiassociates.com/the-kerala-high-courts-interpretation-of-the-immoral-traffic-prevention-act-1956/

K.P.Kirankumar v State, 2025 INSC 1473 (India).

KPMG. (2025). *AI and privacy: A look at biometric tech & data*. KPMG Insights.

K.S. Puttaswamy v. Union of India, (2017) 10 SCC 1 (India).

Li, Q., Cui, T., Zhao, Y., & Wu, Y. (2023). Facial recognition technology: A comprehensive overview. *Academic Journal of Computing & Information Science*, *6*(7), 15–26. DOI: 10.25236/AJCIS.2023.060703

Lok Sabha Secretariat. (n.d.). *Bharatiya Nyaya Sanhita, 2023 (Annex)*. https://sansad.in/getFile/annex/267/AU2227_7QKUFb.pdf

Maharashtra Police. (2023). *Data-driven policing: AI and facial recognition in human trafficking detection*. Government of Maharashtra. https://www.mahapolice.gov.in

Menéndez González, N., & Mobilio, G. (Eds.). (2025). *Next democratic frontiers for facial recognition technology (FRT): The legal, ethical and democratic implications of FRT*. Springer Nature. DOI: 10.1007/978-3-031-89794-8

Ministry of Electronics and Information Technology. (2024). *MeitY annual report on AI governance*. Government of India. https://www.meity.gov.in/

Ministry of Electronics and Information Technology. (2024). *MeitY annual report 2024*. Government of India. https://www.meity.gov.in/

Ministry of Home Affairs, Government of India. (2022). *Crime in India report*. Government of India.

Ministry of Home Affairs, Government of India. (n.d.). *National advisories*. https://www.mha.gov.in/en/commoncontent/advisories-0 Ministry

Ministry of Women and Child Development, Government of India. (2019). *RTI and government affidavits*. Government of India.

Monash University. (2025). *Facial recognition technology: Definition and applications*. Retrieved February 7, 2026, from https://www.monash.edu

Mukherjee, S. (2025). Algorithmic bias and discrimination: Legal accountability of AI systems. *International Journal of IRJMPS, 13*(4), 232659. Advance online publication. DOI: 10.37082/IJIRMPS.v13.i4.232659

Nagpur Police. (2025). Operation Shakti initiative and Garuda Drishti overview; Times of India. (2025, August 27). Cops unleash AI arsenal to crush human trafficking; Nagpurnews.live (2023, July 30)

Nair, P. M. (n.d.). *Ready reckoner on provisions of laws for tackling human trafficking*. Bureau of Police Research and Development, Ministry of Home Affairs, Government of India. https://bprd.nic.in/uploads/pdf/1745497790_31ae803126827f574b39.pdf

. National Academies of Sciences, Engineering, and Medicine. (2024). *Facial recognition technology: Current capabilities, future prospects, and governance*. The National Academies Press.

National Crime Records Bureau. (2021). *Automated facial recognition system: Project tender documents*. Government of India.

National Crime Records Bureau. (2021). *Automated facial recognition system: Tender documents and project architecture*. Government of India.

National Crime Records Bureau. (2022). *AFRS Evaluation Report*. Crime in India 2022

Online, E. T. (2024, September 2). *Popularity of face authentication* [Slideshow]. *The Economic Times*. https://economictimes.indiatimes.com/wealth/save/what-is-aadhaar-face-authentication-these-government-social-protection-programs-use-face-authentication/popularity-of-face-authentication/slideshow/112988712.cms

Online, M. J. I. L. (2024, October 27). *The balancing act: How the European Union's Artificial Intelligence Act frames biometric identification for trafficking*. https://www.mjilonline.org/the-balancing-act-how-the-european-unions-artificial-intelligence-act-properly-frames-the-dangers-and-benefits-of-using-biometric-identification-to-combat-human-trafficking/

Panoptic.in. (2020, October 24). *Delhi Police case study*. https://panoptic.in/case-study/delhi-police

Panoptic.in. (2020, October 24). *Delhi Police case-study*. https://panoptic.in/case-study/delhi-police

Parkman, S., & Stratton, E. C. (2025). A qualitative phenomenological study of the lived experiences of female sex workers in a Bangladesh brothel. *Scandinavian Journal of Caring Sciences, 39*(1), e13316. DOI: 10.1111/scs.13316 PMID: 39775800

Pragya Prasun & Ors. v. Union of India, 2025 INSC 599(India)

Privacy International. (2025, September 30). *Legal frameworks for facial recognition usage.* https://privacyinternational.org/

Pulitzer Center & The Wire. (2025, July 1). As AI took over policing in Delhi, who bore the brunt? https://pulitzercenter.org/stories/ai-took-over-policing-delhi-who-bore-brunt

Rani, M. (2024). Impacts and ethics of using artificial intelligence (AI) by the police force in India. *Emerald Insight*, 27(2), 182–202. https://www.emerald.com/pap/article/27/2/182/1212999/Impacts-and-ethics-of-using-Artificial

Roeloffs, M. (2023, August 9). DHS Says it identified 311 new child sexual exploitation victims after Forbes reports AI facial-recognition push. *Forbes.* https://www.forbes.com/sites/maryroeloffs/2023/08/09/dhs-says-it-identified-311-new-child-sexual-exploitation-victims-after-forbes-reports-ai-facial-recognition-push/

Sadhan Haldar v. State of NCT of Delhi, (2018) Delhi HC (India).

Security Industry Association. (2020, June 25). *Security Industry Association strongly opposes the Facial Recognition and Biometric Technology Moratorium Act.* https://www.securityindustry.org/2020/06/26/security-industry-association-strongly-opposes-the-facial-recognition-and-biometric-technology-moratorium-act-citing-immeasurable-benefits-of-the-proven-technology/

Sharma, R., & Verma, P. (2023). Cybersecurity challenges in emerging digital economies. *Academic Journal of Computing & Information Science*, *6*(7), 15–26. DOI: 10.25236/AJCIS.2023.060703

Smyth, S. M. (2019). *Biometrics, surveillance and the law: Societies of restricted access, discipline and control.* Routledge. DOI: 10.4324/9780429022326

S.S. Rana & Co. (2025, April 27). *Facial recognition technology - A growing challenge for privacy.* https://ssrana.in/articles/facial-recognition-technology-a-growing-challenge-for-privacy/

Supreme Court of India. (2022). *B.N. Srikrishna Committee report.* https://www.sci.gov.in/

. *Takshashila Foundation. (2023).* Regulating AI in Law Enforcement: A Proportionality Analysis

TechGDPR. (2025, May 25). *Comparing the UK and EU framework on facial recognition technology.* https://techgdpr.com/blog/comparing-the-uk-and-eu-framework-on-facial-recognition-technology/

Times of India. (2025, August 28). *Cops unleash AI arsenal to crush human trafficking, prostitution rackets.* https://timesofindia.indiatimes.com/city/nagpur/cops-unleash-ai-arsenal-to-crush-human-trafficking-prostitution-rackets/articleshow/123551729.cms

Tony, H. (2025, April 16). Grubesic, Edward Helderop, Jorge A. Sefair & Dominique Roe- Sepowitz (16 Apr 2025): Human Trafficking: A Scientometric Review of the Knowledge Domain. *Journal of Human Trafficking*, 1–22. Advance online publication. DOI: 10.1080/23322705.2025.2483115

Two Birds. (2025, April 22). *European Union Artificial Intelligence Act: A guide.* https://www.twobirds.com/-/media/new-website-content/pdfs/capabilities/artificial-intelligence/european-union-artificial-intelligence-act-guide.pdf

United Nations Office on Drugs and Crime. (2024). *Global report on trafficking in persons.* https://www.unodc.org/documents/data-and-analysis/glotip/2024/GLOTIP2024_BOOK.pdf

United Nations Office on Drugs and Crime. (2025). *Action against human trafficking and migrant smuggling*. https://www.unodc.org

U.S. Department of Justice. (2025). *Attorney General's annual report to Congress on U.S. government human trafficking projects.* https://www.justice.gov/

U.S. Department of State. (2025). *Trafficking in persons report.* https://www.state.gov/

U.S. Department of Transportation. (2024). *Preventing and addressing human trafficking*. https://www.transportation.gov/

Veena, S. (2023). Automated facial recognition and the Indian criminal justice system: Promise and pitfalls. *Indiana Law Review*, *7*(2), 145–168.

Vidhi Centre for Legal Policy. (2024, March 12). *The landscape of facial recognition technologies in India*. TechPolicy Press. https://www.techpolicy.press/the-landscape-of-facial-recognition-technologies-in-india/

White House Archives. (2024). *National action plan to combat human trafficking*. https://www.whitehouse.gov/

. *Women Safety Division, Ministry of Home Affairs. (2024).* Advisory on Responsible Use of Biometric Technology

Zarnowski, A. (2024, December 23). *INTERPOL identifies over 140 human traffickers in new initiative*. Infosecurity-Magazine. https://www.infosecurity-magazine.com/news/interpol-identifies-140-human/

Zheng, S. (2021). The application of facial recognition in China and India: Potential risks and regulation suggestions. *Journal of Politics and Law*, *18*(3), 125–140. https://www.davidpublisher.com/Public/uploads/Contribute/6123074d2bb20.pdf

Chapter 6

Digital Legal Aid Platforms at the Nexus of Prostitution and Human Trafficking Law

Pranjal Khare
http://orcid.org/0000-0002-9937-9588
Jindal Global Law School, O.P. Jindal Global University, India

ABSTRACT

The global environment for sex work is complex, with three distinct legal models - Prohibitionist, Abolitionist/Nordic, or Legalization/Regulation - that has created an access to justice crisis in consensual sex work and human trafficking. Traditional legal aid rewrites does not work due to financial barriers, geographical isolation, and institutionalized mistrust, with vulnerable populations fearing they have been sanctioned by law enforcement as a criminal. Digital legal aid (DLA) platforms emerge as a lifeline, offering anonymous, secure, and immediately accessible support that can help mediate structural and psychological barriers to safety and justice. Ethical design requires Data Security (end-to-end encryption, data minimization), Stealth Mode features to increase users' safety and nylon protective privacy screening. For sex worker users, DLA constitutes an almost de facto decriminalization of sex work, allowing for immediate Know Your Rights information and collective documentation of police abuse.

DOI: 10.4018/979-8-3373-5841-3.ch006

INTRODUCTION

The international context of sex work is highly complex, legally ambiguous, and full of disastrous human vulnerability. At the heart of the issues related to sex worker is the important legal difference between consensual sex work, where adult participants exchange sexual services for money or goods, vs. human trafficking, which is recognized as the use of coercion, force, or fraud to compel someone to provide labor of services, including sexual services. The legal difference between the two is evident, yet the practical, policy, and law enforcement lines become greatly muddied in practice; ultimately, bringing about a dangerous reach between victims of exploitation and people consensually providing criminalized work. The legal consequences for both parties' labor compromise their access to the most basic legal rights.

The scale of the population affected by sex work prompts its global significance. The International Labour Organization (ILO) estimates there are millions of forced labor victims internationally and a considerable proportion of this comprises commercial sexual exploitation (CSE) as recognized as human trafficking. Human trafficking is a transnational crime totaling billions of dollars a year in profits; conversely, victims to CSE, commonly marginalized or low-socio-economic adults, oppressed communities and migrants/recently arrived folks, CSE industrial workers, put in a situation where an authority does not give them a path to justice. Sex workers, regardless of legality in a context, are typically tied to a large population that is often underground. Regardless of whether sex work is criminalized, regulated, or decriminalized, those who engage in sex work have several unique occupational hazards: violence, non-payment, health risks, and most importantly, chronic legal precarity. The experience of marginalization, criminalization, and fear of accessing state authorities does unite both populations and frames a necessary contextual entry point for thinking about digital solutions to access justice (Hansen & Johansson, 2022).

The tension between consensual acts of criminality and coercive victimization is compounded by the fact that the two acts affect one another on a near daily basis. Sex workers are particularly vulnerable to being exploited by traffickers, and the very laws and policies against trafficking or prohibiting sex work ultimately isolate the very people they seek to protect. Thus, it is important to note that the legal context, guided by different moral and political philosophies across countries, typically does not provide even a post-factum safe route to legal redress, due process, or protection for either group. It is in this precarious and highly complex legal milieu that we are seeing a variety of digital legal aid platforms emerge as quite literally a lifeline to help circumvent barriers to access and bridge geographical distances and to disseminate legal information, services and human resources necessary to mitigate the legal crisis (Firmin et al., 2013).

Distinguishing and Intersecting Legal Frameworks

The challenges associated with applying legal frameworks to the commercial sex industry can be traced directly to the ideological foundation for how states view prostitution and sex work. This ideological foundation can be categorized broadly into three preeminent models, each of which shapes a particular legal landscape with corresponding legal needs (Platt et al., 2018).

The first is the Prohibitionist Model, which is predominant in the United States and other jurisdictions, which regards selling and/or buying sexual services as a criminal act. The Prohibitionist model is tied to a moral aversion to sex work or a stated desire to "end" prostitution by criminalizing it. The principal social consequence of this model is that once sex work is criminalized, any commercial sexual activity goes underground, making it impossible for law enforcement and service providers to distinguish between consensual behavior and coercion, and making both sex workers and trafficking victims more vulnerable as a result. In the case of sex workers, the act of criminalization establishes a perpetual fear of arrest, or exploitation of the fear of arrest, will discourage sex workers from reporting violence or seeking health. Similarly, for trafficked persons, the potential fear of being arrested for prostitution is a powerful disincentive to report to their traffickers and contributes to their silence and ongoing exploitation. The model conflates being trafficked with the act of selling sex.

The second approach is the Abolitionist or Nordic Model (often called the Equality or End Demand Model) and has been adopted by Sweden, Norway, France, and elsewhere. This model makes it illegal to buy sexual services but legal to sell such services or simply does not penalize the seller. The premise behind this approach is that prostitution, itself, is a form of violence against women and by eliminating demand the system of exploitation will cease to exist. Abolitionists typically advocate a model in the spirit of decriminalization that is aimed to lessen the criminal element in sex work. However, when implemented, this model produces its own exploitative outcomes. Since the buyer of sex is criminalized, the work remains hidden and invisible and sex work moves to more unsafe, hidden, and remote "places of business" making it extremely difficult for outreach workers and legal aid to connect with potential clients. With the police enforcement efforts and the direction of the police authorities, although theoretically targeted at buyers, the police often arrest the sex worker to identify and catch the client, when doing outreach and legal work. Therefore, the cycle of police surveillance and harassment to control sex workers and revealing the client as a criminal continues. The abolitionist rhetoric tries to delineate sex workers from criminals but matches them when it pertains to protections for the legal protections and safety (Leon et al., 2025).

The third model is Legalization or Regulation, which has been applied in parts of Australia, Germany, and the Netherlands. This model recognizes sex work as a legitimate, regulated sector for which workers are expected to apply for licenses, health checks, and pay taxes. In theory, this model is intended to improve working conditions, affirm workers' labor rights, and bring the industry under state control for easier monitoring for exploitation. In practice, the reality of regulation is complex. Often, only a small, privileged part of the sector can comply with rigorous legal requirements (e.g., working indoors in regulated areas, facilities). The overwhelming majority of workers, usually migrants or those working in street-based work, prefer this location, are therefore outside of the recognized formal system and pushed into unregulated and criminalized spaces. Finally, in terms of legalization, while it technically separates sex work from trafficking, regulated spaces might then provide cover for trafficking enterprises that operate just outside these formal spaces, meaning that legal aid platforms operating in this context have to deal with heavily labor rights, workplace safety, and compliance issues (Davis & Mavisakalyan, 2024).

The nexus is the crucial juncture at which these models overlap and collapse. In practice, police and prosecutors, no matter which model is in play, often do not properly allocate resources, and instead of simply arresting prostitution, confuse trafficking investigations with low-level arresting. As the models illustrate, this failure to accurately distinguish coercion from consent has a serious social consequence: it undermines the most vulnerable individuals' trust in the legal system and results in a climate in which sex workers and trafficking survivors do not view the state as protective, but rather see the state as a source of further criminalization, punishment, and deportation. Any digital legal aid platform operating in this space must be robust enough to anticipate which legal model governs the immediate reality of its users, then tailored advice, whether it be rights information, defense strategy advice, or victim identification advice, based on that model. This legal and social distrust is precisely what digital, secure, and anonymous pathways are aimed at overcoming.

The Crisis in Access to Justice for Vulnerable Populations

The justice access crisis for populations at this nexus is urgent, complicated, and systemic, arising from a systemic mix of legal, structural, and psychosocial barriers. Although sex workers and trafficking survivors have distinct legal needs, the barriers to accessing the formal legal system are for the most part the same, all often based in pervasive social stigma and state-sanctioned criminalization.

The first and most debilitating barrier is financial and structural exclusion. Legal aid services globally are underfunded at alarming rates, and the few existing services are often not within a reasonable distance, requiring an individual to travel long-distances, take time off from unstable employment, or navigate a sometimes-intimidating public transport system. Geographic isolation is a barrier for trafficking survivors and sex workers who often lack fixed addresses and have unstable housing situations. Traditional legal aid offices with fixed hours and intake processes, cannot function with clients who have fluid unstable lives. Additionally, many of these clients often lack documentation such as identification, or proof of residence, making the first step of applying for state legal service impossible (Jabyn, 2020).

The second, and arguably most pressing, barrier is institutional mistrust and fear. Individuals who have been criminalized for their work like sex workers or suffered trauma/violence such as trafficking victims, have a strong negative association with police, courts, and state agencies. For a trafficking victim, telling their story means not only relieving the trauma but possibly admitting acts that were illegal while they were being exploited, worrying about deportation or, even worse, being re-trafficked. For sex workers, even reporting violence or theft to the police often leads to them being arrested instead, making the victim into the defendant. This fear is understandable and rational, and it leads to a pervasive culture of self-exclusion from the legal system. They simply do not trust the system to protect them; they have learned through experience that it will punish them (Kuran et al., 2020).

The third barrier is information asymmetry and specialized legal complexity. The law concerning human trafficking issues is highly particularized and constantly evolving. For example, T-Visa applications and laws on vacating criminal records for survivors. Sex workers also face a dizzying array of local laws and police enforcement that can change drastically moment to moment or block to block. When an individual's life is at stake, they need accurate legal information immediately, not on a scheduled appointment or a physical piece of paper. They need to know their rights now, for instance, during a police officer stop, or investigate their rights an instant after finding a way to leave a dangerous situation. The current system fails not merely because there aren't enough lawyers, but rather there is a mismatch between the delivery mechanism of justice and the immediate, discreet, and flexible needs of the client population. Digital legal aid is a reaction to this systemic failure, and its objective is to create a safe, anonymous, and immediately accessible bridge over these structural and psychological gaps.

The Emergence of Digital Legal Aid

The global Access to Justice movement has increasingly embraced technology to help address the scale and complexity of the legal aid gap, and this has led to the rapid rise of Digital Legal Aid (DLA) platforms. These are not just digitized versions of "traditional" services, but a significant shift in how justice is delivered, using mobile connectivity, data security, and artificial intelligence to engage populations not engageable before.

DLA, in a basic form, encompasses Information and Education tools; secure websites; encrypted messaging services; and self-help apps providing information about rights and template legal documents. At a more sophisticated level, DLA incorporates Chatbots and AI Triage Systems. These systems use natural language processing (NLP) and machine learning (ML) to process user questions, clinically filter out non-legal questions, and critically for this study, identify indicators of urgency, such as trafficking or coercion, guiding the user to a human lawyer or social worker in real time. The ability to triage is necessary so that scarce human legal resources can focus their time only on the most complicated and urgent cases.

The technology behind DLA holds significant potential for the unique needs of sex workers and victims of trafficking. Anonymity and Safety are the most important. DLA can use advanced end-to-end encryption and can design architectures that do not log actual identifying user data. For a population who has their well-being based on being discreet and not creating digital footprints, technical and digital safety provides a level of trust that may not always exist with actually going to a physical legal office. Second, DLA provides Geographical and Time Flexibility. A mobile app will be available 24/7 from anywhere with a cellular signal. No need to travel, arrange a time, or be physically present will help create those immediate opportunities for someone who is a sex worker working in a remote location, or for a trafficking victim who is being surveilled, to get important information quickly and discreetly. Third, DLA can create Real-time crisis intervention. Picture a "panic button" whereby if it is activated, pre-written text messages are automatically sent to positive contacts, the app records the pertinent information, the user is immediately connected to an available lawyer for short telephone consultation, and all of this is accomplished in a highly secure digital environment (Singh & Upadhyay, 2024).

Moreover, these platforms provide the opportunity to scale support in a way possible for human lawyers to provide. They can likewise provide basic legal assistance (e.g. steps to follow to file a non-payment claim) to thousands of people at once, while using machine learning techniques to identify patterns of violence or exploitation in aggregated, anonymized data. In this regard, the difficulty for developers and lawyers alike is to produce technology that is sophisticated enough to tackle the complexities involved with legal matters at the human trafficking and sex work nexus, that it can give accurate, contextual, and safe assistance, without simply placing a bot in place of the required empathy and qualitative reason to address human rights and criminal defense situations. The true promise of DLA, then, is not to replace human lawyers, but to enhance human lawyers' capacity, in order to use digital tools to support the maximum reach and impact of human legal expertise.

The approach utilized in this analysis is mixed methods, and primarily based on legal and policy analysis, supplemented by case study analysis. The research will first conduct a critical doctrinal analysis of the intersecting national and international legal frameworks (e.g., Palermo Protocol, CEDAW) governing human trafficking and sex work. The research will then conduct a comparative analysis of selected DLA tools currently existing, describing their technical architecture, user interface, and stated ethical protocols. The final stage involves developing policy and technical recommendations grounded in best practices and existing legal ethics.

THE LEGAL AND TECHNICAL ARCHITECTURE OF DIGITAL LEGAL AID

The creation of Digital Legal Aid platforms is based not just on addressing service gaps, but also on core international human rights law, especially the universal Right to Legal Aid and the obligation to Non-Discrimination. The Right to Legal Aid is, most clearly, based on international law in Article 14 of the International Covenant on Civil and Political Rights (ICCPR) which includes the right to a fair trial and having been assigned legal counsel. The relevance of legal assistance has undoubtedly expanded from the narrow scope of criminal defense in court to the equally vital areas of civil and administrative proceedings, such asylum or T-Visa applications, or restorative justice. For human trafficking victims, the denial of immediate and trauma-informed legal assistance to help with victim certification, obtain restitution, or expunge criminal records acquired while being trafficked, is a violation of their basic rights as a survivor. Legal aid for individuals engaging in sex work, is also vital to ensuring robust legal assistance in the event of a criminal defense commence, challenges to police overreach, and other incidents when state actors deny basic precepts of due process while ignoring harassment or wrongful arrest. The main issue for Digital Legal Aid, is finding a way to translate the human right to counsel into a form of accessible and real-time functionality in a digital world that removes the physical and psychological barriers entailed in traditional legal aid systems (Bambal & Deshmukh, 2025).

The principle of Non-Discrimination, established by instruments such as the Universal Declaration of Human Rights and CEDAW, prohibits bias on the basis of profession, social status, and presumed morals. Both sex workers and survivors of trafficking are extremely susceptible to bias based in a systematic way; sex workers are typically subjected to punitive biases, whereas survivors of trafficking, especially victims with marginal identities, e.g., migrant, transgender, or indigenous, are often distrusted by authorities, and risk re-victimization or deportation. DLA architecture must be deliberately created as a counter-discriminatory tool. First, when DLA provides anonymous, standardized access to legal information and discovery, it largely circumvents the human bias that is often an obstacle to justice seeking that affects marginalized peoples in traditional contexts. Therefore, legal justification for DLA relies on the notion that created alternative pathways, are deep access, and allow for enforcement of existing rights in contexts where existing legal structures have been actively hostile or neutral (Fine et al., 2017).

Types of Digital Legal Aid Platforms

Digital legal aid tools operate on a functional spectrum, addressing varied phases of the client's legal experience according to 3 core categories. The first layer is made up of Information and Education Tools, which seek to democratize legal knowledge and information through secure websites, mobile applications, and interactive media. For sex workers, this means providing accurate, localized "Know Your Rights" information regarding specific ordinances around solicitation or loitering, providing responses to questions from law enforcement, and providing step-by-step, anonymous instruction on reporting lines. For human trafficking and exploitation victims, this is a way to provide government rights to protection, confidentiality, or special RV visas like the T-Visa, and translate complex legal terms into easy-to-understand terms with glossaries in multiple languages. Importantly, the technical architecture of I&E tools should prioritize user safety with parameters such as low bandwidth, easily delectable access points, and a 'quick exit' feature to allow the user to quickly change the screen to a generic and non-suspicious screen when being observed (Colleen & Kim, 2025).

Communication and Triage Systems extend beyond providing information about support and services to engage, assess, and provide urgent connections to initial human support. These systems emphasize secure messaging and artificial intelligence to facilitate convenient and anonymous communication, such as secure chat and encrypted helpline services. While not detailed here, these secure chat and encrypted helpline services are often built on end-to-end encrypting protocols that allow individuals to communicate with legal assistance workers or trauma workers. This is particularly valuable for accessing information for individuals who are under coercion and are not able to risk using unencrypted calls or seeing someone in person. AI Chatbots and Triage systems use Natural Language Processing to gather initial information for intake interviews. These bots are trained for the critical function of identifying indicators of coercive trafficking from indicators related to consensual sex work. This triage function saves human legal time by screening out 'routine' inquiries and quickly elevating high-risk cases to human intake or legal workers. These systems must employ strong identity verification processes while ensuring protocols are in place to avoid any personally identifiable information (PII) collected by these systems, as traffickers may then exploit these PII, or hostile elements may use this to entrap (Mowbray et al., 2020).

The most advanced level of DLA integration occurs in case-mapping and document generation platforms, which facilitate the collaborative propulsion of a case. The platforms use Automated Document Assembly to draft routine, but legally critical documents like expungement petitions for sex workers or to pre-fill complex government applications for victims of trafficking who are applying for certifications of victim status or restitution. The platform then acts as a Secure Lawyer Matching portal to match the specific legal needs of the client with the location to ensure that a verified, specialized attorney is assigned to the case. Once the case is assigned, the document platform becomes the main, encrypted Client Communication Portal for privileged communication, document-sharing, status updates, etc., to maintain security and continuity of the legal process.

Technical Challenges and Ethical Imperatives

Using DLA with the sex work/trafficking nexus entails major technical and ethical risk, particularly when users are vulnerable, and a poorly designed platform could harm users. Adherence to the ethical imperatives is not negotiable, starting with Data Security and Privacy. For this population, data safety risk is direct, where an individual's location or prior history could lead to violence, re-trafficking, or deportation should the trafficker or law enforcement become aware of the person's information. Platforms must deploy End-to-End Encryption on all communications and abide by the rigorous Data Minimization principles. This means that platforms only gather personally identifiable information that is necessary to fulfill the legal intervention criteria. In situations where storage is a requirement, PII data stored must be pseudonymized and guarded by jurisdictions with strong data security standards - ideally under litigation protection from state seizure altogether. In addition, DLA must preemptively anticipate the risks of vulnerability to State Surveillance and forensic data dissemination, a concern in jurisdictions less than marginally protective of sex work or trafficking victims (Selkova, 2022).

The cross-border nature of sex work and human trafficking creates complicated Jurisdictional issues. Clients may be seeking services in one country for an event that occurred in another, or they may be interacting with a platform headquartered in yet a third. This raises the necessity for DLA to efficiently create a management system for the Conflict of Laws. This necessitates the creation of geo-aware automated systems which are trained on at least two often contradictory legal systems (Legalization vs. Prohibitionist models). The maintenance of Attorney-Client Privilege becomes more complex due to communication across international borders and the involvement of non-lawyer support staff using DLA Platform, for which clear legal firewalls and client consent protocols are needed to delineate privileged information.

Second, DLA is limited also by Accessibility: Addressing the Digital Divide. The most vulnerable clients are often also those with some of the greatest shortfalls in reliable access to the internet, even access to a reliable device, and access to reliable digital literacy. DLA Platform must be designed and optimized in relation to Device and Bandwidth Constraints, so it works reliably and efficiently on low-cost older mobile devices with less data, because being plugged in is often precarious and very costly. The interface itself must also have an intuitive design, Digital Literacy and Language, so that there is minimal text with clear iconography, makes work for clients with low literacy and will offer multi-language support and low-literacy interfaces. Importantly, while enabling digital reach, DLA should be cautious to not Mitigate Isolation through technology that seeks to transform or replace traditional forms of boots-on-the-ground services and should rather be a conduit to connection to people and to a range of social support.

Case Studies of Existing Digital Legal Aid in other High-Risk Areas

DLA can draw transferable technical feasibility and ethical lessons from DLA applications in similar, high-risk legal contexts. For example, tech companies working with Domestic Violence and Gender-Based Violence (GBV) survivors have incorporated key safety features, given the analogous risk of surveillance and abuse. For example, applications that allow clients to draft and file restraining orders away from the courthouse and to do so safely, demonstrate a 'stealth mode' or 'fake app' cover layer, which conceals the DLA application from service users abusers or traffickers who are companions to the client and watching their phone (Vahedi et al., 2024).

Refugee and Asylum Law cases similarly illustrate the value of automated, localized legal education for clients who often lack PII or may be rapidly traversing multiple jurisdictions. For example, refugee information chatbots, that have large training sets incorporating complex bodies of international law, are a caution to DLA users in terms of maintaining accurate legal content since sudden shifts in policy can render legal advice as old news within hours. Refugee information chatbots help service users apply decentralized methods of identity that do not rely on government IDs.

Finally, platforms pertaining to Public Defense and Criminal Justice Reform have provided lessons in efficiency that directly apply to criminalized sex workers. Tools that automate the complicated process of Record Expungement gather data via a simple Q&A and pre-populate the necessary forms for Court. This is an excellent example of an efficient use of automated processes for a high volume, low complexity legal task like expungement or vacatur petitions for trafficking survivors and allow human lawyers to attend to the high stakes, low complexity cases such as prosecution of traffickers or defense against deportation. The effectiveness of this type of tool relies heavily on the correspondence between the automation tool and the legacy government document structure and court systems.

Using the safety-first design of GBV solutions, the cross-border legal expertise of refugee law, and the automated efficiencies of criminal justice reform can help to build the next generation of DLA platforms to meet the highly specialized requirements of individuals living at the difficult intersection of prostitution and human trafficking law (Kluge, 2025).

DIGITAL AID FOR VICTIMS OF HUMAN TRAFFICKING

A survivor of human trafficking may have one of the most legally complicated profiles in contemporary law today because of their compelling and interrelated legal needs in criminal, civil, and administrative law. Equal to that complexity, it is common that victims are non-citizens in need of Immigration Relief, primarily through the T-Visa in the United States. The T-Visa is a vehicle for legal status that allows individuals, who have been victims of a severe form of trafficking in persons and remain in the United States, to apply for a visa based on their agreed-upon cooperation with law enforcement in the investigation or prosecution of trafficking offenses. Status acquired under T-Visa agreements must show evidence of continuous physical presence and hardship in order to be deemed credible and applicable in compliance with Immigration law. The T-Visa process notoriously takes a long time and is paperwork intensive for both survivors and attorneys alike. Failing to submit or properly document a T-Visa application directly leads to deportation, which forces survivors back into an environment of vulnerability or in the hands of their trafficker. Often, during their time trafficked individuals' survivors are forced into committing crimes such as prostitution, drug offenses, or petty theft. These crimes, or lack of engagement through marriage, directly lead to the creation of a criminal record that severely restricts housing options, employment, and social integration of post-rescue. Currently, Digital Legal Aid is uniquely qualified to automate the initial steps of expungement or vacatur applications with security measures and creates the necessary court forms that could shift a costly, time-intensive human appellate process to an affordable, low-barrier digital process (Stephenson et al., 2025).

Besides immigration and clearance of criminal records, the victims also have urgent needs regarding their civil and financial cases. They have options for Restitution Claims under state and federal criminal law, for lost wages, medical expenses, and a financial value for the exploitation and tactics of exploitation. Given the scale and complexity of these transnational trafficking businesses, determining the full scope of damages will often require forensic accounting and meticulous records, in which DLA can create standardized, encrypted digital financial journals and evidence logs, to collect in a safe way that the survivor can maintain and curate. Additionally, the most substantial, and legally difficult, avenue for recovery is a Civil Suit against traffickers, exploiters, or businesses that indirectly profited from, or turned a blind eye to the trafficking operation, whether located in hotels, labor brokering, or even banking institutions (Polizzi et al., 2024).

It is a priority that these types of cases are evaluated with substantial legal resources, along with expert witnesses so that the innovations are pursued to their maximum potential. Further, DLA platforms must be able to serve as initial intake mechanisms for these high-risk cases, screening for jurisdictional connections, or named defendants, and securely compiling the initial evidentiary packet before human lawyer decides whether to devote substantial pro bono and/or contingency resources. The linking requirement through all of these legal issues is that legal assistance will be timely, discreet, immediate, and trauma-informed practice, where traditional, fixed-location advocacy agencies fail at every level (L'Hoiry et al., 2024).

Designing Platforms for Confidentiality and Safety

The ethical and technical obligations in DLA for trafficking survivors demand an overriding consideration of confidentiality and safety in design and technical conditions. Unlike regular legal aid clients, a survivor's use of a digital platform might literally endanger their safety based on the abuser or trafficker's awareness of the attempt to seek assistance. Thus, the platform has to implement layered protection against abuser/trafficker detection. This begins with technical protection: End-to-End Encryption must be integrated into all communications to assure that no one can read or detect the content of messages, including the DLA provider. Moreover, the DLA provider must adhere firmly to Data Minimization, meaning that only what information is necessary for immediate legal intervention takes place in DLA, and that communication history is deleted immediately or after a predetermined period.

Technical encryption is not enough, however; device security is critically important. The platform needs to provide Stealth Mode and 'Quick Exit' Features. The quick exit feature would permit the user to immediately navigate away from the platform, switching the app screen to a decoy with a single tap, thus allowing a person to return to a safer application and not be caught in a sudden inquiry/detection by an abuser. Additionally, the application should be purposeful in design to mimic an innocuous utility like a budgeting tool or calendar, referred to as a 'Fake App' cover, so that a trafficker has no indication a legal aid resource is present on their device. Location data is another area of risk; the DLA should not use Geolocation

Logging unless the user expressly and with knowledge requests to use a safety or emergency feature because a record of a survivor's location could present a risk if the record is subpoenaed or hacked. Beyond technology, the platform, based on strength, must include some form of user verification that avoids any Personally Identifiable Information. Instead of a name or addresses, the verification should be based on unique randomly generated user IDs or simply multi-factor authentication that is impossible for an abuser to replicate, while manageable and easy for the survivor to modify or remove if compromised. These design implementations take the DLA from simply an informational tool to a truly safe digital space, which establishes the trust a survivor needs in order to disclose their trauma and have some form of support (Alsemairi, 2022).

Role of AI and Machine Learning in Screening and Triage

The vastness of human trafficking worldwide, in connection with the difficulty of spotting the victim, who may be trained or manipulated to deny their status, sets the reason for using AI and ML in Screening and Triage. Intake traditionally involves a human interviewer, which can take up a lot of time, require resources, and be daunting for a traumatized survivor. AI/ML breaks through the identification barrier through the use of sophisticated natural language processing models trained on datasets of the survivor's narratives and indicators of trafficking. These NLP models were not built to replace the human lawyer, rather than to serve as a trauma-informed digital filter. When the survivor speaks with a chatbot or fills out an intake form, the NLP may assess the language patterns, keywords, and the consistency of their story/anecdote to assign a risk score.

An essential purpose of this AI is to detect Subtle Indicators of Coercion. Survivors are often unable to directly state, "I am trafficked". Instead, their story may include disjointed disclosures, minimization of violence, or learned helplessness. ML algorithms, especially deep learning models, are significantly more advanced and able to detect these subtle linguistic and behavioral indicators of control and exploitation than linear triage questions. The AI is not diagnostic, but classificatory; to quickly and accurately differentiate between a user who is in crisis and requires prompt, potentially life-saving assistance and someone who is inquiring about a non-coercive legal issue. After a high-risk score is generated, the AI will Cascade to Connecting to Specialized Legal Supports. This routing function immediately alerts a human legal aid attorney or a trained social worker who specializes in trafficking issues, along with a preliminarily anonymous risk assessment. This prioritization process allows scarce human legal resources to be deployed to the highest risk of individuals who might otherwise be hidden in a larger pool of general inquiries. Ethical application requires, however, the AI to clarify its limits and always make a clear introduction to verbal conversation by human legal professionals so that the trust built in a digital capacity is maintained (Akinsuli, 2022).

Collaboration with Law Enforcement and NGOs

The process of DLA appearing for trafficking victims presents an inevitable challenge to balance the duty to collaborate with law enforcement, and the ethics of preserving client trust and safety. The prosecution of traffickers and access to certain victim benefits probably depends upon some level of cooperation with the police or federal investigators. Conversely, the survivor community approaches legal enforcement with a high degree of distrust and fear of additional victimization, arrest, or deportation. The DLA platform must be able to establish and practice a delicate legal and technical firewall.

This firewall revolves around the question of mandatory reporting laws. Even if a DLA is not considered 'abuse or trafficking', laws exist in many jurisdictions for the requirement of any person, including staff of non-profits or social workers, to report if they suspect child abuse or human trafficking to the authorities. The provision of legal aid of the platform must clearly specify the distinctions of the service and coverage under Attorney/Client Privilege and situations where it would not be. The user agreement for the platform must clearly provide explicit, low-literacy level warnings about the limits to confidentiality and when disclosures can be required and by whom legally.

In addition, DLA must adhere to the consent-first principle: survivor data related to the trafficking case must never be shared with LE or other government partners without the survivor's explicit consent, informed and easily withdrawable. Working with partners at NGOs, such as shelters, health clinics, and social service providers, is important to support a survivor in a comprehensive way. DLA should create opportunities to share data securely and with consent with trusted NGO partners to create a wraparound of services. A survivor who receives legal assistance also requires shelter and therapy. However, the DLA must still create the technical architecture to keep the data isolated and anonymized that was generated in the DLA model. In other words, a Data Firewall to ensure only aggregated and de-identified data is shared with the resulting partner for government policy and resource allocation. All the High-Risk PII and case details will remain secured under legal privilege. This form of balancing, enough cooperation for services and reparations but still sufficient protection of client safety and trust is the other most significant legal and operational challenge for DLA working in this sector.

Effectiveness of Digital Tools

When considering the success of the DLA in addressing the needs of trafficking survivors, it is important to move beyond simple measures of downloads or engagement. Genuine success must be evaluated in tangible ways regarding Legal Outcome Quality and Survivor Stability, and the impact assessment must be multi-faceted.

To begin, success can be measured by the Improved Victim Identification Rates. Evaluation must determine if the AI-based DLA triage is succeeding in identifying individuals who would be otherwise missed by conventional intake methods when they are most isolated or under the tightest control. Second, along with tracking Positive Legal Outcomes, like successful T-Visa applications, vacatur of criminal records, achieving restitution, and the prosecution rate of traffickers who were associated with users of the platform, is a measure of success; to provide this data to the DLA will require a feedback loop where human legal aid lawyers report case dispositions back into DLA for quantifying the DLA's actual impact on some measure of justice.

The most ethically concerning question is how to evaluate impact, which must incorporate enhanced survivor safety and long-term stability. Evaluative metrics must employ post-assistance measures, including documented decrease in re-victimization rates, achievement of stable housing and employment, and access to ongoing support services. An effective DLA platform should be able to demonstrate how it shortens the time it takes for a survivor to progress from the first contact with the service to having their case handled legally. Careful consideration must be given to how this impact will be evaluated, which must be carefully crafted to be non-extractive and centered on survivors, emphasizing the user's safety and well-being over the metrics that institutions are interested in reporting. This frequently involves working with social science researchers to administer anonymous surveys and qualitative interviews to users, assessing the evaluation solely through the survivor's perception of their safety, agency, and access to justice. Centering these nuanced outcomes will prove the model is worth gauging not only as a technological innovation, but also as an important solution for upholding human rights (Ismaidar et al., 2025).

DIGITAL AID AND THE DECRIMINALIZATION/ LEGALIZATION DEBATES FOR SEX WORKERS

Workers in the sex trade are subjected to an isolated, universal cluster of legal vulnerabilities resulting from either the criminalization or intense regulation around their profession, regardless of the regulatory structure of the jurisdiction. These vulnerabilities are compounded by social stigma and institutional bias, which further facilitate a state of constant precarity that DLA platforms, or any social service organization, must be mindful of. The most immediate and common risk of employing sex work is arrest, which can happen even in jurisdictions where sex work is permissible, as 'arrest' can entail arrests for ancillary crime. Notably, even when the incident does not result in a conviction, many arrests will permanently affect housing, work, and education while trapping individuals further into the very margins they are seeking to escape. In addition to ascribing to an individual a permanent criminal record, criminalizing sex work often leads to harassment by police, where many sex workers report unlawful stops, coercive questioning, unlawful searches, and officers stealing or destroying property, even when merely using their perceived ability to remove them as a coercive threat. Additionally, laws targeting drug offenses or public nuisance are certainly weaponized in a location where sex work is been criminalized to both target and control sex workers, regardless of whether the individual is engaged in drug use or public nuisance.

Another major legal mechanism available against sex workers is Property Forfeiture. In many jurisdictions, police can seize any cash, vehicle, or device that they believe is connected to the commission of a crime. For sex workers, this practice can devastate their economic stability by taking away their ability to work and communicate and basically strip their ability to independently survive. Digital Legal Aid platforms must provide solutions to this reality in the form of immediate legal advice on protecting assets and navigating the process for challenging forfeiture, which can be complicated, and sometimes very time sensitive. In addition to issues of criminal justice, sex workers experience serious labor rights violations. Even with regulated models, sex workers generally are not considered valid employees. This means they are not provided the legal protections against wage theft, unsafe working conditions, and sexual assault from clients or managers. Their occupation automatically prevents them from accessing conventional employment tribunals and union protections, as reporting the issue would also constitute admitting to an illegal enterprise or deeply stigmatized profession. Again, DLA should go beyond the narrow concept of criminal defense and refer resources for documenting labor abuses and navigate the complicated options, in the domestic sphere, for pursuing some form of remedy against labor abuses, and possibly civil claims against the perpetrator, or complaints to human rights commissions.

Platforms as Tools for De Facto Decriminalization

Because legislative reforms usually take a long time, mainly because of the politics behind achieving full decriminalization, DLA platforms have a valuable role to play. In this case, we are referring to De Facto Decriminalization. In ordinary terms, De Facto Decriminalization means using technology to provide immediate, actionable legal information and support to reduce harm in real time. More specifically, technology that can meaningfully reduce harm, lower arrest and prosecution rates, and stabilize the legal environment, all without changing the legal status of the act. The center of this function is the provision of real-time legal information to mitigate immediate harm. In other words, technology provides preloaded information that is easily available, and can be referenced immediately, such as at a government interaction such as a police officer stop or a raid. As an illustration, a DLA app could have a script (specific to the jurisdiction) that instructs the user on "what to say during a police interaction", that they have a right to remain quiet, refuse any police request to search, and request to speak with a lawyer, all while not saying anything that would implicate themselves. This serves as real-time legal empowerment, acting as a preventative factor, enhancing the user's level of confidence in following the legal instructions given, and often even causing law enforcement to disengage from unwarranted stops or searches.

Additionally, platforms assist users in contacting emergency legal observers. The platform will typically have a secure, pre-programmed panic function, which informs a network of legal observers or pro bono lawyers about the user's exact position and what is occurring, which is a legal incident rather than a potential illegal arrest. The presence of a legally observed incident prompts greater accountability externally and provides a significant disincentive against police misconduct. DLA is also an important tool for contesting the legal construction of criminality. The platforms will provide publicly available information about legal classifications of categories, for example in the context of solicitation, usually criminal, as contrasted with communication, that can help users declare and exercise rights and challenge the expansive, and often unconstitutional, enforcement of anti-prostitution laws. The objective becomes to make targeting a sex worker a riskier proposition for police, exercising both a shifting in the legal power balance and a near decriminalization in practice, by allowing individuals to consistently invoke and document their rights using technology. This genius solution accepts the understanding that until statutes change, our strongest user defense is to consistently know and quickly verify our existing legal rights as it pertains to the issue at hand (Djuraev et al., 2025).

Digital Tools for Collective Advocacy and Rights Enforcement

In addition to individual protection, DLA platform use is further being seen as an important tool for Collective Advocacy and Rights Enforcement, turning isolated, stigmatized cases of abuse into evidence for systemic change. Documenting police abuse is one of these critical functions of the DLA platforms. Traditional processes to report abuse are ineffective due to sex workers' concerns of retaliation and/or dismissal of their testimony. DLA platforms provide anonymous, safe means for users to document every interaction with law enforcement officers, including date, time, location, officers' names, and type of harassment. These logs, consistent and combined with multiple users over an extended period, change anecdotal reports into evidence for Systemic Data. This Systemic Data is then helpful to advocacy organizations to show systematic abuse and/or enforcement via data and patterns of misconduct. If, for example, they collect several reports of racial profiling, or discriminatory enforcement. This information could be powerful for advocacy organizations to engage and work towards class action lawsuits in certain precincts, lobbying for new laws, and/or other public integrity investigations.

In addition, the platforms also serve as essential mechanisms for organizing policy change. As long as legal aid organizations keep a secure line of communication open with the user base, they can notify them of impending legislative debates, policy hearings, and legal actions. The DLA mainly acts as a secure online town hall, enabling the community to mobilize quickly to engage in lobbying, or public testimony. This becomes especially vital for elevating the participation of highly marginalized and physically dispersed communities in legal processes that will impact their lives. In addition, the accumulated data that the platform collects in the name of Rights Enforcement can assist users in locating lawyers who specialize in specific forms of injustice and allow the organizer to notify multiple users experiencing similar systemic violations to the same identity legal representation. Thus, the DLA offers a pivot from individual defense to collaborative, data-driven systemic change, which is what makes it a critical tool of social justice.

Distinguishing Consent and Coercion on Digital Platforms

The core challenge of running DLA in the tension between sex work and trafficking is the moral and methodological obligation to identify consent and coercion through digital services. DLA must effectively reach people who engage in consensual sex work and want to protect their rights while simultaneously identifying and assisting people who have been trafficked in non-consensual situations requiring immediate response. This challenge necessitates a dual-purpose nuanced screening process. The ethical obligation to screen trafficking is critical; a rights-based platform cannot accidentally perpetuate exploitation by not engaging and flagging survivors in need. This inclusion is through AI-assisted triage like the response for explicit trafficking but designed to be sensitive to the language of autonomy.

The screening must be non-extractive and non-judgmental. Unlike traditional anti-trafficking screening tools that may be extractive, in that they ask deficit-based questions, the DLA triage must use affirmative language that focuses on the user's immediate needs for safety, security, and legal support. The system should recognize any relevant key indicators of coercion but must avoid conflating indicators of sex work with indicators of trafficking. For example, a user reporting that they are being denied wages by a client would be routed to schema for labor rights resources, as opposed to someone reporting a third-party is holding their passport to force a continued work engagement would immediately be routed to high-risk trafficking intervention protocol. In addition, the platform must delicately navigate the privacy of the consent framework. The legal information that is available must be made available to every sex worker, regardless of whether the sex worker has been or is being trafficked, with no requirement to show their current 'non-trafficking' status. The DLA's structure must ensure that merely asking about sex worker information does not lead to a decision to begin a trafficking investigation that cannot be undone in a way that honors the choosing user and secures a clear and accessible route to intervene with the coerced user. This ethical balancing act is the most difficult design challenge in the entire DLA ecology.

Challenge of Serving Marginalized Sex Worker Populations

While the general population of sex workers is heterogenous in nature, potential legal and technical difficulties expand significantly when we narrow our focus on marginalized sex worker populations. This generally includes undocumented migrants, transgender individuals and youth. These populations experience heightened intersectional vulnerabilities including being targets of aggressive police action, discrimination in housing and healthcare, and limited access to technology and legal resources. Undocumented migrants are typically ambivalent to utilizing any platform because of their real fear of immediate deportation if they are required to or exposed. For this group, the DLA has to provide entirely paperless, location-free, and anonymous communication. The emphasis is largely on providing urgent information on immigration raids, asylum resources, and challenging labor exploitation claims completely separate from criminal statutes (Coombes et al., 2022).

Transgender individuals, especially those of color, experience extraordinarily high levels of violence, harassment, and arrest. These issues have often arisen from antiquated laws that have perpetuated gender profiling. DLA must also explicitly be gender-affirming, supportive of proper language, while expeditiously sharing legal information relevant to addressing discriminatory profiling, changing one's name, or accessing gender-affirming health care, when necessary, often due to violence. Both youths need platforms that adhere to child protection laws while offering confidential support. Under DLA users require a protocol that can distinguish between a mature minor requesting legal support, and a victim subject to mandatory reporting laws that often requires immediate and secure transfer to a human trained in child welfare and trauma informed approach to care. Herein lies the true technological conundrum, the solution can be infinitely adaptable for leveraging segmentation features that cater not only to differing laws, but acute safety and legal needs that arise from multiple layers of marginalization and context. Meeting the DLA needs of these populations is, ultimately, the ultimate measure of a platform's commitment to universal justice in this volatile and complex nexus (Kinzer, 2025).

CONCLUSION AND WAY FORWARD

The previous chapters have demonstrated the pressing need for complicated structures of Digital Legal Aid platforms at the difficult intersection of law on prostitution and trafficking in persons. A consideration of the findings indicates that while DLA holds considerable promise to fill systemic access to justice gaps, from obtaining T-Visas for isolated survivors to supporting sex workers in real-time with rights information for responding to police misconduct, potent ethical, regulatory, and financial challenges are also at play. The central promise of DLA is to remove physical and institutional barriers that exist to historically exclude marginalized populations; the central threat is that data collected to assure safety and advocacy can also be used as a weapon against the user when the architecture of the platform is not well designed or the legal protections are inadequate. The future and sustainability of the DLA model must address an immediate holistic recognition that technology is not a neutral arbiter; it is an empowered player needing to be designed under new ethical, legal, and operational imperatives that prioritize user safety and autonomy over measures of efficiency.

The most significant risk involved in DLA is the Ethics of Automation in Legal Advice. While AI is quite adept at high-volume, low-complexity tasks, such as generating expungement forms or identifying basic legal rights, it is still, by definition, ill-suited for high nuance, trauma-informed judgment required in complicated trafficking situations. Decisions related to asylum, the showing of extreme hardship for a T-Visa, the complex distinctions between consensual sex work and coercion require human empathy, human legal experience, and direct, privileged communication. If DLA systems overly rely on automated advice in these situations, they risk engaging in legal malpractice by giving generalized or perhaps harmful advice, which could lead to deportation or re-arrest. Thus, the first ethical requirement is to clarify boundaries for human oversight: automated triage must only serve as a funnel to parse, and all advice involving irreversible legal consequences, must be verified and reviewed by a licensed legal professional. Additionally, DLA providers must assume liability for the automated advice, which ultimately imposes a legal obligation, requiring a procedural revolution of the rules of professional responsibility, in relation to the provision of quasi-digital advice.

This ethical dilemma is further complicated by dual-use concerns, the fear that a DLA platform that works could instead serve as a repository of evidence for ill-intended users. The same rich, geo-tagged, historical data required for collective advocacy by sex workers could be used by law enforcement or anti-trafficking groups for prosecution, surveillance, or enforcement actions. Therefore, platforms must be built with a 'deletion-first' mentality, retain only strictly anonymized data in high-trust jurisdictions, and build technical safeguard against government requests for information, including legal planning for defending against subpoenas as a matter of compelling advocacy based on the principle of derived attorney client privilege. The platform should function as a defensive tool, as opposed to a file for future prosecution.

This challenge highlights glaring regulatory gaps in existing legal frameworks. The internet and AI have significantly outstripped legal ethics and policy. Existing rules around the attorney-client privilege were never designed to account for a situation where a survivor living in one jurisdiction writes to a platform based in a second jurisdiction to obtain advice from a licensed lawyer working in a third jurisdiction. We need dedicated legal tech regulations designed to address the liability of AI non-lawyer agents, the obligations of platforms that provide international and inter-jurisdictional transactions in providing regards to data privacy in these sensitive legal contexts, and recreation of a framework for when a DLA platform can or is required to refuse a state demand for user data. Consideration of these legal gaps will require either international policy harmonization, or as a minimum, the creation of a recognized legal status for digital intermediaries designed to support marginalized communities similar to protect afforded to medical professions or pastoral communities.

Sustainability, Synthesis, and Recommendations

To ensure the long-term viability of DLA, effective Funding and Sustainability Models are essential. There are significant costs associated with developing and operating a secure, multilinguistic website that is regularly a human oversight. Supporting DLA only through sporadic philanthropic funding does not create stability; if you depend only on the support from philanthropy, it threatens continuity of services and, even more importantly, the data of the users may be at risk if a platform business closes. Hybrid funding models are the best solution. Governments and international funders should fund DLA as one component of a rights-based legal aid model and in the same manner that public defenders are funded by the state, with the state supplying the ongoing infrastructure, necessary security, and funding to enable the platform to grow and develop. Operations, however, need to be separated, and to use independent NGOs or collectives of rights-based technologists to manage

DLA. Separation of the source of funding and operational control creates the trust needed and an ethical firewall in case of state intrusion.

In summary, the promise of DLA can only be realized if its architecture encounters a unique legal intersection: it needs to be trauma-informed and safety-first while also being rights-affirming and privacy-focused. The dual imperative is the awkward balancing act of successfully identifying a coerced victim while protecting the anonymity and agency of a consenting sex worker. Success is evidenced in DLA's ability to provide de facto decriminalization, empowering users to claim their rights, and 'preventing the police from causing immediate harm' even when de jure laws are still punitive. Failure will be unavoidable if the technology is developed without external auditing, clear legal liabilities, or meaningful engaged relationships with the communities the technology has a goal of serving.

The next step is to develop robust recommendations for lawyers, technologists, and policymakers. A technologist must develop an open-source architecture to enable community members to scrutinize the architecture. Technologists must conceptualize that a low-bandwidth, easily purgeable, quick-exit interface is possible, and should operate in all global contexts. Legal professionals should push for clear ethical guidelines for using artificial intelligence in client intake and pursue Impact Litigation to challenge subpoenas for DLA data.

Policymakers need to do more than just fund DLA. They should also create a permanent Digital Legal Aid Trust Fund, with a global working group focused on developing binding international protocols related to data-sharing and privilege protection for legal technology resources that support marginalized populations. Ultimately, DLA is an indispensable tool for advancing justice at this difficult juncture, but only if its design is informed by an ethics of radical protection and a policy agenda framed with legal foresight.

REFERENCES

Akinsuli, O. (2022). *AI and the Fight Against Human Trafficking: Securing Victim Identities and Disrupting Illicit Networks.* ResearchGate.

Alsemairi, S. S. (2022). The role of digital technologies in combating cyber-trafficking in persons crimes. *Computer and Information Science*, *16*(1), 49. DOI: 10.5539/cis.v16n1p49

Bambal, S., Deshmukh, J., Bhagat, M., Thakare, S., & Gulhane, S. (2025). Implementation of 'legal aid: Know your rights': A digital platform for legal assistance. *International Journal For Multidisciplinary Research, 7*(2). DOI: 10.36948/ijfmr.2025.v07i02.41889

Colleen V. & Kim, M. (2025). Generative AI and Legal Aid: Results from a Field Study and 100 Use Cases to Bridge the Access to Justice Gap, *Loy. L.A. L. Rev*, 903.

Coombes, E., Wolf, A., Blunt, D., & Sparks, K. (2022). Disabled sex workers' fight for digital rights, platform accessibility, and design justice. *Disability Studies Quarterly*, *42*(2). Advance online publication. DOI: 10.18061/dsq.v42i2.9097

Davis, L. S., & Mavisakalyan, A. (2024). Individualism and the legal status of prostitution. *Journal of Comparative Economics*, *52*(3), 714–732. DOI: 10.1016/j.jce.2024.07.001

Djuraev, I., Baratov, A., Khujayev, S., Yakubova, I., Rakhmonova, M., Mukumov, B., & Abdurakhmanova, N. (2025). The impact of digitization on legal systems in developing countries. *Qubahan Academic Journal*, *5*(1), 81–117. DOI: 10.48161/qaj.v5n1a1246

Fine, J. B., Mayall, K., & Sepúlveda, L. (2017). The Role of International Human Rights Norms in the Liberalization of Abortion Laws Globally. *Health and Human Rights*, *19*(1), 69–80. PMID: 28630542

Firmin, M. W., Lee, A. D., Firmin, R. L., Deakin, L. M., & Holmes, H. J. (2013). Qualitative perspectives toward prostitution's perceived lifestyle addictiveness. *Journal of Behavioral Addictions*, *2*(4), 231–238. DOI: 10.1556/JBA.2.2013.013 PMID: 25215205

Hansen, M. A., & Johansson, I. (2022). Asking about "prostitution", "sex work" and "transactional sex": Question wording and attitudes toward trading sexual services. *Journal of Sex Research*, *60*(1), 153–164. DOI: 10.1080/00224499.2022.2130859 PMID: 36269626

Jabyn, M. (2020). Advancing justice interests and human rights of vulnerable groups through clinical legal education. *Jindal Global Law Review*, *11*(2), 271–288. DOI: 10.1007/s41020-020-00127-0

Kinzer, Q. M. (2025). Policy and platforms: Sex workers' labor experiences under changing online regulation. *Gender, Work and Organization*, *32*(6), 2369–2384. DOI: 10.1111/gwao.70014

Kluge, H. H. P. (2025). Addressing technology-facilitated violence against women: The unique position of health care providers. *The Lancet Regional Health. Europe*, *56*, 101417. DOI: 10.1016/j.lanepe.2025.101417 PMID: 41624088

L'Hoiry, X., Moretti, A., & Antonopoulos, G. A. (2024). Human trafficking, sexual exploitation and digital technologies. *Trends in Organized Crime*, *27*(1), 1–9. DOI: 10.1007/s12117-024-09526-4

Mowbray, A., Chung, P., & Greenleaf, G. (2020). Utilising AI in the legal assistance sector—Testing a role for legal information institutes. *Computer Law & Security Review*, *38*, 105407. DOI: 10.1016/j.clsr.2020.105407

Platt, L., Grenfell, P., Meiksin, R., Elmes, J., Sherman, S. G., Sanders, T., Mwangi, P., & Crago, A.-L. (2018). Associations between sex work laws and sex workers' health: A systematic review and meta-analysis of quantitative and qualitative studies. *PLoS Medicine*, *15*(12), e1002680. DOI: 10.1371/journal.pmed.1002680 PMID: 30532209

Polizzi, G., D'Arcy, J., Harris, R., Yates, S., Cullen, C., & Andrew, B. (2024). Survivors of modern slavery and their digital inclusion: A UK qualitative study from the perspective of survivors and organizations that support them. *Journal of Human Trafficking*, 1–18. DOI: 10.1080/23322705.2024.2393969

Selkova, A. (2022). Would online legal services guarantee the availability of justice and legal aid? *SHS Web of Conferences*, *134*, 00035. DOI: 10.1051/shsconf/202213400035

Singh, M., & Upadhyay, S. N. (2024). Digitization Of Legal Aid Services And Criminal Justice To The Detainees In India. *Law and World*, *10*(1), 37–49. DOI: 10.36475/10.1.4

Stephenson, S., Ramjit, L., Ristenpart, T., & Dell, N. (2025). Digital technologies and human trafficking: Combating coercive control and navigating digital autonomy. *Proceedings of the 2025 CHI Conference on Human Factors in Computing Systems*, 1–21. DOI: 10.1145/3706598.3713544

Syaharani, N., Nurdiana, C., Saputra, D. D., & Haharap, R. N. F. (2025). Legal review of the effectiveness of providing legal aid by advocates through digital media. *Journal Indonesia Law and Policy Review*, *6*(2), 323-329. DOI: 10.56371/jirpl.v6i2.418

Vahedi, L., Stark, L., Ding, R., Masboungi, C., Erskine, D., Poulton, C., & Seff, I. (2024). A qualitative investigation of gender-based violence prevention and response using digital technologies in low resource settings and refugee populations. *European Journal of Psychotraumatology*, *15*(1), 2347106. DOI: 10.1080/20008066.2024.2347106 PMID: 38722768

Chapter 7
Sex Work and Caste Governance in India:
Between Informal Regulation and Legal Apathy

Bharvi Shahi
http://orcid.org/0009-0005-7965-4609
Christ University, India

Shikhar Srivastava
http://orcid.org/0009-0009-2445-7316
National Law University and Judicial Academy, Assam, India

ABSTRACT

Sex work in India occupies a paradoxical position tolerated in practice yet criminalized and morally condemned in law and society. However, this paradox is not merely a product of legal ambiguity; it is deeply entrenched in India's historical caste hierarchies, gender norms, and systems of informal governance. This article critically interrogates the intersection of caste and sex work in India, focusing on how marginalized caste communities engaged in traditional and contemporary forms of sexual labor are governed not only by a punitive legal framework but, more insidiously, through caste-based informal regulation and entrenched social surveillance. The state's neglect, combined with a moralized legal discourse, contributes to what this article terms "legal apathy"- a systemic failure to extend legal rights, protections, or recognition to sex workers, particularly those from oppressed caste locations.

DOI: 10.4018/979-8-3373-5841-3.ch007

INTRODUCTION

The role of sex work in India enjoys an ambiguous status that furthers understanding of the complex relationship of caste hierarchies, colonial pasts and present legal fictions of caste status. While the act of prostitution is technically legal under Indian law and therefore, the act of a working woman selling sex is not criminalized, support actions associated with sex work; establishing a brothel, street solicitation, and deriving sexual commerce income are specifically outlawed within the Immoral Traffic (Prevention) Act (1956). This legal ambiguity creates a relationship we may think of as "tolerated criminalization" in that sex work is worked, policed, and punished by a regime that provides sex workers no legal recourse, yet monitors and invalidates them at the state level. But this inconsistency exists beyond legal absurdity. It finds its roots in the ancient caste system of India that defined communities of labor for sexual and entertainment services. The regulation of sex work, as it exists today, can only be explained through the intervention of colonialism on pre-existing caste based applicable identity, some of which have been subjected to criminality throughout post-independence (India Together).

Traditionally, caste and sexual labor in India were linked to modes of prostitution developed prior to colonialism and were articulated within a larger framework of relations of patronage, ritual performance, and economic exchange. In some orthodox communities, specifically the sex workers from the Devadasi communities in south India, delineated institutionalized sexual and entertainment services as part of religious and artistic offerings in the Indian Temples and, whether under the temple's patronage or outside of it, never relinquished their caste due to the upper consciousness they introduced themselves into. These were systems functioning within established social order which if repressive, also offered a level of protection and social status with one's socio-cultural geography (Shankar & Ganesan, 2021). The devadasi system is a classic example of caste-based sexual labor being organized through religious and economic imperatives wherein women from select lower castes were "dedicated" to temples via ritualized acts that obligated them, as a condition of their caste-dedication, to provide sexual services to upper caste patrons and temple authorities. This indebtedness resulted in a hereditary sexual serf 'age-caste based occupational determination of fate, a tradition that would persist into the colonial and post-colonial period (Harishankar & Mvadha, 2011). Similarly, the Bedia, Nat, Dom, Perna, and Kanjar caste communities were assigned traditional roles as entertainers, acrobats and sex workers in brothel situations sometimes by those members of these communities who took part in additional stigmatized occupational specializations of folk music, dance and fortune telling. These caste communities had complex internal governing structures control entry into types of employment, income division and social ties that transcended or common boundary placement between members of their communities. The research on the Bedia caste community informs us that caste regulated sexual service through painful customs in communities where 'the traditional occupation of this caste was that of prostitution women of community should do prostitution with the concern of family'-meaning that caste regulates sexuality was historically made part of community control and regulatory customs. Gender equity and impotence type assertions on the bifurcation of sexuality as commodity versus virtue and 'bedia communities, in their own ways maintain a sexualized identity' while doing so produces structural violence. The Bedia communities movement away from traditional roles suggested how "the transition from nomadic to established cultures does not terminate their link to sex trade; it merely modifies the terms on which the trade was conducted (Harishankar & Mvadha, 2011). The community of Kanjar is another case of caste coming into contact with sexualized labor because there was a somewhat 'fortunate' coincidence between caste and the structural forms of labor within this community. Ethnographic studies show that "sex work is a traditional occupation with its own subculture that is ingrained in the economic ecology," and informants about community socialization processes discuss how young women are groomed to engage in sexual labor as part of life in the community. These narrower social constructs (local societies) created not necessarily repressive social or cultural institutions that controlled and legitimized sexual labor within the specific social conditions in which they lived. The Nat community had long supplemented their income from entertainment services with sex work, and they developed integrated economic strategies to survive India's inherently invidious caste structure. Colonial interventions, however, disrupted this hierarchy, compelling adjustments that frequently made women more vulnerable and deprived them of the social securities and economic options (Jangir, 2024).

These strategies of colonial governance disrupted pre-existing social networks by instituting Victorian moral codes and bureaucratic categories that criminalized, or opposed, what had previously been socially accepted. The Criminal Tribes Act of 1871 represented the most substantive legislative intervention in this process, criminalizing nomadic, or semi-nomadic, groups that the colonial state had determined a priori were criminal. The Act defined a criminal tribe as "any tribe, gang or class of person habituated to the systematic commission of non-bailable offence" and a criminal tribe could be compelled to settle in a place fixed by the provincial government, resulting in the effective criminalization of whole communities based upon their traditional status. This process of categorization was not merely bureaucratic, however, and revealed more systemic colonial anxieties regarding managing peoples living in conditions beyond sedentary agriculture and private property. The colonial conception of crime was significantly shaped through a process of "enumerative data" and statistical surveillance that sought to eliminate criminal acts through systematic recording and control. Many of the community practices were transformed into statistical categories often tracked, policed, and ultimately criminalized. Thus, commonly "eliminating" crime and generating "success narratives" were instead official tales of violent suppression of real and diverse community ways if collaborating with the realities of how these complicated communities functioned. Throughout the working of this Act, it developed into family as the space for surveillance and control as part of a larger plan to produce `industrious families` that aligned with colonial economic and moral visions. In reshaping these family interventions, it fundamentally altered gender relations and economic relationships in these communities and often rendered women into precarious work such as sex work, or resulted from women engaging in sex work as occupations were rendered criminalized or economically obsolete (Jessica Hinchy, 2020). The implementation was achieved through the process of compulsory registration, placing and entrusting members of the designated criminal tribes into productive labor colonies, thereby restricting their mobility, employment and income-generating enterprise options, which effectively served as an alternative to custodial supervision. Within these communities, women in particular found themselves extremely vulnerable, given that their traditional forms of entertainment and sexual services were banned with few alternative means of income-generating allowed and often with caste-based exclusion, very few, if any, options outside of their live account as employment.

After the Criminal Tribes Act was abolished in 1952, the stigma and marginalization associated with "criminal tribes" continued. These communities became "Denotified Tribes" (DNTs), which still denoted a criminality (albeit without the status of criminality), serving to socially marginalize and economically disempower an entire population. Many of those labeled DNT still faced over-policing and surveillance and were shut out of mainstream economic opportunity, leading many families to engage in illicit or stigmatized labor, including sex work. Recent studies show that "sex work from DNT communities lingers as a shame and they continue to be highly marginalized", experiencing both discriminations based on their caste and their sex work. The marginalization is further institutionalized by a legal framework, i.e., the Immoral Traffic (Prevention) Act, 1956, which criminalize the systems of support that the sex workers need for the safety of life and livelihood. This leads to a situation where the act of sex work is still technically legal, but the means of conducting it safely are criminalized and inevitably forces sex workers into even more harm and exploitation. Research shows that DNT sex workers experience "double stigmatization": for being of a particular caste and for being in the sex trade, leaving them socio-economically marginalized in ways that mainstream policies don't recognize. The surveillance practices and government control mechanisms devised in colonial contexts have not been abandoned but rather continue to be present in policing of these communities in current forms. As communities continue to be officially "denotified," they are continued to be placed under more aggressive police surveillance and likely the first to be accused in all instances while closed accounts record them as innocent the stereotypes that remain result from representing the NDT community as 'criminals by birth' during the British colonial time. This constant surveillance takes a particular toll on Dalit and Adivasi women particularly in sex work who bear the burden of violence against their marginalized caste status and criminalization of sexuality. Their proximity to state attention makes them structurally vulnerable and unable to access legal support in order to challenge exploitative arrangements in their communities.

The nature of modern sex work with caste-marked individuals is shaped by a complex regime of informal regulation regarding the access, economic reward, and manners of socializing. These regimes function contemporaneously with, but typically supersede, formal regulation and create alternative forms of authority that are both legitimate and exploitative. In societies such as the Perna, women's engagement in sex work may be pre-determined to a great extent by ethnic caste tradition whereby sex work is socially accepted primarily as a cost of moving women toward privatization through marriage. Elders and caste panchayats maintain control over sex work, including the conditions of work, distribution of economic gain among family and community relatives, as well as the behavioral expectations for sex work individuals who violate the norms approved by their elders or caste panchayats. Another example of how caste governance systems intersect with sex work is the case of some Bedia community. Both ethnographic research as well as social science research has reported "widespread engagement of women in prostitution with consent of family." In these communities' men in the household will often claim ownership over the economic value of women's sexual labor. This produces systems of economic extraction, in which women's bodies are commodified as income for both family and community and managed through a type of caste-based power, rather than enacted through persons' agency and legal protections.

Research indicates that these systems of informal governance are often oriented by a gendered division of labor and power, where women offer sexual services and men control the transactions and representations in the public sphere of the community. The Kanjar community, in particular, shows that "sex work is a traditional occupation with a separate subculture wedded to economic structure," which both legitimized the routes for women to be pushed into sexual labor and framed men as patrons and exploiters. These arrangements are often enhanced with complicated transactions of family, community, and patron relation that define the terms by which to expect sex work. Women's agency is restrained through community norms, economic dependency and fear of social stigmas of women who are unable to navigate around the established network of relationships (Lama, 2022). The psychosocial dimensions of this caste-based governance comprise what the authors call "inherited stigma trauma," or intergenerational transference of shame, marginalization, and lack of life options which informs women's imagination of possibilities and limitations. This trauma is intensified by "dispossessive" trauma born of historical loss of their traditional occupations and "state abandonment" trauma caused by the lack of legal protections and social welfare provisions.

Theoretical frameworks that seek to analyze interlocking systems of oppression can help us understand the governance of caste-marked sex work. Caste intersectional feminism, a term originally coined by Kimberley Crenshaw while developing theories around double oppression based on her experiences living as a black woman in the U.S., has today been reconstituted and theorized by Dalit feminist scholars to improve the status of caste oppressed (Dalit women) by analyzing the intersectionality of caste with gender, roles, class and other categories of identity. Uma Chakravarti's concept of 'Brahmanical patriarchy' is one possible conceptual anchor for this type of analysis because it shows how ruling power of upper-caste and upper-class men is based on the governance of women's sexuality and the institution of endogamous marriage. Thus, establishing a social hierarchy by which: "upper-caste men have the maximum privilege, upper-caste women have more privilege, Dalit men have more deprivations, and Dalit women have maximum deprivations," (Najar, 2023). In this regard, Dalit women are sexualized bodies that represent a caste landscape, whose emotional bodies guard against an upper caste challenge through sexual violence and exploitation. Aspects of Dalit women's sexuality are regulated by the caste system to maintain its purity while social construct ordains caste-based women as the impure sexual objectified of society. This lens recognizes that most Dalit women do not enter as a sex work choice; they enter because they are outside the structure (either excluded or not included) for work and because the economic system of the country continues to structure certain castes to deliver sex and entertainment services (i.e., caste work-based structure). According to the evidence, Dalit women probably have a sizable proportion of "rural women forced into sex work or sold into urban brothels," which follows the pattern of caste that economically deprives women. Even the Dalit feminists criticize rescue-and-rehabilitation models that privilege upper-caste ideas of honor and deprive Dalit women of their experiences of caste-based exploitation. The failure of these approaches to recognize the agency of Dalit women in sex work is because they assume them to be mere victims in need of moral redemption not workers working under structural limitations for economic survival amidst the lack of better choices.

We refer to "multiple marginalization" to understand qualitatively distinct forms of oppression caste-marked sex workers experience, in which caste oppression is not simply summation of caste plus gender oppression. The intersectionality of these identities creates particular vulnerabilities and lived experiences that must be analyzed and engaged with differently than if these experiences stood alone. This intersectional discrimination confronts caste-marked sex workers in different yet parallel experiences exclusion from the feminist movement which tends to center upper-caste women's experiences and anti-caste movements that are unable to center struggles related to gender. In addition, caste-marked sex workers experience double criminalization by both caste ostracism and state legal sanction for behaviors associated with sex work. The connection between caste and sex work in India has larger implications of occupational segregation, a practice that has historically relegated certain types of work to specific caste groups. Many of these communities, often described as criminal tribes in colonial sentencing, engaged in traditional occupations such as performances, rituals, and sexual services as part of larger economic strategies. Similarly, in the Dommari community in Telangana, when acrobatics lost value with the transition to a free-market economy, "prostitution emerged as the primary livelihood". These two examples illustrate that caste communities attempt to transition their economy in line with the changing economy, yet they remain confined within prescribed caste boundaries with few options for true social mobility, where such communities survive despite their stigmatization (Harasankar Adhekari, 2011).

Caste is closely associated with sex work, as sex work is inherited and constructed by birth (both the profession and stigma). Ethnographic evidence illustrates that in certain communities, such as the Bacchara, girls and young women face "forced choice," as sex work becomes the best option to make a living with police harassment a danger. The "predetermination in sex work" is not an abstract choice, but a systemic organizing of certain caste categories directed towards certain professions. The normativity of sex work within some caste communities allows for complex power dynamics to present as cultural tradition, when in fact the normativity may be a form of accommodation to historical and social exclusion, and contemporary economic deprivation. These accommodations become part of niche community practice/identities, creating forms of internal governance that simultaneously protects and exploits women in those communities.

CASTE GOVERNANCE AND ITS IMPACT ON LOWER-CASTE COMMUNITIES IN SEX WORK

Within low-caste communities in India, and especially for those who are sex workers, the intersections of caste-gender-class create some of the deepest typologies of marginalization and violence. Within Bedia to Nat to Dom communities, the act and choice of sex work is implicated as a tradition of survival, heavily regulated for the communal economy and the communal values, economic extraction supplemented by the domination of caste, and the generation after generation violent pathologizing of a marginalized occupation. Thus, sex work in a lower caste-influenced setting offers the burden not only of social stigma but moreover, a more insidious form of social control and psychological damage of caste patriarchy, dispossession, and inherited social safety. However, these communities have also produced extraordinary forms of resistance and reclamation through collective organizing, litigation, and dignity-rights campaigns. Therefore, economic extraction by caste-marked sex work is not merely a function of governance, but a base logic in communities like the Bedia and Nat. Caste elders, family patriarchy, and community networks oversee a sex worker's entrance, earning and exit from sex work, operating through complex systems of male-controlled distribution of earnings to male family and kin and community leaders. This system is enforced through continuous social surveillance everything a woman does is monitored and evaluated. Everything she does, from where she works and for whom, to how she interacts with her clientele, provides the basis for suggestion and sanction (Harasankar Adhikari, 2011). Surveillance functions at different levels. Women monitor their mobility and income-generating activities within the family. Elders and panchayats administer community discipline, punish those who violate the community's rules and decide, as a community, how to deal with law enforcement or any outside pressure. However, surveillance is not only internal: dominant castes and state authorities reinforce it dynamically, by periodically raiding families, accepting bribes from families and morally surveilling the lower caste sex workers themselves. Therefore, economic extraction is combined with gender and caste-based control mechanisms that establish women's second status and strengthen community relative to the individual (Kumar, 2021).

In many of the lower castes, sex work is a tradition that has been handed down from generation to generation. In Nat and Bedia societies, just like lower caste communities that are more doctrinally religious, predestination is incorporated into the ritual of sex work. The Nat Uthari tradition, for instance, initiates girls into sex work as a part of becoming a woman. Sociological studies show how girls are groomed early on it is part of the family tradition, it is part of the local customs, it is part of the training process supervised by mothers, aunts, and elder sisters who are sex workers. When other ways of earning a living and getting an education are not an option, the burden of tradition becomes heavier. Because lower-caste women in the caste hierarchy are trained to be "naturally inclined" to this profession, many believe they have no choice in the matter since childhood. The "choice" in this context, is not real; they are caught between collective moral obligation, family coercion, and the built environment that precludes them from other kinds of work and social spaces. Caste can be seen as a pipeline which auto Grooms generations of women to be a sex worker- sex work acts as a basic mechanism of survival of women, family and community with no regard of these women and her aspirations and choices (Rana et al., 2020). However, the economic benefits of sex work, generally, are also retained by men, such as breeders and community leaders while the risks, emotional costs, and social consequences are borne by women. This extraction of labor is sanctioned through lived responsibilities for the sake of community expectations. Ethnographic studies have noted the Bedia and the Nat communities, that banned marriage for women as a local community expectation, so sex work would remain an economic activity. The household and the community serve as a site of economic exploitation, where the bodies of women exist for the purpose of exploitation, for everyone else's benefit. Family patriarchs often act as managers or intermediaries, controlling access to clients, for negotiating fees, and maintaining order. Where a woman's earnings from work are not enough, there are not-so-subtle pressures from the community, or domestic violence. All of this is couched in family responsibilities and caste customs that foreclose the possibility of asking for labor rights or demanding agency as an individual. Additionally, community leaders justify this cycle by delegitimizing sexual labor as a productive and appropriate means of social compact, which is (at least) provide some level of income and security from others, while denying any rights or dignity to the individuals themselves (Jha & Sharma, 2015).

Any violations of caste related sex work are met with swift, violent, and harsh punishment. They are at the mercy of an unpredictable caste-based system of retribution that finds women ostracized, gossiped about, shamed in public spaces, and in the worst cases beaten or killed for refusing to engage in the work, attempting to leave the caste, or asking for their share of cash. Today, community elders have the power of informal judication, and the punishments range from ostracism to complete banishment from the community stripping the woman and her entire family of a social and economic lifeline. Research through ethnography and legal research has shown that women trying to leave prostitution or assert their autonomy are subject to violence, social exclusion, coercive debt (in which women are made indebted to the brothel owner or traffickers in a deliberate failure to pay off the debt so they could leave the sex industry), or violence through coercion or manipulation of their children (Human Rights Watch). In addition, this punitive regulatory structure is reinforced by broader caste rules in which the upper caste populace can punish lower caste women for violating sex work traditions through denial of access to public services, violence, or prompting police action. Resistance becomes nearly impossible as women navigate the reality of asserting agency and the need for self-preservation and vulnerability of social exclusion.

Caste governance and sex work have a profound and complex psychological impact. Trauma related specifically to sex work does not only include the direct violence of sex work, harassment, exploitation, and risk of disease, but additionally the slow violence of dispossession, and the generational stigma attached to these communities. Women who are part of a sex work community are particularly socialized from a young age to feel their worth is wrapped up in a commodification, that their bodies are vessels of intergenerational shame, or that options for respite or recovery are scarce. The scholarly literature suggests substantial prevalence rates of depression, anxiety, chronic stress, and post-traumatic symptoms for sex workers classified as "lower caste". The functionality of daily degradation, threat of violence, and ritualizing subordination constantly diminish mental and physical health. The cumulative effect of this degradation, combined with lack of professional and educational opportunities, increases dispossession: for many women, even the most basic rights seem impossible to obtain, based solely on caste and choice of profession. Stigma acquired through inheritance permeates daily life from conversations to community rituals, with fatalism and internalized shame and guilt passed along in some instances as family trauma. The perpetual reminder of the precariousness of their position, only one step away from violence or being marginalized, adds insult to injury, denies healing to trauma, and hides hope for change. Few interventions exist, and when present, they rarely intervene intersectionally in caste, gender and economic deprivation.

Lower-caste sex workers have established effective principles of survival and resistance in the context of great difficulty. In sex worker unions, self-help groups, community forums, and partnerships with civil society, collective organizing creates an opportunity to challenge economic extraction and social regulation, and make a claim to rights. Initiatives from DMSC (Durbar Mahila Samanwaya Committee), VAMP (Veshya Anyay Mukti Parishad), and more recently, the Sangsad (Parliament) of Sex Workers of Bangladesh have focused on legal literacy, resistance to exploitation, and mutual aid networks. To put it simply, legal literacy has opened the door to women to use and access resources and to know about their rights and to challenge the illegal and exploitative practices. Dignity campaigns have attempted to change people's minds, converting people to see sex workers in low castes not as criminals or victims, but as working citizens with a right to respect and safety. Dignity movements are frequently based in Dalit feminist theory, which centers the structural violence of caste and patriarchy while also celebrating local strategies of empowerment. Grassroots advocacy, with the support of national non-governmental organizations and international agencies, has catalyzed and demanded for trauma-informed and caste-sensitive intervention recognizing that healing will need to involve the impact of external oppression and internalized stigma. Over the past few decades, there has been some mobilizing toward affirmative action, land rights, education, and labor protections, however, there are still socio-economic barriers present. Case studies from Tamil Nadu and West Bengal showed that some organized sex workers negotiated collectively to improve pay, working conditions, and self-defense against harassment. However, when caste hierarchy is still accepted as the social order, resistance grows, and community leaders and dominant caste will exclude or be violent toward those collectively organizing. Nevertheless, their stories knit the continuing struggle to reclaim dignity, agency, and justice from an implicit hierarchy.

From the perspective of lower-caste women, the caste system is a systemic and permanent mode of governance of sex work that brings caste, class, and gender together. It establishes a regime of economic extraction and social surveillance, making people predestined by established custom and punishing those who deviate from that regime, and then it extends beyond their generation. Women are subjected to cash and coerced labor, creating a psychological pressure of not just land but the infamy of being single, exclusion, or lack of alternative status. Most legal and social change do not address the multiple exclusionary and violent systems embedded and instead support the separate worlds or create a singular lens into their circumstances operationalizing their experiences against education, land or security. Despite these realities, lower-caste sex workers are engaged in forms of resistance that are quite complex in character, including collective organizing, legal literacy, and campaigns for dignity; all against the many different types of oppression, in the guise of patriarchy or governmental authority. It foregrounds their somewhat contradictory position as both vulnerable and agentic and promotes that the most oppressive structures are not able to entirely extinguish the desire of the individuals they are oppressing to be recognized and compensated for their labor, or for their contribution to the domestic world. Understanding these dynamics is critical in thinking through policy that is responsive but also impactful, in the short term - economic supports should not be reliant on caste-based structures of power and control and support only through trauma informed methods. The words, the sound, and the life must be for them - lower caste sex workers, who will determine what to desire, how to aspire to dignity and rights, citizenship, etc.

LEGAL APATHY AND THE FAILURE OF THE INDIAN STATE

The Indian system's legal indifference for long has exposed caste-oppressed so-called immoral women involved in sex work to chronic victimization, which makes them vulnerable to violence, criminalization, and social exclusion. This chapter suggests that the vagueness in laws, harassment by the police and the conflation of consensual sex work with trafficking within policy enable a process of vulnerability, which denies dignity, rights, and protections to sex workers, notably those from lower castes. The legal status of sex work in India is uncertain and the Immoral Traffic (Prevention) Act (ITPA) is at the center of a different type of ambiguity which enables the indirect criminalization and exclusion of social sex work. For example, the provision in the Act does not criminalize sex work, however, the associated provisions make it illegal to keep a brothel, solicit, or live on the earnings of broader sex work - thus further marginalizing the context of sex work. This indirect provision contributes to a space of legal ambiguity, where sex workers can experience harassment, arrest and extortion by state officials. Other forms of sex work include caste-based forms of work and as for lower caste sex workers, they face exclusion from formal protections or economic opportunities, which means lower caste status often means sex work is largely informal and caste-based. This legal schizophrenia means that sex work is illegal but not illegal, which reinforces a vulnerable community that is subject to police action, harassment and social control that is boundless.

Additionally, ambiguity is compounded by unevenness in enforcement, plus ongoing legal washing. Police frequently arrest workers not for legal violations, but through conclusory or vague phrases that define solicitation and brothel-related activities under the ITPA. However, in their quest to survive, women held networks for mutual aid and protection which led them to suspicion of "living off" the avails of another, further criminalizing community and solidarity. Legal ambiguity, therefore, does not function as a kind of limited tolerance, but as a means of exploitation and abandonment of the state, particularly for lower-caste sex workers who do not possess the social capital and/or legal clarifications to intervene. The criminalization of sex work in India is not an act apart but part of the cycle of raids, extortion, harassment and moral framing of law enforcement that follows sex workers as a second ghost - sometimes more visible than they are. Police raids in the name of enforcement of ITPA or anti-trafficking are commonplace, as noted and documented in many case studies and testimonies by legal aid professionals, who shared stories of sex workers being linked to the charges of ITPA, with no evidence to support legal action, thus failing IMBI. Police bump into the sex industry, granted authority from unspecified complaints. After a raid has occurred, the police may ask for money to release the women, will not act upon alleged infractions, or act to preempt any additional violence against the women. In particular, lower-caste men and women are more easily targeted when dealing with the police while living in a neighborhood where the police are more aggressive against those who are lower caste, and those who belong to dominant caste groups do not protect them (Dasgupta, 2017).

The law is so nebulous, it provides the police with a moral justification: sex work is defined as inherently illegitimate, and the police act as observers of this undesirability that must be eradicated at much lower costs than removal. The moral framing of sex work as a so-called "vice" directs police actions and legitimizes public harassment and discrimination, increasing societal stigmatization and vulnerability of the sex worker experience. Many others have found that the resolution for their assaulted complaints ends in the police ignoring ousting or in the worst part harassing them in turn not only creating an environment in which the worker sex is frightened and made to feel that it is unsafe or impossible to report for themselves. The police are not to be used for protection or for the enforcement of the law but rather to control, discipline and remove profits.

One of the distinctions of legal apathy in India is the inability to disentangle sex work and trafficking, which is a product not only of the design of ITPA but also the tenor of public discourse. Laws assume all sex work is the result of coercive conditions or moral failure, and police, courts and NGOs treat adult sex workers as "victims to be rescued" regardless of the sex workers own avowals of consent and autonomy. The merging of sex work and trafficking gives rise to intrusive "rescue operations," forced institutionalization, and "rehabilitation" into waged labor or family re-integration, and for women from lower-caste communities, these processes can become permanent acts of suspicion and paternalism, with terrible outcomes.

Research literature and policy analysis provide evidence of how conflation creates legal ambiguities and policy contradictions. Anti-trafficking efforts consistently bracket sex workers stated consent, criminalize consensual sex work, and diminish workers' security and safety. Indigenous sex worker organizations and Dalit feminist thinkers critique such models as producing new forms of surveillance and control (i.e., not liberation). Enforcement occurs in the absence of the law to violent imprisoning, forced laboring, or leaving the already marginalized to collegial self-organization to reproduce existing relationships of marginalization and class/caste exclusion. In Budhadev Karmaskar v. State of West Bengal (2022), the Supreme Court passed a bench ruling confirming the violation of sex workers' constitutional rights and dignity. The Court also confirmed a sex worker an Constitutionally guaranteed right to live and liberty under Article 21, as well as protection from police cruelty, unlawful arrest and access to healthcare, and considerations for a sex worker's dignity and right to choice. The Court directed all states to acknowledge the rights and autonomy of sex workers, end arbitrary raids, and give sex workers' access to rights to health, housing and livelihoods. Nevertheless, the significance, the legacy of Budhadev Karamaskar does little more than generate legal ambiguity, state surveillance and social stigma. While the decision establishes a strong judicial precedent, many sex workers, particularly from lower-caste communities, report that daily policing and access to justice has not changed much. This reluctance to enforce constitutional protections by law enforcement, state institutions, and local authorities of all stripes represents an incessant body of legal and social indifference; a divergence between progressive jurisprudence and the lived experiences of citizens throughout the nation.

India ratified the Palermo Protocol in 2011, following an international framework for trafficking with a victim-centered, rights-based approach. The Protocol states, "the state should distinguish between trafficking and consensual sex work, with a respect for the rights and autonomy of adults engaged in sex work" (United Nations Human Rights). However, as seen in many studies and reports, the protocol has generally not been implemented in India. Reports support the viewpoint of established anti-trafficking mechanisms remaining focused on punitive "rescue and rehabilitation" processes that are often difficult to extract from the way the state defines sex work in a broader sense. The overlap of trafficking and adult sex work, without clear legal distinctions or policy to differentiate these, creates clear breaches of rights and forced departures, which have been characterized as harmful and ineffective responses to marginalized women. Reports from work under the Palermo Protocol highlight that the implementation of anti-trafficking law results in policing that is often concerned primarily with policing sex work, with little attention to sex worker right or opinion to guide the police action itself, which carries heavy state and non-state level enforcement against the legal and social exclusion from sex work.

CEDAW GR No.38 (2020) expands upon this by calling on states to "differentiate trafficking from migration for sex work and trafficking from any other dissimilar forms of sex work." And again, "not to punish sex workers, and to also cease actions including criminalization of sex workers and other actions which undermine individual autonomy." The UN further voiced that states should endeavor to not use punitive and harmful approaches that alter the status of sex workers, endeavor to pursue legal recognition and protections of their rights, and work to abolish coercive and paternalistic models. At the very least, this indicates a gap between CEDAW norms and Indian practice. To the contrary, the Indian system continues to examine all sex work through the prism of moral panic and trafficking, a framework that again erases consent and autonomy, let alone the recommendation. This also affects marginalized caste groups in a disparate manner, and in doing so are automatically classified as trafficked victims even though their labor is invisible under the law. The overall denial of rights, dignity, and safety for sex workers is a continued trend in national laws and policy that go against international human rights norms. International covenants, particularly the International Covenant on Civil and Political Rights and the International Covenant on Economic, Social and Cultural Rights guarantee general human rights including privacy, dignity, health and livelihood. These rights have been defined by UN bodies as universal, meaning, they belong to sex workers, independent of caste, station or deed. India consistently performs poorly on the implementation score, as national law does not keep pace with obligations arising from ratified treaties. Others record violations of the ICCPR and ICESCR because of citizenship denial, police violence, and exclusion from health and social services. Whether it be strong sex worker collectives or human rights advocates, the call for full realisation continues to ring out, and there also exists a consistent pattern of state indifference and neglect of the laws that frame our rights.

In view of international and national NGO activism, rescue and rehabilitation models have become major narratives in the Indian prostitution and trafficking framework. But these models are not without coercion and paternalism; adult sex workers - and especially those from impoverished or "renotified" communities - are forcibly removed from their jobs and/or workplaces where they are forced into either "rehab" homes or vocational "rehabilitation" programs that offer little meaningful economic opportunity and are never asked what they need or want. The harm caused by these state-sponsored interventions is severe and entrenched, producing mass incarceration, impoverished communities, and stigma, as demonstrated in both library and ethnographic accounts. Adult sex workers are often violently or sexually abused in rehabilitation centers and are forced back into sex work with far fewer protections against violence in light of their isolation from the community. Many adult sex workers live in communities where sex work is a survival strategy or a caste tradition; in these situations, the action of rescue undermines a livelihood and reinforces systems of structural violence instead of creating a pathway for agency and social mobility.

This legal inaction is not merely a lack of reform from above, of which there should be plenty available, it constitutes a system of social abandonment for caste-oppressed sex workers. This is evidenced through a lack of recognition of continuity of labor through the state not providing clarity over the recognition of the sex worker as a worker, the denial of a right to be protected from violence and denial of the basic social, economic and health rights guaranteed to all under Indian law and various International Covenants. The state of caste biases is compounded by perils facing lower-caste sex workers through predatory police and ostracized neighborhoods, where over-violence and under-justices persist and continue to remain unremedied. They contend that such legal phobia is constitutive and is reproduced as a result of legal vagueness, social stigma, and habitual bureaucratic inertia, but it is also structural, in that it is the collective and compositional responsibility of civil society to provide solutions to significant problems of municipalities. However, despite court decisions that have been progressive from the Supreme Court, most steelworkers (especially those that are battling both caste stigma and occupation stigma) would satisfy all indicators of legal abandonment. They need to be recognized, not as a charity project, but as an issue of justice and constitutional right; otherwise, that failure itself is a violent act and a continued denial of dignity (Chereches, 2021).

The Indian government's enforced legal unawareness constitutes the backbone of systemic violence against sex workers affected by caste-based injustices. The abstraction of the term of criminalization, under the ITPA (Immoral Traffic Prevention Act) hides that a cloak of legitimacy exists around criminalization, while the vague term allows for police sexual exploitation of 'Exploitation Policing,' which in turn has some moral framing, and moral cycles of extortion. The state consummates its disregard for the variability and distinction between trafficking and voluntary sex work, as it collectively points a finger at positioned moral superiority and intrusion into people's lives to pacify the complexity of governmental paternalism. This also exacerbates the knowledge economy of caste oppression by "protecting" a privileged agenda which ignores state violence against voluntarily active sex workers, even if the courts periodically came close as when it said sex workers are better treated, as we saw in Budhadev Karmaskar. Although the required distance is often reinforced by the legal limits, as we know, the gap between law and lived reality is persistently clear. Delayed anchoring of human rights practices that promote sex workers' exclusion in India is furthered by 'rescue', and the 'rehabilitation' of survivors while replicating vulnerabilities and instabilities. There will always be a home for legal indifference as a powerful engine of structural violence until sex work is expressly recognized by all parties in India as labor, legal protections are defined, legal distinctions are made between adult consensual work and trafficking, and an affirmation of dignity and agentic support is encouraged.

BETWEEN INFORMAL REGULATION AND LEGAL APATHY- THE STRUCTURAL VULNERABILITY OF CASTE-OPPRESSED SEX WORKERS

In India, sex workers, as a part of marginalized caste communities, find themselves at the tense junction of both informal caste-based regulation and legal indifference or hostility. This chapter explores the dynamics of caste governance and the gaps in law that in fact come together to create a structural vulnerability that is manifested in being culled the joint experience of economic extraction, social extraction, legal visibilitelessness, and social pollution. It questions dominant punitive feminist narratives that serve to reinforce caste hierarchies, highlights the efforts of sex worker collectives to build resistance, includes comparative explorations from Nepal and Bangladesh, and ultimately presented rights-based, trauma-informed and caste-sensitive recommendations using international human rights law.

In caste-regulated sex work communities such as the Bedia, Nat and Perna, extra-legal caste authorities have strong influence over the bodies of women and the ways they make their livelihoods. Entry into sex work, appropriation of sex work earnings, and compliance with norms are dictated by caste panchayats, family elders and other leaders in the sites of intervention who sanction compliance. This is an informal governance regime of sexuality and labor; however, ultimately it redistributes wealth upwards to male kin and community elites. In conjunction, we see incredible "legal apathy" that has been enabled by the Indian state. Courts have repeatedly affirmed progressive rights; however, because the state has so much latitude with the vague provisions of law – specifically the Immoral Traffic (Prevention) Act (ITPA) – individual police continue to harass, extract bribes from and refuse to protect sex workers from extreme violence (including murder and rape). Thus, caste-based surveillance networks reinforce punitive legal regimes that disregard the rights of sex workers which exacerbates the state of marginalization and vulnerability sex workers are subjected to. This convergence signifies a Democratic failure both jurisprudentially and socio-culturally. The indifference/hostility of states leaves caste communities to bypass any informal or formal control demonstrates this reality, creating a scenario in which sex workers are policed and rendered accountable to both social norms and legal codes. This sort of structural abandonment allows access to no means to salvation and/or justice for caste oppressed sex workers, who become cast as unrecognized illegals; this is how caste oppression genocides socially desiring caste contamination and/or status through acculturation.

In India, well-known discourses of feminism and anti-trafficking discussions are occasionally mocked for a brand of "carceral feminism" that focuses solely on punitive state responses that solely support Brahmanical patriarchal morality. Policy responses are often framed in simply conflating sex work and trafficking, the criminalization of sex workers and those helping them, and an extension of police powers in the name of progress. The methods described perpetuate caste biases in the name of criminal justice, rendering itself a policy that in effect harms caste-minoritarian sex workers and reinforces the notion of the victimized "sex worker" as someone in need of a rescue, all while enabling moral inertia and reinforcing an emphasis on the social hierarchy around "purity" and "honor." Beyond hyperbole, the moralism found in carceral feminism is a driver of caste stigma and grants legitimacy to the invasive policing and marginalization of caste-oppressed sex workers and offers no quasi-protection of sex worker rights and dignity from the law. This critique identifies the need to transform the law and policy away from punishment and towards empowerment, or the recognition of sex workers as rights bearers and citizens rather than simply problems to be solved. As an answer to caste violence and social criminalization of caste, sex workers in India form effective collective community organizations and advocate for legal legitimacy, access to healthcare, and status as citizens with dignity. These collective movements, again, were/is for labor rights and de-stigmatizing sex work and exemplify important components of the struggle from stigma. Specifically, the case of the Durbar Mahila Samanwaya Committee hailing from Kolkata is an example of an enduring sex worker lead organizational engagement, built upon a politics of solidarity, mutual support, and legal supports to re-work the sex worker image away from social paupers to work and social citizenship. Veshya Anyay Mukti Parishad (VAMP) provides sex worker organizational action in Maharashtra that combines sex workers from Dalit and tribal areas, with legal literacy and support including workers bargaining power. Both DMSC and VAMP name and contest the punitive structures of caste and state, which is key to interrupting this stigma, while advocating for sex worker voices to be centered in policy responses. Their success illustrates the potential to do organized resistance to structural violence and develop agency-based positionalities, considerable via numerous networks. (Shreyas Gupta, 2013).

The intertwining of caste or ethnic hierarchies, sex work, and state neglect is not an exclusively Indian phenomenon, but is echoed across South Asia. In Nepal, caste and ethnicity, like in India, organizes the sex work industry in a manner that generates sexual stratification, and renders individuals of lower social status to have near no property rights as a formal matter, coupled with inadequate legal status, to identify as a sex worker. Polo-intersecting the legal delineation between prohibition and harm-reduction is tenuous and convoluted. The policing practices and public stigma in Nepal creates a toxic cycle of vulnerability for sex workers. Despite laws to regulate sex work, ethnic minorities and those from lower caste backgrounds remain socially and legally marginalized in Bangladesh. In India, even government oversight of sex work still reproduces a form of informal community control, coupled with irregular police harassment, social stigma, and economic precariousness.

The cumulative effects of caste hierarchies, coupled with the indifference of Indian law, have resulted in a set system of embedded structural vulnerability. Caste governance creates a fiction of social alienation and legally generated dependence that keeps sex workers purposely in liminal spaces of exclusion where labor rights, social security, or protection from violence could otherwise be considered by the law with indifference. This sweeping emblematic dual and caste governance results in poverty, stigma, and trauma. Sex workers are simultaneously surveilled and punished by law enforcement, as sex workers are rewarded by caste elders. This margin of additional suffering is not by happenstance, it is systemic, since it already reconceptualizes the dehumanizing practice of sex work to make it feasible to capitalize on already institutionalized caste patriarchal historical inequalities, that shape/construct the world of sex work.

RECOMMENDATIONS

There is an urgent need to address legal grey areas that maintain conditions of exploitation and harassment from police and move towards decriminalization of sex work across the board. Decriminalizing sex work will facilitate access to legal protections, safe working conditions, reduced stigma and support health and well-being. The law needs to recognize sexual labour within the Indian legal framework, provide legal protections, protections for a labour right, social justice rights, and allow for organizing in the capacity of workers. Legally defining sexual labour will provide a basis for sex workers to combat the economic and caste limited capacity to work. The legal framework needs to be trauma-informed, caste informed and move towards an understanding of the specific psychological harms caused by caste-based violence and discrimination. We need to empower and dignify agency, not paternalistic control. Lastly, India also needs to commit to and uphold additional international human rights frameworks like CEDAW General Recommendation 38, the Palermo Protocol, and ICCPR and ICESCR obligations to protect sex workers' safety, privacy, health, livelihood and freedom from discrimination.

CONCLUSION

Caste governance and the Indian legal environment operate in a contradictory manner that is manifest in the lived experience of sex workers living in marginalized communities. Throughout this research, it was made abundantly clear that sex work in India exists at the intersection of historically compounded caste logics, competing patriarchal logs, colonial legacies, and a continuum of both ambivalence and neglect towards sex work by the state. These structural conditions held up forms of marginalization that produced stigma, surveillance and economic exploitation while denying sex workers legal recognition, protection, and rights. We already discussed how caste has historically organized sexual labor into hereditary, ritualized occupations such as the Bedia, Nat, Dom, and Perna communities, classified as criminal tribes during colonization, a classification which continues to shape their lives today. While caste elders and community panchayats exercised unimpeded authority over sex worker entry, exit and earnings, they reinforce caste norms in contexts where the law has no influence or has been disowned. In this chapter I argued that the structural relationship between caste and law have co-produced the social and economic situation of the sex workers in this research, and both an intersectional and Dalit feminist perspective are essential to understanding their specific vulnerabilities. Caste governance shapes the existence of sex workers through material effects: socially, through economic exploitation, in caste-based determined sex work, through gender-determined appropriation of earnings, and through punitive consequences for those resisting caste-enabled norms of the community. The caste-ification of the lived experience of sex workers is negotiated through some of the most potent psychological massive dimensions of trauma, in many complex ways, specifically, the trauma of caste patriarchy, forced dispossession, while laboring under inherited stigma; and yet, and importantly, when I began to study sex workers to learn of their integrative oppression, specifically in outreach work, I came to learn of their tremendous capabilities and resiliency to engage with self-organizing, legal literacy, dignity campaigns, and beyond, sex workers have these capacities and resilience historically engrained as a strategy of surviving life to engage in what they lived through. Therefore, this chapter has demonstrated unequivocally that caste is more than social identity, that caste is also political as it sets out material and psychic limitation for already marginalize sex workers. The reform of the Indian legal system addresses sex work through the Immoral Traffic (Prevention) Act (ITPA), which indirectly criminalizes sex work and creates a legal grey area, leaving sex workers (especially from low-caste backgrounds) - to police harassment and exploitation. Anti-trafficking efforts overlap with the decriminalization of sex work to create a legal environment that is especially marked by moralistic involvement and coercive "rescue" operation focused on non-sanitized low-caste sex workers. Although there are protections in law, implementation of the laws is far lacking. The courts, in particular, in the famous Budhadev Karmaskar case, have explicitly stated the dignity and rights of sex workers, but the application of this rights assertion has been a total failure. The chapter also too stock of India's failure to comply with human rights treaties (Palermo Protocol, CEDAW GR 38) and treaties (ICCPR, ICESCR) and further describes an issue separate from compliance, the failure of legal malfeasance, not just failure to act but, alarming degeneration of denial of their rights and entitlementsIn previous chapters, we highlighted the intersectional structural vulnerability that caused by informal caste control and formal legal indifference, criticized harmful carceral feminist frameworks that uphold capitalist moral orders, and documented how sex worker collectives like DMSC and VAMP were important actors in reconstituting sex workers' located identities as political actors as laborers and rights-holders. And in the bordering nation, Nepal and Bangladesh, they also reveal comparative observations of caste, or ethno-caste hierarchies in relation to sex work and relation to state indifference (neglect) across the region. In conclusion, the chapter provided a summary of amending recommendations based on the complete decriminalization and legal recognition of sex workers as work, trauma-informed and caste-sensitives reforms, and integration of international human rights standards into domestic law. This demonstrates that caste-oppressed sex works are not individually or disjointed injustices, but rather manifestations of systems of domination that are deep-rooted and co-constituted, with caste governance in tandem with state law Florida's apathy or lack of interest, and vice versa, reproducing more marginalization and exclusionary exploitative relations. They occupy a legal and social no man's land, obscured by stigma and structurally rendered legally invisible. Addressing this intersectional understanding of oppression will require collective methodologies that disentangle from a carceral law practice and practices, polyphonically disrupt caste hierarchies, and elevate the agency and self-determination of sex workers as respected and informed subjects of their lives. In order to manifest meaningful synergy and solidarity we need to involve enforcement and ultimately enact legal reforms that are human rights and labor informed; involve social welfare policies that are culturally responsive and informed even by situated trauma histories; and facilitate a greater role for grassroots organizing which centers on sex workers as the agents of change in their own futures. Until that time, sex workers oppressed by caste will continue to find themselves in the contradictory position of perpetually being used but never acknowledged, and rights, dignity and citizenship will continue to be structurally denied without being recognized as a category, advocate or project. Only considerable, intersectional and justice-oriented interventions will disrupt these structures of oppression, permitting sex workers to claim identity, empowerment and to be part of social justice in the fullest sense of the term.

REFERENCES

Adhikari, H. (2011, January). Chaste wives and prostitute sisters: Patriarchy and prostitution among the Bedias of India. *Journal of International Women's Studies*. https://vc.bridgew.edu/cgi/viewcontent.cgi?article=1094&context=jiws

Chereches, B. (2021). *The representation of the Dalit community in Indian writing in English* (Master's thesis). Universidad de Zaragoza. https://zaguan.unizar.es/record/145214/files/TESIS-2024-419.pdf

Dasgupta, S. G. (2017, August). Commercial sex work in Calcutta: Past and present. ResearchGate. https://www.researchgate.net/publication/345121397_Commercial_Sex_Work_in_Calcutta_Past_and_Present

Gupta, S. (2013, July). Human rights of sex workers in India: The way forward. SSRN *Electronic Journal*. https://papers.ssrn.com/sol3/papers.cfm?abstract_id=2357167 DOI: 10.2139/ssrn.2357167

Harishankar, V. B., & Mvadha, M. P. (2011). *Exploitation of women as devadasis and its associated evils*. National Commission for Women. https://ncwapps.nic.in/pdfReports/Exploitation_of_Women_as_Devadasis_and_its_Associated_Evils_Report.pdf

Hinchy, J. (2020, February). Gender, family, and the policing of the 'criminal tribes' in nineteenth-century North India. *Modern Asian Studies*. https://www.cambridge.org/core/journals/modern-asian-studies/article/abs/gender-family-and-the-policing-of-the-criminal-tribes-in-nineteenthcentury-north-india/9F9F6EA7FD37138ABB295C7FCF99164B

Human Rights Watch. (2007, February). *Hidden apartheid: Caste discrimination against India's "untouchables"*. https://www.hrw.org/report/2007/02/12/hidden-apartheid/caste-discrimination-against-indias-untouchables

Jangir, H. P. (2024, November). From Sarkivasi (nomadic) to Gaonvasi (villager): The impact of sedentarisation on Rajasthan's stigmatised Nat community. *Heliyon*. https://www.sciencedirect.com/science/article/pii/S2590291124004352

Jha, D., & Sharma, T. (2015, December). Caste and prostitution in India: Politics of shame and of exclusion. *Anthropology*. https://www.longdom.org/open-access/caste-and-prostitution-in-india-politics-of-shame-and-of-exclusion-2332-0915-1000160.pdf

Kumar, A. (2021, October). Sexual violence against Dalit women: An analytical study of intersectionality of gender, caste, and class in India. *Journal of International Women's Studies*. https://www.researchgate.net/publication/366175802_Sexual_Violence_against_Dalit_Women_An_Analytical_Study_of_Intersectionality_of_Gender_Caste_and_Class_in_India

Lama, P. (2022, July). Sexual and gender-based violence against Dalit women and girls in India. COFEM Secretariat. https://cofemsocialchange.org/sexual-gbv-dalit-women-girls-india/

Najar, J. L. (2023, January). Brahmanical patriarchy and the politics of anti-trafficking and prostitution governance: From colonial to contemporary India. *Third World Quarterly*, *44*(4), 667–685. Advance online publication. DOI: 10.1080/01436597.2022.2099824

Rana, U., Sharma, D., & Ghosh, D. (2020). Prostitution in northern Central India: An ethnographical study of Bedia community. *International Journal of Anthropology and Ethnology*, *4*(2), 2. Advance online publication. DOI: 10.1186/s41257-020-0027-5

Shankar, S., & Ganesan, P. (2021). *The devadasis, dance community of South India: A legal and social outlook. International Journal on Minority and Group Rights*. https://www.researchgate.net/publication/354164302_The_Devadasis_Dance_Community_of_South_India_A_Legal_and_Social_Outlook

United Nations General Assembly. (2000). Protocol to prevent, suppress and punish trafficking in persons, especially women and children, supplementing the United Nations Convention against Transnational Organized Crime (Resolution 55/25). United Nations Office of the High Commissioner for Human Rights. https://www.ohchr.org/en/instruments-mechanisms/instruments/protocol-prevent-suppress-and-punish-trafficking-persons

Chapter 8
A Legal and Psychological Study of Migrant Women in Prostitution Under the Immoral Traffic (Prevention) Act in India: Criminalizing the Vulnerable

Kumar Mukul Choudhary
http://orcid.org/0009-0009-8658-9752
Vellore Institute of Technology, Chennai, India

Swarlata Pandey
Vellore Institute of Technology, Chennai, India

Parul Meena
University of Delhi, India

Kavi Shankar
http://orcid.org/0009-0007-4656-4118
Vellore Institute of Technology, Chennai, India

ABSTRACT

India's moral imagination has combined prostitution and trafficking into a single vice that has miserably failed to distinguish the tragic realities of gender vulnerabilities. Colonial notions of morality attempted to control women's sexuality and viewed their bodies as sites of moral decay. The impact of these colonial obsessions can still be seen in legislative policies as well. Inefficient laws fail to protect the fundamental

DOI: 10.4018/979-8-3373-5841-3.ch008

right guaranteed by the Constitution under Article 15(3), leading to constitutional infirmity. The right to life with dignity guaranteed under the Grundnorm feels like a vision deferred to eternity. Presently, the Immoral Traffic (Prevention) Act, 1956 (ITPA) aims to adhere to international commitments under the UN Convention for the Suppression of the Traffic in Persons, but it embodies inconsistencies in India.

INTRODUCTION

Prostitution and trafficking of women, although different concepts have been presumed synonymous to one another in the Indian social and legal order. They are supplementary to one another (Ramchandran, 2025). The legal status and position of prostitutes in India is of ambiguity, neglect and deep-rooted stigma that exist against women in general and them as particular. Prostitution has existed historically in India and was generally considered as marginal professions (Acharya & Azhar, 2025). However, during colonial rule and years after that stigma attached to the profession has expounded significantly. In modern times prostitution is morally unacceptable in society. Although the legal system does not outlaw the profession per se. Yet the Immoral Traffic (Prevention) Act 1956 (the principal anti trafficking statute in India) criminalizes a wide range of activities that is being attached with and surrounds sex work (Dasgupta, 2014), such as soliciting, brothel keeping and living of the earnings of prostitution. The intention of Immoral Traffic (Prevention) Act 1956 was to end prostitution and protect the interests of the victim. However, the punitive framework and characteristic of law targets disproportionately the most vulnerable socially and economically disadvantaged women (Dasgupta, 2014).

The most vulnerable of women who found themselves suffering in prostitution have generally been forced to migrate internally. There are various reasons for the same. Migration and introduction in prostitution and trafficking is generally being affected by rural distress, poverty, caste-based exclusion and development-based displacement (Giles & Giles, 2021). The prominent sufferers in all this are women belonging to lower castes, Dalits and Adivasis. They are being historically discriminated against and forced to leave their land. This creates economic insecurity for them. Due to this many of these women were forced into prostitution(Giles & Giles, 2021). Many cultures even have a tradition of women indulging in prostitution. However, with changing times and trafficking becoming an organised crime have further forced many women of marginality into prostitution. Now criminal groups manipulate women and force women to enter into prostitution and sell them as sex workers (Ramchandran, 2025). The central figure in all this remains the marginalised woman. She is being subjected to subjugation from every side. However, this paper will assert how law too acts as an instrument of suffering and punishment for these women.

The ITPA legislation has been passed to curb prostitution. It does not illegalise prostitution per se. Nevertheless, it outlaws the activities leading to expansion of prostitution. However, the application of law remains questionable. The police and the government agency that were responsible to implement the law focus upon sex workers, instead of people around them who forced such activities. They arrest women indulged in such activities. After these kinds of arrest women are being put into shelter homes and protective institutions without their will. In such institutions they do not have access to legal representation or even autonomy to consent for their decisions (Ramchandran, 2025a) . Essentially this transcends women to the position of criminal rather than a victim. The whole process of police arrest to judicial proceedings does not keep in mind bodily autonomy and personal freedom of women to make choices. The whole process is dehumanising that takes away the agency of women. It considers prostitution as an extended form of trafficking.

The whole criminalisation process brings psychological consequences for women who are victims and yet are being recognised as perpetrators. It creates multiple levels of trauma for women. Furthermore, the unavailability of trauma informed procedures both in criminal adjudication and rescue interventions extends the sufferings of women. Hence, the state actions that should have been taken to protect these women generally leads to harming the women themselves (Ramchandran, 2025a). The intersectionality of gender, class, caste, and marginality is very essential in understanding how women in prostitution experience the criminal justice system. The traditional understanding of victim v criminal must be set aside to understand the complex realities of women who indulge or are being forced into prostitution. Therefore, in this research the researchers will attempt to do the same.

The researchers will critically examine the psychological and legal consequences of criminalisation of women in prostitution. They will further look upon it from the standpoint of intersectional identities and marginalities. The paper will further see how one-dimensional application of ITAP and other criminal laws reproduce trauma in victims and entrench marginality. The paper will not only talk about statutory provisions rather also focus upon institutional biases, implementation gaps and lived experiences of victims. The paper will put insights to rethinking criminal law in a manner that upholds dignity, agency and justice for women.

Objectives of Research

- To critically analyse the legal provisions of the ITPA and BNS sections related to prostitution and how it impacts women who belong to marginalised sections of the society.

- To explore the criminalisation patterns faced by internal migrant women, especially from marginalized castes.
- To assess the psychological impact of anti-trafficking interventions, police actions, and judicial proceedings.
- To recommend legal and policy reforms based on a trauma-informed and intersectional approach to prostitution and trafficking.

Research Question

- How does the Immoral Traffic (Prevention) Act, 1956, and related provisions of BNS shape the legal definition of sex worker and in what ways does it criminalise and affect the women belonging to the marginalised section of the society.
- What role do caste, class, and internal migration status play in the disproportionate criminalization of women in prostitution during police raids, arrests, and prosecutions under anti-trafficking laws?
- How do police, judicial authorities, and legal aid mechanisms implement anti-trafficking laws in cases involving migrant women in prostitution, and to what extent are these processes shaped by discriminatory presumptions and procedural biases?
- To what extent does the current criminal law regime in India conflate consensual sex work with trafficking, and how does this conflation impact the legal and social outcomes for internal migrant women involved in the sex trade?
- What legal and policy reforms are necessary to build a trauma-informed, intersectional, and rights-based approach within Indian criminal law to better protect the dignity and autonomy of marginalized women engaged in prostitution?

Research Methodology

The research will be a mixture of both empirical research and doctrinal research. Statutory provisions will be analysed. Judicial conceptions will be discussed and empirical study will be done through existing data to calibrate and understand how law understands prostitution and trafficking and how these definitions impact women, especially from the marginalised section.

Limitations

The research will be restricted to internal migration and will only focus upon rights and interest of women from the standpoint of criminal law.

HISTORICAL AND LEGAL EVOLUTION OF THE ITPA AND BNS

This chapter attempts to understand Prostitution and trafficking as a concept that exists in Indian legal order. This chapter will attempt to answer these questions with the help of legal reason and legal norms that regulate human trafficking and prostitution in India. However, prior to delving into those concepts we have to first understand What we essentially understand from the term human trafficking and how human trafficking is an umbrella term which includes in itself the concept of prostitution. The term prostitution and human trafficking have to be differentiated. Human trafficking is a wider term that is generally being used to explain scenarios of movement of people without their free will. The term trafficking has been defined in various ways in international instruments. Some of them are as follows- Trafficking has been defined in various international instruments, however the most prominent and acceptable definition of the term has been found in the trafficking protocol (*UNTC*, n.d.). The protocol defines trafficking in comprehensive detail in following words-

Article 3, paragraph (a) of the Protocol states that trafficking in persons

"shall mean the recruitment, transportation, transfer, harbouring or receipt of persons, by means of the threat or use of force or other forms of coercion, of abduction, of fraud, of deception, of the abuse of power or of a position of vulnerability or of the giving or receiving of payments or benefits to achieve the consent of a person having control over another person, for the purpose of exploitation. Exploitation shall include, at a minimum, the exploitation of the prostitution of others or other forms of sexual exploitation, forced labour or services, slavery or practices similar to slavery, servitude or the removal of organs."

Article 3, (b) states that:

"The consent of a victim of trafficking in persons to the intended exploitation set forth in subparagraph (a) of this article shall be irrelevant where any of the means set forth in subparagraph (a) have been used."

Article 3, (c) states that:

"The recruitment, transportation, transfer, harbouring or receipt of a child for the purpose of exploitation shall be considered trafficking in persons even if this does not involve any of the means set forth in subparagraph (a)."

The definition of trafficking under the protocol is comprehensive. It covers every aspect of movement of people and exploitation. The protocol defines trafficking to include movement, recruitment, transportation, transfer, harbouring of people because of force or fraud or any other illegal means. Therefore, the definition does not cover the movement of people done for economic needs or any other purpose. The point of consideration is intention. If the individual intends to move by himself and such intention does not originate because of any fraud or illegal activity then in that case it won't amount to trafficking (*UNTC*, n.d.). However, there is another aspect in recognising act of movement as trafficking. It is exploitation. The movement must have the purpose of exploiting the individual. Exploitation has also been defined comprehensively under the protocol. It includes exploitation of all sorts. Sexual, forced labour, slavery or removal of organs. Therefore, the protocol ensured a comprehensive definition for human trafficking. However, the term found its origin initially in the context of prostitution and sexual slavery (O'Connor et al., 2006). Therefore, human trafficking is considered simultaneous to prostitution and sexual slavery. The protocol attempted to change the same with a wider and acceptable definition. Yet recognition of human trafficking as merely prostitution and sexual slavery has created complex scenarios. It has restricted the states to focus upon only the sexual activities. This in extension creates a scenario, where in the name of prohibiting human trafficking prostitution is being considered and termed as an illegal activity (O'Connor et al., 2006). Due to this, women who indulge into prostitution on their own free will also face the wrath of the state. Hence, this chapter will look up on the issue of how misinterpretation of the term human trafficking has impacted the right of women and how those women who indulge into prostitution or those who recognise prostitution as their profession is being discriminated by the state both in terms of legal recognition of profession as well as violation of rights that these women have. In the next part of the chapter, we will look upon the perspective of the colonial state and how the colonial state has dealt with these women that has led to significant discrimination against women which continues even today.

The contemporary legal regulation to govern sex work or prostitution is historically being adopted during the colonial governance. The rules that are being made by the colonial government are being extended by the Modern Governments. During the colonial times the colonial government adopted policies where it attempted to regulate the sex work and the women who indulge in sex work (Legg, 2009). Under the British law prostitution was never outlawed per se however the Framework was designed in such a manner to control women's bodies for public health, morality and imperial order (Roche, 2017). For this the colonial government passed the contagious disease Act, established locked hospitals under which the women suspected of indulging into prostitution would be examined (Legg, 2009). The purpose of these provisions was to target women and to ensure that Imperial discipline and controls are being maintained in India. Yet it has to be understood that the concern of the colonial state was not women's right but the presence of morality in the society. It was assumed that Indian prostitute women were vectors of moral decay and diseases. Therefore, regulation has to be made to keep them away from the soldiers to keep up the military efficiency (Legg, 2009). The early regulation of prostitution introduced two ideals in the Indian legal regime that even continues today. The first one being the proscription and marginalisation of sex work and second the moralisation of female sexuality. These two ideals were going to influence the position of women, especially those who indulged in prostitution in a very significant way. This would ultimately lead to a scenario where the women who were forced into prostitution would be considered as a perpetrator and not the victim.

Independence in India was a significant event where the new state had the responsibility to protect the right of the people who were converted from subject to citizen (De, 2018). However, after independence the Indian state faced a moral and political dilemma. The question was how this modern state would demonstrate its modernity and its aspiration to achieve international standards of human rights. This modernity has to be achieved in the bounds of conservative society (De, 2018). Therefore, to achieve this modernity at least in the context of prostitution and sexuality, the Indian state passed the suppression of Immoral Trafficking in women and girls Act 1956 (Kotiswaran, 2018). Although the international norms asserted that exploitation has to be ended. however, India's domestic legislation went further by criminalising various sexual acts even though they are consensual. The domestic legislation reflects the anxiety of the state to purify the new nation state. This purification has to be achieved on the bodies of the women where the state would focus upon the rescue and rehabilitation of women and not the autonomy of women. This led to a scenario where the state acted as a parent and a strict one and punished women for being forced into prostitution and attempted only to rehabilitate them once they have decided to move away from it (Kotiswaran, 2018). Therefore, it can be concluded that suppression of Immoral Trafficking in women and girls Act 1956 was the project of disciplining women's sexuality in the independent state.

A shift has been seen in the prostitution and trafficking regime of India. thereby amendments were made in the suppuration of Immortal trafficking Act and its name was changed into immoral trafficking prevention Act 1956. The goal of the state was to modernize the legal regime and to ensure that the anti-trafficking measures are being enhanced. The change primarily increases the punitive powers of the state and the surveillance capacity against the prostitution (Kotiswaran, 2018). The Act prohibits various aspects related to prostitution but not prostitution in itself. It includes brothel keeping, living on the earnings of prostitution, procuring prostitutes and soliciting prostitution in public places. This legal contradiction created by the state creates a paradoxical situation where by prostitution is legal yet the practice of prostitution is impossible to perform without the possibility of violating the legal norms of the state (Kotiswaran, 2018). The 1986 amendment attempted to bring the law within the international legal standards by application of the term 'commercial sexual exploitation' to align the law with modern legal terminology. The focus of the laws was to eliminate Immoral traffic. this shift clearly fails to understand that by this mechanism the state essentially forgets to recognise sex work as a profession. The insertion of word prevention in title of the Act instead of suppuration creates a scenario whereby the state attempts to regulate women's mobility and her sexuality in the name of protecting the right of the women.

When we wish to look upon the logic of the ITP Act, we will realise that the Act is essentially developed upon the views of morality. The act is based on the logical premise of victim and perpetrator. The law believes that a woman can either be a victim or a preparator. She cannot be an independent agent. It has been asserted by the law that a woman indulging in prostitution could either be helpless and need the support of the state or she could be the one who has become immoral and would take other women in the profession. Therefore, the law either must protect or punish her. If you look upon the Section 8 of the act, the Section prohibits soliciting for prostitution (Satish et al., 2021). This provision only affects the workers who take prostitution as her profession and use public spaces to attract the potential customer. The impact of law falls upon those women who are generally poor and marginalised and have no support of the state. The data too agrees with this claim. From 2015 to 2023, 17261 cases were registered under the Act. More than 49000 people were arrested in those cases (Pankaj, 2026). However, 30% of the arrested individuals remains women. Due to this the courts have set aside the arrest of woman under the ITPA law (Pankaj, 2026). Nevertheless, the emphasis of the state on public order and decency makes a moral justification for police raids and arrests. It generally and disproportionately affects women who are at marginality; these women are generally Dalit or migrants (Satish et al., 2021). The effect of this is criminalisation of Survival where poverty and gender labour is looked upon from the lens of immorality. Although the Indian Judiciary is being recognised as Protector of right however the courts have failed to protect the interest of women (Kotiswaran, 2018). In some of the cases the supreme court recognised that sex workers have right to livelihood (Kotiswaran, 2018) however the court reasoning still frames sex workers as a victim which requires rehabilitation from the side of the state rather than recognising them as an independent decision maker. In one of the judgements the Supreme Court has ordered the government to establish a rehabilitation scheme for women in prostitution (Kotiswaran, 2018) and their children. Although the intention of the court was good and it wished to do something good for women, however, this approach only reinforces to the nation that prostitution is a social evil and it must be eradicated. The Judiciary fails to realise that with compassion they bring in moral control in the discussion which essentially take away the right of the women and her free will and agency to take a decision that would affect her life. Therefore, with the state there is also a need for the judiciary to change its approach in terms of women and prostitution.

In 2023 the Indian parliament took a bold step to amend the colonial criminal law with the intent to bring in the modernity in the law (Parliament, 2023). Yet this new legal regime was also based upon the traditional norms of morality and assumptions about gender. This could be seen more specifically in the context of law relating to trafficking. The provision that defines trafficking and specifies what amount to trafficking was in line with the Global definition that we have discussed previously. However, the interesting part was in relation to the definition of the term exploitation. exploitation is being defined in terms of sexual exploitation and not otherwise. due to this trafficking is being recognised as an extension of sexual exploitation and prostitution (Parliament, 2023). Although the new legal regime has shifted from the old definition and the term immoral traffic is being replaced and the Act only uses trafficking, yet the Immoral nature of act presumed in the old law is still there in the new law (Parliament, 2023). Many of the readers may ask that what is wrong in including prostitution within the norms of trafficking it may be possible that prostitution would be a significant cause in human trafficking or trafficking in general. However, when we look upon it from the standpoint of law enforcement, we would realise that although the intention of the law was essentially to protect women as the law has the characteristic of the Protector, it is often being used for the purpose of surveillance and extortion. Police raids are being conducted with the pretext of a rescue operation (Dasgupta, 2014). Yet it frequently results in detention of adult women who are not even being trafficked and are indulging in those acts with their own free will. They are kept in prison for months without any justified legal proceeding due to this their basic liberty and due process is being violated (Dasgupta, 2014). These practices have also been criticised by the National Human Rights Commission and international bodies which essentially argue that these laws are being used not to protect women rather to make them suffer for the choices these women make (Dasgupta, 2014). These laws are against poverty and against those who rely upon sex work for fulfilment of their livelihood. It is essentially against the poor women.

CASTE, CLASS, AND MIGRATION IN THE CRIMINALIZATION OF SEX WORK

In India sex work and prostitution cannot be understood solely through legal provisions. It is deeply rooted in social hierarchies and social norms of caste class and migration. The social structures determine who will enter the trades and how the state will react to that. Although the laws are being made essentially to protect the rights of women and rescue them from these activities. The laws disproportionately affect the lives of Adivasi and migrant women (Jha & Sharma, 2016). Those whose social vulnerability make them more fallible and easily dispensable in the eyes of the legal system. Various feminist and Dalit scholars (Jha & Sharma, 2016) have argued that sex work in India is the mirror to the caste base sexual economy historically developed through social order. Commodified under the traditional social sanctions and shift in economy from feudal to capitalist is yet not taken women away from those historical norms. It has failed to bring them equal dignity and status quo in the society (Jha & Sharma, 2016). The data asserts the same. A major proportion of person trafficked are young adults (Aziz, 2023). Out of them at least 70% of those individuals belong to schedule caste and schedule tribe. Furthermore, 15 to 20% of belong to other backward classes. This Cleary shows that marginalisation in an important factor in trafficking (India - United States Department of State, 2025).

Caste has long organized sexual access and control in India. Social and religious practices such as devadasi in various parts of India have institutionalised the sexual exploitation of socially and economically backward women and specially Dalit and marginalize women (Acharya, 2012). Despite the attempts being made from the side of the state to prohibit activities of devadasi, the structures of caste and sexual servitude persist (Acharya, 2012). Many women who are being dedicated under the system shifted to sex work after the prohibition of those activities because they do not get any other economic opportunities (Acharya, 2012). Police and legal Institutions often believe that even though these women are equal citizens yet they are a fallen subject, a perception that these women cannot be rescued and is responsible for the lack of moral character in the society. Therefore, even under the ITPA regime the individuals who suffer are not the clients rather the marginalised women (Ramchandran, 2025). The scenario of marginality can be better understood even in context of women who rely on sex work for the livelihood. Those women who are not marginalised generally rely on online methods to get their clients which is generally safe and has limited to no impact from the limitations imposed by the state. However, the women who are marginalised generally rely upon streets or traditional brothels to find their clients which generally leads to the situation where if these places are being raided by the police, then these women are being called for and recognised as indulging into illegal activities. Therefore, it can be seen that even the state wishes to impose its morality upon women of marginality. It restricts livelihood only of those women that are at marginality. No provisions are being made essentially to restrict prostitution or sex work that is being done online because the practice is not illegal. However, since the women at marginality can easily be arrested from the streets or from the traditional brothels (the address of which is known by every administrative officer) they are generally the easy targets of the state (Ramchandran, 2025). By attacking these women, the state fulfils its responsibility to enhance morality in the society and make every citizen a moral citizen of the state.

Migration of women also plays an important role in ensuring women's entry into sex work. It enhances their vulnerability and criminalisation. Economic distress that these women face when they shift to a new place and the displacement and lack of employment opportunities which they have faced in their homelands have forced these women to indulge into sex activities for economic benefit (Jha & Sharma, 2016). Women who come from these marginalised backgrounds generally lack any legal identity in the new place and do not have stable housing or any social network, factors that make them susceptible to both police harassment and rescue operation (Ragavender, 2024). The legal regime also fails to protect these women because law does not look upon the economic vulnerability faced by these women, rather it always presumed migrant sex workers as trafficked women disregarding their agency or their consent. Even leading to be rescued by the state. This effectively destroys and ends marginalised women's labour mobility. Anti trafficking laws generally wish to treat all migrant women as being trafficked sex workers disregarding their agency to decide on their own behalf. Although it is based on the humanitarian perspective of protecting the women, the state through its legal regime controls both the mobility as well as sexuality of women. Empirical studies on the subject of marginality, gender and prostitution have shown that profiling plays an important role in detention and suffering of women (Ragavender, 2024). The data shows that Police raids are often based on profiling of women rather than any evidence of them being trafficked. Dark skin poor looking and marginalised women are generally being arrested under section 3 to Section 8 of the Act. This intersection of caste coded appearance and class code space guides the logic of suspicion (Ragavender, 2024). In contrast, the clients and the brothel owners who generally belong to well of social section of the society are generally not being arrested or convicted by the police and legal system. These patterns tell us how morality is being implemented through the criminal justice system in certain spaces which are essentially public spaces, such as streets, parks and cheap lodges which are generally recognised as Immoral zones. Whereas elite spaces remain private and invisible to moral surveillance of the state. This tells us that the legal regime of India is essentially based on the idea of morality of spaces rather than morality of actions. Caste class and migration are essentially the centre for criminalisation of India sex work regime. The ITPA and various provisions of BNS do not target sexual commerce rather they target specific sections of the society. These sections are marked by poverty, caste symbol and mobility. In the next part of the paper, we will attempt to see how these stigmas extend to institutional practice of policing adjudication and legal aid.

POLICING, JUDICIAL PROCESS, AND LEGAL AID BIASES

The State is the protector of every citizen and has the responsibility to protect everyone equally. With this intention each and every law is being made by the Parliament and adopted by the state. The law must never be discriminatory or must never target any group for their specific marginality or identity. At least on paper this is true for the ITPA regime and provisions of BNS, that target prostitution and trafficking. However, when we look deeper specifically in context of implementation of law, we will realise that the scenarios are completely different. During the process of implementation of law both by the executive in form of police or by the judiciary in form of decision makers essentially create a situation which leads to discrimination against marginalised women or women who are at vulnerable positions in the society. In this chapter we will attempt to look up on this issue and to understand how the implementation process essentially fails to understand the position of marginalized women and instead of recognising them as a victim, recognises them as a perpetrator.

The ITPA was adopted with the intention of protecting women. Therefore, the focus of the law was on rescuing women and not arresting women. Yet the methods used by the police administration mirror any other criminal raid. Empirical research shows that in arrest, the cases of women that are being arrested in certain states of India, a significant proportion of them have never been trafficked and are working in prostitution with their own will (Dasgupta, 2014). Yet under the provisions of the law these women are being sent to protection homes without considering their own will or without following the due process of law. Police discretion determines who shall be recognised as a victim and who shall be criminalised. The NGOs have studied the scenarios on field and found out that women who attempt to register their free will or their agency to choose are being reckoned as criminals (Dasgupta, 2014). Cases are being registered against them as solicitors or brothel keepers. The migrant women face additional discrimination as their accent and their lack of documentation make them a suspect of law and due to this they were generally being arrested by the police. This shows us how the law that was made with the intention to protect women has essentially collapsed and extended itself to restrict women in application of their free will through punitive control.

An important organ of any democratic structure is the judiciary. In India the judiciary is being considered as the backbone of modern democratic structures. It is expected from the Judiciary that they would protect the interest of citizens and vulnerable groups of the society. We hope that the judiciary would not follow the views of the government and act independently of any bias. However, in the case of women who are being discriminated against by the state and who are being considered as immoral prostitutes and sex workers, the judiciary generally follows the bias of the state (Kotiswaran, 2018). The judiciary in many of its judgments has framed women prostitutes as fallen helpless or morally degraded women. while many of the judgement of the Supreme Court has recognised the dignity of the women and asserted the state to protect the dignity of those (Kotiswaran, 2018). Yet in many of the other judgements the supreme court has observed that these women have no moral standards and therefore it is the responsibility of the state to rescue them from prostitution and resettle them in some different profession (Kotiswaran, 2018). Similar to other agencies of the state the courts as well are of the bias against these women who are in prostitution. The courts believe that these women are generally being forced into prostitution and they have no free will to be part of such a profession. This presumption originates from the view that prostitution or sex work is essentially an immoral act which normal human being would never do. Moral structure and codes expect everyone to be part of that moral social order. If anyone fails to stand in those moral values then in that case the state presumes that the morality of that person has fallen and he is a threat to the society. The same views are being accepted by the Judiciary where initially the Judiciary tries to rescue women from those Immortal activities and if it fails to do so then it recognises that Person to be a preparator which would continue indulge in immoral activity and also make others part of similar Immortal activities (Kotiswaran, 2018). In circumstances when the Judiciary acquit a woman of ITPA charges the judgement rarely critics the method used by the police for arresting the woman or raids that are being done against such marginalised women. instead, the court say that women's presence in sex work is economic necessity and a misfortune which should be changed by the policies of the state. It would make the life of women better. The Judiciary always favours the moral view point over the constitutional rights. The judiciary mostly never attempts to make the position of women better. The judiciary rarely asserts that a woman has free will and she may choose whatever may feel just and necessary to her (Kotiswaran, 2018). Therefore, it could be concluded that the Judiciary has similar beliefs as legislature and executive. It does not provide free will to the women and similar to other organs of the state try to find morality within the body of women by taking away the right of female to choose her profession. All the organs of states recognise women as a vulnerable being who is being forced by the society to do Immoral activities which she herself do not want to do and she is dependent on the state for her rescue.

Another important aspect of the Indian legal system is it provides legal Aid to the weakest section of the society so that no one could face lack of representation before the court of law. In this line similar provisions are there for women who are being detained under ITP Act. However, the surveys have found out that those women who are being detained under these legislations have no access to legal aid. One of the surveys has found out that women who are being detained for indulging into prostitution have no access to lawyers for the first 48 hours and if ever they get access to the lawyer, it is only in exceptional circumstances (Ramchandran, 2025). Furthermore, similar to other agencies of the state, lawyers who provide legal aid have a complex moral ideology whereby they then self believe that the legal aid is being provided to the morally fallen women. Due to this they rarely take interest in these cases and do not work properly for the protection of the rights of the women

(Ramchandran, 2025). On many occasions it has been found out that the lawyers who are providing legal advice generally advise women to go for rehabilitation rather than to seek their right to follow the profession. These lawyers assert that the courts generally protect those women who go for rehabilitation instead of those who wish to follow the profession and ask for freedom and free will (Ramchandran, 2025). Therefore, all the institutions including state as well as non-state actors generally ask women to move away from the profession and to rescue herself from these immoral activities rather than recognising her choice, her free will and her belief to continue with the profession which provides her the livelihood.

Women who indulge in sex work are also being discriminated by legal procedures that are being provided under the Indian criminal law regime. It has been found during research that on many occasions the evidence that is being used for the purpose of detention and for the purpose of determination of guilt of any particular woman is being forged (Ramchandran, 2025). Since these women are easily dispensable in the eyes of the state therefore no one looks upon their circumstances and the suffering that they have to constantly go through and the discrimination that they have to face. Similar to these procedural discriminations there is also a separate industry which is established with the help of NGOs that only focuses upon the rescue of women (Ramchandran, 2025). Although many of the NGOs are working to rescue the women because of their concern towards them, however, many NGOs in this area do not recognise the consent of women and do not consider whether the women actually want to move away from the industry or not. Therefore, these NGOs, similar to the biased views of the state, are expanding the moral view and forcing the women to accept those moral views. They want women to behave according to those moral viewpoints (Ramchandran, 2025). At the end it can be concluded that both state as well as non-state actors see women from the perspective of morality and not from her own perspective or from her own agency. All of them attempt to impose a sense of morality upon her character and expect that she would behave as per the character that is expected from her by the society. That she would always be ready to lose her agency and to act as per the wishes of the society.

CONFLATION OF SEX WORK AND TRAFFICKING IN LAW AND PRACTICE

We have explained and understood the complex dichotomy that exists between the state and the women in terms of her choice to indulge in any sexual activity even for commerce and economic benefit. However, this dichotomy has created a situation whereby the distinction between prostitution and trafficking has been lost. In the Indian legal system, both trafficking and prostitution are considered interchangeable. Due to this the legal regime that is being adopted in India not only proscribes trafficking but also prohibits prostitution. Due to this even those women who indulge in prostitution with their own free will suffer the wrath of the state and are generally detained in prisons. However, in this chapter the authors will try to resolve this conflict that exists between trafficking and prostitution and to assert that the Indian legal system has recognised both of them as equal. Due to this the rights of women are being violated. By the end of the chapter, we will attempt to argue that a distinction is necessary between the two and prostitution shall not be considered similar to trafficking.

The confusion between prostitution and trafficking arise because of the overlapping that exists in the definition of two under the Indian legal system. Both the ITPA and BNS provide definitions of trafficking and prostitution which essentially makes them interchangeable. Section 5 of the ITPA penalises procuring any person for prostitution (Parliament of India, 1956). However, such procurement does not require proof of deception or coercion. Similar to those lines the BNS talks about trafficking and human trafficking. However, when it defines exploitation, it restricts itself to only sexual exploitation (Parliament, 2023). Although these definitions are not in line with the global standard yet when we look up on it separately, we also realise that these definitions in itself are the reason why there is complexity and confusion between prostitution and trafficking. Even when the BNS talks about sexual exploitation it does not mention any deception or coercion or any other fraud by which such sexual exploitation is being committed. However, it only talks about sexual exploitation which includes both kinds of sexual exploitation whether intentional or unintentional, with will or without will, forced or unforced. Due to this even in those scenarios where a woman indulges in the prostitution with her own will, all of her actions are considered as part of trafficking. It is being presumed from the side of the state that she has lost her way and she is being trafficked. That is the reason why she has indulged prostitution. However, this view point is completely wrong and does not recognise the will of the women and force her to the marginality. It creates a scenario where the state essentially takes away her choice and makes her follow the moral and social beliefs of the state. Even the judicial interpretation upon it follows similar viewpoints. It has been seen in the judgements of various courts; these courts have concluded that adult women are the victims of trafficking even though they engage in sex work through their own will. Such a ruling reflects the complex beliefs of the Indian Courts that no woman could choose prostitution as a profession. A presumption which is deeply rooted in patriarchal morality of the state.

India's approach to trafficking laws has been influenced by international norms as well as the American abolitionist approach. The central influences to Indian trafficking laws are essentially US trafficking victim Protection Act 2000 (*Victims of Trafficking and Violence Protection Act of 2000*, n.d.) and The Palermo protocol

2000 *UNTC*.(n.d.). both instruments have been critiqued at the global level for their approach to recognising prostitution and trafficking as interchangeable terms (Zimmerman, 2005). The Indian legal system did not look upon these difficulties and adopted these two norms to resolve trafficking in India. The Indian state went a step further by including the norms of morality and purity in women's sexuality within these norms. The state believes that in India the role of women is to protect the family. Hence, if she becomes immoral the family will lose its value. Therefore, they considered trafficking and prostitution as interchangeable acts. This discourse has helped the Indian state in moving away from its domestic anxieties over urban moral disorder and migration. The result was that the Indian law is global in vocabulary but local in disciplinary logic. For the state, trafficking has become a flexible category through which the state can control prostitution, migration and sexuality of women.

A group of women that faced difficulty from this understanding of legal regime are the migrant women. These women essentially came from villages and countryside due to the lack of economic opportunities. They believed that they would get these opportunities in the cities. However, it was always difficult to settle down in cities and to ensure that they have sufficient economic resources. Due to this many women indulge into sex work so to fulfil their economic requirements (Jha & Sharma, 2016). Many of them are of the view that this will help them in settling down in the cities and that they are indulging in these activities of their own free will. However, it is the belief of the state and the interpretation of law that leads to the complex conclusion that these women are essentially indulging into prostitution because they have been trafficked from their villages and home towns and now in the new city it is the responsibility of the state to protect them from sexual exploitation. Yet the state fails to fulfil its duty of rescuer when it sends those women to rescue homes so as to ensure that the interests of these women are being protected. However, these rescue homes become the centre of re victimization where the women are being forced to indulge in prostitution (Ramachandran, 2023) and on many occasions, they are being surveillanced or forced by the state machinery to suffer because of her marginality (Ramachandran, 2023). Even the judicial discourse has failed to recognise the complex situation which these migrant movements found themselves and the court always believe that the position taken by the state by rescuing these women is not against poverty but for protecting the interest and sexuality of women (Ramachandran, 2023). Hence the point of rescue becomes indistinguishable from the state control over the mobility and sexuality of poor woman. Through these controls the state, even though not able to protect them from poverty and provide economic support to the individual, attempts to protect their sexuality which the individual intends to use through their own free will. This narrative of equalling prostitution to trafficking is important for the state as it allows the state to present criminalisation as protection and compassion by denying women's capacity for consent. Through this legal regime the state introduces and reasserts patriarchal norms. While it does not recognise structural inequalities such as caste discrimination and labour exploitation. This ideological function is also visible in judicial and policy language where the same law is being used for protection as well as punishment. It is ultimately upon the implementation of the law and the institution that is responsible to implement the law to determine whether a woman should be protected or she should be punished. These norms put marginalized women in a complex scenario where there is no certainty whether the state would protect her or it would punish her.

The feminist groups do not agree with the view point of the state as well as the Judiciary. Therefore, in the last decade they have put in significant effort essentially to argue before the state institutions that sex work should not be considered similar to trafficking, that both sex work as well as trafficking are different domain and originate from different circumstances (Shah, 2007). it was the effort of these feminist groups that in later years the supreme court itself recognised that trafficking and sex work are completely different and cannot be equated as same by the state (Shah, 2007). The supreme court further directed the state that they should focus upon the health and well-being of women who indulge in sex work and to provide them best of medical facilities. However, the courts restricted the state from intervening or restricting women indulging into those activities with her own free will. Therefore, it can be asserted that over the years attempt have been made by feminist groups and NGOs to protect the right of women and to recognise sex work as a legitimate profession and only in last few years the court has recognised that sex work can be a separate profession and can be practice by women by her own will. The courts have shown that they can go beyond the traditional norms of morality established in the Indian social order.

TOWARDS A RIGHTS-BASED, TRAUMA-INFORMED REFORM FRAMEWORK

In the last few chapters, we have looked upon how Immoral Trafficking Prevention Act 1956 functions less as an anti-trafficking statute and more as a norm of social and moral control. The implementation of the legislation reveals that structural entanglement of caste, class, gender and migration are central to the governance of sexuality of women. This legislation is based on moral economic underpinnings and essentially can be termed as bio political control that regulates sexuality of women through law. This chapter attempts to resolve these difficulties and to go ahead with suggestions as to how things could be made better for women. The chapter explore how India can move away from its traditional morality driven approach to a right based intersectional approach where the focus of the state shall not be upon protecting the morality of the citizens rather to protect the dignity of the women and to show that even though she is indulged in sex work, her recognition as an equal citizen should always be there. Therefore, in this chapter we will attempt to provide suggestions as to how Indian legal order can move away from traditional social and moral norms to an intersectional right based approach.

The core difficulty in India's anti trafficking law is its equalising of sex work and trafficking. If a right based approach is being adopted in India, then in that case the first thing that the legislation has to focus upon is to create a distinction between voluntary adult sex work and trafficking involving fraud, coercion or deception. Some critics may argue that decriminalising consensual sex may legalise coercion. However, it's a wrong presumption and it should be understood that decriminalising consensual sex essentially leads to protection of dignity under article 21 and protection of profession under article 19 of the Indian constitution. Furthermore, India will not be the first country who would have adopted this approach. A similar approach has been adopted by countries like New Zealand (*Stopping People Trafficking*, n.d.) and South Africa, where they have defined trafficking in distinction with the consensual sex and it has led to positive results. The change in law has distinguished between prostitution and trafficking. The law has focused more upon trafficking (*Immigration New Zealand's Commitment to Combatting Trafficking in Persons*, n.d.). The attempts were made to restrict the same. The change in approach has improved health safety and legal accountability without increasing trafficking. Data shows that trafficking has dropped significantly in these countries due to the change in legal norm. If a similar approach is being adopted in India, then in that case significant amendment has to be made in section 3 to Section 8 of the ITP Act. Furthermore, a revision has to be made in the BNS Act. It is also necessary that when sexual exploitation is being talked about as a crime it must have clear evidence of coercion or deceit. This would ensure that consensual sex would not be recognised as trafficking. Furthermore, it is necessary that separate mechanisms for trafficking in labour and traffic in exploitation are being developed. One cannot be equated with another. This will give state institutions the opportunity to put more time and effort on sexual trafficking.

The mainstream anti trafficking discourse in India is generally being regulated by the upper class, upper caste urban, English-speaking feminist. These women have different perspectives towards prostitution. They believe that prostitution is violence against all women. However, it should be understood that the experience of an upper caste would be completely different from the experience of a lower caste Dalit woman. In that context intersectionality becomes important as it has to be understood that Dalit migrant women might experience legal harm completely different from upper caste women and their scenarios or their views should not be considered equal. Intersectional feminist jurist also recognises this point where they demand that law should not only create equality but should also account for subordination, caste patriarchy, economic patriarchy and migration status as all these identities shape women's interaction with the law (Ramchandran, 2025). Therefore, if change is being made in the law it has to be kept in mind that the change shall bring out the perspective of both upper caste feminist as well as the Dalit feminist. It essentially means that when law defines trafficking it has to be separated from prostitution as prostitution is an economic activity that is generally being done by a Dalit or migrant women, sometimes by choice and sometimes because of economic necessity. Therefore, equating the two by the upper caste feminist essentially creates a scenario that leads to suffering for a Dalit or migrant woman.

The Indian anti trafficking regime also suffered from that problem of trauma reproduction. The institutions that are responsible to prohibit or check trafficking essentially create more trauma than to reduce. women are being subjected to raids detention and involuntary rehabilitation which ultimately leads to humiliation, social ostracization and traumatization. They are further being humiliated by forcing them to be detained and given a medical test. Therefore, if institutions wish to protect the interest of women, then in that case a new trauma informed model has to be adopted. This model should be as follows. This model shall require mandatory Gender and caste sensitivity training for all law enforcement agencies and institutions that are essentially dealing with this sort of scenario and women who are going through trauma. Prohibition shall also be done on unwanted detentions and protective homes which do not recognise the consent of women and force them to change their approach rather than to understand her will. Furthermore, the community should also play an important part in reducing harm and allowing these women to become part of the society. If these reforms are being done then in that case it would bring the Indian laws in line with article 14 of the Constitution as well as article 21 which protect dignity and equality of the women. In the new model a change has to be done in terms of understanding of term rescue and rehabilitation. The failure of current anti trafficking mechanism is essentially the presumption that each and all women in sex work need rehabilitation and therefore, the law and state institutions forces each and every woman to move away from it. Even those who are there with their own will. However, the new model as suggested by the researchers asserts that first differentiation has to be made in terms of understanding of term rescue and Rehabilitation. where the institutions have to ensure that rehabilitation has to be given to only those who require such rehabilitation and want to move away from the job. Those who wish to continue with sex work for them the work environment has to be made safe and they should be allowed to have access to better health care. If any women want to have rehabilitation, then the approach of the state shall not be to send them to protection homes rather to ensure that there is economic integration of these women in the society. They must have access to micro credit housing and social security. For them recognition of sex work as informal labour shall be done and Labour protection regime has to be applied to prostitution as well. Public health care system should be developed so that these women who are part of sex work shall have easy access to medical health care system for their Physical health and mental health. Framing rehabilitation through a right based approach instead of morality-based approach will align it with India's directive principle of State Policy where the state is responsible for the protection of livelihood and to provide a better working environment to the workers. In this new model the Judiciary is also an important stakeholder. We have discussed previously in this chapter that although some change is being accepted by the Judiciary where the Judiciary has adopted the rights-based approach instead of the morality-based approach. However, all of this is provisional and rare. Therefore, in the new model the Judiciary must absolutely shift away from the morality-based approach to the right based approach and try to ensure that right of the women who indulge in sex work has to be protected. It has to ensure that the transformative character of the Constitution should also be seen in the case of sex workers who are the most vulnerable section of the Indian society. For them also the Indian Constitution must act as a transformative document through which the Indian courts must protect their rights and give them new freedom. In this new model state Institutions and enforcement authorities shall also change. In the new model it is being expected from the institution and state in general that they will move away from their protector of morality approach to a right based approach. where instead of ensuring and forcing morality in the lives of people the state would start to look upon the rights of the people. Through its institutions the state shall ensure that each and every individual of the society has access to these rights. If these changes are being done then it can be visible in the lives of the women who are in prostitution. Their lives would improve and trafficking as a crime would decrease significantly as it would ensure that everything would not be looked through the lens of morality rather from the lens of right which each individual has under Indian Constitution.

CONCLUSION

When the Indian constitution was adopted on 26th of January 1950 the goal was to transform the subject into citizens. This could only be done when the state machinery does not have any bias in its mind against any of its citizens irrespective of what identities they hold, what they do, how they behave or what section of the society they are part of. However, this prospective is not found in context of prostitution and sex work. The ITP Act is essentially a moral legal regime that disciplines women's bodies through intersecting identities of caste, class and migration. The

Act was implemented in such a manner that boundaries between victimhood and criminality would effectively perish. Therefore, all that is left is social vulnerability and economic marginality. Through this paper we can conclude that Dalit and Adivasi women continue to occupy the most stigmatized position within the society. These women rely upon sexuality for their livelihood. Yet the law chose to criminalize the poorest section of the society. The migrant women too face similar difficulties. They are being punished for their wish to have a better life with better economic standards. The state institutions too play a crucial role in this. They continue to discriminate against these women because of their identity and their vulnerability. Therefore, reforms are a must. The reforms must be multi-dimensional that shall breach boundaries of institutions. Executive, legislature and judiciary, all of them require significant reform. The most significant change that has to be done is in the idea of protection and the role of state in protection. In Indian democracy time has come when the state shall recognise the autonomy and free will of women.

The story of Immoral Trafficking Prevention Act 1956 is not mearly the story of prostitution or the sex work rather it is the story of anxiety Indian state holds towards morality and protection of morality. The law's obsession with rescuing women reveals an unwillingness of law as well as the state to recognise the independent choices of women and the freedom that the woman always wishes to have. A truly transformative legal order must understand that freedom and dignity are not granted through protection rather recognition of freedom and rights. Caste, class and migration are not the problem of trafficking rather they are the foundations of it. It could only be made better by departing from the traditional norms and recognising that these are not the problems but the sectors in which reforms are necessary. The Indian state wants to move away from the colonial laws by way of transforming its criminal law. However, it is not yet able to move away from its traditional responsibilities of ensuring morality in the society. If the Indian state is able to do so then it would be beneficial for everyone including women who have to constantly fight for their choices against the might of the state.

REFERENCES

Acharya, A., & Azhar, S. (2025). "We are Treated as Outsiders in Our Own City": Lived Experiences of Intersectional Stigma Against Sex Workers in Kolkata, India. *Sexuality Research & Social Policy*, *22*(3), 1417–1429. DOI: 10.1007/s13178-024-01054-8

Acharya, A. R. K. (2012). Impact of cultural and religious practices of prostitution on the trafficking of women in India. In *TRAYECTORIAS: Vol. AÑO 14, NÚM. 33-34* (pp. 95–114) [Journal-article].

Aziz, S. (2023, August 22). In India, human traffickers target tribal women and girls. *Voice of America*. https://www.voanews.com/a/in-india-human-traffickers-target-tribal-women-and-girls/7235083.html

Dasgupta, S. (2014). Sovereign silence: Immoral Traffic (Prevention) Act and legalizing sex work in Sonagachi. *Political and Legal Anthropology Review*, *37*(1), 109–125. DOI: 10.1111/plar.12053

De, R. (2018). A people's constitution. In *Princeton University Press eBooks*. DOI: 10.23943/princeton/9780691174433.001.0001

Giles, M., & Giles, M. (2021, February 11). Human trafficking in India: How the colonial legacy of the Anti-Human Trafficking Regime undermines Migrant and Worker Agency - LSE Human Rights. *LSE Human Rights - A student-led blog from LSE Human Rights*. https://blogs.lse.ac.uk/humanrights/2021/02/11/human-trafficking-in-india-how-the-colonial-legacy-of-the-anti-human-trafficking-regime-undermines-migrant-and-worker-agency/

Immigration New Zealand's commitment to combatting trafficking in persons. (n.d.). Immigration New Zealand. https://www.immigration.govt.nz/about-us/news-centre/immigration-new-zealands-commitment-to-combatting-trafficking-in-persons/

India - United States Department of State. (2025, January 6). United States Department of State. https://www.state.gov/reports/2023-trafficking-in-persons-report/india

Jha, D., & Sharma, T. (2016). Caste and Prostitution in India: Politics of shame and of exclusion. *Anthropology; a Guide to First Degree Courses in UK Universities*, *04*(01). Advance online publication. DOI: 10.4172/2332-0915.1000160

Kotiswaran, P. (2018, July 18). *How did we get here? Or a short history of the 2018 trafficking bill*. Economic and Political Weekly. https://www.epw.in/engage/article/how-did-we-get-here-or-short-history

Legg, S. (2009). Governing prostitution in colonial Delhi: From cantonment regulations to international hygiene (1864–1939). *Social History*, *34*(4), 447–467. DOI: 10.1080/03071020903257018

O'Connor, M., & Healy, G. Coalition Against Trafficking in Women (CATW), & European Women's Lobby (EWL). (2006). *The Links between Prostitution and Sex Trafficking: A Briefing Handbook.* https://catwinternational.org/wp-content/uploads/2019/09/The-Links-between-Prostitution-and-Sex-Trafficking-A-Briefing-Handbook.pdf

Pankaj, J. (2026, January 21). Datanomics: Women constitute 30% of trafficking arrests in India. www.business-standard.com. https://www.business-standard.com/india-news/datanomics-women-constitute-30-of-trafficking-arrests-in-india-126012100831

Parliament. (2023). THE BHARATIYA NYAYA SANHITA, 2023. In *THE BHARATIYA NYAYA SANHITA*. https://www.mha.gov.in/sites/default/files/250883_english_01042024.pdf

Parliament of India. (1956). THE IMMORAL TRAFFIC (PREVENTION) ACT, 1956. In *THE IMMORAL TRAFFIC (PREVENTION) ACT, 1956*. https://www.indiacode.nic.in/bitstream/123456789/15378/1/the_immoral_traffic_%28prevention%29_act%2C_1956.pdf

Ragavender, D. (2024). *Female migration and migrant women harassment in INDIA*. Chyren Publication.

Ramachandran, V. (2023). From 'house of horrors' to 'sensitive' governance: Sex workers' shelter detention in India. *Contemporary South Asia*, *32*(2), 223–241. DOI: 10.1080/09584935.2023.2268559

Ramchandran, A. (2025). A tale of two rescues. In *Cambridge University Press eBooks* (pp. 41–69). DOI: 10.1017/9781009490313.004

Roche, M. M. (2017). *Dis*. Placing Empire., DOI: 10.4324/9781315264189

Satish, A. H., Rao, K. A., Bhushan, B., Chouhan, H., & Shah, J. H, L. J., Mohapatra, M., & G.D, N. (2021). *Gender, human rights and law* (S. E. Thomas, Ed.; Vol. 9). Centre for Women and the Law, National Law School of India University. https://www.nls.ac.in/wp-content/uploads/2021/10/GHRL-Vol-9-11-10-2021.pdf

Shah, S. P. (2007). Distinguishing poverty and trafficking: Lessons from field research in Mumbai. *Georgetown Journal on Poverty Law & Policy*, *14*(3), 441–454.

Stopping people trafficking. (n.d.). Immigration New Zealand. https://www.immigration.govt.nz/about-us/our-strategies-and-programmes/stopping-fraud-and-exploitation/stopping-people-trafficking/

UNTC.(n.d.). https://treaties.un.org/pages/ViewDetails.aspx?src=TREATY&mtdsg_no=XVIII-12-a&chapter=18

Victims of Trafficking and Violence Protection Act of 2000. (n.d.). U.S. Department of State. https://2009-2017.state.gov/j/tip/laws/61124.htm

Zimmerman, Y. C. (2005). Situating the Ninety-Nine: A critique of the Trafficking Victims Protection Act. *Journal of Religion & Abuse*, *7*(3), 37–56. DOI: 10.1300/J154v07n03_03

Chapter 9

The Legal Vacuum: Women's Customary Practices and Failure of Justice in Bundelkhand, Madhya Pradesh

Priyamvada Bhargava
http://orcid.org/0009-0006-0642-9707
Sri Sathya Sai Law College for Women, Bhopal, India

ABSTRACT

In many rural areas of India, women find that legal protections exist mostly in theory, not practice. This study examines the situation in Sagar and Damoh districts of Madhya Pradesh, revealing how the inability of police, courts, and legal aid to enforce women's rights forces reliance on patriarchal, informal systems. Through interviews with women, legal aid workers, and officials, it documents how this legal vacuum increases economic hardship, worsens health outcomes, and allows cycles of vulnerability to continue across generations. The research calls for urgent reforms to strengthen the justice system and ensure women's rights are honored not just in law but in daily life.

1. INTRODUCTION

The intersection of gender, law, and culture within tribal societies in India presents one of the most compelling, yet fraught, arenas for socio-legal inquiry. Despite a constitutional vision that champions equality and social justice, the daily lives of tribal women remain profoundly shaped by historical marginalization, economic precarity, and entrenched customary norms. Madhya Pradesh—situated in the Central Indian Plateau—uniquely embodies this paradox. It is a landscape where ancient

DOI: 10.4018/979-8-3373-5841-3.ch009

traditions coexist with modern governance, and where the reach of formal law often falters before the authority of local custom. Within this context, tribal women must negotiate their identities and rights amidst overlapping systems of power: the state, the community, and the patriarchy.

1.1. The Research Problem: The "Legal Vacuum"

This chapter explores this negotiation by examining the interaction between formal legal frameworks and customary practices in the Bundelkhand districts of Sagar and Damoh. While the Indian Constitution provides robust affirmative measures under the Fifth Schedule and through legislation like the Panchayats (Extension to the Scheduled Areas) Act (PESA), 1996, and the Forest Rights Act, 2006, the lived experience of women in these districts suggests that these guarantees remain aspirational rather than transformative. At the grassroots level, customary laws exert a profound influence on tribal life. These customs, while integral to community identity, often reinforce patriarchal authority and circumscribe women's agency. Local dispute resolution is frequently handled by informal councils (*panchs*), whose decisions prioritize communal harmony and traditional "honour" over individual gender justice. Issues such as inheritance, domestic violence, and sexual exploitation are rarely reported to formal authorities, as doing so is frequently branded an act of communal disloyalty.

This tension creates what this study identifies as a "legal vacuum"—a socio-legal space where neither formal justice mechanisms nor traditional systems adequately address women's grievances. Formal laws fail to penetrate these regions due to structural barriers like illiteracy, spatial remoteness, and a deep-seated mistrust of state institutions. Conversely, customary practices, though locally legitimate, are seldom equipped—or willing—to dismantle gender-based violence or economic inequality. The Bedia community offers a particularly poignant example of this vacuum; traditionally stigmatized due to historical associations with the sex trade, Bedia women occupy a precarious position where state laws against trafficking clash with informal economies shaped by generational necessity and community custom.

1.2. Scope and Methodology

The rationale for focusing on Sagar and Damoh lies in their representative character. Both districts exhibit the broader patterns of underdevelopment and patriarchal kinship systems prevalent in Bundelkhand, yet each reveal unique localized dynamics in how welfare schemes and legal awareness are navigated. To capture these nuances, this study utilizes a multi-layered ethnographic and socio-legal framework:

- **Targeted Qualitative Consultations (N=22):** Primary narratives were collected to understand how justice is perceived "from below." The study is grounded in *22 qualitative consultations* conducted with stakeholders in the Bundelkhand region, including:
- **Legal & Administrative Stakeholders (N=8):** Consultations with lawyers from the District Legal Services Authority (DLSA), protection officers, and NGO workers specializing in tribal rights.
- **Community Narratives (N=14):** Targeted discussions with community elders and women from rural settlements in Sagar and Damoh to map the prevalence of *Wirasat* (patrilineal inheritance) and *Chuttachar* (informal divorce).

1.3. Documentary and Legal Analysis:

A review of *National Family Health Survey (NFHS-5)* data and *Agriculture Census* statistics alongside an analysis of constitutional provisions and judicial precedents to assess the gap between normative law and practical enforcement.

1.4. Interpretive Synthesis and Ethical Reflexivity:

Situating the findings within the broader discourse of legal pluralism, examining how multiple normative orders state, custom, and morality—intersect and conflict.

1.5. Ethics:

Given the sensitive nature of ritualized exploitation and domestic violence, all personal identifiers have been pseudonymized. The research adheres to a *"Do No Harm"* protocol, focusing on the state's failure to provide "internal exit options" for women rather than a critique of community identity.

1.6. Significance and Structure

Understanding this relationship is not merely an academic exercise in feminist legal theory; it is a practical necessity for crafting policies that are responsive to the social fabric of tribal India. By prioritizing the "lived realities" of women who find themselves sidelined by both the courtroom and the *panchayat*, this study seeks to bridge the epistemic gap between the state's idea of justice and the indigenous experience of it.

The chapter is organized to move progressively from theory to evidence. Section 2 establishes the legal and theoretical framework, defining the "paradox of multicultural vulnerability" and the mechanics of legal pluralism. Section 3 provides the essential socio-economic and cultural grounding of the Sagar and Damoh districts. Section 4 presents the empirical core of the study—the case studies and fieldwork findings regarding property, violence, and the Bedia community. Finally, Section 5 synthesizes these insights to offer recommendations for filling the "legal vacuum" through cultural engagement and institutional accountability.

Having established the theoretical and legal contradictions inherent in the Indian tribal context, the next section examines the specific legal frameworks and pluralistic theories that define the boundaries of state and customary authority.

2. LEGAL AND THEORETICAL FRAMEWORK

The lives of Bedia women in the Sagar and Damoh districts of Madhya Pradesh unfold within a world shaped as much by tradition as by law. Their everyday realities are influenced not by a single legal system, but by a web of overlapping rules, beliefs, and customs that have evolved over generations. While the Constitution of India promises equality and protection to every citizen, these ideals often remain out of reach for women whose lives are still guided by unwritten community codes and inherited practices.

For many women in these regions, *law exists in theory more than in practice.* Official protections—such as those related to domestic violence, inheritance, or property rights—often fail to reach them. Instead, local customs and community decisions continue to define their roles, rights, and responsibilities. This creates what can only be described as a *legal vacuum*: a space where state law fades into the background, and social customs quietly dictate how justice is understood and delivered.

To make sense of this situation, it becomes essential to look at how *state law, personal law, and customary norms* interact in the lives of Bedia women. Each of these systems holds its own authority, yet together they often produce contradictions that leave women caught between competing worlds. On one hand, the state's legal system aspires to equality; on the other, personal and customary laws frequently uphold patriarchal values that restrict women's autonomy.

Legal pluralism—the coexistence of multiple systems of law—is often seen as a marker of India's cultural richness. Yet, in practice, it can also deepen inequalities when community customs are allowed to override constitutional values. In such cases, the promise of equality becomes conditional, shaped by who you are, where you live, and which tradition claims you.

At the same time, Bedia women are not merely victims of this imbalance. Within their families and communities, many continue to *negotiate, resist, and reinterpret* the norms that limit them. Their acts of resilience—whether asserting property rights, seeking education, or confronting domestic abuse—show how agency survives even within restrictive systems. These everyday negotiations make visible the strength of women who continue to seek dignity and justice despite the law's absence or silence.

This framework also draws attention to the *broader legal and ethical context.* India's commitments under the *Convention on the Elimination of All Forms of Discrimination against Women (CEDAW)* and the *International Covenant on Civil and Political Rights (ICCPR)* obligate the state to ensure equality and non-discrimination in both law and practice. Yet translating these global standards into meaningful protection at the local level remains an uphill task. In communities like the Bedia, where traditional authority still carries more weight than state institutions, the challenge is not just to enforce laws but to bridge the distance between *universal rights and local realities.*

In essence, this section offers a framework for understanding how *law, custom, and gender intersect* in the everyday lives of Bedia women. It reveals how the absence of effective legal protection deepens vulnerability, yet also how these women continue to assert their agency and self-worth within the limited spaces available to them. Their stories remind us that justice, in such contexts, is not only a matter of law—it is also a matter of *voice, recognition, and dignity.*

2.1. The Interplay of State Law, Personal Law, and Custom

India's legal landscape is defined by its plural character. The Constitution coexists with multiple layers of personal and customary laws, producing a complex system where the meaning of "law" varies according to context and community (Menski, 2003). This pluralism, while meant to preserve cultural diversity and autonomy, often creates *contradictory spaces of justice*—particularly for women in marginalized and tribal societies. The lives of Bedia women in Sagar and Damoh districts illustrate how these overlapping systems of law and tradition shape both protection and vulnerability in daily life.

At the heart of this complexity lies the *tension between state law and local practice.* The Indian Constitution guarantees equality before law (Article 14)[1], non-discrimination on grounds of sex (Article 15)[2], and protection of life and personal liberty (Article 21)[3]. These guarantees are reinforced through legislative measures such as the *Hindu Succession (Amendment) Act, 2005*, which grants daughters equal rights in ancestral property, and the *Protection of Women from Domestic Violence Act, 2005*, which recognizes physical, sexual, emotional, and economic abuse as violations of law. Despite this strong normative foundation, the impact of these reforms remains limited in regions such as Bundelkhand, where *customary norms and patriarchal authority* often hold greater sway than formal legal mechanisms (Agnes, 2012).

For many Bedia women, the reach of the state's legal apparatus is weakened by *social distance and institutional inaccessibility.* Legal aid, awareness campaigns, and judicial mechanisms rarely penetrate rural settlements. The law, when it appears at all, is often mediated through local police officials or informal intermediaries, making justice appear remote or intimidating. As a result, women frequently rely on *customary mechanisms* such as community panchayats or informal arbitration led by male elders (Bhattacharyya, 2019). While these systems promise speed and familiarity, they tend to reproduce traditional hierarchies and silence women's voices, particularly in disputes involving marriage, sexual autonomy, or inheritance.

The *personal law system*, which operates alongside state legislation, adds another layer to this complexity. Personal laws—based on religious identity—govern intimate matters such as marriage, divorce, and inheritance. Although reforms in Hindu and Christian personal laws have aimed to promote gender equity, others, including aspects of Muslim and tribal customary law, remain resistant to change (Parashar, 1992) The Bedia community, which lies outside formal religious law frameworks, follows customary rules similar to personal law principles in determining kinship, marital alliances, and family property. These customs carry a sense of legitimacy and continuity, yet they often marginalize women's claims in favour of collective or male authority (Sarin, 2020).

Custom, in this context, becomes the most powerful yet least codified form of law. Among the Bedia of Sagar and Damoh, customary practices regulate marriage negotiations, dowry arrangements, and sanctions for social deviance. Decisions made by local elders or caste councils are viewed as binding, even when they contradict constitutional protections. In many cases, *women's access to justice is mediated through community morality*, where ideals of purity, family honour, and obedience define the limits of acceptable female behaviour (Kaushal & Sharma, 2024). The customary system thus provides both belonging and constraint: it maintains social cohesion but also enforces gendered hierarchies that limit women's autonomy and participation in decision-making.

The interplay between these layers—state law, personal law, and custom—creates what scholars call *"negotiated legality"* (Merry, 1988). Women navigate these systems not passively but strategically, moving between different forums depending on what offers the greatest sense of protection or resolution. For instance, some Bedia women invoke state law when facing domestic violence or property disputes, especially when they seek outside intervention. Others prefer community-based resolutions to avoid stigma or retaliation. This strategic engagement highlights both the *resilience and vulnerability* of women who must operate within overlapping systems of authority.

The judiciary has occasionally acted to bridge the gap between constitutional ideals and personal or customary law. In *Shayara Bano v. Union of India* (2017)[4] the Supreme Court struck down the practice of instant triple talaq as unconstitutional, asserting that constitutional morality must override religious customs that violate fundamental rights. Similarly, in *Vineeta Sharma v. Rakesh Sharma* (2020)[5], the Court reaffirmed daughters' equal coparcenary rights, extending the principle of gender equality within Hindu law. Yet, despite such landmark rulings, the *translation of constitutional promises into lived experience* remains partial and uneven, especially for women in rural and tribal contexts (Desai, 2021).

In the Bundelkhand region, including Sagar and Damoh, these contradictions are starkly visible. The state's legal protections coexist with deep-rooted patriarchal practices and customary systems that continue to define gender relations. The "legal vacuum" that emerges is not simply the absence of law but the *failure of legal recognition and enforcement* where it is most needed. For the Bedia women, justice becomes a matter of negotiation—between law and custom, rights and duties, autonomy and acceptance. Their experiences remind us that gender justice in India is not achieved merely through formal reform but through the *constant dialogue between legal ideals and social realities.*

i. Strategic Agency: Negotiated Legality and Selective Appropriation

The interaction between state law and customary practice in Sagar and Damoh is often framed as a site of normative conflict in which women appear trapped between two competing systems (Tschalaer, 2009). However, the empirical material emerging from this study suggests a more nuanced reality. Women are not merely passive subjects navigating legal pluralism; they engage with it strategically. Their experiences reflect what may be described as *negotiated legality*—a conscious, situational movement between formal and informal forums depending on the nature of harm, the urgency of relief required, and the social consequences likely to follow (Chakraborty, 2019; Mishra, 2024).

In a region marked by what this chapter identifies as a "legal vacuum," justice is not accessed through a single institutional pathway (Singh, 2025). Instead, women assess which system—state law or customary authority—offers the most viable protection in a given circumstance. This assessment is rarely abstract or ideological. It is shaped by practical considerations: enforceability, cost, speed, community acceptance, and long-term survival within existing social networks.

When confronted with severe domestic violence, forced dispossession, or abandonment, some women turn to formal legal institutions (Mishra, 2024). This shift typically occurs when customary forums either refuse intervention or reinforce patriarchal authority. In such situations, women approach police stations, Protection Officers, or district courts not necessarily out of faith in constitutional morality, but because state law carries coercive power that customary bodies lack. The possibility of criminal sanction, arrest, or judicial order introduces accountability in ways that community mediation often cannot. Importantly, engagement with formal law does not always culminate in sustained litigation. In several instances, the mere act of filing—or threatening to file—a complaint alters intra-family negotiations. State law thus becomes leverage, reshaping power relations even if the dispute ultimately returns to informal settlement.

At the same time, many women consciously choose to resolve disputes within customary forums such as village panchayats or caste councils. These bodies are immediate, socially embedded, and procedurally simple. They do not require travel, legal literacy, or significant financial expenditure. More importantly, they allow women to remain within the relational framework that sustains everyday life. For those who depend on kinship networks for shelter, subsistence, and childcare, complete reliance on formal courts may carry heavy social costs, including ostracization. A negotiated settlement within the village—however imperfect—often preserves social belonging. In this context, justice is not defined solely by rights enforcement but also by the ability to maintain social continuity.

An emerging pattern within the study is the subtle blending of these systems. Women increasingly invoke the language of formal law within informal settings. Rather than immediately pursuing prosecution under the Bharatiya Nyaya Sanhita or other statutory frameworks, they reference these provisions during community negotiations. By making the authority of the state visible within customary deliberations, they recalibrate their bargaining position. This hybrid strategy neither abandons tradition nor wholly submits to it. Instead, it reflects a pragmatic effort to draw strength from multiple normative sources. Formal law becomes a background presence that influences outcomes without necessarily displacing community structures.

Women's choices remain constrained by economic dependency, limited literacy, stigma, and institutional bias. Strategic engagement operates within structural inequality; it does not eliminate it. In the case of the Bedia community, where customary practices intersect with systemic exploitation, the scope for meaningful exit is particularly restricted. Actions such as seeking NGO assistance, delaying ritual practices, or negotiating terms within the community may reflect resilience, but they occur within a deeply entrenched socio-economic framework. Agency in such contexts often signifies adaptation and harm reduction rather than complete emancipation.

Nevertheless, the presence of negotiated legality complicates simplistic narratives of victimhood. Women in Sagar and Damoh are neither wholly subordinated to custom nor fully protected by state law. They inhabit the space between these systems, moving across them with caution and calculation. Their strategies illuminate the central tension underpinning this chapter: the coexistence of constitutional guarantees of equality with socially embedded hierarchies that continue to shape everyday life.

This analysis strengthens the broader argument of the study by demonstrating that the "legal vacuum" is not merely a failure of statutory design or enforcement. It is sustained by the layered interaction between formal law, cultural authority, economic vulnerability, and community belonging. At the same time, the growing invocation of rights language within customary forums suggests that pluralism is not static. Constitutional norms are gradually entering local discourse, even if unevenly and selectively.

The experiences of these women therefore reveal both limitation and possibility. Justice in legally plural settings is not linear; it is negotiated, situational, and relational. Women turn to the state when protection becomes urgent, rely on custom when belonging is essential, and increasingly attempt to reshape both. In doing so, they expose the fragility of the divide between law and life, and highlight the ongoing challenge of reconciling constitutional equality with deeply rooted social authority without sacrificing women's dignity in the process.

2.2. Critiques of Legal Pluralism and Its Impact on Gender Justice

Legal pluralism, though intended to honour India's cultural and social diversity, has often reinforced rather than reduced gender hierarchies. It is often noted that when *state law, personal law, and customary law* co-exist, the result is not always empowerment but often *fragmented justice* (Choudhury, 2019). In many contexts, including among the Bedia community of Sagar and Damoh, the coexistence of legal orders leaves women navigating conflicting expectations—constitutional equality on one side and patriarchal customs on the other.

Feminist critiques argue that pluralism sustains *male-dominated community control*, particularly where personal and customary laws regulate marriage, inheritance, or sexuality (Agnes, 2012; Rao, 2021). The state's reluctance to intervene in "private" or "cultural" domains often leaves women without effective protection, reinforcing a *de facto legal vacuum* (N. Kundal, 2023)[6]. For instance, disputes involving domestic violence or inheritance are frequently resolved by local panchayats rather than through formal courts, privileging community harmony over women's rights (Bhattacharyya, 2019).

Judicial attitudes have been ambivalent. While decisions such as *Shayara Bano v. Union of India* (2017) assert constitutional supremacy over discriminatory practices, the broader system remains uneven. In regions like Bundelkhand, informal justice forums still dominate, shaping women's access to legal recourse. This imbalance reveals how pluralism, without a gender-sensitive framework, can perpetuate inequality rather than foster inclusion.

For the Bedia women, law is both protective and distant—symbolizing rights in theory but rarely in lived experience. True justice demands a *transformative pluralism*, one that acknowledges cultural diversity while actively challenging customs that undermine women's autonomy and dignity.[7]

However, the most significant challenge within this pluralistic framework remains the critical tension between group-differentiated rights and individual gender justice. While the state recognizes the distinct cultural identities of tribal communities through the Fifth Schedule and Acts like PESA, this often grants a 'cultural shield' to traditional institutions that are fundamentally patriarchal. Critics argue that by prioritizing community autonomy to preserve 'tradition,' the state inadvertently validates the authority of male elders who may suppress the individual constitutional rights of women in the name of group cohesion. Consequently, for Bedia women, the 'right to culture' can become a 'right to discriminate,' where the preservation of customary identity takes precedence over the universal guarantees of equality and dignity. This creates what scholars describe as the *'paradox of multicultural vulnerability,'* where state-sanctioned group autonomy risks trapping 'internal minorities'—specifically women—within oppressive traditional frameworks (Shachar, 2001).

2.3. The Paradox of Multicultural Vulnerability: Identity vs. Individual Rights

While the Indian legal framework attempts to honour the country's diverse social fabric through legal pluralism, this coexistence often creates a profound "paradox of multicultural vulnerability". This paradox arises when the state's efforts to protect the collective cultural identity of marginalized groups inadvertently leave the most vulnerable members—specifically women—without protection from the community itself.

In the context of tribal and semi-tribal regions like Sagar and Damoh, this tension manifests in several critical ways:

- **The "Cultural Shield" of Autonomous Governance**: Under the Fifth Schedule of the Constitution and the *Panchayats (Extension to the Scheduled Areas) Act (PESA), 1996*, the state recognizes and protects the distinct cultural identities and traditional management systems of tribal communities. However, by granting a "cultural shield" to these traditional institutions, the state often validates the authority of male-dominated customary councils. These bodies frequently prioritize group cohesion and "tradition" over the individual constitutional rights of women.
- **The Right to Culture as a "Right to Discriminate"**: For Bedia and other tribal women, the "right to culture" can effectively transform into a "right

to discriminate". When the preservation of customary identity—such as the Bedia's *Khandani Pesha*—takes precedence over universal guarantees of equality and dignity, women are trapped within oppressive traditional frameworks sanctioned by their own group's autonomy.

- **Internal Minorities and State Deference**: The state's reluctance to intervene in what are deemed "private" or "cultural" domains often leaves women as "internal minorities" within their communities. This institutional deference to patriarchal elders creates a de facto legal vacuum where the state's commitment to multiculturalism ends up reinforcing local gender hierarchies rather than dismantling them.
- **Conflict with Universal Standards**: This local dynamic stands in direct opposition to international standards like *CEDAW*, which obligates the state to modify or abolish discriminatory customs. In practice, however, efforts to challenge these oppressive traditions are frequently framed by community leaders as external intrusions into tribal life, further slowing the implementation of gender-sensitive reforms.

Ultimately, this paradox reveals that pluralism without a robust, gender-sensitive framework can perpetuate inequality. True justice in regions like Bundelkhand requires a "transformative pluralism" that respects cultural diversity without allowing it to shield practices that undermine a woman's fundamental right to a life of dignity and autonomy.

i. International Human Rights Standards vs. Local Context (CEDAW, ICCPR)

International human rights instruments such as the *Convention on the Elimination of All Forms of Discrimination against Women (CEDAW, 1979)* and the *International Covenant on Civil and Political Rights (ICCPR, 1966)* establish global norms for equality, dignity, and non-discrimination. India's ratification of these treaties reflects its commitment to upholding gender justice and protecting women from cultural or structural subordination. Yet, in practice, the translation of these global principles into *local realities*—particularly in rural and tribal regions like Sagar and Damoh—remains uneven and incomplete (Choudhury, 2019).

While CEDAW obligates states to modify or abolish discriminatory customs and traditions, local governance structures in many parts of Madhya Pradesh still allow *customary norms* to dominate dispute resolution and moral regulation. For Bedia women, whose socio-economic lives are shaped by both poverty and entrenched patriarchal codes, the international guarantees of autonomy and equality often feel distant and abstract (Rao, 2021). Awareness of such rights is minimal, and institutional mechanisms—such as legal aid centres or women's protection officers—rarely reach remote villages.

Moreover, the *tension between universal human rights and cultural relativism* continues to shape India's policy approach. Efforts to challenge oppressive customs are often perceived as external intrusions into community life, especially in tribal areas where identity and tradition are closely intertwined (Garg, 2022). This dynamic creates a *cultural defensiveness* that slows the implementation of gender-sensitive reforms.

Despite these challenges, India's judiciary and civil society have invoked international human rights standards to expand women's rights within domestic law. In *Vishaka v. State of Rajasthan* (1997)[8], the Supreme Court explicitly relied on CEDAW to frame guidelines against workplace harassment—demonstrating how international norms can fill domestic legislative gaps. However, such progressive interpretations rarely filter down to marginalized communities like the Bedia, where access to justice is mediated by social stigma, illiteracy, and customary control.

The gap between *international commitments and local enforcement* illustrates a deeper paradox: legal rights exist, but they are often *inaccessible to those most in need.* Bridging this divide requires not only institutional outreach but also cultural engagement—ensuring that global norms of equality are reinterpreted within local idioms of justice, dignity, and belonging.

2.4. Constitutional Mandates and Protective Indian Legislation

The Indian Constitution provides the main foundation for women's equality and justice. It guarantees *equality before the law (Article 14)*, prohibits *discrimination on the grounds of sex (Article 15)*, and protects every person's *right to life and personal liberty (Article 21).* These principles form the moral core of India's legal system and aim to create a society where women can live with dignity and freedom. For *Bedia women in the Sagar and Damoh districts of Madhya Pradesh*, these promises represent hope—yet their real impact on everyday life remains limited.

To make these rights meaningful, India has introduced several *protective laws.* The *Protection of Women from Domestic Violence Act (PWDVA), 2005* recognizes not only physical abuse but also emotional, verbal, and economic violence. The *Hindu Succession (Amendment) Act, 2005* gave daughters equal rights in ancestral property, marking a significant move toward gender equality (Agnes, 2012)[9]. However, for many rural and tribal women, such as those from the Bedia community, *awareness of these laws is low*, and access to legal help is difficult (Rana, 2020)

In practice, many disputes in rural Bundelkhand are still resolved through *customary panchayats or community councils*, which tend to prioritize social order over women's rights. This often pushes women back into silence, even when the law is on their side (Mookerji, 2011). The gap between *what the law promises* and *what it delivers* creates a "legal vacuum" where formal protections exist but are not effectively enforced.

Indian courts have made important strides in strengthening women's rights. In *Lata Singh v. State of Uttar Pradesh* (2006)[10] and *Shayara Bano v. Union of India* (2017)[11], the Supreme Court held that women's equality and freedom must prevail over social customs or patriarchal control. Yet, these progressive rulings rarely reach women in remote or marginalized communities. For Bedia women, legal justice still feels distant, overshadowed by everyday struggles of poverty, social stigma, and community pressure.

To truly uphold constitutional ideals, laws must *connect with the realities of women's lives*. This means spreading awareness, improving access to justice, and creating safe spaces where women can assert their rights without fear. For Bedia women, genuine equality will come not just through new laws, but through the courage to challenge harmful customs and claim the rights already guaranteed to them.

2.5. Bridging the Gap: Towards a Gender-Responsive Legal Framework

Despite the constitutional promises and a range of gender-focused legislations, the reality for many women in India—especially those from marginalized and semi-tribal groups like the *Bedia women of Sagar and Damoh*—remains far removed from the spirit of equality envisioned in law. The everyday lives of these women continue to be governed by a mix of *state laws, personal laws, and customary norms*, each carrying its own biases and boundaries. While the law on paper appears progressive, its reach often stops at the threshold of rural and tribal settlements, leaving women caught between formal rights and lived realities (Jhaveri, 2024).

Creating a *gender-responsive legal framework* begins with listening to women's experiences and understanding the social worlds they inhabit. Legal reform alone cannot change the conditions of women's lives if the *structures of power and patriarchy* remain untouched. Many Bedia women, for instance, hesitate to approach the police or courts despite facing violence or exploitation, not because the law is absent, but because the system feels alien and unresponsive to their needs. The fear of social backlash, lack of legal literacy, and deep-rooted mistrust of formal institutions further silence them (Kanta & Sharma, 2025).

To bridge this disconnect, the law must work *with* communities rather than *over* them. Strengthening *local legal aid systems*, deploying *mobile courts*, and training *gender-sensitive police officers* can bring justice closer to women's everyday realities. Equally important is encouraging *community-driven change*—where women are empowered as *paralegal volunteers, educators, and mediators* who reinterpret law within their cultural context. When law becomes a familiar language of dialogue rather than distant authority, it begins to transform the ground it stands on (Bhattacharyya, 2019).

India's international commitments, especially under *CEDAW*, emphasize the need to challenge social and cultural practices that perpetuate gender inequality. Aligning domestic legal initiatives with these global principles ensures that justice reaches beyond urban centers to women in rural and tribal regions (Kapur, 2012).

Ultimately, a gender-responsive legal order must aim not only for *legal equality* but for *transformative justice*—a framework that recognizes women as active agents of change. For Bedia women, this means being heard in the making and application of laws that affect their lives. Bridging the gap between law and life, therefore, is not just a policy goal but a *shared responsibility* that calls for empathy, participation, and structural change.

2.6. Critical Synthesis: Reconciling Custom, Constitution, and Gender Justice

The preceding analysis of the Sagar and Damoh districts reveals that the "legal vacuum" is not merely a gap in statutory drafting but a persistent failure of institutional recognition and socio-legal translation. This synthesis addresses the core tensions that emerge when universal constitutional promises meet the deeply embedded customary realities of rural and tribal Central India.

2.6.1. The Threshold of Unconstitutionality and the "Cultural Shield"

A critical debate within Indian legal pluralism is identifying when the state's deference to custom becomes unconstitutional. While the state recognizes distinct cultural identities through the Fifth Schedule and PESA (1996), this study highlights a *"paradox of autonomy."* As argued by scholars like *Shachar (2001)*, state-sanctioned group rights often create a "cultural shield" that allows dominant males within a community to govern "internal minorities"—specifically women—without state interference.

In the Bedia context, the *Khandani Pesha* is shielded by an appeal to cultural distinctiveness, effectively creating a zone where Articles 14, 15, and 21 of the Constitution are suspended. True *constitutional morality*, as articulated in *Justice K.S. Puttaswamy (2017)*, must dictate that individual dignity is the "core of the constitutional edifice" and cannot be sacrificed at the altar of group autonomy.

2.6.2. The Failure of Vernacularization: Judicial vs. Community Change

While landmark rulings such as *Shayara Bano (2017)*[12] and *Vineeta Sharma (2020*[13]*)* assert the supremacy of gender equality, their impact in Bundelkhand is hindered by a lack of *"vernacularization." Merry (2006)* posits that for human rights to be effective, they must be translated into local cultural imagery.

In Sagar and Damoh, formal law remains an "alien language." Fieldwork suggests that women do not view the High Court as a viable alternative to the Panchayat; rather, they engage in *"negotiated legality."* This is where women strategically invoke the *idea* of formal rights—threatening to go to the police or a lawyer—to recalibrate their bargaining power within informal forums. Thus, the vacuum is not filled by the arrival of a judge, but by the local empowerment of women to speak the language of rights within their own relational frameworks.

2.6.3. Methodological Reflexivity and Ethical Caution

Studying "shadow populations" like the Bedia involves navigating significant *social distance*. Reviewing sensitive topics such as ritualized trafficking (*Nathni Utarna*) requires a move away from "extractive" research toward *reflexive ethnography*. This study acknowledges the "social cost" of testimony: for a Bedia woman, speaking against custom is not just a legal act but a survival risk that may lead to the loss of her only economic and social safety net. Ethical research in this vacuum must prioritize "do no harm" protocols, ensuring that the pursuit of academic rigor does not exacerbate the vulnerability of the subjects.

2.6.4. Filling the Vacuum: Beyond Institutional Deference

The legal vacuum in Sagar and Damoh is sustained by *"institutional deference,"* where the police and administration treat violence and exploitation as "private family matters" to avoid local friction. Filling this vacuum requires a shift toward *institutional accountability*. As *Flavia Agnes (2011)* notes in her critique of personal laws, the state cannot remain a "silent spectator" to customary injustice. Reconciling custom and constitution requires an *intercultural dialogue*: reinterpreting tribal identity not as an exemption from equality, but as a framework that can evolve to honour both local wisdom and universal dignity.

However, the 'legal vacuum' described above is not a theoretical abstraction; it is a lived reality carved into the specific geography and history of Central India. To understand how 'institutional deference' and 'customary injustice' manifest in practice, one must move from the doctrinal framework to the physical terrain of

Bundelkhand. The following section provides the necessary socio-cultural grounding in Sagar and Damoh districts, examining the demographic and economic structures that allow these customary practices to persist in the shadow of the state.

3. THE SOCIO-CULTURAL LANDSCAPE OF SAGAR AND DAMOH

Understanding the everyday realities of Bedia women requires looking beyond statutes and judicial interpretations to the *social worlds they inhabit*. The districts of *Sagar and Damoh*, located in the *Bundelkhand region of Madhya Pradesh*, offer a complex picture of continuity and change. While the state's legal and policy frameworks have gradually expanded their reach, the *structures of caste, patriarchy, and economic dependency* still shape women's lives in powerful ways. These districts are marked by *deep-rooted traditional hierarchies, agrarian livelihoods, and slow-paced modernization*, making them a telling microcosm of rural gender relations in central India.

The *Bedia community*, the focal group of this study, occupies a liminal position—both socially and culturally. Historically categorized among semi-tribal or denotified groups, their identity has long been shaped by stigma, poverty, and cultural marginalization. For Bedia women, questions of law and justice are not abstract legal debates but daily negotiations within families, communities, and local power structures. To understand these negotiations, it is essential to trace the *demographic, institutional, and economic contours* of the region.

3.1. The Shadow of the Past: From "Criminal by Birth" to De-notified

The history of DNTs is rooted in the Criminal Tribes Act (CTA) of 1871, a piece of colonial legislation that didn't just penalize acts, but identities. Under this law, over 200 communities were labeled "hereditary criminals."

- The Colonial Logic: The British viewed these nomadic and forest-dwelling communities as threats to settled, taxable agriculture and social order.
- The Stigma: Membership in these tribes meant mandatory registration, restricted movement, and the crushing psychological weight of being told—and told by the state—that your very existence was a crime.

In 1952, the Act was finally repealed, and these tribes were "De-notified." However, the celebration was short-lived. The Habitual Offenders Act (1952) was swiftly introduced, essentially pouring the old colonial wine into a new "democratic" bottle, allowing police to continue profiling these groups under the guise of crime prevention.

3.1.1. The "Legal Vacuum": Administrative Invisibility

Despite their repeal from the "Criminal" list, DNTs fell into a unique and devastating legal vacuum. Unlike Scheduled Castes (SC) or Scheduled Tribes (ST), DNTs lack a uniform, nationwide constitutional category.

Table 1.

The Issue	The Consequence
Categorization Chaos	A single tribe might be listed as SC in one state, ST in another, and OBC in a third—or not listed at all.
Identity Erasure	Without a clear category, they are often excluded from reservation quotas and targeted welfare schemes.
Lack of Protection	Many DNTs do not fall under the SC/ST (Prevention of Atrocities) Act, leaving them without specific legal recourse against hate crimes and systemic bias.

This administrative chaos is not unique to the Bedia; it mirrors the experiences of the Bachara in Mandsaur and the Nat in Rajasthan, where legal definitions vary wildly across state lines.

3.1.2. The Jabali Yojana Paradox

This administrative confusion has direct consequences for state-led intervention. A prime example is the *Jabali Yojana*, a specialized scheme launched by the Madhya Pradesh government specifically for the social and economic rehabilitation of the Bedia, Bachara, and Nat communities. While the policy exists on paper to provide education, healthcare, and alternative livelihoods, it remains largely inaccessible in the rural pockets of Sagar and Damoh. Because the scheme is tied to specific "caste/tribe" certificates, the "Categorization Chaos" mentioned above acts as a bureaucratic barrier. Women who cannot produce proof of their specific DNT status—often due to historical nomadism and lack of documentation—are effectively erased from the state's radar, leaving the "legal vacuum" unfilled despite the presence of targeted welfare.

3.1.3. Gendered Exploitation: The Double Burden

The intersection of historical stigma and legal invisibility creates a unique landscape of violence for DNT women. Because the state views their communities as "criminal," the standard protections of the law are often inverted into tools of harassment (Rana, 2020).

3.1.4. Police Violence as Control

DNT women are frequently the primary targets of police raids. In the absence of the men (who often flee to avoid arbitrary arrest), women face custodial torture, verbal abuse, and sexual assault used as "pressure tactics" to extract information or bribes.

3.1.5. Economic Marginalization and Sex Work

The "criminal" label makes formal employment nearly impossible. This economic dead-end, combined with the loss of traditional nomadic livelihoods, has pushed some communities toward subsistence-level sex work. This creates a vicious cycle where the state uses the "immorality" of their survival to justify further criminalization (Dalla et al., 2022).

3.1.6. Social Ostracization

Because DNTs are often nomadic or live in peripheral settlements, women lack access to safe housing, clean water, and maternal healthcare. Their perceived "criminality" acts as a barrier to empathy from mainstream society, making them "un-victimmable" in the eyes of the public and the judiciary.

3.1.7. The Reality

For a DNT woman, the law is not a shield; it is the primary source of her insecurity. Her struggle is not just against poverty, but against a century-old narrative that marks her body and her lineage as inherently illegal.

3.2. Demographic Profile: Caste, Tribe, and Economic Indicators

Sagar and Damoh together represent the *socio-cultural core of Bundelkhand*, characterized by rich historical heritage yet persistent poverty and ecological fragility. Both districts are predominantly rural—over *75% of the population lives in villages*, relying heavily on land-based occupations (Census of India, 2011). The demographic composition reflects India's layered social fabric: a mixture of upper-caste agrarian groups, backward classes, Scheduled Castes, and Scheduled Tribes. According to census data, *Scheduled Castes constitute about 23% of the population in Sagar and 22% in Damoh*, while *Scheduled Tribes make up roughly 14% and 13%, respectively*.

Within this diversity, the *Bedia community* remains numerically small but socially significant. Often positioned at the margins of both caste and tribe, their historical livelihood practices have contributed to social stigmatization and exclusion from mainstream development. Access to *education, healthcare, and formal employment* remains extremely limited. Literacy rates, though improving, reveal stark gender disparities—female literacy in many villages remains below 50%, particularly among denotified and semi-tribal groups (Government of Madhya Pradesh, 2021).

The economic landscape mirrors these inequalities. The majority of families depend on *subsistence farming or daily wage labour*, with few alternative livelihood options. Landholding patterns are skewed; a small segment of upper-caste families controls most cultivable land, while lower-caste and tribal groups survive on marginal plots or sharecropping. This unequal distribution of resources reinforces *class and caste hierarchies*, leaving women—especially from the Bedia community—at the intersection of multiple vulnerabilities.

3.2.1. The Gendered Reality of Land Ownership: Law vs. Customary Wirasat

Within the demographic and economic landscape of Sagar and Damoh, land is the primary source of survival, yet its ownership remains almost exclusively a male domain. For women from the Gond, Bhil, and Baiga communities, the promise of economic independence through land rights is frequently stalled at the intersection of state law and tribal tradition.

- **The Promise of the Hindu Succession (Amendment) Act, 2005**: In a formal legal sense, the 2005 Amendment was a landmark shift, granting daughters equal coparcenary rights in ancestral property. This law should, in theory, empower tribal women to claim their share of family land, providing a critical buffer against the poverty and agrarian distress that define the Bundelkhand region.
- **The Barrier of Customary 'Wirasat'**: Despite this statutory foundation, the actual transfer of land continues to follow the unwritten code of Wirasat (patrilineal inheritance). Among the Gonds, Bhils, and Baigas, land is viewed

as an ancestral asset that must remain within the male kinship line to prevent it from passing to another clan through marriage.

- **Social Pressure and Relinquishment**: Because daughters are traditionally considered *paraya dhan* (another's wealth), they are often coerced by family elders and community panchayats to sign "relinquishment deeds". These women frequently waive their legal rights under the Hindu Succession Act not out of choice, but to maintain social ties and avoid being seen as "disloyal" to their brothers and the wider community.
- **Impact on Vulnerability**: This systematic exclusion from land titles leaves tribal women invisible in the eyes of the state's agricultural support systems. While they perform the majority of agricultural labor—from sowing to harvesting—the lack of an independent land title prevents them from accessing formal credit, government subsidies, or crop insurance. For widows or childless women, this exclusion can lead to Niyog (levirate marriage), where they are pressured to marry a male relative just to ensure the land remains under patriarchal control.

Ultimately, the persistent dominance of *Wirasat* creates a "legal vacuum" where the 2005 Amendment exists on paper but is effectively nullified by local practice. For women in the tribal heartland of Madhya Pradesh, justice is not found in the statute books, but in the difficult, often impossible, negotiation against deep-seated customary norms that prioritize collective male ownership over individual female rights.

3.3. Dominant Community Structures and Traditional Power Holders (Panchayats, Caste Elders)

The *social organization of villages in Sagar and Damoh* continues to be governed by deeply entrenched customary institutions. *Caste panchayats*, *jati sabhas*, and *village elders* operate as moral and disciplinary authorities, shaping decisions about marriage, sexuality, inheritance, and social conduct. These informal structures are often perceived as legitimate and culturally appropriate, even when they contradict statutory law (Vashishth, 2024).

For women, however, these traditional bodies can act as both protectors and oppressors. In the Bedia community, social harmony is often maintained through decisions taken by male elders who adjudicate disputes and prescribe sanctions. Women rarely participate directly in these deliberations; their voices are mediated through male relatives. When women attempt to assert autonomy—by choosing their partners, seeking legal recourse, or challenging caste norms—they risk *public humiliation, social ostracization, or violent retribution*.

Although the *Constitution's 73rd Amendment (1992)* introduced the *Panchayati Raj system* with mandatory representation for women, the coexistence of these formal and informal systems creates a duality. Statutory panchayats exist in parallel with customary institutions, but the latter often command greater cultural legitimacy. In sensitive matters—such as sexual relationships, property disputes, or inter-caste unions—*customary law prevails* over formal justice mechanisms. This overlap limits the transformative potential of legal reforms, particularly for women who lack the social capital or confidence to approach formal courts (Rao, 2017).

In practice, the authority of caste and community remains the *primary determinant of women's choices*. Law, even when available, is filtered through the lens of local morality. The result is a hybrid system where *custom continues to dominate*, shaping the moral and legal boundaries of women's lives in rural Bundelkhand.

3.4. Economic Context: Agrarian Dependency and Migration as a Factor of Vulnerability

The economy of Sagar and Damoh is deeply *agrarian and climate-sensitive*, relying primarily on monsoon rains. The region's *semi-arid conditions* and erratic rainfall patterns contribute to recurring crop failures and agrarian distress (National Sample Survey Office, 2020). With limited irrigation and low productivity, most families depend on *subsistence farming or casual labour*, leading to cycles of debt and poverty.

Women constitute a major share of the agricultural workforce, yet their contribution remains *invisible and undervalued.* They perform crucial tasks—sowing, weeding, harvesting, and livestock care—but rarely hold land titles. This lack of ownership limits their bargaining power both within the household and in the community (India Development Review, 2025).

In recent decades, *migration has emerged as a coping strategy.* Men often migrate seasonally to nearby cities or industrial centres in search of work, leaving behind women to manage domestic responsibilities, care for children, and sustain small farms. This feminization of rural responsibility exposes women to new forms of vulnerability. Without male support, many women face *economic insecurity, increased workload, and heightened social scrutiny.* For Bedia women, the pressures are compounded by their community's marginal status—informal employment, lack of documentation, and social stigma restrict their access to welfare schemes and credit (Dalla, 2022).

Migration also disrupts family structures, leading to *unstable relationships and heightened risks of exploitation.* The absence of men sometimes forces women to enter precarious labour markets or depend on local intermediaries, exposing them to trafficking and abuse. Moreover, the migration of young men affects community dynamics—traditional hierarchies tighten control over women's movement and behavior to preserve "honour" in the face of perceived social change.

Thus, the *economic fragility of agrarian life*, combined with *migration-induced social stress*, creates a landscape where gendered inequalities deepen. For Bedia women, survival often means navigating between the obligations of tradition and the uncertainties of a changing economy.

3.5. Postcolonial Feminist Critique: Legal Pluralism as a Site of Power Struggle

The "legal vacuum" observed in Sagar and Damoh is not merely an absence of law, but a manifestation of what postcolonial feminist scholars describe as the paradox of legal pluralism. In tribal India, the coexistence of statutory law and customary practice is often framed as "respect for diversity." However, a critical lens reveals that this pluralism frequently functions as a site of active power struggle where women's bodies and rights are the primary currency.

3.5.1. The "Community" as a Patriarchal Construct

Postcolonial feminists like Ratna Kapur (2005) and Nivedita Menon (2004) argue that the state often treats "the community" as a homogenous, monolithic block. By doing so, the state recognizes the voices of male elders (the *Jati Sabhas* or *Panchayats*) as the authentic voice of the tribe.

- *The Gendered Cost:* When the state defers to "customary law" to preserve tribal identity, it effectively subsidizes internal patriarchies. For Bedia women, the "community" is not always a site of protection; it is often the very entity that enforces the "hereditary" nature of their exploitation to maintain social and economic boundaries.

3.5.2. Selective Sovereignty and the "Victim" Narrative:

Scholars such as Rajeshwari Sunder Rajan (2003) point out that the postcolonial state often oscillates between "protectionism" and "neglect." In the context of DNTs, the state uses the "criminal" history of the tribe to justify intrusive policing, yet uses "respect for custom" to avoid intervening when women are denied land rights or subjected to customary sanctions.

- *The Power Struggle:* This creates a "selective sovereignty" where the law is hyper-present when it seeks to punish (the Habitual Offenders Act) but becomes a "vacuum" when it is needed to empower (the Hindu Succession Act).

3.5.3. Custom as a "Reinvented" Tool of Control:

Contrary to the idea that "custom" is ancient and unchanging, postcolonial critique suggests that customary practices are often reinvented to serve modern patriarchal interests.

- *Example:* The rigid enforcement of *Wirasat* (patrilineal inheritance) in Bundelkhand is often framed as "preserving tradition." However, as Bina Agarwal (1994) argues, this is often a modern economic strategy to prevent the fragmentation of landholdings in a market-driven economy. Custom is thus weaponized to ensure that women remain "landless labourers" on their own ancestral soil, making them more vulnerable to the precarious labour markets and sex trade discussed in Section 3.3.

3.5.4. Moving Beyond "Agency vs. Victimhood":

A postcolonial feminist reading of the Bedia community avoids the trap of seeing these women as mere victims of "backward" traditions. Instead, it analyzes their "negotiations" as a form of subaltern agency. When a Bedia woman navigates the demands of her caste elders while simultaneously seeking the "promise" of state welfare, she is operating within a "legal vacuum" that forces her to be a strategist for her own survival.

- *Summary Critique:* The "legal vacuum" in Sagar and Damoh is a political choice. By allowing customary law to trump constitutional rights without providing "internal exit options" for women, the state maintains a fragile peace with local power-holders. For the Bedia woman, the struggle is not just against "tradition," but against a postcolonial legal structure that finds her rights inconvenient to enforce.

3.6. Visual Aids

The Bedia community occupies a complex socio-legal space in India. Their traditional practices—historically rooted in performance and, in some segments, hereditary sex work—often collide with modern statutes aimed at protecting women and tribal autonomy. Below is a chronological mapping of how key Indian statutes and judicial precedents interact with the customary realities of the Bedia community.

3.6.1. Mapping Statutes, Precedents, and Customary Conflicts

Table 2.

Year	Statute / Judicial Precedent	Key Legal Framework	Specific Bedia Customary Conflict
1996	PESA Act	Grants Gram Sabhas the power to safeguard traditions and manage resources in Scheduled Areas.	Self-Governance vs. Reform: While PESA empowers tribal councils, Bedia customary councils (*Panchayats*) have historically sanctioned exploitative practices like *Nathni Utarai*, creating a clash between "customary autonomy" and human rights.
1997	*Vishaka v. State of Rajasthan*	Established guidelines against sexual harassment; emphasized the right to dignity.	Normalization of Exploitation: The "Rai" dance tradition often blurs the line between cultural performance and sexual exploitation, directly challenging the "dignity" standards set by the court.
2005	PWDVA (Domestic Violence Act)	Protects women from physical, emotional, and economic abuse within the household.	Economic Exploitation: In some Bedia families, women are the primary earners through sex work. PWDVA is often underutilized because the "abuse" (forcing entry into sex work) is culturally institutionalized.
2006	Forest Rights Act (FRA)	Recognizes the rights of forest-dwelling tribes to land and resources.	Displacement & Vulnerability: As a traditionally nomadic or marginalized group, many Bedias lack land titles. Failure to implement FRA forces further reliance on traditional (often exploitative) occupations for survival.
2011	*Budhadev Karmaskar v. State of West Bengal*	The Supreme Court ruled that sex workers have a right to live with dignity under Article 21.	Rehabilitation vs. Tradition: This precedent supports Bedia women seeking to exit the trade, but implementation is hindered by the community's reliance on the income generated by the "oldest daughter" tradition.
2022	*Budhadev Karmaskar (Directions)*	The Court directed states to issue Aadhaar cards to sex workers without requiring proof of residence.	Identity & Inclusion: Crucial for the Bedia community, as their historical marginalization often left them without the documentation needed to access social welfare and exit exploitative cycles.

3.6.2. Key Tensions in the Bedia Context

The intersection of law and custom for the Bedia community is rarely a straight line. It's more of a tug-of-war between three distinct forces:

- Constitutional Morality: The courts prioritize the individual rights of women to dignity and bodily autonomy (Article 21).
- Customary Preservation: PESA and other tribal protections aim to keep state interference out of community traditions, which can inadvertently shield exploitative practices.
- Economic Survival: Statutes like the FRA are vital because, without land or alternative livelihoods, legal prohibitions on traditional Bedia occupations often lead to poverty rather than "liberation."

Note on "Criminal Tribes" Legacy: It is important to remember that the Bedia community was once classified under the Criminal Tribes Act of 1871. Although repealed, the "habitual offender" stigma persists in local policing, often leading to the misapplication of anti-trafficking laws against the community as a whole.

3.7. Structural Silences in Tribal Empowerment: The Gender Gaps in PESA and FRA

While the Panchayats (Extension to the Scheduled Areas) Act (PESA), 1996 and the Scheduled Tribes and Other Traditional Forest Dwellers (Recognition of Forest Rights) Act, 2006 (FRA) are hailed as landmark legislations for tribal self-governance, they contain "structural silences" regarding gender that deepen the legal vacuum for women in Sagar and Damoh (Sharma, 2018; Bhatia, 2020). These acts aim to shift power from the state to the community, but without explicit gender-sensitive mechanisms, they often inadvertently shift that power into the hands of traditional male elites.

- **The Gram Sabha and the Myth of Neutrality:** Under PESA, the *Gram Sabha* is the soul of village governance, empowered to manage local resources and settle disputes. However, in the Bundelkhand region, these assemblies are often extensions of patriarchal *jati sabhas*. While the law mandates women's presence, it does not guarantee their voice. In practice, the "consensus" reached in these meetings usually reflects the will of male elders, while women—burdened by the "culture of silence" and social stigma—remain peripheral to the decision-making process.
- **The Forest Rights Act and the "Joint Title" Barrier**: The FRA was a revolutionary step in recognizing the rights of forest-dwelling communities. While the Act provides for joint titling of land in the names of both spouses, its implementation on the ground remains dismal for women in Madhya Pradesh (Pathak, 2015; Krishnan, 2019). Customary notions of *Wirasat* (patrilineal inheritance) often override the FRA's gender-neutral language, as community leaders often view individual women's claims as a threat to collective tribal landholdings.
- **Decentralization without Democratization:** For women in the Bedia and other tribal communities, PESA and FRA have often resulted in "decentralized patriarchy." By granting legal shield to "customary law" without providing safeguards against discriminatory practices, the state allows male-dominated local bodies to act as a *de facto* judiciary. This traps women in a cycle where they must choose between their community identity and their individual constitutional rights to equality and dignity (Chakraborty, 2019; Upadhyay, 2021).

Ultimately, the failure of these acts to address the internal power dynamics of tribal societies means that the "legal vacuum" is not just an absence of law, but a presence of laws that are blind to the gendered realities of the people they seek to empower.

4. THE SPECTRUM OF THE LEGAL VACUUM: FROM ECONOMIC EXCLUSION TO BODILY EXPLOITATION

The legal vacuum in Sagar and Damoh is not a uniform void; it is a stratified system of displacement where customary law progressively replaces constitutional protections. This section maps the "spectrum" of this vacuum, moving from the pervasive denial of property rights affecting the majority of rural women to the extreme, institutionalized exploitation of the Bedia community.

4.1. The Foundation of the Vacuum: Property and the 'Wirasat' System

While the Hindu Succession (Amendment) Act, 2005 theoretically dismantled patrilineal inheritance, fieldwork in Sagar and Damoh reveals that the custom of *Wirasat* remains the de facto law.

- **Customary Relinquishment**: Daughters are socialized as *Paraya Dhan* (another's wealth). This cultural ideology is codified through "relinquishment deeds," where women legally waive their coparcenary rights to avoid social ostracization.
- **Data Grounding**: This qualitative finding is mirrored in Agriculture Census data for Madhya Pradesh, which indicates that despite the 2005 Amendment, female landholding remains disproportionately low (often below 15% in rural pockets), validating the "vacuum" between statutory intent and customary outcome.
- **Niyog (Levirate Marriage) as Land Control**: The practice of *Niyog* (pressuring a widow to marry her brother-in-law) functions as a strategic customary tool to prevent land fragmentation. By re-characterizing the widow as a "custodian" of the lineage rather than an independent title-holder, the family ensures that property remains under patriarchal control, effectively nullifying the widow's rights as a Class I heir.

4.2. Marital Security: Chuttachar and the Shadow of the Court

The legal vacuum in domestic life is sustained by a preference for "internal settlements" over judicial intervention.

- **Informal Divorce (Chuttachar):** In most non-Bedia communities, marriage dissolution is managed by the Caste Panchayat. While *Chuttachar* provides social finality, it offers no legal standing.
- **The Maintenance Trap:** Because these divorces are not legally recorded, women are ineligible for state schemes like the *Mukhyamantri Jan-Kalyan Sambal Yojana*. Furthermore, the acceptance of a lump-sum *Guzara* (settlement) under social pressure effectively prevents women from later seeking statutory maintenance under Section 144 of the BNSS.
- **Statistical Context:** According to NFHS-5 data for Madhya Pradesh, over 75% of women in rural districts justify family-led dispute resolution, highlighting how the "vacuum" is reinforced by a deep-seated distrust of formal judicial delays.

4.3. The Extreme Manifestation: Institutionalized Exploitation in the Bedia Community

The Bedia case represents the "total nullification" of the criminal code. Here, the vacuum is not merely an absence of property rights, but the transformation of the female body into the primary economic asset of the kinship group.

- **Khandani Pesha and Ritualized Crime**: The transition from child to sex worker is formalized via the Nathni Utarna ritual. This community-sanctioned ceremony functions as a parallel "license," which local authorities often fail to challenge due to a "Legal Vacuum of Deference"—where police prioritize social friction management over the enforcement of the POCSO Act and ITPA.
- **Intergenerational Limbo**: The deliberate erasure of fatherhood leads to a lack of birth and caste certificates. This "legal invisibility" ensures that Bedia children cannot access the very education or state benefits that might facilitate an exit from the custom.

4.4. Critical Synthesis: Why the Vacuum Persists

The resilience of these customs suggests a tension between Constitutional Morality and Cultural Autonomy. In the tribal and rural contexts of Central India, the state often retreats, viewing customary law as a "stabilizing" force.

- **Feminist Critique of Pluralism**: Following the scholarship of Sally Engle Merry, this vacuum persists because "human rights" have not been "vernacularized." To a woman in Damoh, the Panchayat is a present, immediate reality, while the High Court is a distant, expensive abstraction.
- **The Samjhauta (Compromise) Culture**: The institutional deference of the police—referring cases back to the Panchayat for "compromise"—is the structural mechanism that maintains the vacuum. It prioritizes community "honour" over individual gender justice.

4.5. Puncturing the Vacuum: Emerging Nuances

It is essential to note that the vacuum is not absolute. Recent years have seen "localized punctures":

- **Education and NGOs**: Increased enrollment of Bedia girls in residential schools has begun to disrupt the cycle of *Khandani Pesha.*
- **Judicial Activism**: Local legal aid clinics are increasingly helping women bypass *Chuttachar* settlements to file for formal maintenance, though these cases remain the exception rather than the rule.

4.4. The Manifestation of the Legal Vacuum

The "legal vacuum" for women in accessing justice, particularly in rural and disadvantaged settings, is a complex phenomenon shaped by a combination of practical, cultural, and institutional hurdles. These barriers prevent women from effectively utilizing the formal legal system, thus denying them their fundamental right to justice (Singh, 2025).

5.1. Methodological Ethics: Navigating the "Wall of Silence"

Researching the "legal vacuum" within the Bedia community presents ethical complexities that go far beyond standard academic inquiry. When a researcher enters these settlements, they are not just documenting a "legal issue"—they are entering a space where the very practices being studied (trafficking and ritualized prostitution) are the primary sources of community survival.

5.1.1. Cultural Defensiveness:

One of the greatest challenges is the "wall of silence" or cultural defensiveness erected by community elders. Because the Bedia have been historically criminalized first under colonial law as a "Criminal Tribe" and now by modern anti-trafficking statutes—there is a deep-seated distrust of any outsider asking about "rights" or "law." Any attempt to suggest reform is often framed by community leaders as an attack on their tribal identity, which significantly slows down the implementation of government interventions.

5.1.2. The Ethics of Observation:

The researcher must navigate the thin line between being an objective observer and a witness to systemic exploitation. Collecting data becomes a sensitive act of balancing the need for truth with the duty to ensure that the women who speak out are not further marginalized or endangered within their own kinship networks.

5.1.3. Data vs. Lived Reality:

Traditional data collection (surveys/interviews) often fails to capture the nuance of "negotiated legality." A woman might tell a researcher she is "happy" with her custom because she fears the state's "rehabilitation" centers, which she views as prisons. Therefore, the methodology must rely on deep ethnographic immersion to understand that her "silence" is often a strategic survival mechanism.

5.2. Structural Barriers

Structural barriers are the systemic and practical obstacles inherent in the legal and physical infrastructure that restrict access to courts and legal services.

5.2.1. Geographical Distance from Courts

In rural and remote areas, the sheer *geographical distance* to the nearest functional court, police station, or legal aid office presents a significant deterrent. The lack of reliable and affordable transport, coupled with limited mobility for many women due to patriarchal social norms, transforms a trip to a court into a major, often insurmountable, logistical and security challenge (Madhya Pradesh State Legal

Services Authority, 2025). This physical inaccessibility effectively excludes a large segment of the female population from the formal justice system.

5.2.2. Cost of Litigation

Despite constitutional provisions for free legal aid, the *financial constraints* associated with pursuing a case remain a substantial barrier. These costs extend beyond lawyer fees to include court expenses, travel, loss of daily wages for both the litigant and any accompanying family member, and potential informal payments. For women who are often economically dependent on male family members, these costs are prohibitive and can be a direct cause of their inability to seek redressal, particularly in cases of domestic disputes where they may risk losing all financial support (Steinert et al., 2023).

5.2.3. Complexity of Legal Procedures

The formal legal process is notoriously *complex and time-consuming*, involving intricate procedures, copious documentation, and a specialized language that is incomprehensible to those with limited legal literacy. The lengthy judicial delays, often spanning years, are frustrating and discouraging, leading many women to abandon their pursuit of justice. The difficulty in navigating the bureaucratic application procedures for legal aid further exacerbates this issue (Chiongson et al., 2011).

5.2. Attitudinal Barriers

Attitudinal barriers are the socio-cultural and psychological deterrents that arise from ingrained biases, stereotypes, and a lack of awareness, deeply affecting a woman's decision to seek justice and her subsequent experience within the system.

5.2.1. Fear of Social Ostracization

A pervasive *fear of social ostracization* and victim-blaming discourages women from reporting crimes, especially sexual or domestic violence. In many communities, a woman's 'honour' is tied to the family's reputation, and pursuing legal action, particularly against a family member or community elder, is seen as bringing shame upon the entire family (Singh, 2024). This social stigma can lead to a withdrawal of community support, threats of retaliation, and intense family pressure to withdraw the complaint, resulting in the denial of justice for the sake of 'family honour' (Madhya Pradesh State Legal Services Authority, 2025).

5.2.2. Lack of Legal Literacy Among Women

A widespread *lack of legal literacy*—or awareness of their rights and available legal resources—is a fundamental barrier. Many women, particularly in rural and marginalized communities, remain uninformed about laws designed to protect them, such as those concerning domestic violence, property rights, or inheritance. This lack of awareness limits their ability to recognize an abuse of their rights and to access the existing, albeit inadequate, support structures (Shukla & Bhat, 2022).

5.2.3. Institutional Bias (Police and Lower Judiciary)

The formal justice system itself is often marred by *institutional bias*. Within the police and lower judiciary, *gender bias and patriarchal attitudes* are prevalent (Tyagi, 2024). Police may be reluctant to register complaints (known as 'non-registration of FIRs'), may display insensitive or sceptical attitudes towards female complainants, or may be influenced by local power structures. Judicial pronouncements can also reflect gender stereotypes, with some judges questioning the character or morality of female victims, which can lead to unjust rulings or a failure to ensure justice (Deshpande, 2022). This systemic lack of gender-sensitivity erodes women's trust in the formal institutions.

5.3. The Parallel Justice System

The shortcomings of the formal system—its cost, distance, and complexity—have led to the emergence of a *parallel justice system* at the grassroots level, primarily embodied by the *Gram Panchayat* (village council) and, where they exist, the *Nyay Panchayat* (village-level judicial body). While customary systems like the *Caste Panchayat* often reinforce gendered hierarchies, they are not solely instruments of oppression; they also present a *complex paradox of belonging*. In the remote regions of Sagar and Damoh, where formal courts are geographically and financially inaccessible, these informal forums offer a "familiar language of justice" that is immediate and inexpensive. For some women, the *Panchayat* may provide a level of social mediation or physical security—such as enforcing basic shelter or food-sharing within a kinship network—that the distant and slow-moving formal legal system cannot guarantee. This "negotiated legality" suggests that women may strategically choose community-based resolutions not only out of fear but because they offer a path to social reintegration that does not result in the total ostracization often triggered by an FIR or a formal lawsuit.

5.3.1. The Gram Panchayat and Nyay Panchayat as the De Facto Judiciary

Due to the inaccessibility of formal courts, these local bodies become the *de facto judiciary* in rural India. They are often the first and only forum that villagers approach for dispute resolution. The Gram Panchayat, as an institution of local self-governance, and the *Nyay Panchayat* (if constituted), may take on the mantle of local arbitrators and mediators. This system is preferred by the local population because it is accessible, quick, and inexpensive (Chauhan & Deshta, 2024).

5.3.2. Prioritizing Social Harmony over Individual Justice for Women

The primary objective of these parallel systems is *prioritization of social harmony and community consensus* rather than the impartial non-enforcement of codified law or the delivery of individual rights-based justice (Ghosh, 2014). Disputes are resolved through mediation and arbitration that focus on maintaining the *status quo* and restoring peace within the community structure.

For women, this often means that their individual claims, especially those challenging family or patriarchal structures (such as domestic violence or property rights), are consistently *subordinated to the needs of the larger community or family*. The decisions often reinforce traditional gender roles and biases, pressuring the woman to compromise her legal rights for the sake of reconciliation and family unity. While Gram Panchayats are constitutional bodies and can play a positive role in development (UNFPA India, n.d.), their function as an informal court in gender disputes frequently results in the denial of full, rights-based justice for women, cementing the legal vacuum at the grassroots.

6. CONSEQUENCES OF THE LEGAL VACUUM: HEIGHTENED VULNERABILITY

The systemic failure to provide accessible and impartial justice creates a vacuum that deepens the vulnerability of women, translating the non-enforcement of law into concrete, measurable costs related to their well-being and future.

6.1. Economic Dispossession and Indebtedness

When the legal system fails to secure a woman's right to property or maintenance, it directly leads to her economic marginalization and dependence.

6.1.1. Failure to Secure Property and Assets:

Despite codified laws, such as the Hindu Succession Act (amended in 2005) granting equal inheritance rights, *judicial non-enforcement* and pressure from community forums coerce women into relinquishing their claims to marital property or land (Equality Now, 2020). This leaves women *dispossessed* of their rightful economic base, hindering their ability to seek justice independently (Singh, 2024).

6.1.2. Indebtedness and Financial Dependence:

The failure to secure timely and sufficient court-mandated maintenance or alimony forces women into economic precarity. To meet basic needs and raise children, they must take on *low-wage, informal sector jobs* or accrue significant *debt* (Madhya Pradesh State Legal Service Authority, 2025). This financial dependency becomes a barrier to escaping abuse, as the cost of prolonged litigation and independent survival is often unsustainable.

6.2. Physical and Mental Health Impacts (Violence and Stress)

The prolonged exposure to an unresponsive justice system exacerbates the physical and psychological harm caused by the violence itself.

6.2.1. Compounded Physical Health Consequences:

The lack of legal consequence often allows the cycle of violence to continue or escalate. Studies show that abused women experience significantly higher rates of chronic health issues, including *gastrointestinal disorders, chronic pain syndromes, and injuries* (Panday et al., 2018; WHO, 2024). The chronic stress associated with fighting a hostile system while remaining in a vulnerable environment compounds these physical ailments.

6.2.2. Mental Health Crisis:

The psychological toll of seeking justice amid systemic delays, police bias, and victim-blaming is severe. Survivors exhibit alarmingly high rates of *depression, anxiety, Post-Traumatic Stress Disorder (PTSD)*, and significantly increased *suicidal ideation* compared to non-abused women (Sharma et al., 2019; WHO, 2024). This pervasive distress is a direct consequence of the legal vacuum, where the system itself becomes a source of secondary trauma.

6.3. The Intergenerational Transfer of Vulnerability (Impact on Daughters)

The mother's failed quest for justice transmits vulnerability to the next generation, perpetuating the cycle of gender inequality.

6.3.1. Reduced Investment in Daughters:

The mother's economic dispossession, resulting from the lack of legal recourse, directly limits the resources available for her children's development. Research suggests that the mother's lower bargaining power and asset base are associated with *worse health outcomes and fewer years of completed schooling* for her children (Bhat, 2022). Daughters, in particular, may see their education or health compromised, creating a new generation of economic vulnerability.

6.3.2. Normalisation of Violence and System Mistrust:

Children, especially girls, who witness their mother's rights being ignored, her suffering trivialised, and her abusers remain unpunished, internalize a deep *mistrust of the formal justice system* (Equality Now, 2020). This exposure normalizes patriarchal authority and the community's acceptance of gender-based violence, making daughters less likely to seek legal protection when they themselves face abuse later in life (UNFPA, 2010).

7. CONCLUSION AND RECOMMENDATIONS

"As one community stakeholder in Damoh observed during our consultations, *'The law stays in the books at the Thana (police station), but our lives are decided in the courtyard of the Panchayat.'* This simple statement captures the essence of the 'legal vacuum' explored in this chapter. It reminds us that for the women of Sagar and Damoh, justice is not a matter of constitutional theory, but a daily negotiation with traditions that often view their autonomy as a threat to community stability. The data presented in these pages—from the systemic exploitation of the Bedia community to the informal exclusion of women from *Wirasat* (inheritance)—reveals a landscape where the state's 'institutional deference' acts as a silent endorsement of customary injustice."

7.1. Summary of Findings: The Systemic Failure to Bridge the Law–Custom Divide

The case of the Bedia tribes in Sagar and Damoh districts highlights a persistent gap between formal legal protections and entrenched customary practices. Despite constitutional guarantees of equality (Articles 14, 15, and 21) and progressive laws such as the *Hindu Succession (Amendment) Act, 2005*, the *Protection of Women from Domestic Violence Act, 2005*, and the *Bharatiya Nyaya Sanhita* (BNS) and *Bharatiya Nagarik Suraksha Sanhita* (BNSS) of 2023, the everyday realities of tribal and denotified women remain largely excluded from these frameworks (Das & Lakshmana, 2020).

Customary systems—dominated by panchayats and patriarchal elders—function as parallel justice mechanisms, perpetuating practices like *wirasat* (patrilineal inheritance), *Chhorna/Chuttachar* (informal divorce), and *Nata Pratha* (informal cohabitation), which deny women legal and economic rights. Most alarming is the *institutionalized forced prostitution* among Bedia women, socially legitimized as a "customary livelihood." Despite relevant BNS provisions against trafficking and sexual exploitation (Sections 63–76, 67–72), law enforcement often remains ineffective due to cultural acceptance and administrative inertia (India Today, 2013; The New Indian Express, 2017).

This persistent 'legal vacuum', however, is increasingly being challenged by modern socio-economic shifts and civil society interventions. Recent field observations indicate that young Bedia women are beginning to utilize alternative livelihood pathways facilitated by NGOs like Samvedna and Action-Aid India, moving away from the *Khandani Pesha* through vocational training and higher education. Furthermore, the introduction of Mahila Desks and gender-sensitive policing has shown localized success in breaking the 'culture of silence,' allowing some women to leverage the threat of formal criminal action under the BNS to negotiate better settlements within their customary councils. These instances of successful 'rights-based mediation' demonstrate that when formal law is made accessible through community intermediaries, it can effectively bridge the reality gap and transform the status of women from 'vulnerable subjects' to 'rights-bearing citizens'. This shift necessitates a re-evaluation of current policy frameworks to ensure these localized successes are scaled into sustainable institutional changes (Anuja, 2022).

7.2. Policy and Legal Recommendations

To address this persistent disjunction between *law and custom*, an integrated strategy combining *legal reform, institutional accountability, and community participation* is essential.

7.2.1. Strengthening Legal Awareness and Access:

7.2.1.1. Legal Aid and Outreach:

The Madhya Pradesh State Legal Services Authority (MPSLSA) should conduct targeted legal literacy campaigns under the Legal Services Authorities Act, 1987, focusing on tribal and denotified communities in Sagar and Damoh. Periodic camps with para-legal volunteers and women police officers can raise awareness about rights under the BNS and BNSS, especially regarding maintenance (Section 144 BNSS), domestic violence, and sexual offences (National Legal Services Authority, 2023).

7.2.1.2. Mobile Legal Clinics:

Establish mobile legal aid vans in collaboration with NGOs such as *Samvedna* and *ActionAid India* to provide on-ground legal counselling for women in vulnerable communities (The Better India, 2015).

7.2.2. Institutional Reforms and Procedural Safeguards

7.2.2. Mandatory Registration of Customary Divorces and Marriages:

Amend state-level registration rules to make it compulsory for all customary marriages and divorces to be registered with local authorities, ensuring documentation and access to maintenance and inheritance rights.

7.2.3. Community-Level Vigilance Committees:

Under the supervision of the *District Collector*, such committees should include women representatives and social workers to monitor instances of trafficking, coercion, or customary exploitation in the name of tradition.

7.2.4. Special Monitoring Cells:

The *Women and Child Development Department* should constitute special monitoring cells at the block level to track violations of women's rights in tribal regions and coordinate with police and social welfare officers.

7.3. Criminal Justice Enforcement

7.3.1. Effective Application of BNS Provisions:

Police and magistrates must be trained to apply the BNS sections on sexual exploitation, trafficking, and unlawful compulsion in contexts of customary coercion.

For example: *Section 63 BNS* (sexual intercourse by deceitful means), *Section 70 BNS* (human trafficking), *Section 73 BNS* (exploitation of trafficked persons), and *Section 144 BNSS* (maintenance obligations). Sensitisation must emphasize that "custom" cannot justify an offence under national law.

7.3.2. Gender-Sensitive Policing:

Local police stations should deploy *Mahila Desks* with trained women officers to handle complaints of domestic abuse, sexual exploitation, and coercive customs with confidentiality and empathy (Ministry of Home Affairs, 2024).

7.3. Recommendations for Civil Society and Community Engagement

Civil society plays a pivotal role in bridging the normative gap between *state law and community practice*. In the case of the Bedia tribe, social transformation requires sustained dialogue and alternatives to exploitative customs.

7.3.1. Community-Based Sensitisation:

Conduct *awareness workshops* within Bedia settlements focusing on women's rights, education, and the illegality of coercive customs. Promote *gender sensitisation programs* in schools and local institutions to reshape perceptions of women's roles beyond traditional confines.

7.3.2. Economic Empowerment and Rehabilitation

7.3.2.1. Alternative Livelihood Programs:

Collaborate with the *National Rural Livelihood Mission (NRLM)* and *Madhya Pradesh State Skill Development Mission (MPSSDM)* to create vocational and microfinance initiatives for Bedia women, helping them transition away from the hereditary sex trade (NRLM, 2023).

7.3.2.2. Rehabilitation and Education of Children:

Ensure that daughters of Bedia women are enrolled in residential schools under *Beti Bachao, Beti Padhao* and *Kasturba Gandhi Balika Vidyalaya* schemes to break the cycle of forced prostitution (Ministry of Women and Child Development, 2023).

7.3.3. Collaborative Governance

7.3.3.1. Encourage *partnerships between district administrations, NGOs, and academic institutions* for continuous documentation, research, and monitoring of gender justice in tribal regions.

7.3.3.2. Establish *Community Women's Collectives* within Bedia settlements to represent women's voices in panchayat meetings, land disputes, and welfare claims.

7.4. Concluding Observation

The study concludes that *customary law must not be allowed to operate as an instrument of oppression.* The challenge lies not merely in legal reform but in reimagining justice as a lived reality for tribal and denotified women. Bridging the law–custom divide demands more than the presence of statutes—it requires *cultural engagement, institutional accountability, and empowerment of women as rights-bearing citizens.*

Only when state machinery, community leaders, and civil society act in concert can the "legal vacuum" be filled, transforming the lived experience of women in Sagar and Damoh from one of inherited vulnerability to one of dignity and autonomy.

Ultimately, the resolution of the legal vacuum in Central India is not merely a local administrative challenge; it is a test of India's commitment to international human rights standards. The systematic failure to protect Bedia and tribal women from customary exploitation stands in direct tension with the principles of the *Convention on the Elimination of All Forms of Discrimination Against Women (CEDAW)* and the *International Covenant on Civil and Political Rights (ICCPR),* to which India is a signatory.

True progress requires moving beyond 'doctrinal hope' to 'institutional accountability.' By aligning local governance with these global benchmarks for dignity and equality, the state can ensure that the women of Sagar and Damoh are no longer forced to choose between their community identity and their fundamental rights. The goal is a future where the 'legal vacuum' is filled not by the weight of oppressive custom, but by the robust presence of a gender-just constitution."

REFERENCES

Bhatia, R. (2020). Empowering tribal women through PESA in Bastar. International Journal of Novel Research and Development. https://ijnrd.org/papers/IJNRD2509132.pdf

Agnes, F. (2012). *Law, Justice and Gender: Family Law and Constitutional Provisions in India.* Oxford University Press. DOI: 10.1093/acprof:oso/9780198072201.003.0005

Agnes, F. (2012). *Law, Justice and Gender: Family Law and Constitutional Provisions in India. Oxford University Press; Rao, A. (2021). Custom, Gender, and the Politics of Legal Pluralism in South Asia.* Cambridge University Press. DOI: 10.1093/acprof:oso/9780198072201.003.0005

Anuja, A. (2022). "Stigma, Sex Work and State: A Study of Bedia Community in India." Journal of Exclusion Studies.

Bhat, B. A. (2022). *The intergenerational effects of marital transfers: Evidence from India.* Indian Statistical Institute.

Bhattacharyya, D. (2019). *Empire and ecology in the Bengal Delta: The making of Calcutta.* Cambridge University Press.

Census of India. (2011). Present and predicted literacy rate in Madhya Pradesh. Government of Madhya Pradesh. http://www.lbp.world/UploadedData/4860.pdf

Chakraborty, S. (2019). Cultural hegemony and victimisation of Bedia women in Central India. Academia.edu. https://www.academia.edu/90728622/Cultural_Hegemony_and_Victimisation_of_Bedia_Women_in_Central_India

Chakraborty, S. (2019). Cultural hegemony and victimisation of Bedia women in Central India. Academia.edu. https://www.academia.edu/90728622

Upadhyay, R. (2021). Decentralization without democratization in tribal governance. Drishti IAS. https://www.drishtiias.com/daily-news-analysis/panchayat-extension-to-scheduled-areas-pesa-act-1996

Chauhan, S. P., & Deshta, S. (2024). Access to justice: The role of panchayat facilitated mediation in resolution of disputes. Paripex - Indian Journal of Research, 13(4), 1–4.

Chiongson, R. A., Desai, D., Marchiori, T., & Woolcock, M. (2011). *Role of law and justice in achieving gender equality. Background paper prepared for the World Bank World Development Report 2012 "Gender Equality and Development.".* The World Bank.

Choudhury, N. (2019). *Women and the Weight of Legal Pluralism in India: Gendered law and Cultural Identity*. Routledge.

Dalla, R. L. (2022). A life-course perspective of sex trafficking among the Bedia of rural Madhya Pradesh, India. *Advances in Life Course Research, 54*, 100517. DOI: 10.1016/j.alcr.2022.100517 PMID: 36651617

Dalla, R. L., Kreimer, R., & Cole, A. (2022). A life-course perspective of sex trafficking among the Bedia caste of northern Central India. *Advances in Child Development and Behavior, 63*, 107–135.

Das, A., & Lakshmana, C. M. (2020). The implementation of domestic violence act in India: A state-level analysis. *International Journal of Social Science and Economic Research, 5*(4), 1234–1245. https://www.isec.ac.in/wp-content/uploads/2023/07/WP-499-Anamika-Das-and-C-M-Lakshmana-Final.pdf

Desai, M. (2021). *The Limits of Law: Social Reform and the Politics of Gender Justice in India*. Routledge.

Deshpande, A. (2022, November 13). A patriarchal protocol: Judicial stereotyping of survivors of gender-based violence in India. *The Fletcher Forum*.

Garg, R. K. (2022). Cultural Relativism via-a-vis Woman's Human Rights in India: Legal and Constitutional Perspective. Part 1 Indian J. *Integrated Rsch. L., 2*, 1.

Ghosh, P. (2014). Restorative justice: The new paradigm in the province of justice in India? *SSRN, 1*(4), 88–96. DOI: 10.2139/ssrn.2467373

India, U. N. F. P. A. (n.d.). Advancing the Rights of Women and Girls Panchayats Leading the Way. Retrieved October 26, 2025, from https://india.unfpa.org/sites/default/files/pub-pdf/unfpa_compendium_panchayat_mopr.pdf

India Development Review. (2025, September 3). Indian agriculture can't thrive without women farmers. https://idronline.org/article/agriculture/indian-agriculture-cant-thrive-without-women-farmers/

Jhaveri, D. (2024). "Empowering Tribal Women: A comprehensive exploration of rights, challenges and the way forward." Journal of Political Science. Empowering Tribal Women: A comprehensive exploration of their roles and participation in local government

Kanta, C., & Sharma, A.K. (2025). "Analyzing the Impact of Legal Reforms and Cultural Barriers in Rural Rajasthan." The Academic, Volume 3, Issue 4

Kapur, R. (2012). Gender, alterity and human rights: Freedom in a fishbowl. *Economic and Political Weekly, 47*(39), 67–75.

Kaushal, A., & Sharma, R. (2024). Law and gender inequality in India: A socio legal perspective. *International Journal of Law Management and Humanities*, *7*(6), 118–136. https://doij.org/10.10000/IJLMH.118461

Madhya Pradesh State Legal Services Authority. (2025). Providing legal aid and support for women victims of domestic violence in Madhya Pradesh. Retrieved from https://www.mpslsa.gov.in

Menski, W. (2003). *Hindu law: Beyond tradition and modernity*. Oxford University Press.

Merry, S. E. (1988). Legal Pluralism. *Law & Society Review*, *22*(5), 869–896. DOI: 10.2307/3053638

Merry, S. E. (2006). *Human rights & gender violence: Translating international law into local justice*. University of Chicago Press.

Ministry of Home Affairs. (2024). *Guidelines on Women's Safety and Gender-Sensitive Policing*. Government of India.

Ministry of Women and Child Development. (2023). *Beti Bachao, Beti Padhao Scheme: Annual report 2022–23*. Government of India.

Mookerji, N. (2011). "Women Empowerment and Panchayati Raj in Bundelkhand. Women Empowerment and Panchayati Raj in Bundelkhand | PDF | Empowerment | Society

National Legal Services Authority. (2023). *Legal Services to Women: Outreach and Awareness Initiatives*. NALSA.

National Rural Livelihood Mission. (2023). *Empowering rural women through livelihoods: Annual progress report 2022–23*. Government of India.

Now, E. (2020). Justice denied: Sexual violence & intersectional discrimination – Barriers to accessing justice for Dalit women and girls in Haryana, India. Retrieved from https://equalitynow.org/news/press-releases/india_caste_system_preventing_justice_nov2020/

Panday, P., Khan, R., & Singh, A. K. (2018). Consequences of violence against women on their health and well-being: An overview. *Journal of Medical Science and Clinical Research*, *6*(10), 570–577.

Parashar, A. (1992). *Women and Family Law Reform in India: Uniform Civil code and Gender Equality*. Sage Publications.

Pathak, V. (2015). FRA implementation challenges for tribal women. Tribal Affairs Ministry reports; Krishnan, S. (2019). Forest rights and gender justice in tribal India. Open access tribal.nic.in repository.

Rana, U. (2020). Cultural hegemony and victimisation of Bedia women in Central India (U. Rana, Trans.). *Space and Culture, India*, *8*(2), 96–105. DOI: 10.20896/saci.vi0.798

Rao, N. S. (2017). Interface of tribal self-governance institutions and statutory panchayats: A study in the Scheduled Areas of Andhra Pradesh. National Institute of Rural Development & Panchayati Raj. http://nirdpr.org.in/nird_docs/srsc/srsc230217-19.pdf

Sarin, M. (2020). Customary Practices and Women's Property Rights in India: A Regional Perspective. *Indiana Law Review*, *4*(2), 145–168. DOI: 10.1080/24730580.2020.1715749

Shachar, A. (2001). *Multicultural jurisdictions: Cultural differences and women's rights*. Cambridge University Press. DOI: 10.1017/CBO9780511490330

Sharma, K. (2018). PESA and women's participation gaps. Vishnu IAS Academy analysis.

Shayara Bano v. Union of India, (2017) 9 SCC 1 (SC)

Shukla, S., & Bhat, A. (2022). Legal awareness and utilization of empowerment services among rural women: A study from Dharwad district. *International Journal of Food and Agricultural Nutrition Sciences*, *5*(2), 45–55. https://ijfans.org/uploads/paper/5646f9187d3fba14c24e15834e01dcf5.pdf

Sidhu Kundal, N. (2023). Land rights of tribal women in India. *International Journal for Multidisciplinary Research*, *5*(6), 1–15. https://www.ijfmr.com/papers/2023/6/9351.pdf

Singh, D. (2024). Challenges women face in accessing justice in India. *International Journal of Research Publication and Reviews*, *5*(11), 6032–6037.

Singh, R. (2025). Customary law vs state law in tribal jurisprudence – Harmony or conflict. International Journal of Law and Legal Research. https://www.ijllr.com/post/customary-law-vs-state-law-in-tribal-jurisprudence-harmony-or-conflict

Steinert, J. I., Valli, E., Chan, J. K., & Brahmbhatt, H. (2023). Evidence from focus group discussions on economic abuse against women in India. *BMJ Global Health*, *8*(10), e012576. https://gh.bmj.com/content/8/10/e012576. DOI: 10.1136/bmjgh-2023-012576 PMID: 37798047

Supreme Court of India. (2006). Lata Singh v. State of Uttar Pradesh, (2006) 5 SCC 475.

The Better India. (2015, June 12). The Bedia Community Prostitutes its girls. An NGO, Samvedna, is changing that. Retrieved from https://www.thebetterindia.com/

The New Indian Express. (2017, August 29). Madhya Pradesh woman fights to protect daughters from forced prostitution. Retrieved from https://www.newindianexpress .com/

Tschalaer, M. (2009). Women entering the legal landscape: Negotiating legal gender reforms in a 'tribal' women's forum. Commission on Legal Pluralism. https://clp .thebestwebshop.org/system/commission-on-legal-pluralism/volumes/60/tschalaer -art.pdf

Tyagi, K. (2024). Gender bias in the criminal justice system: Analyzing the treatment of female offenders in India. *International Journal of Finance and Management Research*, *6*(6), 1–12. https://www.ijfmr.com/papers/2024/6/31306.pdf

UNFPA. (2010). Violence against women in India. Retrieved from https://india .unfpa.org/sites/default/files/pub-pdf/435.pdf

United Nations. (1966). International Covenant on Civil and Political Rights. Treaty Series, 999 U.N.T.S. 171.

United Nations. (1979). Convention on the Elimination of all forms of Discrimination Against Women. Treaty Series, 1249 U.N.T.S. 13.

Vashishth, K. (2024). Khap Panchayat system in India – A detailed analysis. *Indian Journal of Integrated Research in Law*, *IV*(III), 494–500. https://ijirl.com/wp -content/uploads/2024/05/KHAP-PANCHAYAT-SYSTEM-IN-INDIA-%E2%80 %93-A-DETAILED-ANALYSIS.pdf

Vineeta Sharma v. Rakesh Sharma, (2020) 9 SCC 1 (SC)

Vishaka v. State of Rajasthan, (1997) 6 SCC 241 (SC).

ENDNOTES

1 The Constitution of India, art. 14 (1950)

2 The Constitution of India, art. 15 (1950)

3 The Constitution of India, art. 21 (1950)

4 Shayara Bano v. Union of India, (2017) 9 SCC 1 (SC)

5 Vineeta Sharma v. Rakesh Sharma, (2020) 9 SCC 1 (SC)

6 Sidhu Kundal, N. (2023). Land rights of tribal women in India. *International Journal for Multidisciplinary Research, 5*(6), 1–15. https://www.ijfmr.com/papers/2023/6/9351.pdf

7 See Note ix.

8 Vishaka v. State of Rajasthan, (1997) 6 SCC 241 (SC).

9 See note v.

10 Supreme Court of India. (2006). *Lata Singh v. State of Uttar Pradesh*, (2006) 5 SCC 475.

11 See note xi.

12 Shayara Bano v. Union of India, (2017) 9 SCC 1 (India)

13 Vineeta Sharma v. Rakesh Sharma, (2020) 9 SCC 461 (India)

Chapter 10
Breaking the Cycle of Child Labor in Dehradun: A Multidimensional Study on Causes and Challenges

S. Srinivasan
http://orcid.org/0009-0002-0179-9849
Department of Humanities and Social Sciences, Graphic Era University, Dehradun, India

Tushar Bhatia
http://orcid.org/0009-0000-7532-0488
Political Sciences, Department of Humanities and Social Sciences, Graphic Era University, Dehradun, India

Jipson Joseph
http://orcid.org/0009-0005-1795-5051
School of Law, Christ University, Banglore, India

R. N. Ravikumar
http://orcid.org/0009-0009-3705-1681
Department of Computer Engineering, Marwadi University, Rajkot, India

ABSTRACT

Child labor remains a critical issue, particularly in developing nations like India, where millions of children are deprived of their right to education and safe childhood due to poverty, marginalization, and inadequate policy implementation. This study explores the underlying causes, occupational patterns, and harmful consequences of child labor in Dehradun, Uttarakhand. It highlights that children are primarily engaged in agriculture, domestic work, and small industries, often facing physical

DOI: 10.4018/979-8-3373-5841-3.ch010

and mental exploitation. Despite existing legal frameworks and initiatives like the Child Labor (Prohibition and Regulation) Act and National Child Labor Projects, enforcement challenges persist. The study uses cross-sectional and triangulation methods to analyze data from 42 child laborers and suggests a holistic approach, including poverty alleviation, quality education, community empowerment, and rehabilitation services, as key to combating child labor. It emphasizes the need for multi-stakeholder participation to ensure child rights and reduce labor dependency among vulnerable families.

INTRODUCTION

Child labor is the exploitation of children's childhood through work that exceeds their potential, dignity, and affects them physically, mentally, socially, and morally. Such exploitation is prohibited by laws worldwide. According to the International Labor Organization report, approximately 138 million children were engaged in labor in the year 2024 (Mohammadi et al., 2024). However, as per the International Labor Organization and the United Nations International Children's Emergency Fund, out of the 138 million, around 54 million are working in hazardous sites, which seriously impact their health, mental well-being, and safety. According to recent data from both UN agencies, agriculture remains the largest sector for child labor (61%), followed by services such as markets and domestic work (27%), and the manufacturing and mining industries (13%) (Safdar & Kataria, 2024).

The latest records demonstrate a reduction of over 22 million in child labor since 2020. This shows a positive trend, and the majority of poor and developing countries have framed policies to reduce child labor. Notwithstanding, a large number of children are still forced to engage in labor in poor countries at present, in 2025 (Sebates-Wheeler & Sumberg, 2022). As far as data from different continents is concerned, the child labor rate in Asia and Pacific countries has dropped from 5.6% to 3.1% since 2020 to the present year. Likewise, Latin American and Caribbean countries achieved a reduction rate from 11% to 8%, as per world organizations UNICEF and ILO. But child labor has continued to increase in Sub-Saharan African countries due to poverty and increasing population (Gebregziabher et al., 2023). Every two-thirds of all children are involved in the labor market—around 87 million. Despite all this, UNICEF reiterated that "Boys and girls are equally likely to be involved in child labor, but in different responsibilities and roles (Hoque, 2023).

Poverty, discrimination, marginalization, and children born into vulnerable societies are the main drivers of child labor. According to the government, India has been taking various proactive policies to eliminate child labor. But education is a proven strategy for reducing child labor (Nayar et al., 2014). Lack of access to education keeps the cycle of illiteracy, exploitation, and poverty going in the future. The family members of the children depend upon child labor for the family's livelihood. The family's earnings and savings are spent only on food security throughout their lives. Due to this, the economic conditions of child labor families are unable to be upgraded for the upcoming generation (Chukwudeh & Oduaran, 2021). On the other hand, girls are also engaged in labor, but inside the home, doing domestic work without pay. In addition to this, however, children drop out of school during early primary education and after the completion of primary education. According to Child Rights and You (CRY), early marriages, inadequate school facilities, gender disparities, lack of parental involvement, and improper guidance and counselling are contributing factors (Udoh, 2024). The government recently amended the law to introduce a balance between the need for education and employment without exploitation. Further, Indian laws have abolished the employment of adolescents below the age of 14 years in any hazardous industry. But the improper implementation of policies remains a significant issue for the Indian political system and higher executive authorities (Ahmad, 2011).

Child Labour

Child labour involves children in work that harms their physical, mental, and social development and interferes with their education. It often leads to irregular school attendance or early dropout and is mainly concentrated in informal sectors such as agriculture, domestic work, construction, and small-scale industries, especially in developing countries.

Poverty

Poverty is a major cause of child labour, as low household income, unemployment, debt, and lack of social protection force families to rely on children's earnings. It also restricts access to education, creating an intergenerational cycle of deprivation.

Education

Education is a key factor in preventing child labour by improving skills and future employment prospects. However, high costs, poor infrastructure, distance to schools, and low perceived returns discourage school participation, increasing children's vulnerability to labour.

CONSTITUTIONAL AND LEGAL SAFEGUARDS AGAINST CHILD LABOUR

The Supreme Courts have an effective way to protect children and must provide proper education. It is a fundamental right to increase the holistic development of society. Child labour is one of the major worldwide challenges. To eliminate child labor, the state government must take responsibility and implement policies with effective utilization.

As per the Indian Constitution, Article 24 prohibits the employment of children under 14 years in hazardous work. The article clearly illustrates Article 21A; it provides guarantees of free and compulsory education for children in the age group between 6 and 14 years. Article 39 explains further mandates for the State to protect children from exploitation. The Child and Adolescent Labour (Prohibition and Regulation) Act, 1986, prohibits child labour. This might restrict children and youth from hazardous work at worksites; violations can result in penalties. The enforcement mechanisms mention the use of standard operating procedures by the Ministry of Labour and Employment and the use of the PENCIL online complaint platform. The lower number of cases registered under this Act highlights the need for stronger measures and may increase proactive enforcement of the law.

Local-Level Implementation of Child Labour Laws

The elimination of child labour depends on the effectiveness of the government and its implementation by the local administration team. Especially at the district level, to enforce the laws and monitor compliance to provide rehabilitation services for education and social welfare schemes. The district-level child protection officers and labour inspectors must ensure and inspect all the workplaces. To identify the various violations and take legal action, particularly for the informal sector. The Child Welfare Committees (CWCs) ensure the protection of children and rehabilitation services. To provide various services such as counselling, education, and family reintegration support services. The effective implementation of the law and enforcement provides strong coordination among local and district authorities. To involve various stakeholders such as NGOs, the police department, and local communities, involvement is necessary.

Rehabilitation and Reintegration of Rescued Child Laborers

Rehabilitation and reintegration provide a better way to eliminate child labor. It is effective implementation for rehabilitation to provide immediate care and support, counseling services, educational support, and skill training. Find out school dropout children for enrolment in schools, along with remedial support and various life skills training for the children. The training must prevent re-entry into the workplace in child labour.

Influence of Migration and Urbanisation on Child Labour in Dehradun

Migration and rapid urbanisation contribute significantly to child labour in Dehradun. Seasonal migration from rural and hill regions exposes children to informal work due to poor housing, limited schooling access, and weak social support. Urban labour demand further increases vulnerability, highlighting the need for migrant-inclusive education, social protection, and coordinated local governance.

Child labour in the informal sector is a serious concern due to weak regulation and limited legal oversight. Children are engaged in domestic work, agriculture, street vending, construction, and small family enterprises, often in unsafe and unmonitored conditions. This exposes them to exploitation, long working hours, and low or unpaid wages. The informal sector restricts access to education, healthcare, and social protection, reinforcing poverty and social exclusion. Weak law enforcement, poor employer accountability, and economic pressures on families sustain child labour. Effective prevention requires stronger legal enforcement, community monitoring, quality education, family livelihood support, and coordinated action by government agencies, NGOs, and local communities.

CHILD LABOUR IN INDIA: CONSTITUTIONAL PROVISIONS, LEGAL STATUTES, AND GOVERNMENT SCHEMES

Constitutional Provisions

The Indian Constitution provides a strong normative framework to protect children from economic exploitation and hazardous employment:

Article 21A: Guarantees the *Right to Free and Compulsory Education* for children aged 6–14 years, thereby directly discouraging child labour by mandating school attendance.

Article 23: Prohibits trafficking in human beings and forced labour, which includes bonded and exploitative child labour.

Article 24: Explicitly prohibits the employment of children below the age of 14 years in factories, mines, and other hazardous occupations.

Article 39(e) and 39(f) (Directive Principles of State Policy): Direct the State to ensure that children are not forced by economic necessity to enter vocations unsuited to their age and strength and that childhood is protected against exploitation and moral abandonment.

Article 45: Emphasizes early childhood care and education, strengthening the preventive approach against child labour.

Together, these provisions establish child protection as a constitutional obligation of the State.

Legal Statutes

India has enacted several laws to operationalize constitutional mandates against child labour:

Child and Adolescent Labour (Prohibition and Regulation) Act, 1986 (Amended in 2016)

I. Prohibits employment of children below 14 years in all occupations and processes.
II. Prohibits adolescents (14–18 years) from working in hazardous occupations.
III. Allows limited exceptions for family enterprises and artists under strict conditions.
IV. Introduces stricter penalties for employers violating child labour laws.

Juvenile Justice (Care and Protection of Children) Act, 2015

Criminalizes the employment of children in hazardous occupations, trafficking, and forced labour. Treats working children as *children in need of care and protection*, emphasizing rehabilitation over punishment.

Bonded Labour System (Abolition) Act, 1976

Abolishes bonded labour practices, a major contributor to child labour in informal sectors.

- *Right of Children to Free and Compulsory Education (RTE) Act, 2009*
    - o Makes education a legal entitlement and places responsibility on the State to ensure school enrolment and retention.
- *Factories Act, 1948 and Mines Act, 1952*
    - o Restrict and regulate the employment of children and adolescents in industrial and mining sectors.

Government Schemes and Policy Interventions

The Government of India has implemented multiple schemes to prevent child labour and promote rehabilitation:

National Child Labour Project (NCLP) Scheme

A. Focuses on the identification, rescue, and rehabilitation of child labourers.
B. Provides special training centres, bridge education, vocational training, mid-day meals, and stipends.
C. Facilitates mainstreaming of rescued children into formal education.

Samagra Shiksha Abhiyan

Integrates child labour prevention through universal access, retention, and quality education. Supports children from vulnerable and migrant families.

Integrated Child Protection Scheme (ICPS) / Mission Vatsalya

Strengthens child protection systems at district and state levels. Supports Child Welfare Committees (CWCs), shelter homes, and rehabilitation services.

PENCIL Portal (Platform for Effective Enforcement for No Child Labour)

A digital platform for reporting, monitoring, and coordinating child labour rescue and rehabilitation.

Mid-Day Meal Scheme (PM POSHAN)

Improves school attendance and retention, indirectly reducing child labour driven by poverty.

RELATIONSHIP BETWEEN SOCIO-ECONOMIC FACTORS AND CHILD LABOUR

Socio-economic factors are central to the persistence of child labour. Poverty is the primary driver, as households with low and unstable incomes often depend on children's earnings for survival. Parental education and occupation also influence child labour, with children from poorly educated parents engaged in informal or low-paid work being more vulnerable to labour participation. Large family size and high dependency ratios further increase economic pressure and limit educational investment. Limited access to quality education strengthens this link. School-related costs, poor learning outcomes, migration, and insecure living conditions contribute to dropout and irregular attendance, pushing children into work. Social norms and community acceptance, especially in informal and family-based occupations, normalize child labour, while gender roles shape its visibility—boys in wage labour and girls in unpaid domestic work.

Research Objectives

1. To understand the demographic details of the children.
2. To identify the core reasons for children dropping out of school.
3. To find out the current occupation of the children.
4. To assess workplace violations experienced by children while laboring.
5. To examine government policies at the union, state, and local levels for the protection of child rights.

Research Questions

1. What are the family background conditions of the children?
2. What are the socio-economic conditions of the children?
3. What are the primary reasons for children dropping out of school?
4. How does poverty impact children's access to education and their likelihood of engaging in child labor?
5. In which occupational sectors are children laboring?
6. What is the range of challenges faced by children while laboring at occupational sites?
7. How do workplace conditions affect the physical and mental health of child laborers?
8. Are child laborers provided with adequate safety equipment and training?
9. How do the three-dimensional government policies at the union, state, and local levels benefit children?
10. How are governments policies executed to provide benefits that prevent children from engaging in labor?

Background of the study

The early historical study of child labor focused more on the socio-economic and cultural conditions of families whose children were laboring under the proletariat class or industrial class. This has happened due to poverty, vulnerable families, and disadvantaged sections of society running their livelihood through labor. Moreover, the background study is limited to geographical areas where poverty, discrimination, and marginalization are at a high level (Sohel et al., 2024). Also, the study examines the various sectors where children are employed. These kinds of studies did not provide a holistic understanding of the deep-rooted causes of increasing child labor, even though strict Indian laws prohibit it. Now, the focus of the study has shifted towards human rights and child rights concerns (Ali et al., 2017).

India has a federal form of government, and labor laws come under the Concurrent List, where both the Union and State governments have the power to make laws. The various past laws are: the Factories Act, 1948; the Mines Act, 1952; the Child Labor (Prohibition and Regulation) Act, 1986; and the Right of Children to Free and Compulsory Education Act, 2009 (Dasgupta, 2018). Besides this, various government projects, schemes, and programs have been initiated to eliminate child labor in India, supported by NGOs, societal awareness, and the involvement of professional faculties and lawyers to raise awareness among civil societies. Since 1988, the Ministry of Labor and Employment has implemented 100 industry-specific National Child Labor Projects to rehabilitate child workers (Milczarek-Desai, 2024).

Additionally, the Child Labor (Prohibition and Regulation) Amendment Act, 2016 completely banned child labor and introduced initiatives involving vocational training, mid-day meals, special schools for recently rehabilitated children, and poverty alleviation programs (Roberts, 2015). The various social schemes are: the National Family Benefit Scheme, Janani Suraksha Yojana, and Jan Dhan Yojana, which provide indirect benefits to poor families and ultimately encourage children to join or rejoin school (Pradhan et al., 2024).

LITERATURE REVIEW

Although India has many legal laws that prohibit child labor, enforcement still remains a challenge for the government despite legal frameworks such as the Child Labor (Prohibition and Regulation) Act. As many children continue to work in industrial and hazardous conditions, there are many Indian states such as Uttar Pradesh, Bihar, Madhya Pradesh, Andhra Pradesh, and Odisha where child labor is highly prevalent in various sectors like agriculture, services, and the manufacturing industry (Miller & Bush, 2004). However, several NGOs, non-state actors, and institutional studies suggest that awareness and interventions are required to improve access to education and provide economic support to families. In fact, during the COVID pandemic, the child labor problem increased as family members became jobless. Over the last two decades, India has articulated its commitment to addressing child labor through numerous policies like the Right of Children to Free and Compulsory Education Act, 2009 (Abdullah et al., 2022).

All children between 6–14 years receive free education. After that, the Child Labor (Prohibition and Regulation) Amendment Act, 2016 prohibited the employment of children below 14 years, and the National Education Policy, 2020 advocated for universal access to quality early childhood care and education, as well as equitable and inclusive education for all (Hamenoo et al., 2018). Related to the educational system, psychological evidence shows that participation in life skills education programs reduces school discontinuation among children. As poverty and illiteracy are the main drivers of child labor, in the case of India, child labor may be difficult to abolish; however, exploitation can be prevented through the combined efforts of the government, non-government organizations, civil societies, public-private partnerships, and professional bodies (Sasmal & Guillen, 2015).

However, in India, numerous forms of deprivation exist against children while laboring. Even experts and child-care specialists refer to it as Modern Slavery, which includes the recruitment and exchange of children for labor in informal industrial sectors, as well as their harboring and movement through the use of force, coercion, abuse, and deception (Thévenon & Edmonds, 2019). Even this modern slavery has expanded its form to include sexual abuse, domestic servitude, harassment, torture, forced marriage, and blackmail. Many times, even after completing their regular working hours, children continue laboring extra hours without any pay (Wood, 2020). UNICEF has standardized the working hours of children at the global level based on age, type of work, hours of work, and working conditions, as follows:

Age 5–11 years – At least 1 hour of economic work or 21 hours of unpaid household services per week.
Age 12–14 years – At least 14 hours of economic work or 21 hours of unpaid household services per week.
Age 15–17 years – At least 43 hours of economic work or unpaid domestic services per week.

Different kinds of exploitation occur in different working patterns. Like in India, the agriculture sector employs the largest number of children as laborers for farming and agriculture-related activities with their family members, but they face work-related hazards which affect their health (Moayad et al., 2021). In construction sites, children are employed at different locations based on requirements, exchange of children, extra working hours, and migration. Hence, there is no permanent laboring zone for children, which impacts their health (Kadir et al., 2019). In small industries within the urban sector, skilled child laborers are exploited by owners through low wages, no fixed working hours, no pay for extra working hours, and lack of safety equipment. Therefore, exploitation occurs in the form of health issues, mental stress and weakness, inadequate earnings, and no festival holidays (Řimnáčová & Kajanová, 2019).

Child Labour: An Overview

Lack of education and poverty are the significant causes that force families to make their children work for livelihood purposes. Due to this, most of the children dropped out before or during primary school (Hasan & Chaitee, 2022). However, at the global level, many countries have their own laws to promote education and eliminate child labor. Especially in developing countries, child labor has been a serious issue (Radfar et al., 2018). Additionally, millions of children have always been working in hazardous conditions, which impact their health. As per the International Labor Organization, it is estimated that over 130 million children between the ages of five and fourteen work twelve hours a day. In the case of India, the estimated number of child laborers is around 70–80 million at present (Scott & Pocock, 2021). Moreover, in rural India, almost 80% of child laborers are engaged in the agricultural sector, while the remaining 20% work in urban areas across different sectors such as domestic work, workshops, small-scale industries, hotels, restaurants, gig industries, and numerous informal industries. Besides these, child labor is also found in hazardous industries in developing states, such as tea plantations in West Bengal and Assam, carpet weaving and the sports industry in Uttar Pradesh, employment in fireworks in Tamil Nadu, and diamond cutting in Gujarat (Sharma, 2009; Tandon et al., 2022).

Furthermore, most child labor emerges from those states where the middle class is not in the majority. It means the existence of upper and lower class divisions has promoted poverty among the working class. As a result, lower-class families are forced to make their children work for survival and livelihood (Bourdilon, 2018). Through this, the lower class migrated to other states to earn more to meet its basic requirements for the family. Therefore, all family members become breadwinners in different ways according to their gender, age, and health. As a result, children from poor and vulnerable communities never attend school or mostly drop out after completing primary education. If this continues for the long term, the situation will become worse due to persistent poverty and lack of education (Borrell et al., 2008; Kim, 2019).

In such cases, international agencies like the International Labor Organization (ILO) and the United Nations International Children's Emergency Fund (UNICEF) have taken milestone steps toward the elimination of child labor at the global level. In 1992, both organizations launched the International Programme on the Elimination of Child Labor (IPEC) to fight against child labor through awareness campaigns, promote education, encourage the direct involvement of communities to motivate children to attain higher education, and urge the government to formulate favorable policies for vulnerable children willing to attend educational institutions. Actually, all these policies and programs can be achieved through the role of multiple stakeholders, such as NGOs, trade unions, public-private partnerships, civil society, and individuals, coming together to contribute in terms of socio-economic support, psychological support, and the establishment of rehabilitation centers to encourage children to access education again.

It has also been argued that minor children engage in criminal activities due to inhumane and torturous treatment while employed in informal or unregistered industries. Indeed, juvenile illegal and criminal activities have increased nowadays. To address this, there are many child protection laws, but their practical execution is far from being half as effective as the legislation (Baidawi et al., 2020). Although the Indian Constitution clearly prohibits child labor below the age of fourteen in any dangerous, hazardous, or life-threatening activities, as stated in Article 24. Besides all these, under the Directive Principles of State Policy, Articles 39 and 47 focus on the protection and development of children in an inclusive manner (Bajpai, 2012). Above all, the 86th Amendment Act, 2002, included Article 21A of the Indian Constitution, which provides for free and compulsory elementary education for children between 6 and 14 years of age. But unfortunately, in a democratic country like developing India, child labor is officially recorded as having decreased compared to the 2011 child labor statistics. As per recent 2020 reports, it is mentioned that approximately 60 lakh children are engaged in child labor, but there are no records regarding informal sectors, such as the construction sector (Yadav, 2019; Das, 2022).

Nonetheless, various historical legislations such as the Mines Act, Factories Act, Minimum Wages Act, and the Child Labor (Prohibition and Regulation) Act exist. The implementation of all these parliamentary laws at the ground level has been unable to eliminate child labor. Even many times, official secretaries and policymakers reform laws, which demonstrate a lack of serious and in-depth study regarding child employment and its impact on family members (Khan et al., 2007). Ultimately, poverty alleviation programs and child development policies have not been compatible with empowering women, children, and deprived communities. However, there are many state administrative laws that do not comply with union laws; indicating that law-making and implementation at the grassroots level have not been successfully achieved. This is also the reason that child rights and protections still remain largely on paper (Liebel, 2012).

Notwithstanding, the Union government announced many centrally sponsored and central sector schemes for people coming from below the poverty line (BPL), but unfortunately, both the Union and state governments have not succeeded in increasing the number of children admitted to government educational institutions. Moreover, both the government and civil society have faced failure while trying to transform the mindset of poor families who deliberately drop their children out of education and force them into labor (Rathod & Koli 2015). Through this, illiteracy, unorthodox thinking, increased vulnerabilities, hunger, poverty, juvenile crime, and eventually an immoral civil society directly or indirectly perpetuate child labor. As an outcome, child discrimination, the digital divide between rural and urban areas, and the continuation of class divisions weaken society, and internal security becomes threatened due to clashes of civilizations in a multi-diverse society like India (Yousaf et al., 2025). Actually, children are easily controlled, inexpensive, and accept orders without complaining, performing extra work without demanding money. Therefore, most small enterprises and informal sector industries prefer child labor. As a result, children face exploitation, health impacts, loss of childhood, and separation from their families (Ilyas et al., 2020).

The United Nations reported that approximately 220 million children are still engaged in child labor. In the case of India, child labor has consistently reduced, but it may have increased in other sectors such as the gig industry, construction, and informal industries. As mentioned earlier, 5–6 million children are engaged in labor, which persistently indicates that socio-economic discrimination and inequalities are also increasing (Kumar & Srivastava, 2024). This highlights the urgent requirement for free and proper elementary education without prejudice, to strengthen policy-making and simultaneously implement strategic planning for better education and community awareness programs (Eden et al., 2024). Actually, if we understand the problem from a historical background, during the early 18th and 19th centuries, children were exploited due to the Industrial Revolution in European countries. During that time, the agricultural economic society was gradually depleted, and the vulnerable situation of poor families became even worse. Children from already poor families were forced to be employed in hazardous industries (Woolf, 2002).

After such events, during the period of the 1900s, one-fourth of children from poor families lost everything and died due to harmful diseases. All rights and liberties were in the hands of the land-owning class. Similarly, in the USA, over five million children were engaged in labor under dangerous conditions, such as glass factories, bangle industries, the beverage industry, and industries involving harmful chemicals and dyes (Saeed & Qureshi, 2024). During that period, similar conditions occurred all over the world due to colonial rule. Moreover, in the agricultural sector, the health of most children deteriorated due to exposure to dangerous fertilizers and chemicals while being employed to increase the production of pulses and wheat. This was dangerous for children's lungs and eyes because of their lack of skill (Roberts et al., 2012).

In such situations, children had no right to education because most poor families were engaged in bonded labor. Even in Asian and African countries under colonial rule, children, women, and poor families were forced to migrate to other countries as bonded laborers. Further, according to the International Labor Organization report, violations of child rights due to labor are not only outside the home. Even within the four walls, female child laborers face prejudice, discrimination, torture, hatred, and physical abuse (Parson, 2010). Indeed, in large landowner properties and households, female child laborers were treated as slaves, which is considered heinous domestic violence. If such situations continue for a long period, children themselves may turn to illegal activities and, in certain cases, may even join terrorist groups (Eteng & Nnam, 2022). Besides all this, while working, children face various challenges such as sexual exploitation and torture. Sometimes, elder laborers kidnap female child laborers, and ultimately, the family is forced to marry their daughter to the person who committed the assault (Huang, 2017).

In 1989, the United Nations Children's Fund (UNICEF) was the first global organization to sign the Convention on the Rights of the Child. After that, the situation changed worldwide, and parents began recognizing children's rights and liberties. For the first time ever, all countries, despite having different political ideologies, realized that children, irrespective of religion, race, caste, sex, or place of birth, have rights and liberties. As time passed, child labor changed its form, manifesting as torture in the context of drug trafficking, forced involvement in pornography, and human trafficking for the sale of child labor (Greenbaum, 2021).

Ethical aspects of Child Labor

From a moral and ethical viewpoint, freedom, justice, liberty, privacy, beneficence, equality, and rights—none of these characteristics are observed during child labor. Actually, parents manipulate children to work so that, through their earnings, elder children can meet the needs of younger siblings (Teixeira, 2024). If children initially agree to give consent to their parents for labor at an early age, after 4–5 years, they realize that exploitation began at an early stage. Indeed, after reaching 14–15 years of age, children are unable or unwilling to access education. The reason behind this lack of interest in studying is their focus on earning more through extra effort and time (Greenbaum, 2014). This is referred to as an ethical challenge for children, where they want to go to school but feel internally compelled to earn more. In such conditions, no one is left to provide support or proper counseling, so that he or she can make informed choices. Uneducated children are suggested to undergo skill-based manual training, while young child laborers are advised to return to school and complete at least upper primary education (Pirzada et al., 2020).

As time passed, many educationists and specialists observed that while children were engaged in labor, employers or head managers tried to exert hegemonic control by offering incentives, which ultimately led children to continue working for many years. In a general context, as in the case of India, migrated child laborers and their families work in different places across the country (McKinney, 2015). Ethical exploitation and domination also occur in such a way that basic facilities, rights, and liberties are not provided during working hours. The Union government's policies and schemes periodically provide labor codes and rights during working hours, but employers or managers do not implement these government provisions. Moreover, families and child laborers are often unaware of government schemes, policies, and codes for labor communities (Rioux et al., 2020).

Additionally, overpopulation and poverty are complementary to each other in promoting child labor. People who have been laboring since childhood are not interested in learning skill training after reaching adulthood, and moreover, family members pressure girls to marry. Through this, more burden falls upon males if a married female is underage; as a result, conflicts arise due to immaturity. Many times, female child laborers in households face challenges similar to those faced by males in outside labor (Makinde et al., 2021).

During female laboring in households, homeowners torture them in many ways, such as not giving monthly wages on time, assigning extra work, and making them spend unnecessary extra hours, and they face inhumane treatment like beating, verbal abuse, and sexual harassment (Fawole, 2008). Unfortunately, most girl child laborers are unable to share all these issues with their families due to owner intimidation. Besides this, sometimes females remain silent because of the greater responsibility to fulfill the requirements of their family livelihoods. At the international level, Asia has the highest child labor at over 61%, followed by Africa at 41% and Latin America at 17%. In the last ten years, child labor has reduced in India, but laboring practices are still ongoing in the informal and unorganized sectors (Webbink et al., 2012). The union government has been unable to cancel licenses in informal sectors where the majority of employees are children. It means the Indian government is only focused on increasing GDP through all sectors like IT, industrial, corporate, agriculture, livestock, textile, fishing, and SMEs, etc. But child labor in agriculture, industrial, SMEs, and informal sectors does not consider the vulnerable and deprived situations of children (Maksud et al., 2024).

Cultural aspects and the child labor

As in the case of cultural perspectives, it also contributes to the expansion and promotion of child labor in Asian countries like India. In India, the majority of the population, irrespective of religion, race, caste, sex, or place of birth, believes that work is a prayer or karma. Additionally, the Indian community asserts that all work is equal and whatever work we are doing has already been decided by God (Begum & Gill, 2023). We are here to do such kind of work as we are able to do it in an honest manner. If we honestly do labor, our efforts and God are always happy. Moreover, this traditional and orthodox thinking, without using rationalism and empiricism, naturally and gradually leads children to follow the footsteps of their family and its elder members. Through this, children mostly join labor in the early stages of adolescence (Osthaus, 2004).

Similarly, in cultures followed by female children, even family members more heavily pressure the female child to learn domestic labor. People also endeavor to employ the female child in domestic labor before males. Indeed, parents never think about girls' education compared to boys (Assaad et al., 2010). Moreover, many families who really desire to put their children in educational institutions do not have enough money or have fewer saving; therefore, unnecessary children go into labor. From a socio-cultural perspective in India, there are many prejudices, discrimination, and separation issues in social evils, which impact girls' development and growth due to laboring and torturing (Rafferty, 2013).

From religion perspective and the child labor

In general, every parent wants their children to enjoy life and achieve more development and success than they did. Definitely, parents have the rights and duties to provide all kinds of facilities to their children so that they experience growth and development in all aspects. In doing so, children are indirectly motivated by their parents, such as through hard work day and night, saving money, and providing food for their children (Harvey, 2016). In this way, their children realize their duties and responsibilities from early childhood, and children feel that supporting parents and families is only through labor. Many times, religion plays a major role in introducing more manual work throughout life. For example, Muslim people follow Islamic principles, such as that Allah or God loves those who engage in honest manual work (AI-Hawary et al., 2023). It means a person's body must work while earning money, through activities like laboring, agriculture, handmade work, skilled work, etc. In that manner, gradually Muslim children, in early childhood or at a young age, start earning for themselves and their families. This, in some way, indirectly promotes child labor. Mostly, experts and researchers have observed that some Muslim parents have enough money to spend on education but try to avoid investing in it, specifically for girls (Dyson, 2014).

Likewise, more or less, in other religions where the situation and culture are different, they also encourage child labor based on class, caste, race, and cultural factors. But compared to the Muslim religion, the Christian community in Western European countries has generally avoided having their children do labor, in fact, due to the class divisions at their peak during the 18th and 19th centuries (Razack, 2004).

In 2001, the UN Millennium Development Goals issued a declaration at the global level to eliminate poverty on a large scale in a permanent manner. In this way, the UN Sustainable Development Goals clearly mentioned the elimination of poverty, zero hunger, free education, decent work, and economic growth with sustainable development for all people (Leal Filho et al., 2021). Regarding this, the International Program on the Elimination of Child Labor (IPEC) works with many stakeholders from different countries to conduct and campaign awareness programs through the involvement of public authorities, private business players, civil societies, and NGOs to abolish child labor and poverty, while at the same time promoting free and compulsory education for all children (Alberto & Yamamoto, 2017). IPEC is also engaged in and directly involved with policies and political decisions in underdeveloped and developing countries, particularly with political members who are unwilling to make favourable policies for children regarding education, development, and employment.

Moreover, it is also actively engaged in capacity-building program initiatives, which are useful and helpful in encouraging civil society and countries to abolish poverty, thereby gradually reducing child labor on a large scale. Actually, during the capacity-building process conducted at the national level, volunteers and stakeholders recognized the deep problems and various circumstances of families, and ultimately, community members are likely to understand that the root cause of child labor is directly related to poverty (Morgan, 2016).

Many government institutions, like the National Commission on Human Rights and the National Commission on Women and Child Development, collaborated with private institutions to identify and report informal sectors where child labor is still occurring. After this, the Union Government of India warned against employing children in hazardous factories and industries (Amon et al., 2012). At the same time, the Labor Code Policy, 2020 provides economic, professional, socio-economic, cultural, and legal security and protection in an inclusive and holistic manner. Besides this, the government established the Juvenile Justice and Protection Board under the direct control of the District Magistrate to protect minor children who are illegally imprisoned on false allegations (D'Agostino, 2024).

The Role of Multi-Stakeholders and Child Labor

Education is significant not only for getting a job and earning, but it is also a lifelong process that continues to help the intellectual development of human beings. Due to child labor, their learning capacity is downgraded, and as they age, the willingness to learn new things is lost (Ray, 2014). The negative stakeholders pursue their interests by hiring child labor at a cheap cost. They not only damage childhood but also weaken psychological strength by giving excessive physical burdens and causing mental torture. Despite the specific enforcement of laws in India, children still easily engage in labor in agriculture and the unorganized informal sector. However, at the global level, UN agencies conduct awareness campaigns to abolish child labor. In reality, there are no common child rights laws globally, as different countries have different laws regarding child rights and liberties (Reading et al., 2009).

Above all, while education is emphasized, India is still limited in ensuring the completion of primary education for all children as free and compulsory. However, India must also revise its child rights policies. To establish inclusive education, child education policies must be expanded to include specific training that is helpful in the demand-supply market to meet human resource needs in IT and many allied sectors (Thapa & Sarkar, 2019). However, some multi-stakeholders want to sustain old traditions of employing child labor. This is the main hindrance to the development of children and an obstacle to the elimination of child labor. Similarly, in rural areas, child labor in the education sector is reduced by using organic farming, which does not require fertilizers. Actually, migrant child laborers used fertilizers to increase production (Gumus & Wingenbach 2016). While using fertilizers is harmful to child health, organic farming is better as it helps contribute to sustainable development, such as eliminating child labor, maintaining soil fertility, providing more vitamins and minerals, and producing good quality food (Islam et al., 2024).

Child Labor and the Need for Integrated Policy Action

Child labor is a social and public health issue that has been producing negative outcomes over the last five decades. The reduction of child labor is a remarkable achievement, but certain new challenges and obstacles have emerged due to the new economic market and the entry of new entrepreneurs in the export-import and other sector markets (Kutscher et al., 2025). Therefore, child labor is still happening in informal sectors and on gig platforms. According to an ILO report, poverty is the most significant underlying cause of poverty, hunger, and the food crisis. In this way, the government must allocate more funds to eliminate child labor, and any emerging solutions should be immediately implemented to remove social evils that exist in different sectors (Dammert et al., 2018). At the same time, the government must make policies reliable and favorable for vulnerable communities and ensure their implementation reaches the grassroots level. The Ministry of Education and the Ministry of Labor must build proper cooperation and coordination at all levels, from the highest to the lowest. Additionally, the protection of juvenile rights and liberties while addressing minor children requires rehabilitation and mitigation to combat poverty in all spheres of life (Umejiaku, 2024).

Persistent Inequalities and Systemic Failures in Addressing Child Labor

Child labor is driven by family conditions in such a manner that children are compelled to work in various sectors. However, marginalized families often belong to rural or deprived sections due to historical, cultural, and caste backgrounds. All these families are basically engaged in manual labor; even then, they are not able to do skilled work (Srivastava, 2019). The family conditions are so poor that they cannot afford to spend on skilled training for their children to learn skills that would improve their earnings and savings for the future. However, above all, in urban areas, children and their family members living in slum areas mostly belong to scheduled caste and tribal backgrounds. These communities also face similar kinds of problems and challenges (Fonseka & Malhotra, 2020). Actually, labor-class people know about government schemes and labor policies, but their execution at the ground level is never fully achieved. Additionally, urban children from the labor class are not interested in actively participating or striking against the moral corruption activities of such government bodies (Kesküla, 2018).

SOCIOECONOMIC VULNERABILITIES, EXPLOITATION, AND POLICY GAPS IN ADDRESSING CHILD LABOR

Minority communities of child labor, who have little awareness about programs and government labor policies, try to convince labor communities to provide financial support so that they are able to enroll their children in government educational institutions and provide basic public facilities such as roads, hospitals, and transportation. It has been noted that labor families, whether above or below the poverty line, are interested in enrolling their children in schools. These communities are even capable of earning enough to pay school fees on time. Unfortunately, society, neighbors, and factory owners force the children to work under the influence of factors such as increasing daily wages, providing intoxicating substances, and exploiting girls for sexual purposes (Edmonds & Shrestha, 2014).

Moreover, the primary reasons for children dropping out are as follows: poverty as the main cause, poor quality of education in government schools, high costs, labor families being unable to take responsibility for their children's studies, migration problems, and various cultural factors (Boyden, 2018).

Furthermore, there is a range of challenges while working at occupational sites, such as no fixed working hours and no basic food facilities like tea, coffee, biscuits, or energy drinks. Every day, children face verbal and non-verbal violence in the workplace, sexual harassment, and can be easily removed or replaced by another child employee. As a result, physical and mental weakness impacts child health, which may affect the growth and development of children (Briganti et al., 2020). However, there is no safety equipment or training for children before starting work in hazardous industries. Therefore, union, state, and district labor codes must comply with each other so that it becomes easier to provide all such facilities to the labor class and to eliminate child labor, while also ensuring free education and adequate nutrition. Programs like the mid-day meal and the National Child Labor Project aim to rescue, rehabilitate, and counsel children to pursue education (Shendell et al., 2016).

RESEARCH METHODOLOGY

The research study on child labor employs a cross-sectional analysis and a triangulation analysis approach. It utilizes a combination of qualitative and quantitative methods, aiming to analyze the purposive sample of exactly 42 child laborers in Dehradun city. The study using tools and techniques like a self-prepared questionnaire and semi-structured interviews. Further, the study also presents statistical analysis using frequency and correlation.

LIMITATION

"This study primarily focuses on child labor below the age of 18 years within the geographical location of Dehradun city, Uttarakhand. The study analyzes child labor in occupational sites only. The study is limited by specific purposive sampling, which might involve a chance of bias and variability. To avoid or reduce this, interviews and questionnaires are conducted to find out the rational reasons why children drop out of school and become involved in laboring. Although, the study is less focused on the psychological and health conditions of the children while laboring in the workplace.

RESULT

Figure 1. Age

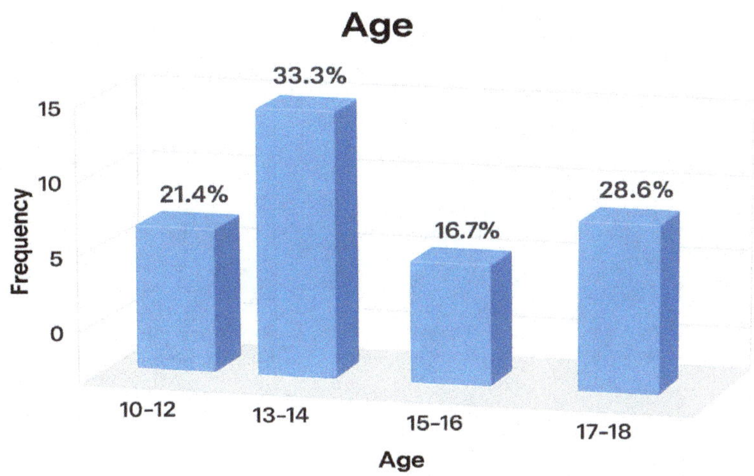

The age-wise distribution indicates that most respondents (33.3%) belong to the *13–14 years* age group, suggesting a predominance of early adolescents. This is followed by *17–18 years* (28.6%), representing a considerable number of late adolescents. In the age group between 10 years and above, 21.4% belong to the younger group. The age group between 15 and 16 years old accounts for 16.7% of adults. The results show different age groups of children and adults. The 13–14 years age group, which falls under the middle school stage, is affected in terms of their future career.

Figure 2. Demographic and socioeconomic profile of respondents

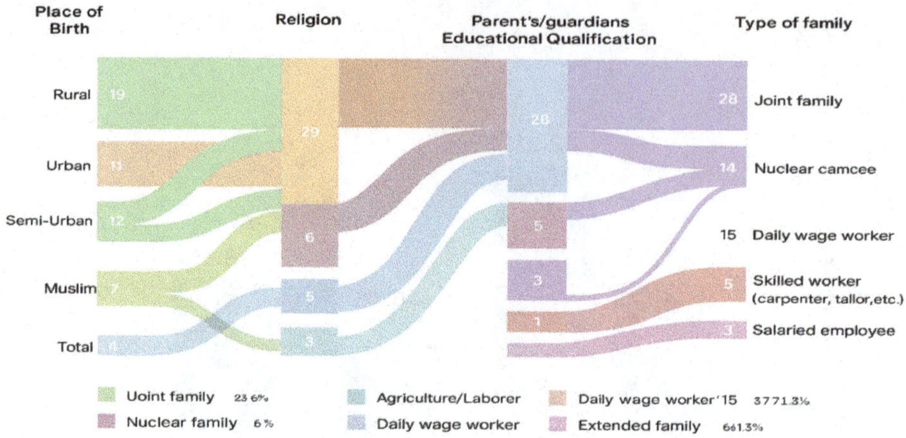

The Sankey diagram provides the social and economic conditions of the children. The maximum number of respondents are located in rural areas (45.2%), followed by those living in semi-urban and urban areas (26.2%) who shifted for work purposes. The remaining respondents are located in rural backgrounds. The majority of the children's religion is Hindu (69%), followed by Muslim (16.7%) and Christian (14.3%), representing smaller groups. It shows that all religious groups are involved in child labour activities. This is one major concern to avoid such circumstances. The community of the respondents shows that the maximum group comprises Scheduled Caste (SC) children involved in various types of jobs. Scheduled Tribe accounts for nearly 11.9%, and the Other Backward Class involved in labour work accounts for 14.3%. A total of 7.1% are involved in the General category. The results pertaining to the educational status of most parents and guardians show that nearly the majority of them have primary education (47.6%). Nearly 28.6% of them are illiterate, which shows a lack of literacy. Some of the respondents' parents (16.7%) have secondary education, and a very minimal proportion (7.2%) have higher secondary or graduate degrees. This mainly emphasizes the low level of educational qualifications among parents, which leads children to engage in labour employment activities and contributes to child labour.

The occupational condition of the parents shows that the majority are daily wage workers, accounting for nearly 35.7% of the respondents. 33.3% of them are involved in agricultural activities and agricultural daily wage work. A small proportion of them are skilled and salaried employees, accounting for nearly 23.8%. Other respondents are involved in business and trade, with nearly 7.1% engaged in their own small-scale industrial activities. It reflects that child labour is one of the main reasons affecting children due to low economic conditions, and the majority of their parents are involved in unorganized working conditions. The family condition of the majority shows that they belong to joint families, accounting for nearly 66.7% of the respondents. The extended family accounts for nearly 14.3% of them. 19% of the respondents belong to nuclear families, which reflects that due to a higher number of family members, economic reasons lead children to be involved in labour work.

Figure 3. Monthly family income

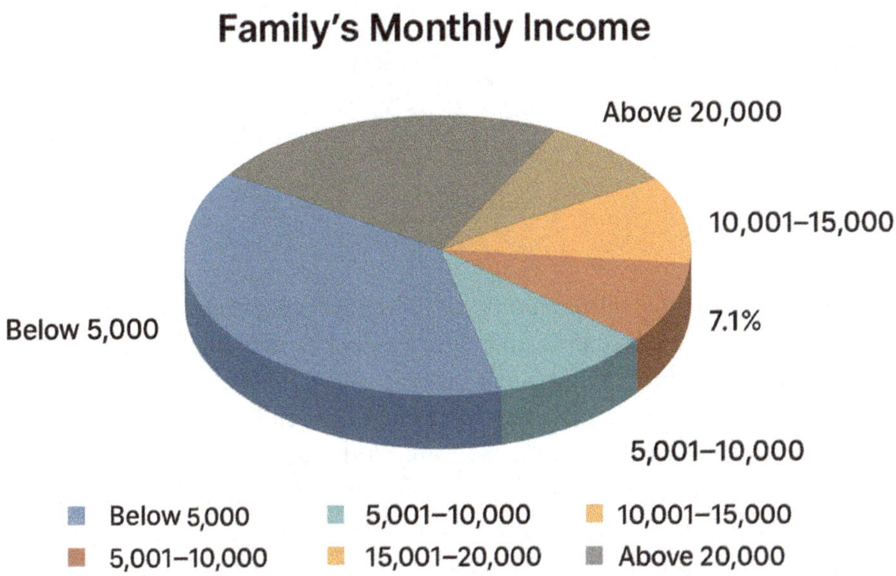

Children's family income helps identify the reasons for the pull factors involved in child labour. Most of the family income is below Rs. 5,000, which reflects a very low financial background. 31% of them have a monthly family income of Rs. 5,000 to Rs. 10,000, which indicates that these households are economically weak and belong to low-income groups. A very small group (7.1%) has a family income ranging between Rs. 10,001 to Rs. 15,000, Rs. 15,001 to Rs. 20,000, and above Rs. 20,001. Fewer respondents belong to middle-income household conditions. This reflects that the economic vulnerability of the respondents affects their education and leads them to be involved in labour activities.

Figure 4. Current working sectors

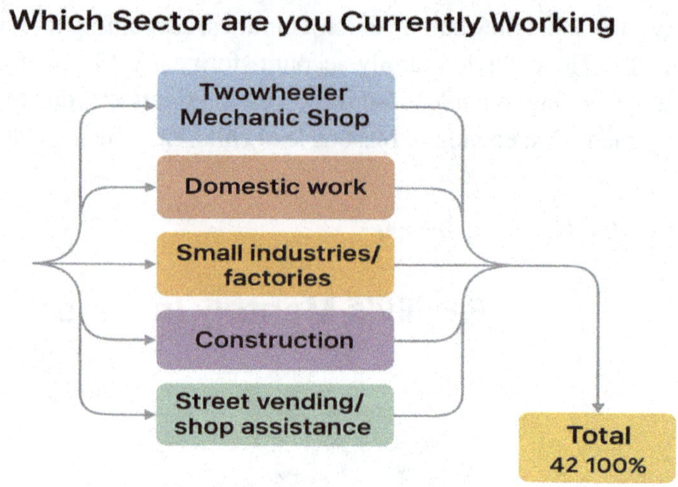

The figure provides information on children working in various sectors. 28.6% of the children are involved in small industries, such as manufacturing-related work. 26.2% of them are involved in street vending and roadside selling of products or edible items. These are informal activities in which children are mostly involved. 19% of the children are involved in mechanic work, such as assisting in two-wheeler shops. 14.3% of them are involved in home-based work such as cleaning, gardening, and maintenance work. This indicates that low levels of income push the child labour force into workplaces. 11.9% of them are working at construction sites, which might affect their physical health and future career. Most of the children work for daily wages, which is more useful for the family.

Table 1. Socioeconomic conditions, work patterns, and awareness of child welfare policies among respondents

Descriptions	Options	Frequency	%
Basic facilities at home (electricity, water, sanitation)	Yes, all	24	57.1
	Partially	12	28.6
	No	6	14.3
	Total	42	100
Currently Attending School	Yes	20	47.6
	No	22	52.4
	Total	42	100

continued on following page

Table 1. Continued

Descriptions	Options	Frequency	%
If not attending school, what is the reason	Financial problems	2	9.1
	Need to work and support family	4	18.2
	Lack of interest in studies	7	31.8
	Distance of school/transport issues	2	9.1
	Health problems	5	22.7
	Family pressure/tradition	2	9.1
	Total	22	100
Poverty has affected your Education	Yes, completely	23	54.8
	Yes, partially	10	23.8
	No	9	21.4
	Total	42	100
Are you working to support your family income	Yes, full-time	12	28.6
	Yes, part-time	21	50
	No	9	21.4
	Total	42	100
Hours of work per day	Less than 4 hours	5	11.9
	4–6 hours	8	19
	7–8 hours	15	35.7
	8-9 hours	9	21.4
	More than 10 hours	5	11.9
	Total	42	100
Challenges Face while Working	Long working hours	13	31
	Physical strain	9	21.4
	Unsafe environment	6	14.3
	Harassment/abuse	9	21.4
	Low wages	5	11.9
	Total	42	100
Are you provided with safety equipment (gloves, masks, shoes, etc.	Always	14	33.3
	Sometimes	21	50
	Never	7	16.7
	Total	42	100
Have you received any training for your work	Yes	8	19
	No	34	81
	Total	42	100

continued on following page

Table 1. Continued

Descriptions	Options	Frequency	%
Are you aware of any government schemes for child welfare/education	Yes	11	26.2
	No	31	73.8
	Total	42	100
If yes, which schemes do you know about	Mid-day meal scheme	2	18.2
	Free education/RTE Act	2	18.2
	Scholarships	3	27.3
	Child labor rehabilitation schemes	3	27.3
	5	1	9.1
	Total	11	100
Has your family received any benefits from these schemes	Yes, regularly	3	30
	Yes, occasionally	3	30
	No	4	40
	Total	10	100
Do you think government policies (union/state/local) are effective in preventing child labor	Yes	5	12.2
	No	31	75.6
	Partly	5	12.2
	Total	41	100
How are these policies executed in your area	Very effectively	7	16.7
	Somewhat effectively	9	21.4
	Poorly implemented	9	21.4
	Not implemented at all	17	40.5
	Total	42	100

The majority of them do not have basic facilities, accounting for nearly 57.1%. Electricity, water, and sanitation facilities are very limited in the households. 28.6% and 14.3% of them have partial facilities. There is an even split in school attendance, with 47.6% of the respondents attending school and 52.4% not attending school. Among the 22 not attending, the leading reasons are lack of interest (31.8%) *and* health problems (22.7%), followed by work (18.2%) *and* financial or access barriers (each ≈9.1%). Poverty strongly affects education: 54.8% say poverty has completely affected their education and another 23.8% say partially. Most children are working: 78.6% (12 full-time + 21 part-time = 33/42) contribute to family income. Work patterns concentrate in typical full-day ranges (modal 7–8 hrs, 35.7%), but long hours are a common challenge.

Working conditions show important risks: top problems are long working hours (31%), physical strain (21.4%), and harassment/abuse (21.4%); 14.3% report unsafe environments and 11.9% low wages. Safety equipment is inconsistent — only 33.3% always receive it, while 50% sometimes and 16.7% never do. Training is rare: just 19% have received work training. Awareness and benefits from government schemes are low. Only 26.2% are aware of child-welfare/education schemes; among those aware the commonly named schemes include mid-day meal, free education, scholarships and rehabilitation. Very few families report regular benefit receipt. Public confidence in policy is weak: 75.6% say policies are not effective (only 12.2% say effective), and 40.5% report policies are *not implemented at all* locally.

Practical priorities: (1) strengthen school retention and access (financial support, flexible hours, outreach for health-related barriers); (2) expand awareness campaigns so families can access existing schemes; (3) enforce child-labour protections, improve monitoring and provision of safety equipment; (4) provide vocational training and safe, regulated part-time options that do not disrupt schooling; (5) ensure benefits reach families (simplify delivery and monitoring).

Notes & limitations: sample = 42 (small). A few minor data inconsistencies appear (one question totals 41; scheme-benefit responses mismatch by one), and all measures are self-reported. Interpret results as indicative, not definitive.

Figure 5. Daily working hours

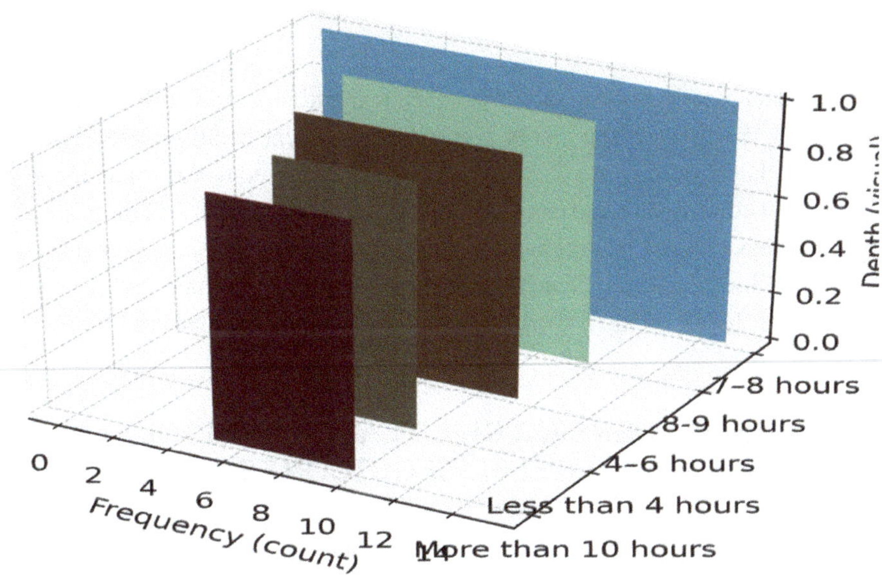

Most respondents (n = 42) work a conventional day: 15 (35.7%) report 7–8 hours. Estimated mean ≈ 7.12 hrs (SD ≈ 2.26); 27/42 (64.1%) fall between 4–9 hrs, while extremes (<4 and >10) are 11.9% each. The figure illustrates that the majority of the families have women who are widows due to economic and financial conditions. Economic dependence affects children's involvement in the labour force, and they are all engaged in daily working hours.

Figure 6. Impact of work on respondents' physical and mental health

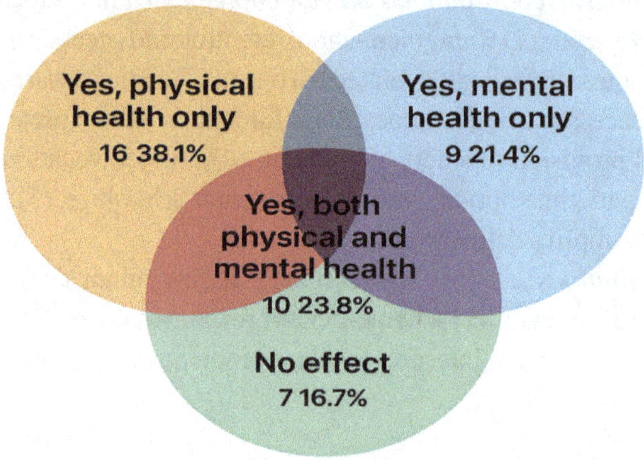

The data clearly explain children's physical and mental health conditions, with nearly 38.1% of the respondents affected by physical health–related issues. This indicates that children have less physical strain compared to the younger age group. This might affect health and cause injuries in some cases. 23.8% of them are affected by both physical and mental health–related problems. 21.4% of them are affected by mental health–related issues, which impact their emotional and psychological well-being. 16.7% of them work without any health-related issues.

FACTORS INFLUENCING CHILD LABOR, SCHOOL ATTENDANCE, AND WELFARE OUTCOMES

The study provides a comprehensive understanding of the children's living conditions and the nature of their workplaces. Every individual is born and brought up with equal potential for health, influenced by family situations and environmental conditions. For various reasons, they become child laborers due to financial dependency. There are children who work in specific fields and under long working hours. Children must face various challenges at the workplace, including risks and consequences related to the work environment. Access to basic home facilities is positively associated with school attendance, type and hours of work, and provision of safety equipment, and negatively associated with challenges faced while working. Attending school is more likely among children with better home facilities, formal work arrangements, longer work hours, and safety support, but is strongly hindered by poverty. The reasons for not attending school are closely linked to place of birth, type of work, and longer working hours, with fewer reported challenges reflecting intense work obligations that prevent schooling. Working to support family income is negatively associated with school attendance, while sector of work strongly determines working conditions, hours, exposure to risks, and provision of safety equipment. Hours worked per day are positively related to place of birth, home facilities, sector of work, and health impacts, but negatively associated with challenges, suggesting structured work reduces reported difficulties. Children with better home conditions or benefits from schemes report fewer challenges, and proper safety equipment is linked to formalized work, school attendance, and reduced health risks. Training is associated with formal work, longer hours, and awareness of government schemes, which, along with benefits received, enhance confidence in policy effectiveness. Health impacts are largely determined by work intensity and type, while areas with effective policy execution support formal work, welfare, and child protection.

DISCUSSION

Child Labor: Causes, Impacts, and Policy Perspectives

Child labor exploits children through work beyond their capacity, depriving them of childhood, education, and dignity. In 2024, 138 million children were engaged in labor globally, with 54 million in hazardous work—mainly agriculture (61%), services (27%), and manufacturing/mining (13%) (Mohammadi et al., 2024; Safdar & Kataria, 2024). Although declining by 22 million since 2020, child labor remains high in Sub-Saharan Africa; Asia and Latin America show improvements. Boys and girls are equally involved, with differing roles.

Poverty, marginalization, discrimination, and lack of education drive child labor. Families often depend on children for income, perpetuating illiteracy and vulnerability (Chukwudeh & Oduaran, 2021; Nayar et al., 2014). Girls are disproportionately in unpaid domestic work; early school dropouts, early marriages, and poor educational access worsen the problem (Udoh, 2024). In India, laws such as the Factories Act (1948), Mines Act (1952), Child Labor (Prohibition and Regulation) Act (1986, amended 2016), and Right to Education Act (2009), along with programs like the

National Child Labor Project and mid-day meals, target child labor (Roberts, 2015; Pradhan et al., 2024). Enforcement is inconsistent, especially in informal and hazardous sectors; high-incidence states include Uttar Pradesh, Bihar, Madhya Pradesh, Andhra Pradesh, and Odisha.

Child labor negatively affects health, mental well-being, and social development. Children face long hours, unsafe conditions, harassment, and abuse; girls face additional risks of sexual exploitation (Moayad et al., 2021; Fawole, 2008). Cultural and religious norms, such as "karma" and family labor traditions, also contribute (Begum & Gill, 2023; AI-Hawary et al., 2023). Global initiatives, including ILO's IPEC and UN SDGs, stress education, poverty reduction, and multi-stakeholder engagement (Alberto & Yamamoto, 2017; Leal Filho et al., 2021). Holistic strategies combining education, enforcement, community engagement, and poverty alleviation are essential to protect children's rights and development.

The age-wise distribution shows a slight concentration of early adolescents (13–14 years, 33.3%), with balanced representation across other age groups. Most respondents come from rural areas (45.2%), predominantly Hindu (69%) and from marginalized communities (66.7% SC), with low parental education and income, and a majority living in joint families. Parents are mainly daily wage laborers or agricultural workers, reflecting economic vulnerability. Respondents work largely in informal or semi-skilled sectors, including factories, street vending, mechanics, domestic work, and construction. While most households have basic facilities, school attendance is nearly split, with absenteeism driven by lack of interest, health issues, work obligations, and poverty. Most children contribute to family income, often working 7–8 hours per day, facing challenges such as long hours, physical strain, harassment, unsafe environments, and low wages. Safety equipment and training are limited, and awareness of government schemes is low, with weak confidence in policy implementation.

CONCLUSION

Eliminating child labour is one of the major concerns for the development of the nation. Providing free and compulsory education ensures children's well-being and a safe future. Various implementations and policies are involved in actively protecting children's rights (Aufseeser et al., 2018). The government takes various policy measures to eliminate child labor, actively participating to reduce poverty and promote access to education (Ngutuku, 2025). Various factors are involved in child labour, including age group, working hours, nature of work, and working conditions. Children must face various challenges and consequences when involved in labour activities. This involves responsibilities to prevent child labour from the perspectives of society, family and relatives, and corporate social responsibility must also be engaged to stop child labour (Wahito, 2024).

REFERENCES

Abdullah, A., Huynh, I., Emery, C. R., & Jordan, L. P. (2022). Social norms and family child labor: A systematic literature review. *International Journal of Environmental Research and Public Health, 19*(7), 4082. DOI: 10.3390/ijerph19074082

Ahmad, N. (2011). Child labour: Ground realities of Indian labour laws. *Commonwealth Law Bulletin, 37*(1), 61–74. DOI: 10.1080/03050718.2010.524287

Al-Hawary, S. I. S., Kumar, T., Pallathadka, H., Alshahrani, S. H., Al-Tamimi, H. A. N. M., Muda, I., & Singer, N. (2023). The education of children in an Islamic family based on the Holy Qur'an. *Hervormde Teologiese Studies, 79*(2), 8273.

Alberto, M. D. F. P., & Yamamoto, O. H. (2017). When education is not the solution: Public policy in the fight against child labor. *Trends in Psychology, 25*, 1677–1691. DOI: 10.9788/TP2017.4-10Pt

Ali, M. A., Ali, M. V., & Abbas, F. (2017). Hidden hazardous child labor as a complex human rights phenomenon: A case study of child labor in Pakistan's brick-making industry. *Cogent Social Sciences, 3*(1), 1369486. DOI: 10.1080/23311886.2017.1369486

Amon, J. J., Buchanan, J., Cohen, J., & Kippenberg, J. (2012). Child labor and environmental health: Government obligations and human rights. *International Journal of Pediatrics, 2012*(1), 938306. DOI: 10.1155/2012/938306

Assaad, R., Levison, D., & Zibani, N. (2010). The effect of domestic work on girls' schooling: Evidence from Egypt. *Feminist Economics, 16*(1), 79–128. DOI: 10.1080/13545700903382729

Aufseeser, D., Bourdillon, M., Carothers, R., & Lecoufle, O. (2018). Children's work and children's well-being: Implications for policy. *Development Policy Review, 36*(2), 241–261. DOI: 10.1111/dpr.12215

Baidawi, S., Sheehan, R., & Flynn, C. (2020). Criminal exploitation of child protection-involved youth. *Children and Youth Services Review, 118*, 105396. DOI: 10.1016/j.childyouth.2020.105396

Bajpai, A. (2012). Protecting India's children: Vulnerabilities and challenges. *Macalester International, 29*(1), 8.

Begum, H., & Gill, A. K. (2023). Understanding the experiences of British South Asian male survivors of child sexual abuse. In *Child Sexual Abuse in Black and Minoritised Communities: Improving Legal, Policy and Practical Responses* (pp. 59–113). Springer International Publishing., DOI: 10.1007/978-3-031-06337-4_3

Borrell, C., Muntaner, C., Solè, J., Artazcoz, L., Puigpinos, R., Benach, J., & Noh, S. (2008). Immigration and self-reported health status by social class and gender: The importance of material deprivation, work organisation and household labour. *Journal of Epidemiology and Community Health, 62*(5), e7–e7. DOI: 10.1136/jech.2006.055269

Boyden, J. (2018). 'We're not going to suffer like this in the mud': Educational aspirations, social mobility and independent child migration among populations living in poverty. In *Education, Mobilities and Migration* (pp. 26-46). Routledge.

Briganti, P., Mele, S., & Varriale, L. (2020). New technologies for preventing and reducing verbal and non-verbal assaults against healthcare professionals within hospitals: The state of art. *Digital Transformation and Human Behavior: Innovation for People and Organisations*, 281-297. DOI: 10.1007/978-3-030-47539-0_19

Chukwudeh, O. S., & Oduaran, A. (2021). Liminality and child labour: Experiences of school aged working children with implications for community education in Africa. *Social Sciences (Basel, Switzerland), 10*(3), 93. DOI: 10.3390/socsci10030093

D'Agostino, A. (2024). What Goes Up But Never Comes Down? Juvenile Punitive Practice Within The United States. *California Western International Law Journal, 54*(1), 8.

Dammert, A. C., De Hoop, J., Mvukiyehe, E., & Rosati, F. C. (2018). Effects of public policy on child labor: Current knowledge, gaps, and implications for program design. *World Development, 110*, 104–123. DOI: 10.1016/j.worlddev.2018.05.001

Das, K. S. (2022). Child labour and its determinants in India. *Children and Youth Services Review, 138*, 106523. DOI: 10.1016/j.childyouth.2022.106523

Dasgupta, S. (2018). Child Labour in India: Literary Representations along the Trajectory of Nation. *International Research in Children's Literature, 11*(2), 160–172. DOI: 10.3366/ircl.2018.0272

Dyson, J. (2014). *Working childhoods: Youth, agency and the environment in India.* Cambridge University Press. DOI: 10.1017/CBO9781107415706

Eden, C. A., Chisom, O. N., & Adeniyi, I. S. (2024). Education policy and social change: Examining the impact of reform initiatives on equity and access. *International Journal of Science and Research Archive, 11*(2), 139-146. I: DOI: 10.30574/ijsra.2024.11.2.0372

Edmonds, E. V., & Shrestha, M. (2014). You get what you pay for: Schooling incentives and child labor. *Journal of Development Economics, 111*, 196–211. DOI: 10.1016/j.jdeveco.2014.09.005

Eteng, M. J., & Nnam, M. U. (2022). Gender and Modern-Day Slavery: Aggression and Violence in the Context of a Nigerian Focus. *An International Collection of Multidisciplinary Approaches to Violence and Aggression, 21.*

Fawole, O. I. (2008). Economic violence to women and girls: Is it receiving the necessary attention? *Trauma, Violence & Abuse*, *9*(3), 167–177. DOI: 10.1177/1524838008319255

Fonseka, L., & Malhotra, D. D. (2020). India: Urban poverty, children and participation. In *Urban Children Distress* (pp. 161-215). Routledge.

Gebregziabher, K., Hadush, M., & Abrha, K. (2023). Child labor and its determinants: An empirical test of the luxury axiom-cum the wealth paradox theory. *Cogent Economics & Finance*, *11*(2), 2282890. DOI: 10.1080/23322039.2023.2282890

Greenbaum, J. (2021). Child labor and sex trafficking. *Pediatrics in Review*, *42*(12), 639–654. DOI: 10.1542/pir.2020-001396

Greenbaum, V. J. (2014). Commercial sexual exploitation and sex trafficking of children in the United States. *Current Problems in Pediatric and Adolescent Health Care*, *44*(9), 245–269. DOI: 10.1016/j.cppeds.2014.07.001

Gumus, S. G., & Wingenbach, G. (2016). The child labor problem in Turkish agriculture: What can we do? *Social Indicators Research*, *127*(3), 1193–1215. DOI: 10.1007/s11205-015-0999-1

Hamenoo, E. S., Dwomoh, E. A., & Dako-Gyeke, M. (2018). Child labour in Ghana: Implications for children's education and health. *Children and Youth Services Review*, *93*, 248–254. DOI: 10.1016/j.childyouth.2018.07.026

Harvey, K. (2016). "When I go to bed hungry and sleep, I'm not hungry": Children and parents' experiences of food insecurity. *Appetite*, *99*, 235–244. DOI: 10.1016/j.appet.2016.01.004

Hasan, M. J., & Chaitee, N. N. (2022). Reasons behind the Drop out of Street Children from Non-formal Primary Education Program. *International Journal for Educational and Vocational Studies*, *4*(2), 81–88. DOI: 10.29103/ijevs.v0i0.5612

Hoque, M. M. (2023). Understanding the role of structural factors and realities in normalizing child labour in urban slums of Bangladesh. *Cogent Social Sciences*, *9*(2), 2272319. DOI: 10.1080/23311886.2023.2272319

Huang, L. (2017). The trafficking of women and girls in Taiwan: Characteristics of victims, perpetrators, and forms of exploitation. *BMC Women's Health*, *17*(1), 104. DOI: 10.1186/s12905-017-0463-2

Ilyas, A., Shahid, M. S., & Ali Hassan, R. (2020). Evaluating the motives of child labourers in the informal economy. *The International Journal of Sociology and Social Policy, 40*(3/4), 409–424. DOI: 10.1108/IJSSP-01-2019-0001

Islam, M. R., Promity, J. F., Afroz, K. M., Kaniz, S. M., Hassan, M. R., & Islam, K. F. (2024). Nutritional Status and Food Habits of Child Labor in Rangpur City, Bangladesh. *Health Dynamics, 1*(9), 316–323. DOI: 10.33846/hd10901

Kadir, A., Battersby, A., Spencer, N., & Hjern, A. (2019). Children on the move in Europe: a narrative review of the evidence on the health risks, health needs and health policy for asylum seeking, refugee and undocumented children. *BMJ paediatrics open, 3*(1), bmjpo-2018. DOI: 10.1136/bmjpo-2018-000364

Kesküla, E. (2018). Miners and their children: The remaking of the Soviet working class in Kazakhstan. In *Industrial labor on the margins of capitalism: precarity, class, and the neoliberal subject* (pp. 61–84). Berghahn., DOI: 10.2307/j.ctvw04hxm.7

Khan, F. R., Munir, K. A., & Willmott, H. (2007). A dark side of institutional entrepreneurship: Soccer balls, child labour and postcolonial impoverishment. *Organization Studies, 28*(7), 1055–1077. DOI: 10.1177/0170840607078114

Kim, S. W. (2019). Left-behind children: Teachers' perceptions of family-school relations in rural China. *Compare: A Journal of Comparative Education, 49*(4), 584–601. DOI: 10.1080/03057925.2018.1438885

Kumar, K., & Srivastava, R. (2024). Educational and Vocational Aspirations of Child Labourers with Special Reference to Patna. *Global Journal of Enterprise Information System, 16*(4), 57–63. https://www.gjeis.com/index.php/GJEIS/article/view/836

Kutscher, L., Notté, E., & Anderson, K. (2025). Child Labour in the Extraction of Strategic Raw Materials: A Review and Risk Assessment. *Green Health, 1*(2), 14. DOI: 10.3390/greenhealth1020014

Leal Filho, W., Lovren, V. O., Will, M., Salvia, A. L., & Frankenberger, F. (2021). Poverty: A central barrier to the implementation of the UN Sustainable Development Goals. *Environmental Science & Policy, 125*, 96–104. DOI: 10.1016/j.envsci.2021.08.020

Liebel, M. (2012). Grassroots Children's Rights. In *Children's Rights from Below: Cross-Cultural Perspectives* (pp. 125-142). London: Palgrave Macmillan UK. DOI: 10.1057/9780230361843_9

Makinde, C. O. B., Daib, O. A., Arogundade, T. O., & Adeoye, A. (2021). Forced marriage and child labor: A gender outlook during COVID 19 pandemic. *Journal of Humanities Therapy, 12*(2), 127–150. DOI: 10.33252/jht.2021.12.12.2.127

Maksud, A. K. M., Hossain, K. R., Sayed, S., & Aked, J. (2024). Informal Economy Perspectives on the Prevalence of Worst Forms of Child Labour in Bangladesh's Leather Industry. DOI: 10.19088/CLARISSA.2024.005

McKinney, K. (2015). Situating corporate framings of child labor: Toward grounded geographies of working children in globalized agriculture. *Geoforum*, *59*, 219–227. DOI: 10.1016/j.geoforum.2014.10.018

Milczarek-Desai, S. (2024). (Hidden) in Plain Sight: Migrant Child Labor and the New Economy of Exploitation. *Arkansas Law Review*, *77*(2), 345. DOI: 10.54119/alr.pmgv5144

Miller, M. E., & Bush, D. (2004). Review of the Federal Child Labor Regulations: Updating hazardous and prohibited occupations. *American Journal of Industrial Medicine*, *45*(2), 218–221. DOI: 10.1002/ajim.10329

Moayad, S. J., Kamal, S. H. M., Sajjadi, H., Vameghi, M., Harouni, G. G., & Alamdari, S. M. (2021). Child labor in Tehran, Iran: Abuses experienced in work environments. *Child Abuse & Neglect*, *117*, 105054. DOI: 10.1016/j.chiabu.2021.105054

Mohammadi, F., Masoumi, S. Z., Oshvandi, K., Borzou, S. R., Cheraghi, F., & Karkhanei, B. (2024). Dignity: The cornerstone of psychological health among victims of child labor, a qualitative study. *BMC Research Notes*, *17*(1), 259. DOI: 10.1186/s13104-024-06911-8

Morgan, J. (2016). Participation, empowerment and capacity building: Exploring young people's perspectives on the services provided to them by a grassroots NGO in sub-Saharan Africa. *Children and Youth Services Review*, *65*, 175–182. DOI: 10.1016/j.childyouth.2016.04.012

Nayar, U. S., Stangl, A. L., De Zalduondo, B., & Brady, L. M. (2014). Reducing stigma and discrimination to improve child health and survival in low-and middle-income countries: promising approaches and implications for future research. *Journal of health communication, 19*(sup1), 142-163. DOI: 10.1080/10810730.2014.930213

Ngutuku, E. (2025). *Children's Lived Experience of Poverty and Vulnerability in Kenya: Going Beyond Multi-dimensionality*. Taylor & Francis., DOI: 10.4324/9781003356769

Osthaus, C. R. (2004). The Work Ethic of the Plain Folk: Labor and Religion in the Old South. In *The Best American History Essays 2006* (pp. 89-122). New York: Palgrave Macmillan US. DOI: 10.1007/978-1-137-06580-3_5

Parson, N. (2010). "I am not [just] a rabbit who has a bunch of children!": Agency in the midst of suffering at the intersections of global inequalities, gendered violence, and migration. *Violence Against Women*, *16*(8), 881–901. DOI: 10.1177/1077801210376224

Pirzada, G., Muhammad, Y., & Anis, F. (2020). Perspectives of working children on their education and life goals: A case study. *Research Journal of Social Sciences and Economics Review*, *1*(4), 122–132. DOI: 10.36902/rjsser-vol1-iss4-2020(122-132)

Pradhan, J., Ray, S., & Nielsen, M. O. (2024). Social protection schemes for mother and children in Odisha: A matched-gap analysis. *SN Social Sciences*, *4*(10), 185. DOI: 10.1007/s43545-024-00984-9

Radfar, A., Asgharzadeh, S. A. A., Quesada, F., & Filip, I. (2018). Challenges and perspectives of child labor. *Industrial Psychiatry Journal*, *27*(1), 17–20. DOI: 10.4103/ipj.ipj_105_14

Rafferty, Y. (2013). International dimensions of discrimination and violence against girls: A human rights perspective. *Journal of International Women's Studies*, *14*(1), 1–23.

Rathod, G. R., & Koli, V. L. (2015). Child labour and school dropout. *Scholarly Research Journal for Interdisciplinary Studies*, *3*(16), 3199–3207.

Ray, R. (2014). Education and child labor: a global perspective. In *The World of Child Labor* (pp. 118–126). Routledge.

Razack, S. H. (2004). Imperilled Muslim women, dangerous Muslim men and civilised Europeans: Legal and social responses to forced marriages. *Feminist Legal Studies*, *12*(2), 129–174. DOI: 10.1023/B:FEST.0000043305.66172.92

Reading, R., Bissell, S., Goldhagen, J., Harwin, J., Masson, J., Moynihan, S., Parton, N., Pais, M. S., Thoburn, J., & Webb, E. (2009). Promotion of children's rights and prevention of child maltreatment. *Lancet*, *373*(9660), 332–343. DOI: 10.1016/S0140-6736(08)61709-2

Řimnáčová, Z., & Kajanová, A. (2019). Stress and the working poor. *Human Affairs*, *29*(1), 87–94. DOI: 10.1515/humaff-2019-0008

Rioux, S., LeBaron, G., & Verovšek, P. J. (2020). Capitalism and unfree labor: A review of Marxist perspectives on modern slavery. *Review of International Political Economy*, *27*(3), 709–731. DOI: 10.1080/09692290.2019.1650094

Roberts, J. R., Karr, C. J., Paulson, J. A., Brock-Utne, A. C., Brumberg, H. L., Campbell, C. C., Lanphear, B. P., Osterhoudt, K. C., Sandel, M. T., Trasande, L., & Wright, R. O. (2012). Pesticide exposure in children. *Pediatrics, 130*(6), e1765–e1788. DOI: 10.1542/peds.2012-2758

Roberts, J. W. (2015). Comparative Approaches to Myanmar's Child Labor Epidemic: The Role of Compulsory Education. *Emory Int'l L. Rev., 30*, 661.

Sabates-Wheeler, R., & Sumberg, J. (2022). Breaking out of the policy enclave approach to child labour in sub-Saharan African agriculture. *Global Social Policy, 22*(1), 46–66. DOI: 10.1177/1468018121991813

Saeed, S., & Qureshi, M. B. (2024). Health Issues Faced by Home Based Women Bangle Workers of Hyderabad Sindh, Pakistan. *Research Mosaic, 4*(1), 37–52. DOI: 10.64428/rm/v4.i1.5

Safdar, R., & Kataria, J. R. (2024). Exploring the Causes of Child Labor and its Implications on their Mental Well-Being. *Pakistan Social Sciences Review, 8*(2), 707–721. DOI: 10.35484/pssr.2024(8-II-S)62

Sasmal, J., & Guillen, J. (2015). Poverty, educational failure and the child-labour trap: The Indian experience. *Global Business Review, 16*(2), 270–280. DOI: 10.1177/0972150914564419

Scott, N. B., & Pocock, N. S. (2021). The health impacts of hazardous chemical exposures among child labourers in low-and middle-income countries. *International Journal of Environmental Research and Public Health, 18*(10), 5496. DOI: 10.3390/ijerph18105496

Sharma, S. (2009). Trends, Causes and Consequences of Child Labour in India. *The Indian Journal of Public Administration, 55*(2), 220–236. DOI: 10.1177/0019556120090205

Shendell, D. G., Noomnual, S., Chishti, S., Sorensen Allacci, M., & Madrigano, J. (2016). Exposures resulting in safety and health concerns for child laborers in less developed countries. *Journal of Environmental and Public Health, 2016*(1), 3985498. DOI: 10.1155/2016/3985498

Sohel, M. S., Alam, S., Rahman, M. M., Obaidullah, M., Anam, A. S. M. T., Hossain, B., & Hossain, M. A. (2024). Exploring the multifaceted vulnerabilities of female street child labor in the capital city of Bangladesh. *Heliyon, 10*(18), e37302. https://www.cell.com/heliyon/fulltext/S2405-8440(24)13333-6. DOI: 10.1016/j.heliyon.2024.e37302

Srivastava, R. N. (2019). Children at work, child labor and modern slavery in India: An overview. *Indian Pediatrics*, *56*(8), 633–638. DOI: 10.1007/s13312-019-1584-5

Tandon, N., Basu, P., Krishnan, O., & RV, B. (2022). *Emerging work trends in Urban India: COVID-19 and beyond*. Routledge India.

Teixeira, P. N. (2024). Between ethics and science: Economic and political arguments against child labor in the progressive period. *Review of Political Economy*, *36*(1), 76–96. DOI: 10.1080/09538259.2023.2181063

Thapa, R., & Sarkar, K. K. (2019). Universal elementary education in India: Barriers and persistent challenges. *Social Change*, *49*(2), 257–275. DOI: 10.1177/0049085719844105

Thévenon, O., & Edmonds, E. (2019). Child labour: Causes, consequences and policies to tackle it. *OECD Social, Employment, and Migration Working Papers*, (235), 4-82.

Udoh, E. (2024). The Effect of Gender Inequality and Early Marriage on Girl-Child Education in Ikot Ekpene Senatorial District. *AKSU Annals of Sustainable Development*, 29-39. DOI: 10.60787/AASD-1-1-6

Umejiaku, N. (2024). Multidimensional Child Poverty and Its Implication on Juvenile Justice System. *Journal of Commercial and Property Law*, *11*(4), 177–186.

Wahito, N. (2024). Mutuality and Power: An Analysis of Non-State Actors' Influence in Mitigating the Negative Consequences of State Response to COVID-19 on Adolescent Girls in Kenya. *Leadership and Developing Societies*, *9*(1), 49–65. DOI: 10.47697/lds.38380014

Webbink, E., Smits, J., & De Jong, E. (2012). Hidden child labor: Determinants of housework and family business work of children in 16 developing countries. *World Development*, *40*(3), 631–642. DOI: 10.1016/j.worlddev.2011.07.005

Wood, L. C. (2020). Child modern slavery, trafficking and health: A practical review of factors contributing to children's vulnerability and the potential impacts of severe exploitation on health. *BMJ Paediatrics Open*, *4*(1), e000327. DOI: 10.1136/bmjpo-2018-000327

Woolf, A. D. (2002). Health hazards for children at work. *Journal of Toxicology. Clinical Toxicology*, *40*(4), 477–482. DOI: 10.1081/CLT-120006750

Yadav, M. A. (2019). Implementation of Right to Education: A Constitutional overview. *International Journal of Research in Social Sciences*, *9*(3), 1.

Yousaf, M. N., Khan, A., Hayat, U., & Ahmad, A. (2025). Socioeconomic Perspective and Analysis of the Linkage of Education and Child Labor in Pakistan: Challenges and Prospects. *Journal of Religion and Society*, *3*(02), 25–39.

Chapter 11
Exploiting Crisis:
How Traffickers Thrive in Global Conflicts

Kavya Tyagi
http://orcid.org/0009-0003-4284-4324
Amity University, India

Arvind P. Bhanu
http://orcid.org/0000-0001-9392-3354
Amity University, India

ABSTRACT

Human trafficking takes on devastating dimensions in times of global conflicts. This chapter explores how war, displacement and the collapse of governance create fertile conditions for trafficking in persons to flourish. Drawing on legal and psychological perspectives, the chapter also examines how weakened institutions, fragmented law enforcement, and humanitarian failures perpetuate cycles of impunity and abuse. It analyses the gaps in international legal frameworks alongside the practical barriers to victim identification and prosecution in crisis zones. Three case studies which are of Syria, Haiti, and Gaza illustrate these dynamics through concrete evidence of exploitation in conflict and post-conflict settings. The chapter concludes with recommendations for stronger legal accountability, survivor centred rehabilitation and the integration of anti-trafficking norms within humanitarian and peacebuilding frameworks.

DOI: 10.4018/979-8-3373-5841-3.ch011

INTRODUCTION

Human trafficking is one of the most dreadful violations of human rights, thriving wherever governance collapses and weakened law mechanisms prevail. It is a global crime transcending borders that takes on horrible forms during armed conflicts and humanitarian crises. The United Nations Office on Drugs and Crime (UNODC, 2022) identifies armed conflict as one of the main drivers of trafficking, noting that violence, displacement, and economic collapse intersect to create such fertile land for exploitation. In such circumstances, traffickers, capitalize on this chaos to recruit, transport, and exploit vulnerable populations for labour, sexual servitude, and forced combat. While human trafficking has existed across historical periods, its manifestation has developed significantly over the past decades, particularly following large-scale conflicts in the Balkans, Iraq, Syria and more recently Ukraine and Gaza. These contexts reveal how trafficking adapts to shifting geopolitical, economic, and humanitarian conditions.

The Palermo Protocol (United Nations, 2000) defines trafficking as the "recruitment, transportation, transfer, harbouring or receipt of persons" through coercion, fraud, or abuse of vulnerability for the purpose of exploitation. However, in conflict times, these coercive elements often blend with the survival or livelihood behaviours. The International Organization for Migration (IOM, 2023) emphasizes that forced migration blurs the line between voluntary movement and coercion particularly when individuals flee without any documentation, protection, or access to basic needs.

The escalation of trafficking in recent crises and conflicts highlights this intersection between vulnerability and conflict. For example, *Europol (2022)* reported that criminal networks engaging in trafficking in human beings were targeting Ukrainian refugees especially women and children with sexual and labour exploitation as well as forced criminality and begging. Since the Taliban has returned to power in Afghanistan, reports have documented forced and early marriages, sexual slavery, and recruitment of children (U.S. Department of State, 2025*). Similarly, Research by the* Global Survivors Fund (2023) shows that in Myanmar's conflict regions, the survivors of sexual violence including many displaced Rohingya women face ongoing trafficking risks tied to displacement and lack of access to reparations, reinforcing how exploitation flourishes where justice and relief systems are absent. This chapter later explores these patterns in greater depth through focused case studies from Syria, Haiti, and Gaza.

Conflict does not simply create vulnerability; it reshapes the very meaning of safety, law, and survival. When families flee bombed homes, when borders close, and when basic governance collapses, the social fabric that once offered protection dissolves. In these moments, the line between consent and coercion becomes almost invisible. What begins as a desperate act to survive a journey, a job, a promise of marriage can quickly become entrapment. Women, children, and displaced men are caught in an impossible calculus between hunger, violence, and exploitation. Yet, behind each instance of trafficking lies a broader truth: that systems meant to protect the vulnerable often collapse first in crisis. When the rule of law is replaced by the rule of force, exploitation becomes the language of power. Trafficking in these contexts is not random; it is organized, adaptive, and sustained by global demand that transcends the battlefield. Through war economies and illicit labour markets, armed groups and transnational criminal networks generate sustained demand for exploitation, embedding trafficking within the political and economic dynamics that shape and sustain crisis and displacement. The crime endures because it thrives on invisibility, shame, and silence factors amplified by war and displacement. Understanding trafficking in conflict, therefore, requires confronting not just the traffickers themselves but the global systems of inequality, displacement, and indifference that allow it to persist.

This chapter establishes trafficking as not merely an opportunistic crime but as a structural outcome of crisis that is driven by the erosion of the rule of law, economic fragmentation, and the collapse of safety nets. It builds upon both legal and psychological perspectives to argue that conventional anti-trafficking mechanisms, which were once designed for peacetime governance and stable institutions, are ill-suited to contexts of global conflict and humanitarian collapse. By examining the legal architecture, enforcement gaps, and the psychological impact on survivors, this chapter offers a comprehensive understanding of how crisis not only transforms trafficking into a crime of opportunity but also embeds it within systems of survival and exploitation. The subsequent sections explore the mechanisms through which conflict fuels trafficking, followed by detailed case studies from Syria, Haiti, and Gaza that exemplify these global dynamics and reveal the urgent need for integrated, survivor-centred, and justice-oriented responses. In doing so, this chapter also critically assesses why existing legal and policy responses fail in crisis settings and outlines pathways for developing conflict-responsive, survivor-centred interventions that are tailored to conditions of instability and displacement.

I. HOW GLOBAL CONFLICTS FUEL HUMAN TRAFFICKING?

Global conflicts fundamentally reshape the landscape in which human trafficking occurs. Warfare destroys economies, displaces millions, and dismantles institutions responsible for enforcing laws and protecting citizens. Historically, similar patterns were observed in post-conflict Balkans during the 1990s, where trafficking networks expanded rapidly in the absence of effective policing and judicial oversight. As the UNODC (2022) notes, the weakening of state structures and social systems in conflict and post-conflict settings "creates environments of impunity where traffickers operate with limited risk." In these circumstances, the vulnerability of civilians increases exponentially particularly for women, children, refugees, and internally displaced persons (IDPs).

Crisis driven displacement is a key accelerator of trafficking. The IOM (2023) notes that during displacement, migrants often lose access to documentation, employment, and social networks, which heightens their vulnerability to exploitation in informal labour markets. Refugees may engage smugglers to cross borders but later find themselves trapped in forced labour or sexual servitude. In protracted crises such as those in Libya and Yemen, trafficking has become embedded in war economies. As a result, trafficking related abuses are frequently normalized within war economies rather than treated as criminal offenses. Militias and armed groups systematically exploit civilians for revenue generation through forced labour, sexual exploitation, and ransom schemes *(U.S. Department of State, 2025).*

The European experience with Ukrainian refugees provides a contemporary example of how organized crime adapts rapidly to crises. *(Europol, n.d.)* documented an increase in trafficking networks targeting women fleeing the war, using deceptive online advertisements for employment or housing.

Similarly, UNHCR (2024) reported that the combination of inadequate protection mechanisms, language barriers, and financial insecurity exposed refugees to traffickers in transit and destination countries. These patterns are mirrored globally from child recruitment in the Sahel to forced marriages in the Afghanistan highlighting that the traffickers are deeply intertwined with geopolitical instability and displacement.

Furthermore, conflicts transform traditional gender dynamics, amplifying the vulnerability of women and girls. The *Research by the* Global Survivors Fund (2023) and *Europol (2022)* both confirm that sexual violence, slavery, and forced marriages have been systematically used as tools of domination by armed actors. When the access to justice collapse, survivors face stigma, retraumatization, and impunity for perpetrators. In many conflict settings, survivors are unable to pursue legal remedies due to fear of retaliation, lack of evidence, or the absence of functioning courts.

Ultimately, conflict functions not merely as a backdrop but as both a catalyst and an ecosystem for trafficking. It dismantles the protective frameworks that uphold law, security, and human dignity, transforming exploitation from an exception into a norm of survival. In war-torn environments, people make impossible choices like selling their labour, bodies, or even family bonds in exchange for safety or food. Such coercive contexts blur moral and legal boundaries, making trafficking not only predictable but preventable. When the rule of law collapses, traffickers do not simply emerge; they take root, building parallel economies of control and profit that persist long after ceasefires are declared. Therefore, trafficking in persons during conflict cannot be treated as a secondary humanitarian concern. It is a barometer of systemic failure and an early warning of deeper governance decay. Recognizing this nexus is vital to crafting responses that go beyond rescue or prosecution. Anti-trafficking protections must be integrated into every stage of humanitarian intervention i.e. from emergency aid distribution to peace negotiations and post-conflict reconstruction. This means embedding accountability, survivor participation, and gender-sensitive safeguards within humanitarian and peacebuilding operations. To address trafficking in crisis settings is, at its core, to defend the principle that even amid war and ruin, human life retains its inalienable worth. Combating this crime, therefore, is not solely a matter of justice but a necessary foundation for lasting peace.

II. LEGAL LANDSCAPE

Under the international law, trafficking in persons is prohibited by a network of treaties, conventions and customary norms. However, in times of crisis, even these frameworks lose their operational strength, resulting in the proliferation of trafficking networks and widespread impunity. Gallagher (2010) argues that although the international legal architecture addressing trafficking is extensive, its effectiveness depends entirely on domestic implementation and institutional capacity. Likewise, Obokata (2006) observes that the erosion of governance and the breakdown of human rights protection during crises create fertile ground for traffickers to operate. Together, these insights underscore that the fragmentation of legal systems in conflict zones does more harm than weaken enforcement as it fundamentally dismantles the very foundations upon which anti-trafficking norms depend.

The primary international legal instrument addressing human trafficking is the *United Nations Protocol to Prevent, Suppress and Punish Trafficking in Persons, Especially Women and Children* (2000), commonly referred to as the *Palermo Protocol*. It supplements the *United Nations Convention against Transnational Organized Crime* and obliges States Parties to criminalize trafficking, protect victims, and promote international cooperation. While the Palermo Protocol has achieved near universal ratification, its efficacy in crisis-affected areas remains severely limited (Gallagher & David, 2014). They note that legal and institutional capacity are critical for the Protocol's success and many States Parties lack the infrastructure and political stability required to give effect to their treaty obligations, particularly in contexts of weak governance, crisis and corruption.

The very institutions necessary for enforcing anti-trafficking provisions namely judiciary, police officials, and other law enforcement institutions are often non-functional or weak and corrupt which enable trafficking to flourish. (Aronowitz, 2009, 2017).

Courts and investigative bodies may cease to function, and displaced populations are stripped of legal personhood through the loss of documentation or nationality. The resulting misidentification of victims as irregular migrants or offenders, rather than persons entitled to protection, is a recurring failure within international migration governance (Guild, Grant, & Groenendijk, 2019). Humanitarian emergencies also complicate the legal distinction between forced migration, migrant smuggling and trafficking in persons. It is often observed that individuals escaping conflict may initially move voluntarily but can later be subjected to coercion, deception, or exploitation that satisfies the legal elements of trafficking. The inability of weakened institutions to detect and respond to such transitions underscores the urgent need for crisis-responsive frameworks capable of maintaining rule of law protections even amid displacement and instability.

International humanitarian law (IHL) and international human rights law reinforce the prohibition of trafficking in persons. Under the *Rome Statute of the* International Criminal Court (1998), acts such as enslavement and sexual slavery amount to *crimes against humanity* and *war crimes* when committed in armed conflict (*International Criminal Court [ICC], 1998, arts. 7–8*). Similarly, the *Geneva Conventions (1949)* and their *Additional Protocol II (1977)* prohibit slavery and the slave trade in all their forms as grave breaches of international humanitarian law (*International Committee of the Red Cross [ICRC], n.d.*). The *ICC Office of the Prosecutor's Policy on Slavery Crimes (2024)* further clarifies that slavery crimes encompass practices such as forced labour, trafficking in persons, or servile status, thereby situating these abuses within the broader framework of crimes against humanity and war crimes (*ICC Office of the Prosecutor [ICC OTP], 2024, p. 13*). This recognition expands the Court's prosecutorial reach to include exploitative labour and trafficking under the broader framework of slavery crimes. However, despite these foundations, enforcement remains limited in the crisis driven zones. As Allain (2012) observes, despite the jus cogens status of the prohibition of slavery, prosecutions for such abuses remain rare in conflict zones due to evidentiary challenges, jurisdictional limitation, and political reluctance to hold perpetrators accountable. Consequently, trafficking and related forms of exploitation often become entrenched in wartime economies, perpetuating impunity.

The collapse of legal order during crises also distorts how victims of trafficking are classified and treated. In the absence of effective mechanisms for identification, many trafficked persons are mistakenly classified as irregular migrants, criminals, or even combatants rather than victims entitled to protection. This systemic failure is rooted in immigration centric responses that prioritise border control over human-rights safeguards [*(OHCHR), 2017, (UNODC), n.d.*]. In conflict zones, the lack of coordination between law enforcement agencies, immigration authorities and humanitarian institutions further enables traffickers to succeed. These interlinked institutional weaknesses will be analyzed in more depth in the following subsection on Obstacles to Identification, Investigation, and Prosecution.

Parallel to these enforcement challenges there are fundamental deficiencies within the international legal framework itself. Although the principal treaties on trafficking are broad in scope and widely ratified, they remain heavily dependent on state implementation which is a condition rarely satisfied in fragile or transitional states (Gallagher, 2010). In such settings, inconsistent ratification, weak domestic incorporation of international standards, and inadequate monitoring mechanisms create exploitable gaps that traffickers easily exploit. Moreover, a persistent lack of conceptual and legal clarity between trafficking and related offenses such as migrant smuggling, forced marriage or sexual slavery has resulted in fragmented legal responses. The forthcoming subsection, "Gaps in the International Framework," will analyze these shortcomings in greater detail along with also shedding light onto the jurisdictional ambiguities and enforcement asymmetries in crisis affected regions.

In sum, the legal landscape of crisis-driven trafficking reveals a paradox i.e. while international law provides a robust normative framework against it, the same lacks the adaptive capacity to function in conditions of conflict and humanitarian collapse. This chapter therefore contends that the fight against trafficking in global crisis settings requires not merely stringent laws but more resilient institutions, integrated with humanitarian and peacebuilding efforts. Without this intersectional approach, international law will continue to offer protection only on paper, leaving the world's most vulnerable populations trapped between displacement and exploitation.

A. Gaps in the International Framework

The cornerstone of the international legal regime, the United Nations *Protocol to Prevent, Suppress and Punish Trafficking in Persons, Especially Women and Children* (2000), commonly known as the *Palermo Protocol* has been widely regarded as a landmark in codifying trafficking as a transnational crime (United Nations, 2000). It supplements the *United Nations Convention against Transnational Organized Crime (UNTOC)* and obliges States Parties to criminalize trafficking, protect victims, and promote cooperation. The Protocol's overemphasis on criminal justice mechanisms and state-centric implementation has often led to inadequate victim protection, weak preventive measures, and limited attention to the socio-economic root causes of exploitation (Gallo & Thinyane, 2020). The *United Nations University's 20-year review* underscores that, despite extensive legislative reforms, most anti-trafficking strategies inspired by the Protocol have failed to achieve sustainable long term change (UNU, 2020). These systemic weaknesses are further magnified in fragile or transitional states, where enforcement institutions are weakest and jurisdictional mechanisms often fail to operate effectively (Gallagher, 2010).

The Palermo Protocol provides the foundational definition of human trafficking, yet its distinction from related phenomena such as smuggling and irregular migration remains ambiguous (United Nations Office on Drugs and Crime *[UNODC], 2004*). This lack of clarity complicates the identification of trafficking victims in humanitarian crises, where displacement and population movement are widespread, and increases the risk that vulnerable individuals may not receive the protection to which they are entitled (Obokata, 2024).

The *United Nations Global Plan of Action to Combat Trafficking in Persons (2010)* represents a significant step toward coordinating international efforts under the four pillars of *prevention, protection, prosecution,* and *partnership*. However, its *non-binding nature* and reliance on *voluntary state cooperation* have substantially limited its impact. The Plan does not establish any enforcement or accountability mechanisms, leaving implementation dependent on domestic political will and available resources. While it encourages data sharing and capacity building through the United Nations Office on Drugs and Crime (UNODC) and the Inter-Agency Coordination Group against Trafficking in Persons (ICAT), these initiatives remain largely programmatic rather than legally obligatory. Consequently, the Global Plan functions more as a *policy framework* than a *binding legal instrument*, reflecting the broader fragmentation of international anti-trafficking governance (United Nations General Assembly [UNGA], 2010; UNODC, 2010).

Efforts to strengthen victim-centered approaches, such as the Council of Europe Convention on Action against Trafficking in Human Beings (2005), and the monitoring mechanisms established through the Group of Experts on Action against Trafficking in Human Beings (GRETA), have yielded progress but also reveal persistent challenges. GRETA reports highlight ongoing deficiencies in victim assistance, limited access to support services, and low conviction rates, particularly in states affected by conflict or weak institutional capacity (Council of Europe, 2019). These gaps underscore the difficulty of implementing international standards effectively in contexts where state structures are disrupted and trafficking networks exploit instability.

At the regional level, the African Union's Ouagadougou Action Plan to Combat Trafficking in Human Beings, Especially Women and Children (2006) provides a comprehensive strategy linking trafficking with migration and development. This plan emphasizes a three-pronged approach i.e. prevention, protection, and prosecution, aiming to address the root causes and consequences of trafficking within the African context (African Union, 2006).

The ASEAN Convention Against Trafficking in Persons, Especially Women and Children (2015) has advanced harmonization efforts across Southeast Asia but faces uneven domestic transposition and persistent gaps in victim-centred practices. While all ASEAN member states have ratified the Convention, disparities in national frameworks and limited capacity for victim protection continue to hinder effective regional cooperation (ASEAN-Australia Counter Trafficking, 2022).

Another critical structural deficiency lies in the absence of explicit legal linkages between international humanitarian law (IHL) and international anti-trafficking frameworks. The Palermo Protocol and its parent instrument, the United Nations Convention against Transnational Organized Crime, were primarily designed to address transnational organized crime in peacetime governance settings rather than the realities of armed conflict or humanitarian emergencies (Gallagher, 2010). As a result, trafficking committed in situations of conflict frequently falls through jurisdictional and institutional gaps. Domestic systems often lack the capacity to integrate humanitarian norms such as the protection of civilians and prohibition of enslavement with criminal justice obligations (IOM, 2016). Gallagher and David (2014) further emphasize that the implementation of international anti-trafficking obligations is weakest in fragile or transitional states, where the rule of law is undermined and enforcement mechanisms are either inoperative or complicit. The outcome is a fragmented legal architecture: one that formally recognizes trafficking as a serious international crime but fails to secure accountability or protection when states are in crisis or transition.

Other related frameworks, including the ILO Forced Labour Conventions (Nos. 29 and 105), CEDAW (1979), and regional instruments such as the SAARC Convention (2002), also reveal significant limitations. While normatively valuable, they suffer from narrow definitions, non-binding implementation, and limited integration with contemporary trafficking law.

In sum, while the international community has developed a broad set of instruments to combat trafficking, the persistence of definitional inconsistencies, weak enforcement and limited integration with humanitarian and human rights law allows traffickers to exploit legal vacuums. These gaps are further compounded by political breakdown, fragmented regional cooperation, and inadequate victim-centred frameworks which collectively hinder accountability and effective protection.

B. Obstacles to Identification, Investigation, and Prosecution

Identification of trafficking victims is the critical first step in any protection-led response, but it routinely fails in crisis and displacement settings. Frontline responders immigration officials, camp staff, law enforcement and humanitarian personnel frequently lack training to recognise indicators; as a result, victims may be missed or misclassified as irregular migrants or criminals (IOM, n.d.; UNODC, 2022). The UNODC Global Report documents persistent under-identification even as crises increase vulnerability, noting that fewer victims are being formally detected in contexts where needs are growing and that men and boys remain less likely to be identified because of gendered stereotypes and service gaps (UNODC, 2022). National Referral Mechanisms (NRMs) and standard operating procedures exist in some jurisdictions, but GRETA and other monitoring bodies repeatedly report weak implementation, inconsistent use of indicators, and gaps in referrals between humanitarian and criminal-justice actors (*Council of Europe, 2022; GRETA reports*).

UNHCR–IOM guidance explicitly call for joint standard operating procedures because asylum and reception processes frequently prioritize registration and border control over proactive victim screening; where reception authorities lack trafficking expertise, survivors remain invisible and may be detained, deported, or pushed into secondary exploitation (UNHCR/IOM, 2020*;* EUAA, 2022). Recent field reporting confirms this dynamic: for example, UN experts have documented cases in which clear indicators of sexual exploitation were overlooked in migrant reception facilities, demonstrating systemic failures in screening and referral (Reuters, 2024).

Evidence collection in crisis zones is hampered by insecurity, population movement, loss of documentation, and the destruction or inaccessibility of crime scenes and records (UNODC, 2022). Trauma and coercive control further complicate investigations: many victims distrust authorities, fear reprisals, or dissociate from traumatic memories, undermining their willingness or ability to provide coherent testimony (IOM, n.d.; Allain, 2012). The forensic capacity of domestic systems like DNA analysis, financial tracing, digital forensics is often limited in fragile states, reducing the ability to link perpetrators to criminal networks or to establish chains of illicit profit (Gallagher, 2010; UNODC, 2022).

Trafficking networks commonly operate transnationally, while victims and evidence traverse multiple legal systems; weak mutual legal assistance, incompatible evidentiary standards, and slow extradition procedures frequently stall investigations (Gallagher & David, 2014). In conflict settings, states may lack effective control over territory or borders, and non-state armed groups sometimes implicated in trafficking are not readily subject to domestic prosecution, producing effective impunity (ICC OTP, 2024; Allain, 2012). For example, in *Prosecutor* v. *Kunarac et al.* (International Criminal Tribunal for the former Yugoslavia [ICTY], 2001), the Tribunal recognised enslavement and sexual exploitation in armed conflict as crimes against humanity, yet such findings remain exceptional and difficult to replicate in contemporary trafficking prosecutions involving non-state armed groups. Similarly, the European Court of Human Rights in *Rantsev v. Cyprus and Russia* (European Court of Human Rights [ECtHR], 2010) affirmed states' positive obligations to investigate trafficking; however, such standards are rarely met in crisis or post-conflict environments where institutional capacity is severely constrained.

Corruption and complicity among local officials or security personnel further erode the prospects of identification and prosecution. Reports and monitoring bodies have documented instances where officials in detention or reception facilities either ignored indicators or participated in exploitation themselves, discouraging victim disclosure and obstructing investigative pathways (GRETA, 2022; UNODC press release, 2023). Where corruption is entrenched, victims who attempt to cooperate with investigators face retribution, and evidence trails are actively disrupted.

Traffickers exploit social media, encrypted messaging apps, and online marketplaces to recruit, advertise, and manage victims, often across jurisdictions; while digital footprints can be evidentially valuable, investigators in many affected states lack capacity, legal frameworks, or cross-border access to pursue technology-facilitated crimes (GRETA, 2022; UNODC, 2022).

Finally, prosecution and conviction rates for trafficking offences remain low worldwide, reflecting the cumulative effect of these identification and investigative barriers. UNODC's analysis shows that only a small fraction of detected trafficking flows result in successful prosecutions, and that judicial outcomes are highly uneven across regions (UNODC, 2022). Practical impediments victim re-traumatization risks in court, weak witness protection programmes, plea bargaining that spares higher-level facilitators, and political reluctance to prosecute powerful actors further depress outcomes (Allain, 2012; Gallagher & David, 2014). In conflict or post-disaster contexts, the combination of destroyed institutions, security risks for witnesses, and competing political priorities makes meaningful prosecution especially rare (ICC OTP, 2024; IOM, n.d.).

Taken together, these obstacles show that identification, investigation, and prosecution are not discrete failures but interlinked systemic deficiencies. Overcoming them requires investing in multi-agency training and NRMs, ensuring proactive screening in migration and humanitarian settings, strengthening forensic and digital investigative capacities, developing robust witness protection, and improving cross-border judicial cooperation measures repeatedly recommended in international guidance and monitoring reports (UNODC, 2022; UNHCR/IOM, 2020; GRETA, 2022).

III. PSYCHOLOGICAL FALLOUT

The psychological effects of human trafficking are profound and often enduring, particularly when exploitation occurs amid armed conflict or humanitarian emergencies. Survivors experience multiple and intersecting traumas exposure to violence, coercion, displacement, loss of family, and prolonged abuse which create complex mental-health outcomes extending well beyond immediate rescue or return (*Zimmerman et al., 2012*). Studies consistently show high prevalence rates of post-traumatic stress disorder (PTSD), depression, anxiety, and substance-use disorders among trafficking survivors, often exceeding those found in survivors of single-incident trauma (Hossain et al., 2010; Oram et al., 2012).

In conflict-affected settings, these harms are compounded by the breakdown of health systems and the normalization of violence. Trafficked persons especially women and children are repeatedly exposed to sexual violence, forced labour, and captivity under militia or criminal control, producing cumulative and complex PTSD symptoms such as emotional dysregulation, intrusive memories, dissociation, and chronic feelings of guilt or shame (United Nations Office on Drugs and Crime [UNODC], 2022; International Organization for Migration [IOM], 2019). Forced recruitment of children into armed groups creates distinct developmental trauma patterns marked by disrupted attachment, aggressive behaviour, and identity fragmentation (Betancourt et al., 2013).

Psychological distress is exacerbated by post-trafficking realities: stigma, fear of retaliation, and social rejection frequently hinder disclosure and help-seeking (Zimmerman & Kiss, 2017). In many humanitarian contexts, psychosocial support services are either unavailable or poorly integrated into protection mechanisms. Mental-health care is often treated as a secondary concern within anti-trafficking or refugee programming, despite evidence that trauma symptoms directly affect survivors' capacity to participate in legal processes or reintegration programmes (World Health Organization [WHO], n.d.; IOM, 2019). Consequently, untreated trauma not only impairs recovery but can perpetuate cycles of vulnerability, increasing the risk of re-trafficking or further exploitation.

Emerging neuroscience research confirms that chronic captivity and coercion can produce neurobiological changes similar to those observed in prisoners of war, altering stress-response systems and reinforcing psychological dependence on perpetrators. Such findings underscore the necessity of trauma-informed care and survivor-centred approaches. Evidence from post-conflict recovery programmes indicates that community-based psychosocial interventions, peer-support groups, and culturally adapted therapies are among the most effective tools for rebuilding resilience and reducing PTSD and depression symptoms among trafficking survivors (IOM, 2019; WHO, n.d.).

Ultimately, addressing the psychological fallout of crisis-driven trafficking requires integrating mental health and psychosocial support (MHPSS) into all stages of humanitarian and justice responses. This means ensuring immediate access to psychological first aid, long-term trauma-specific therapy, and survivor-led participation in service design. Beyond clinical treatment, survivors need safe spaces, community reintegration programs, and culturally sensitive healing practices that restore agency and dignity. Building the capacity of local practitioners, empowering survivor networks, and embedding MHPSS within legal and reintegration frameworks are critical steps toward sustainable recovery. Without sustained psychological healing, legal and social rehabilitation efforts remain incomplete, making the recognition of mental health care not merely a humanitarian obligation but a central pillar of justice, empowerment, and recovery.

IV. CASE STUDIES: TRAFFICKING IN SPECIFIC CRISIS CONTEXTS

The erosion of state institutions and enforcement mechanisms, mass displacement, and the collapse of rule of law institutions leave populations acutely vulnerable to exploitation. The United Nations Office on Drugs and Crime (UNODC, 2022) emphasizes that conflict and post-conflict zones present "fertile ground for traffickers," as civilians seek safety or livelihood in conditions where governance and protection mechanisms have disintegrated. Similarly, the International Organization for Migration (IOM, 2023) has documented a consistent pattern in which displacement caused by persecution, war, or disaster heightens exposure to trafficking for purposes of sexual exploitation, forced labour, and servitude.

Recent crises have underscored the magnitude of this phenomenon. *Europol (2022)* noted that Ukrainian refugees, particularly women and children, face risks of sexual and labour exploitation, forced criminality, and begging. In Afghanistan, the Taliban's return has led to reports of forced marriages, sexual slavery, and child recruitment (*U.S. Department of State, 2025*), while in Myanmar, survivors of sexual violence especially displaced Rohingya women remain vulnerable to trafficking due to insecurity and lack of reparations (Global Survivors Fund, 2023).

In Libya and Yemen both designated as "Special Cases" in the *2025 Trafficking in Persons Report* due to ongoing conflict and the absence of unified governance armed groups, militias, and transnational traffickers have committed acts of rape, forced labour, and sexual slavery with near-total impunity amid widespread humanitarian collapse (*U.S. Department of State, 2025*). The convergence of war economies, migration routes, and the absence of judicial oversight sustains cycles of exploitation that are inseparable from the dynamics of conflict itself.

These global patterns reveal that trafficking in persons during armed conflict is not an incidental by-product but a structural outcome of insecurity, displacement, and economic desperation. The following case studies of Syria, Haiti, and Gaza illustrate the diverse manifestations of this nexus between conflict and trafficking. Each demonstrates how institutional breakdown, displacement, and poverty transform vulnerability into commodification, and how weak enforcement, stigma, and international inaction perpetuate impunity.

Together, they highlight the urgent need to integrate anti-trafficking protections within humanitarian, peacebuilding, and reconstruction frameworks, ensuring that responses to crisis address not only immediate protection needs but also the deeper structural inequalities that enable exploitation.

A. Syria

The protracted conflict in Syria has severely shattered the social structures, rule of law, and protection systems, creating conditions in which human trafficking can flourish. More than half of Syria's pre-war population has been displaced internally or across borders, while governance and service delivery have fractured among competing state and non-state authorities. Within this environment of insecurity and economic collapse, exploitation becomes both opportunistic and systemic. The U.S. Department of State Trafficking in Persons Report (2025) notes that the Syrian government does not effectively identify or protect trafficking victims and that both government and non-state actors have been implicated in forced labour, sexual exploitation, and child soldier recruitment.

Women and girls are particularly vulnerable to abuse in displacement settings. Humanitarian organizations report that families facing economic desperation increasingly resort to early and forced marriages framed as "marriage for protection," which in practice can amount to sexual exploitation or servitude (*World Vision, 2020;* UNICEF, 2017*;* UNFPA, 2024). Similar patterns are observed in refugee-hosting areas of Lebanon and Jordan, where informal marriage arrangements expose women and adolescent girls to coercion and abuse. Armed groups operating in Syria have also recruited and used children in hostilities. Human Rights Watch (2024) *and* Anadolu Agency (2024) confirm that the Syrian Democratic Forces and other militias have continued to enlist minors despite international prohibitions, while the Syrian government has imposed forms of forced and indefinite conscription under threat of detention or harm. The 2025 US State Department report verifies that both the Assad regime and other militias "forced citizens to serve indefinitely under threats of detention, torture, familial reprisal, or death". NGOs further document the recruitment and deployment of children as young as six, not only in combat, but also as domestic servants, spies, or forced brides

Reports from humanitarian protection clusters further document incidents of sexual exploitation and extortion at checkpoints, where officials or armed actors demand sexual acts or bribes in exchange for passage, documentation, or employment (UNFPA, 2024). The collapse of judicial mechanisms has left victims with little recourse, and those subjected to trafficking are often criminalized as irregular migrants or offenders rather than recognized as victims of serious crime. Although

Syria is a party to major international anti-trafficking instruments, including the 2000 Palermo Protocol, domestic enforcement remains negligible.

Taken together, these findings illustrate how conflict transforms trafficking from an opportunistic crime into a structural component of wartime economies. In the absence of functioning legal and protective institutions, trafficking in persons becomes normalized as a survival mechanism and as an instrument of control exercised by armed and political actors (UNFPA, 2024; HRW, 2024). Strengthening accountability and protection frameworks in such contexts requires not only criminal justice reform but also humanitarian interventions that restore documentation, livelihoods, and survivor-centred support. This approach must integrate social protection, community rebuilding, and psychosocial care to ensure that recovery addresses both structural vulnerabilities and the lived realities of those most affected.

B. Haiti

In Haiti, one of the most entrenched and tragic forms of child exploitation is the *restavèk* system which is a longstanding practice in which impoverished rural families send their children to live with wealthier urban households under the promise of food, shelter, and education. In theory, it was supposed to provide poor rural children with food, shelter, and education by keeping them in more affluent families in the cities. In reality, it has been an exploitative system (Ciza et al., 2018). Children living as restavèks often work long hours performing household chores, are denied education, and experience high rates of physical, psychological, and sexual abuse. These conditions satisfy the international legal elements of child trafficking and forced labour under the Palermo Protocol and ILO Forced Labour Conventions. The *Violence Against Children Survey* found that restavèk children are far more likely to be beaten, sexually assaulted, or neglected than other Haitian children (Ciza et al., 2018).

The 2021 earthquake and subsequent political upheaval displaced hundreds of thousands of families and deepened already severe poverty (*Human Rights Watch [HRW], 2025*). Amid this instability, traffickers and organized gangs reportedly infiltrated temporary shelters and displacement camps, posing as aid workers or recruiters and promising children education or jobs abroad, often in the Dominican Republic. Many of these children were later found in forced labor or street begging situations, while others simply disappeared (*U.S. Department of State, 2025*).

The Haitian National Police, under-resourced and overextended, faces armed gangs that control large parts of Port-au-Prince and major transport routes (HRW, 2025). This has rendered rescue operations and law enforcement interventions extremely dangerous. Although Haiti has enacted *Law No. CL/2014-0010* on the fight against human trafficking to align with the Palermo Protocol, enforcement remains inconsistent, and implementation largely depends on international aid and nongovernmental organizations (*U.S. Department of State, 2025*). Victim support services are minimal: only a handful of shelters operate nationwide, and many depend on unstable foreign funding. Delays in victim identification and reintegration further expose survivors to cycles of re-trafficking and abuse.

The Haitian experience demonstrates that human trafficking does not always stem from armed conflict alone. Unlike Syria, where trafficking is driven by armed conflict, Haiti illustrates how chronic governance failure, poverty, and disaster can generate trafficking in the absence of formal war. The restavèk system, once rationalized as a survival strategy, has become a normalized mechanism of exploitation that traps tens of thousands of children in domestic servitude. As the *U.S. Department of State (2025) and* Human Rights Watch (2025) both emphasize, durable progress requires more than legal reform, it demands sustained social investment in child protection systems, economic resilience, and education. Haiti's case underscores that economic collapse and recurring disasters can erode human security as profoundly as warfare itself, turning vulnerability into a permanent condition of exploitation.

C. Gaza

The Gaza Strip has long endured protracted conflict, economic collapse, and isolation that have eroded its legal and social protection systems. Decades of blockade and recurring hostilities have created chronic humanitarian fragility, but the escalation of violence in 2024–2025 produced an unprecedented crisis. According to the *United Nations Office for the Coordination of Humanitarian Affairs (*OCHA, 2025*)*, more than 1.9 million Palestinians, nearly 85 percent of Gaza's population were displaced, many seeking refuge in overcrowded schools, temporary shelters, or makeshift encampments with limited access to food, clean water, and medical care. This breakdown of social cohesion and infrastructure generated conditions of desperation and insecurity that traffickers have exploited.

The United Nations Population Fund's (UNFPA, 2025) *Gender-Based Violence Snapshot: Gaza* reported tens of thousands of survivors receiving assistance for sexual violence, forced marriage, and coerced labour during the 2024–2025 escalation. Many were widowed, displaced, or separated from their families. Traffickers and smugglers have exploited this vulnerability by offering false promises of escape to Egypt or Israel in exchange for payment or future labour, often trapping victims in debt bondage or coercive marriages that quickly devolve into exploitation (UNFPA, 2025*;* Zaher et al., 2025). Once across the border, victims are frequently isolated, undocumented, and unable to access legal assistance or consular protection.

UNFPA (2025) *and* OCHA (2025) report that several safe houses for women and children have closed due to insecurity and lack of funding. Humanitarian organizations face severe resource shortages, leaving thousands of survivors without access to emergency shelter, counselling, or medical care. The *U.S. Department of State (2025) Trafficking in Persons Report* confirms that law enforcement in Gaza is fragmented among competing authorities the Palestinian Authority, Hamas, and the Israeli military administration resulting in near-complete impunity for traffickers. Despite the Palestinian Authority's adoption of *Law No. 7 of 2019 on Combating Human Trafficking*, enforcement remains limited, and jurisdictional ambiguity undermines prosecutions. Victims often refrain from reporting abuse for fear of retaliation, stigma, or disbelief.

Trafficking in Gaza cannot be viewed merely as criminal exploitation; it is a manifestation of survival under siege. Families facing destitution and displacement may feel compelled to accept exploitative arrangements sending a child away for safety, agreeing to marriage for protection, or accepting work under coercive conditions. As Zaher et al. (2025) observe, the interplay between occupation, blockade, and humanitarian crisis has normalized transactional relationships that blur the line between coping and coercion.

Ultimately, the Gaza experience demonstrates how conflict and prolonged occupation dismantle not only physical infrastructure but also human agency and legal protection. In such a context, trafficking functions simultaneously as a symptom of systemic collapse and a desperate survival strategy for populations stripped of mobility, security, and dignity. Without sustained international accountability and inclusive recovery mechanisms, the cycle of vulnerability and abuse will continue to regenerate across generations, undermining any prospect of genuine peace or justice.

V. HUMANITARIAN FAILURES

While humanitarian organizations are often perceived as the primary safeguard for populations in crisis, the international aid system has repeatedly demonstrated structural weaknesses and at times complicity in perpetuating trafficking and exploitation. Reports from various places reveal persistent cases in which peacekeeping personnel, aid contractors, and local humanitarian staff engaged in sexual exploitation and abuse (SEA) of those they were mandated to protect. Such misconduct not only violates international law but also erodes survivors' trust in institutions that are intended to deliver safety and care.

Investigations into UN peacekeeping operations in the Central African Republic, the Democratic Republic of Congo, and Haiti documented instances where peacekeepers exchanged food, shelter, or humanitarian aid for sexual acts, including with minors (Beber et al., 2017). In Haiti, allegations of SEA by UN personnel following the 2010 earthquake prompted significant scrutiny into the absence of effective complaint mechanisms and disciplinary accountability (King et al., 2021). Similarly, *The New Humanitarian and the Thomson Reuters Foundation (2020)* jointly exposed widespread sexual exploitation of women by aid workers during the Ebola response in the Democratic Republic of Congo, many of whom were affiliated with major international NGOs and UN agencies. These cases illustrate how crisis environments, marked by dependence on humanitarian aid and lack of oversight, can enable new forms of coercion and trafficking-like exploitation. When aid or protection is made contingent directly or indirectly upon sexual access or labour, such practice meets core elements of trafficking under international law, including abuse of power, exploitation of vulnerability, and extraction of benefit.

The failures are not limited to individual misconduct but extend to institutional responses. The United Nations' zero-tolerance policy toward sexual exploitation and abuse, first articulated in the early 2000s, has often lacked robust implementation and follow-up (United Nations, 2025). Survivors rarely receive compensation or psychosocial support, while perpetrators frequently avoid criminal prosecution due to jurisdictional immunity frameworks or weak referral mechanisms between international organizations and host-state authorities.

Humanitarian operations often rely on rapid deployment models that prioritize logistical delivery over ethical accountability. Scholars argue that emergency aid frameworks, built on short-term funding cycles and contractor-based labour, inherently weaken internal checks and survivor feedback systems (Independent Commission for Aid Impact [ICAI], 2022). This operational fragility contributes to a widely documented "protection paradox" in which humanitarian assistance can inadvertently reproduce the same patterns of exploitation it seeks to prevent.

Addressing these humanitarian failures requires more than reactive disciplinary measures. A paradigm shift is needed i.e. one that embeds anti-trafficking and survivor-protection mechanisms within humanitarian mandates, emphasizes independent oversight, and ensures legal accountability for international personnel. Integrating trauma-informed approaches, gender-sensitive training, and transparent reporting structures is essential to rebuilding trust and ensuring that humanitarian action does not become another vector of vulnerability for those already displaced and traumatized by conflict. This transformation also demands stronger collaboration between humanitarian, legal, and psychosocial actors to create systems of protection that prioritize dignity, agency, and long-term resilience over short-term relief.

VI. RECOMMENDATIONS FOR LEGAL AND PSYCHOLOGICAL REFORM

Addressing the intersection of human trafficking and conflict requires reforms that strengthen both the legal framework and psychosocial support for survivors. Legally, it is crucial to integrate anti-trafficking norms into humanitarian and post-conflict governance systems. This alignment ensures that protection mechanisms are accessible to displaced and conflict-affected populations, particularly through flexible identification standards, cross-border referrals, and non-criminalization safeguards.

Improving *cross-border cooperation* remains central to combating trafficking networks that exploit jurisdictional fragmentation. Strengthening mutual legal assistance treaties (MLATs), improving extradition practices, and establishing rapid information-sharing systems among national focal points can help close enforcement gaps. The European Union's Directive 2011/36/EU offers a working model for regional coordination by requiring member states to harmonize criminal definitions, share data, and ensure victim protection (European Union, n.d.). Similar approaches have been encouraged in Africa under the AU's *Ouagadougou Action Plan* and in Southeast Asia through the ASEAN Convention Against Trafficking in Persons.

A key reform priority is *survivor participation* in the design and implementation of policies. Survivor-led initiatives have proven to enhance both identification and long-term recovery outcomes. Research by the International Organization for Migration (IOM, 2022) and Zimmerman and Kiss (2017) shows that programs incorporating survivor consultation are more responsive and sustainable. Survivor engagement helps policymakers identify practical barriers to access such as stigma, lack of legal documentation, or fear of reprisal and design remedies accordingly. Including survivor representation in national coordination mechanisms and monitoring bodies ensures that protection measures remain grounded in lived experience.

Psychological rehabilitation is equally vital. Evidence consistently shows that trafficking survivors especially those emerging from conflict settings face high rates of post-traumatic stress disorder (PTSD), depression, and anxiety (Oram et al., 2012; Hossain et al., 2010). The World Health Organization (WHO, n.d.) recommends trauma-informed care that integrates mental health and psychosocial support (MHPSS) with social reintegration and livelihood assistance. Coordinating mental health services with legal assistance such as witness protection or compensation schemes creates a holistic framework for recovery. Without psychological stabilization and trauma-informed support, the survivors' ability to engage with legal processes, provide testimony or pursue remedies is significantly compromised.

At a broader policy level, sustainable prevention depends on the effective realization of the *2030 Agenda for Sustainable Development*, particularly Goal 16 on peace, justice, and strong institutions and Goal 8.7 on eradicating forced labour and human trafficking (United Nations, 2015). Preventing conflict and strengthening governance are among the most reliable strategies for reducing trafficking risks in fragile states. As United Nations Secretary-General António Guterres (2025) stated on the *World Day Against Trafficking in Persons*, dismantling the "business model" of trafficking requires ending impunity, cutting illicit profits, and reinforcing justice systems. His statement reinforces that trafficking prevention is inseparable from the pursuit of peace, accountability, and socioeconomic stability.

Ultimately, meaningful reform must bridge legal and psychological dimensions. Legal mechanisms should ensure accountability, protection, and cooperation, while psychosocial services must restore dignity and resilience. Integrating these domains advances a rights-based, survivor-centred approach i.e. one that moves beyond punitive models toward prevention, recovery, and justice in the face of crisis-driven trafficking. This integrated framework must also prioritize survivor participation in policy design, and invest in capacity-building for frontline responders. Only by uniting legal strength with psychological healing can anti-trafficking efforts achieve lasting impact and transformative justice.

CONCLUSION

Human trafficking in conflict and crisis settings is not a peripheral human rights issue but a central indicator of systemic collapse. It reveals the fractures in international law, humanitarian accountability, and collective moral responsibility. Across Syria, Haiti, and Gaza, as well as in Ukraine, Afghanistan, and Myanmar, a consistent pattern emerges wherever war and instability destroy governance, traffickers fill the vacuum. Legal frameworks, while comprehensive on paper, falter in implementation amid fractured institutions and competing jurisdictions. Humanitarian mechanisms, though vital, too often replicate the hierarchies of power and dependency that allow exploitation to thrive.

To confront trafficking effectively, states and international institutions must move beyond episodic responses and adopt holistic, survivor-centred, and context-sensitive strategies that link protection to peacebuilding and reconstruction. It requires sustained political will, coordinated international cooperation, and genuine accountability for both perpetrators and complicit systems.

Trafficking in these crisis zones does not emerge in isolation; it is the direct consequence of a long chain of failures political, economic, and ethical. When governance collapses, the line between protector and exploiter blurs. Yet, these crimes persist not merely because of conflict but because of a collective complacency that treats them as an unfortunate side effect of war rather than a deliberate outcome of neglect.

The rebuilding of war-torn societies must therefore include more than the restoration of infrastructure it must rebuild trust, justice, and dignity. A truly survivor-centred approach demands that those who have endured exploitation be heard not only as victims but as experts of lived experience. Their testimonies hold the moral and practical blueprint for reform. Justice mechanisms should move beyond prosecution alone and integrate reparative, psychological, and social dimensions that restore autonomy to survivors.

Furthermore, anti-trafficking efforts must be embedded within peacebuilding frameworks from the very outset of reconstruction. Disarmament and reintegration programs, transitional justice commissions, and post-conflict legal reforms must all incorporate provisions to identify, protect, and rehabilitate trafficked persons. When peace negotiations or humanitarian missions exclude gender specialists, psychosocial experts, or survivor advocates, they inadvertently allow the same vulnerabilities to persist that traffickers exploit. International cooperation must also evolve beyond the rhetoric of shared responsibility. True coordination requires harmonizing laws, exchanging intelligence, and establishing clear jurisdictional channels that prevent traffickers from exploiting legal loopholes between states. This involves training border officials, police, and humanitarian workers not merely to recognize trafficking indicators but to act with trauma-informed sensitivity. Too often, victims who escape captivity face detention or deportation upon arrival in "safe" territories, their pleas dismissed as irregular migration. Protection should never depend on geography it must follow the individual not the passport.

At the same time, humanitarian actors must confront their own blind spots. Aid systems that depend on unequal power relations can, unintentionally, reproduce patterns of dependency and control. Cases of sexual exploitation and abuse by peacekeepers or aid personnel have exposed how authority without accountability transforms assistance into another vector of harm. Embedding accountability mechanisms within humanitarian operations independent reporting lines, survivor-led oversight, and zero-tolerance enforcement is crucial to restoring faith in protection systems.

Psychological rehabilitation, too, must be re-imagined as an integral component of justice. The trauma of trafficking in conflict zones is multilayered it fuses the violence of war with the intimate violence of exploitation. Survivors require long-term, culturally attuned mental-health support that addresses shame, loss, and fractured identity. Community-based healing programs, survivor peer networks, and creative therapy initiatives can offer spaces for recovery where formal institutions cannot reach.

Ultimately, ending crisis-driven trafficking is not a matter of drafting new treaties but of breathing life into existing ones. To protect the most vulnerable is to reaffirm the very essence of civilization that even in the ruins of war, human dignity is not negotiable. The path forward demands more than reform; it demands remembrance that behind every statistic stands a life interrupted, a story unfinished, a future waiting to be reclaimed.

As United Nations Secretary-General António Guterres (2024) reminded the world on the occasion of the World Day Against Trafficking in Persons, *"Human trafficking is a crime that exploits the most vulnerable. In times of crisis, we must act with unity and urgency to end impunity, strengthen justice, and restore dignity."* This call encapsulates the spirit of this chapter: the fight against trafficking is not only a legal obligation but a moral imperative—an affirmation that even amid war and chaos, the worth of every human life must remain inviolable.

REFERENCES

African Union. (2006). *Ouagadougou action plan to combat trafficking in human beings, especially women and children.* https://www.warnathgroup.com/wp-content/uploads/2020/05/2006-Ouagadougou-Action-Plan-to-Combat-Trafficking-In-Human-Beings-Especially-Women-and-Children.pdf

Allain, J. (2012). *Slavery in international law: Of human exploitation and trafficking.* Martinus Nijhoff.

Anadolu Agency. (2024, June 25). US's PKK-linked partners in northeastern Syria continue to recruit children: State Department. https://www.aa.com.tr/en/middle-east/uss-pkk-linked-partners-in-northeastern-syria-continue-to-recruit-children-state-department/3257206

Aronowitz, A. A. (2009). *Human trafficking, human misery: The global trade in human beings.* Praeger.

Aronowitz, A. A. (2017). *Human trafficking: A reference handbook* (2nd ed.). Routledge. DOI: 10.5040/9798400667497

Beber, B., Gilligan, M. J., Guardado, J., & Karim, S. M. (2017). Peacekeeping, compliance with international norms, and transactional sex in Monrovia, Liberia. *International Organization, 71*(1), 1–30. DOI: 10.1017/S0020818316000242

Betancourt, T. S., Borisova, I., Williams, T. P., Meyers-Ohki, S. E., Rubin-Smith, J. E., Annan, J., & Kohrt, B. A. (2013). Research review: Psychosocial adjustment and mental health in former child soldiers—A systematic review of the literature and recommendations for future research. *Journal of Child Psychology and Psychiatry, and Allied Disciplines, 54*(1), 17–36. DOI: 10.1111/j.1469-7610.2012.02620.x PMID: 23061830

Ciza, D., Dominique, K., Kyambile, B., & Nkurunziza, J. (2018). Results from the Violence Against Children Survey: Haiti. *Child Abuse & Neglect, 76*, 409–418. DOI: 10.1016/j.chiabu.2017.10.009 PMID: 29112856

Council of Europe. (2019). *Assistance to victims of human trafficking.* https://rm.coe.int/assistance-to-victims-of-thb/1680a521f5

Council of Europe—GRETA. (2022). *GRETA reports and general activities.* https://www.coe.int/en/web/anti-human-trafficking

European Union Agency for Asylum (EUAA). (2022). *Identifying and supporting survivors of human trafficking—Asylum report 2022*. https://euaa.europa.eu/asylum-report-2022/55-identifying-and-supporting-survivors-human-trafficking

European Union. (n.d.). Preventing and combating trafficking in human beings (Amending Directive (EU) 2024/1712). EUR-Lex. https://eur-lex.europa.eu/EN/legal-content/summary/preventing-and-combating-trafficking-in-human-beings.html

Europol. (2022, March). *Early warning notification: War in Ukraine – refugees arriving to the EU from Ukraine at risk of exploitation as part of trafficking in human beings* (Ref. No. 2022-340). https://www.europol.europa.eu/cms/sites/default/files/documents/Early_Warning_Notification__War_in_Ukraine_%E2%80%93_refugees_arriving_to_the_EU_from_Ukraine_at_risk_of_exploitation_as_part_of_THB.pdf

Europol. (n.d.). *Trafficking in human beings situational report*. https://www.europol.europa.eu/sites/default/files/documents/thb_situational_report_-_europol.pdf

Gallagher, A. T. (2010). *The international law of human trafficking*. Cambridge University Press. DOI: 10.1017/CBO9780511761065

Gallagher, A. T., & David, F. (2014). *The international law of migrant smuggling*. Cambridge University Press. DOI: 10.1017/CBO9781139059619

Gallo, F., & Thinyane, H. (2020, November 15). The Palermo Protocol turns 20: Failures of the past and shifting paradigms for the future. United Nations University Institute in Macau. https://unu.edu/macau/news/palermo-protocol-turns-20-failures-past-and-shifting-paradigms-future

Global Survivors Fund. (2023, March). *Myanmar: Study on opportunities for reparations for survivors of conflict-related sexual violence* [Global Reparations Study]. https://www.globalsurvivorsfund.org/fileadmin/uploads/gsf/Documents/Resources/Global_Reparation_Studies/GSF_Report_MYANMAR_EN_March2023_WEB.pdf

Guild, E., Grant, S., & Groenendijk, C. A. (Eds.). (2019). *Human rights of migrants in the 21st century*. Routledge., https://www.routledge.com/Human-Rights-of-Migrants-in-the-21st-Century/Guild-Grant-Groenendijk/p/book/9781138503397

Hossain, M., Zimmerman, C., Abas, M., Light, M., & Watts, C. (2010). The relationship of trauma to mental disorders among trafficked and sexually exploited girls and women. *American Journal of Public Health*, *100*(12), 2442–2449. DOI: 10.2105/AJPH.2009.173229 PMID: 20966379

Human Rights Watch. (2020, January 11). *UN peacekeeping has a sexual abuse problem*. https://www.hrw.org/news/2020/01/11/un-peacekeeping-has-sexual-abuse-problem

Human Rights Watch. (2024, October 2). *Northeast Syria: Military recruitment of children persists.* https://www.hrw.org/news/2024/10/02/northeast-syria-military-recruitment-children-persists

Human Rights Watch. (2025). *World report 2025: Haiti* (pp. 2–6). https://www.hrw.org/world-report/2025

Independent Commission for Aid Impact (ICAI). (2022, February 24). *The UK's approach to safeguarding in the humanitarian sector: Literature review* [Report]. https://icai.independent.gov.uk/html-version/the-uks-approach-to-safeguarding-in-the-humanitarian-sector-3/

International Committee of the Red Cross. (n.d.). Rule 94: Slavery and the slave trade (Customary IHL Database). https://ihl-databases.icrc.org/es/customary-ihl/v2/rule94

International Criminal Court. (1998). *Rome Statute of the International Criminal Court.* https://www.icc-cpi.int/resource-library/documents/rs-eng.pdf

International Criminal Court, Office of the Prosecutor. (2024, December). *Policy on slavery crimes.* https://www.icc-cpi.int/sites/default/files/2024-12/policy-slavery-web-eng.pdf

International Organization for Migration (IOM). (2016). *Addressing human trafficking and exploitation in times of crisis: Evidence and recommendations for further action to protect vulnerable and mobile populations.* International Organization for Migration. https://publications.iom.int/books/addressing-human-trafficking-and-exploitation-times-crisis

International Organization for Migration (IOM). (2019). *Caring for trafficked persons: Guidance for health providers* (2nd ed.). https://publications.iom.int/books/caring-trafficked-persons-guidance-health-providers

International Organization for Migration (IOM). (2022). *Study and toolkit: Monitoring and evaluation – Executive summary.* https://publications.iom.int/system/files/pdf/pub2022-114-el-study-and-toolkit-monitoring-exec-sum.pdf

International Organization for Migration (IOM). (2023)... *World Migration Report, 2024,* •••. https://www.iom.int/wmr

International Organization for Migration (IOM). (n.d.). *Trafficking victim identification (practical resources).* https://www.iom.int/sites/g/files/tmzbdl486/files/iscm/materials/traffickingvictimidentification.pdf

King, C., Ferraro, G., Wisner, S. C., Etienne, S., Lee, S., & Bartels, S. A. (2021). "MINUSTAH is doing positive things just as they do negative things": Nuanced perceptions of a UN peacekeeping operation amidst peacekeeper-perpetrated sexual exploitation and abuse in Haiti. *Conflict Security and Development, 21*(6), 749–779. DOI: 10.1080/14678802.2021.1997453

New Humanitarian & Thomson Reuters Foundation. (2020, September 29). More than 50 women accuse aid workers of sexual exploitation during Ebola crisis in Congo. https://longreads.trust.org/item/congo-ebola-aid-workers-accused-demanding-sex-for-jobs

Obokata, T. (2006). *Trafficking of human beings from a human rights perspective: Towards a holistic approach.* Martinus Nijhoff Publishers. DOI: 10.1163/ej.9789004154056.i-247

Obokata, T. (2024). Report of the Special Rapporteur on contemporary forms of slavery, including its causes and consequences. United Nations General Assembly. https://docs.un.org/en/A/HRC/57/46/Add.1

Office for the Coordination of Humanitarian Affairs (OCHA). (2025, March 29). *Gaza humanitarian response update: 16–29 March 2025.* https://www.ochaopt.org/content/gaza-humanitarian-response-update-16-29-march-2025

Office of the High Commissioner for Human Rights (OHCHR). (2017). *In search of dignity: Report on the human rights of migrants at Europe's borders.* https://www.ohchr.org/sites/default/files/Documents/Publications/FS36_en.pdf

Office of the United Nations High Commissioner for Human Rights. (2023). *Recommended principles and guidelines on human rights and human trafficking: 20 years on.* https://www.ohchr.org

Oram, S., Stöckl, H., Busza, J., Howard, L. M., & Zimmerman, C. (2012). Prevalence and risk of violence and the health impact of human trafficking: Systematic review. *PLoS Medicine, 9*(5), e1001224. DOI: 10.1371/journal.pmed.1001224 PMID: 22666182

Prosecutor v. Kunarac, Kovač & Vuković, Case No. IT-96-23 & IT-96-23/1-A, Judgment (Int'l Crim. Trib. for the Former Yugoslavia Feb. 22, 2001) https://www.icty.org/x/cases/kunarac/acj ug/en/

Rantsev v. Cyprus and Russia, App. No. 25965/04, Judgment (Eur. Ct. H.R. July 1, 2010). https://hudoc.echr.coe.int/eng#%22itemid%22:[%22001-96549%22]

Reuters. (2024, December 2). Greece failed to identify sex trafficking victims in migrant centre, UN expert alleges. https://www.reuters.com/world/europe/greece-failed-identify-sex-trafficking-victims-migrant-centre-un-expert-alleges-2024-12-02/

UNHCR & IOM. (2020). *Framework on developing standard operating procedures to facilitate the protection of trafficked persons.* https://www.refworld.org/policy/opguidance/unhcr/2020/en/123233

UNICEF. (2017, March 7). *Syrian children forced to quit school and marry early to survive.* https://www.unicef.org/stories/syrian-children-forced-quit-school-marry-early-survive

United Nations. (2000). *Protocol to prevent, suppress and punish trafficking in persons, especially women and children, supplementing the United Nations Convention against Transnational Organized Crime.* https://www.ohchr.org/en/instruments-mechanisms/instruments/protocol-prevent-suppress-and-punish-trafficking-persons

United Nations. (2025). *Report of the Secretary-General on special measures for protection from sexual exploitation and abuse: A new approach* (A/79/789). https://conduct.unmissions.org/sites/default/files/report_of_the_secretary-general_on_special_measures_for_protection_from-sexual-exploitation-and-abuse_a79789.pdf

United Nations Entity for Gender Equality and the Empowerment of Women (UN Women). (2024, January 19). *Gender alert: The gendered impact of the crisis in Gaza.* https://www.unwomen.org/en/digital-library/publications/2024/01/gender-alert-the-gendered-impact-of-the-crisis-in-gaza

United Nations High Commissioner for Refugees (UNHCR). (2024, September 30). *New study on vulnerability to trafficking in persons in the context of the war in Ukraine.* https://www.unhcr.org/europe/news/announcements/new-study-vulnerability-trafficking-persons-context-war-ukraine

United Nations Office on Drugs and Crime (UNODC). (2010, September). *United Nations launches global plan of action against human trafficking.* https://www.unodc.org/unodc/en/frontpage/2010/September/un-launches-global-plan-of-action-against-human-trafficking.html

United Nations Office on Drugs and Crime (UNODC). (2022). *Global report on trafficking in persons 2022.* https://www.unodc.org/documents/data-and-analysis/glotip/2022/GLOTiP_2022_web.pdf

United Nations Office on Drugs and Crime (UNODC). (2023, January). Press release: Global report on trafficking in persons 2022 — crises shift trafficking patterns. https://www.unodc.org/unodc/press/releases/2023/January/global-report-on-trafficking-in-persons-2022.html

United Nations Office on Drugs and Crime (UNODC). (n.d.). *A/CONF.222/11: Global and national data on trafficking victims* (para. 18). United Nations. https://www.unodc.org/documents/congress/Documentation/A-CONF.222-11/ACONF222_11_e_V1500612.pdf

United Nations Population Fund (UNFPA). (2024). *Voices from Syria 2024: Gender-based violence and protection assessment.* https://arabstates.unfpa.org/en/publications/voices-syria-2024

United Nations Population Fund (UNFPA). (2025, April). *Gender-based violence snapshot: Gaza.* https://palestine.unfpa.org/sites/default/files/pub-pdf/2025-04/GBV-Snapshot-2025-Final.pdf

United Nations Relief and Works Agency for Palestine Refugees in the Near East (UNRWA). (2025, July 4). *UNRWA situation report #178 on the humanitarian crisis in the Gaza Strip and the West Bank, including East Jerusalem.* https://www.unrwa.org/resources/reports/unrwa-situation-report-178-situation-gaza-strip-and-west-bank-including-east-jerusalem

United States Department of State. (2025). *Trafficking in persons report 2025.* https://www.state.gov/reports/2025-trafficking-in-persons-report/

United States Department of State. (2025a). *Trafficking in persons report 2025: Afghanistan.* https://www.state.gov/reports/2025-trafficking-in-persons-report/afghanistan/

United States Department of State. (2025b). *Trafficking in persons report 2025: Syria.* https://www.state.gov/reports/2025-trafficking-in-persons-report/syria

United States Department of State. (2025c). *Trafficking in persons report 2025: Israel, West Bank, and Gaza.* https://www.state.gov/reports/2025-trafficking-in-persons-report/israel

United States Department of State. (2025d). *Trafficking in persons report 2025: Haiti.* https://www.state.gov/reports/2025-trafficking-in-persons-report/haiti

World Health Organization (WHO). (n.d.). *Mental health & psychosocial support (MHPSS).* https://wkc.who.int/our-work/health-emergencies/knowledge-hub/mental-health-psychosocial-support-%28mhpss%29

World Vision International. (2020). *Stolen future: War and child marriage in Northwest Syria.* https://www.wvi.org/sites/default/files/2020-07/Stolen%20Future-War%20and%20Child%20Marriage%20in%20Northwest%20Syria-Online.pdf

Zaher, S., Khalil, H., & Rustom, A. (2025). Beyond borders and blockades: Human trafficking risks among vulnerable Palestinian populations under occupation. *BMC Public Health, 25*(1), 3544. DOI: 10.1186/s12889-025-24893-5 PMID: 41120982

Zimmerman, C., Hossain, M., & Watts, C. (2011). Human trafficking and health: A conceptual model to inform policy, intervention and research. *Social Science & Medicine, 73*(2), 327–335. DOI: 10.1016/j.socscimed.2011.05.028 PMID: 21723653

Zimmerman, C., & Kiss, L. (2017). Human trafficking and exploitation: A global health concern. *PLoS Medicine, 14*(11), e1002437. DOI: 10.1371/journal.pmed.1002437 PMID: 29166396

Chapter 12
Reframing Accountability for Human Trafficking Along the India–Bangladesh Border:
A Securitization and Fragmented Governance Approach

Susmita Paul
http://orcid.org/0009-0004-7484-8503
Christ University, India

ABSTRACT

This research investigates the persistence of human trafficking along the India–Bangladesh border through the combined theoretical lenses of securitization and fragmented governance. While existing literature and policy frameworks often approach trafficking as an issue of migration management, social welfare, or criminal justice, this study argues that such interpretations inadequately address the structural and political dynamics that shape state responses. The research posits that the framing of trafficking as a national security threat—rather than a social or human rights concern—has produced a system where accountability is diffuse, bureaucratic, and performative rather than substantive.

INTRODUCTION

One of the longest and most densely inhabited international borders in the world is the 4,096-kilometer border between Bangladesh and India. Unlike borders pri-

DOI: 10.4018/979-8-3373-5841-3.ch012

marily created by colonial conquest or geopolitical rivalry, this boundary traverses historically linked social, economic, and cultural landscapes. As van Schendel (2005) explains in *The Bengal Borderland: Beyond State and Nation in South Asia*, communities on both sides of the border have historically shared linguistic, familial, and labor networks that precede the contemporary nation-state. In the past, cross-border travel was considered routine, especially in rural and riverine areas such as the Sundarbans, North 24 Parganas, and Cooch Behar.

The creation of the border through the Partition of British India in 1947 fundamentally disrupted these patterns. Mass displacement, shattered local economies, and strict territorial sovereignty imposed on formerly flexible social spaces were all consequences of partition. In *The Spoils of Partition*, Chatterji (1999) shows how the hasty, poorly managed boundary-making process created long-term risks, especially for vulnerable rural populations. These vulnerabilities did not go away with time; instead, they were made worse by later political events, such as the 1971 Bangladesh Liberation War, which, according to Government of India statistics and UNHCR historical assessments, forced an estimated 10 million people into India.

Against this historical backdrop, trafficking emerged not as an aberration but as a structural outcome of disrupted livelihoods, gendered labor markets, and weak social protection. According to recent studies like Rina Chowdhury's *Trafficking, Migration and Border Governance in Eastern India* (Chowdhury, 2020), trafficking networks take advantage of poverty, the need for informal labor, and restricted access to documents. Particularly in situations where domestic employment, unofficial manufacturing, and the entertainment sector operate outside of effective regulation, women and children are disproportionately impacted.

Though the socioeconomic factors that contribute to human trafficking are widely known, the ways in which state interventions influence susceptibility and survivor outcomes have received less attention. Trafficking along the border between Bangladesh and India has been viewed more and more through the prism of national security throughout the last thirty years. Cross-border mobility has increasingly been associated with organized crime, illegal migration, and infiltration in political rhetoric in both Bangladesh and India. This reframing reflects a broader global trend in which migration-related phenomena are securitized, thereby legitimizing exceptional governance measures.

Barry Buzan, Ole Wæver, and Jaap de Wilde, in *Security: A New Framework for Analysis* (Buzan et al., 1998), define securitization as a process whereby political actors construct an issue as an existential threat requiring emergency action beyond routine political procedures. Once securitized, an issue is removed from the realm of deliberative policy-making and placed under the authority of security institutions. Applied to trafficking, securitization shifts the policy center of gravity away from welfare and rights-based interventions toward border control, surveillance, and enforcement.

According to empirical data, this change has had a significant impact on how trafficking is regulated along the border between Bangladesh and India. In order to fight human trafficking and illegal migration, border fencing, more patrols, biometric identification technology, and increased authority for border security forces have all been justified. According to the United Nations Office on Drugs and Crime, detections of trafficking victims decreased globally in 2020, with notably fewer victims identified in low- and medium-income countries, which may reflect challenges in law enforcement capacities rather than improved survivor outcomes. Increased enforcement activities in these areas do not necessarily lead to better identification of victims or improved access to post-rescue services.

This paradox lies at the heart of the accountability problem this paper addresses. While states can demonstrate action through arrests, rescues, and border infrastructure, these metrics do not capture whether survivors are able to access justice, rebuild livelihoods, or avoid re-trafficking. The emphasis on visible enforcement allows governments to claim success without addressing long-term harms. As a result, accountability is measured in outputs rather than outcomes.

At the same time, governance of trafficking along the India–Bangladesh border is highly fragmented. Numerous players, including border security forces, state police, anti-human trafficking units, welfare departments, judicial bodies, and non-governmental groups, share responsibility for prevention, rescue, rehabilitation, prosecution, and reintegration. Each is driven by different political incentives, resource limitations, and mandates. Bob Jessop's *State Power: A Strategic-Relational Approach* (Jessop, 2007) conceptualizes such arrangements as fragmented governance systems, in which authority is dispersed, and responsibility is often diffused.

In reality, this fragmentation results in what is known as institutional uncertainty. NGOs offer frontline assistance but lack formal authority; border security forces prioritize maintaining territorial integrity and preventing crime; welfare departments focus on providing services but lack enforcement authority; and legal procedures move slowly across jurisdictions. The porous border between India and Bangladesh and the widely scattered checkpoints and security staff contribute to the challenges of addressing human trafficking along the border.

Importantly, fragmentation and securitization are not separate processes. Instead, they support each other. Securitization marginalizes welfare-oriented actors while strengthening the power of security institutions. By limiting their function to interception and rescue, fragmentation in turn enables security organizations to escape accountability for long-term survivor outcomes. When these factors come together, there is a lack of accountability, meaning no organization is clearly in charge of ensuring survivors' safety once they are rescued.

This paper contends that addressing trafficking along the India–Bangladesh border requires moving beyond enforcement-centric narratives toward a human security framework. According to the UNDP's Human Development Report from 1994, human security emphasizes independence from want and fear, moving the focus of security from the state to the individual. When it comes to trafficking, a human security approach puts survivor agency, dignity, and long-term wellness ahead of territorial control.

Despite rhetorical commitments to victim-centered approaches in policy documents, implementation remains limited. Survivor perspectives are often invoked symbolically rather than operationally. Although case studies of survivor-led projects in districts such as Murshidabad and North 24 Parganas show the promise of participatory methods, official government systems continue to overshadow them. According to research published in 2019 by the Institute of Development Studies on Participatory Accountability in Anti-Trafficking Governance, survivor participation works best when integrated into institutional decision-making processes rather than treated as an afterthought.

This research paper aims to redefine accountability in analytically accurate, policy-relevant terms by situating trafficking within the overlapping mechanisms of securitization, fragmented governance, and historical borderland vulnerability. The more important question is whether current governance systems can provide survivors with genuine protection and reintegration, rather than whether states are doing enough to combat trafficking.

SITUATING THE STUDY: THEORETICAL FRAMEWORK AND RESEARCH GAPS

Over the past 20 years, scholarly interest in human trafficking along the India-Bangladesh border has grown dramatically, encompassing fields such as international law, criminology, development economics, migration studies, and gender studies. Nevertheless, despite this expanding corpus of work, current research frequently remains analytically dispersed, reflecting the governance issues it aims to clarify. A large portion of the literature ignores issues of power, securitization, and institutional responsibility in favor of concentrating on the legal and policy frameworks or the socioeconomic factors that contribute to human trafficking. This section explains the article's distinctive contribution, places the current work within these discussions, and highlights critical conceptual constraints in previous research.

Early scholarship on trafficking in South Asia primarily framed the issue through poverty, gender inequality, and labor market informality. Studies such as Siddharth Kara's *Sex Trafficking: Inside the Business of Modern Slavery* (Kara, 2009) emphasized the economic rationality of trafficking networks and the profitability of exploitation. While such analyses were instrumental in drawing attention to the scale and brutality of trafficking, they often treated the state as either a neutral enforcer or a passive failure, rather than as an active producer of governance conditions that shape vulnerability. Similarly, development-oriented analyses, including UNDP's *Human Development Report 2009: Overcoming Barriers,* highlighted structural inequality and lack of employment as primary drivers, but offered limited insight into how border governance itself mediates these risks.

More recent scholarship has begun to interrogate the state's role more critically. Research on migration securitization has demonstrated how borders are not merely sites of regulation but are actively produced through political narratives and institutional practices. According to Didier Bigo's *Security and Immigration: Toward a Critique of the Governmentality of Unease* (Bigo, 2002) and Jef Huysmans' *The Politics of Insecurity* (Huysmans, 2006), securitization turns migrants into objects of suspicion, which justifies repressive governance. Despite these studies primarily focusing on Europe, non-Western contexts are increasingly drawing on their theoretical insights.

Securitization has taken on several forms across South Asia, shaped by regional geopolitics and the postcolonial state-creation process. In *The Marginal Nation,* Samaddar (1999) discusses how border communities are frequently portrayed as security threats rather than as citizens with rights. Along the India-Bangladesh border, where political discourse commonly conflates trafficking, illegal migration, and demographic change, this framing is especially salient. Such narratives obscure the daily realities of border communities while justifying increased surveillance, as Anasua Basu Ray Chaudhury contends in *Bordering Practices and Migration Control in Eastern India* (Basu Ray Chaudhury, 2018).

Despite these observations, much of the research on securitization overlooks how institutional design and security logics interact to shape policy outcomes. Securitization provides an explanation for the dominance of enforcement, but it falls short in explaining the displacement or diffusion of the duty to protect survivors. Scholarship on fragmented governance, which looks at the distribution of power among various actors and scales, fills this vacuum.

In his book *State Power: A Strategic-Relational Approach,* Jessop (2007) argues that governance is a dynamic process wherein state and non-state actors operate within naturally unequal power relations. Coordination failures in fragmented systems are inherently generated rather than unintentional. When this concept is applied to the governance of trafficking, it becomes clear how various agencies—such as police, border forces, welfare departments, and non-governmental organizations—operate independently rather than collaboratively. According to the IOM's *Cross-Border Human Trafficking Between India and Bangladesh* (2021), survivors often fall through institutional cracks as a result of a lack of standardized referral mechanisms and data-sharing protocols.

Legal scholarship has also brought implementation gaps to light. In its different iterations, *India's Trafficking in Persons (Prevention, Care and Rehabilitation) Bill* promises extensive victim protection; yet detractors point out that it places a strong focus on law enforcement. According to *A Critical Review of India's Anti-Trafficking Bill* (2021) by the Centre for Law and Policy Research, rehabilitation provisions are still inadequately funded and poorly implemented. Bangladesh is dealing with similar issues. Ministry of Home Affairs (India) (2022) reports, such as the National Action Plan to Combat Human Trafficking 2018–2022, set high standards but offer few mechanisms for cross-border accountability.

Although these gaps are recognized in legal and policy assessments, they are often treated as technical issues rather than as expressions of more fundamental governance logics. Borderland studies provide crucial information in this regard. *The Bengal Borderland* by van Schendel (2005) illustrates how sovereignty in this area has always been erratic, negotiated, and dependent. Borders are social structures that allocate rights and vulnerabilities rather than just lines on a map. Additionally, Itty Abraham's *How India Became Territorial* (Abraham, 2014) argues that, particularly in frontier areas, postcolonial states frequently prioritize territorial sovereignty over social well-being.

These observations are especially pertinent to comprehending the governance of trafficking. What Abraham refers to as "graduated sovereignty," in which the state uses coercive power without providing comprehensive social protection, is frequently experienced by inhabitants of borderlands. Due to this circumstance, trafficking networks are able to take advantage of both legal ambiguity and economic precarity. Despite the relevance of borderland theory, many trafficking studies regard borders as static backgrounds rather than as active producers of vulnerability.

Survivors' viewpoints represent another significant gap in current knowledge. Although "victim-centered" approaches are frequently mentioned in policy texts, there is still little actual research on survivor agency. Researchers studying participatory governance and feminist scholars have long maintained that the efficacy of policies is compromised when impacted groups are excluded. Survivor-led monitoring enhances service delivery and fosters trust, according to the Institute of Development Studies (2019) paper *Participatory Accountability in Anti-Trafficking Governance.* Similar to this, Paul G. Harris contends in *Ethics and Global Politics* (Harris, 2018) that effective governance goes beyond just shielding impacted groups as passive recipients and calls for their inclusion in decision-making processes.

In Bangladesh and India, survivor-led initiatives in places such as Murshidabad and North 24 Parganas have demonstrated promise in peer monitoring, prevention, and reintegration support. However, rather than assessing the scalability or integration of these efforts into formal governance systems, previous research often portrays them as isolated success stories. This strategy strengthens the distinction between community-based and state-led programs and reduces their policy relevance.

Comparative viewpoints further highlight these restrictions. The potential and limitations of international cooperation are illustrated by regional frameworks such as the ASEAN Convention Against Trafficking in Persons (ACTIP). Despite advancements in legal harmonization, institutional capacity, and domestic affairs, politics will remain essential for successful implementation, according to the UNODC's ACTIP Implementation Review (2022). Similar issues may be seen in South Asia, where underutilized frameworks like BIMSTEC and SAARC exist.

The entire body of literature points to several persistent problems. First, governance theory is not sufficiently taken into account in assessments of trafficking, which are often portrayed solely as security or socioeconomic issues. Second, accountability is typically seen as an implicit outcome rather than the primary analytical focus. Third, although survivor agency and borderland dynamics are recognized, explanations do not always account for them.

By creating an integrated analytical framework that connects securitization, fragmented governance, and borderland theory to empirical data from the India–Bangladesh border, this research paper fills in the identified gaps. Instead of concentrating only on policy outputs, the analysis places responsibility as the primary analytical concern, giving survivor-centered outcomes priority. The argument advanced is that effective anti-trafficking reform requires a fundamental reorientation in how border governments conceptualize security, sovereignty, and responsibility, alongside the adoption of stricter legislation and enhanced cooperation.

HISTORICAL FORMATION OF THE INDIA–BANGLADESH BORDER AND THE PRODUCTION OF VULNERABILITY

Understanding current trends in human trafficking along the India-Bangladesh border requires a close look at the historical processes that created and maintained the border. Instead of emerging on its own, trafficking in this area is entwined with a larger history of displacement, upended livelihoods, and unequal governmental presence. Beyond merely separating two independent states, the border has served as a socially constructed area influenced by political choices, economic shifts, and changing regimes. These historical factors continue to influence vulnerability and limit the effectiveness of anti-trafficking measures.

After British India was divided in 1947, the Bengal region saw tremendous disruption. Villages, farmlands, rivers, and family networks that had previously operated as cohesive social units were split apart by the Radcliffe Line, which was established quickly and with little local input. The partition of Bengal was marked by long-term administrative upheaval, violence, and displacement, as Joya Chatterji details in *The Spoils of Partition* (Chatterji, 1999). Despite generations of residence, many border villages were abruptly labeled as "migrants" or "minorities" within newly constituted national areas.

Beyond the immediate humanitarian catastrophe, Partition had far-reaching effects. Due to the extensive displacement that disrupted the rural economy and informal labor markets, many households were forced to rely on seasonal or circular migration for subsistence. Samaddar (1999) argues in *The Marginal Nation* that the post-Partition government in eastern India established "zones of abandonment," where the state employed intermittent coercive control but was unable to provide consistent social support. These regions, particularly border districts, become essentially vulnerable to exploitation.

These dynamics became much more intense during the Bangladesh Liberation War in 1971. It is estimated that ten million people have been displaced by the unrest, mainly to West Bengal, Assam, and Tripura in India. The war solidified trends in cross-border migration and informal settlement, despite many refugees subsequently returning. According to UNHCR historical evaluations and Indian government documents, during this time, short-term confinement was given precedence over long-term integration in refugee management. Due to their persistent lack of access to safe documentation and state services, many relocated families were more susceptible to exploitation by unofficial labor brokers.

Cross-border travel continued as a means of subsistence rather than as a criminal activity in the decades after Bangladesh gained its independence. Particularly among underprivileged and landless people, seasonal migration for domestic work, construction, agriculture, and informal manufacturing persisted. Willem van Schendel's 2005 book *The Bengal Borderland* highlights that, despite the border's metaphorical hardening, it remained porous in reality. While the state's involvement remained selective and uneven, local economies nevertheless relied on cross-border trade (van Schendel, 2005).

Trafficking networks progressively established themselves under this historically accepted framework of migration. Early types of trafficking frequently coexisted with the recruitment of unorganized labor, making it difficult to distinguish between exploitation and migration. According to Rina Chowdhury's *Trafficking, Migration and Border Governance in Eastern India* (Chowdhury, 2020), dishonest hiring practices usually function through reliable social networks, making detection and deterrence especially difficult. Current policy solutions that aim to establish clear legal distinctions between "legitimate" migration and "criminal" trafficking are complicated by this historical overlap.

However, the management of the border between Bangladesh and India started to change significantly in the late 1980s. Particularly in India, worries about illegal immigration, demographic shifts, and national security have taken center stage in political discourse. The border was gradually reinterpreted as a place of danger rather than a site of trade. The development of border infrastructure, such as floodlighting, fencing, and improved surveillance systems, coincided with this change.

This change, according to academics, is part of a larger post-Cold War trend toward the securitization of borders. Both internal politics and regional geopolitics influenced securitization in the Indian setting. In *Bordering Practices and Migration Control in Eastern India* (2018), Anasua Basu Ray Chaudhury makes the case that trafficking and migration have become more and more enmeshed in security narratives, which have given legitimacy to extraordinary governance measures. For border communities, this reframing had profound effects because they were perceived more as suspicious than as citizens.

The tightening of border measures did not prevent cross-border movement. Instead, it altered its situation. As movement became riskier and more costly, reliance on intermediaries increased. Traffickers adjusted by taking advantage of unofficial crossings, corruption, and surveillance flaws. Restrictive border policies frequently boost the profitability of trafficking by increasing the risks and benefits involved with illegal migration, according to the UNODC's Global Report on Trafficking in Persons 2022.

Securitization also changed institutional priorities. While welfare-oriented organizations continued to play a supporting role in border governance, border security forces were given more power. According to Bob Jessop's *State Power: A Strategic-Relational Approach* (Jessop, 2007), political priorities are reflected in governance systems; social protection takes a backseat when security takes precedence.

The historical evolution of the border thus produced a layered vulnerability. First, the Partition and post-Partition displacement disrupted livelihoods and documentation. Second, securitization criminalized mobility without addressing its structural drivers. Third, fragmented governance diffused responsibility for protection and reintegration. Together, these factors created conditions in which trafficking could flourish despite increased enforcement.

Many people point to the 2015 Land Boundary Agreement (LBA) between Bangladesh and India as a historic attempt to address past irregularities along the boundary, especially the enclave problem. Although thousands of inhabitants had their citizenship status clarified and enclaves transferred formally under the LBA, its implementation exposed the limitations of legal settlement in the absence of governance unification. ActionAid's *Post-LBA Rehabilitation and Trafficking Vulnerability* (ActionAid, 2019) reports on delays in former enclave residents' access to welfare programs, documentation, and livelihood assistance. These gaps made many people susceptible to human trafficking, highlighting the systemic risk that persists long after official territorial settlement.

Crucially, there is an unequal distribution of historical vulnerability. The intersections of gender, caste, religion, and class have an impact on exposure to human trafficking. Social norms that limit mobility and educational opportunities, as well as gendered work demands, put women and girls from vulnerable groups at higher risk. In areas with inadequate educational infrastructure, child trafficking for domestic work and informal labor is nevertheless common. UNICEF's *Child Trafficking in South Asia: Regional Analysis* (2020), which emphasizes the relationship between poverty and social exclusion, documents these trends.

It is evident from placing modern trafficking within this historical framework that enforcement-centric solutions are not enough. The accumulated vulnerabilities created by decades of marginalization, displacement, and unequal governance are not addressed by policies that only concentrate on interception and rescue. As this paper argues, accountability must therefore be understood not only in legal terms but as a historical and institutional obligation to address the conditions that render specific populations exploitable.

This historical analysis provides the foundation for the sections that follow. Having established how the border and its vulnerabilities were produced, the following section examines how these dynamics manifest empirically across specific trafficking corridors and governance arrangements.

METHODOLOGICAL APPROACH, CASE SELECTION, AND ANALYTICAL STRATEGY

This research study employs a qualitative, interpretive research design to examine how securitization and fragmented governance influence accountability in anti-trafficking initiatives along the India–Bangladesh border, building on the preceding historical and structural analysis. Qualitative methods are particularly effective for capturing institutional dynamics, policy implementation gaps, and lived experiences that are often obscured in aggregate data due to the complex and context-dependent nature of trafficking. Rather than seeking to measure prevalence or produce statistically generalizable findings, the study aims to generate analytically grounded insights into the practical functioning of governance arrangements and the reasons they yield specific outcomes.

Critical policy analysis and borderland studies, both of which emphasize situating institutional practices within their socio-political contexts, serve as the foundation for this paper's analytical perspective. Policies should be viewed as collections of practices, discourses, and power dynamics rather than just formal documents, as

Shore et al. (2011) contend *in Policy Worlds: Anthropology and the Analysis of Contemporary Power*. This viewpoint is especially pertinent to trafficking governance, where there is frequently a significant disconnect between the intention of policies and their actual application.

The study uses a variety of secondary sources, including government reports, policy documents, peer-reviewed academic literature, and publications from civil society organizations and international organizations. Reports from the International Organization for Migration, UNICEF, Human Rights Watch, the United Nations Office on Drugs and Crime, and national ministries in Bangladesh and India are important sources. Documented case studies and program evaluations created by non-governmental organizations that directly assist victims of human trafficking are included to these resources. The study makes considerable use of empirically supported sources that reflect realities on the ground, though it does not contain any new original fieldwork data.

Both practical and ethical factors are reflected in this reliance on secondary qualitative data. Concerning consent, retraumatization, and secrecy, primary research with trafficking survivors presents serious moral issues. Survivor-centered research must put participant welfare ahead of data gathering, as stressed in the UNODC's *Ethical and Safety Recommendations for Interviewing Trafficked Persons* (2008). By engaging with existing ethically reviewed studies and reports, this research avoids duplicating harm while still incorporating survivor perspectives into the analysis.

To structure the empirical discussion, the study adopts a corridor-based case analysis. Three trafficking corridors along the India–Bangladesh border are examined in detail: (1) North 24 Parganas–Jessore, (2) Cooch Behar–Lalmonirhat, and (3) the Sundarbans–Khulna route. Three criteria were used to select these routes. First, they are frequently mentioned as essential trafficking routes in scholarly research and policy papers. Second, they reflect a variety of geographical and socioeconomic circumstances, such as border zones that are close to cities, places that were once enclaves, and coastal regions that are vulnerable to climate change. Third, they enable comparative research within a single border regime by illuminating different governance issues.

It has long been known that the North 24 Parganas–Jessore corridor is a prominent trafficking route, especially for women and children who are trafficked for informal labor, domestic work, and sexual exploitation. It is a key location for traffickers due to its proximity to Kolkata, dense population, and established transportation systems. The corridor is extensively documented in Rina Chowdhury's *Trafficking, Migration and Border Governance in Eastern India* (Chowdhury, 2020) and in the UNODC's *Assessment of Trafficking Routes in South Asia* (2018). Analyzing this corridor allows for examination of how urban labor demand intersects with border enforcement practices.

A different example is the Cooch Behar–Lalmonirhat region, which was shaped by the implementation of the 2015 Land Boundary Agreement and the legacy of enclaves. The LBA settled long-standing issues of citizenship and geographical sovereignty, but social and economic integration did not follow. According to ActionAid's *Post-LBA Rehabilitation and Trafficking Vulnerability* (ActionAid, 2019), new types of vulnerability were brought about by delays in documentation, welfare access, and livelihood support. This corridor is especially helpful for examining the ways in which legal resolution without coordinated governance may unintentionally increase the risk of human trafficking.

A growing trafficking landscape, influenced by environmental change, is evident along the Sundarbans–Khulna route. Erosion, salinization, and cyclones gradually affect the low-lying deltaic Sundarbans. These environmental pressures have led to an upsurge in distress migration, particularly among women. According to the International Organization for Migration's *Environmental Migration and Trafficking Risk in Coastal South Asia* (International Organization for Migration, 2021b), traffickers take advantage of conditions created by climate-induced displacement. By incorporating this corridor, the study may evaluate whether current governance frameworks can accommodate new forms of vulnerability and account for changing trafficking drivers.

Three interconnected dimensions are examined in these cases: (1) institutional roles and coordination; (2) policy implementation and accountability mechanisms; and (3) survivor outcomes, specifically reintegration and danger of re-trafficking. This analytical structure reflects the paper's core argument: accountability cannot be assessed solely through legal compliance or enforcement outputs. Still, it must be evaluated in terms of how governance arrangements affect survivor trajectories over time.

Analyzing the policies and procedures of key players, such as border security forces, law enforcement, anti-human trafficking units, welfare departments, and non-governmental organizations, enabled examination of institutional responsibilities. Particular attention is paid to delineating responsibilities and identifying any gaps or overlaps. Reintegration outcomes are influenced by survivor-centered solutions, according to studies such as UNODC's *Trafficking data harmonization in South Asia: Gaps and challenges* (2022) and the Institute of Development Studies (2019) *Participatory Accountability in Anti-Trafficking Governance*. These sources also highlight the detrimental consequences of inadequate follow-up, including re-trafficking and social marginalization.

Throughout the analysis, care is taken to avoid presenting case studies as exceptional or unusual. Instead, they are used to illustrate broader governing patterns and to assess the explanatory power of the conceptual framework developed earlier. Rather than making statistical generalizations, the goal is to demonstrate analytically how securitization and fragmentation operate under different conditions within the same border regime. According to the IOM's *Cross-Border Human Trafficking Between India and Bangladesh* (2021), uncertain jurisdiction and accountability frequently cause delays in rescue, repatriation, and service delivery.

Formal promises and observable practices are contrasted to evaluate the effectiveness of policy implementation. This means looking at regional groups such as SAARC and BIMSTEC, as well as bilateral organizations such as the India-Bangladesh Joint Task Force. The approach examines how institutional incentives, resource limitations, and political agendas shape these mechanisms' operation, rather than treating them as static institutions. This strategy addresses complaints that discussions of regional cooperation frequently focus too much on aspirations and not enough on practicality.

The third and most important aspect of analysis is survivor outcomes. The study examines livelihoods, education, psychosocial support, legal assistance, access to shelter, and program evaluations and qualitative research.

Lastly, the methodological approach admits its shortcomings. When secondary sources are used, the analysis is influenced by the goals and viewpoints of previous research. However, the study aims to reduce bias and improve robustness by triangulating across many sources and disciplines. Furthermore, the emphasis on governance and accountability enhances rather than replaces current prevalence-focused research.

The empirical analysis that follows is predicated on this methodological framework. In order to show how historical vulnerability, securitization, and fragmentation coincide in particular situations, the paper's following section focuses on a thorough analysis of trafficking routes and governance methods.

EMPIRICAL ANALYSIS I: TRAFFICKING CORRIDORS, BORDER ENFORCEMENT, AND GOVERNANCE FAILURES

Building on the historical and methodological foundations established earlier, this section examines how securitization and fragmented governance operate empirically across key trafficking corridors along the India–Bangladesh border. Rather than treating trafficking as a uniform phenomenon, the analysis focuses on how local institutional arrangements, enforcement practices, and socio-economic conditions interact to shape patterns of exploitation and survivor outcomes. The corridors discussed here—North 24 Parganas–Jessore and Cooch Behar–Lalmonirhat—illustrate how intensified border control and weak coordination can coexist with persistent trafficking, revealing fundamental limitations in current governance approaches.

It has long been known that one of the busiest human trafficking routes between Bangladesh and India is the North 24 Parganas–Jessore corridor. Its strategic importance stems from its proximity to Kolkata, dense population, extensive transportation networks, and long-standing patterns of cross-border labor migration. Women and children are regularly recruited for domestic work, informal manufacturing, agricultural labor, and sexual exploitation along this corridor. These patterns are well documented in Rina Chowdhury's *Trafficking, Migration and Border Governance in Eastern India* (Chowdhury, 2020) and the UNODC's *Assessment of Trafficking Routes in South Asia* (2018).

Despite ongoing police operations in this area, trafficking networks have proven resilient. Instead of being prevented by a border wall, additional police, or monitoring technology, illegal crossings have altered trafficking strategies. Restrictive border regimes frequently increase reliance on intermediaries and boost the expenses of transportation, which increases traffickers' control over victims, as the UNODC points out in the *Global Report on Trafficking in Persons 2022*. Traffickers in North 24 Parganas sometimes use unofficial crossings, bribes, and falsified documents, swiftly adapting to shifting enforcement trends.

Securitization has a significant influence on the governance response in this corridor. With responsibilities focused on maintaining territorial integrity and preventing crime, border security personnel play an essential role. Official narratives may emphasize rescue missions, but they pay much less attention to rehabilitation and reintegration. *Trigger Happy: Excessive Use of Force at the India–Bangladesh Border* (2010), a report by Human Rights Watch, explains how enforcement actions can cause harm to civilians without addressing underlying vulnerabilities. Although the report focuses primarily on use-of-force concerns, it also underscores a broader governance problem: security institutions are not equipped, nor mandated, to address the long-term needs of trafficking survivors.

Fragmentation further compounds these challenges. After rescue, survivors are often transferred between multiple agencies, including police, child welfare committees, shelter homes, and NGOs. Each transition introduces delays and uncertainty. Inconsistent access to services is sometimes caused by a lack of established referral systems, according to the International Organization for Migration's *Cross-Border Human Trafficking Between India and Bangladesh* (International Organization for Migration, 2021a). Survivors may remain in shelters for extended periods of time without knowing if they will be repatriated or face legal action, which can worsen their psychological state and make them more susceptible to human trafficking.

Coordination in these situations is meant to be facilitated by the India-Bangladesh Joint Task Force against Trafficking. Empirical assessments, however, indicate that its primary focus is still on rescue and repatriation rather than reintegration. According to program evaluations referenced in UNODC's *Victim-Centered Justice in Trafficking Cases* (2022), data on survivor outcomes are not routinely gathered, and long-term follow-up is uncommon. Because there is no outcome-based accountability, institutions are able to claim success without proving a significant impact.

The Cooch Behar–Lalmonirhat corridor presents a different, yet equally revealing, governance landscape. This region was historically characterized by enclaves—small pockets of territory belonging to one country but surrounded by territory belonging to the other. Residents of the enclave lived in a state of legal uncertainty for many years, without access to official jobs or essential amenities. By trading enclaves and offering citizenship to residents, the 2015 Land Boundary Agreement (LBA) between Bangladesh and India aimed to address these irregularities.

Even while the LBA is frequently hailed as a diplomatic triumph, its application highlights the limitations of using the legal system in isolation from integrated governance. Significant delays in the delivery of identity cards, land records, and welfare benefits to former enclave residents are documented in ActionAid's *Post-LBA Rehabilitation and Trafficking Vulnerability* (ActionAid, 2019). During this transitional period, many households faced acute economic insecurity. Traffickers exploited these conditions by offering deceptive employment opportunities, particularly to women and adolescents.

The governance response in this corridor illustrates a different dimension of fragmentation. In contrast to North 24 Parganas, where security institutions predominate, administrative coordination is the main issue here. Rehabilitation was divided among several departments, including revenue, social welfare, rural development, and local government agencies. No single entity was responsible for guaranteeing all-encompassing support because there was no central coordinating authority. Therefore, legal inclusion did not result in economic or social protection.

However, institutional priorities were still shaped by securitization. While livelihoods remained unstable, border enforcement remained stringent. Former residents of the enclave had fewer alternatives because they risked detention or harassment if they tried to cross the border for employment. These dynamic underscores what Abraham (2024) refers to as postcolonial governance's preference for territorial sovereignty over social welfare in *How India Became Territorial* (2014). The state asserts control but does not assume responsibility for the socio-economic consequences of that control.

Both variance and convergence are evident when comparing these two corridors. Trafficking continues despite strict enforcement in North 24 Parganas–Jessore; in Cooch Behar–Lalmonirhat, it arises amid administrative change and legal ambiguity. However, there is still little accountability for survivor outcomes in both situations.

Instead of focusing on long-term gains in survivor health, institutions gauge success by actions, such as rescues, border security, and agreements signed.

Crucially, capacity limitations cannot be the only reason for these failures. They reflect deeper governing logics shaped by fragmentation and securitization. While welfare agencies have little power and resources, security institutions are motivated to show control. NGOs close essential gaps, but their efforts are frequently project-based and reliant on outside funding. In the meantime, survivors must negotiate a system that views them more as objects of rescue than as agents with rights.

The empirical evidence from these corridors thus reinforces the central argument of this paper. Anti-trafficking governance along the India–Bangladesh border is characterized by a misalignment between institutional priorities and survivor needs. Without mechanisms to integrate enforcement, welfare, and accountability, trafficking networks continue to adapt, and survivors remain at risk.

EMPIRICAL ANALYSIS II: EMERGING RISKS, SURVIVOR AGENCY, AND STAKEHOLDER DYNAMICS

The Sundarbans–Khulna route demonstrates how new risks combine with pre-existing institutional flaws to create new types of vulnerability, while the trafficking corridors covered in the previous section show historical governance shortcomings. This corridor, which crosses the ecologically delicate Sundarbans delta, shows how a combination of environmental change, livelihood precarity, and government fragmentation alters trafficking dynamics. By looking at this area, the research study can go beyond well-known paths and account for how trafficking governance needs to change in response to evolving circumstances.

Millions of people who rely on agriculture, fishing, and forest-based livelihoods reside in the Sundarbans region, which is shared by Bangladesh and India. It is home to one of the largest mangrove ecosystems in the world. Over the past 20 years, cyclones, erosion, salinization, and rising sea levels have contributed to increased environmental stress in the region. These forces have weakened traditional means of subsistence, and distressed migration has increased. Environmental displacement disproportionately impacts women, who frequently migrate in dangerous conditions in pursuit of employment, according to the International Organization for Migration's *Environmental Migration and Trafficking Risk in Coastal South Asia* (International Organization for Migration, 2021b).

Trafficking networks have adapted to this situation by focusing on populations that have been displaced by the environment. In urban areas, women from the Sundarbans are regularly hired for informal labor and household chores, frequently under false pretenses of steady employment. According to IndiaSpend's investigative study *Cli-*

mate Crisis in the Sundarbans Makes Women Vulnerable to Trafficking (IndiaSpend, 2024), recruiters take advantage of the despair and lack of other livelihoods brought on by climate change. These trends highlight the shortcomings of anti-trafficking policies that focus solely on border security, rather than on the root causes.

The Sundarbans' governance solutions exhibit well-known trends of fragmentation and securitization. Welfare and adaptation efforts lag behind, yet border controls are strictly enforced. Despite their obvious ties, anti-trafficking programs and climate resilience projects are frequently carried out independently. The UNDP characterizes these institutional silos as a failure to integrate human security across policy domains in their *Human Development Report 2022: Uncertain Times, Unsettled Lives*. People who are relocated due to environmental change consequently fall within the governance of migration, climate change, and human trafficking.

The Sundarbans example also shows how current accountability deficiencies are made worse by new threats. Mechanisms for rescue and repatriation are still reactive; they only step in after exploitation has taken place. Support for long-term reintegration is scarce, especially for survivors going back to locations with poor environmental conditions and few employment opportunities. Re-trafficking is still very likely in the absence of consistent financial assistance. Reintegration failure is a significant predictor of recurrent exploitation, according to program assessments included in UNODC's *Global Report on Trafficking in Persons 2022*.

One recurring feature across all three corridors this study examined is that governance procedures do not adequately incorporate survivor agency. Despite the growing use of "victim-centered" and "survivor-centered" methods in policy texts, these ideas are frequently more rhetorical than practical. Survivors are rarely involved in decision-making processes that influence the creation or application of policies and are only occasionally consulted, if at all.

Nonetheless, empirical evidence suggests that survivor-led initiatives can play a critical role in prevention and reintegration. In districts such as North 24 Parganas and Murshidabad, survivor collectives have engaged in peer monitoring, community awareness, and livelihood support. Institute of Development Studies (2019) details these efforts and shows how survivor involvement enhances communication, trust, and early detection of trafficking threats. However, these programs often operate outside established governance frameworks and are supported by donor funding and NGO facilitation.

The underutilization of survivor-led models is a reflection of larger power imbalances in the governance of human trafficking. While survivors and community organizations have firsthand information but no official authority, governments and security agencies have coercive power and resources. In *Ethics and Global Politics*, Harris (2018) argues that institutionalizing involvement rather than treating it as optional is necessary to rebalance these imbalances and ensure ethical governance.

Survivor-centered initiatives run the risk of becoming symbolic gestures rather than significant reforms in the absence of such rebalancing.

Accountability is made more difficult by stakeholder interactions. Numerous entities working at various scales are involved in governance along the India-Bangladesh border, including national governments, state and municipal authorities, security forces, international organizations, non-governmental organizations, and community groups. Different incentives and mandates apply to each actor. International organizations stress coordination but rely on government collaboration; welfare agencies focus on providing services; border security forces prioritize territorial control; and NGOs offer vital assistance but lack authority.

Asymmetries between Bangladesh and India further influence these processes. Although the two nations are frequently portrayed as equal partners in bilateral discourse, their enforcement capabilities, economic clout, and diplomatic clout differ significantly. The conditions of collaboration are shaped by India's greater resources and regional clout, especially in areas such as border management and data exchange. Realistic policy design requires acknowledging these inequalities. Symmetrical frameworks used to asymmetrical circumstances sometimes fail to yield equitable results, as noted by regional governance researchers.

The India-Bangladesh Joint Task Force best shows these difficulties. The Task Force offers a forum for cooperation and discussion, but its operational scope is still constrained. According to assessments referenced in UNODC's *Victim-Centered Justice in Trafficking Cases* (2022), the Task Force prioritizes rescue and repatriation over monitoring or reintegration. The lack of comprehensive data collection on long-term survivor outcomes makes it challenging to evaluate efficacy or assign blame.

In a similar vein, the SAARC and BIMSTEC regional mechanisms remain primarily aspirational. Despite conventions and action plans expressing commitments to collaboration, their implementation varies. Political rivalries, resource constraints, and lack of enforcement mechanisms limit their impact. Regional frameworks are only effective when combined with monitoring mechanisms and specialized funding, according to comparative analysis with ASEAN, especially the ASEAN Convention Against Trafficking in Persons (ACTIP). The significance of institutional follow-through is emphasized in the UNODC's *ACTIP Implementation Review* (2022), a lesson that is still underutilized in South Asia.

Trafficking along the India-Bangladesh border continues not due to a lack of activity but rather to a lack of accountability. While fragmented governance distributes accountability among organizations, securitization places a higher priority on border control than human security. Systems that are already underprepared to provide comprehensive protection are further strained by emerging threats such as climate change.

This analysis also points toward the limits of advocacy divorced from implementation. Normative commitments to human-centered approaches are insufficient without concrete institutional mechanisms. Survivor participation must be embedded within governance structures, not appended as an afterthought. Regional cooperation must be grounded in political and administrative realities, not idealized aspirations.

REFRAMING ACCOUNTABILITY: ANALYTICAL SYNTHESIS AND THEORETICAL IMPLICATIONS

Empirical analyses reveal a central paradox in anti-trafficking governance along the India–Bangladesh border: trafficking persists despite sustained institutional engagement, and survivor outcomes remain unstable. Conventional explanations, such as lax enforcement or criminal adaptability, do not fully account for this anomaly. Instead, the findings suggest a more profound lack of accountability resulting from the interplay of securitization, fragmented governance, and historically unequal sovereignty. Accountability in this context should be reframed by assessing how governance institutions allocate authority, responsibility, and protection, rather than focusing solely on enforcement outcomes.

The securitization of human trafficking constitutes the primary cause of this accountability deficit. Securitization theory highlights how political actors invoke existential threats to redefine institutional authority and justify extraordinary measures. Findings across the three studied routes demonstrate that trafficking is consistently integrated into broader security narratives concerning organized crime, illicit migration, and border infiltration. This framing deprioritizes welfare-oriented interventions and elevates border control and surveillance. Consequently, agencies with coercive mandates gain prominence, while those tasked with rehabilitation and reintegration receive diminished resources and authority.

Empirical data from North 24 Parganas–Jessore illustrate this dynamic. Trafficking networks persist despite stringent border controls, adapting their strategies to evolving security measures. Although rescue operations are obvious and politically salient, they are not matched by systematic reintegration support. This pattern aligns with critiques in the UNODC's *Global Report on Trafficking in Persons 2022*, which observes that securitized interventions often emphasize outputs rather than substantive outcomes. In such contexts, accountability becomes performative rather than meaningful.

Fragmented governance further intensifies this issue. Multiple organizations with diverse mandates and operational scales are involved in anti-trafficking efforts. Rather than simply reflecting administrative complexity, such fragmentation actively shapes political outcomes by dispersing responsibility, as Jessop (2007) argues in *State Power: A Strategic-Relational Approach*. The case studies reveal that institutions may exploit this dispersal to avoid accountability. Welfare departments cite capacity limitations, NGOs address service gaps without formal mandates, and border security forces claim success based on interceptions. Survivors, meanwhile, must navigate a disjointed and incoherent system.

The Cooch Behar–Lalmonirhat corridor demonstrates that, without unified governance, accountability cannot be achieved solely through judicial mechanisms. While the Land Boundary Agreement resolved territorial disputes, it did not establish protocols for coordinated post-settlement support. Although former enclave residents obtained formal citizenship, their socioeconomic conditions remained precarious. This outcome corroborates findings from borderland studies, such as Willem van Schendel's *The Bengal Borderland* (2005), which show that social protection does not automatically follow from sovereignty. From this perspective, accountability encompasses both legal status and institutional responsibility for well-being.

Environmental change introduces additional complexity to the accountability landscape, particularly in the Sundarbans–Khulna corridor, where climate-induced displacement heightens vulnerability to trafficking. However, anti-trafficking, migration governance, and climate adaptation initiatives remain siloed. The UNDP, in its *Human Development Report 2022*, describes this fragmentation as a failure to operationalize human security across policy sectors. The findings suggest that accountability frameworks must become adaptive, integrating emerging threats rather than responding only after exploitation occurs.

Across all cases, survivor agency emerges as a significant yet underutilized resource. While victim-centered approaches are increasingly referenced in policy discussions, empirical evidence indicates that survivor participation is not systematically institutionalized. Despite their demonstrated benefits in prevention and reintegration, survivor-led initiatives remain marginal within formal governance structures. This gap highlights a tension between practical implementation and ethical commitments. As Harris (2018) contends in *Ethics and Global Politics*, ethical governance necessitates recognizing individuals as agents capable of shaping policy outcomes, in addition to ensuring their protection.

A conceptual shift is required to effectively rethink accountability. It cannot be confined to bilateral cooperation or legal compliance. Instead, accountability should be understood as a multidimensional responsibility encompassing prevention, rehabilitation, sustained reintegration, and protection. From a human security perspective, accountability is measured by the extent to which governance structures restore agency and reduce vulnerability. This reframing challenges securitized approaches that prioritize territorial control over individual well-being.

These findings also have significant implications for regional collaboration. Although entities such as the India-Bangladesh Joint Task Force, BIMSTEC, and

SAARC offer platforms for dialogue, their effectiveness is constrained by insufficient enforcement and oversight. A comparative analysis of ASEAN's ACTIP framework indicates that targeted resource allocation, outcome-oriented metrics, and explicit accountability mechanisms are essential for effective regional cooperation. In the absence of these elements, regionalism risks remaining aspirational rather than transformative.

In sum, the analytical synthesis demonstrates that accountability failures are structurally generated rather than incidental. Securitization reduces responsibility, fragmentation disperses it, and historical marginalization exacerbates vulnerability. Addressing trafficking along the India-Bangladesh border thus necessitates a fundamental rethinking of how security, sovereignty, and accountability are conceptualized and implemented, rather than relying on incremental reforms.

CONCLUSION

This article aimed to investigate the persistence of human trafficking along the India–Bangladesh border despite comprehensive legal frameworks, bilateral initiatives, and heightened border enforcement. The analysis contends that trafficking endures not due to deficiencies in capacity or intent, but because governance structures prioritize border control over human security and diffuse accountability across multiple institutions. This argument draws on securitization theory, analyses of fragmented governance, and insights from borderland studies.

Historical analysis in this study demonstrates that displacement, partition, and uneven state presence have produced enduring vulnerabilities that continue to shape human trafficking dynamics. Empirical case studies from the Sundarbans–Khulna corridor, North 24 Parganas–Jessore, and Cooch Behar–Lalmonirhat illustrate how securitization and fragmentation impede reintegration and heighten the risk of re-trafficking. Emerging threats, such as climate-induced displacement, further challenge institutions that are already ill-equipped to deliver comprehensive protection.

The principal contribution of this study is the identification of accountability as the critical missing element in anti-trafficking governance. It advocates for a human-security-centered approach that prioritizes survivor outcomes, institutional coordination, and participatory governance, rather than relying solely on enforcement metrics or legal formalism. This framework underscores the importance of integrating survivor agency into decision-making and aligning welfare, adaptability, and migration policies with anti-trafficking strategies.

This reconceptualization carries direct policy implications. First, anti-trafficking governance should move away from securitized approaches that conflate trafficking with irregular migration. Second, accountability mechanisms must be designed to track long-term survivor outcomes, not merely rescue statistics. Third, regional collaboration should be grounded in realistic assessments of institutional capacity and power dynamics, supported by explicit monitoring and enforcement protocols. Finally, survivor-led initiatives should be formally integrated, recognizing experiential knowledge as a valuable form of governance expertise.

While the India-Bangladesh border serves as the primary case, the study's conclusions are relevant to other securitized borders characterized by state control, historical migration, and socioeconomic marginalization. Future research could extend this approach through primary fieldwork, longitudinal studies of reintegration outcomes, and cross-regional comparative analysis. Such efforts would further elucidate the diverse contexts in which accountability can be effectively operationalized.

In conclusion, redefining accountability in anti-trafficking governance necessitates a transition from border management to a focus on human security. Without this shift, survivors will remain subject to interventions that prioritize rescue over restoration, and policies will continue to address symptoms rather than root causes. Beyond its ethical imperative, a human-security-centered approach offers a practical pathway to more effective and accountable governance.

REFERENCES

Abraham, I. (2014). *How India became territorial: Foreign policy, diaspora, geopolitics*. Stanford University Press.

ActionAid. (2019). *Post-LBA rehabilitation and trafficking vulnerability in border enclaves: A situational analysis*. ActionAid India.

Basu Ray Chaudhury, A. (2018). Bordering practices and migration control in eastern India. *Economic and Political Weekly*, *53*(31), 45–53.

Bigo, D. (2002). Security and immigration: Toward a critique of the governmentality of unease. *Alternatives*, *27*(1), 63–92. DOI: 10.1177/03043754020270S105

Buzan, B., Wæver, O., & de Wilde, J. (1998). *Security: A new framework for analysis*. Lynne Rienner.

Chatterji, J. (1999). *The spoils of partition: Bengal and India, 1947–1967*. Cambridge University Press.

Chowdhury, R. (2020). Trafficking, migration and border governance in eastern India. *Journal of Southeast Asian Studies*, *43*(2), 245–262.

Harris, P. G. (2018). *Ethics and global politics*. Edinburgh University Press.

Huysmans, J. (2006). *The politics of insecurity: Fear, migration and asylum in the EU*. Routledge. DOI: 10.4324/9780203008690

IndiaSpend. (2024). *Climate crisis in the Sundarbans makes women vulnerable to trafficking*.

Institute of Development Studies. (2019). *Participatory accountability in anti-trafficking governance*.

International Organization for Migration. (2021a). *Cross-border human trafficking between India and Bangladesh*.

International Organization for Migration. (2021b). Environmental migration and trafficking risk in coastal. *South Asia*.

Jessop, B. (2007). State power: A strategic-relational approach. *Polity*.

Kara, S. (2009). *Sex trafficking: Inside the business of modern slavery*. Columbia University Press.

Ministry of Home Affairs (India). (2022). *Annual report on anti-human trafficking*.

Samaddar, R. (1999). The marginal nation: Transborder migration from Bangladesh to West Bengal. *Sage (Atlanta, Ga.).*

Shore, C., Però, D., & Wright, S. (2011). Policy worlds: Anthropology and the analysis of contemporary power.

UNDP. (1994). *Human development report 1994: Human security.*

UNDP. (2009). *Human development report 2009: Human mobility and development.*

UNDP. (2022). *Human development report 2021/2022: Uncertain times, unsettled lives.*

United Nations Office on Drugs and Crime. (2008). *Ethical and safety recommendations for interviewing trafficked persons.*

United Nations Office on Drugs and Crime. (2018). *Assessment of trafficking routes in South Asia.*

United Nations Office on Drugs and Crime. (2020). *Global report on trafficking in persons.*

United Nations Office on Drugs and Crime. (2022). *Global report on trafficking in persons.*

United Nations Office on Drugs and Crime (UNODC). (2022). *Trafficking data harmonization in South Asia: Gaps and challenges.* UNODC Regional Office for South Asia.

van Schendel, W. (2005). *The Bengal borderland: Beyond state and nation in South Asia.* Anthem Press.

Chapter 13
Sex Work, Trafficking, and the Law:
Intersectional and Comparative Approaches to Rights and Resistance

Shikha Tiwary
http://orcid.org/0009-0001-2839-7922
Chanakya National Law University, India

Rohit Tiwari
http://orcid.org/0009-0001-1445-1510
Chanakya National Law University, India

B. Ravi Narayan Sarma
http://orcid.org/0009-0006-5033-2857
Chanakya National Law University, India

Anil Kumar Tiwari
http://orcid.org/0009-0000-8516-639X
PG Department of Economics, Tilka Manjhi Bhagalpur University, India

ABSTRACT

The complexity of intersection of sex work, trafficking and legal systems continues to introduce legal, ethical and systems challenges to the world. This paper examines the intersections between sex work, trafficking, and legal systems on the basis of intersectional and comparative approaches. It highlights how gender, race, immigration status, socioeconomic status, and other identities affect sex workers, notably in terms of criminalisation and stigma. This study provides a wide rang-

DOI: 10.4018/979-8-3373-5841-3.ch013

ing and critical examination of the collaboration between sex work and the law. Flexible comparative approaches highlight the diverse national approaches and unintended repercussions of so-called protecting laws, emphasising the need for multifaceted and context-dependent policies based on directly affected people's views. Intersectionality emphasises comprehending diverse forms of marginalisation and promoting collective action and social change beyond legal reform. The study examines how sex workers realign themselves under current law, future regulations, and the lack of legal discourse.

INTRODUCTION

Intersection of sex work, human trafficking and legal frameworks have evolved into an extremely intricate and controversial field of research, policy making, and lobbying. Sex work and trafficking as terms that have been used interchangeably in societal contexts are indicative of two vastly different realities, though they have been treated under the same legal and political framework. The misconception has led to the adoption of laws aimed at fighting trafficking and consequently criminalizes consensual adult sex workers, hence denying them their rights, safety and autonomy. The international legal environment offers a scale of regulatory measures to sex work, such as full criminalization, decriminalization, legalization and rights-based measures. Simultaneously, the Western-centric, moralistic or paternalistic discourses of global anti-trafficking frameworks have amended national legislation to the detriment of populations that are already disadvantaged, including migrant employees, transgender individuals, radicalized communities and those living in poverty. In this proposal, the distinction between the terms victim, criminal and worker in sex trade and trafficking will be examined and also be regulated by the laws and policies based on particular cultural, colonial and moral history. The exploitative nature of sex work has concealed the resistance and freedom of choice mechanisms employed by sex workers. Globally, sex workers have formed unions, cooperatives, and activist coalitions to address the issue of criminalization, shame, and marginalization. To this inquiry, their voices are necessary, especially the Global South and people who have historically been overlooked in policy making. The present discussion will be based on comparative, intersectional approach to the analysis of the way in which the legal frameworks used by different jurisdictions draw a distinction between exploitation and labor, criminality and consent, and the ways in which they are influenced by the larger socio-political contexts. The research is eventually meant to move the discussion towards focus on rights, body autonomy and social justice as opposed to carceral control or moral panic. This is a timely and a needed study. With policies worldwide considering sex work and trafficking, increasingly sophisticated evidence-based and community-knowledge research, not hurting anyone, and allowing the most affected individuals to speak out is increasingly demanded. The given project enhances our knowledge about sex work and trafficking in the 21st century by synthesizing legal theory, feminist criticism, and grassroots activism. It promotes an intersectional, more fair and neocolonial perspective.

There are laws regarding sex work in the world that are highly fragmented. Laws consider and address sex work in a wide number of ways. Others are full criminalization, legalization, decriminalization, and the Nordic model also called end-demand or abolitionist approach. All these models possess their objectives and outcomes, some of which are scheduled and others which are not. We have example of nations such as Sweden, Norway and Canada have adopted the Nordic framework that criminalizes the act of buying sex but decriminalizes the act of selling sex, and the rationale behind the model is to reduce demand, and put off the sale of human bodies as a commodity. Germany and Netherlands have legalized and regulated sex work and it is now possible to have brothels and registered sex workers operating within some restrictions. In New Zealand, this has been achieved through complete decriminalization of sex work where it is now legal employment and accounted in the workers' rights and health and safety at work systems. Meanwhile, such countries as the US and South Africa penalize sex workers and their customers, and it often results in arrests, jailing, and humiliation of sex workers. In India, sex work and trafficking is enshrined in a complicated socio-legal context that tends to confuse the distinction between a legal sex work and trafficking. The primary legislation that regulates this field is the Immoral Traffic (Prevention) Act of 1956 (ITPA). It attempts to prevent trafficking and exploitation but does not criminalize sex work. Nevertheless, the trauma of confounding trafficking with voluntary sex work in legal and social discussions tend to result in police harassment and social stigma of sex workers. Laws in the Indian Penal Code concerning trafficking and exploitation of the minors are frequently made illegal, yet they tend to criminalize the things that seemingly belong to sex work. The poor people are most vulnerable due to gender, caste, class, and migration of sex workers who are mostly women and transgender people. The fact that they are stigmatized makes them even more difficult to access health care, legal services, and social services. In India, sex workers are trying to legalize sex work and ensure rights of sex workers are met through the efforts of sex worker rights groups such as All-India Network of Sex Workers and Veshya Anyay Mukti Parishad. They are also propagating the necessity to isolate trafficking and consensual sex work.

These various legal systems are influenced by historical, cultural, religious and political aspects. Policy is a major effect of feminist discourse. There is also an abolitionist opinion, which is expressed by some groups, that sex work is another exploitation of women and violence. Others are concerned with the agency, bodily autonomy, the right to work, dignity and as well as the protection of labor. The national governments have also been compelled by international anti-trafficking documents such as the 2000 UN Palermo Protocol to enact laws against trafficking. International legal framework serves to make us see in detail, what is working and what is not, concerning enhancing the rights, health, and safety of sex workers. Prostitution Reform Act of 2003 of New Zealand also made it legal and enabled sex workers to report cases of violence, access medical treatment, and exercise their labor rights without the dread of arrest. This policy has been lauded by researchers and advocacy groups due to the fact that it has eased such things to the sex workers. There are weaknesses in the system and particularly concerning the treatment that the migrant workers receive, lacking the benefit of the law. It, however, demonstrates that alternative to criminalization, fairer results may be achieved. Abolitionist feminists and certain international entities have lauded the Swedish model; however, sex workers and human rights organizations have criticized it because the model drives the business into the shadows, creating a heightened stigma and exposing workers to more risk. Legalization in Germany has already resulted in a controlled industry, which is said to be biased towards brothel owners and not workers. This demonstrates that other types of exploitation could be brought about by legalization devoid of high worker protection. Such instances highlight the need to adopt a policy-based approach that is inclusive and rights-based and incorporates the perspectives and experiences of sex workers. This paper seeks to analyze various legal systems through a comparative analysis and to seek the interplay between law, gender, ethnicity, migration, and class in defining the experiences of sex workers around the world. It will use legal texts, policy documents, interviews with sex workers and advocacy organizations, and media analysis in terms of assessing the tangible effects of various methodologies. The research aims to give subtle information on how the government can fight exploitation and trafficking without being punitive on the consensual sex workers. The researcher in this paper seeks answers to the following research questions across various segments.

- In what manner do various legal systems delineate and govern sex work and trafficking?
- What are the implications of these legal frameworks for marginalized groups within the sex industry?
- How does mixing sex work with trafficking affect laws, enforcement, and how people see it?
- What insights can be derived from comparing international methodologies to formulate more equitable and efficient policies?

The group of sex workers comprises a wide group of individuals who request and provide services to their clients in a number of settings, such as the web, escort agencies, third-party facilities such as brothels or massage rooms, and even open spaces. Sex work is highly stigmatized across the world and the general policy response to this is criminalization and policing. The overlapping of criminalization and stigmatization systems continue to subject sex workers to poor working conditions which subject them to more risks of violence and poor health, thus hindering their ability to enjoy their full human rights such as occupational health and safety, police protection and accessing the law. Because the criminalization of sex work has numerous negative impacts on the human rights of sex workers, it increases their levels of violence, and exacerbates health risks, such as HIV and STD susceptibility. Human trafficking, particularly, sexually, is a crime against the human rights, both at the national and international scale. It has been established to be a pressing global population health issue impacting almost all nations in the world. It is important to highlight that there was no uniform legal definition of human trafficking until 2000, when the United Nations gave one. The UN definition includes "recruitment, transportation, transfer, or receipt of persons," utilising threats, force, "or other forms of coercion, of abduction, of fraud, of deception, of the abuse of power," or the exchange of remuneration or perks for permission and eventual exploitation. In this sense, exploitation refers to forced or coerced prostitution or other forms of manipulation or abuse, including "forced labour, slavery or practices akin to slavery, servitude, or organ removal." Several researchers have criticised this definition, arguing that it obscures the understanding of the lives and choices of individuals who are trafficked. Instead, this definition conflates sex trafficking with illegal immigration and implies that victims are coerced into their work. However, once the UN urged people to gain knowledge about the many other ways people are trafficked, the media focused on sex trafficking in particular, as shown in movies, books, and other art forms. Human trafficking affects over 40.3 million people worldwide with women and girls constituting approximately 99% of the commercial sex industry and 58% of victims of other trafficking forms. It is also important to recognise that preconceptions about women, especially women of colour, and important human rights concerns like sexual abuse and sex trafficking have been made up by society, including in mainstream and social media over time.

Conceptual structure

Over 40.3 million individuals are affected by human trafficking globally, with women and girls constituting approximately 99% of the commercial sex sector and 58% of victims in other trafficking categories. It is also significant that preconceptions of women, especially women of colour, along with pertinent human rights issues (such as sexual abuse and sex trafficking), have been socially produced, including in mainstream and social media throughout history. An integrative intersectional, and trauma-informed approach will be employed to examine the social and mainstream media conceptualisations of sex work and trafficking, as well as their effects on the understanding, prevention, and intervention of sex trafficking across many levels. This integrated paradigm necessitates that sex trafficking be recognised not just as organised criminality but also that human trafficking is fundamentally perceived as a human rights violation that disproportionately affects individuals vulnerable to many types of institutional oppression (Intersectionality: Crenshaw (1989). Moreover, sex trafficking infringes against fundamental universal human rights, including the right to freedom and the autonomy of one's own body. This text examines intersectionality and trauma to analyse historical and contemporary attitudes of victims and survivors of sex trafficking, as well as the implications for prevention and intervention strategies. The historical context of the issue within the framework of the interdisciplinary approach is essential to understanding the complex and multidimensional aspects of the challenging issue of sex trafficking, its representations, and the action that should be taken to prevent it and address it (Crenshaw, 1989).

Intersectionality theory

According to intersectionality theory, a number of social structures and stereotypes have a direct bearing on how different identities including those regarding race, ethnicity, gender, age, and other traits like aptitude and financial status are interconnected. An intersectional framework is required to examine the ways that the multi-level impacts of racism, sexism, classism, and other types of bias vary depending on different identities. In order to better understand and actively confront complicated and widespread social issues like sex trafficking, what is required to handle it holistically, and how social action may further critical analysis, intersectionality can be viewed as a critical social theory.

Applying a critical intersectional lens emphasises the examination of connections between intersecting social systems and their effects on individuals, such as survivors of sex trafficking, while also highlighting how intersectional advocacy can enhance our current comprehension of sex trafficking (Crenshaw, 1989; Cho et al., 2013). When employing intersectionality as a critical social theory to comprehend intricate and socially stigmatised issues such as sex trafficking, a fundamental aspect that should be emphasised is the "practices of theorising that generate those concepts," or "the processes by which these ideas are formulated and utilised." This requires an extensive analytical self-reflection and direct experience with diverse at-risk and survivors to gain a better understanding and confront the complex problem of sex trafficking, and clarify ways of how a deeper understanding of it and corresponding social action are intertwined. It is important to know how social theories may cause multi-level harm because the theories are usually developed and applied to support or challenge the traditional paradigms of society and the modern practices. An intersectional perspective entails recognising the specific devaluation of women of colour as victims of sexual exploitation, attributed to heightened risks of being perceived as embodying perversions of desire and being systematically regarded as a lower class than their white counterparts. Consequently, intersectionality advocates for an antiracist framework in comprehending and tackling issues by scrutinising and enlightening efforts to rectify structural injustices, namely identifying deficiencies in historical and contemporary policies, rather than interrogating the character of individuals (Crenshaw, 1989). The emphasis is on methods to combat structural intersectional prejudice arising from systemic discrimination and oppression, which can be altered through activism and multi-tiered efforts.

Modern trauma theory

Individuals who have survived sex trafficking or are at heightened risk of being trafficked for sex frequently endure multi-faceted and intersectional oppression, accompanied by associated violence and trauma (Crenshaw, 1989; Herman, 1992). Contemporary trauma theory serves as a framework for comprehending the impact of traumatic events or events that disrupt a general sense of equilibrium in the absence of perceived or actual support on multi-level functioning, within the context of psychological or physical injury as a legitimate response and a necessity for assistance and recovery. Instead of blaming victims or survivors for what happened to them or the trauma that came from it, a trauma-informed approach focusses on the urgent need for a multi-level understanding of trauma, such as the trauma that sexual abuse survivors go through and the trauma of sex trafficking. A trauma-informed framework is a "philosophy or cultural point of view that integrates awareness and understanding of trauma." Consequently, it is imperative to prioritise the recognition and comprehension of the trauma stemming from sex trafficking, to promote awareness of its traumatic nature, and to investigate both current and necessary strategies to mitigate such trauma, thereby enhancing the agency, well-being, and resilience of survivors and individuals at risk. Utilising an integrative intersectional and trauma-informed framework necessitates a focus on various forms of oppression that heighten the risks of sex trafficking, alongside an examination of historical trauma, specifically the enduring effects of oppression and violence on individuals who have faced intersectional oppression, such as women of colour. This analysis also needs to make clear the differences between prostitution and sex trafficking. People who are willing to have sex for money are usually thought to be involved in prostitution because of inequity, trauma, or their own choice. Human trafficking, on the other hand, entails a pimp or trafficker using threats or violence to get what they want. Also, trafficking people is against the law. Still, the main difference between prostitution and trafficking can be hard to explain. It has to do with agreement versus coercion or force.

One reason it can be hard to tell the difference between the two is because both prostitution and sex trafficking are seen as exploitative. Also, among scholars and practice, two simplistic perspectives on the issue of prostitution vs. trafficking exist, which greatly influences the interpretation of prostitution and sex trafficking. The former school of thought proposes that by legalising prostitution, one is condoning gender inequality and exploitation whereas the latter school of thought argues that prostitution is a profession worth being recognised as respectable and as much as it is rooted in inequality and as exploitative as it is (MacKinnon, 1989; Weitzer, 2012).

HISTORICAL PERSPECTIVE ON THE SOCIAL CONSTRUCTIONS AND PARADIGMS THAT HAVE INFLUENCED THE ISSUE OF SEX TRAFFICKING

The knowledge regarding the social construction of prostitutes can be traced back to Biblical times. The ancient prostitutes were either referred to as "brothel worker," "brothel slave," or "streetwalker." Courtesans were portrayed as infiltrating upper social status groups, whereas sex slaves were associated with a significantly lower social status; they did not evoke the same sentiment or affection. In contrast to courtesans, sex slaves were not regarded as charming, quick-witted, or highly valued; rather, they were typically despised. Rather than engaging in a limited number of committed relationships, sex slaves were represented as engaging in sexual intercourse with a multitude of strangers. Women were portrayed as sexually available, uninhibited, and deviant. In Southeast Asia between 1500 and 1800, women of low socio-economic status who were slaves of ex-slaves were also identified as sources of domestic and sex labour. As a result of intersectional systematic oppression, they were not accorded the same level of respect as women in higher socioeconomic classes. Consequently, Southeast Asian sex slaves were socially constructed as promiscuous and undeserving of assistance, a stereotype that was subsequently applied to black individuals who were enslaved in the United States, similar to the jezebel stereotype that was previously mentioned. The emergence of patriarchy, foreign influence, capitalism, and subsequent imbalances of power, internalised discrimination, and trauma are all factors that have contributed to the development of sex trafficking trends in Africa, North and South America, and Southeast Asia. It has been observed that images are a potent tool for influence, capable of eliciting intense emotions, when investigating historical social constructions. In particular, it is crucial to acknowledge the presence of images of women and sex trafficking survivors throughout history, as individuals of colour are more frequently trafficked for sex than white women and girls. It is also crucial to evaluate the potential motivations behind these images in relation to power, privilege, sexism, racism, and enduring intersectional, race-based, and sexual trauma.

The safety and rights of sex workers are being neglected in favour of other matters. The growing tide of anti-sex legislation around the world is a reflection of this tendency.

A growing body of research from disciplines such as academia, medicine, intersectional feminism, and human rights has lent credence to calls to decriminalise sex work. Many believe that the greatest way to protect the health, safety, and human rights of sex workers is to decriminalise the industry. On the other hand, criminalisation has been the focal point of more backward political and legislative initiatives. Although sex trade legislation differs from one jurisdiction to the next, the vast majority treat the profession as a criminal offence. Every jurisdiction has a criminal framework in place to control sex work to some extent; the only exceptions being New Zealand, New South Wales, and Victoria in Australia, and, most recently, Belgium. Legal regulation of the sex business is an ongoing and contentious topic, and sex work is a polarising subject within contemporary feminism (Weitzer, 2012; Donovan & Barnes, 2017). Gender equality, human trafficking, immigration, public health, sex worker safety and rights, globalisation, and globalised sex markets are among topics that are discussed in relation to the regulation of sex work.

Beginning in 1999 in Sweden, the Global North has experienced a widespread implementation of End Demand-style laws over the past two decades. The purported objective of these laws is to reduce the sex industry by criminalising the purchase of sex and conveying a symbolic message that sex work is unacceptable, thereby ending the demand for commercial sex. Numerous jurisdictions, including Israel and Northern Ireland, have explicitly designed these statutes to combat trafficking. The Fight Online Sex Trafficking Act (FOSTA) and Stop Enabling Sex Traffickers Act (SESTA) were enacted with the supposedly similar objective of reducing sex trafficking in the United States. These laws criminalised all websites that advertised any form of sex work. Research has demonstrated that the criminalisation of sex work, regardless of whether it involves sex workers, clients, third parties, or platforms, diminishes the capacity of sex workers to manage risks and work securely. Despite the fact that legal and regulatory frameworks exist in a variety of forms, there has been a lack of attention to the ways in which the law, beyond criminal law, affects the daily lives of sex workers. This is a critical inquiry, as the legal discourse surrounding sex work frequently centres on the distinctions between regulatory approaches, despite the fact that evidence indicates that contrasting legal approaches frequently yield similar outcomes. There has been a significant amount of discussion regarding the harm reduction benefits of decriminalisation and the hazards of criminalisation. However, neither of these ideological opposites, nor the partially criminalised framework or legalisation model, has the ability to reduce, eliminate, or increase the number of individuals who sell sex. In fact, sex worker activists frequently emphasise that individuals are not impeded from purchasing or selling sex by differing degrees of criminalisation. Therefore, it may be time to reconsider the laws that we assess and, in addition, to query the relevance of law in the first place. It was crucial for us to consider the complexities of law and sex work by incorporating the knowledge of academics, activists, and, particularly, sex workers from around the world when assembling this special edition. In doing so, we recognise that expertise is found in a variety of forms and that the lived experience of sex workers must be prioritised in order to comprehend the realities of sex work and its relationship with regulation.

ANALYSIS OF VARIED LEGISLATIVE STRATEGIES

Each country analysed in this study employs a version of one of three approaches to prostitution: criminalisation, legalisation, and decriminalisation.

Criminalisation signifies that engaging in prostitution lawfully is either difficult or almost impossible. This strategy aims to diminish or eradicate prostitution and can be categorised into three subcategories.

- Prohibitionism aims to eradicate prostitution by criminalising every facet of the practice. The perception sees prostitution as a violation of human rights. The criminal law and effective enforcement of law are considered as important tools that would reduce the numbers of people involved in the prostitution business.
- Abolitionism is often described as a middle ground to prohibitionism and legalisation. Advocates of this strategy claim that as much as sex workers can choose to become members of the trade, it is still a social problem. They claim that the governments should take action to allow prostitution as long as it does not interfere with safety and order of people.
- Neo-abolitionism asserts that prostitution is intrinsically violent, viewing all kinds of prostitution as the commodification and exploitation of human bodies. Neo-abolitionists advocate for the decriminalisation of sex workers' activities while seeking the criminalisation of all other facets of prostitution, including the roles of pimps and clients.

Decriminalisation entails the abrogation of laws pertaining to prostitution, but maintaining general criminal statutes and other regulations to govern the sector. Although certain basic restrictions pertaining to prostitution may be established, the aim is to regard prostitution as any other profession.

Legalization refers to the specific regulation of prostitution through criminal law, labour law or other legislation. This approach treats prostitution as a legal occupation that is nevertheless controlled by a set of rules to govern who can work and under what circumstances they can do so. Typically, governments that have adopted the legalization approach regulate the trade through work permits, licensing and/or tolerance zones.

NORDIC MODEL

The Nordic Model, referred to as the Swedish or Gender Equality Model, was implemented in Sweden in 1999 and has since served as a significant political strategy in combating prostitution and human trafficking. The main principle of this model is that prostitutes should be decriminalised, whereas the sex consumers and brothel owners should be prosecuted, and exit programs and preventative measures should be developed. The aim is to reduce the necessity of sex work and protect women during crisis times. The model is based on four key aspects. The four pillars must be incorporated, as they would bring together both criminal and social activities to reduce the prostitution systematically and promote equality. One of the primary requirements is to not criminalise the prostitutes but rather offer them protection. The laws on prostitution often require them to be registered, which may lead to a punishment or imprisonment in case of violation. This penalizes the prostitution victims. It aims at accommodating those who have been affected into the legal system in the most efficient way and not punishing them.

Criminalising customers- dealing with demand.

The criminalisation of sex work is the main process of the rule of law. Through the demand control, the market of prostitution and sex trafficking ought to reduce. The notion defines clients as sexual service perpetrators instead of consumers. This sends a very strong social message i.e sex is not a commodity.

Efficient aid aligned with human rights

It is not enough to prohibit the purchase of sex only, and so there is an urgent need to provide departure strategies. These include the counselling services, financial assistance, housing assistance, and medical assistance. Without such programs, prostitutes will be left in a poor economic situation. Austria has a wide range of support programs to help people who were affected by prostitution or human trafficking to build an independent life devoid of exploitation.

Education and prevention

It is very important for people to learn about how exploitation works and what happens when someone becomes a prostitute. This includes campaigns and programs to raise awareness in schools.

LEGISLATIVE APPROACH IN NEW ZEALAND

New Zealand has one of the most advanced legal systems in the world when it comes to prostitution. It also has strict laws and punishments for human trafficking and exploitation. Prostitution in New Zealand is decriminalised pursuant to the Prostitution Reform Act 2003 (PRA), which supplanted previous bans with a rights-oriented regulatory framework. Such legislative measures are a reaction to the criticism that the previous system in New Zealand was sluggish in prosecution and sometimes promoted too light sentences. These changes have been supported by child advocacy and anti-trafficking organisations, including ECPAT Child Alert Trust and World Vision New Zealand, which highlight the importance of more actions and more clarifications, especially with regard to forced labour, servitude, sexual exploitation, and slavery, so that they can successfully prosecute and provide support to the victims (ECPAT & World Vision New Zealand, 2022).The current studies on the present-day slavery highlight that effective monitoring and enforcement can only be achieved by proper definition and quantification of the vice. At the same time, the New Zealand officials have suspended the recognition of the dangerous foreign adoptions following the discovery of data that showed shortcomings in the screening of the adoptive parents in terms of criminal or child abuse backgrounds. There have also been incidences of neglected or abused children who were adopted internationally and were found in New Zealand, and urgent changes were required to ensure vulnerable minors were not exploited and trafficked.

According to Prostitution Reform Act 2003 Act, adult sex work such as brothel-keeping, benefiting off prostitution and soliciting on the streets that are not forced, is legalised when under the age of eighteen (New Zealand Legislation, 2003). The act resulted out of a coalition of pressure groups and academicians and health activists who saw the need to reduce harm and empower sex workers. Prior to the enactment of this act, the Massage Parlours Act 1978 had allowed brothels to operate covertly, but sex workers would face strict registration and the danger of being prosecuted. With the introduction of the Prostitution Reform Act, the key shift was made and the criminal law regulation of the consensual adult prostitution way was replaced with the civil and local jurisdiction regulation. Sex workers gained the skills to refuse services and employment disputes can be resolved either through labour agency or Disputes Tribunal. With the help of the New Zealand Prostitutes' Collective, the Ministry of Health changed health and safety regulations and made a substantial contribution to occupational safety programs, advocating healthy sex and support services (New Zealand Ministry of Health, 2023). Whereas voluntary adult sex work is legal, there are still many limitations sexual service contracts are accepted but cannot be enforced in cases of non-compliance by a provider, advertising is limited and non-residents or visa holders cannot work or invest in the sex sector, where deportation is the penalty in case of violation. The law enforcers have strict prohibitions on the involvement of minors; the people who induce, facilitate or profit off sexual activities between minors and those who are below the age of eighteen face severe criminal punishments and it is also illegal to obtain sexual services of anyone who is less than eighteen years.

The existing debates in the country revolve around street sex work, zoning of brothels, especially around learning institutions and the safety, employment and welfare of the marginalised groups such as the transgender children. Local authorities, like Manukau and Auckland, often seek tighter by-law policies towards prostitution, particularly street solicitation but national government evaluations invariably point to local outreach and multi-stakeholder programmes as being more effective than prohibitions. Reports by organisations and scholarly research following reforms show that sex workers report improved safety and health results, police have become more responsive to violence and exploitation, and that stigma remains a barrier and challenge to integrating sex work within the traditional labour systems. Despite occasional controversy and calls to criminalize or restrict it, the evidence of what has been collected by the government in terms of assessment has shown that decriminalization did not increase the amount of sex workers or heightened street sex workers. Opponents claim that it is accompanied by negative effects and community nuisance, claims that are often refuted by the knowledgeable commissions that cite consistent or falling figures on the street sex industry and challenges exaggerated arguments of massive trafficking within the industry.

New Zealand has an elaborate dual-framework. Put differently strict anti-trafficking laws that criminalise all forms of exploitation and follow the international best practice, coupled with a decriminalised model of prostitution aimed at addressing the rights of adults, harm reduction, health and safety. The protection of children is one of the major priorities, as stringent laws and intersectoral operations have been set to ensure the fight against underage exploitation, trafficking, and unsafe adoptions.

The changing laws show the commitment of New Zealand towards individual autonomy of adults and creating strong safeguards about the vulnerable children, with the aim of establishing a social paradigm that eradicates exploitation but upholds the freedom of choice to engage in consensual adult relationships.

INDIA'S LEGISLATIVE APPROACH

Laws that regulate the problem of human trafficking and prostitution in India are established through constitutional provisions, judicial opinions and the legislation, with the Immoral Traffic (Prevention) Act, 1956 (ITPA) as the main part of the regulation. This legal framework is trying to find a delicate balance between victim protection and rehabilitation, prosecution of criminals, and the rights of sex workers, but it is full of grey areas and the constantly changing arguments of personal freedoms and social justice.

Constitutional and Legal Basis

Laws that regulate the problem of human trafficking and prostitution in India are established through constitutional provisions, judicial opinions and the legislation, with the Immoral Traffic (Prevention) Act, 1956 (ITPA) as the main part of the regulation. This legal framework is trying to find a delicate balance between victim protection and rehabilitation, prosecution of criminals, and the rights of sex workers, but it is full of grey areas and the constantly changing arguments of personal freedoms and social justice.

Legality and Courts Interpretation

The peculiar feature of the Indian model is that prostitution is not a crime. The act is aimed at criminalizing acts of abetting, facilitating or leading to sexual exploitation in the quest of commercial gain. Bombay High Court has reiterated that prostitution is not outlawed in the country, only those acts that are related to commercial sexual exploitation or solicitation in the streets is punishable. In a case of Budhadev Karmaskar v. State of West Bengal, (2022), it has been ruled by the Supreme Court that consensual adult sex work is a valid profession, and dignity and legal security should be granted to sex workers. Consenting adult sex workers can thus not be subjected to criminal prosecution by police authorities but the majority of activities surrounding them are illegal under ITPA.

Salient Features and Provisions

The ITPA punishes a range of activities, including:

- Keeping a brothel or allowing premises to be used as a brothel.
- Procuring, inducing, or detaining persons for prostitution.
- Living off the earnings of prostitution.
- Soliciting in or near public places.
- Seducing for purposes of prostitution.

The ITPA has been criticized for its ambiguous language, limited scope, and lack of holistic victim support. Its definition of "victim" excludes male and transgender persons, reflecting a gendered approach that leaves many unprotected (Immoral Traffic (Prevention) Act [ITPA], 1956). The criminalization of those living off prostitution earnings may inadvertently result in arresting the children or relatives of sex workers, who may be financially dependent. Further, the Act does not offer psychological, economic, or educational support for survivors an essential aspect of effective rehabilitation.

Despite courts recognizing prostitution as a profession, the act maintains a prohibitionist stance, making it nearly impossible for sex workers to operate within the law even if they do so voluntarily. Amendments in 2006 and subsequent draft bills like the Trafficking in Persons (Prevention, Care & Rehabilitation) Bill, 2021 seek to address these lacunae, aiming to expand protections for victims, include new categories of offenders, and offer comprehensive care and rehabilitation. India faces a lot of difficult problems, such as cyber slavery, child exploitation, and forced labour trafficking. It is still very important for the government to keep making changes to the law and the courts. The new anti-trafficking bill will include more people, including transgender people, and set up national anti-trafficking committees. It will also make it easier for victims to get help. India's laws and policies are slowly changing to better balance deterrence, justice, and the rights of vulnerable groups thanks to these kinds of changes.

AN DEVASTATING CRISIS IN BANGLADESH

Bangladesh's response to human trafficking and prostitution is still very bad. Victims are still being exploited, and the system for protecting them and enforcing the law is still broken. The Prevention and Suppression of Human Trafficking Act, 2012 (PSHTA) gives the country a strong legal framework on paper, but in real life, victims of trafficking and people who work in prostitution are still in a very bad situation. In Bangladesh, human trafficking and forced prostitution are widespread and affect women, children, and other groups that are already on the fringes of society. Traffickers take advantage of victims from both Bangladesh and other countries. Bangladeshi men, women, and children are trafficked within the country and to other countries, especially India, Pakistan, the Gulf States, and Southeast Asia. Trafficking thrives in places where people are poor, homeless, stigmatised, and don't have access to education. In Bangladesh's large red-light districts, children are even more vulnerable. Many of them are born to sex workers and are stuck in brothels, where they are rarely able to escape sexual exploitation. In the garment, fishing, and domestic sectors, children as young as twelve are forced to work and abused. An estimated 120,000 children work in terrible conditions in industrial areas like Keraniganj.

Legal and Policy Failures

The PSHTA makes many types of trafficking illegal and sets harsh punishments, such as life in prison or death. However, enforcement is weak, and the number of convictions has dropped sharply in recent years. Bangladeshi courts only convicted 103 traffickers in 2025, down from 407 the year before. Political unrest and court closures made things even worse. The government's approach tends to put too much emphasis on international labour trafficking, while ignoring a lot of other issues, like child sex trafficking, bonded labour, and internal trafficking.

There aren't enough efforts to find victims, and protection and reintegration services are still very bad, especially for Rohingya refugees and migrant workers who are coming back to their home countries. The crisis is made worse by labour inspectors not having enough power, corruption that never goes away (with some officials allegedly helping traffickers), and the fact that migrant workers are still being recruited through debt. There are more than a million Rohingya refugees living in Bangladesh who are in danger. Armed groups and traffickers take advantage of the refugees' desperation by forcing children and adults to work or have sex for money, both in their own country and across borders. Government rules that make it hard for refugees to get legal jobs push many of them to take dangerous illegal migration routes, which makes them more likely to be trafficked or kidnapped.

Ongoing Exploitation in Prostitution

Even though prostitution is technically legal for consenting adult women who register with magistrates, it is still stigmatised and very exploitative. Sex trafficking, often of minors, happens in legal brothels, many illegal brothels, and private hotels. The cyclical nature of exploitation where daughters of sex workers are drawn into commercial sex remains almost unbreakable due to lack of real intervention, education, or avenues for escape.

International Critique and Required Action

International organisations, such as the US State Department, have consistently placed Bangladesh in Tier 2 for anti-trafficking measures. This means that the country doesn't meet basic standards, even though some things have gotten better. Some of the most important suggestions are to make law enforcement stronger, hold labour recruiters accountable, offer more help to victims, and deal with both internal and Rohingya trafficking right away. Bangladesh's current circumstances vividly illustrate a persistent humanitarian crisis. Trafficking and exploitative prostitution can thrive because of systemic policy and capacity failures, ongoing corruption, and a lack of victim care those focusses on trauma. Without quick legal and social changes that focus on human rights, as well as real money for law enforcement and survivor support, many weak Bangladeshis, especially children and refugees, will keep being abused in brothels, workplaces, and at the borders.

HUMAN TRAFFICKING LEGISLATION IN USA

The federal government has a strong set of laws and policies in place to fight human trafficking and manage prostitution. Each state also has its own set of laws that add to this. The Trafficking Victims Protection Act (TVPA) of 2000 and its many reauthorisations, such as the Frederick Douglass Trafficking Victims Prevention and Protection Act of 2025, set the stage for intervention, victim protection, prosecution of offenders, and cooperation between countries. The TVPA is the main federal law in the US that deals with human trafficking. It defines sex trafficking and labour trafficking, makes a lot of related activities illegal, and gives traffickers harsh punishments, with sentences ranging from long prison terms to life in prison in the worst cases. The Act says that "severe forms of trafficking in persons" include sex trafficking that is forced, fraud, or coerced, or that involves a child under 18, as well as labour trafficking that is forced, fraud, or coerced.

Key features of US trafficking legislation include:

- A three-pronged "3P" approach: Prevention, Protection, and Prosecution.
- The requirement for victim-centred policies: legal status, access to shelter and medical care, immigration relief (like T-visas), and federal funding for services for victims.

- Setting up task forces, the Human Smuggling and Trafficking Centre, and making sure that all agencies work together.
- Ongoing changes and reauthorisations, such as the 2025 Frederick Douglass Act, keep adding protections for survivors, improving law enforcement training, and getting more money for anti-trafficking efforts across federal agencies and partnerships with states.

Prostitution Laws

Prostitution laws in the US vary considerably by state:

- Prostitution is not explicitly criminalised at the federal level; however, various activities associated with sex work, including the operation of businesses that sell sex, child prostitution, and interstate trafficking for commercial sex, are prosecutable under federal law.
- In most states, prostitution is illegal. This means that people who trade sexual services for money can be arrested, fined, and even convicted of a felony if they do it again.
- There are only a few places where this is true: legal brothels are only open in a few counties in Nevada, and there is a lot of discussion about decriminalisation and reform models like the "Equality Model," which partially decriminalises sex work and provides support services for workers but punishes buyers and third-party recruiters.
- In the past few years, lawmakers have tried to seal records of prostitution convictions (especially in Illinois), require police to get training to stop sex workers from being exploited, and create a "sex workers' Bill of Rights" in some places. However, decriminalisation has not happened on a national level.

Enforcement and Challenges

The US government actively investigates and prosecutes trafficking and commercial sexual exploitation crimes. It does this with the help of special federal and state law enforcement units, specialised prosecutors, and public awareness campaigns. But even with strong legal tools, there are still problems:

- Disparities in state laws lead to inconsistent protection and criminalization of sex workers.
- Reports of marginalized migrant populations, runaway youth, and LGBTQ+ individuals being disproportionately targeted by traffickers.

- Ongoing debate over the balance between victim protection and criminal enforcement, particularly regarding consensual adult sex work.

In sum, the United States has a combination of the powerful federal enforcement tools, including the powerful TVPA and reauthorizations, and the variety of state legislation to deal with human trafficking and prostitution. Although the work has been advanced in the area of protecting victims and prosecuting them, changing legal regulations and pressure campaigns are still guiding the federal response, especially in terms of vulnerable population support and decriminalization models of consensual sexual work in adults.

CONCLUSION

The various ways of defining and controlling sex work and human trafficking are different in relation to the legal systems that are established worldwide. The consequences of these decisions are enormous towards populations that already are at the outskirts of the sex industry. Criminalization models are the most frequent in numerous locations, such as the US, South Asia, most part of Africa, and Eastern Europe. It implies that not only the act of selling and purchasing sex but also such activities as brothel-keeping, solicitation, or third-party facilitation are all illegal. These models claim to be attempting to prevent exploitation, yet in fact, they only exacerbate stigma, drive sex workers into unsafe and underground spaces and make it more difficult to access justice, health services, and financial support. Participation of some criminalization seen in other countries including India and the UK criminalizes certain activities but still permits the underlying act of criminalization hence perpetuating social exclusion and exposing the most vulnerable to more vulnerability. The Nordic model that is applied in the Nordic countries (Sweden, Norway, and France) argues that the criminals are the clients, and sellers are not. It makes this industry more confidential and does not create a clear distinction between consensual work and coercion. This leaves sex workers, in particular migrants, LGBTQ+ individuals, and ethnic minorities, at a higher risk of being surveilled, segregated and assaulted. In legal systems or regulatory systems, such as those in Germany or the Netherlands, brothels are legalized or established and they must be registered, health-examined, and licensed. Nevertheless, they usually exclude undocumented migrants, trans workers, and individuals who are not able to fulfill bureaucratic prerequisites, which results in parallel illegal markets and a continuous threat. Full decriminalization, as practiced in New Zealand and adopted in the proposals of leading rights organizations, on the contrary, eliminates criminal penalties against consensual sex work among adults but maintains strong legislation against trafficking, coercion, and child abuse. It has been demonstrated that decriminalization allows sex workers to access health and legal assistance more easily, have more control over their lives, and report and end trafficking and exploitation. The reason is that the risks of arrest and stigmatization are minimized, and third parties, who are harmful, could be filtered.

These frameworks have a big impact on people in the sex industry who are already on the outside. Criminalisation, whether total or partial, disproportionately affects migrant workers, transgender and gender-nonconforming individuals, ethnic minorities, and those living in poverty. These groups are at risk of arrest, police abuse, detention, and extortion. They are also left out of housing, banking, healthcare, and the legal system. Stigma and the fear of being punished for their actions push sex workers into more dangerous situations, hurt their sense of community, and make it harder for them to fight for their safety, fair pay, or group rights. In regulatory models, bureaucratic barriers keep undocumented migrants, trans and gender-nonconforming workers, and people with criminal records on the edge of legality. This pushes them into unregulated areas where abuse is common and there is no way to get help. This cycle keeps discrimination going and makes social and economic inequalities worse.

There is a substantial policy challenge posed by the fact that sex work is being confused with trafficking in both laws and practice and in the popular imagination. When consensual adult sex work is not legally differentiated by force or child labor, police tend to over-classify or save sex workers against their wishes, destabilize necessary support networks, and generate statistics that conceal the reality of the traffic of people into exploitative or political activities. This misunderstanding makes aggressions, evictions, and policies that sanction all the people engaged in the sex trade irrespective of the consent and situation acceptable. This exacerbates violence, complicates the process of contacting and minimizing harm, and negatively affects the health and safety of individuals that the law is designed to protect. Furthermore, this conflation affects the general understanding and forms the discourse that all sex work is exploitative in nature and the workers are all victims who are shamed or infantilized, instead of being viewed as people with agency that can articulate their needs and experiences.

Comparative studies of the strategies of these countries show that decriminalization, with effective protection against violence, labor exploitation, and human trafficking, have always led to better social, economic, and overall health outcomes, of sex workers and survivors of human trafficking. It has been demonstrated that under the New Zealand model, the way to make it safer, healthier and more rights-respecting is to eliminate penalties against consensual adult sex work without raising trafficking or exploitation. Regulatory systems offer certain benefits, however, leaving those people who cannot comply with the requirements susceptible to systematic abuse. The Nordic model, wherein the main aim is to punish clients further drives sex worker even more underground. It can reduce the sex work on the street, yet it causes the most vulnerable individuals to suffer the most and little is done to prevent the actual trafficking. The lesson to be learned universally is that there must be a distinction between consensual sex work and trafficking in the fair and effective policies. They must also emphasize human rights in legislation and actions, involve the affected groups in the process formulation of decisions and reallocate enforcement resources, which were formerly centered on consensual economic activity to the ones which are based on exploitation, coercion, and violence. Societies must dismantle systemic punishments, address the factors that make people vulnerable, and empower sex workers in order to effectively address trafficking and exploitation. This will foster health, dignity and justice to all.

REFERENCES

Cho, S., Crenshaw, K. W., & McCall, L. (2013). Toward a field of intersectionality studies: Theory, applications, and praxis. *Signs (Chicago, Ill.), 38*(4), 785–810. DOI: 10.1086/669608

Crenshaw, K. (1989). Demarginalizing the intersection of race and sex: A Black feminist critique of antidiscrimination doctrine, feminist theory and antiracist politics. *University of Chicago Legal Forum, 1989*(1), 139–167.

Herman, J. L. (1992). Complex PTSD: A syndrome in survivors of prolonged and repeated trauma. *Journal of Traumatic Stress, 5*(3), 377–391. DOI: 10.1002/jts.2490050305

U.S. Congress. (2018). *Allow States and Victims to Fight Online Sex Trafficking Act of 2017* and *Stop Enabling Sex Traffickers Act* (FOSTA-SESTA), Pub. L. No. 115-164, 132 Stat. 1253 (2018).

Chapter 14
Global Legal Approaches to Prostitution:
Evaluating Policy Models and the Way Forward for India

Alisha Verma
http://orcid.org/0000-0001-6735-3829
Symbiosis International University, Pune, India

Gargi
Amity University, Noida, India

ABSTRACT

This research critically evaluates global prostitution laws and their effects on Indian policy reform. Criminalisation, legalisation, decriminalisation, and the neo-abolitionist approach towards sex work reflect different moral, social, and gender values. The comparative and rights-based study examine how different approaches affect sex worker safety, public health, and human dignity. It illustrates that punishing individuals, like India's Immoral Traffic (Prevention) Act, 1956, mixes prostitution with trafficking and doesn't address poverty and gender inequality. The study claims that India's framework violates its constitutional and human rights obligations. The paper concludes that India adopts a rights-based framework like the neo abolitionist model (Nordic approach), which decriminalises sex sales but criminalises purchases. This technique is fair and humanitarian since it moves legal responsibility from the exploited to the exploiters and punishes demand with significant support for sex workers' rehabilitation, education, and livelihoods.

DOI: 10.4018/979-8-3373-5841-3.ch014

INTRODUCTION

Prostitution represents a persistent global challenge that intersects with issues of gender inequality, economic vulnerability, and human rights. In India, it exists in a legal grey zone, which is neither wholly prohibited nor formally recognized as labour. The existing legal framework, embodied in the Immoral Traffic (Prevention) Act, 1956 (ITPA), criminalizes associated activities such as brothel keeping and solicitation while leaving private sex work itself unregulated. This fragmented approach perpetuates exploitation and fails to uphold the dignity of those involved. Since past few decades, prostitution has become a global problem. The issue has gotten worse and more complicated with the expansion of urbanisation and industry.

In laws passed in the nineteenth and twentieth centuries, the term "prostitution" was frequently used to refer to sex work (Sanger, 2022; Scott, 2014). Advocates for sex workers believe that the labels "prostitution" and "prostitute" stigmatise sex workers because of their negative connotations. All adults who sell or exchange sex for money, products, or services are referred to as "sex workers"(Chernick & Sweeting, 2025). The phrase is used to describe sex workers, including willing transgender, male, and female individuals who routinely or sporadically accept payment or products in exchange for sexual services.

Prostitution has often been described as "the world's oldest profession," and there is evidence of prostitution occurring throughout history in all societies. Early forms of prostitution involved "sacred prostitution," in which the sexual act was performed for a religious purpose with a person other than one's spouse (Neethi & Kamath, 2025). Perceptions of prostitution are based on culturally determined values that differ between societies.

United Nations considers the practice violative of basic human rights of women (Alsalem, 2025). It is considered one of many ways of exploitation of women. Prostitution nevertheless poses a social problem despite a sophisticated legal system designed to control and treat the practise. States are required to uphold International human rights standards as reflected in the Universal Declaration of Human Rights (UDHR) (Alsalem, 2025) and other core human rights instruments. Sex workers are entitled to recognition of fundamental human rights (regardless of domestic laws that criminalize sex work), including rights to non-discrimination and equal treatment before the law consistent with the *International Covenant on Civil and Political Rights* (ICCPR), and the right to the highest attainable standard of health (including HIV prevention, treatment, care and support) consistent with the *International Covenant on Economic Social and Cultural Rights* (ICESCR) (Abdirasulovich & Alisherovich, 2025; Karlebach, 2008).

Different societies react differently, based on values and ideologies. There are various approaches to govern the sex worker legislations and different countries adopt different approaches according to the cultural uniqueness and social, economic and political factors. The following part deals with different approaches and a few examples of the country abiding by such approach are listed.

CONCEPTUAL AND THEORETICAL FRAMEWORK

History of prostitution

The term prostitute has been derived from the Latin word *prostibula or proseda* (Roy, 2019). This terminology describes prostitution as the association with the idea of public display and commercial exchange of sex. Prostitution is not a recent phenomenon rather; its roots are deeply buried in the past. This practice has no bounds and has been seen globally in different formats. It is rather difficult to identify all factors contributing to prostitution because it has often been argued that prostitution has its roots deep in the fabric of society.

Prostitution is deemed to be the world's oldest profession, but it could not have emerged before the emergence of trade (Tarlow & Spencer, 2025). Earlier, prostitutes exchanged their services for goods and later with emergence of money, they exchanged their services for money. In the pre-historic days one can find references of prostitutes even in religious literature like sacred prostitution linked with temples of *Ishtar/Inanna* in the *Mesopotamian* religion and *Kamasutra (3rd century CE)* although often secularised, it was rooted in Hindu philosophy and discusses courtesans (Karlebach, 2008). Sacred prostitution has been considered as one of the oldest forms of prostitution (Blanchette et al., 2020). A few countries have more prominent history than others based not only on religion but also on the approach in drafting the legal framework (Balogh & Juhász, 2025).

Prostitution is, perhaps, coeval with human society. It was found in all societies, all over the world, and in all ages. Through literature, art, paintings and sculptures, the presence of prostitutes had been documented in the most ancient civilizations (Bhattacharjee, 2025). In some places ordinary respectable women went to temple and has intercourse with the priest or with a casual stranger (Tarlow & Spencer, 2025).

In *Mesopotamia* during the Sumerian society women's prostitution was regarded with grave concern and was punishable by death if found out (Lerner, 1986). Since women were only expected to have sexual relations with their own husbands, this was a cultural norm. During the Babylonian period, women were labelled as a man's most prized possession (Lerner, 1986). *Herodotus* was considered one of the most offensive customs during this period (*The Melammu Project*, n.d.). It stated that at least once in a woman's lifetime, she must visit the Aphrodite temple and expose herself to a foreign man (*The Melammu Project*, n.d.). *Myletta rite* of ancient

Babylon, where every female was required to sit in the temple of the goddess and accept coitus from the first male who threw silver coin in her lap (Lerner, 1986; *The Melammu Project*, n.d.). Later in Assyrian civilisation, Hammurabi rules in their retrieved form were applied, in which women were classified according to the types of sexual activities they engaged in (Lerner, 1986; *The Melammu Project*, n.d.).

In ancient *Isreal* society prostitution was considered as sin and there was legislation in the law of *Moses* (*Ancient History - Was Prostitution Legal in the Kingdom of Israel during the Reign of Solomon? - History Stack Exchange*, n.d.). Women were considered their father's property and later handed over to her husband as his property (Bhattacharjee, 2025). Thus, adultery would mean violation of another man's property. As per the ancient society prostitutes were at the bottom of the social ladder and stayed outside the marriage contract (Bhattacharji, 1987).

The *Greek* mythology was filled with spirit of morals initially penalized rape, adultery or seduction but later by *Solon* formally established various houses filled with female slaves which was known as *Dicteria* (Taylor, 2025). These female slaves were deemed as public servants and the revenue generated was utilized in building of temple dedicated to Venus the courtesans. The ancient history of *Greece* mentions *Symonides* of Amorgos (7th century BCE) portrayed women as inherently uncontrollable in their sexuality, arguing that they drained men's strength, food, and wealth (Scott, 2014; Taylor, 2025). Jane McIntosh Syder in his poem on women, compared women to animals such as pigs, foxes, and horses, emphasizing their supposed destructive influence on male order and society (King & Snyder, 1990). *Hetairai* in classical Greece were distinct from common prostitutes (*pornai*), as they were usually free women who provided companionship, conversation, and entertainment in addition to sexual relations (King & Snyder, 1990). They played a visible role in the intellectual and social life of elite men, particularly within the symposium culture (Taylor, 2025).

In the *Egyptian* culture man was disguised as God and during the period of God *Amoun* beautiful girls were sent to Amoun's temple as prostitutes as sacred women (Shousha & Taha, 2025). The Old Testament mentions about extensive prevalence of sexual vices and prostitution in *Palestine* of old puritan days (Lerner, 1986). But all the same the laws of Moses for the Jews were very strict in matters of sex. Penalty for adultery was death (Sanger, 2022).

The prostitution in *United States of America* also faced a war between the sex industry and the religious personalities. Prostitution was banned at some periods and at some it was legal. It 1670s till 1700s it was legally banned in US (Scott, 2014). Again in 1970, the profession of prostitution was declared illegal (Bhattacharjee, 2025). On the other hand, the popular conception of a prostitute as a woman who temporarily loans the use of her body to a miscellany of men in return for money is obviously too narrow and restricted; as is also Webster's dictionary definition, "to give up to lewdness for hire" (*Prostitute Definition by Webster's at Smart Define Dictionary*, n.d.). In colonial times it was rare and tightly policed, but by the 19th century urban migration, low wages for women, and military mobilization created thriving red light districts (Scott, 2014). For many women, sex work was a means of survival or independence, even as it exposed them to violence, disease, and stigma. Prostitution also flourished in the early 20th century when immigration had peaked and since then various social activist have been working on criminalization of prostitution (Sanger, 2022; Scott, 2014; Taylor, 2025). Finally in 1970, the profession of prostitution was declared illegal (Bhattacharjee, 2025). Prostitution was legally banned that is it was criminalized but yet the prostitution continued to flourish.

In ancient India, prostitution and related practices were embedded within wider social and political frameworks. King maiden gifts were a show of alliance, friendship, and loyalty (Bhattacharji, 1987). The *Arthashastra*, written by *Kautilya* in around 300 BCE, is one of the most extensive treatments of prostitution regulation, emphasising official monitoring (Bhattacharji, 1987; Karlebach, 2008; Sanger, 2022). This shows the practice's ubiquity and incorporation into administrative and commercial institutions. Vatsayana's Kamasutra, written about 225 BCE, also mentions courtesans and clients (Neethi & Kamath, 2025). It details how courtesans were kept in distinct city areas and who they attracted from professors and philosophers to rogues and less refined men (Bhattacharji, 1987; Neethi & Kamath, 2025; Scott, 2014). The *Kamasutra* maintains a wealth of knowledge on early Indian prostitution's cultural, social, and economic aspects ("Sex Worker as the Juridical Subject," n.d.). Sex labour helped many women, especially from underprivileged origins, survive and gain the patronage of powerful men. Prostitution developed and became more institutionalised in Mughal culture. Mughals' sponsorship of courtesans boosted musicians, dancers, and entertainers, blending sex labour with art and culture (Bhattacharji, 1987; "Sex Worker as the Juridical Subject," n.d.). Emperor Jahangir's *harem*, renowned for its large number of mistresses, symbolized both power and prestige (Bhattacharji, 1987; Sanger, 2022). The tradition of the *tawaif*, women trained in poetry, dance, etiquette, and refined arts emerged during this era, distinguishing courtesans from those merely labelled as prostitutes, though society at large often grouped them together as immoral women who threatened conventional norms (Bhattacharji, 1987; Sanger, 2022; "Sex Worker as the Juridical Subject," n.d.).

Following India's independence, the dynamics of sex work shifted dramatically. Once confined largely to red light districts, the industry diversified into new forms such as escort services, call girls, street-based prostitution, and the rapidly growing field of pornography. These transformations reflect not only changes in social structures and urban economies but also the continued tension between regulation, stigma, and the persistence of sex work as both a livelihood and a contested social institution.

Legal Policy Models

Decriminalization

Decriminalisation acknowledges prostitution as a legitimate enterprise by abolishing laws that prohibit it (Goyal & Ramanujam, 2014). Prostitutes are governed by the same norms and legislation as employees in other sectors; for example, they are required to pay taxes, adhere to working hours, undergo periodic health examinations, and register brothels and sex workers. Decriminalisation seeks to grant prostitutes equivalent rights to other workers to avert the clandestine nature of sex work.

Decriminalisation has been implemented in many states across Australia, New Zealand, and additional regions (Nde Fon & Balogh, 2025). The Prostitution Reform Act was enacted in New Zealand in 2003, permitting women to operate in groups for enhanced security and mandating licenses for external operators (Balogh & Juhász, 2025). Following its enactment, 60% of sex workers report more empowerment to refuse clients, while 95% assert that their rights have been more effectively protected (Goyal & Ramanujam, 2014; Nde Fon & Balogh, 2025).

Criminalization

Criminalization refers to a legal framework that makes sex workers and related activities, such as soliciting in public or on the street, advertising, sharing space with other indoor sex workers, engaging in other buying related activities, such as kerb crawling, running a brothel, or facilitating or profiting from sex work, illegal (Gonzalez-Recio et al., 2025). Under this approach buying and selling or pimping, brothel keeping are criminalized. Criminalization makes prostitution illegal subject to the domestic laws of a nation. The basic aim for criminalization is to create a sense of deter in the minds of people who are engaged in the work of prostitution either by way of buying, selling or pimping, brothel keeping etc (Gonzalez-Recio et al., 2025; Goyal & Ramanujam, 2014).

Numerous nations prohibit prostitution, either by criminalising the act of engaging in it or by banning the purchase of sexual services. This strategy is primarily motivated by the intent to avert exploitation and human trafficking, as well as to diminish the demand for prostitution (Gonzalez-Recio et al., 2025). Prostitution is deemed illegal when it is criminalised and regulated by the statutes specified in a nation's Criminal Code. Trading might be rendered illegal if the acts of certain or all merchants are deemed unlawful; criminalisation seeks to diminish the accessibility of prostitutes. Three subtypes of criminalisation may be identified: "prohibitionist," "abolitionism," and "neo abolitionism" (Gonzalez-Recio et al., 2025).

Abolitionism seeks to eradicate prostitution by criminalising associated activities outside prostitution itself, including pimping, operating brothels, and procuring (Tyler, 2021). This method advocates for the limitation of public solicitation, highlighting the detrimental effects of overt engagement in the profession. Abolitionists say that prostitution is intrinsically violent and that no community should endorse such conduct (Tarlow & Spencer, 2025). Criminalisation seeks to deter persons from entering and participating in the industry by establishing a fear of arrest. Limited data, however, substantiates the efficacy of the three criminalisation tactics.

The prohibition of prostitution frequently engenders more problems than it alleviates. Women suspected of prostitution or associated charges in prohibitionist and abolitionist regimes frequently face punishment or detention. An arrest or fine may inadvertently promote prostitution instead of acting as a deterrent (Nde Fon & Balogh, 2025). Women sometimes return to prostitution after obtaining a reference due to insufficient cash to pay the fine and the potential hindrance of a criminal record in securing legitimate employment in the future (Bateman, 2021; Gonzalez-Recio et al., 2025; Tyler, 2021).

The Nordic/Swedish model is analogous to Neo-abolitionism. The neo abolitionist perspective, unlike abolitionism, aims to criminalise the procurement of sexual services (Tandon & Nayak, 2025). Neo rationale abolitionism posits that reducing the demand for prostitution may be achieved by focussing on the client (Tandon & Nayak, 2025). This hypothesis, which has gained prominence in several nations and areas, including Sweden, France and Izrael are predicated on the belief that reducing the demand for sex work will result in a proportional decline in the provision of sexual services (Tandon & Nayak, 2025; Tyler, 2021). Only persons willing to violate the law would seek the services of a prostitute.

Legalization

This approach takes into account prostitution as legal only under some circumstances. Controls and requirements that are specifically outlined by the state for prostitution are important markers of legalised regimes. Licencing, registration, and required health exams are a few examples (Rathor, 2023). Legalization if often confused with decriminalization, whereas decriminalization involves removal or absence of laws and former includes introduction of laws to oppress sex workers (Rathor, 2023). Legalization is not immune to scrutiny. In various countries like Netherlands and Dutch law prostitution is legal but the government impose strict restrictions and limitations on various matters like control of brothels, background check of owners and operators, safety regulations, etc (Balogh & Juhász, 2025; Martin, 2025; Rathor, 2023) . In countries such as Germany, the Netherlands, Austria,

Greece, Turkey, Senegal, the USA (State of Nevada), and some Australian states, sex work is legal (Balogh & Juhász, 2025).

INTERNATIONAL ORGANISATIONS AND THE GLOBAL FRAMEWORK ON PROSTITUTION

The United Nations (UN) has repeatedly characterised prostitution and sex trafficking as infringements of human rights, encouraging nations to safeguard women and children from commercial sexual exploitation (Tarlow & Spencer, 2025). Foundational treaties, including the International Convention for the Suppression of the Traffic in Women and Children (1921) and the White Slave Traffic Convention (1910), criminalised trafficking while underscoring the importance of cooperation, prevention, and addressing socio economic factors such as poverty and gender inequality (Abdirasulovich & Alisherovich, 2025). The principles were codified in the Convention for the Suppression of the Traffic in Persons and of the Exploitation of the Prostitution of Others (1949), which continues to serve as the foundation of international anti exploitation legislation (Abdirasulovich & Alisherovich, 2025).

Subsequent instruments, specifically the Convention on the Elimination of All Forms of Discrimination against Women (CEDAW) (1979) and its Optional Protocol (1999), explicitly classify prostitution as a manifestation of gender-based discrimination, obligating states to implement policies that tackle both demand and structural inequality (Alsalem, 2025). The Palermo Protocol (2000) enhanced this by delineating trafficking, guaranteeing victim protection, and advocating for coordinated international efforts to combat the commercial sex trade (Abdirasulovich & Alisherovich, 2025; Alsalem, 2025; Tarlow & Spencer, 2025).

Numerous UN affiliated and international networks bolster these commitments. The International Women's Rights Action Watch-Asia Pacific (IWRAW-AP) oversees compliance with CEDAW and champions state accountability, whereas the Global Network of Sex Work Projects (NSWP) and Sex Workers' Rights Advocacy Network (SWAN) advocate for the inclusion of sex workers in policymaking, particularly regarding HIV/AIDS prevention (Balogh & Juhász, 2025; Basu et al., 2004). The Office of the UN High Commissioner for Human Rights (OHCHR) and the Global AIDS Strategy (2021-2026) emphasise the connection among human rights, health, and non-discrimination (Abdirasulovich & Alisherovich, 2025). The International Labour Organisation (ILO) mandates, via the Forced Labour Convention (1930) and the Worst Forms of Child Labour Convention (1999), that nations eradicate exploitation and offer viable alternatives via education, rehabilitation, and employment opportunities (Tyler, 2021). The World Health Organisation (WHO) supports this rights-based approach, promoting universal access to preventative healthcare, HIV services, and social protection for sex workers (Basu et al., 2004; Spyra, 2025).

Collectively, these global frameworks advocate for a human right focused, demand reduction strategy that aligns with the philosophy of the Nordic model, decriminalizing the exploited, penalising the exploiters, and fostering rehabilitation. For India, conforming to this worldwide consensus will enhance adherence to its international commitments under CEDAW and the Palermo Protocol, while also establishing a moral and legal basis for implementing a contextualised Nordic framework that safeguards dignity and mitigates exploitation.

COMPARATIVE ANALYSIS OF DIFFERENT MODELS

True gender equality cannot coexist with legalised prostitution. Racism, class, and gender inequity underpin the idea that men should have sexual access to women (Balogh & Juhász, 2025). It violates international law and cannot be questioned. The incapacity to fight legalised prostitution threatens every human rights concept requiring dignity and equality. European countries like the Netherlands and Germany have legalised or decriminalised prostitution, including pimps, brothels, and customers or johns (buyers) (Megías et al., 2025). Brothels and the buying of women for commercial sexual exploitation are theoretically legal in Thailand, although they are tolerated, especially in sex tourism (Balogh & Juhász, 2025; Tandon & Nayak, 2025). Sweden decriminalised prostitutes but penalised consumers (Tandon & Nayak, 2025).

These reasons apply to all state-sponsored prostitution, including the full legalisation of brothels and pimping, the decriminalisation of the sex trade, the regulation of prostitution through laws like registering or requiring health checks for prostitutes, or any system that recognises prostitution as "sex work" or encourages it as a viable employment option (Bateman, 2021). The difficulties of different models of law related to prostitution are examined under this section. Thorough review of literature and reports after the enforcement of respective laws has shown certain concerns. This scholarship has discussed it as follows:

(a) Legalisation has benefitted pimps, traffickers, and the sex industry: Netherlands licenses all aspects of the sex industry, including consumers, suppliers, and pimps, who become sexual entrepreneurs and third-party businesses (Tandon & Nayak, 2025). When the sex business is legalised or decriminalised, brothels, sex clubs, massage parlours, and other prostitution-related sites can lawfully grow commercial sexual activity. Some believe that legalising or decriminalising prostitution elevates prostitutes. Seeing prostitution as work advances the sex business, not women (Megías et al., 2025).

People often forget that decriminalisation impacts the whole sex industry, not just women. They also haven't addressed the consequences of acknowledging pimps as sex businessmen or third-party businesses or that men who buy women for sex are suddenly legitimate sex clients (Bateman, 2021). Fighting for the decriminalisation of prostitution in countries where it is illegal is crucial. No woman should pay for her servitude. However, decriminalising brothels, other sex establishments, buyers, procurers, and pimps is never wise.

(b) Encourages sex trafficking: Prostitute legalisation is a major cause of sex trafficking. Legalising prostitution in the Netherlands was justified by the exploitation of defenceless immigrant women transported there. Research shows that 80% of Dutch brothel women were transported there illegally (Balogh & Juhász, 2025). In 1994, "nearly 70% of trafficked women were from Central and Eastern European Countries (CEEC)" in the Netherlands, according to the IOM.

The Dutch government promotes anti-trafficking programs despite legalising pimping, procuring, and brothels (Bateman, 2021). The Dutch Ministry of Justice supported a legal quota of foreign "sex workers" in 2000 because the prostitution sector needed a variety of "bodies" (*Government policies and sex work realities*, 2017). In 2000, the Dutch government requested and received a European Court judgement recognising prostitution as an economic activity (Balogh & Juhász, 2025). This permitted EU and former Soviet bloc women to work as "sex workers" in the Dutch sex industry if they could prove they were self-employed (*Government policies and sex work realities*, 2017).

European non-governmental groups say traffickers use work permits to recruit foreign women into the Dutch prostitution industry and educate them to identify as independent "migrant sex workers" (Tandon & Nayak, 2025). Twelve victim support groups claimed that the number of foreign victims has not reduced since the Netherlands repealed its brothel prohibition, while eight Dutch victim support organisations reported an increase in trafficking victims (Post et al., 2019; Tandon & Nayak, 2025). 43 of 348 Dutch towns (12%) have a no-brothel policy, however the Minister of Justice warns that it may violate the "right to free choice of work"(Post et al., 2019) . In 1984, Victoria's (Australia) Labour government legalised brothel prostitution (Bateman, 2021). The 1994 Prostitution Control Act culminated later Australian governments' prostitution legalisation efforts (Balogh & Juhász, 2025). The US Department of State linked Australia's legalisation of prostitution to human trafficking: "East Asian women are being trafficked for the sex trade, and antitrafficking enforcement is difficult due to lax regulations, including legalised prostitution in some regions (Rathor, 2023).

(c) Decriminalisation leads to more prostitution: The Netherlands' sex business grew by 25% over the previous ten years after pimping and brothels were legalised in 2000 (Post et al., 2019; Tandon & Nayak, 2025).
(d) Legalising prostitution in Victoria, Australia, boosted the sex business. Other forms of sexual exploitation, such as table-top dance, peep shows, phone sex, and pornography, have also become more profitable (*10 Reasons for Not Legalizing Prostitution – CASAC*, n.d.). The Schengen agreement facilitates national border crossings, so it's likely that countries with state-sponsored prostitution act as conduits for large numbers of women to other European countries (*Government policies and sex work realities*, 2017).
(e) Legalisation increases the prevalence of prostitution: Legalised prostitution was intended to move prostitutes indoors, into brothels and clubs, where they would be less vulnerable. However, many women engage in street prostitution to avoid being manipulated and taken advantage of by pimps, who have become sex traders (Megías et al., 2025). Esohe Aghatise opposed an Italian proposal to legalise prostitution by arguing that brothels rob women of any protection they may have on the street by keeping them in enclosed areas where they have little chance of encountering outreach workers or other people who could help them leave prostitution (Abdirasulovich & Alisherovich, 2025).
(f) Prostitution is legal or decriminalised in the Netherlands, but women who engage in it say it is stigmatised (Tandon & Nayak, 2025). Women are more likely to be labelled "whores," and they must register and give up their privacy, so most continue to do so clandestinely and illegally. Chief Inspector Nancy Pollock, Scotland's highest-ranking female police officer, founded Glasgow's street liaison squad for prostitution-related women in 1998.
(g) Legalising or decriminalising prostitution would "simply abandon women to do what has to be the most demeaning job in the world" (*10 Reasons for Not Legalizing Prostitution – CASAC*, n.d.). Number of researchers have agreed that women could engage in prostitution in safer settings, citing sauna prostitution as an example (Tarlow & Spencer, 2025). Few street women engage in anal or non-condom intercourse. Sauna owners choose what the women do, which is often anal intercourse without a condom, because they don't want unhappy clients (Nde Fon & Balogh, 2025). The argument that strict sector management will eliminate the sex industry's criminal underbelly is unfounded. The illegal market has grown most since it became legal in Australia (*10 Reasons for Not Legalizing Prostitution – CASAC*, n.d.). Unregistered brothels in Victoria grew

from 1998 to 1999 and remain unchecked (*Legalization - Mary Lucille Sullivan, Sheila Jeffreys, 2002*, n.d.). New South Wales legalised prostitution in 1995, and by 1999, Sydney had 400–500 brothels, most of which were unregistered to advertise or conduct business (*Whore Laws of Yore: How New South Wales Decriminalised Sex Work 1979-1995*, n.d.). Due to police corruption, local councils and planning agencies took over unlawful prostitution (Bateman, 2021).

(h) Child prostitution increases: Another argument was that legalising prostitution in the Netherlands would end child prostitution. In the 1990s, Dutch child prostitution skyrocketed. From 4,000 children in 1996 to 15,000 in 2001, more than 300% more youngsters were prostituted, according to Amsterdam-based KidsRight (Haynes, 2025; Tarlow & Spencer, 2025). They estimate that at least 5,000 Dutch prostitutes are victims of international child trafficking, including many Nigerian girls ("Migrant Crisis," 2016).

(i) Prostitutes are not protected: In two studies of 186 victims of commercial sexual exploitation, women indicated that prostitution facilities, legal or illegal, did not protect them. A woman said, "The only time they protect anyone is to protect the customers" (*10 Reasons for Not Legalizing Prostitution – CASAC*, n.d.; Haynes, 2025). One study interviewed 146 trafficking victims from 5 countries (*10 Reasons for Not Legalizing Prostitution – CASAC*, n.d.). Whether they were trafficked internationally or locally, 80% of the women interviewed had experienced physical abuse from pimps and buyers, as well as similar and multiple health effects from sexual exploitation (*Legalization - Mary Lucille Sullivan, Sheila Jeffreys, 2002*, n.d.). Second research on American prostitutes found the following: women who claimed that working in the sex business protected them said no "protector" was ever in the room (Megías et al., 2025). One on-call prostitute said: "The driver was a bodyguard, when you arrive, you should call to make sure everything went as planned. However, they aren't watching from the outside while you're inside, so anything could happen (*Legalization - Mary Lucille Sullivan, Sheila Jeffreys, 2002*, n.d.; Megías et al., 2025). Surveillance cameras in brothels protect customers and the brothel, not the women (Abdirasulovich & Alisherovich, 2025).

(j) Encourages demand: Prostitution has become legal in nations where the sex business is no longer illegal, and many men who wouldn't have risked paying women for sex do so today (Post et al., 2019). Legalisation sends the message to younger men and boys that women are sexual commodities and prostitution is harmless entertainment (Abdirasulovich & Alisherovich, 2025). Victoria's roads are lined with advertisements that promote women as sexual objects (Bateman, 2021).

(k) Does not improve women's health: Medical screenings and certification are often required in legalised prostitution systems, but only for sellers, not for buyers

(Gonzalez-Recio et al., 2025; Nde Fon & Balogh, 2025). Since monitoring prostituted women does not protect them from HIV/AIDS or STDs, health exams or testing for women but not for men makes no sense in terms of public health. In one survey, 47% of prostitution-related women in the US said that men expected intercourse without a condom; 73% said that men offered to pay extra for sex without a condom; and 45% said that men were aggressive if they requested condoms (Basu et al., 2004; Cole, 2025; Gore et al., 2020). This suggests that enforceable condom rules in legalised brothels or other "controlled" prostitution facilities protect women. In reality, each prostitute enforced the condom law, and the urge to accept more money was constant. If more money came in, the condom would be thrown out the window.

"Safety policies" did not protect women in brothels, where customers and, occasionally, brothel proprietors and their associates watched by "bouncers," according to the allegations (Alsalem, 2025; "Sex Worker as the Juridical Subject," n.d.). Women endured violence from purchasers even when someone intervened to temporarily stop it.

(l) One survey found that 67% of law enforcement officers believed women did not become prostitutes willingly (Blanchetteç, 2022; Tarlow & Spencer, 2025). If the distinction between forced and consensual prostitution can be used to legalise prostitution, pimping, and brothels, the sector will have more legal protection and market stability. Women who want to file claims against pimps and other offenders must prove they were "forced." How will disadvantaged women prove coercion? Some former prostitutes say it took them years to realise that prostitution was not a free choice because to reject one's own ability for choice is to deny oneself (Gonzalez-Recio et al., 2025). According to a 1998 International Labour Organisation (ILO) report, prostitution is one of the most alienating forms of work. Women who prostituted did so "with a heavy heart," "felt forced," or were "conscience-stricken," and had negative self-identities (Gonzalez-Recio et al., 2025). A large percentage said they would quit if they could (Gonzalez-Recio et al., 2025).

People are becoming more aware that a woman is not there freely when she stays in an abusive relationship with a boyfriend who beats her or justifies his behaviour. When forced into prostitution, abused women may lie about their abuse if given no other options. Women's opposition: In the interviews the researcher has watched online, most trafficked and prostituted women strongly believed that prostitution should not be legalised and considered a legitimate job and warned that legalisation would increase the risks and harm for women from already violent clients and pimps.

Applying evaluative criteria shows that India's current approach criminalizes vulnerability while ignoring demand. The Nordic model offers a solution by penalizing clients, addressing structural gender inequality, and aligning with constitutional principles of dignity and equality.

It balances compassion with accountability recognizing sex workers as victims of systemic forces rather than offenders and creates legal deterrence for exploiters and buyers.

THE INDIAN LEGAL FRAMEWORK AND JUDICIAL INTERPRETATION

Constitutional Provisions

The Indian Constitution does not explicitly address prostitution; however, various provisions collectively establish the framework for understanding the matter. Article 21 ensures the protection of life and personal freedom, with judicial interpretations extending this to encompass the right to live with dignity (Goyal & Ramanujam, 2014; Rathor, 2023). Article 23 forbids the trafficking of individuals and forced labour practices such as *begar* and other analogous forms of coercion (Karlebach, 2008). The Directive Principles of State Policy, specifically Articles 38, 39(e), and 39(f), mandate that the State must guarantee that individuals are not compelled by financial constraints into occupations that undermine human dignity, and that children are safeguarded against abuse and exploitation (Verma & Bohra, 2024).

The Bharatiya Nyaya Sanhita, 2023

The Bhartiya Nyaya Sanhita, 2023, has brought prostitution and trafficking laws up to date and made them more consistent, while still keeping the spirit of the old laws that wanted to do rid of them. The BNS, which replaced the Indian Penal Code, nevertheless makes it a crime to trade people for sexual exploitation under Section 144, which is quite similar to the old Sections 370 and 370A of the IPC (Tandon & Nayak, 2025). It generally defines trafficking as recruiting, transporting, harbouring, or receiving people through threats, coercion, abduction, or deceit for purposes such as prostitution, enslavement, or organ trade (Verma & Bohra, 2024). The law says that the punishment should be harsher if the crime involves juveniles, women, or public officials (Tandon & Nayak, 2025). This shows that India is still committed to ending commercial sexual exploitation. The BNS does not make prostitution a legal job, instead it strengthens the idea that trafficking and exploitation, whether they are physical, financial, or mental, are abuses of human dignity (Verma & Bohra,

2024). The new code is in line with Article 23 of the Constitution and supports the goals of the Immoral Traffic (Prevention) Act, 1956 by making the punishment for systematic sexual exploitation stronger instead of making sex work legal(Verma & Bohra, 2023).

Legislative Context

The Immoral Traffic (Prevention) Act of 1956 is the main law governing prostitution in India, prohibiting pimping and related practices that violate prostitutes' human rights (Rathor, 2023). The act does not criminalize prostitution itself, but it addresses various forms of commercial sexual exploitation, including prostitution in all its manifestations, as well as the trafficking of women and children (Verma & Bohra, 2023).

Key provisions of the Act include, Section 3 criminalizes various forms of prostitution and related activities, making it an offence to knowingly carry on or help in carrying on prostitution or brothel-keeping (Verma & Bohra, 2024).

Section 4 deals with living off earnings of any other person's prostitution, making individuals over 18 years old liable for living off the earnings on prostitution done by someone else (Goyal & Ramanujam, 2014). Section 5 criminalizes prostitution and other types of exploitation facilitated by human trafficking (Goyal & Ramanujam, 2014). Section 6 makes it an offence to detain a person in premises where prostitution is carried on (Goyal & Ramanujam, 2014; Verma & Bohra, 2024). In Budhadev Karmaskar v. State of West Bengal 2011, the supreme court transformed the jurisprudence on prostitution by locating sex worker's rights within Article 21. The court held that sex workers are entitled to dignity, equality, and constitutional protection, further the court clarified that prostitution per se is not illegal under Indian law. Emphasising the socio-economic compulsions underlying sex work, the court imposed a positive obligation on the State to provide rehabilitation, vocational training, and social reintegration.

Section 7 criminalizes the carrying on of prostitution in the vicinity of a public place, with punishments ranging from 3 months to 7 years in certain cases (Goyal & Ramanujam, 2014; Verma & Bohra, 2023). Section 8 criminalizes seducing and soliciting in public, with punishments up to 1 year and fine (Rathor, 2023). Section 9 criminalizes aiding or abetting seduction intended for sexual exploitation when the accused has the care and custody of such person, with punishments ranging from 7 years to lifetime imprisonment (Verma & Bohra, 2024). Section 10A introduces the provision for detention of a woman found guilty under sections 7 and 8 in a corrective institution, creating mutual exclusive between imprisonment and detention in the institution (Goyal & Ramanujam, 2014; Verma & Bohra, 2024).

Special police officers are appointed to deal with offences under the Act, and Section 15 empowers them to search reported premises without a warrant (Verma & Bohra, 2024). Section 19 allows individuals being coerced into prostitution to be kept in protective homes, with records produced by the court (Verma & Bohra, 2024). Section 20 empowers magistrates to issue show cause notices to individuals carrying on prostitution in specific areas, violating citizens' right to life (Verma & Bohra, 2024). In case of Gaurav Jain v. Union of India 1997, a public interest litigation was filed concerning the plight of children born to sex workers and the failure of the State to implement rehabilitation and welfare measures under the ITPA. The Supreme Court held that the purpose of the ITPA is not merely punitive but rehabilitative and preventive and the victims of prostitution must be treated with dignity. The State must create protective homes, vocational training, and social integration programmes. The court also held that mere raids and arrests are insufficient. The Court further directed the formulation of comprehensive welfare schemes.

Despite being criticized for being too harsh on sex workers and failing to address the root causes of trafficking and exploitation, the Act remains vital in India's ongoing fight against human trafficking and commercial sexual exploitation. Court rulings highlight the Act's ultimate goal of ending women's trafficking for commercial benefits (Verma & Bohra, 2024). The Act's reach is somewhat restricted, with authorities targeting prostitutes during raids, police and government personnel being plagued by corruption (Rathor, 2023). Inadequate facilities for reform and rehabilitation of prostitutes are another issue. Many victims are unable to find stable housing, forcing them to return to criminal behaviour (Nde Fon & Balogh, 2025).

Amendments and Reform Attempts

The Indian government has attempted to introduce amendments to the Immoral Traffic (Prevention) Act, 1956 in 2006, 2018, and 2021, but none of these bills were passed. The 2006 bill was referred to the standing committee and lost after its report, while the 2018 bill was passed by the lower house of Indian Parliament but never debated in the Rajya Sabha.

The Prevention of Immoral Traffic Amendment Bill, 2006, changed the Act, which has been criticized for being too harsh on sex workers and failing to address the root causes of trafficking and exploitation. The bill punishes anyone who visits a brothel with the intent of sexually exploiting trafficked people, including those found guilty of trafficking in persons for sexual exploitation (Verma & Bohra, 2024). The statute authorizes both the central government and states to take action against human trafficking.

The Trafficking of Persons (Prevention, Protection and Rehabilitation) Bill, 2018, deleted sections 8 and 20 from the Act, creating a legal framework for the identification, prevention, and treatment of victims of human trafficking. The Bill also penalizes property owners or lessors who knowingly permit trafficking to occur on their property, violating Article 21 of the Constitution (Verma & Bohra, 2024).

The Trafficking of Persons (Prevention, Care and Rehabilitation) Bill, 2021, was introduced by the Ministry of Women and Child Development to combat the trafficking of people for sexual or physical exploitation. The Bill expanded the definition of "victims" to include transgender people and other people, and extended its coverage to offenses with international repercussions. It proposed preventative and beneficial measures. The Sex Workers (Rehabilitation and Social Security) Bill, 2015, addresses the rights of commercial sex workers in place of human rights, including chapters on equality, healthcare, education, financial security, and penalties for exploitation. The bill captures the need for better services and living conditions for commercial sex workers.

The Children of Pavement Dwellers and Sex Workers (Prevention of Abuse and Welfare Measures) Bill, 2001 & 2019, aims to protect the rights and welfare of children in India who are the children of sex workers and those who live on the streets (Verma & Bohra, 2024). It calls for the establishment of rehabilitation facilities and educational institutions to promote their entire development and ensure access to school, healthcare, and other necessities (Basu et al., 2004).

Judicial Developments in India so far

State of Uttar Pradesh v. Kaushalya,1964 included dispute about Kanpur-based sex workers (Verma & Bohra, 2024). The local magistrate summoned the women to "show cause, why they should not be forced to remove themselves from the premises." Defendants objected to invalid proceedings. The High Court upheld the revision petition and overturned SITA, 1956 Section 20. It disagrees with the High Court's verdict; thus, the state appealed to the Supreme Court. The respondents asserted that a section 13 special police officer should furnish the magistrate with information under section 20 of the SITA act. The court reasoned that the Act would have plainly declared that the Legislature did not intend for Special Police officers to obtain specific information. The court stated that "well established law" states that legislation can be lawful if they classify persons logically and have a purpose. Section 20 does not infringe Article 14 since it prevents moral decay in a public place.

In *Vishal Jeet v. Union of India, other States & UTs,1990* a Supreme Court of India advocate filed a public interest litigation to order the CBI inquiry against the police officers under whose jurisdiction commercial sex work and *Devadasi* and *Jogins* are still practiced. The court noted that commercial sex work has existed since ancient times and that poverty and illiteracy drive women to it. The court also discussed Section 13 of the Juvenile Justice Act of 2000, which allows police or other persons to take custody of a neglected juvenile and bring them before a board that decides their foster care or adoption. Despite legal provisions and rehabilitation plans, the state has failed to achieve its goals. The court rejected the petitioner's claim and ordered pimps, brokers, and brothel operators to suffer hefty penalties to end the flesh trade. The Supreme Court of India advised state and union territory governments and law enforcement to address the child prostitution situation immediately. It advised each state and union territory to form an Advisory Committee of welfare departments, law departments, criminologists, sociologists, and women's welfare organizations to propose measures to end the trade of children as prostitutes and implement social welfare services to care for, protect, treat, and rehabilitate young victims. All state governments were advised to create medical and social worker-staffed rehabilitation institutions. The union government was instructed to form a committee to create and implement victim welfare measures. Central, state, and union territory administrations should create distinct mechanisms to implement committee recommendations.

Gaurav Jain v. Union of India & Ors, 1997 required the Supreme Court of India to outline government agency rules and procedures in this area. Separating prostitutes' children from the general population in schools and dorms would harm them and society, the court decided. The court also ordered the creation of secure and nurturing homes for the female victims' children.

The committee recognised 10 prostitution types: streetwalkers, religious prostitution, brothels, singing and dancing girls, nude bars, massage parlours, and call girls. Poverty and unemployment drove prostitute recruitment. The committee noted that brothel mothers generally cannot work or attend school. This perpetuates slavery and bondage by forcing women to borrow from brothel keepers to support their children. The lack of alternative money and society's acceptability prohibits these women from leaving the profession. Poverty, societal intolerance, health concerns, lack of economic assistance, and family rejection were the main reasons women entered prostitution, according to the committee. NGOs are vital to re-establishing and educating sex worker children. The court stressed that the state must rehabilitate women forced to work in trades due to social and financial concerns. The court recommended *counselling, cajoling*, and *compelling* to adopt ITPA and JJ Acts to protect women and children from the trade. The court ordered the Central and State governments to organise an Advisory Committee to address child prostitution and make suggestions on how to care for, protect, and rehabilitate minor victims in May 1990.

Established rules by judiciary so far:

(a) Sex workers should not be discriminated against in laws; the age of majority and informed consent should be equal. Police cannot interfere or commit crimes if the sex worker is an adult and gives their consent consciously and freely.
(b) Sex workers who have been sexually assaulted should receive emergency medical care.
(c) Raids should not imprison sex workers.
(d) State governments may be pushed to survey all ITPA Protective Homes to speed up the evaluation and discharge of adult women incarcerated against their will.
(e) Police reportedly employ disproportionate force and hostility towards sex workers. Law enforcement and other government personnel should be informed on the rights of sex workers and refuse to verbally or physically harass or pressure them into sexual actions.
(f) The Press Council of India should set regulations for reporting on sex workers' names following arrest, raid, and rescue operations and penalise the media for posting photographs of them with their customers under the guise of a rescue mission.

In *Sahyog Mahila Mandal v. State of Gujarat, 2004* the Indian Supreme Court declared that the Immoral Traffic (Prevention) Act, 1956, did not violate Articles 14, 19, and 21 of the Indian Constitution. The court found that Sections 7(1)(b), 14 and 15 of the Act do not violate the right to equality by criminalising prostitution in public places since they aim to abolish it and are not discriminatory or arbitrary.

In *Manoj Kumar Shaw V. State of West Bengal, 2019* the court ordered an investigating officer to file a notice under Section 41A of the Code of Criminal Procedure against a health spa owner who employed young girls for prostitution. The court stated that where an offence involves a seven-year sentence or longer, the investigating officer should carefully consider all the circumstances before providing the notification required by Section 41A of the Code of Criminal Procedure, 1973.

In *Kajal Mukesh Singh & Ors. V. State of Maharashtra, 2019* the court declared the victims guilty after a year of detention. Both lower courts ignored Section 17 of the Immoral Trafficking (Prevention) Act and handled the issue lightly. The court emphasised that the Act prohibits the Magistrate from detaining victims for more than three weeks without a court order.

The court further stated that the statute punishes sexual exploitation, commercial sex, and brothel operation or enticement, not prostitution. Court stressed that victims have the same rights as other people and should obtain their consent before being placed in a correctional facility. The court found that Indian courts now prioritise prostitutes' rights and well-being. Indian governments must develop "red-light districts" where prostitution is legal and prostitutes have access to social amenities including healthcare, according to the Supreme Court.

KEY ISSUES AND IMPLEMENTATION CHALLENGES

The positions of several governments on prostitution have faced criticism for prioritising the penalisation of sex workers over those of customers. This tactic has impeded sex workers' access to healthcare and protection against abuse and exploitation. This policy fails to address the primary causes of prostitution, including poverty, illiteracy, and insufficient work opportunities.

(a) Stigma and discrimination: The stigma that is attached to sex workers in India is well ingrained, which contributes to the perpetuation of social exclusion and restricts access to healthcare, housing, and justice. Although the court acknowledged their right to dignity in *Budhadev Karmaskar v. State of West Bengal, 2022,* law enforcement frequently handles them as offenders rather than victims.

(b) Economic insecurity and lack of livelihood alternatives: Poverty, gendered unemployment, or coercive socio-economic constraints are the primary factors that lead the majority of women to engage in prostitution. In the absence of comprehensive livelihood initiatives, criminalising purchasers alone (as in the Nordic model) would not be sufficient; it is vital to provide supplementary rehabilitation and skill-building opportunities.

(c) Limited data and research on prostitution dynamics: There is no official database that has all of the information on the number of sex workers in India, their working conditions, or their demographics. Methodology has a significant impact on the estimates, which range anywhere from six to ten lakh workers. It has been emphasised by both the World Bank and UN Women that the absence of reliable data contributes to the perpetuation of invisibility and affects the design of rehabilitation programs (Scoular, 2010). Policy discussions continue to be based on moral principles rather than empirical evidence, which results in legislation that is ineffectual.

(d) Political and moral opposition to decriminalization of sellers: The public and political discourse in India continues to moralise prostitution, associating it with immorality or criminality instead of recognising its inherent value. Numerous reform attempts are typically met with opposition from religious and conservative organisations, which portray sex work as a danger to the social order. There were significant ideological differences that were represented in the arguments that took place in the Parliament about the Trafficking of Persons (Prevention, Protection and Rehabilitation) Bill, 2018, which eventually prevented the bill from being passed. The United Nations Special Rapporteur on Violence against Women (2022) advised India to adopt a rights-based, pragmatic strategy that focusses on demand reduction rather than moral policing.

CONCLUSION AND THE WAY FORWARD: A CONTEXTUALISED NORDIC MODEL FOR INDIA

Core Pillars of Reform

(a) Decriminalize selling sex while criminalizing purchase and trafficking: The legal system of India needs to change its attention from prosecuting those who engage in prostitution due to economic necessity to punishing those who exploit, trade, and buy prostitutes. The Nordic approach, which was successfully adopted in Sweden and Norway, was able to successfully reframe prostitution as a form of gender-based violence and reduce street prostitution by addressing demand (Ekberg & Wahlberg, n.d.).

(b) Establish rehabilitation, education, and livelihood programs: It is necessary for rehabilitation to extend beyond the confines of rescue homes and incorporate long-term social and economic reintegration. Community-based rehabilitation and vocational training are two of the recommendations that the Ministry of Women and Child Development (MWCD) has included in its draft of the Trafficking in Persons (Prevention, Care and Rehabilitation) Bill for the year 2021 (Verma & Bohra, 2024). Through successful implementation in the Nordic region, exit programs and employment opportunities sponsored by the state have been shown to minimise re-entry into prostitution (Post et al., 2019).

(c) Introduce demand reduction and public awareness campaigns: Raising awareness among the general public is essential to the success of the Nordic model. There was a discernible shift in cultural norms as a result of campaigns in Sweden, such as "Don't Buy Sex," which reframed the act of purchasing sexual services as socially undesirable (Scoular, 2010). Similarly, India has to make investments in ads that target demand, gender stereotypes, and patriarchal conceptions of entitlement among its population.

(d) Strengthen institutional coordination across ministries and NGOs: This act, which was passed in 1956, should be amended or replaced in order to include Nordic ideals. It should clearly decriminalise vendors while criminalising purchasers, traffickers, and brothel owners. In order to supervise implementation, data gathering, and coordination among states, a National Anti-Demand and Rehabilitation Board should be established so that it falls within the jurisdiction of the MWCD. It is important to provide Vocational Training, Housing, and Microcredit Schemes in order to facilitate reintegration, particularly via conjunction with existing schemes such as PM-DAKSH and the National Skill Development Corporation (NSDC). In accordance with the recommendations made by the United Nations Special Rapporteur on Violence against Women

(2022), provide training for the police and the judiciary on gender sensitivity, human rights norms, and the strategy that is based on the Nordic model.

Expected Outcomes

In order to improve rehabilitation, comprehensive social protection and livelihood initiatives should be implemented. Create opportunities for disadvantaged women by integrating them into the education and job systems of the mainstream society. To advance gender justice in accordance with India's constitutional protections (Articles 14, 15, 21) and international commitments under the Convention on the Elimination of All Forms of Discrimination Against Women (CEDAW) and the Palermo Protocol. According to Levy and Jakobsson (2014), empirical data from Nordic nations reveals that there has been a continuous drop in street prostitution, better gender equality indices, and public consensus against sexual exploitation. It would be possible for India to make the transition from a punishing morality to a caring governance system if it adopted a similar strategy. Punitive legal frameworks have failed to eliminate exploitation or provide safety to women in the trade. The Nordic model offers a balanced alternative one that penalizes demand, protects dignity, and promotes social reintegration. Adopting a contextualized Nordic model would align India's policy with its constitutional values of equality and dignity, marking a decisive shift from moral condemnation to compassionate, rights-based governance.

REFERENCES

Abdirasulovich, K. A., & Alisherovich, E. O. (2025). ANALYSIS OF INTERNATIONAL LEGAL NORMS ESTABLISHING LIABILITY FOR CERTAIN OFFENSES AGAINST MORALITY, SUCH AS MAINTAINING A BROTHEL OR ENGAGING IN PROSTITUTION. *The Conference Hub*, 89–93. https://theconferencehub.com/index.php/tch/article/view/280

Alsalem, R. (2025). Response to a Political Critique and Personal Attack Against a United Nations Report that Presented New Evidence About Prostitution as a Cause and Consequence of Violence Against Women and Girls. *Dignity: A Journal of Analysis of Exploitation and Violence, 10*(1), 6.

Ancient history—Was prostitution legal in the Kingdom of Israel during the reign of Solomon? - History Stack Exchange. (n.d.). Retrieved October 24, 2025, from https://history.stackexchange.com/questions/10884/was-prostitution-legal-in-the-kingdom-of-israel-during-the-reign-of-solomon

Balogh, L., & Juhász, B. (2025). Debates on Legal Models Regarding Prostitution, with a Focus on the Role of Terminology. *MTA LAW WORKING PAPERS, 1*(1), 1–15.

Basu, I., Jana, S., Rotheram-Borus, M. J., Swendeman, D., Lee, S.-J., Newman, P., & Weiss, R. (2004). HIV Prevention Among Sex Workers in India. *Journal of Acquired Immune Deficiency Syndromes (1999), 36*(3), 845–852.

Bateman, V. (2021). How Decriminalisation Reduces Harm Within and Beyond Sex Work: Sex Work Abolitionism as the "Cult of Female Modesty" in Feminist Form. *Sexuality Research & Social Policy, 18*(4), 819–836. DOI: 10.1007/s13178-021-00612-8

Bhattacharjee, B. (2025). The Muffled Memories: Tracing the Traumatic History of the Comfort Women of World War II through Jan Ruff O'Herne's Memoir Fifty Years of Silence. In Soman, N., Padmanabhan, B., & Kudale, K. M. (Eds.), *Between Trauma and Memory* (pp. 3–16). Springer Nature Singapore., DOI: 10.1007/978-981-96-8375-8_1

Bhattacharji, S. (1987). Prostitution in ancient India. *Social Scientist (New Delhi), 15*(2), 32–61. DOI: 10.2307/3520437

Blanchette, T. G., Simões, S. S., Paula da Silva, A., & Murray, L. R. (2020). The Prostitute, the City, and the Virus. *SSRN, 3608567*, •••. https://papers.ssrn.com/sol3/papers.cfm?abstract_id=3608567. DOI: 10.2139/ssrn.3608567

Blanchetteç, T. G. (2022). A Place at the Table: Sex Workers and Allies in the Redefinition of Brazil's Anti-Trafficking Law. *Social Sciences (Basel, Switzerland), 11*(11), 11. Advance online publication. DOI: 10.3390/socsci11110530

Chernick, K., & Sweeting, K. D. (2025). Beyond Ingrained Stigma: A Critical Intersectional Analysis of Sex Work, Social Equity, and Canada's PCEPA Legislation. *Sexuality Research & Social Policy*. Advance online publication. DOI: 10.1007/s13178-025-01158-9

Cole, K. (2025). Evaluating Public Attitudes and Arguments for Sex Work Decriminalization: Insights From a Vignette Experiment. *Criminal Justice Policy Review, 36*(5), 187–212. DOI: 10.1177/08874034251334353

Ekberg, G. S., & Wahlberg, K. (n.d.). 10. Twenty-five Years of Enforcing the Ban against the Purchase of Sexual Services in Sweden. *Law, Ideology, and the Experiences of Sex Workers and Clients*, 195.

Gonzalez-Recio, P., Armstrong, L., Alonso-Colón, M., Padilla, M., Bustillos, A., Belza, M. J., & Moreno-García, S. (2025). "We want back the dignity they stole from us": Epistemic injustice, sex work criminalization and trans sex workers' mental health. *International Journal of Transgender Health*, •••, 1–14. DOI: 10.1080/26895269.2025.2573833

Gore, M., Narayanan, P., & Juvekar, S. (2020). Does fear for infection affect condom use and HIV testing? A study of female sex workers in Pune city. *Clinical Epidemiology and Global Health, 8*(2), 562–566. DOI: 10.1016/j.cegh.2019.12.003

Government policies and sex work realities: Human trafficking in the regulated sex industry (with Verhoeven, M. A.). (2017). publisher not identified.

Goyal, Y., & Ramanujam, P. (2014). Ill-conceived laws and exploitative state: Toward decriminalizing prostitution in India. *Akron Law Review, 47*, 1071.

Haynes, J. (2025). International human rights law's complicity in status subordination: A postcolonial critique of treaty bodies' engagement with human trafficking. *Leiden Journal of International Law*, •••, 1–33.

Karlebach, N. J. (2008). Recognizing women's worth: The human rights argument for ending prostitution in India. *Boston College Third World Law Journal, 28*(2), 483–510.

King, K. C., & Snyder, J. M. (1990). The Woman and the Lyre: Woman Writers in Classical Greece and Rome. *Tulsa Studies in Womens Literature, 9*(2), 323. DOI: 10.2307/464231

Legalization—Mary Lucille Sullivan, Sheila Jeffreys, 2002. (n.d.). Retrieved October 26, 2025, from https://journals.sagepub.com/doi/10.1177/107780102401101773

Lerner, G. (1986). The Origin of Prostitution in Ancient Mesopotamia. *Signs (Chicago, Ill.), 11*(2), 236–254. DOI: 10.1086/494218

Martin, A. (2025). Prostitution as Profession: Histories of 'Work-Shy' Labour in a Welfare State, West Germany between 1949 and 1974. *Contemporary European History, 34*(3), 1–18. DOI: 10.1017/S0960777325000013

Megías, J. L., Thon, P., Siebler, F., & Bohner, G. (2025). Attitudes Toward Prostitution in Norway, Spain, and Germany: Association With the Legal Context and Susceptibility to Persuasion. *Scandinavian Journal of Psychology, 66*(2), 253–265. DOI: 10.1111/sjop.13082 PMID: 39528352

Migrant crisis: Child trafficking on rise in EU. (2016, May 19). *BBC News*. https://www.bbc.com/news/world-europe-36338022

Nde Fon, N., & Balogh, L. (2025). *The Impact of Decriminalisation on Sex Work: A Global Meta-synthesis of Health, Safety, and Societal Perceptions from the Perspective of Sex Workers*. https://www.diva-portal.org/smash/record.jsf?pid=diva2:1984543

Neethi, P., & Kamath, A. (2025). Turbulent transformations and urban undesirables: Revanchist urban transition and street-based sex work in Bangalore. In *Mapping Legalities* (pp. 141–158). Routledge., https://www.taylorfrancis.com/chapters/edit/10.4324/9781003384816-9/turbulent-transformations-urban-undesirables-neethi-anant-kamath

Post, C., Brouwer, J. G., & Vols, M. (2019). Regulation of Prostitution in the Netherlands: Liberal Dream or Growing Repression? *European Journal on Criminal Policy and Research, 25*(2), 99–118. DOI: 10.1007/s10610-018-9371-8

Prostitute Definition by Webster's at Smart Define dictionary. (n.d.). Retrieved October 25, 2025, from https://www.smartdefine.org/prostitute/definitions/2050132

Rai, S. (2024). Interested Gazes and Invisible Audiences: Judicial Narratives on Sex Work. *Indian Journal of Gender Studies, 31*(2), 159–176. DOI: 10.1177/09715215241235346

Rathor, M. (2023). The Regulation and Legalisation of Prostitution in India with Emphasis on Socio-Legal Effects. *Issue 1 Indian JL & Legal Rsch., 5*, 1.

10Reasons for Not Legalizing Prostitution – CASAC. (n.d.). Retrieved October 26, 2025, from https://casac.ca/10-reasons-for-not-legalizing-prostitution/

Roy, P. K. R. K. (2019). *The role of state in Prostitution: An anthropological exploration in a frontier city of Bangladesh. 2*(9), 14–28. DOI: 10.5281/ZENODO.3386549

Sanger, W. W. (2022). *The history of prostitution: Its extent, causes, and effects throughout the world.* DigiCat. https://books.google.com/books?hl=en&lr=&id=9AxzEAAAQBAJ&oi=fnd&pg=PT10&dq=history+of+prostitution+&ots=ejVinmiQqu&sig=hEb4PTZZNLdJMA8LsFfCLDkBAIk

Scott, G. R. (2014). *A history of prostitution: From antiquity to the present day.* Routledge. https://www.taylorfrancis.com/books/mono/10.4324/9781315828091/history-prostitution-george-ryley-scott

Scoular, J. (2010). What's Law Got To Do With it? How and Why Law Matters in the Regulation of Sex Work. *Journal of Law and Society, 37*(1), 12–39. DOI: 10.1111/j.1467-6478.2010.00493.x

Sex Worker as the Juridical Subject: Interrogating the Violence of Legal Interpretation. (n.d.). *Journal of Indian Law and Society.*

Shousha, N. M., & Taha, D. M. (2025). Sacred Bonds, Silent Pain: Understanding Women's Perceptions and Experiences of Marital Rape in Egypt. *Journal of Family Violence*. Advance online publication. DOI: 10.1007/s10896-025-00902-4

Spyra, J. Z. (2025). Jewish Prostitution in the Archives: Reflections on Stigma, Access, and Anonymization. *Journal of Jewish Identities, 18*(2), 307–332. DOI: 10.1353/jji.2025.a966367

Tandon, B., & Nayak, P. (2025). Reconsidering criminalisation of prostitution: A comparative critical study of the models in vogue in India, Sweden and the Netherlands. *International Journal of Public Law and Policy, 11*(2), 210–231. DOI: 10.1504/IJPLAP.2025.145307

Tarlow, P. E., & Spencer, A. (2025). From Slavery to Prostitution: Entrance to Human and Sex Trafficking. In *Human Trafficking and the Tourism Industry* (pp. 83–111). Emerald Publishing Limited. https://www.emerald.com/insight/content/doi/10.1108/978-1-83797-929-520251004/full/html

Taylor, C. (2025). Women in the ancient Greek world: History and historiography. *The Journal of Hellenic Studies, 145*, 1–13. DOI: 10.1017/S0075426925100414

The Melammu Project. (n.d.). Retrieved October 24, 2025, from http://www.melammu-project.eu/database/gen_html/a0000237.html

Tyler, M. (2021). All roads lead to abolition? Debates about prostitution and sex work through the lens of unacceptable work. *Labour & Industry: A Journal of the Social and Economic Relations of Work, 31*(1), 66–86. DOI: 10.1080/10301763.2020.1847806

Verma, A., & Bohra, S. (2023). The vague perception of commercial sex work and exploitation of women: The Indian legal framework. *International Journal of Human Rights and Constitutional Studies, 10*(2), 176. DOI: 10.1504/IJHRCS.2023.130016

Verma, A., & Bohra, S. (2024). The rights of commercial sex workers in India: A critical analysis of the legislative and judicial trends. *International Journal of Human Rights and Constitutional Studies, 11*(2), 169–185. DOI: 10.1504/IJHRCS.2024.137723

Whore Laws of Yore: How New South Wales Decriminalised Sex Work 1979-1995. (n.d.). Retrieved October 26, 2025, from https://www.tiki-toki.com/timeline/entry/754853/-Whore-Laws-of-Yore-How-New-South-Wales-Decriminalised-Sex-Work-1979-1995/

Chapter 15
From Criminalization to Protection:
Reimagining Prostitution Laws Through the Lens of Women's Rights

Anuj Kumar Singh
http://orcid.org/0009-0002-1760-6685
GLA University, Mathura, India

Ankita Sharma
http://orcid.org/0009-0007-6276-3926
GLA University, Mathura, India

ABSTRACT

This chapter analyzes India's semi-criminalized legal framework on prostitution and its failure to safeguard women's rights. It argues that conflating consensual sex work with trafficking perpetuates stigma, exploitation, and systemic exclusion. Using a feminist doctrinal and comparative method, the paper highlights that countries adopting regulated or decriminalized models ensure better health, labor protection, and social inclusion for sex workers. It concludes that India must replace moralistic criminalization with rights-based regulation that acknowledges sex work as legitimate labor, ensuring dignity, safety, and equality for women engaged in the trade.

INTRODUCTION

Sex work has existed in India since time immemorial, with evidentiary references found in various historical texts. Despite its longstanding presence, it has remained a

DOI: 10.4018/979-8-3373-5841-3.ch015

contested and stigmatized issue. In the modern era, sex work has generated debates surrounding law and morality, public health, human rights, and gender justice. The debate regarding the legalization of sex work gained momentum with increasing recognition of sex workers' rights as human rights (Amnesty International, 2016).

Advocates supporting legalization argue that criminalizing sex work forces the industry underground, increasing violence, human trafficking, and sexually transmitted infections. Conversely, opponents argue that sex work inherently involves exploitation, gender inequality, and objectification of women. The Indian sex industry is considered a multi-billion-dollar sector, rapidly expanding and often associated with organized and clandestine criminal activities (World Bank, 2020).

Empirical data indicates that approximately 40% of sex workers fall between 18 and 25 years of age, while nearly 70% operate in urban areas. Trafficking accounts for nearly 60% of entry into sex work among women, while poverty and illiteracy remain primary contributing factors. Sex workers frequently encounter health risks and violence. HIV prevalence among female sex workers remains significantly higher than the general adult population. According to the National AIDS Control Organization, HIV prevalence among female sex workers during 2020-21 was 1.9%, compared to 0.21% among the general adult population (National AIDS Control Organization [NACO], 2021).

Globally, forced labor remains a major concern. The International Labour Organization estimated that 27.6 million individuals were subjected to forced labor in 2022, including 6.3 million in forced sexual exploitation (International Labour Organization, 2022). In India, crime data shows 1,769 cases registered under the Immoral Traffic (Prevention) Act, 1956, in 2023, involving 1,544 adult women and 833 minor girls. Additionally, 2,250 cases were registered under Section 370 of the Indian Penal Code, with conviction rates ranging between 30% and 35% (National Crime Records Bureau, 2023).

International organizations distinguish between consensual adult sex work and trafficking. The Joint United Nations Programme on HIV/AIDS defines sex work as consensual sexual service exchange between adults and differentiates it from trafficking (UNAIDS, 2012). Similarly, the World Health Organization defines sex workers as individuals who receive money or goods in exchange for sexual services and emphasizes the importance of public health interventions and HIV prevention (World Health Organization, 2013).

The International Labour Organization does not explicitly endorse sex work but considers it within the informal economy and emphasizes decent work and non-discrimination principles while distinguishing forced sexual exploitation from voluntary participation (International Labour Organization, 2010). The Palermo Protocol defines trafficking as recruitment, transportation, or harboring individuals through coercion or deception for exploitation and clarifies that consent becomes irrelevant when coercion exists (United Nations, 2000).

Amnesty International advocates complete decriminalization of consensual adult sex work to protect human rights (Amnesty International, 2016). In May 2022, the Supreme Court of India affirmed that sex workers are entitled to equal protection under Article 21, guaranteeing dignity and protection from harassment, though brothel-related activities remain criminalized (Budhadev Karmaskar v. State of West Bengal, 2022).

The Law Commission of India recognized prostitution as a persistent social phenomenon and stated that complete prohibition would likely prove ineffective, as prostitution would continue to reappear within society (Law Commission of India, 1975). Additionally, economic analyses highlight that poverty and unemployment significantly influence individuals' entry into prostitution (World Bank, 2020). Scholars argue that sexuality constitutes a fundamental aspect of human existence, and excessive criminalization suppresses individual autonomy, pushing the trade underground and increasing exploitation.

Regulation of prostitution would enable state authorities to implement mandatory medical checkups and safety protocols, thereby reducing sexually transmitted infections, including HIV/AIDS. Sex workers residing in red-light areas often experience unsafe and unsanitary living conditions and are frequently treated as public nuisances. Regulation would impose obligations on governments to improve living standards and facilitate social inclusion. Additionally, it would address disparities between high-end escort services and economically vulnerable red-light area workers, thereby promoting parity and ensuring consumer and worker safety.

Regulation may further empower women by enabling them to seek legal remedies against harassment and exploitation. However, it is argued that customers should not be treated as consumers under the Consumer Protection Act, as the human body should not be treated as a commodified service. Instead, legal provisions should ensure accountability for customers engaging in abusive or exploitative conduct.

The present study presupposes that lack of regulation ultimately jeopardizes the interests of women engaged in sex work. Although the Supreme Court has recognized prostitution as a form of livelihood, comprehensive legal protection remains absent. The study therefore aims to analyze India's regulatory framework concerning prostitution and propose legal reforms to protect women's rights and prevent trafficking. It argues that India must reform prostitution laws to provide protective mechanisms, formal recognition, and social acceptance of sex workers as part of mainstream society.

LITERATURE REVIEW

In the study titled *Regulating Prostitution: A Comparative Law and Economic Approach*, researchers examined regulatory impacts on market efficiency, public health, safety outcomes, human rights, and public order across different regulatory regimes including criminalization, legalization, decriminalization, and the Nordic model (Cunningham & Shah, 2018).

The study compared the criminalization model prevalent in parts of the United States, legalization models in Germany and the Netherlands, decriminalization in New Zealand, and the Nordic model, which criminalizes clients rather than sex workers. The study applied economic analysis, conceptualizing prostitution as a market transaction between consenting adults. It also examined state intervention in cases of market failure, particularly public health risks, moral concerns, and externalities, and evaluated how legal skepticism affects entry barriers and operational safety for female sex workers.

The study concluded that criminalization reduces labor protections and creates black markets, thereby increasing violence, disease transmission, and exploitation. Enforcement costs are also significantly high. Conversely, legalization improves access to health services, social welfare benefits, and transaction transparency. Decriminalization reduces stigma and increases social acceptance of voluntary sex work as legitimate labor. The Nordic model reduced visible street prostitution but increased hidden and online sex work (Cunningham & Shah, 2018).

Another comparative law and economics study analyzing prostitution regulation evaluated social welfare outcomes under prohibition, regulation, and decriminalization models. The prohibition model was associated with unsafe working conditions, black markets, and increased enforcement expenditure. Decriminalization improved worker safety, health outcomes, and transparency. Legalization through licensing reduced worker harm but created regulatory burdens that excluded marginalized workers. The Nordic model aimed to reduce demand but often displaced prostitution into hidden markets (Weitzer, 2012).

The authors concluded that decriminalization combined with selective regulation achieves the most effective balance between protecting sex workers' rights and promoting social welfare. Economic reasoning supports regulation and decriminalization over prohibition, emphasizing policy frameworks focused on protecting voluntary sex workers, ensuring labor and health rights, and combating trafficking and coercion.

The paper titled *Legalization of Prostitution: Defining New Boundaries for the 21st Century* examines the contemporary status of prostitution with particular emphasis on human rights and gender equality. The study argues in favor of legalization and regulatory frameworks, suggesting that such models provide a more humane and justified approach. It asserts that state recognition, licensing, and formal regulation of prostitution can ensure protection against coercion and trafficking while providing labor rights and social security benefits. However, the study cautions that over-regulation may force workers underground and recommends a balanced legalization model emphasizing dignity, safety, and equality of sex workers (Weitzer, 2012).

The study titled *The Impact of Decriminalization of Sex Work in New Zealand: Report to the Prostitution Law Review Committee* evaluates the consequences of decriminalization in improving health, safety, and working conditions of sex workers while reducing trafficking. Based on surveys of sex workers, interviews with police and health authorities, and comparative pre- and post-legislation analysis, the study found that decriminalization empowered sex workers by enabling them to refuse clients, access healthcare services, and report violence. Importantly, the study concluded that decriminalization did not increase the overall number of sex workers but significantly improved workplace safety and health standards, although special protection remains necessary for migrants and vulnerable groups (Prostitution Law Review Committee, 2008).

The report titled *Trafficking in Nine Countries: An Update on Violence and Post-Traumatic Stress Disorder* examines the prevalence of violence and trauma among sex workers across multiple countries. Based on structured interviews and surveys, the study identified high levels of physical and sexual violence and widespread psychological harm, including post-traumatic stress disorder. The study argues that even in cases categorized as voluntary sex work, coercion and structural vulnerabilities remain prevalent. It strongly recommends anti-violence measures and comprehensive exit and rehabilitation support services for sex workers (Farley et al., 2004).

The paper *The Social Construction of Sex Trafficking: Ideology and Institutionalization of a Moral Crusade* argues that sex trafficking has often been socially constructed and politicized, leading to policy confusion between trafficking and consensual sex work. Through content analysis of media and academic literature and comparative legal approaches, the study concludes that trafficking debates are frequently influenced by moral panic and incomplete empirical evidence. The paper advocates evidence-based policymaking that clearly distinguishes coercion from voluntary sex work to prevent human rights violations (Weitzer, 2007).

The work titled *Militarized Humanitarianism Meets Carceral Feminism: The Politics of Sex, Rights and Freedom* critically examines feminist anti-trafficking campaigns that rely heavily on criminal enforcement mechanisms. The author argues that such approaches, described as "carceral feminism," promote punitive policing, prosecution, and deportation measures that often undermine human rights protections. Using case studies, feminist theory, and policy analysis, the study demonstrates that criminalized anti-trafficking frameworks frequently expand state control mechanisms while neglecting structural causes such as poverty and migration restrictions. The study recommends non-punitive protection measures, labor rights frameworks, and social welfare interventions (Bernstein, 2010).

The collection *Prostitution, Power and Freedom* analyzes conceptual and empirical distinctions between sex work and trafficking. Using ethnographic research, critical legal theory, and qualitative fieldwork, the study highlights that rigid binary classifications between consensual sex work and trafficking overlook structural determinants such as economic necessity, labor market exclusion, and immigration status. The study recommends policy interventions focusing on labor protection and social rights alongside targeted anti-trafficking enforcement (Doezema, 2010).

The paper *Dangerous Sex, Invisible Labor: Sex Work and Law in India* examines the Indian legal framework governing prostitution and argues that Indian law treats sex work primarily as a moral and criminal issue rather than labor. Based on doctrinal legal analysis, interviews, and field research involving sex workers, NGOs, and law enforcement authorities, the study demonstrates that conflation of voluntary sex work with trafficking leads to harmful raid and rescue operations. The study finds that lack of recognition of sex work as labor deprives sex workers of fair wages, workplace safety, social security, and protection from exploitative intermediaries. It recommends decriminalization of voluntary adult sex work and recognition of sex work as labor to ensure social protection and collective bargaining rights (Kotiswaran, 2011).

The paper *Law, Sex Workers and the State in India* critically reviews India's semi-criminalized legal framework and argues that it results in serious human rights violations without effectively addressing trafficking or exploitation. Using doctrinal analysis of the Immoral Traffic (Prevention) Act, Indian Penal Code provisions, and judicial decisions along with empirical NGO data, the study applies feminist legal theory to criticize the moralistic foundation of current laws. The study finds that criminalization of brothel-keeping and solicitation forces sex workers into unsafe working conditions, increases police violence and extortion, and results in involuntary detention in rescue homes. It recommends decriminalization, regulatory labor welfare policies, and inclusion of sex workers in policymaking processes (Agnes, 2013).

The paper *Sex Work, Labour and Human Rights* challenges victim-centric and morality-driven approaches within Indian and international human rights law. Using feminist legal theory and doctrinal analysis of statutory and constitutional frameworks, the study argues that rescue-oriented policies undermine autonomy, livelihood rights, bodily integrity, and privacy. It suggests that India's legal framework reflects colonial moral assumptions and abolitionist feminist influences that often harm sex workers. The study recommends decriminalization of voluntary sex work, recognition of sex work as legitimate labor, and amendment of the Immoral Traffic (Prevention) Act to focus exclusively on coercion and trafficking (Kotiswaran, 2014).

The study *Trafficking, Sex Work and Law Reform in India* examines the Immoral Traffic (Prevention) Act in light of India's international obligations under global anti-trafficking frameworks. Using doctrinal and comparative analysis supported by NGO field data and interviews, the study finds that Indian law conflates trafficking with consensual adult sex work, resulting in criminalization and underground operations that restrict healthcare access and legal protection. The study proposes a two-tier legal framework emphasizing strict anti-trafficking laws targeting coercion and minors alongside decriminalization and regulation of voluntary adult sex work as an economic activity (Sangram, 2012).

The paper *Decriminalizing Sex Work in India: Constitutional Promises and Judicial Developments* examines constitutional protections available to sex workers, particularly following the Supreme Court judgment in *Budhadev Karmaskar v. State of West Bengal*. Using doctrinal constitutional analysis and comparative human rights frameworks, the study argues that dignity, privacy, and livelihood rights under Articles 21 and 19(1)(g) extend to consensual adult sex work. The study concludes that the Immoral Traffic (Prevention) Act conflicts with constitutional guarantees and recommends repeal or comprehensive reform of penal provisions that criminalize consensual adult sex work (Chandrachud, 2022).

METHODOLOGY

This paper adopts a qualitative doctrinal research design to test the hypothesis that the reluctance of the State to regulate prostitution ultimately leads to the detriment of women's rights particularly autonomy, self-determination, and privacy guaranteed under the Constitution of India (1950). The doctrinal approach involves systematic study of primary and secondary legal sources, including legislation, case laws, government reports, and academic literature. The study evaluates statutory frameworks through a feminist perspective to determine their implications for women's autonomy, self-determination, and right to privacy (Law Commission of India, 1975).

MODELS / APPROACHES OF DIFFERENT NATIONS TO DEAL WITH PROSTITUTION

Various countries adopt different regulatory models balancing human rights, morality, and public order.

The legalization model exists in the Netherlands, Germany, and New Zealand. In the Netherlands, brothels were legalized through amendments to the Dutch Penal

Code to regulate sex work through licensing and registration requirements (Government of Netherlands, 2000). Germany legalized prostitution through statutory labour protections and social welfare entitlements (Government of Germany, 2002, 2017). New Zealand adopted complete decriminalization focusing on safeguarding human rights and protection against exploitation (Government of New Zealand, 2003).

The criminalization model is followed in the United States and Saudi Arabia. In the United States, prostitution is generally punishable, although certain counties in Nevada allow licensed brothels (LegaleagleWeb, 2022). Saudi Arabia imposes a complete ban on prostitution under religious law.

Australia follows a decriminalization model that varies across states. New South Wales decriminalized prostitution through statutory amendments, while states like Victoria and Queensland regulate prostitution through licensing.

The Nordic Model is followed in Sweden, Norway, and France. Sweden criminalizes buyers rather than sellers to reduce demand and support exit strategies for sex workers (Government of Sweden, 1999). Norway adopted similar reforms through penal law amendments (Government of Norway, 2009). France also adopted buyer criminalization combined with educational programs (Government of France, 2016).

Canada follows a hybrid model under which selling sex is decriminalized but purchasing and brothel operations remain illegal (Government of Canada, 2014). South Africa currently criminalizes prostitution but has proposed legislative reforms through policy debates (Government of South Africa, 1957).

India follows a partial criminalization model where prostitution itself is not illegal, but related activities are penalized under the Government of India's Immoral Traffic (Prevention) Act, 1956 (Government of India, 1956). In India, activities such as keeping a brothel, carrying out prostitution near public places, and soliciting for prostitution are punishable under statutory law (Government of India, 1956).

ANALYSIS OF LEGAL FRAMEWORK RELATING TO PROSTITUTION

Historically, prostitution in ancient India was treated as a social phenomenon rather than a criminal activity. Ancient Hindu texts such as the Dharamshastra and the statecraft principles reflected in the Arthashastra recognized prostitution as an activity that could be regulated through taxation and administrative supervision (Kautilya, 1915). The *Arthashastra* recommended licensing, surveillance, and even the strategic use of courtesans for intelligence gathering and revenue purposes. Although social stigma was attached to prostitution, certain provisions recognized courtesans and extended regulatory and legal protection to them. During the medieval period, religious and customary frameworks, including Islamic legal influences, further regulated prostitution. Later, colonial legal reforms reframed prostitution as both a criminal and public health issue, shaping modern Indian legal policy.

Article 23 of the Constitution of India explicitly prohibits human trafficking and forced exploitation for commercial purposes (Constitution of India, 1950). Clause (2) further provides that any individual engaging in trafficking shall be punishable by law. The Government of India criminalizes trafficking involving coercion and exploitation while not criminalizing prostitution per se. Sections 143–145 of the statute contain provisions addressing trafficking and exploitation of persons forced into commercial sexual activity (Government of India, 2023).

The Government of India was enacted to suppress trafficking and exploitation in prostitution (Government of India, 1956). According to reports published by Reuters, a significant proportion of individuals involved in commercial sex work originate from trafficking networks and marginalized socio-economic backgrounds (Reuters, n.d.). Under the Act, prostitution is defined as the commercial exploitation or abuse of persons. While prostitution itself is not criminalized, the Act penalizes brothel-keeping, trafficking, and living on the earnings of prostitution. The law also restricts prostitution near public places, thereby indirectly regulating the trade.

The statutory framework suggests that legislative intent does not declare prostitution illegal but isolates it from mainstream societal and labour protection mechanisms. This partial criminalization often results in vulnerability among women engaged in sex work. The lack of comprehensive regulation and labour recognition creates conditions in which intermediaries and traffickers dominate the trade. Scholars and policy reports have observed that women involved in prostitution often remain economically and socially marginalized due to absence of clear regulatory and protective mechanisms (Law Commission of India, 1975).

The legislative intent in India does not explicitly criminalize prostitution; rather, it segregates prostitution from mainstream society. The Government of India neither completely bans nor formally recognizes prostitution as a legitimate occupation. Instead, it indirectly regulates prostitution by prohibiting brothel-keeping, solicitation, and prostitution near public places (Government of India, 1956). The statute does not adequately address issues of autonomy, self-determination, or privacy of women engaged in sex work. The constitutional mandate of equality suggests that social exclusion of sex workers increases their vulnerability and marginalization (Constitution of India, 1950).

In developing societies, socio-economic inequalities often compel women to engage in prostitution due to lack of alternative livelihood opportunities. The absence of regulatory protection results in exploitation by intermediaries who capture a significant share of earnings. Although the Act prohibits living on the earnings of prostitution, marginalized women frequently refrain from lodging complaints to safeguard their subsistence. The statute recognizes prostitution as a form of sexual exploitation but fails to acknowledge the compulsive socio-economic realities that force women into this occupation. Such regulatory gaps have direct adverse consequences on the rights and dignity of women engaged in sex work (Law Commission of India, 1975).

The Constitution of India guarantees the right to live with dignity through Articles 21, 38, 39, 41, 42, 43, and 47, which collectively emphasize social welfare, health, livelihood, and humane working conditions (Constitution of India, 1950). However, the absence of comprehensive legislative protection for sex workers undermines the principle of equal protection of laws. Article 19(1)(g) guarantees the freedom to practice any profession, subject to reasonable restrictions based on morality and public order. Judicial interpretation has increasingly emphasized constitutional morality rather than social morality, underscoring democratic values of liberty, equality, and rule of law.

Despite constitutional guarantees, sex workers continue to experience severe human rights violations. Reports from the Walk Free Foundation indicate that India accounts for a significant proportion of persons subjected to forced sexual exploitation globally (Walk Free Foundation, 2023). Article 21 protections extend not only to citizens but also to foreign nationals trafficked into India. Studies show that sex workers frequently suffer from physical and mental health challenges, including trauma, anxiety, and increased vulnerability to communicable diseases. Weak bargaining power often prevents them from negotiating safer working conditions, including protection against health risks.

Sex workers are also frequently subjected to unlawful police action and custodial violence. Judicial safeguards relating to arrest and detention procedures have been emphasized by the Supreme Court of India in *D.K. Basu v. State of West Bengal*, which laid down procedural protections against custodial abuse. Nevertheless, reports suggest that these guidelines are not consistently followed in cases involving sex workers (Supreme Court of India, 1997). Such violations highlight the urgent need for legal reform and regulatory protection.

Although brothel-keeping is criminalized, brothels continue to operate informally. Management of such establishments is often controlled by male intermediaries who exploit sex workers financially. Since sex work is not recognized as an industry under labour laws, sex workers are unable to form legitimate trade unions or claim fair wages and social security benefits. Additionally, sex workers do not fall within the statutory definition of workmen under existing labour legislation, thereby excluding them from labour welfare protections.

Judicial interpretation in *Unni Krishnan v. State of Andhra Pradesh* recognized the broader scope of the right to health and medical care as an essential component of the right to life under Article 21 (Supreme Court of India, 1993). Extending such protections to sex workers would require legislative reforms recognizing sex work as labour, thereby ensuring access to social security, healthcare, and dignified working conditions.

REPORTS OF LAW COMMISSION ON PROSTITUTION

In 1975, the first report of the Law Commission on prostitution-related laws was introduced. It evaluated the *Suppression of Immoral Traffic in Women and Girls Act, 1956* and found that the legislation was ineffective due to inconsistent enforcement. The Commission recommended clearer definitions of the terms "prostitution," "brothel," and "living on the earnings of prostitution." It further emphasized rehabilitation and social reintegration as policy goals (Law Commission of India, 1975).

The second Law Commission report dealt with arbitrary police arrests relating to prostitution. The Commission observed that the police often abused their powers of arrest under preventive laws and the *Immoral Traffic (Prevention) Act, 1956.* It noted that sex workers were frequently detained and harassed in the name of public order. The Commission proposed statutory guidelines for arrest procedures and recommended gender-sensitive enforcement under judicial supervision (Law Commission of India, 1993).

The third report indirectly related to sex workers by examining the scope of rape laws under Sections 375–376 of the Indian Penal Code. The report emphasized that sex workers are entitled to equal legal protection and rejected the notion that payment of money amounts to consent. It recommended that lack of consent should be the sole criterion for determining rape, irrespective of the victim's occupation. The report also suggested expanding rape protection to custodial and institutional contexts where sex workers are frequently detained (Law Commission of India, 2000).

The fourth Law Commission report, submitted in 2008, addressed the issue titled *Laws on Prostitution and Allied Offences.* The report comprehensively examined existing prostitution laws while considering India's obligations under international human rights instruments such as CEDAW and the Palermo Protocol. It recognized prostitution as a socio-economic issue rather than merely a criminal or moral problem. The Commission suggested partial decriminalization of sex work, asserting that sex work itself should not be criminalized, while trafficking, child prostitution, and coercion should remain punishable offences. It also recommended removing Sections 7 and 8 of the *Immoral Traffic (Prevention) Act, 1956* where only sex workers are involved. The report advocated vocational training, healthcare support, social security schemes, and dignified working conditions for sex workers. Although these recommendations were not fully implemented, they significantly influenced judicial interpretation, particularly in *Budhadev Karmaskar v. State of West Bengal* (Law Commission of India, 2008; Budhadev Karmaskar v. State of West Bengal, 2011).

The fifth report in 2015 addressed discrimination against women in guardianship and custody of minor children. Though not directly related to prostitution, it examined discrimination faced by women engaged in non-traditional occupations, including sex work. The report criticized stereotypical moral judgments that often label sex workers as unfit guardians. It emphasized that guardianship decisions must be based solely on the welfare of the child rather than the occupation of the parent. The principles of dignity and equality emphasized in the report were later reflected in the 2022 follow-up directions in *Budhadev Karmaskar v. State of West Bengal* (Law Commission of India, 2015; Budhadev Karmaskar v. State of West Bengal, 2022).

Overall, several Law Commission reports, though not exclusively focused on prostitution, have had significant implications for sex work jurisprudence. Report No. 64 (1975) marked a shift from criminalization toward rehabilitation. Report No. 146 (1993) emphasized procedural safeguards and rights-based arrest practices. Report No. 172 (2000) promoted equal protection for sex workers under sexual assault laws. Report No. 205 (2008) advocated partial decriminalization and a human rights-based model. Report No. 256 (2015) highlighted occupational neutrality in child custody matters and promoted substantive equality (Law Commission of India, 1975, 1993, 2000, 2008, 2015).

CASE LAWS ADVOCATING RIGHTS OF WOMEN INVOLVED IN SEX WORK

In *Laxmi Kant Pandey v. Union of India*, the issue of child prostitution through inter-country adoption was raised before the Supreme Court. The Court emphasized the State's responsibility to protect children from sexual exploitation and directed the government to frame regulatory guidelines to prevent trafficking and abuse through adoption processes (Laxmi Kant Pandey v. Union of India, 1984).

In *State of Maharashtra v. Madhukar Narayan Mardikar*, the Supreme Court examined whether the testimony of a woman of so-called "easy virtue" could be considered reliable. The Court strongly affirmed that even a sex worker is entitled to constitutional protection, including equality before the law and the right to dignity. The Court held that a sex worker has the right to privacy and that her consent must be respected. Although the case did not directly recognize sex work as a legitimate occupation, it contributed significantly to the jurisprudence recognizing the human dignity of sex workers (State of Maharashtra v. Madhukar Narayan Mardikar, 1991).

In *Prajan Welfare Association v. State of Tamil Nadu*, a Public Interest Litigation (PIL) was filed seeking regulation and rehabilitation of sex workers, particularly in relation to controlling the spread of sexually transmitted diseases. The Madras High Court marked an important shift from a punitive approach toward a welfare-based approach. The Court directed the government to implement welfare measures, including education and rehabilitation programs for children of sex workers, healthcare facilities for sex workers, and preventive measures against trafficking and coercion. The judgment attempted to balance public health concerns, morality, and individual rights (Prajan Welfare Association v. State of Tamil Nadu, 1996).

In *Gaurav Jain v. Union of India*, a journalist and social activist filed a PIL before the Supreme Court highlighting the vulnerability of sex workers and their children. The petitioner sought State intervention to provide education, rehabilitation, and alternative employment opportunities for sex workers, along with protection against exploitation of their children. The Supreme Court directed the government to formulate rehabilitation schemes for sex workers and emphasized that children of sex workers must not be deprived of education and equal opportunities because of their parent's occupation. The Court observed that sex workers are often victims of socio-economic circumstances rather than criminals. This landmark judgment recognized the importance of social rehabilitation and affirmed the right to live with dignity under Article 21 of the Constitution (Gaurav Jain v. Union of India, 1997).

In *S. Khushboo v. Kanniammal*, the actor Khushboo publicly supported premarital relationships, which resulted in multiple criminal complaints alleging obscenity. Although the case was not directly related to prostitution, it addressed the broader issues of sexual autonomy and public morality. The Supreme Court held that criminal prosecution cannot be based solely on moral disapproval. The Court emphasized that society must tolerate alternative viewpoints of morality unless such views cause public harm. The judgment reinforced the principle that constitutional morality prevails over social morality (S. Khushboo v. Kanniammal, 2010).

In *Budhadev Karmaskar v. State of West Bengal*, a sex worker was brutally murdered by a client, and the accused was sentenced to life imprisonment by the Calcutta High Court. Upon appeal, the Supreme Court expanded the scope of the case to examine the fundamental rights and dignity of sex workers. The Court held that sex workers are entitled to the same constitutional protections as other citizens, particularly the right to life and dignity under Article 21 of the Constitution. The Court directed the constitution of a panel to recommend rehabilitation measures to ensure that sex workers are able to live with dignity. The judgment approached the issue from a human rights perspective and laid the foundation for future judicial interventions (Budhadev Karmaskar v. State of West Bengal, 2011).

In the follow-up directions issued in 2022, the Supreme Court provided detailed guidelines to safeguard the rights of sex workers. The Court directed that police authorities should not arrest or harass consenting adult sex workers except in cases involving trafficking or exploitation. It further held that children of sex workers should not be separated from their mothers solely on the basis of their occupation. The Court emphasized that the privacy, dignity, and livelihood of sex workers must be protected under Article 21. Additionally, the Court directed the media to respect the confidentiality and dignity of sex workers. The judgment strongly supported the protection of sex work conducted between consenting adults from unnecessary criminal interference (Budhadev Karmaskar v. State of West Bengal, 2022).

CONCLUSION

Based on the analysis of existing legal frameworks and scholarly research, India does not formally regulate prostitution, although it has acquired a de facto presence in certain regions. Indian law permits consensual sexual relations between adults; however, the absence of a comprehensive regulatory policy creates uncertainty regarding the rights of sex workers. The State's reluctance to clearly recognize or regulate prostitution contributes to the growth of illegal human trafficking and exploitation. Since prostitution does not have de jure recognition, women engaged in sex work often remain uncertain about their legal rights and protections.

The lack of regulatory clarity has enabled middlemen and organized networks to dominate the industry, often resulting in exploitation and financial deprivation of women involved in sex work. The emergence of escort and call-girl systems in urban and elite social structures further demonstrates the transformation of prostitution into a widespread yet unregulated trade. The absence of regulation jeopardizes the autonomy and dignity of women and perpetuates male dominance within the industry.

If prostitution is appropriately regulated by the State, it may reduce crimes related to sexual exploitation and provide a safer environment for women engaged in such work. Individuals with excessive sexual impulses may be less likely to engage in criminal behaviour if lawful and regulated alternatives exist. Legal scholarship and policy analysis suggest that the absence of regulation threatens personal autonomy and privacy, which form intrinsic components of the right to life under Article 21 of the Constitution.

If a woman chooses sex work due to compelling socio-economic circumstances and operates within the boundaries of law, such a choice reflects her autonomy and should be respected. Where barriers restrict the exercise of such autonomy, it becomes the responsibility of the State to provide support mechanisms to protect the dignity, safety, and fundamental rights of women engaged in sex work.

REFERENCES

Agnes, F. (2013). *Law, justice and gender: Family law and constitutional provisions in India*. Oxford University Press.

Amnesty International. (2016). *Policy on state obligations to respect, protect and fulfil the human rights of sex workers*. https://www.amnesty.org

Bernstein, E. (2010). Militarized humanitarianism meets carceral feminism: The politics of sex, rights, and freedom. *Signs (Chicago, Ill.)*, *36*(1), 45–71. DOI: 10.1086/652918 PMID: 20827852

Budhadev Karmaskar v. State of West Bengal, (2011) 11 SCC 538 (India).

Budhadev Karmaskar v. State of West Bengal, 2022 SCC OnLine SC 704 (India).

Budhadev Karmaskar v. State of West Bengal, (2022) Supreme Court of India.

Budhadev Karmaskar v. State of West Bengal, Writ Petition (Criminal) No. 135 of 2010, Order dated May 19, 2022 (India).

Chandrachud, G. (2022). Decriminalizing sex work in India: Constitutional promises and judicial developments. *Indiana Law Review*, *6*(2), 145–168.

Constitution of India. (1950). Government of India.

Cunningham, S., & Shah, M. (2018). Decriminalizing indoor prostitution: Implications for sexual violence and public health. *The Review of Economic Studies*, *85*(3), 1683–1715. DOI: 10.1093/restud/rdx065

Dharamshastra. (Various authors). *Ancient Hindu legal and normative texts*.

Doezema, J. (2010). *Sex slaves and discourse masters: The construction of trafficking*. Zed Books. DOI: 10.5040/9781350222502

Farley, M., Cotton, A., Lynne, J., Zumbeck, S., Spiwak, F., Reyes, M., Alvarez, D., & Sezgin, U. (2004). Prostitution and trafficking in nine countries: An update on violence and posttraumatic stress disorder. *Journal of Trauma Practice*, *2*(3–4), 33–74. DOI: 10.1300/J189v02n03_03

Gaurav Jain v. Union of India, (1997) 8 SCC 114 (India).

Government of Canada. (2014). *Protection of Communities and Exploited Persons Act*.

Government of France. (2016). *Law penalizing purchase of sexual services*.

Government of Germany. (2002). *Prostitution Act*. Prostitutionsgesetz.

Government of Germany. (2017). *Prostitute Protection Act.*

Government of India. (1956). *Immoral Traffic (Prevention) Act, 1956.*

Government of India. (1956). *The Immoral Traffic (Prevention) Act, 1956.*

Government of India. (2023). *The Bharatiya Nyaya Sanhita, 2023.*

Government of Netherlands. (2000). *Amendments to the Dutch Penal Code relating to brothel legalization.*

Government of New Zealand. (2003). *Prostitution Reform Act.*

Government of Norway. (2009). *Amendments to Norwegian Penal Code relating to purchase of sexual services.*

Government of South Africa. (1957). *Sexual Offences Act.*

Government of Sweden. (1999). *Sex Purchase Act.*

International Labour Organization. (2010). *Recommendation concerning HIV and AIDS and the world of work.* ILO.

International Labour Organization. (2022). *Global estimates of modern slavery: Forced labour and forced marriage.* ILO, Walk Free, & IOM.

Kautilya. (1915). *Arthashastra* (R. Shamasastry, Trans.). Mysore Government Press. (Original work published ca. 3rd century BCE).

Kotiswaran, P. (2011). *Dangerous sex, invisible labor: Sex work and the law in India.* Princeton University Press.

Kotiswaran, P. (2014). Sex work, labour and human rights. *Economic and Political Weekly, 49*(22), 52–59.

Law Commission of India. (1975). *Sixty-fourth report on the Suppression of Immoral Traffic in Women and Girls Act, 1956.* Government of India.

Law Commission of India. (1975). *Sixty-fourth report on the Suppression of Immoral Traffic in Women and Girls Act, 1956.* https://lawcommissionofindia.nic.in/51-100/Report64.pdf

Law Commission of India. (1993). *One hundred forty-sixth report on custodial crimes.* Government of India.

Law Commission of India. (2000). *One hundred seventy-second report on review of rape laws.* Government of India.

Law Commission of India. (2008). *Two hundred fifth report on laws on prostitution and allied offences*. Government of India.

Law Commission of India. (2015). *Two hundred fifty-sixth report on elimination of discrimination against women in matters relating to guardianship and custody of minor children*. Government of India.

Laxmi Kant Pandey v. Union of India, (1984) 2 SCC 244 (India).

LegaleagleWeb. (2022, May 26). *Supreme Court recognises sex work as a profession*. https://legaleagleweb.com

National AIDS Control Organization. (2021). *India HIV estimations 2020–21*. Ministry of Health and Family Welfare, Government of India.

National Crime Records Bureau. (2023). *Crime in India 2023 statistics*. Ministry of Home Affairs, Government of India.

Prajan Welfare Association v. State of Tamil Nadu, 1996 (Madras High Court, India).

Prostitution Law Review Committee. (2008). *Report of the prostitution law review committee on the operation of the Prostitution Reform Act 2003*. Government of New Zealand.

Reuters. (n.d.). *Reports on trafficking and commercial sexual exploitation*. https://www.reuters.com

S. Khushboo v. Kanniammal, (2010) 5 SCC 600 (India).

Sangram. (2012). *Trafficking, sex work and law reform in India*. Sangram Policy Report.

State of Maharashtra v. Madhukar Narayan Mardikar, (1991) 1 SCC 57 (India).

Supreme Court of India. (1993). *Unni Krishnan, J.P. v. State of Andhra Pradesh*, AIR 1993 SC 2178.

Supreme Court of India. (1997). *D.K. Basu v. State of West Bengal*, (1997) 1 SCC 416.

UNAIDS. (2012). *UNAIDS guidance note on HIV and sex work*. Joint United Nations Programme on HIV/AIDS.

United Nations. (2000). *Protocol to prevent, suppress and punish trafficking in persons, especially women and children*. Palermo Protocol.

Walk Free Foundation. (2023). *Global slavery index 2023*. https://www.walkfree.org

Weitzer, R. (2007). The social construction of sex trafficking: Ideology and institutionalization of a moral crusade. *Politics & Society, 35*(3), 447–475. DOI: 10.1177/0032329207304319

Weitzer, R. (2012). *Legalizing prostitution: From illicit vice to lawful business.* New York University Press.

World Bank. (2020). *Poverty and shared prosperity report.* World Bank.

World Health Organization. (2013). *Prevention and treatment of HIV and other sexually transmitted infections for sex workers.* WHO.

Chapter 16
Framed as Victims, Treated as Offenders:
The Legal and Psychological Fallout of India's Anti-Trafficking Response to CSEC

Sushmita Singh
http://orcid.org/0009-0001-7821-9323
Chanakya National Law University, India

ABSTRACT

Women and children who are trafficked for sexual or labour exploitation are often prosecuted despite statutory promise of non-criminalisation. This chapter makes three contributions and shows how trafficked individuals are imprisoned, charged, or deported instead of receiving assistance. First, it shows how government institutions prioritise illegality, immigration control and prosecution rather than human rights, leading to the criminalisation of victims. Second, it contends that this punitive tendency is gendered, with women and girls disproportionately placed in immigration detention or custodial "care" under the guise of protection. Third, it contrasts the current legal framework in India with the experience of the United Kingdom to demonstrate how both countries struggle, albeit in different ways, with the same fundamental contradiction. The recommendations made in this chapter correspond to decoupling trafficking enforcement from immigration policing, emphasising the non-punishment principle and rights-based remedies in prosecutorial, policing and judicial practice.

DOI: 10.4018/979-8-3373-5841-3.ch016

1. INTRODUCTION

Human trafficking is widely described as a contemporary form of enslavement and a violation of core human rights (United Nations Office on Drugs and Crime, 2024). Across jurisdictions, governments formally condemn it, and legislators promise "zero tolerance." At the same time, global data continue to show expansion, diversification, and increased brutality in trafficking flows. The 2024 UNODC Global Report on Trafficking in Persons—covering 156 countries—documents that detected trafficking victims rose by 25% between 2019 and 2022, with cases of forced labour increasing sharply during and after the COVID-19 period. A shift is witnessed toward forced criminality and technology-enabled exploitation. In other words, trafficking is not receding; rather, it is mutating.

Yet, and this is the central idea driving this article, States frequently respond to trafficked persons not as injured parties, or holders of rights, but as offenders, "illegal migrants," or public order problems. Malloch (2015) shows, for the United Kingdom, that even after the introduction of anti-trafficking directives and victim protection guidance, trafficked men, women, and children were routinely detained in immigration centres or prisons, being accused of offences such as identity fraud, irregular entry, benefit fraud, or cannabis cultivation—offences they often committed under threat, coercion, or direct instruction from exploiters. The paradox is brutal. A person who is trafficked into forced labour can be arrested in that same workplace, prosecuted for conduct arising from the coercion, and then deported as a status offender. Meanwhile, the trafficker remains structurally insulated. This is not a problem unique to Britain. Versions of it appear in Europe, North America, Southeast Asia, and India. In India, for example, the Immoral Traffic (Prevention) Act, 1956 (ITPA) was drafted with the objective of suppressing "immoral traffic," especially the exploitation of women and girls in prostitution.

Over time, the ITPA has frequently been used to police sex work, raid brothels, and confine women to "protective homes," without targeting organisational and financial structures behind such exploitation. It has been argued by the opponents that this approach ultimately punishes those in prostitution—who are often themselves trafficked—under the grounds of obscenity, solicitation, and loitering. They are treated as vectors of immorality rather than individuals who may have survived physical coercion, debt bondage, or deception.

India has recently overhauled its criminal laws. The Bharatiya Nyaya Sanhita, 2023 (BNS), which replaces the Indian Penal Code, 1860 (IPC) and consolidates trafficking offences in Sections 143 and 144. These provisions define trafficking, build upon and expand the preceding Sections 370 and 370A of the IPC and permit harsher punishment, including rigorous imprisonment for life, specially when minors are implicated or in cases of trafficking of multiple persons. The Indian government has publicly described these measures as evidence of a strengthened national stance against trafficking. But the structural question remains: will these laws protect victims from being criminalised, or will they continue, like the ITPA in practice, to police and discipline the bodies they claim to protect?

This article advances three aims. First, it maps how criminalisation of victims of trafficking operates in practice in the United Kingdom, drawing heavily on Malloch's documentation of detention, prosecution, and "protective" custody. Second, it reads that UK experience alongside global trends: the post-pandemic upsurge in detected trafficking cases, the rise in forced labour, and the expansion of "forced criminality." Third, it turns to India, examining how the two Indian legal instruments—the ITPA and the BNS—handle trafficking and related exploitation.

2. CONCEPTUAL AND LEGAL FRAMEWORK

2.1 Victimhood, credibility, and the "deserving/undeserving" binary

Anti-trafficking law rests on a principle: if you are trafficked, you will be recognised as a victim and protected from punishment. That promise collapses in practice because such recognition is conditional. Prosecutors, immigration officers, and police draw a line between the "genuine victim" and the "false claimant." The result is a screening culture in which the burden shifts to the individual to prove a status of extreme victimhood—docile, passive, non-resistant, grateful—under conditions of trauma, fear of reprisals, language barriers, and custody. This reasoning is similar to previous distinctions in asylum adjudication between "economic migrants" and "genuine refugees," where only the most legible suffering is deemed legitimate.

2.2 Crimmigration

Crimmigration describes the increasing overlap between criminal law and immigration control. Immigration enforcement has absorbed the tools, rhetoric, and punishment logics of criminal justice, while criminal law has started to treat immigration status itself as an indicator of dangerousness. The UK illustrates crimmigration in action: individuals trafficked into cannabis cultivation or forced labour are arrested as offenders in crimes tied to drugs or identity fraud, then assessed through an immigration lens that treats them as removable aliens rather than injured parties.

Crimmigration originated as a framework to explain how states increasingly govern mobility through punitive criminal law tools (Stumpf, 2010). In Western contexts, migrants are often treated as potential offenders, whereby we find the blending of immigration enforcement with criminal justice. This concept, though developed elsewhere, strongly resonates with India's governance of marginalisation, mobility and trafficking. Wacquant (Wacquant, 2008; Wacquant, 2009), in his work on the expansion of carceral institutions, argues that in modern times, States use detention centres, prisons and punitive welfare institutions to manage social disorder and poverty. In India, shelter homes, protective homes, and moral policing institutions often function as extensions of the State's carceral institutions. Bauman's (1998) concept of 'liquid fear' describes how societies project anxiety onto those who appear to be unstable, mobile or outside societal norms – such as tribal migrants, women travelling alone, women working in the hospitality and entertainment industry, transgenders and undocumented foreign nationals, requiring surveillance.

Cohen's (2001) "states of denial" further explains how societies acknowledge exploitation rhetorically while simultaneously enabling punitive systems that harm victims. This contradiction is illustrated in India's anti-trafficking system, where police, ministries and NGO's emphasise 'victim protection,' survivors tend to face coercive raids, forceful rescue, custodial rehabilitation and charges under immigration laws.

Anderson and Andrijasevic (2008) argue that states *manufacture illegality* through documentation requirements, bureaucratic barriers, and selective enforcement. Such illegality is often constructed through bureaucratic practices which classify individuals as morally suspect. In India, such illegality is shaped by caste, gender, religion and also by immigration law. India's anti-trafficking laws and related practices often treat survivors as offenders: criminalisation is embedded within social, moral and administrative structures.

India's crimmigration system is rooted in four primary legal instruments, including:

i. Immoral Traffic (Prevention) Act, (ITPA, 1956),
ii. the Foreigners Act (1946),
iii. the Passport Act (1967) and
iv. Bharatiya Nyaya Sanhita (BNS, 2023)

Immoral Traffic (Prevention) Act, (ITPA, 1956)

ITPA was enacted to suppress the 'immoral traffic in men' and continues to blur the boundaries between trafficking and commercial sex work. Sections 17 to 21 of the ITPA contain several provisions related to involuntary 'rescue,' institutional detention for up to three years, confinement based on moral assessments, and limited judicial oversight, thus highlighting the absence of due-process safeguards. The language of the Act is moralistic, making the assumption that the presence of a brothel implies victimhood and deviance. It is understood that sex workers, whether voluntary, coerced, or economically deprived, are in fact vulnerable to raids, 'rescue,' and forced rehabilitation. This form of punitive welfare aligns more closely with Wacquant's (2009) analysis of the state's imposition of coercive assistance on marginalised groups.

Foreigners Act (1946) and Passport Act (1967)

Trafficking survivors, especially from Nepal, Bangladesh, Myanmar, and Nigeria, are routinely arrested for irregular entry, overstaying visas, and possession of forged documents. UNODC reports (2022, 2024) show that police often register immigration offences before screening for trafficking indicators, which leads to arrest, remand, prolonged confinement and transfer to shelter homes and eventual deportation. This treatment embodies the crimmigration logic that sees mobility—and particularly foreign mobility.

Bharatiya Nyaya Sanhita (BNS, 2023)

The Bharatiya Nyaya Sanhita, 2023 enhances penalties for trafficking but does not incorporate the non-punishment principle. Victims who were forced into crimes for the purpose of solicitation, forged document use, or border crossing can still be prosecuted and undergo punishment. Thus, India's new criminal code does not prevent survivors from being penalised for acts directly linked to exploitation.

Policing Practices That Reproduce Crimmigration

Legal provisions alone do not create crimmigration; it is policing practices that bring them to life. The *raid-rescue model* was reinforced in India by Prajwala v. Union of India (2015). Raids in India are carried out in forceful manner, many times driven by media, indiscriminate in nature, often traumatic, and rarely based on credible information. After raids, these women are moved to protective homes where they explicitly state that they are adults acting voluntarily. This reflects what Bosworth and Guild (2008) call *governing through suspicion*.

Police across Indian states rely heavily on *surveillance and profiling* based on language like Bengali, Nepali, tribal dialects, class markers mainly clothing, occupation, caste identity, religion. We find that gender, caste, class and religion are often seen as different filters of crimmigration which disproportionately target those who are already marginalised.

Muslim women and Rohingya refugees, transgender persons and women on the basis of their mobility patterns especially those travelling alone are considered vulnerable capable of destabilising social order, suspected and targeted. Women belonging to Dalit, Adivasi, or low-income backgrounds are readily labelled "at risk" and subjected to rescue or detention. These practices align with Bauman's (1998) view that marginalised groups are often projected with fear and disorder.

The Border Security Force (BSF) plays a major role in shaping crimmigration. At the eastern and north-eastern borders of India touching Bangladesh, minors are treated as illegal entrants, victims are charged under immigration law and put in shelter homes and repatriation takes years. One can locate Anderson and Andrijasevic's (2008) concept of bureaucratic bordering where illegality is produced through late screening, administrative delay, and institutional neglect.

Caste also operates as a domestic border. Dalit and Adivasi women working in construction, brick kilns, as domestic labour, in the hospitality and entertainment industry are targeted disproportionately by police and welfare authorities. Their labour mobility is interpreted as deviance or risk. Wacquant's (1999) idea of managing "dangerous classes" translates easily into India's caste hierarchy. Though India's vast informal sector produces significant vulnerabilities that resemble trafficking conditions. Its policing often criminalises informal workers, treats migration as illegal and targets precarious labourers instead of exploitative employers. Thus, we find that Cohen's (2001) theory of state denial explains how structural exploitation is ignored while the exploited are punished.

2.3 Non-punishment principle

International instruments and laws promote the "non-punishment principle": trafficked persons should not be prosecuted for unlawful acts they were compelled to commit. This principle is reflected in domestic law and prosecutorial guidance in the UK. At least on paper, it looks humane. In practice, two problems are identified: frontline actors do not consistently know, understand, or apply the guidance; and "public interest" language gives prosecutors discretion to proceed even where trafficking is credibly alleged.

2.4 Protective custody and gendered control

Confinement of trafficked women and girls is frequently justified by states as being required for moral rescue, witness protection, or rehabilitation. Some jurisdictions hold women who have been "rescued" from trafficking circumstances in immigration detention centers or "protective" institutions that resemble prisons. These facilities may have no term restrictions, little legal protections, and a disciplinary system that regulates their mobility and sexuality. The Indian practice under the ITPA is somewhat comparable to this.

3. THE UNITED KINGDOM: HOW VICTIMS BECOME OFFENDERS

3.1 Detention and prosecution despite formal protections

The UK government claims to prohibit the punishment of trafficking victims. Yet, in practice, victims continue to be arrested, charged, convicted, and imprisoned. According to monitoring groups and inquiries, trafficked persons are punished for activities such as cannabis cultivation, identity fraud, benefit fraud, and involvement in informal economies controlled by organised criminal groups. While some of these "crimes" are the result of direct compulsion, others are post-escape survival tactics.

3.2 The National Referral Mechanism (NRM) and its limits

It is the responsibility of the NRM to locate possible victims of human trafficking and provide them with protection and assistance. However, there is ample evidence of recurring identification errors during the arrest and charging phases. Even when referrals happen and decisions are positive, women often have already spent months in custody. Arresting officers often approach suspects as offenders first, not as potential victims, and do not consider themselves responsible for making proactive trafficking referrals.

3.3 Prosecutorial discretion and the "public interest"

Prosecutorial guidance acknowledges that coerced criminality is a known feature of trafficking and that, in principle, the justice system should not punish a person for an act directly compelled by their trafficker. However, prosecutors can only consider these protections if they are told that the accused may be a victim, and the "public interest" test gives prosecutors residual discretion to continue with charges in cases viewed as serious. The result is that the principle of non-punishment is most needed in the hardest cases, yet those are the cases most likely to trigger the instinct to prosecute.

3.4 Immigration detention and "welfare" custody

Trafficked women are routinely placed into immigration detention in the UK, where they face removal proceedings rather than stabilisation and recovery. This continues despite UN recommendations that detention of trafficking victims should be avoided and that protective measures should prioritise dignity, recovery, and safety from reprisals. Detention undermines cooperation and trust, and the system ends up producing a revolving door: arrest the coerced worker, process them, deport them, and claim success.

4. GLOBAL PATTERNS: FORCED LABOUR, FORCED CRIMINALITY, AND EXPANDING DETENTION

In Southeast Asia, recent studies have highlighted that victims trafficked into online scam operations in Myanmar, Cambodia, and Laos are frequently prosecuted under cybercrime or immigration laws (United Nations Office on Drugs and Crime, 2024). In Thailand and Malaysia, women trafficked into the sex industry or domestic work are often detained and deported under immigration provisions without access to legal recourse (Asia Pacific Refugee Rights Network, 2022). In the same manner, irrespective of the Directive 2011/36/EU's emphasis on non-punishment, it has been observed by GRETA (2023) and the European Commission that there is continued detention and criminalisation of trafficked victims for offences related to their exploitation, like drug trafficking or theft. In Italy, trafficking survivors apprehended at sea are at times prosecuted as facilitators of smuggling activities (GRETA, 2023). According to the International Labour Organisation (2023), over three million people worldwide are trapped in various forms of forced criminal labour, while less than one per cent are identified as victims of trafficking. Such findings reveal a structural failure of recognition within international criminal justice systems. An emerging issue is the digitisation and privatisation of immigration control, in which algorithms risk determining detention and deportation priorities, and private security firms handle border management. These technologies reinforce existing biases and hinder individualised assessments, leading to automated exclusion in place of protection. In essence, the United Kingdom's contradictions echo a global trend: anti-trafficking laws and measures continue to be weaponised as tools of security and moral governance and not human rights protection (Malloch, 2015).

4.1 Post-pandemic shifts

The patterns of trafficking did not return to a pre-pandemic "normal." Instead, the exploitation adapted itself to crises. A surge has been witnessed in trafficking for forced labour, and traffickers have increasingly compelled victims to participate in criminal operations such as online scams, cyberfraud rings, forced begging, and drug cultivation. Forced criminality is not a marginal feature anymore; it is now central to many trafficking economies.

4.2 Who is identified as a victim?

Global detection reveals enduring gender trends. While men and boys are more commonly reported in categories related to forced work, women and girls continue to make up the majority of trafficking victims found globally, particularly in relation to sexual exploitation. At the same time, minors now make up a significant portion of those victims that have been identified. However, despite the fact that more victims are being found worldwide, there is still a disproportionate number of prosecutions and convictions, with labour and forced criminality receiving fewer investigations and prosecutions.

4.3 Protective detention as governance

Mass imprisonment of women and girls in "protective" or "rehabilitation" facilities is occasionally the outcome of "rescue" operations against human trafficking, especially in Asia. These facilities serve as semi-carceral areas. Indefinite stays, restricted freedom of movement, and communication restrictions may be imposed on residents if they are deemed necessary for their safety or the further prosecution of traffickers. The reasoning allows the state to monitor and regulate female sexuality and movement while simultaneously reassuring the public that "something is being done."

4.4 Digital Crimmigration

In an effort to improve efficiency, coordination, and intelligence-led policing, India's anti-trafficking framework has progressively included technology-driven enforcement tools. To enhance detection and interstate coordination in trafficking investigations, platforms like the National Automated Fingerprint Identification System (NAFIS), the Crime and Criminal Tracking Network and Systems (CCTNS), and growing facial recognition databases are being developed (Ministry of Home Affairs, 2009; NCRB, 2022). These technologies run the risk of exacerbating the fundamental contradiction of anti-trafficking legislation, which is that children who are framed as victims are really treated as criminals in cases of Commercial Sexual Exploitation of Children (CSEC).

Digital recording of children through biometric capture, photo databases, and case-tracking systems is a common outcome of rescue efforts. These tactics are similar to criminal intake procedures even though they are marketed as preventative measures. The rescued youngster becomes a data subject within a monitoring infrastructure that was initially created for criminal control after they are entered into centralised databases. It becomes difficult to distinguish between policing and protection.

Pattern identification, behavioural indicators, and predicted risk assessments are becoming more and more important in AI-assisted profiling tools (Lum & Isaac, 2016).

In the context of CSEC, these systems might indicate:

- Repeated "rescues" from the same geographic location
- Return to exploitative environments
- Inconsistent statements
- Refusal to cooperate with law enforcement
- Contact with alleged traffickers

These behaviours are not shocking or incriminating from a trauma-informed standpoint. A child's reactions are often influenced by trauma bonding, coercive dependency, economic weakness, and fear of reprisals. Avoidance, memory fragmentation, ambivalence toward exploiters, and emotional numbness are recognised as typical symptoms in the clinical literature on Complex PTSD (van der Kolk, 2014). However, algorithmic systems consider data points that deviate from typical victim conduct to be aberrant. Trauma reactions are digitally labelled as risk indicators, which is a subtle but significant outcome.

Algorithmic distrust is ingrained in decision-support systems, as opposed to overt police scepticism. Children may be classified as "habitual absconders," "non-cooperative," or "repeat cases" by case management software. Cases that statistically resemble previous failed prosecutions may receive a lower investigative priority according to predictive analytics. Therefore, attrition trends that already afflict anti-trafficking enforcement may be institutionalised by technology. When rescued juveniles are arrested under municipal laws, immigration policies, or public order laws before their status as victims is officially acknowledged, the dilemma becomes more acute. The identity of the juvenile circulates within policing databases when biometric data is gathered under such accusations. Even if the individual is subsequently determined to be a victim under child protection laws or the Immoral Traffic (Prevention) Act, the digital trail remains. To put it another way, the child is first categorised as an offender and is only thereafter reclassified as a victim.

The use of automated sequencing has psychological effects. When someone is photographed, fingerprinted, and interrogated in a detention center, internalised stigma is strengthened. When children think they are being treated like criminals, anti-trafficking laws lose their ability to be rehabilitative. The system communicates distrust rather than security.

The situation is further complicated by algorithmic prejudice. AI systems make predictions based on historical police data. If previous enforcement disproportionately targeted marginalised groups, particularly migrant populations, Dalit and tribal communities, and girls from lower socioeconomic backgrounds, training datasets may contain biases. Therefore, automated systems may disproportionately label children from communities already under surveillance as “high-risk,” “likely to reoffend,” or “prone to absconding.” Anticipatory suspicion becomes structural vulnerability as a result. Because of the epistemic power of technology, these categories seem objective. Police officers and child welfare officials may disregard digital risk indicators without taking into account their socioeconomic or psychological backgrounds. Furthermore, courts could unwittingly rely on structured risk assessments without challenging the trauma-informed validity of the underlying models (Dutton & Painter, 1993). The primary source of danger with technology is not the technology itself, but rather the normative framing of it. Anti-trafficking strategies have traditionally placed a strong emphasis on enforcement. The punishing logic of an architecture that already criminalises is amplified by digital tools. Surveillance systems designed for crime prevention are not suitable for child protection unless they undergo a major reorientation (Kempadoo, 2015).

CSEC's victim-centric philosophy necessitates specific protections in technology implementation: 1. Criminal database input is prohibited before victim identification 2. Tight restrictions on rescued kids' biometric capturing 3. Required trauma-informed training for cops who use artificial intelligence 4. Independent evaluations of algorithmic discrimination across class, gender, and caste 5. Procedures for deleting data after official victim identification. In the absence of these steps, technology modernisation runs the risk of strengthening the institutional mistrust that children who are rescued from exploitation face, which is similar to criminal processing. Thus, the anti-trafficking state must make a morally and constitutionally sound decision. Technology can either automate the very stigmas that reform aims to eradicate or provide coordinated protection and rehabilitation (Justice K.S. Puttaswamy v. Union of India 2017). The margin for error is especially high in the situation of CSEC, because victims are children whose agency has been substantially limited. The promise of victim protection turns into a farce if anti-trafficking legislation keeps using logic based on surveillance without being recalculated in light of trauma. In statutory terminology, children will continue to be framed as victims, but in practical reality—now with algorithmic reinforcement—they will be handled as perpetrators.

4.4.1 AI-Driven Profiling and the Criminalisation of Victims in Coerced Cyber-Scam Operation

In order to identify suspected fraud networks, recent law enforcement responses to international cyber-fraud have depended more and more on AI-driven profiling tools like behavioural risk-scoring, anomaly detection, and network-link analysis. Although the goal of these technologies is to increase the effectiveness of investigations, their use in scam-compound operations has created a concerning risk of misclassifying trafficked individuals as cybercriminals. According to international enforcement assessments, a significant percentage of people working in scam centers in Southeast Asia are victims of forced labour and human trafficking who are forced to commit online financial fraud under conditions of debt bondage, violence, and imprisonment (INTERPOL, 2024; United Nations Office on Drugs and Crime, 2025).

High-volume messaging, VoIP use, cryptocurrency transactions, anonymised digital identities, or access to multiple financial accounts are examples of behavioural indicators that AI-assisted investigative systems commonly rely on. These patterns are equally consistent with coerced participation in fraud operations. These algorithmically generated suspicion indicators may cause law enforcement agencies to arrest or detain returned victims based solely on their digital footprints in the absence of a structured trafficking-vulnerability assessment at the intake stage. Trafficked workers leave behind substantial electronic traces that resemble deliberate criminal participation because to the industrialised structure of scam-center ecosystems, as noted by United Nations Office on Drugs and Crime (2025). This increases the possibility of secondary victimisation through prosecution rather than protection.

Although Section 143 of India's post-Bharatiya Nyaya Sanhita (BNS) legal framework recognises human trafficking as a separate crime, the process of classifying returned scam center employees as either victims of trafficking or accused individuals in cyber-fraud investigations is still dependent on frontline screening procedures. Indian nationals have been transported overseas under false pretences and then forced to participate in online scams by threats of physical harm and movement restrictions, according to national agency investigations into trafficking-related cyber-fraud networks (Hindustan Times, 2025). When AI-driven profiling is used in these situations without a parallel assessment of coercion, victims whose seeming involvement in cyber-fraud is a direct outcome of coerced criminality may be wrongfully detained.

According to victimology, this phenomena is a modern example of the “criminalisation of victim behaviour,” in which involvement in illegal action brought on by trauma or coercion is viewed as proof of guilt rather than exploitation. Financial institutions may further solidify this status by limiting access to banking or communication services even after rescue or repatriation through automated account freezes, digital blacklisting, and algorithmic risk-flagging (Press Information Bureau, 2025). Since trafficking victims face custodial or regulatory penalties while traffickers avoid prosecution, AI-mediated enforcement techniques run the danger of escalating a structural inequality that is already evident in NCRB data on trafficking-related rescues and convictions.

These advancements highlight how urgently mandated trafficking vulnerability screening procedures must be incorporated into AI-assisted cybercrime investigations. The rise of algorithmic profiling in fraud detection without these protections could unintentionally reinforce institutional biases that confuse forced involvement with choice criminality, undermining the victim-centered approach of modern anti-trafficking legislation.

4.4.2 Institutional Containment of Victims: From ART Trafficking to Coerced Cyber-Scam Operations

The ongoing trend in anti-trafficking enforcement to place victims in regulatory custody after rescue operations is further highlighted by judicial developments in 2024. The Kerala High Court investigated the interstate recruitment and transportation of women for oocyte donation through middlemen and financial inducements in proceedings stemming from a police raid on an Assisted Reproductive Technology (ART) facility in Ernakulam. The court noted that the practice may constitute a "classic case" of human trafficking despite claims of voluntary participation (Kerala High Court, 2024).

An important example of the paradoxical confinement of trafficked individuals inside protectionist frameworks is the fact that the women, who were discovered as prospective victims during enforcement action, were later held in institutional shelters while they were investigated (Times of India, 2024). The limitations of formal agreement in situations of structural vulnerability are highlighted by the Court's doubts about the voluntariness of their involvement in light of linguistic obstacles and orchestrated recruitment. In cases involving transnational cyber-scam compounds, where trafficked individuals forced to commit online financial fraud are often identified through AI-assisted behavioural profiling systems that rely on indicators like high-volume messaging patterns, cryptocurrency transactions, or anonymised digital accounts. This custodial response is strikingly similar to new enforcement practices (INTERPOL, 2024; United Nations Office on Drugs and Crime, 2025).

Algorithmic suspicion indicators could lead to the arrest or detention of returned victims based only on their digital footprints in the absence of required trafficking vulnerability screening, hence criminalising forced involvement in fraud schemes. As a result, a same institutional logic is shown by both ART-related trafficking cases and compelled cyber-scam trials, where victimhood is mediated through correctional surveillance rather than legal action against exploiters, and rescue is followed by containment. This structural asymmetry supports worries about the secondary victimisation of trafficked individuals under modern anti-trafficking regimes, as evidenced by NCRB data showing a significant discrepancy between the number of trafficking victims "rescued" and the number of traffickers ultimately convicted.

5. INDIA: BETWEEN MORAL POLICING AND MODERNISATION OF TRAFFICKING LAW

Indian jurisprudence on trafficking and prostitution presents a complex interplay between protection, morality, and criminalisation. The Supreme Court in Gaurav Jain v. Union of India (1997) acknowledged the need to rehabilitate children of sex workers and directed the establishment of protective homes.

Despite progressive intent, the decision reinforced the belief that sex work itself is intrinsically exploitative. In contrast, Budhadev Karmaskar v. State of West Bengal (2011) established sex work as a legitimate employment and upheld that sex workers are entitled to the right to dignity under Article 21 of the Indian Constitution. These two landmark cases demonstrate how India oscillates between moral paternalism and rights-based recognition (Menon, 2019).

In reality, the implementation of the Immoral Traffic (Prevention) Act, 1956 (ITPA) continues to criminalise those it purports to protect. Women who are apprehended in raids under Sections 7 and 8 are frequently detained in protective homes for indefinite time, many times without consent or judicial review (HAQ Centre for Child Rights, 2021). Additionally, Sections 143 and 144 of Bharatiya Nyaya Sanhita, 2023 (BNS), which replaces the Indian Penal Code, redefines trafficking in alignment with the Palermo Protocol. Though the BNS significantly enhances penalties for traffickers, including imprisonment for life in aggravated cases, it lacks a non-punishment provision (United Nations Office on Drugs and Crime, 2022). This omission suggests that victims who are coerced into engaging in unlawful activities—like begging, drug trafficking, or sex work—may still be prosecuted. Courts in India have begun to address these inconsistencies. The Delhi High Court highlighted in Court on Its Own Motion v. State (2019) that victims of human trafficking shouldn't experience "double victimization"—first by traffickers and then by the government. In a similar vein, the Bombay High Court ruled that it is unconstitutional to place adult women in protective homes without their consent (XYZ v. State of Maharashtra 2021). Under the UN Bangkok Rules (2010), which places a strong emphasis on voluntary rehabilitation and gender-sensitive justice, these rulings allign with international best practices. Nonetheless, institutional inertia is still evident in the continuation of police-led moral raids and the poor execution of survivor-oriented programs like the Ujjawala Program (National Commission for Women, 2023). Without operationalising the non-punishment principle, India risks perpetuating punitive protectionism under a new legal guise.

5.1 The Immoral Traffic (Prevention) Act, 1956

India's first significant national law intended to prevent exploitation related to prostitution was the ITPA. It makes it illegal to operate a brothel, live off the proceeds of prostitution, acquire, detain, and solicit in public. The Act appears to target traffickers, brothel owners, and pimps. However, in reality, it has also been used to police women who sell sex in public or semi-public areas, frequently in accordance with laws against solicitation and loitering. Women who are "rescued" during police raids are frequently taken into custody and placed in "protective homes" for "rehabilitation," which might resemble closed institutions. This is similar to other "protective custody" models.

5.2 The Bharatiya Nyaya Sanhita, 2023: A new penal framework

The Indian Penal Code is replaced by the BNS, which also reclassifies a number of offences, including human trafficking. BNS Sections 143 and 144 address trafficking, which was previously regulated under IPC Sections 370 and 370A. These clauses identify trafficking as a crime and inflict severe punishments, such as life in prison for aggravated cases and for victims who are children. The BNS recognises recruitment, transportation, harbouring, and coercive means of exploitation when describing trafficking in terms that align with international standards. If properly executed, this change could lessen the tendency to penalise the trafficked individual for "immoral conduct" and instead concentrate on structured networks.

5.3 Does BNS cure the problem of criminalising victims?

Although the BNS toughens punishments for traffickers, the fundamental issue is not just with the laws but also with the way they are enforced. The classification of an individual as a victim to be protected, a witness to be managed, or an offender to be jailed is still up to the police, prosecutors, and lower courts. Women who are "rescued" from brothel raids under the ITPA are frequently kept in protective custody with little control. The answer runs the risk of merely renaming the cage if survivor autonomy, due process, and independent legal representation are not incorporated.

5.4 Victim Handling vs Trafficker Convictions in India (NCRB Baseline, Pre-BNS)

Table 1.

Year	Victims Rescued* (NCRB)	Trafficking Cases Resulting in Conviction	Victims per Conviction (Approx.)
2020	4,680	49	96: 1
2021	6,213	32	194: 1
2022	6,693	131	51: 1

Source: NCRB Anti-Human Trafficking Unit (AHTU) data tables (latest publicly available national series).

Note: *"Rescued" victims frequently enter institutional custody (e.g., protective homes/shelters) under anti-trafficking enforcement frameworks. The Bharatiya Nyaya Sanhita (BNS) came into force on 1 July 2024; NCRB's post-BNS (2024–2025) conviction data under the new statutory mapping is awaited.*

6. JUDICIAL PIVOT POINTS

6.1 Who is framed as dangerous?

In the UK, migrants who are forced to grow cannabis or who are the victims of identity fraud are frequently portrayed as offenders first, migrants second, and victims last. Instead of being portrayed as individuals who might be subject to financial bondage, deceit, or coercion, women in prostitution in India are frequently portrayed as carriers of "immorality," public annoyance, or societal disorder. In both situations, the visible, manageable subject takes center stage over the trafficker. Similar to India's usage of protective houses under ITPA and the raid-rescue-rehabilitation paradigm, the UK places trafficked women in immigration detention or prison-like settings for "processing." Both nations defend this by claiming that custody is necessary for the victim's protection, to stop them from escaping, or to guarantee their availability as a witness. However, from the individual's point of view, it remains involuntary incarceration. Identification is the key that unlocks protection in both nations. The non-punishment concept is never applied in the UK because police and prosecutors fail to identify trafficking at first contact. Following a brothel raid in India, a woman's fate frequently rests on classification decisions that might change depending on local court sentiments, police narratives, and moral presumptions. Credibility is shaped by linguistic obstacles, caste, class, nationality, immigration status, and gender norms.

6.2 Bridge to the Preceding Framework

This section examines how courts convert anti-trafficking laws into thriving principles, building on the legal foundations explored previously. Even progressive laws are only legitimate when they are interpreted in accordance with due process and human dignity. Thus, judicial reasoning shapes how nations strike a balance between protection and punishment by converting abstract obligations into enforceable rights. The analysis that follows looks at how the non-punishment principle, the right to autonomy, and gender-sensitive rehabilitation have been refined gradually in the United Kingdom and India, two common-law jurisdictions with shared colonial legacies, while still battling the persistent logic of control ingrained in anti-trafficking enforcement.

6.3 From Legal Text to Judicial Action

A shift from paternalism to rights recognition can be seen in the judicial development of anti-trafficking legislation. Courts increasingly see trafficked people as agents entitled to constitutional and international protections, while earlier they were regarded as recipients of charity or moral rescue. However, implementation still oscillates between these poles. (Malloch 2015). The immigration procedures, forced rehabilitation, or stigmatising confinement, systems that purport to protect victims nevertheless criminalise them. Analysing seminal rulings reveals how courts have sought to balance human vulnerability with state sovereignty, advocating the concepts of proportionality, consent, and due diligence that serve as the cornerstones of contemporary anti-trafficking rhetoric of modern times.

6.4 The United Kingdom: From R v. O to V.C.L. & A.N.

6.4.1 Early Jurisprudence and the Duty to Inquire

The 2008 decision in R v. O is still valid. Despite her exploitative position, a Vietnamese youngster was found guilty of using a counterfeit passport. The Court of Appeal reversed the conviction and chastised the prosecution and defence for their failure to recognise trafficking signs. The decision was significant because it established the prosecution's duty to investigate trafficking symptoms and ascertain if coercion or deception negated criminal intent. This idea portrayed trafficked people as victims of systemic failure rather than criminals (Malloch, 2015).

6.4.2 Codification of the Non-Punishment Principle

Following this, the *Crown Prosecution Service (CPS, 2011)* and the *Public Prosecution Service for Northern Ireland (2013)* implemented policies acknowledging that prosecution is not in the public interest when there is credible evidence of compulsion. These regulations were in line with the now-universal *non-punishment principle*, which was established by Article 26 of the *Council of Europe Convention on Action against Trafficking in Human Beings (2005)*. Practice, however, trailed rhetoric: Malloch's inquiry showed that trafficked individuals, particularly illegal migrants, were nonetheless deported or imprisoned under immigration laws instead of being acknowledged as victims.

6.4.3 Modern Slavery Act 2015 and Judicial Interpretation

Section 45 of the Modern Slavery Act 2015 (MSA), which combined earlier provisions, offered a legislative defence for people forced to commit crimes through exploitation. The Court of Appeal made it clear in R v. L & Others (2017) that defendants just had to provide evidence of a plausible connection between the offence and their exploitation. In spite of this development, defendants still had the burden of proof, which went against the protective aim of the principle. Section 45 of the Modern Slavery Act 2015 (MSA), which included previous laws, provided a legislative defence for people who were coerced into committing crimes through exploitation. In R v. L & Others (2017), the Court of Appeal clarified that defendants only needed to establish a plausible link between the crime and their exploitation. Despite this development, the defendants continued to bear the burden of proof, which went against the developed principle's protective objective.

The rationale in *R v. O* was further extended to a subsequent decision in *R v. Matela (2013)*. The convictions of asylum seekers who had used forged documents were quashed by the Court, noting the fact that systemic ignorance of trafficking indicators constituted procedural injustice. Together, these rulings have established the principle that criminal proceedings involving potential trafficking must begin with an inquiry into coercion and a failure to do so could render the proceedings catastrophic and contrary to Articles 4 and 6 of the European Convention on Human Rights (ECHR).

6.4.4 European Oversight and the V.C.L. & A.N. Judgment

These principles were unified by the European Court of Human Rights in *V.C.L. & A.N. v. United Kingdom* (2021). Two Vietnamese nationals who were forced into cannabis cultivation were prosecuted irrespective of the police's knowledge of allegations of trafficking. The Court held that by failing to recognise them as victims before prosecution UK has violated Article 4 (prohibition of slavery). The ruling affirmed that State bears a *positive duty* to ensure early identification in order to prevent the victims from being criminalized. In addition, it expanded the procedural dimension by linking the non-punishment principle to *due-process guarantees* (OSCE, 2014).

In response to this judgment, the UK government revised its Modern Slavery Statutory Guidance (2022), thereby improving the procedure of identification under the National Referral Mechanism (NRM). However, GRETA's 2023 review criticised persisting irregularities and the overuse of immigration detention. These developments show that while the UK has achieved doctrinal maturity, border control politics continue to limit its implementation.

6.5 Indian Jurisprudence: From Moral Paternalism to Rights-Based Protection

6.5.1 Early Reformative Approach

India's anti-trafficking jurisprudence evolved under the shadows of the Immoral Traffic (Prevention) Act, 1956 (ITPA), which was initially drafted to suppress prostitution rather than address the issue of trafficking in a human-rights framework. In *Gaurav Jain v. Union of India* (1997), the Supreme Court directed the establishment of rehabilitation homes for the children of sex workers, reinforcing a welfare-state narrative that combined morality with protection. Though the ruling did not address the coercive aspect of "protective custody," but it did recognise social rehabilitation as a state duty.

The jurisprudential shift towards constitutional dignity began with *Budhadev Karmaskar v. State of West Bengal* (2011), where the Apex Court held that sex workers are entitled to the right to livelihood and dignity under Article 21 of the Constitution. This ruling moved the conversation away from moralism and toward autonomy: the law should focus on exploitation rather than consenting, voluntary adult sex employment (Menon, 2019). The Court's focus on dignity established the constitutional foundation for later rulings that declared forceful "rescue" tactics to be unconstitutional.

6.5.2 High-Court Developments and Judicial Empathy

The Delhi High Court addressed the paradox of victims being re-victimized by the criminal justice system in *Court on Its Own Motion v. State* (2019). The court ruled that it is against Articles 14 and 21 to hold rescued women in protective homes against their will and promoted voluntary and informed rehabilitation. The Bombay

High Court reiterated this logic in *XYZ v. State of Maharashtra* (2021), holding that adult women cannot be imprisoned for just performing sex work. The Madhya Pradesh High Court applied these principles to the digital realm in *Prachi Jain v. Union of India* (2023), highlighting the need for coordinated cyber-surveillance against online trafficking and promoting alignment with India's commitments under SDG-5 and SDG-8 as well as the Palermo Protocol.

Another important intervention occurred in *Prajwala v. Union of India* (2015), where the Supreme Court addressed widespread issue of cross-border trafficking and ordered the formulation of a comprehensive victim-centred rehabilitation policy. This was another significant intervention which catalysed the drafting of the Trafficking of Persons (Prevention, Protection and Rehabilitation) Bill, 2018, and influenced subsequent proposals reviewed by NITI Aayog (2021). While the Bill has not yet been passed, judicial advocacy in *Prajwala* showed how courts can encourage legislative reform.

6.5.3 Constitutional Doctrines in Anti-Trafficking Jurisprudence

Courts of India have grounded their reasoning in the three constitutional doctrines discussed below:

a) **Substantive Due Process:** The right to personal liberty under Article 21 can only be curtailed by procedures that are just, fair, and reasonable. When protective custody is applied without consent it fails this standard under ITPA.
b) **Proportionality:** This principle which has been derived from international human-rights jurisprudence requires that state intervention be the least restrictive means to accomplish legitimate and justifiable goals. The judicial intervention in *XYZ* and *Court on Its Own Motion* illustrates that "rescue" cannot be used as an excuse for unlawful detention.
c) **Judicial Empathy:** The courts have invoked empathy as a constitutional method through judgments like *Budhadev Karmaskar*—giving recognition to marginalised persons not as subjects of moral reform but as citizens with agency.

Collectively, these principles have shifted India from a paternalistic to a rights-centric framework, though implementation gaps persist.

6.5.4 Bharatiya Nyaya Sanhita, 2023: New Codification and Old Omissions

The Bharatiya Nyaya Sanhita (BNS, 2023) has modernised the Penal Code and includes extended provisions on trafficking under sections 143–147 and 149. It contains punishment for labour exploitation, forced organ trade and organised trafficking networks. However, it says nothing about the non-punishment principle, leaving the judiciary to infer this protection from Article 21 and international agreements. The absence of a specific statutory defence similar to Section 45 of the UK's Modern Slavery Act represents the continued reliance on constitutional adjudication rather than legislative clarity.

6.6 International Doctrinal Anchors and Comparative Lessons

At the international level, three legal instruments influence judicial and policy interpretation:

a) **The Palermo Protocol (2000)** codified the "3P" paradigm—*prevention, prosecution, protection*—and established the *non-punishment clause* under Article 26, now widely acknowledged as a norm of customary international law.
b) **The OHCHR Recommended Principles and Guidelines (2002) reinterpreted** the clause as a *right* rather than a prosecutorial discretion, mandating the states to ensure that victims are identified and protected prior to any criminal proceedings.
c) **The Bangkok Rules (2010)** insist on voluntary participation, reinforcing gender-sensitive, non-custodial rehabilitation measures for women victims.

The gap between law and execution is highlighted in both the UNODC Global Report (2024) and the Group of Experts on Action against Trafficking in Human Beings(GRETA, 2023). While praising UK statutory reforms, GRETA highlighted inconsistent identification and ongoing immigration detention. As per UNODC, India's "protective homes" model often undermines rehabilitation by confusing care with control.

In the UK, defence is codified in statute, whereas in India it is inferred from the Constitution through judicial reasoning. The difference demonstrates two pathways to the same principle: one legislative and procedural, the other moral and constitutional. However, both depend on enforcement and administrative sensitivity. Harmonising these strategies into an integrated rights-based framework is crucial to the future of international anti-trafficking justice.

6.7 Emerging Themes and Future Directions

Certain themes have been crystallised across jurisdictions. They have been discussed below:

a) **Positive Duty to Identify:** Before initiating prosecution, the States must proactively screen for trafficking indicators. The duty extends to immigration officers, police and prosecutors.
b) **Autonomy and Consent:** It is important to note that rehabilitation cannot be coercive. The courts in India increasingly reject custodial models, while in the UK, non-detention alternatives are expanding through local partnerships.
c) **Gender-Sensitive Adjudication:** The courts are adopting humanitarian reasoning and are identifying women's autonomy within sex work and migration.
d) **Judicial Accountability:** The decision of the courts in *V.C.L. & A.N.* and *Prajwala* lays emphasis on institutional responsibility, and any failure to identify victims or guarantee humane rehabilitation may itself constitute a human-rights violation.
e) **Proportionality and Procedural Fairness:** Both systems put strong emphasis on proportional response—criminal justice measures must not duplicate the coercion they intend to remedy.

The convergence of these themes tracks the emergence of a transnational judicial consensus that any fight against trafficking cannot rely on punitive paternalism but must be based on respect for autonomy, consent, and due process.

6.8 Concluding Reflections

The anti-trafficking legislation in India and the UK has been consistently humanised, according to comparative jurisprudence. The court has acknowledged that victim protection and punishment cannot coexist, as evidenced by its rulings in instances such as *R v. O. and V.C.L. & A.N. to Budhadev Karmaskar and XYZ.* Now a pillar of both domestic and international jurisprudence, the non-punishment concept upholds the constitutional protections of liberty and dignity. The continued use of immigration detention and "custodial rehabilitation" implies that institutional and cultural change must accompany legislative reform. Despite being progressive, court interventions need to be supported by victim identification protocols, procedural protections, and gender-sensitive training for law enforcement. Lastly, anti-trafficking initiatives frequently reinforce the very structures they purport to dismantle, according to Malloch (2015). Real progress arises when victims are acknowledged as active participants in the justice process rather than only being saved from exploitation. Replacing control with care, compassion, and moral oversight with constitutional empathy is the challenge facing society, courts, and governments.

7. CONCLUSIONS AND RECOMMENDATIONS: POLICY GAPS AND HUMAN RIGHTS IMPLICATIONS

The Palermo Protocol (2000) created the integrated framework of protection, prosecution, and prevention. Nation-states, however, have prioritised these factors to differing degrees, and in reality, protection has been subordinated to punishment and prevention. The United Nations Rules for the Treatment of Women Prisoners (2010) and the Office of the High Commissioner for Human Rights (2002) established the non-punishment principle, which is nevertheless enforced unevenly. While there is no equivalent defence in India's criminal procedure structure, prosecutorial discretion still determines if trafficking indicators indicate case withdrawal in the UK (Crown Prosecution Service, 2011).

Incoherent institutional coordination further erodes policy coherence. GRETA (2023) claims that delays in victim recognition are caused by the UK's National Referral Mechanism's lack of legislative force. In India, contradictory mandates arise from the Ministry of Women and Child Development, the Ministry of Home Affairs, and state police departments' overlapping responsibilities. Although it has not yet been signed into law, the NITI Aayog Draft Trafficking in Persons Bill (2021) suggests establishing national and district anti-trafficking committees. Financial deficiencies make the problem worse: India's Prajjwala Scheme is underfunded and has a narrow scope, while UK victim support programs primarily rely on short-term philanthropic financing (NCW, 2023).

Both institutions ultimately embody what academics and scholars call 'rescue without justice'– a framework that saves lives but silences critics (Doezema, 2010). Only when the non-punishment concept is incorporated into statutes, independent victim identification processes are ensured, and trauma-informed judicial practices are adopted can true reform be accomplished. States must redefine trafficking as a human rights issue rather than a law-and-order issue if they are to fulfil their obligations under the Sustainable Development Goals and the Palermo Protocol.

7.1 The erosion of the non-punishment principle

In addition to causing personal injustice, the judicial system undermines the legitimacy of anti-trafficking policies when a trafficked person is charged for a coerced behaviour. The state says it "protects victims" on a worldwide scale, but it imprisons the same victims at police stations and magistrates' courts for identity crimes or public solicitation. Future prosecutions against traffickers are weakened by this credibility issue as survivors are correctly informed that revelation results in jail.

7.2 Criminalisation as migration management

The enforcement of trafficking laws is entwined with border and migration concerns in both the UK and India. Immigrants forced into illicit work flows are initially viewed as illegal entrants in the UK. In India, labour or sex work movement is framed through the perspective of "trafficking," but enforcement on the ground frequently takes the form of anti-begging campaigns, immigration policing, or moral policing instead of survivor-centered care.

7.3 Gendered paternalism

The paternal script that underpins protective custody regimes is that women must be subdued "for their own good." Institutional assertions concerning the welfare of adult women are frequently given more weight than their expressed wishes, agency, or agreement. This is carceral paternalism, not survivor-centered treatment.

7.4 Economic and racialised sorting

Detention, prosecution, and labelling are not neutral. They track lines of race, class, caste, and nationality. In the UK, Vietnamese nationals were overrepresented in cannabis cultivation arrests that in many cases involved trafficking indicators. In India, Dalit, Adivasi, and migrant women and girls are disproportionately vulnerable to being "rescued" and institutionalised under ITPA.

Recommendations: The state condemns trafficking and promises protection. Yet, at the point of contact, trafficked persons are often treated as criminals, irregular migrants, immoral women, or administrative burdens. This contradiction persists because anti-trafficking law has been layered on top of older systems of migration control, vice policing, and moral governance.

a) Codify and operationalise the non-punishment principle, including mandatory, reviewable screening for trafficking indicators at arrest and before charge approval.
b) Decouple trafficking enforcement from immigration enforcement and vice policing; treat trafficking as serious exploitation crime.
c) Replace custodial "protection" with rights-based support, ensuring voluntary safe housing, independent legal aid, and trauma-informed services
d) Train and constrain prosecutorial discretion with presumptions in favour of non-punishment when credible indicators are present.
e) Centre the economic and structural drivers of trafficking by targeting recruitment networks, debt bondage structures, and exploitative intermediaries.

REFERENCES

Aayog, N. I. T. I. (2021). Draft anti-trafficking policy framework: Review and recommendations. New Delhi.

All Party Parliamentary Group on Refugees, & All Party Parliamentary Group on Migration. (2015). The report of the inquiry into the use of immigration detention in the United Kingdom. House of Commons.

Amnesty International. (2008). *Scotland's slaves: An Amnesty International briefing on trafficking in Scotland*. Amnesty International Scotland.

Amnesty International. (2009). *Jailed without justice: Immigration detention in the USA*. Amnesty International.

Anderson, B., & Andrijasevic, R. (2008). Sex, slaves and citizens: The politics of anti-trafficking. *Soundings*, *40*(40), 135–145. DOI: 10.3898/136266208820465065

Bauman, Z. (1998). Globalization: The human consequences. *Polity*.

Bharatiya Nyaya Sanhita. (2023).

Bosworth, M., & Guild, M. (2008). Governing through migration control: Security and citizenship in Britain. *British Journal of Criminology*, *48*(6), 703–719. DOI: 10.1093/bjc/azn059

Budhadev Karmaskar v. State of West Bengal, (2011) 11 SCC 538 (India).

Cohen, S. (2001). States of denial: Knowing about atrocities and suffering. *Polity*.

Council of Europe. (2005). *Convention on action against trafficking in human beings*.

Court on Its Own Motion v. State, (2019) Delhi HC (India).

Crown Office and Procurator Fiscal Service. (2010). *Guidance on human trafficking offences*. COPFS.

Crown Prosecution Service. (2011). *CPS policy for prosecuting cases of human trafficking*. CPS Strategy and Policy Directorate.

Doezema, D. J. (2010). *Sex slaves and discourse masters: The construction of trafficking*. Bloomsbury Publishing.

Dutton, D. G., & Painter, S. (1993). Emotional attachments in abusive relationships: A test of traumatic bonding theory. *Violence and Victims*, *8*(2), 105–120. DOI: 10.1891/0886-6708.8.2.105 PMID: 8193053

Equality and Human Rights Commission Scotland. (2013). *Inquiry into human trafficking in Scotland: Follow-on report.* EHRC.

Foreigners Act. (1946).

Gaurav Jain v. Union of India, (1997) 8 SCC 114 (India).

Government of India. (2023). *The Bharatiya Nyaya Sanhita, 2023*, §143.

Group of Experts on Action against Trafficking in Human Beings (GRETA). (2023). Report concerning the implementation of the Council of Europe Convention on Action against Trafficking in Human Beings by the United Kingdom. Strasbourg.

Hindustan Times. (2025). *NIA chargesheet against accused in Myanmar human-trafficking cyber scam case.*

HM Chief Inspector of Prisons. (2013). Yarl's Wood Immigration Removal Centre. Her Majesty's Inspectorate of Prisons.

HM Inspectorate of Prisons & Independent Chief Inspector of Borders and Immigration. (2012). *The effectiveness and impact of immigration detention casework.* HMIP.

Home Office. (1998). *Fairer, faster and firmer: A modern approach to immigration and asylum.* HMSO.

Immoral Traffic (Prevention) Act. 1956 (India).

INTERPOL. (2024). *Human Trafficking-Fuelled Scam Centres: Crime Trend Update.*

Kempadoo, K. (2015). The modern-day white (wo) man's burden: Trends in anti-trafficking and anti-slavery campaigns. *Journal of Human Trafficking*, *1*(1), 8–20. DOI: 10.1080/23322705.2015.1006120

Kerala High Court. (2024).

Lum, K., & Isaac, W. (2016). To predict and serve? *Significance*, *13*(5), 14–19. DOI: 10.1111/j.1740-9713.2016.00960.x

Malloch, M. (2015). *Criminalising victims of human trafficking: State responses and punitive practices.* Cambridge University Press.

Menon, N. (2019). *Recovering subversion: Feminist politics beyond the law.* Permanent Black.

Organization for Security and Co-operation in Europe. (2012). *Report by OSCE Special Representative and Co-ordinator for Combating Trafficking in Human Beings, following her visit to the UK, 7–10 March 2011.* OSCE.

Organization for Security and Co-operation in Europe. (2014). *Ending exploitation.* OSCE.

Passport Act. (1967).

Prajwala v. Union of India, (2015) 8 SCC 380 (India).

Press Information Bureau. (2025). *Government initiatives to counter rising cyber financial frauds in India.*

Prison Reform Trust. (2012). *No way out: A briefing paper on foreign national women in prison in England and Wales.* Prison Reform Trust.

Public Prosecution Service for Northern Ireland. (2013). *Policy for prosecuting cases of human trafficking. PPS. • RACE in Europe. (2013). Victim or criminal? Trafficking for forced criminal exploitation in Europe – UK chapter.* ECPAT UK.

R v. L & Others, (2017). EWCA Crim 2128 (UK Ct App).

R v. Mateta, (2013). EWCA Crim 1372 (UK Ct App).

R v. O, (2008). EWCA Crim 2835 (UK Ct App).

Sales, R. (2002). The deserving and the undeserving? Refugees, asylum seekers and welfare in Britain. *Critical Social Policy, 22*(3), 456–478. DOI: 10.1177/026101830202200305

Secretary of State for the Home Department. (2014). *The government response to the report from the Joint Committee on the Draft Modern Slavery Bill.* Home Office.

Stumpf, J. (2010). The justice of crimmigration law and the security of home. In Hudson, B., & Ugelvik, S. (Eds.), *Justice and security in the 21st century* (pp. 43–63). Routledge.

Times of India. (2024).

United Nations. (2000). *Protocol to prevent, suppress and punish trafficking in persons, especially women and children (Palermo Protocol).* United Nations.

United Nations. (2010). *United Nations rules for the treatment of women prisoners and non-custodial measures for women offenders (the Bangkok Rules).* United Nations.

United Nations High Commissioner for Human Rights. (2002). *Recommended principles and guidelines on human rights and human trafficking.* Office of the High Commissioner for Human Rights.

United Nations Office on Drugs and Crime. (2022). *Global report on trafficking in persons 2022.* UNODC.

United Nations Office on Drugs and Crime. (2024). *Global report on trafficking in persons 2024*. UNODC.

United Nations Office on Drugs and Crime. (2025). *Inflection Point: Global Implications of Scam Centre Expansion*.

Van der Kolk, B. (2014). The body keeps the score: Brain, mind, and body in the healing of trauma. *New York, 3*, 14-211.

V.C.L. & A.N. v. United Kingdom. (2021). App. Nos. 77587/12 & 74603/12 (ECHR).

Wacquant, L. (1999). "Suitable enemies": Foreigners and immigrants in the prisons of Europe. *Punishment & Society, 1*(2), 215–222. DOI: 10.1177/14624749922227784

Wacquant, L. (2009). *Punishing the poor: The neoliberal government of social insecurity*. Duke University Press.

XYZ v. State of Maharashtra, (2021) Bom HC (India).

Compilation of References

Aayog, N. I. T. I. (2021). Draft anti-trafficking policy framework: Review and recommendations. New Delhi.

Aayog, N. I. T. I. (2024). *Responsible AI: #AIForAll—Ethical principles in India.* https://www.niti.gov.in/sites/default/files/2024-06/document.pdf

Abdirasulovich, K. A., & Alisherovich, E. O. (2025). ANALYSIS OF INTERNATIONAL LEGAL NORMS ESTABLISHING LIABILITY FOR CERTAIN OFFENSES AGAINST MORALITY, SUCH AS MAINTAINING A BROTHEL OR ENGAGING IN PROSTITUTION. *The Conference Hub*, 89–93. https://theconferencehub.com/index.php/tch/article/view/280

Abdullah, A., Huynh, I., Emery, C. R., & Jordan, L. P. (2022). Social norms and family child labor: A systematic literature review. *International Journal of Environmental Research and Public Health, 19*(7), 4082. DOI: 10.3390/ijerph19074082

Abel, G. (2010) *Decriminalisation: A harm minimisation and human rights approach to regulating sex work.* PhD thesis. University of Otago. Available at: https://ourarchive.otago.ac.nz/handle/10523/475

Abel, G. M. (2014). A decade of decriminalization: Sex work 'down under'but not underground. *Criminology & Criminal Justice, 14*(5), 580–592. DOI: 10.1177/1748895814523024

Abraham, I. (2014). *How India became territorial: Foreign policy, diaspora, geopolitics.* Stanford University Press.

Acharya, A. R. K. (2012). Impact of cultural and religious practices of prostitution on the trafficking of women in India. In *TRAYECTORIAS: Vol. AÑO 14, NÚM. 33-34* (pp. 95–114) [Journal-article].

Acharya, A., & Azhar, S. (2025). "We are Treated as Outsiders in Our Own City": Lived Experiences of Intersectional Stigma Against Sex Workers in Kolkata, India. *Sexuality Research & Social Policy*, *22*(3), 1417–1429. DOI: 10.1007/s13178-024-01054-8

ActionAid. (2019). *Post-LBA rehabilitation and trafficking vulnerability in border enclaves: A situational analysis*. ActionAid India.

Adhikari, H. (2011, January). Chaste wives and prostitute sisters: Patriarchy and prostitution among the Bedias of India. *Journal of International Women's Studies*. https://vc.bridgew.edu/cgi/viewcontent.cgi?article=1094&context=jiws

African Union. (2006). *Ouagadougou action plan to combat trafficking in human beings, especially women and children*. https://www.warnathgroup.com/wp-content/uploads/2020/05/2006-Ouagadougou-Action-Plan-to-Combat-Trafficking-In-Human-Beings-Especially-Women-and-Children.pdf

Agnes, F. (2012). *Law, Justice and Gender: Family Law and Constitutional Provisions in India*. Oxford University Press. DOI: 10.1093/acprof:oso/9780198072201.003.0005

Agnes, F. (2013). *Law, justice and gender: Family law and constitutional provisions in India*. Oxford University Press.

Ahmad, N. (2011). Child labour: Ground realities of Indian labour laws. *Commonwealth Law Bulletin*, *37*(1), 61–74. DOI: 10.1080/03050718.2010.524287

Akanksha, S. (2025, April 18). *Facial recognition technology and the right to privacy in India*. Lawful Legal. https://lawfullegal.in/facial-recognition-technology-and-the-right-to-privacy-in-india/

Akinsuli, O. (2022). AI and the Fight Against Human Trafficking: Securing Victim Identities and Disrupting Illicit Networks. ResearchGate. https://www.researchgate.net/publication/386209967_AI_and_the_Fight_Against_Human_Trafficking_Securing_Victim_Identities_and_Disrupting_Illicit_Networks

Alberto, M. D. F. P., & Yamamoto, O. H. (2017). When education is not the solution: Public policy in the fight against child labor. *Trends in Psychology*, *25*, 1677–1691. DOI: 10.9788/TP2017.4-10Pt

Al-Hawary, S. I. S., Kumar, T., Pallathadka, H., Alshahrani, S. H., Al-Tamimi, H. A. N. M., Muda, I., & Singer, N. (2023). The education of children in an Islamic family based on the Holy Qur'an. *Hervormde Teologiese Studies*, *79*(2), 8273.

Ali, M. A., Ali, M. V., & Abbas, F. (2017). Hidden hazardous child labor as a complex human rights phenomenon: A case study of child labor in Pakistan's brick-making industry. *Cogent Social Sciences, 3*(1), 1369486. DOI: 10.1080/23311886.2017.1369486

All Party Parliamentary Group on Refugees, & All Party Parliamentary Group on Migration. (2015). The report of the inquiry into the use of immigration detention in the United Kingdom. House of Commons.

Allain, J. (2012). *Slavery in international law: Of human exploitation and trafficking*. Martinus Nijhoff.

Alsalem, R. (2024). Report of the Special Rapporteur on violence against women and girls, its causes and consequences: Prostitution and violence against women and girls (Vol. A). United Nations Human Rights Council., HRC/56/48.

Alsalem, R. (2025). Response to a Political Critique and Personal Attack Against a United Nations Report that Presented New Evidence About Prostitution as a Cause and Consequence of Violence Against Women and Girls. *Dignity: A Journal of Analysis of Exploitation and Violence, 10*(1), 6.

Alsemairi, S. S. (2022). The role of digital technologies in combating cyber-trafficking in persons crimes. *Computer and Information Science, 16*(1), 49. https://doi.org/10.5539/cis.v16n1p49DOI: 10.5539/cis.v16n1p49

Amnesty International. (2008). *Scotland's slaves: An Amnesty International briefing on trafficking in Scotland.* Amnesty International Scotland.

Amnesty International. (2009). *Jailed without justice: Immigration detention in the USA*. Amnesty International.

Amnesty International. (2016). *Policy on state obligations to respect, protect and fulfil the human rights of sex workers.* https://www.amnesty.org

Amnesty International. (2016). *Policy on State Obligations to Respect.* Protect and Fulfil the Human Rights of Sex Workers.

Amnesty International. (2024). *Surveillance, discrimination and human rights: The dangers of unregulated AI.* Amnesty International.

Amon, J. J., Buchanan, J., Cohen, J., & Kippenberg, J. (2012). Child labor and environmental health: Government obligations and human rights. *International Journal of Pediatrics, 2012*(1), 938306. DOI: 10.1155/2012/938306

Anadolu Agency. (2024, June 25). US's PKK-linked partners in northeastern Syria continue to recruit children: State Department. https://www.aa.com.tr/en/middle-east/uss-pkk-linked-partners-in-northeastern-syria-continue-to-recruit-children-state-department/3257206

Ancient history—Was prostitution legal in the Kingdom of Israel during the reign of Solomon? - History Stack Exchange. (n.d.). Retrieved October 24, 2025, from https://history.stackexchange.com/questions/10884/was-prostitution-legal-in-the-kingdom-of-israel-during-the-reign-of-solomon

Anderson, B., & Andrijasevic, R. (2008). Sex, slaves and citizens: The politics of anti-trafficking. *Soundings*, *40*(40), 135–145. DOI: 10.3898/136266208820465065

Anuja, A. (2022). "Stigma, Sex Work and State: A Study of Bedia Community in India." Journal of Exclusion Studies.

Armstrong, L. (2011) *Managing Risks of Violence in Decriminalised Street-Based Sex Work: A Feminist (Sex Worker Rights) Perspective.* Victoria University of Wellington. PDF

Armstrong, L. (2021) '"I can lead the life that I want to lead": Social harm, human needs and the decriminalisation of sex work in Aotearoa/New Zealand', *Sexuality Research and Social Policy*. Available at: https://link.springer.com/article/10.1007/s13178-021-00605-7

Armstrong, L. (2024) *"In an ideal world, it would be fully decriminalised": Stigma, Discrimination, and Sex Work Laws in Scotland, Aotearoa New Zealand, and the Republic of Ireland.* Victoria University of Wellington. Available at: https://openaccess.wgtn.ac.nz/articles/report/Stigma_Discrimination_and_Sex_Work_Laws_Insights_from_Aotearoa_New_Zealand_Scotland_the_Republic_of_Ireland/26778190

Armstrong, L., Phillips, J., & Ryan, B. (2024) '"I've just schooled you, so you can't shame me": Stigma, discrimination, and healthcare access among sex workers in Scotland, the Republic of Ireland, and Aotearoa/New Zealand', *Open Access Victoria University of Wellington*. Available at: https://openaccess.wgtn.ac.nz/articles/journal_contribution/_I_ve_just_schooled_you_so_you_can_t_shame_me_Stigma_Discrimination_and_Healthcare_Access_among_Sex_Workers_in_Scotland_the_Republic_of_Ireland_and_Aotearoa_New_Zealand/28138067

Aronowitz, A. A. (2009). *Human trafficking, human misery: The global trade in human beings.* Praeger.

Aronowitz, A. A. (2017). *Human trafficking: A reference handbook* (2nd ed.). Routledge. DOI: 10.5040/9798400667497

Ashok, M., Madan, R., Joha, A., & Sivarajah, U. (2022). Ethical framework for artificial intelligence and digital technologies. *International Journal of Information Management, 62*, 102433. Advance online publication. DOI: 10.1016/j.ijinfomgt.2021.102433

Assaad, R., Levison, D., & Zibani, N. (2010). The effect of domestic work on girls' schooling: Evidence from Egypt. *Feminist Economics, 16*(1), 79–128. DOI: 10.1080/13545700903382729

Aufseeser, D., Bourdillon, M., Carothers, R., & Lecoufle, O. (2018). Children's work and children's well-being: Implications for policy. *Development Policy Review, 36*(2), 241–261. DOI: 10.1111/dpr.12215

Awaken. (2019). *Here's why Nevada is not safe for women.*

Aziz, S. (2023, August 22). In India, human traffickers target tribal women and girls. *Voice of America.* https://www.voanews.com/a/in-india-human-traffickers-target-tribal-women-and-girls/7235083.html

Baidawi, S., Sheehan, R., & Flynn, C. (2020). Criminal exploitation of child protection-involved youth. *Children and Youth Services Review, 118*, 105396. DOI: 10.1016/j.childyouth.2020.105396

Bajpai, A. (2012). Protecting India's children: Vulnerabilities and challenges. *Macalester International, 29*(1), 8.

Balogh, L., & Juhász, B. (2025). Debates on Legal Models Regarding Prostitution, with a Focus on the Role of Terminology. *MTA LAW WORKING PAPERS, 1*(1), 1–15.

Bambal, S., Deshmukh, J., Bhagat, M., Thakare, S., & Gulhane, S. (2025). Implementation of 'legal aid: Know your rights': A digital platform for legal assistance. *International Journal For Multidisciplinary Research, 7*(2). https://doi.org/10.36948/ijfmr.2025.v07i02.41889

Barry, K. (1997). Prostitution of sexuality: A cause for new international human rights. *Journal of Personal and Interpersonal Loss, 2*(1), 27–48. DOI: 10.1080/10811449708414404

Basu Ray Chaudhury, A. (2018). Bordering practices and migration control in eastern India. *Economic and Political Weekly, 53*(31), 45–53.

Basu, I., Jana, S., Rotheram-Borus, M. J., Swendeman, D., Lee, S.-J., Newman, P., & Weiss, R. (2004). HIV Prevention Among Sex Workers in India. *Journal of Acquired Immune Deficiency Syndromes (1999), 36*(3), 845–852.

Bateman, V. (2021). How Decriminalisation Reduces Harm Within and Beyond Sex Work: Sex Work Abolitionism as the "Cult of Female Modesty" in Feminist Form. *Sexuality Research & Social Policy*, *18*(4), 819–836. DOI: 10.1007/s13178-021-00612-8

Bauman, Z. (1998). Globalization: The human consequences. *Polity*.

Beber, B., Gilligan, M. J., Guardado, J., & Karim, S. M. (2017). Peacekeeping, compliance with international norms, and transactional sex in Monrovia, Liberia. *International Organization*, *71*(1), 1–30. DOI: 10.1017/S0020818316000242

Begum, H., & Gill, A. K. (2023). Understanding the experiences of British South Asian male survivors of child sexual abuse. In *Child Sexual Abuse in Black and Minoritised Communities: Improving Legal, Policy and Practical Responses* (pp. 59–113). Springer International Publishing., DOI: 10.1007/978-3-031-06337-4_3

Benoit, C., Jansson, M., Smith, M., & Flagg, J. (2018). Prostitution Stigma and Its Effect on the Working Conditions, Personal Lives, and Health of Sex Workers. *Journal of Sex Research*, *55*(4–5), 457–471. DOI: 10.1080/00224499.2017.1393652 PMID: 29148837

Bernstein, E. (2007). The Sexual Politics of the "New Abolitionism". *Differences: A Journal of Feminist Cultural Studies*, *18*(3), 128–151. DOI: 10.1215/10407391-2007-013

Bernstein, E. (2010). Militarized humanitarianism meets carceral feminism: The politics of sex, rights, and freedom. *Signs (Chicago, Ill.)*, *36*(1), 45–71. DOI: 10.1086/652918 PMID: 20827852

Betancourt, T. S., Borisova, I., Williams, T. P., Meyers-Ohki, S. E., Rubin-Smith, J. E., Annan, J., & Kohrt, B. A. (2013). Research review: Psychosocial adjustment and mental health in former child soldiers—A systematic review of the literature and recommendations for future research. *Journal of Child Psychology and Psychiatry, and Allied Disciplines*, *54*(1), 17–36. DOI: 10.1111/j.1469-7610.2012.02620.x PMID: 23061830

Bharatiya Nyaya Sanhita. (2023).

Bhat, B. A. (2022). *The intergenerational effects of marital transfers: Evidence from India*. Indian Statistical Institute.

Bhatia, R. (2020). Empowering tribal women through PESA in Bastar. International Journal of Novel Research and Development. https://ijnrd.org/papers/IJNRD2509132.pdf

Bhatia, S. (2025). AI-driven facial recognition: Human rights concerns and regulatory challenges. *MAGLAW, IV(1)*, 1–16. https://maglaw.puchd.ac.in/index.php/maglaw/article/download/345/74/1298

Bhattacharjee, B. (2025). The Muffled Memories: Tracing the Traumatic History of the Comfort Women of World War II through Jan Ruff O'Herne's Memoir Fifty Years of Silence. In Soman, N., Padmanabhan, B., & Kudale, K. M. (Eds.), *Between Trauma and Memory* (pp. 3–16). Springer Nature Singapore., DOI: 10.1007/978-981-96-8375-8_1

Bhattacharji, S. (1987). Prostitution in ancient India. *Social Scientist (New Delhi), 15*(2), 32–61. DOI: 10.2307/3520437

Bhattacharyya, D. (2019). *Empire and ecology in the Bengal Delta: The making of Calcutta*. Cambridge University Press.

Bigo, D. (2002). Security and immigration: Toward a critique of the governmentality of unease. *Alternatives, 27*(1), 63–92. DOI: 10.1177/03043754020270S105

Blanchetteç, T. G. (2022). A Place at the Table: Sex Workers and Allies in the Redefinition of Brazil's Anti-Trafficking Law. *Social Sciences (Basel, Switzerland), 11*(11), 11. Advance online publication. DOI: 10.3390/socsci11110530

Blanchette, T. G., Simões, S. S., Paula da Silva, A., & Murray, L. R. (2020). The Prostitute, the City, and the Virus. *SSRN, 3608567*, •••. https://papers.ssrn.com/sol3/papers.cfm?abstract_id=3608567. DOI: 10.2139/ssrn.3608567

Borak, M. (2025, November 7). *EU lawmakers approve regulation to expand Europol's capabilities in biometric data processing*. BiometricUpdate. https://www.biometricupdate.com/202511/eu-lawmakers-approve-regulation-to-expand-europols-capabilities-in-biometric-data-processing

Borrell, C., Muntaner, C., Solè, J., Artazcoz, L., Puigpinos, R., Benach, J., & Noh, S. (2008). Immigration and self-reported health status by social class and gender: The importance of material deprivation, work organisation and household labour. *Journal of Epidemiology and Community Health, 62*(5), e7–e7. DOI: 10.1136/jech.2006.055269

Bosworth, M., & Guild, M. (2008). Governing through migration control: Security and citizenship in Britain. *British Journal of Criminology, 48*(6), 703–719. DOI: 10.1093/bjc/azn059

Bouché, V., Robichau, R. W., Tipton, T., Metcalf, M., & Clark, T. A. (2025). Human Trafficking Policy Evolution: Analyzing Punctuated Diffusion Across Two Decades. *Journal of Human Trafficking*, 1–16. DOI: 10.1080/23322705.2025.2529713

Bourgeois, R. (2015). Colonial exploitation: The Canadian state and the trafficking of Indigenous women and girls in Canada. *UCLA Law Review. University of California, Los Angeles. School of Law, 62*, 1426–1463.

Boyden, J. (2018). 'We're not going to suffer like this in the mud': Educational aspirations, social mobility and independent child migration among populations living in poverty. In *Education, Mobilities and Migration* (pp. 26-46). Routledge.

Brents, B. G., & Hausbeck, K. (2005). Violence and legalized brothel prostitution in Nevada: Examining safety, risk, and prostitution policy. *Journal of Interpersonal Violence, 20*(3), 270–295. DOI: 10.1177/0886260504270333 PMID: 15684138

Briganti, P., Mele, S., & Varriale, L. (2020). New technologies for preventing and reducing verbal and non-verbal assaults against healthcare professionals within hospitals: The state of art. *Digital Transformation and Human Behavior: Innovation for People and Organisations*, 281-297. DOI: 10.1007/978-3-030-47539-0_19

Brouwers, L.H.E. (2022) *"I feel safe when I'm working with her": Sex Workers' Experiences of Management and Wider Work Relations.* University of Leeds. PDF

Brown, W. (2021). *In the Ruins of Neoliberalism: The Rise of Anti-Democratic Politics in the West.* Columbia University Press.

Budhadev Karmaskar v. State of West Bengal, (2011) 10 SCC 283 (India).

Budhadev Karmaskar v. State of West Bengal, (2011) 11 SCC 538 (India).

Budhadev Karmaskar v. State of West Bengal, (2022) Supreme Court of India.

Budhadev Karmaskar v. State of West Bengal, 2022 SCC OnLine SC 704 (India).

Budhadev Karmaskar v. State of West Bengal, Writ Petition (Criminal) No. 135 of 2010, Order dated May 19, 2022 (India).

Butler, Y. (2024). Silencing the Sex Worker [PDF]. *UCLA Law Review. University of California, Los Angeles. School of Law, 71*(2), 501–542.

Buzan, B., Wæver, O., & de Wilde, J. (1998). *Security: A new framework for analysis*. Lynne Rienner.

Carnegie Endowment for International Peace. (2024, November 20). *India's advance on AI regulation.* https://carnegieendowment.org/research/2024/11/indias-advance-on-ai-regulation?lang=en

CEDAW Committee. (1992). *General recommendation No. 19: Violence against women* (CEDAW/C/GC/19). United Nations.

CEDAW Committee. (2004). *General recommendation No. 25 on the core obligations of States parties under article 2 of the Convention* (CEDAW/C/GC/25). United Nations.

CEDAW Committee. (2020). *General recommendation No. 38 on trafficking in women and girls in the context of global migration* (CEDAW/C/GC/38). United Nations.

Census of India. (2011). Present and predicted literacy rate in Madhya Pradesh. Government of Madhya Pradesh. http://www.lbp.world/UploadedData/4860.pdf

Chakraborty, S. (2019). Cultural hegemony and victimisation of Bedia women in Central India. Academia.edu. https://www.academia.edu/90728622

Chakraborty, S. (2019). Cultural hegemony and victimisation of Bedia women in Central India. Academia.edu. https://www.academia.edu/90728622/Cultural_Hegemony_and_Victimisation_of_Bedia_Women_in_Central_India

Chandrachud, G. (2022). Decriminalizing sex work in India: Constitutional promises and judicial developments. *Indiana Law Review*, *6*(2), 145–168.

Charlesworth, H., Chinkin, C., & Wright, S. (1991). Feminist approaches to international law. *The American Journal of International Law*, *85*(4), 613–645. DOI: 10.2307/2203269

Chatterjee, P. (2017). *Negotiating sex work in the global South*. Zubaan Books.

Chatterji, J. (1999). *The spoils of partition: Bengal and India, 1947–1967*. Cambridge University Press.

Chauhan, S. P., & Deshta, S. (2024). Access to justice: The role of panchayat facilitated mediation in resolution of disputes. Paripex - Indian Journal of Research, 13(4), 1–4.

Chereches, B. (2021). *The representation of the Dalit community in Indian writing in English* (Master's thesis). Universidad de Zaragoza. https://zaguan.unizar.es/record/145214/files/TESIS-2024-419.pdf

Chernick, K., & Sweeting, K. D. (2025). Beyond Ingrained Stigma: A Critical Intersectional Analysis of Sex Work, Social Equity, and Canada's PCEPA Legislation. *Sexuality Research & Social Policy*. Advance online publication. DOI: 10.1007/s13178-025-01158-9

Chiongson, R. A., Desai, D., Marchiori, T., & Woolcock, M. (2011). *Role of law and justice in achieving gender equality. Background paper prepared for the World Bank World Development Report 2012 "Gender Equality and Development."*. The World Bank.

Cho, S., Crenshaw, K. W., & McCall, L. (2013). Toward a field of intersectionality studies: Theory, applications, and praxis. *Signs (Chicago, Ill.)*, *38*(4), 785–810. DOI: 10.1086/669608

Cho, S.-Y., Dreher, A., & Neumayer, E. (2013). Does legalized prostitution increase human trafficking? *World Development*, *41*, 67–82. DOI: 10.1016/j.worlddev.2012.05.023

Choudhury, N. (2019). *Women and the Weight of Legal Pluralism in India: Gendered law and Cultural Identity*. Routledge.

Chowdhury, M. (2022). MEASUREMENT OF HEALTH DIMENSION OF SEX-WORKERS'CHILDREN: A COMPARATIVE ANALYSIS ON THE BASIS OF NORTHERN AND SOUTHERN RED LIGHT AREAS OF WEST BENGAL.

Chowdhury, R. (2020). Trafficking, migration and border governance in eastern India. *Journal of Southeast Asian Studies*, *43*(2), 245–262.

Christoffersen, A., & McCabe, L. (2025). Operationalising Intersectionality in Equality and Domestic Abuse Policy in Scotland: Contradictions, Contestations and Erasure. *Critical Social Policy*, *45*(2), 234–258. Advance online publication. DOI: 10.1177/02610183241249696

Chukwudeh, O. S., & Oduaran, A. (2021). Liminality and child labour: Experiences of school aged working children with implications for community education in Africa. *Social Sciences (Basel, Switzerland)*, *10*(3), 93. DOI: 10.3390/socsci10030093

Ciza, D., Dominique, K., Kyambile, B., & Nkurunziza, J. (2018). Results from the Violence Against Children Survey: Haiti. *Child Abuse & Neglect*, *76*, 409–418. DOI: 10.1016/j.chiabu.2017.10.009 PMID: 29112856

CLPR. (2022). Voluntary sex work is legal: Supreme Court clarifies sex workers' rights. *Centre for Law and Policy Research*. https://clpr.org.in/blog/voluntary-sex-work-is-legal-supreme-court-clarifies/

Cohen, S. (2001). States of denial: Knowing about atrocities and suffering. *Polity.*

Cole, K. (2025). Evaluating Public Attitudes and Arguments for Sex Work Decriminalization: Insights From a Vignette Experiment. *Criminal Justice Policy Review*, *36*(5), 187–212. DOI: 10.1177/08874034251334353

Colleen V. & Kim, M. (2025). Generative AI and Legal Aid: Results from a Field Study and 100 Use Cases to Bridge the Access to Justice Gap, *Loy. L.A. L. Rev*, 903. https://digitalcommons.lmu.edu/llr/vol57/iss4/2

Committee on Economic. Social and Cultural Rights. (2000). *General comment No. 14: The right to the highest attainable standard of health (Art. 12)* (E/C.12/2000/4). United Nations.

Committee on Economic. Social and Cultural Rights. (2009). *General comment No. 20: Non-discrimination in economic, social and cultural rights (Art. 2(2))* (E/C.12/GC/20). United Nations.

Connelly, M. T. (2018). *The response to prostitution in the progressive era*. UNC Press Books.

Constitution of India. (1950). Government of India.

Convention on the Elimination of All Forms of Discrimination against Women. (1979). Dec. 18, 1979, 1249 U.N.T.S. 13.

Convention on the Rights of Persons with Disabilities. (2006). Dec. 13, 2006, 2515 U.N.T.S. 3.

Convention on the Rights of the Child (CRC). (1989). Nov. 20, 1989, 1577 U.N.T.S. 3.

Coombes, E., Wolf, A., Blunt, D., & Sparks, K. (2022). Disabled sex workers' fight for digital rights, platform accessibility, and design justice. *Disability Studies Quarterly*, *42*(2). Advance online publication. https://doi.org/10.18061/dsq.v42i2.9097DOI: 10.18061/dsq.v42i2.9097

Council of Europe—GRETA. (2022). *GRETA reports and general activities*. https://www.coe.int/en/web/anti-human-trafficking

Council of Europe. (2005). *Convention on action against trafficking in human beings*.

Council of Europe. (2019). *Assistance to victims of human trafficking*. https://rm.coe.int/assistance-to-victims-of-thb/1680a521f5

Court on Its Own Motion v. State, (2019) Delhi HC (India).

Crenshaw, K. (1989). Demarginalizing the intersection of race and sex: A Black feminist critique of antidiscrimination doctrine, feminist theory and antiracist politics. *University of Chicago Legal Forum*, *1989*(1), 139–167.

Crown Office and Procurator Fiscal Service. (2010). *Guidance on human trafficking offences*. COPFS.

Crown Prosecution Service. (2011). *CPS policy for prosecuting cases of human trafficking*. CPS Strategy and Policy Directorate.

D'Agostino, A. (2024). What Goes Up But Never Comes Down? Juvenile Punitive Practice Within The United States. *California Western International Law Journal, 54*(1), 8.

Dalla, R. L. (2022). A life-course perspective of sex trafficking among the Bedia of rural Madhya Pradesh, India. *Advances in Life Course Research, 54*, 100517. DOI: 10.1016/j.alcr.2022.100517 PMID: 36651617

Dalla, R. L., Kreimer, R., & Cole, A. (2022). A life-course perspective of sex trafficking among the Bedia caste of northern Central India. *Advances in Child Development and Behavior, 63*, 107–135.

Dammert, A. C., De Hoop, J., Mvukiyehe, E., & Rosati, F. C. (2018). Effects of public policy on child labor: Current knowledge, gaps, and implications for program design. *World Development, 110*, 104–123. DOI: 10.1016/j.worlddev.2018.05.001

Dari, S. S., Ali, L., & Jadhav, B. (2025). AI-powered criminal identification in India: Evaluating human rights concerns in automated identification systems. *SGS - Humanities & Management*, 1(1). https://spast.org/index.php/sgshm/article/download/5302/479/10424

Das, A., & Lakshmana, C. M. (2020). The implementation of domestic violence act in India: A state-level analysis. *International Journal of Social Science and Economic Research, 5*(4), 1234–1245. https://www.isec.ac.in/wp-content/uploads/2023/07/WP-499-Anamika-Das-and-C-M-Lakshmana-Final.pdf

Dasgupta, S. G. (2017, August). Commercial sex work in Calcutta: Past and present. ResearchGate. https://www.researchgate.net/publication/345121397_Commercial_Sex_Work_in_Calcutta_Past_and_Present

Dasgupta, S. (2014). Sovereign silence: Immoral Traffic (Prevention) Act and legalizing sex work in Sonagachi. *Political and Legal Anthropology Review, 37*(1), 109–125. DOI: 10.1111/plar.12053

Dasgupta, S. (2018). Child Labour in India: Literary Representations along the Trajectory of Nation. *International Research in Children's Literature, 11*(2), 160–172. DOI: 10.3366/ircl.2018.0272

Das, K. S. (2022). Child labour and its determinants in India. *Children and Youth Services Review, 138*, 106523. DOI: 10.1016/j.childyouth.2022.106523

Das, S., & Pande, A. (2021). Agency and Consent in the Global Sex Trade: Beyond Victim Narratives. *Global Gender Studies, 9*(1), 15–34.

Data Security Council of India. (2024). *Cross-border collaborations on privacy-by-design protocols and bias auditing tools.* https://www.dsci.in/

Davidson, C. (2023). *Feminism, Statecraft and Sex Work: Legal Narratives and Marginalised Voices.* Policy Praxis Press.

Davis, L. S., & Mavisakalyan, A. (2024). Individualism and the legal status of prostitution. *Journal of Comparative Economics, 52*(3), 714–732. https://doi.org/10.1016/j.jce.2024.07.001DOI: 10.1016/j.jce.2024.07.001

De, R. (2018). A people's constitution. In *Princeton University Press eBooks.* DOI: 10.23943/princeton/9780691174433.001.0001

Delhi Police. (2018). *Facial recognition initiatives: Implementation of automated facial recognition systems for child protection.* Government of India.

Desai, M. (2021). *The Limits of Law: Social Reform and the Politics of Gender Justice in India.* Routledge.

Deshpande, A. (2022, November 13). A patriarchal protocol: Judicial stereotyping of survivors of gender-based violence in India. *The Fletcher Forum.*

Dharamshastra. (Various authors). *Ancient Hindu legal and normative texts.*

Dixit, A. (2025). Digital surveillance and the right to privacy: Reassessing human rights in the age of technology. *Human Rights Law Review.*

Djuraev, I., Baratov, A., Khujayev, S., Yakubova, I., Rakhmonova, M., Mukumov, B., & Abdurakhmanova, N. (2025). The impact of digitization on legal systems in developing countries. *Qubahan Academic Journal, 5*(1), 81–117. https://doi.org/10.48161/qaj.v5n1a1246DOI: 10.48161/qaj.v5n1a1246

Doezema, D. J. (2010). *Sex slaves and discourse masters: The construction of trafficking.* Bloomsbury Publishing.

Doezema, J. (2010). *Sex Slaves and Discourse Masters: The Construction of Trafficking.* Zed Books. DOI: 10.5040/9781350222502

Dutton, D. G., & Painter, S. (1993). Emotional attachments in abusive relationships: A test of traumatic bonding theory. *Violence and Victims, 8*(2), 105–120. DOI: 10.1891/0886-6708.8.2.105 PMID: 8193053

Dworkin, A. (1993). Prostitution and male supremacy. *Michigan Journal of Gender & Law, 1*(1), 1–12.

Dyson, J. (2014). *Working childhoods: Youth, agency and the environment in India.* Cambridge University Press. DOI: 10.1017/CBO9781107415706

Easton, H.J. (2023) *Contested Discourses: A Feminist Socio-Legal Examination of Legal Responses to Prostitution in the UK*. Macquarie University. PDF

Eden, C. A., Chisom, O. N., & Adeniyi, I. S. (2024). Education policy and social change: Examining the impact of reform initiatives on equity and access. *International Journal of Science and Research Archive, 11*(2), 139-146. I: DOI: 10.30574/ijsra.2024.11.2.0372

Edmonds, E. V., & Shrestha, M. (2014). You get what you pay for: Schooling incentives and child labor. *Journal of Development Economics, 111*, 196–211. DOI: 10.1016/j.jdeveco.2014.09.005

Ekberg, G. S., & Wahlberg, K. (n.d.). 10. Twenty-five Years of Enforcing the Ban against the Purchase of Sexual Services in Sweden. *Law, Ideology, and the Experiences of Sex Workers and Clients*, 195.

Equality and Human Rights Commission Scotland. (2013). *Inquiry into human trafficking in Scotland: Follow-on report*. EHRC.

Eteng, M. J., & Nnam, M. U. (2022). Gender and Modern-Day Slavery: Aggression and Violence in the Context of a Nigerian Focus. *An International Collection of Multidisciplinary Approaches to Violence and Aggression, 21*.

European Parliament. (2014, February 26). *Resolution on sexual exploitation and prostitution and its impact on gender equality* (2013/2103(INI)) (P7_TA(2014)0162).

European Parliament. (2021). *Regulating facial recognition in the EU: 2021/698021*. https://www.europarl.europa.eu/RegData/etudes/IDAN/2021/698021/EPRS_IDA(2021)698021_EN.pdf

European Union Agency for Asylum (EUAA). (2022). *Identifying and supporting survivors of human trafficking—Asylum report 2022*. https://euaa.europa.eu/asylum-report-2022/55-identifying-and-supporting-survivors-human-trafficking

European Union. (2025, February 1). *Article 5: Prohibited AI practices. EU Artificial Intelligence Act*. https://artificialintelligenceact.eu/article/5/

European Union. (2025, March 31). *Understanding the EU AI Act: A security perspective. ASIS Online*. https://www.asisonline.org/security-management-magazine/monthly-issues/security-technology/archive/2024/april/Understanding-the-EU-AI-Act/

European Union. (n.d.). Preventing and combating trafficking in human beings (Amending Directive (EU) 2024/1712). EUR-Lex. https://eur-lex.europa.eu/EN/legal-content/summary/preventing-and-combating-trafficking-in-human-beings.html

Europol. (2022, March). *Early warning notification: War in Ukraine – refugees arriving to the EU from Ukraine at risk of exploitation as part of trafficking in human beings* (Ref. No. 2022-340). https://www.europol.europa.eu/cms/sites/default/files/documents/Early_Warning_Notification__War_in_Ukraine_%E2%80%93_refugees_arriving_to_the_EU_from_Ukraine_at_risk_of_exploitation_as_part_of_THB.pdf

Europol. (2025, November 6). *EU lawmakers approve regulation to expand Europol's capabilities*. https://www.europol.europa.eu/newsroom/news/eu-lawmakers-approve-regulation-to-expand-europol%E2%80%99s-capabilities

Europol. (n.d.). *Trafficking in human beings situational report*. https://www.europol.europa.eu/sites/default/files/documents/thb_situational_report_-_europol.pdf

Facia. (2024, May 17). *Human face recognition vs. human trafficking: Protecting human lives through real time liveness detection*. https://facia.ai/blog/human-face-recognition-vs-human-trafficking-protecting-human-lives-through-real-time-liveness-detection/

Family First New Zealand. (2023). *Prostitution law review: Benefits exaggerated, shortcomings ignored, denied or hidden.*

Farley, M., Cotton, A., Lynne, J., Zumbeck, S., Spiwak, F., Reyes, M. E., Alvarez, D., & Sezgin, U. (2003). Prostitution and trafficking in nine countries: An update on violence and post-traumatic stress disorder. *Journal of Trauma Practice*, *2*(3–4), 33–74. DOI: 10.1300/J189v02n03_03

Fateh Chand v. State of Haryana, Crim. App. No. 1096 of 2004 (2009) (India).

Fawole, O. I. (2008). Economic violence to women and girls: Is it receiving the necessary attention? *Trauma, Violence & Abuse*, *9*(3), 167–177. DOI: 10.1177/1524838008319255

Fine, J. B., Mayall, K., & Sepúlveda, L. (2017). The Role of International Human Rights Norms in the Liberalization of Abortion Laws Globally. *Health and Human Rights*, *19*(1), 69–80. PMID: 28630542

Firmin, M. W., Lee, A. D., Firmin, R. L., Deakin, L. M., & Holmes, H. J. (2013). Qualitative perspectives toward prostitution's perceived lifestyle addictiveness. *Journal of Behavioral Addictions*, *2*(4), 231–238. https://doi.org/10.1556/jba.2.2013.013DOI: 10.1556/JBA.2.2013.013 PMID: 25215205

FitzGerald, S., O'Neill, M., & Wylie, G. (2020). Social justice for sex workers as a "politics of doing": Research, policy and practice. *Irish Journal of Sociology*, *28*(1), 44–60. DOI: 10.1177/0791603520911344

Fonseka, L., & Malhotra, D. D. (2020). India: Urban poverty, children and participation. In *Urban Children Distress* (pp. 161-215). Routledge.

Footer, K. H., White, R. H., Park, J. N., Decker, M. R., Lutnick, A., & Sherman, S. G. (2020). Entry to sex trade and long-term vulnerabilities of female sex workers who enter the sex trade before the age of eighteen. *Journal of Urban Health, 97*(3), 406–417. DOI: 10.1007/s11524-019-00410-z PMID: 32034655

Foreigners Act. (1946).

Foucault, M. (1980). *Power/Knowledge: Selected Interviews and Other Writings 1972–1977*. Pantheon.

Freelaw. (2024, October 31). The impact of AI and facial recognition on criminal investigations. https://www.freelaw.in/legalarticles/The-Impact-of-AI-and-Facial-Recognition-on-Criminal-Investigations

Fussey, P., & Murray, D. (2025). *Facial recognition surveillance: Policing and human rights in the age of artificial intelligence*. Oxford University Press. DOI: 10.1093/9780191979927.001.0001

Gallagher, A. T. (2010). *The international law of human trafficking*. Cambridge University Press. DOI: 10.1017/CBO9780511761065

Gallagher, A. T., & David, F. (2014). *The international law of migrant smuggling*. Cambridge University Press. DOI: 10.1017/CBO9781139059619

Gallo, F., & Thinyane, H. (2020, November 15). The Palermo Protocol turns 20: Failures of the past and shifting paradigms for the future. United Nations University Institute in Macau. https://unu.edu/macau/news/palermo-protocol-turns-20-failures-past-and-shifting-paradigms-future

Garg, R. K. (2022). Cultural Relativism via-a-vis Woman's Human Rights in India: Legal and Constitutional Perspective. Part 1 Indian J. *Integrated Rsch. L., 2*, 1.

Gaurav Jain v. Union of India, (1997) 8 SCC 114 (India).

Gaurav Jain v. Union of India, AIR 1997 SC 3021 (India).

Gebregziabher, K., Hadush, M., & Abrha, K. (2023). Child labor and its determinants: An empirical test of the luxury axiom-cum the wealth paradox theory. *Cogent Economics & Finance, 11*(2), 2282890. DOI: 10.1080/23322039.2023.2282890

Ghosh, P. (2014). Restorative justice: The new paradigm in the province of justice in India? *SSRN, 1*(4), 88–96. DOI: 10.2139/ssrn.2467373

Giametta, C., & Bail, H. L. (2023). The national and moral borders of the 2016 French law on sex work: An analysis of the 'prostitution exit programme'. *Critical Social Policy*, *43*(2), 214–233. DOI: 10.1177/02610183221101167

Giles, M., & Giles, M. (2021, February 11). Human trafficking in India: How the colonial legacy of the Anti-Human Trafficking Regime undermines Migrant and Worker Agency - LSE Human Rights. *LSE Human Rights - A student-led blog from LSE Human Rights.* https://blogs.lse.ac.uk/humanrights/2021/02/11/human-trafficking-in-india-how-the-colonial-legacy-of-the-anti-human-trafficking-regime-undermines-migrant-and-worker-agency/

Global Survivors Fund. (2023, March). *Myanmar: Study on opportunities for reparations for survivors of conflict-related sexual violence* [Global Reparations Study]. https://www.globalsurvivorsfund.org/fileadmin/uploads/gsf/Documents/Resources/Global_Reparation_Studies/GSF_Report_MYANMAR_EN_March2023_WEB.pdf

Gonzalez-Recio, P., Armstrong, L., Alonso-Colón, M., Padilla, M., Bustillos, A., Belza, M. J., & Moreno-García, S. (2025). "We want back the dignity they stole from us": Epistemic injustice, sex work criminalization and trans sex workers' mental health. *International Journal of Transgender Health*, •••, 1–14. DOI: 10.1080/26895269.2025.2573833

Gore, M., Narayanan, P., & Juvekar, S. (2020). Does fear for infection affect condom use and HIV testing? A study of female sex workers in Pune city. *Clinical Epidemiology and Global Health*, *8*(2), 562–566. DOI: 10.1016/j.cegh.2019.12.003

Government of Canada. (2014). *Protection of Communities and Exploited Persons Act.*

Government of France. (2016). *Law penalizing purchase of sexual services.*

Government of Germany. (2002). *Prostitution Act.* Prostitutionsgesetz.

Government of Germany. (2017). *Prostitute Protection Act.*

Government of India, Ministry of Home Affairs. (2023). *Crime analysis and predictive policing reports.* Government of India. https://www.mha.gov.in

Government of India. (1956). *Immoral Traffic (Prevention) Act, 1956.*

Government of India. (1956). *The Immoral Traffic (Prevention) Act, 1956.*

Government of India. (1956). *The Immoral Traffic (Prevention) Act, 1956.* https://www.indiacode.nic.in/bitstream/123456789/15378/1/the_immoral_traffic_(prevention)_act,_1956.pdf

Government of India. (2023). *The Bharatiya Nyaya Sanhita, 2023*, §143.

Government of India. (2023). *The Bharatiya Nyaya Sanhita, 2023.*

Government of Netherlands. (2000). *Amendments to the Dutch Penal Code relating to brothel legalization.*

Government of New Zealand. (2003). *Prostitution Reform Act.*

Government of Norway. (2009). *Amendments to Norwegian Penal Code relating to purchase of sexual services.*

Government of South Africa. (1957). *Sexual Offences Act.*

Government of Sweden. (1999). *Sex Purchase Act.*

Government Offices of Sweden. (2014). *Sweden's follow-up of the Platform for Action from the UN's Fourth World Conference on Women in Beijing 1995—covering the period between 2009–2014.* Government Offices of Sweden.

Government policies and sex work realities: Human trafficking in the regulated sex industry (with Verhoeven, M. A.). (2017). publisher not identified.

Goyal, Y., & Ramanujam, P. (2014). Ill-conceived laws and exploitative state: Toward decriminalizing prostitution in India. *Akron Law Review, 47*, 1071.

Gozdziak, E. M., & Bump, M. N. (2008). *Data and research on human trafficking: Bibliography of research-based literature.* Georgetown University. https://t.ly/UUdYu

Grant, M. G. (2014). *Playing the whore: The work of sex work.* Verso.

Greenbaum, J. (2021). Child labor and sex trafficking. *Pediatrics in Review, 42*(12), 639–654. DOI: 10.1542/pir.2020-001396

Greenbaum, V. J. (2014). Commercial sexual exploitation and sex trafficking of children in the United States. *Current Problems in Pediatric and Adolescent Health Care, 44*(9), 245–269. DOI: 10.1016/j.cppeds.2014.07.001

Grenfell, P., Stuart, R., Eastham, J., Gallagher, A., Elmes, J., Platt, L., & O'Neill, M. (2023). 'Policing and Public Health Interventions into Sex Workers' Lives: Necropolitical Assemblages and Alternative Visions of Social Justice'. *Critical Public Health, 33*(1), 97–112. DOI: 10.1080/09581596.2022.2096428

Group of Experts on Action against Trafficking in Human Beings (GRETA). (2023). Report concerning the implementation of the Council of Europe Convention on Action against Trafficking in Human Beings by the United Kingdom. Strasbourg.

Guild, E., Grant, S., & Groenendijk, C. A. (Eds.). (2019). *Human rights of migrants in the 21st century*. Routledge., https://www.routledge.com/Human-Rights-of-Migrants-in-the-21st-Century/Guild-Grant-Groenendijk/p/book/9781138503397

Gumus, S. G., & Wingenbach, G. (2016). The child labor problem in Turkish agriculture: What can we do? *Social Indicators Research, 127*(3), 1193–1215. DOI: 10.1007/s11205-015-0999-1

Gupta, S. (2013, July). Human rights of sex workers in India: The way forward. SSRN *Electronic Journal*. https://papers.ssrn.com/sol3/papers.cfm?abstract_id=2357167 DOI: 10.2139/ssrn.2357167

Halley, J., Kotiswaran, P., Shamir, H., & Thomas, C. (2006). From the International to the Local in Feminist Legal Responses to Rape, Prostitution/Sex Work, and Sex Trafficking: Four Studies in Contemporary Governance Feminism. *Harvard Journal of Law & Gender, 29*(2), 335–423.

Hamenoo, E. S., Dwomoh, E. A., & Dako-Gyeke, M. (2018). Child labour in Ghana: Implications for children's education and health. *Children and Youth Services Review, 93*, 248–254. DOI: 10.1016/j.childyouth.2018.07.026

Hanscamp, E. (2023) *Developing an Intersectional Feminist Trauma- and Violence-Informed Practice Framework for Mental Health Services for Women in Sex Work*. RMIT University. PDF

Hansen, M. A., & Johansson, I. (2022). Asking about "prostitution", "sex work" and "transactional sex": Question wording and attitudes toward trading sexual services. *Journal of Sex Research, 60*(1), 153–164. https://doi.org/10.1080/00224499.2022.2130859DOI: 10.1080/00224499.2022.2130859 PMID: 36269626

Harding, R. (2020). Regulating Sex Work in the Neoliberal City. *Urban Studies (Edinburgh, Scotland), 57*(4), 845–861. DOI: 10.1177/0042098019857953

Harishankar, V. B., & Mvadha, M. P. (2011). *Exploitation of women as devadasis and its associated evils*. National Commission for Women. https://ncwapps.nic.in/pdfReports/Exploitation_of_Women_as_Devadasis_and_its_Associated_Evils_Report.pdf

Harris, P. G. (2018). *Ethics and global politics*. Edinburgh University Press.

Harvey, K. (2016). "When I go to bed hungry and sleep, I'm not hungry": Children and parents' experiences of food insecurity. *Appetite, 99*, 235–244. DOI: 10.1016/j.appet.2016.01.004

Hasan, M. J., & Chaitee, N. N. (2022). Reasons behind the Drop out of Street Children from Non-formal Primary Education Program. *International Journal for Educational and Vocational Studies*, *4*(2), 81–88. DOI: 10.29103/ijevs.v0i0.5612

Haynes, J. (2025). International human rights law's complicity in status subordination: A postcolonial critique of treaty bodies' engagement with human trafficking. *Leiden Journal of International Law*, •••, 1–33.

Herman, J. L. (1992). Complex PTSD: A syndrome in survivors of prolonged and repeated trauma. *Journal of Traumatic Stress*, *5*(3), 377–391. DOI: 10.1002/jts.2490050305

Hill, A. and Macleod, J. (2023). *Beyond Consent: Carceral Feminism and Gender-Based Violence Services in Scotland.* Policy Report.

Hinchy, J. (2020, February). Gender, family, and the policing of the 'criminal tribes' in nineteenth-century North India. *Modern Asian Studies.* https://www.cambridge.org/core/journals/modern-asian-studies/article/abs/gender-family-and-the-policing-of-the-criminal-tribes-in-nineteenthcentury-north-india/9F9F6EA7FD37138ABB295C7FCF99164B

Hindustan Times. (2025). *NIA chargesheet against accused in Myanmar human-trafficking cyber scam case.*

HM Chief Inspector of Prisons. (2013). Yarl's Wood Immigration Removal Centre. Her Majesty's Inspectorate of Prisons.

HM Inspectorate of Prisons & Independent Chief Inspector of Borders and Immigration. (2012). *The effectiveness and impact of immigration detention casework*. HMIP.

Holistic, A. I. (2024, August 5). *Navigating prohibited practices under the AI Act.* https://www.holisticai.com/blog/prohibitions-under-eu-ai-act

Home Office. (1998). *Fairer, faster and firmer: A modern approach to immigration and asylum.* HMSO.

Hoque, M. M. (2023). Understanding the role of structural factors and realities in normalizing child labour in urban slums of Bangladesh. *Cogent Social Sciences*, *9*(2), 2272319. DOI: 10.1080/23311886.2023.2272319

Hossain, M., Zimmerman, C., Abas, M., Light, M., & Watts, C. (2010). The relationship of trauma to mental disorders among trafficked and sexually exploited girls and women. *American Journal of Public Health*, *100*(12), 2442–2449. DOI: 10.2105/AJPH.2009.173229 PMID: 20966379

Hounga v Allen [2014] UKSC 47.

Huang, L. (2017). The trafficking of women and girls in Taiwan: Characteristics of victims, perpetrators, and forms of exploitation. *BMC Women's Health, 17*(1), 104. DOI: 10.1186/s12905-017-0463-2

Human Rights Committee. (1988). *General comment No. 16: Article 17 (Right to privacy)* (HRI/GEN/1/Rev.1). United Nations.

Human Rights Committee. (1989). *General comment No. 18: Non-discrimination* (HRI/GEN/1/Rev.1). United Nations.

Human Rights Committee. (1992). *General comment No. 20: Article 7 (Prohibition of torture or other cruel, inhuman or degrading treatment or punishment)* (HRI/GEN/1/Rev.1). United Nations.

Human Rights Committee. (1994). *Toonen v. Australia* (Communication No. 488/1992) (CCPR/C/50/D/488/1992). United Nations Human Rights Committee.

Human Rights Committee. (2004). *General comment No. 31: The nature of the general legal obligation imposed on States parties to the Covenant* (CCPR/C/21/Rev.1/Add.13). United Nations.

Human Rights Watch. (2007, February). *Hidden apartheid: Caste discrimination against India's "untouchables"*. https://www.hrw.org/report/2007/02/12/hidden-apartheid/caste-discrimination-against-indias-untouchables

Human Rights Watch. (2020, January 11). *UN peacekeeping has a sexual abuse problem*. https://www.hrw.org/news/2020/01/11/un-peacekeeping-has-sexual-abuse-problem

Human Rights Watch. (2024, October 2). *Northeast Syria: Military recruitment of children persists*. https://www.hrw.org/news/2024/10/02/northeast-syria-military-recruitment-children-persists

Human Rights Watch. (2025). *World report 2025: Haiti* (pp. 2–6). https://www.hrw.org/world-report/2025

Huysmans, J. (2006). *The politics of insecurity: Fear, migration and asylum in the EU*. Routledge. DOI: 10.4324/9780203008690

Ilyas, A., Shahid, M. S., & Ali Hassan, R. (2020). Evaluating the motives of child labourers in the informal economy. *The International Journal of Sociology and Social Policy, 40*(3/4), 409–424. DOI: 10.1108/IJSSP-01-2019-0001

Immigration New Zealand's commitment to combatting trafficking in persons. (n.d.). Immigration New Zealand. https://www.immigration.govt.nz/about-us/news-centre/immigration-new-zealands-commitment-to-combatting-trafficking-in-persons/

Immoral Traffic (Prevention) Act. 1956 (India).

Independent Commission for Aid Impact (ICAI). (2022, February 24). *The UK's approach to safeguarding in the humanitarian sector: Literature review* [Report]. https://icai.independent.gov.uk/html-version/the-uks-approach-to-safeguarding-in-the-humanitarian-sector-3/

India - United States Department of State. (2025, January 6). United States Department of State. https://www.state.gov/reports/2023-trafficking-in-persons-report/india

India Development Review. (2025, September 3). Indian agriculture can't thrive without women farmers. https://idronline.org/article/agriculture/indian-agriculture-cant-thrive-without-women-farmers/

India, U. N. F. P. A. (n.d.). Advancing the Rights of Women and Girls Panchayats Leading the Way. Retrieved October 26, 2025, from https://india.unfpa.org/sites/default/files/pub-pdf/unfpa_compendium_panchayat_mopr.pdf

Indian Express. (2023, August 3). *SC directions on sex workers: History of the case and where it stands now*. https://indianexpress.com/article/explained/sc-directions-on-sex-workers-history-of-the-case-and-where-it-stands-now-7940364/

IndiaSpend. (2024). *Climate crisis in the Sundarbans makes women vulnerable to trafficking*.

Inspeq, A. I. (2025, February 5). EU AI Act: Prohibited practices—European Commission guidelines (Article 5). https://inspeq.ai/blog/eu-ai-act-prohibited-practices-european-commission-guidelines-article-5

Institute of Development Studies. (2019). *Participatory accountability in anti-trafficking governance*.

Inter-American Commission on Human Rights. (2019). *Missing and murdered Indigenous women in British Columbia, Canada* (OEA/Ser.L/V/II. Doc. 30/14).

Inter-American Court of Human Rights. (2006). *Miguel Castro-Castro Prison v. Peru* (Merits, Reparations and Costs), Series C No. 160.

International Committee of the Red Cross. (n.d.). Rule 94: Slavery and the slave trade (Customary IHL Database). https://ihl-databases.icrc.org/es/customary-ihl/v2/rule94

International Covenant on Civil and Political Rights (ICCPR). (1966). Dec. 16, 1966, 999 U.N.T.S. 171.

International Covenant on Economic, Social and Cultural Rights. (1966). Dec. 16, 1966, 993 U.N.T.S. 3.

International Criminal Court, Office of the Prosecutor. (2024, December). *Policy on slavery crimes.* https://www.icc-cpi.int/sites/default/files/2024-12/policy-slavery-web-eng.pdf

International Criminal Court. (1998). *Rome Statute of the International Criminal Court.* https://www.icc-cpi.int/resource-library/documents/rs-eng.pdf

International Criminal Tribunal for the former Yugoslavia (ICTY). (1998). *Prosecutor v. Furundžija* (Trial Chamber Judgment), IT-95-17/1-T.

International Labour Organization. (2010). *Recommendation concerning HIV and AIDS and the world of work.* ILO.

International Labour Organization. (2022). *Global estimates of modern slavery: Forced labour and forced marriage.* ILO, Walk Free, & IOM.

International Organization for Migration (IOM). (2016). *Addressing human trafficking and exploitation in times of crisis: Evidence and recommendations for further action to protect vulnerable and mobile populations.* International Organization for Migration. https://publications.iom.int/books/addressing-human-trafficking-and-exploitation-times-crisis

International Organization for Migration (IOM). (2019). *Caring for trafficked persons: Guidance for health providers* (2nd ed.). https://publications.iom.int/books/caring-trafficked-persons-guidance-health-providers

International Organization for Migration (IOM). (2022). *Study and toolkit: Monitoring and evaluation – Executive summary.* https://publications.iom.int/system/files/pdf/pub2022-114-el-study-and-toolkit-monitoring-exec-sum.pdf

International Organization for Migration (IOM). (2023)... *World Migration Report, 2024,* •••. https://www.iom.int/wmr

International Organization for Migration (IOM). (n.d.). *Trafficking victim identification (practical resources).* https://www.iom.int/sites/g/files/tmzbdl486/files/iscm/materials/traffickingvictimidentification.pdf

International Organization for Migration. (2021a). *Cross-border human trafficking between India and Bangladesh.*

International Organization for Migration. (2021b). Environmental migration and trafficking risk in coastal. *South Asia.*

Internet Freedom Foundation. (2023). *AI, surveillance and privacy in India: Human rights in the age of technology.* Oxford Human Rights Hub. https://ohrh.law.ox.ac.uk/ai-surveillance-and-privacy-in-india-human-rights-in-the-age-of-technology/

INTERPOL. (2024). *Human Trafficking-Fuelled Scam Centres: Crime Trend Update.*

INTERPOL. (2024, October 7). *Facial recognition system.* INTERPOL. https://www.interpol.int/en/operations/facial-recognition-system

INTERPOL. (2025, July 10). *Operation Global Chain.* INTERPOL. https://www.interpol.int/en/operations/global-chain

INTERPOL. (2025, March). *Statement to UNODC.* https://www.interpol.int/en

INTERPOL. (n.d.). *Facial recognition.* https://www.interpol.int/en/How-we-work/Forensics/Facial-Recognition

INTERPOL. *Facial recognition.* https://www.interpol.int/en/How-we-work/Forensics/Facial-Recognition

Islam, M. R., Promity, J. F., Afroz, K. M., Kaniz, S. M., Hassan, M. R., & Islam, K. F. (2024). Nutritional Status and Food Habits of Child Labor in Rangpur City, Bangladesh. *Health Dynamics, 1*(9), 316–323. DOI: 10.33846/hd10901

Jabyn, M. (2020). Advancing justice interests and human rights of vulnerable groups through clinical legal education. *Jindal Global Law Review, 11*(2), 271–288. https://doi.org/10.1007/s41020-020-00127-0DOI: 10.1007/s41020-020-00127-0

Jain, A. (2025, November 4). *NCRB's National Automated Facial Recognition System.* Panoptic. https://panoptic.in/case-study/ncrbs-national-automated-facial-recognition-system

Jain, S. (2023). Algorithmic bias and rights of marginalized populations. *Jindal Global Law Review, 14*(2), 145–168.

Jangir, H. P. (2024, November). From Sarkivasi (nomadic) to Gaonvasi (villager): The impact of sedentarisation on Rajasthan's stigmatised Nat community. *Heliyon.* https://www.sciencedirect.com/science/article/pii/S2590291124004352

Jessop, B. (2007). State power: A strategic-relational approach. *Polity.*

Jha, D., & Sharma, T. (2015, December). Caste and prostitution in India: Politics of shame and of exclusion. *Anthropology.* https://www.longdom.org/open-access/caste-and-prostitution-in-india-politics-of-shame-and-of-exclusion-2332-0915-1000160.pdf

Jha, D., & Sharma, T. (2016). Caste and Prostitution in India: Politics of shame and of exclusion. *Anthropology; a Guide to First Degree Courses in UK Universities, 04*(01). Advance online publication. DOI: 10.4172/2332-0915.1000160

Jhaveri, D. (2024). "Empowering Tribal Women: A comprehensive exploration of rights, challenges and the way forward." Journal of Political Science. Empowering Tribal Women: A comprehensive exploration of their roles and participation in local government

Joulaei, H., Zarei, N., Khorsandian, M., & Keshavarzian, A. (2021). Legalization, Decriminalization or Criminalization; Could We Introduce a Global Prescription for Prostitution (Sex Work). *International Journal of High Risk Behaviors & Addiction, 10*(3), e106741. DOI: 10.5812/ijhrba.106741

Jyotish, K. (2025, November 4). *The legal and ethical challenges of AI surveillance in India: Balancing national security and privacy.* International Journal of Legal and Law Research. https://www.ijllr.com/post/the-legal-and-ethical-challenges-of-ai-surveillance-in-india-balancing-national-security-and-privacy

K.P.Kirankumar v State, 2025 INSC 1473 (India).

K.S. Puttaswamy v. Union of India, (2017) 10 SCC 1 (India).

Kadir, A., Battersby, A., Spencer, N., & Hjern, A. (2019). Children on the move in Europe: a narrative review of the evidence on the health risks, health needs and health policy for asylum seeking, refugee and undocumented children. *BMJ paediatrics open, 3*(1), bmjpo-2018. DOI: 10.1136/bmjpo-2018-000364

Kamaruddin, M. S., Chong, S. K., Mohamad Taha, M., Murad, F. A., & Ma'rof, A. A. (2025). Online pornography consumption: Examining its role in sexual motivation, arousal, gratification, and problematic use. *Journal of Cognitive Sciences and Human Development, 11*(1), 110–126. DOI: 10.33736/jcshd.8829.2025

Kanta, C., & Sharma, A.K. (2025). "Analyzing the Impact of Legal Reforms and Cultural Barriers in Rural Rajasthan." The Academic, Volume 3, Issue 4

Kapur, R. (2005) 'Travel Plans: Border Crossings and the New World Order of Feminism', *Harvard Journal of Gender & Law*, 28(2), pp. 321–354. https://harvardjlg.com/print/volume-28/

Kapur, R. (2012). Gender, alterity and human rights: Freedom in a fishbowl. *Economic and Political Weekly, 47*(39), 67–75.

Kara, S. (2009). *Sex trafficking: Inside the business of modern slavery.* Columbia University Press.

Karlebach, N. J. (2008). Recognizing women's worth: The human rights argument for ending prostitution in India. *Boston College Third World Law Journal, 28*(2), 483–510.

Kaushal, A., & Sharma, R. (2024). Law and gender inequality in India: A socio legal perspective. *International Journal of Law Management and Humanities*, *7*(6), 118–136. https://doij.org/10.10000/IJLMH.118461

Kautilya. (1915). *Arthashastra* (R. Shamasastry, Trans.). Mysore Government Press. (Original work published ca. 3rd century BCE).

Kelly, L. (1988). *Surviving sexual violence*. University of Minnesota Press.

Kempadoo, K. (1999). Slavery or work? Reconceptualizing third world prostitution. *Positions*, *7*(1), 225–237. DOI: 10.1215/10679847-7-1-225

Kempadoo, K. (2015). The modern-day white (wo) man's burden: Trends in anti-trafficking and anti-slavery campaigns. *Journal of Human Trafficking*, *1*(1), 8–20. DOI: 10.1080/23322705.2015.1006120

Kerala High Court. (2024).

Kesküla, E. (2018). Miners and their children: The remaking of the Soviet working class in Kazakhstan. In *Industrial labor on the margins of capitalism: precarity, class, and the neoliberal subject* (pp. 61–84). Berghahn., DOI: 10.2307/j.ctvw04hxm.7

Khan, F. R., Munir, K. A., & Willmott, H. (2007). A dark side of institutional entrepreneurship: Soccer balls, child labour and postcolonial impoverishment. *Organization Studies*, *28*(7), 1055–1077. DOI: 10.1177/0170840607078114

Kim, S. W. (2019). Left-behind children: Teachers' perceptions of family-school relations in rural China. *Compare: A Journal of Comparative Education*, *49*(4), 584–601. DOI: 10.1080/03057925.2018.1438885

King, C., Ferraro, G., Wisner, S. C., Etienne, S., Lee, S., & Bartels, S. A. (2021). "MINUSTAH is doing positive things just as they do negative things": Nuanced perceptions of a UN peacekeeping operation amidst peacekeeper-perpetrated sexual exploitation and abuse in Haiti. *Conflict Security and Development*, *21*(6), 749–779. DOI: 10.1080/14678802.2021.1997453

King, K. C., & Snyder, J. M. (1990). The Woman and the Lyre: Woman Writers in Classical Greece and Rome. *Tulsa Studies in Womens Literature*, *9*(2), 323. DOI: 10.2307/464231

Kingston, S., & Thomas, T. (2019). No model in practice: A "Nordic model" to respond to prostitution? [Link]. *Crime, Law, and Social Change*, *72*(2), 139–157. DOI: 10.1007/s10611-018-9795-6

Kinzer, Q. M. (2025). Policy and platforms: Sex workers' labor experiences under changing online regulation. *Gender, Work and Organization, 32*(6), 2369–2384. https://doi.org/10.1111/gwao.70014DOI: 10.1111/gwao.70014

Kluge, H. H. P. (2025). Addressing technology-facilitated violence against women: The unique position of health care providers. *The Lancet Regional Health. Europe, 56*, 101417. https://doi.org/10.1016/j.lanepe.2025.101417DOI: 10.1016/j.lanepe.2025.101417 PMID: 41624088

Komal Ahuja. (2024, January 3). *The Kerala High Court's interpretation of the Immoral Traffic (Prevention) Act, 1956*. Bhatt & Joshi Associates. https://bhattandjoshiassociates.com/the-kerala-high-courts-interpretation-of-the-immoral-traffic-prevention-act-1956/

Kotiswaran, P. (2018, July 18). *How did we get here? Or a short history of the 2018 trafficking bill.* Economic and Political Weekly. https://www.epw.in/engage/article/how-did-we-get-here-or-short-history

Kotiswaran, P. (2011). *Dangerous sex, invisible labor: Sex work and the law in India*. Princeton University Press.

Kotiswaran, P. (2014). Sex work, labour and human rights. *Economic and Political Weekly, 49*(22), 52–59.

KPMG. (2025). *AI and privacy: A look at biometric tech & data*. KPMG Insights.

Kraus, I. (2018). The German Model, 17 years after the liberalization of prostitution. *Speech by Dr. Ingeborg Kraus at the Italian parliament in Rom, 28*, 2018.

Kumar, A. (2021, October). Sexual violence against Dalit women: An analytical study of intersectionality of gender, caste, and class in India. *Journal of International Women's Studies*. https://www.researchgate.net/publication/366175802_Sexual_Violence_against_Dalit_Women_An_Analytical_Study_of_Intersectionality_of_Gender_Caste_and_Class_in_India

Kumar, K., & Srivastava, R. (2024). Educational and Vocational Aspirations of Child Labourers with Special Reference to Patna. *Global Journal of Enterprise Information System, 16*(4), 57–63. https://www.gjeis.com/index.php/GJEIS/article/view/836

Kutscher, L., Notté, E., & Anderson, K. (2025). Child Labour in the Extraction of Strategic Raw Materials: A Review and Risk Assessment. *Green Health, 1*(2), 14. DOI: 10.3390/greenhealth1020014

L'Hoiry, X., Moretti, A., & Antonopoulos, G. A. (2024). Human trafficking, sexual exploitation and digital technologies. *Trends in Organized Crime*, *27*(1), 1–9. https://doi.org/10.1007/s12117-024-09526-4DOI: 10.1007/s12117-024-09526-4

Lama, P. (2022, July). Sexual and gender-based violence against Dalit women and girls in India. COFEM Secretariat. https://cofemsocialchange.org/sexual-gbv-dalit-women-girls-india/

Lamas, M. (2016). Client Criminalization and the Limits of Feminist Governance. *Social Politics*, *23*(2), 240–265.

Langford, M., & Skilbrei, M. L. (2021). *Branding the Nordic Model of Prostitution Policy*. Routledge. PDF. DOI: 10.4324/9781003156925-11

Law Commission of India. (1975). *Sixty-fourth report on the Suppression of Immoral Traffic in Women and Girls Act, 1956*. Government of India.

Law Commission of India. (1975). *Sixty-fourth report on the Suppression of Immoral Traffic in Women and Girls Act, 1956*. https://lawcommissionofindia.nic.in/51-100/Report64.pdf

Law Commission of India. (1993). *One hundred forty-sixth report on custodial crimes*. Government of India.

Law Commission of India. (2000). *One hundred seventy-second report on review of rape laws*. Government of India.

Law Commission of India. (2008). *Two hundred fifth report on laws on prostitution and allied offences*. Government of India.

Law Commission of India. (2015). *Two hundred fifty-sixth report on elimination of discrimination against women in matters relating to guardianship and custody of minor children*. Government of India.

Laxmi Kant Pandey v. Union of India, (1984) 2 SCC 244 (India).

Leal Filho, W., Lovren, V. O., Will, M., Salvia, A. L., & Frankenberger, F. (2021). Poverty: A central barrier to the implementation of the UN Sustainable Development Goals. *Environmental Science & Policy*, *125*, 96–104. DOI: 10.1016/j.envsci.2021.08.020

LegaleagleWeb. (2022, May 26). *Supreme Court recognises sex work as a profession*. https://legaleagleweb.com

Legalization—Mary Lucille Sullivan, Sheila Jeffreys, 2002. (n.d.). Retrieved October 26, 2025, from https://journals.sagepub.com/doi/10.1177/107780102401101773

Legg, S. (2009). Governing prostitution in colonial Delhi: From cantonment regulations to international hygiene (1864–1939). *Social History, 34*(4), 447–467. DOI: 10.1080/03071020903257018

Lerner, G. (1986). The Origin of Prostitution in Ancient Mesopotamia. *Signs (Chicago, Ill.), 11*(2), 236–254. DOI: 10.1086/494218

Levitt, S. D., & Venkatesh, S. A. (2007). *An empirical analysis of street-level prostitution* (pp. 1-29). University of Chicago working paper–B.

Levy, J. (2015). *Criminalising the Purchase of Sex: Lessons from Sweden*. Routledge.

Liebel, M. (2012). Grassroots Children's Rights. In *Children's Rights from Below: Cross-Cultural Perspectives* (pp. 125-142). London: Palgrave Macmillan UK. DOI: 10.1057/9780230361843_9

Li, Q., Cui, T., Zhao, Y., & Wu, Y. (2023). Facial recognition technology: A comprehensive overview. *Academic Journal of Computing & Information Science, 6*(7), 15–26. DOI: 10.25236/AJCIS.2023.060703

Lok Sabha Secretariat. (n.d.). *Bharatiya Nyaya Sanhita, 2023 (Annex)*. https://sansad.in/getFile/annex/267/AU2227_7QKUFb.pdf

Lorde, A. (1984). *Sister Outsider: Essays and Speeches*. Crossing Press.

Lum, K., & Isaac, W. (2016). To predict and serve? *Significance, 13*(5), 14–19. DOI: 10.1111/j.1740-9713.2016.00960.x

Lux, K. (2009). Work, violence, or both? Framing the sex trade and setting an agenda for justice. In *Advocates' Forum, 2009.*

Macioti, P. G., Power, J., & Bourne, A. (2023) 'The health and well-being of sex workers in decriminalised contexts: A scoping review', *Sexuality Research and Social Policy*. Available at: https://link.springer.com/article/10.1007/s13178-022-00779-8

MacKinnon, C. A. (1989). *Toward a feminist theory of the state*. Harvard University Press.

MacKinnon, C. A. (2007). *Women's lives, men's laws*. Harvard University Press.

MacKinnon, C. A. (2011). Trafficking, prostitution, and inequality. *Harvard Civil Rights-Civil Liberties Law Review, 46*(2), 271–309.

Madhya Pradesh State Legal Services Authority. (2025). Providing legal aid and support for women victims of domestic violence in Madhya Pradesh. Retrieved from https://www.mpslsa.gov.in

Maharashtra Police. (2023). *Data-driven policing: AI and facial recognition in human trafficking detection*. Government of Maharashtra. https://www.mahapolice.gov.in

Makinde, C. O. B., Daib, O. A., Arogundade, T. O., & Adeoye, A. (2021). Forced marriage and child labor: A gender outlook during COVID 19 pandemic. *Journal of Humanities Therapy, 12*(2), 127–150. DOI: 10.33252/jht.2021.12.12.2.127

Maksud, A. K. M., Hossain, K. R., Sayed, S., & Aked, J. (2024). Informal Economy Perspectives on the Prevalence of Worst Forms of Child Labour in Bangladesh's Leather Industry. DOI: 10.19088/CLARISSA.2024.005

Malloch, M. (2015). *Criminalising victims of human trafficking: State responses and punitive practices*. Cambridge University Press.

Martin, A. (2025). Prostitution as Profession: Histories of 'Work-Shy' Labour in a Welfare State, West Germany between 1949 and 1974. *Contemporary European History, 34*(3), 1–18. DOI: 10.1017/S0960777325000013

McConnell, O. (2019) *Assessing the Impact of the Nordic Model of Combating Prostitution*. Florida State University. PDF

McKeown, C. (2021) *Surveillance, In/visibility, Resistance: Searching for Beauty in Scottish Feminist Campaigns to End Men's Violence Against Women*. University of Stirling. PDF

McKinney, K. (2015). Situating corporate framings of child labor: Toward grounded geographies of working children in globalized agriculture. *Geoforum, 59*, 219–227. DOI: 10.1016/j.geoforum.2014.10.018

Megías, J. L., Thon, P., Siebler, F., & Bohner, G. (2025). Attitudes Toward Prostitution in Norway, Spain, and Germany: Association With the Legal Context and Susceptibility to Persuasion. *Scandinavian Journal of Psychology, 66*(2), 253–265. DOI: 10.1111/sjop.13082 PMID: 39528352

Menéndez González, N., & Mobilio, G. (Eds.). (2025). *Next democratic frontiers for facial recognition technology (FRT): The legal, ethical and democratic implications of FRT*. Springer Nature. DOI: 10.1007/978-3-031-89794-8

Menon, N. (2019). *Recovering subversion: Feminist politics beyond the law*. Permanent Black.

Menski, W. (2003). *Hindu law: Beyond tradition and modernity*. Oxford University Press.

Merry, S. E. (1988). Legal Pluralism. *Law & Society Review, 22*(5), 869–896. DOI: 10.2307/3053638

Merry, S. E. (2006). *Human rights & gender violence: Translating international law into local justice*. University of Chicago Press.

Migrant crisis: Child trafficking on rise in EU. (2016, May 19). *BBC News*. https://www.bbc.com/news/world-europe-36338022

Milczarek-Desai, S. (2024). (Hidden) in Plain Sight: Migrant Child Labor and the New Economy of Exploitation. *Arkansas Law Review*, *77*(2), 345. DOI: 10.54119/alr.pmgv5144

Miller, M. E., & Bush, D. (2004). Review of the Federal Child Labor Regulations: Updating hazardous and prohibited occupations. *American Journal of Industrial Medicine*, *45*(2), 218–221. DOI: 10.1002/ajim.10329

Ministry of Electronics and Information Technology. (2024). *MeitY annual report 2024*. Government of India. https://www.meity.gov.in/

Ministry of Electronics and Information Technology. (2024). *MeitY annual report on AI governance*. Government of India. https://www.meity.gov.in/

Ministry of Home Affairs (India). (2022). *Annual report on anti-human trafficking*.

Ministry of Home Affairs, Government of India. (2022). *Crime in India report*. Government of India.

Ministry of Home Affairs, Government of India. (n.d.). *National advisories*. https://www.mha.gov.in/en/commoncontent/advisories-0 Ministry

Ministry of Home Affairs. (2024). *Guidelines on Women's Safety and Gender-Sensitive Policing*. Government of India.

Ministry of Women and Child Development, Government of India. (2019). *RTI and government affidavits*. Government of India.

Ministry of Women and Child Development. (2023). *Beti Bachao, Beti Padhao Scheme: Annual report 2022–23*. Government of India.

Moayad, S. J., Kamal, S. H. M., Sajjadi, H., Vameghi, M., Harouni, G. G., & Alamdari, S. M. (2021). Child labor in Tehran, Iran: Abuses experienced in work environments. *Child Abuse & Neglect*, *117*, 105054. DOI: 10.1016/j.chiabu.2021.105054

Mohammadi, F., Masoumi, S. Z., Oshvandi, K., Borzou, S. R., Cheraghi, F., & Karkhanei, B. (2024). Dignity: The cornerstone of psychological health among victims of child labor, a qualitative study. *BMC Research Notes*, *17*(1), 259. DOI: 10.1186/s13104-024-06911-8

Monash University. (2025). *Facial recognition technology: Definition and applications*. Retrieved February 7, 2026, from https://www.monash.edu

Mookerji, N. (2011). "Women Empowerment and Panchayati Raj in Bundelkhand. Women Empowerment and Panchayati Raj in Bundelkhand | PDF | Empowerment | Society

Moore, L., Chersich, M. F., Steen, R., Reza-Paul, S., Dhana, A., Vuylsteke, B., Lafort, Y., & Scorgie, F. (2014). Community empowerment and involvement of female sex workers in targeted sexual and reproductive health interventions in Africa: A systematic review. *Globalization and Health, 10*(1), 47. DOI: 10.1186/1744-8603-10-47 PMID: 24916108

Morgan, J. (2016). Participation, empowerment and capacity building: Exploring young people's perspectives on the services provided to them by a grassroots NGO in sub-Saharan Africa. *Children and Youth Services Review, 65*, 175–182. DOI: 10.1016/j.childyouth.2016.04.012

Mowbray, A., Chung, P., & Greenleaf, G. (2020). Utilising AI in the legal assistance sector—Testing a role for legal information institutes. *Computer Law & Security Review, 38*, 105407. https://doi.org/10.1016/j.clsr.2020.105407DOI: 10.1016/j.clsr.2020.105407

Mukherjee, S. (2025). Algorithmic bias and discrimination: Legal accountability of AI systems. *International Journal of IRJMPS, 13*(4), 232659. Advance online publication. DOI: 10.37082/IJIRMPS.v13.i4.232659

Nagpur Police. (2025). Operation Shakti initiative and Garuda Drishti overview; Times of India. (2025, August 27). Cops unleash AI arsenal to crush human trafficking; Nagpurnews.live (2023, July 30)

Nair, P. M. (n.d.). *Ready reckoner on provisions of laws for tackling human trafficking*. Bureau of Police Research and Development, Ministry of Home Affairs, Government of India. https://bprd.nic.in/uploads/pdf/1745497790_31ae803126827f574b39.pdf

Najar, J. L. (2021). *Human trafficking in India: how the colonial legacy of the anti-human trafficking regime undermines migrant and worker agency. London School of Economics (LSE).* Human Rights.

Najar, J. L. (2023, January). Brahmanical patriarchy and the politics of anti-trafficking and prostitution governance: From colonial to contemporary India. *Third World Quarterly, 44*(4), 667–685. Advance online publication. DOI: 10.1080/01436597.2022.2099824

Najar, K. (2023). Nordic Model in Practice: Criminalisation, Control, and the Politics of Rescue. *European Journal of Criminology*, *20*(1), 45–63.

National AIDS Control Organization. (2021). *India HIV estimations 2020–21*. Ministry of Health and Family Welfare, Government of India.

National Crime Records Bureau. (2021). *Automated facial recognition system: Project tender documents*. Government of India.

National Crime Records Bureau. (2021). *Automated facial recognition system: Tender documents and project architecture*. Government of India.

National Crime Records Bureau. (2022). *AFRS Evaluation Report*. Crime in India 2022

National Crime Records Bureau. (2023). *Crime in India 2023 statistics*. Ministry of Home Affairs, Government of India.

National Legal Services Authority. (2023). *Legal Services to Women: Outreach and Awareness Initiatives*. NALSA.

National Rural Livelihood Mission. (2023). *Empowering rural women through livelihoods: Annual progress report 2022–23*. Government of India.

Nayar, U. S., Stangl, A. L., De Zalduondo, B., & Brady, L. M. (2014). Reducing stigma and discrimination to improve child health and survival in low-and middle-income countries: promising approaches and implications for future research. *Journal of health communication, 19*(sup1), 142-163. DOI: 10.1080/10810730.2014.930213

Nde Fon, N., & Balogh, L. (2025). *The Impact of Decriminalisation on Sex Work: A Global Meta-synthesis of Health, Safety, and Societal Perceptions from the Perspective of Sex Workers*. https://www.diva-portal.org/smash/record.jsf?pid=diva2:1984543

Neethi, P., & Kamath, A. (2025). Turbulent transformations and urban undesirables: Revanchist urban transition and street-based sex work in Bangalore. In *Mapping Legalities* (pp. 141–158). Routledge., https://www.taylorfrancis.com/chapters/edit/10.4324/9781003384816-9/turbulent-transformations-urban-undesirables-neethi-anant-kamath

New Humanitarian & Thomson Reuters Foundation. (2020, September 29). More than 50 women accuse aid workers of sexual exploitation during Ebola crisis in Congo. https://longreads.trust.org/item/congo-ebola-aid-workers-accused-demanding-sex-for-jobs

Ngutuku, E. (2025). *Children's Lived Experience of Poverty and Vulnerability in Kenya: Going Beyond Multi-dimensionality*. Taylor & Francis., DOI: 10.4324/9781003356769

Nield, L. (2024) 'UK Prostitution Legislation and the Implementation of the Nordic Model', *Student Law Journal*, 3, pp. 1–25. https://doi.org/DOI: 10.24377/LJMU.SLJ.vol3article2205

Now, E. (2020). Justice denied: Sexual violence & intersectional discrimination – Barriers to accessing justice for Dalit women and girls in Haryana, India. Retrieved from https://equalitynow.org/news/press-releases/india_caste_system_preventing_justice_nov2020/

NSWP. (2015). *Community Guide*. The Real Impact of the Swedish Model on Sex Workers.

NSWP. (2024). *Decriminalisation vs. legalization: Understanding Key Differences in Sex Work Legislation.*

O'Connor, M., & Healy, G. Coalition Against Trafficking in Women (CATW), & European Women's Lobby (EWL). (2006). *The Links between Prostitution and Sex Trafficking: A Briefing Handbook*. https://catwinternational.org/wp-content/uploads/2019/09/The-Links-between-Prostitution-and-Sex-Trafficking-A-Briefing-Handbook.pdf

Obokata, T. (2024). Report of the Special Rapporteur on contemporary forms of slavery, including its causes and consequences. United Nations General Assembly. https://docs.un.org/en/A/HRC/57/46/Add.1

Obokata, T. (2006). *Trafficking of human beings from a human rights perspective: Towards a holistic approach*. Martinus Nijhoff Publishers. DOI: 10.1163/ej.9789004154056.i-247

Office for the Coordination of Humanitarian Affairs (OCHA). (2025, March 29). *Gaza humanitarian response update: 16–29 March 2025*. https://www.ochaopt.org/content/gaza-humanitarian-response-update-16-29-march-2025

Office of the High Commissioner for Human Rights (OHCHR). (2017). *In search of dignity: Report on the human rights of migrants at Europe's borders*. https://www.ohchr.org/sites/default/files/Documents/Publications/FS36_en.pdf

Office of the High Commissioner for Human Rights. (2011). Guiding principles on business and human rights: Implementing the United Nations "Protect, Respect and Remedy" framework. United Nations., HR/PUB/11/04.

Office of the High Commissioner for Human Rights. (2012/2021). *The corporate responsibility to respect human rights: An interpretive guide.* United Nations. New Zealand Parliament. (2003). *Prostitution Reform Act 2003,* Public Act 2003 No 28.

Office of the United Nations High Commissioner for Human Rights. (2023). *Recommended principles and guidelines on human rights and human trafficking: 20 years on.* https://www.ohchr.org

Online, E. T. (2024, September 2). *Popularity of face authentication* [Slideshow]. *The Economic Times.* https://economictimes.indiatimes.com/wealth/save/what-is-aadhaar-face-authentication-these-government-social-protection-programs-use-face-authentication/popularity-of-face-authentication/slideshow/112988712.cms

Online, M. J. I. L. (2024, October 27). *The balancing act: How the European Union's Artificial Intelligence Act frames biometric identification for trafficking.* https://www.mjilonline.org/the-balancing-act-how-the-european-unions-artificial-intelligence-act-properly-frames-the-dangers-and-benefits-of-using-biometric-identification-to-combat-human-trafficking/

Oram, S., Stöckl, H., Busza, J., Howard, L. M., & Zimmerman, C. (2012). Prevalence and risk of violence and the health impact of human trafficking: Systematic review. *PLoS Medicine, 9*(5), e1001224. DOI: 10.1371/journal.pmed.1001224 PMID: 22666182

Organization for Security and Co-operation in Europe. (2012). *Report by OSCE Special Representative and Co-ordinator for Combating Trafficking in Human Beings, following her visit to the UK, 7–10 March 2011.* OSCE.

Organization for Security and Co-operation in Europe. (2014). *Ending exploitation.* OSCE.

Osthaus, C. R. (2004). The Work Ethic of the Plain Folk: Labor and Religion in the Old South. In *The Best American History Essays 2006* (pp. 89-122). New York: Palgrave Macmillan US. DOI: 10.1007/978-1-137-06580-3_5

Palermo Protocol. (2000). *Protocol to Prevent, Suppress and Punish Trafficking in Persons, Especially Women and Children, supplementing the United Nations Convention against Transnational Organized Crime,* Nov. 15, 2000, 2237 U.N.T.S. 319.

Panday, P., Khan, R., & Singh, A. K. (2018). Consequences of violence against women on their health and well-being: An overview. *Journal of Medical Science and Clinical Research, 6*(10), 570–577.

Pankaj, J. (2026, January 21). Datanomics: Women constitute 30% of trafficking arrests in India. www.business-standard.com. https://www.business-standard.com/india-news/datanomics-women-constitute-30-of-trafficking-arrests-in-india-126012100831

Panoptic.in. (2020, October 24). *Delhi Police case study.* https://panoptic.in/case-study/delhi-police

Panoptic.in. (2020, October 24). *Delhi Police case-study.* https://panoptic.in/case-study/delhi-police

Parashar, A. (1992). *Women and Family Law Reform in India: Uniform Civil code and Gender Equality.* Sage Publications.

Parkman, S., & Stratton, E. C. (2025). A qualitative phenomenological study of the lived experiences of female sex workers in a Bangladesh brothel. *Scandinavian Journal of Caring Sciences, 39*(1), e13316. DOI: 10.1111/scs.13316 PMID: 39775800

Parliament of India. (1956). THE IMMORAL TRAFFIC (PREVENTION) ACT, 1956. In *THE IMMORAL TRAFFIC (PREVENTION) ACT, 1956.* https://www.indiacode.nic.in/bitstream/123456789/15378/1/the_immoral_traffic_%28prevention%29_act%2C_1956.pdf

Parliament. (2023). THE BHARATIYA NYAYA SANHITA, 2023. In *THE BHARATIYA NYAYA SANHITA.* https://www.mha.gov.in/sites/default/files/250883_english_01042024.pdf

Parson, N. (2010). "I am not [just] a rabbit who has a bunch of children!": Agency in the midst of suffering at the intersections of global inequalities, gendered violence, and migration. *Violence Against Women, 16*(8), 881–901. DOI: 10.1177/1077801210376224

Passport Act. (1967).

Pathak, V. (2015). FRA implementation challenges for tribal women. Tribal Affairs Ministry reports; Krishnan, S. (2019). Forest rights and gender justice in tribal India. Open access tribal.nic.in repository.

Patnaik, A. (2023). Sex Work, Knowledge, and the Carceral State: Epistemic Violence in Policy Making. *Feminist Review.*

Peng, I. (2009). Of course they claim they were coerced: On feminism, 'choice,' and the sex industry. *Bridgewater Review*, 28(2), 8–13. https://vc.bridgew.edu/br_rev/vol28/iss2/6/

Persson, H. (2022) 'Prostitution and trafficking: Does the Nordic Prostitution Model decrease the amount of sex trafficking?', *Working Paper Series, Uppsala University*. PDF

Pirzada, G., Muhammad, Y., & Anis, F. (2020). Perspectives of working children on their education and life goals: A case study. *Research Journal of Social Sciences and Economics Review*, *1*(4), 122–132. DOI: 10.36902/rjsser-vol1-iss4-2020(122-132)

Platt, L., Grenfell, P., Meiksin, R., Elmes, J., Sherman, S. G., Sanders, T., Mwangi, P., & Crago, A.-L. (2018). Associations between sex work laws and sex workers' health: A systematic review and meta-analysis of quantitative and qualitative studies. *PLoS Medicine*, *15*(12), e1002680. https://doi.org/10.1371/journal.pmed.1002680DOI: 10.1371/journal.pmed.1002680 PMID: 30532209

Polizzi, G., D'Arcy, J., Harris, R., Yates, S., Cullen, C., & Andrew, B. (2024). Survivors of modern slavery and their digital inclusion: A UK qualitative study from the perspective of survivors and organizations that support them. *Journal of Human Trafficking*, •••, 1–18. https://doi.org/10.1080/23322705.2024.2393969DOI: 10.1080/23322705.2024.2393969

Post, C., Brouwer, J. G., & Vols, M. (2019). Regulation of Prostitution in the Netherlands: Liberal Dream or Growing Repression? *European Journal on Criminal Policy and Research*, *25*(2), 99–118. DOI: 10.1007/s10610-018-9371-8

Pradhan, J., Ray, S., & Nielsen, M. O. (2024). Social protection schemes for mother and children in Odisha: A matched-gap analysis. *SN Social Sciences*, *4*(10), 185. DOI: 10.1007/s43545-024-00984-9

Pragya Prasun & Ors. v. Union of India, 2025 INSC 599(India)

Prajan Welfare Association v. State of Tamil Nadu, 1996 (Madras High Court, India).

Prajwala v. Union of India, (2015) 8 SCC 380 (India).

Press Information Bureau. (2025). *Government initiatives to counter rising cyber financial frauds in India*.

Preston, S. (2024) *Perspectives on Reform: A Cross-Border Analysis of Sex Work Policy in New Zealand*. MA thesis. University of Regina. Available at: https://ourspace.uregina.ca/bitstreams/e5dbfa43-ce1d-44ec-9a80-84ba93cfddef/download

Prison Reform Trust. (2012). *No way out: A briefing paper on foreign national women in prison in England and Wales*. Prison Reform Trust.

Privacy International. (2025, September 30). *Legal frameworks for facial recognition usage*. https://privacyinternational.org/

Prosecutor v. Kunarac, Kovač & Vuković, Case No. IT-96-23 & IT-96-23/1-A, Judgment (Int'l Crim. Trib. for the Former Yugoslavia Feb. 22, 2001) https://www.icty.org/x/cases/kunarac/acj ug/en/

Prostitute Definition by Webster's at Smart Define dictionary. (n.d.). Retrieved October 25, 2025, from https://www.smartdefine.org/prostitute/definitions/2050132

Prostitution Law Review Committee. (2008). *Report of the Prostitution Law Review Committee on the operation of the Prostitution Reform Act 2003* (Vol. 121). New Zealand Ministry of Justice.

Prostitution Law Review Committee. (2008). *Report of the prostitution law review committee on the operation of the Prostitution Reform Act 2003*. Government of New Zealand.

Public Prosecution Service for Northern Ireland. (2013). *Policy for prosecuting cases of human trafficking. PPS. • RACE in Europe. (2013). Victim or criminal? Trafficking for forced criminal exploitation in Europe – UK chapter*. ECPAT UK.

Pulitzer Center & The Wire. (2025, July 1). As AI took over policing in Delhi, who bore the brunt? https://pulitzercenter.org/stories/ai-took-over-policing-delhi-who-bore-brunt

R v SK (2011). EWCA Crim 1691.

R v. L & Others, (2017). EWCA Crim 2128 (UK Ct App).

R v. Mateta, (2013). EWCA Crim 1372 (UK Ct App).

R v. O, (2008). EWCA Crim 2835 (UK Ct App).

Radfar, A., Asgharzadeh, S. A. A., Quesada, F., & Filip, I. (2018). Challenges and perspectives of child labor. *Industrial Psychiatry Journal*, *27*(1), 17–20. DOI: 10.4103/ipj.ipj_105_14

Rafferty, Y. (2013). International dimensions of discrimination and violence against girls: A human rights perspective. *Journal of International Women's Studies*, *14*(1), 1–23.

Ragavender, D. (2024). *Female migration and migrant women harassment in INDIA*. Chyren Publication.

Rai, S. (2024). Interested Gazes and Invisible Audiences: Judicial Narratives on Sex Work. *Indian Journal of Gender Studies*, *31*(2), 159–176. DOI: 10.1177/09715215241235346

Ramachandran, V. (2023). From 'house of horrors' to 'sensitive' governance: Sex workers' shelter detention in India. *Contemporary South Asia, 32*(2), 223–241. DOI: 10.1080/09584935.2023.2268559

Ramberg, M. S. (2021). *A Comparative Study of Norway and Scotland's Effort to Address and Counter the Threat of Organised Crime in a Globalised World.* PDF.

Ramchandran, A. (2025). A tale of two rescues. In *Cambridge University Press eBooks* (pp. 41–69). DOI: 10.1017/9781009490313.004

Ramirez, T. (2023). *Sex worker criminalization in the United States: A landscape analysis of the criminalization health effects on the sex worker population in the United States.* AIDS United.

Rana, U. (2020). Cultural hegemony and victimisation of Bedia women in Central India (U. Rana, Trans.). *Space and Culture, India, 8*(2), 96–105. DOI: 10.20896/saci.vi0.798

Rana, U., Sharma, D., & Ghosh, D. (2020). Prostitution in northern Central India: An ethnographical study of Bedia community. *International Journal of Anthropology and Ethnology, 4*(2), 2. Advance online publication. DOI: 10.1186/s41257-020-0027-5

Rani, M. (2024). Impacts and ethics of using artificial intelligence (AI) by the police force in India. *Emerald Insight*, 27(2), 182–202. https://www.emerald.com/pap/article/27/2/182/1212999/Impacts-and-ethics-of-using-Artificial

Rantsev v. Cyprus and Russia, App. No. 25965/04, Judgment (Eur. Ct. H.R. July 1, 2010). https://hudoc.echr.coe.int/eng#%22itemid%22:[%22001-96549%22]

Rao, N. S. (2017). Interface of tribal self-governance institutions and statutory panchayats: A study in the Scheduled Areas of Andhra Pradesh. National Institute of Rural Development & Panchayati Raj. http://nirdpr.org.in/nird_docs/srsc/srsc230217-19.pdf

Rathod, G. R., & Koli, V. L. (2015). Child labour and school dropout. *Scholarly Research Journal for Interdisciplinary Studies, 3*(16), 3199–3207.

Rathor, M. (2023). The Regulation and Legalisation of Prostitution in India with Emphasis on Socio-Legal Effects. *Issue 1 Indian JL & Legal Rsch., 5*, 1.

Ray, R. (2014). Education and child labor: a global perspective. In *The World of Child Labor* (pp. 118–126). Routledge.

Razack, S. H. (2004). Imperilled Muslim women, dangerous Muslim men and civilised Europeans: Legal and social responses to forced marriages. *Feminist Legal Studies, 12*(2), 129–174. DOI: 10.1023/B:FEST.0000043305.66172.92

Reading, R., Bissell, S., Goldhagen, J., Harwin, J., Masson, J., Moynihan, S., Parton, N., Pais, M. S., Thoburn, J., & Webb, E. (2009). Promotion of children's rights and prevention of child maltreatment. *Lancet, 373*(9660), 332–343. DOI: 10.1016/S0140-6736(08)61709-2

Reilly, J., Khan, A., & Mbatha, T. (2021). Criminalising Clients, Endangering Workers: An Evaluation of End-Demand Legislation. *Justice Quarterly, 38*(5), 690–712.

Reuters. (2024, December 2). Greece failed to identify sex trafficking victims in migrant centre, UN expert alleges. https://www.reuters.com/world/europe/greece-failed-identify-sex-trafficking-victims-migrant-centre-un-expert-alleges-2024-12-02/

Reuters. (n.d.). *Reports on trafficking and commercial sexual exploitation.* https://www.reuters.com

Rhodes, T., Wagner, K., Strathdee, S. A., Shannon, K., Davidson, P., & Bourgois, P. (2011). Structural violence and structural vulnerability within the risk environment: theoretical and methodological perspectives for a social epidemiology of HIV risk among injection drug users and sex workers. In *Rethinking social epidemiology: Towards a science of change* (pp. 205–230). Springer Netherlands.

Řimnáčová, Z., & Kajanová, A. (2019). Stress and the working poor. *Human Affairs, 29*(1), 87–94. DOI: 10.1515/humaff-2019-0008

Rioux, S., LeBaron, G., & Verovšek, P. J. (2020). Capitalism and unfree labor: A review of Marxist perspectives on modern slavery. *Review of International Political Economy, 27*(3), 709–731. DOI: 10.1080/09692290.2019.1650094

Roberts, J. R., Karr, C. J., Paulson, J. A., Brock-Utne, A. C., Brumberg, H. L., Campbell, C. C., Lanphear, B. P., Osterhoudt, K. C., Sandel, M. T., Trasande, L., & Wright, R. O. (2012). Pesticide exposure in children. *Pediatrics, 130*(6), e1765–e1788. DOI: 10.1542/peds.2012-2758

Roberts, J. W. (2015). Comparative Approaches to Myanmar's Child Labor Epidemic: The Role of Compulsory Education. *Emory Int'l L. Rev., 30*, 661.

Roche, M. M. (2017). *Dis*. Placing Empire., DOI: 10.4324/9781315264189

Roeloffs, M. (2023, August 9). DHS Says it identified 311 new child sexual exploitation victims after Forbes reports AI facial-recognition push. *Forbes*. https://www.forbes.com/sites/maryroeloffs/2023/08/09/dhs-says-it-identified-311-new-child-sexual-exploitation-victims-after-forbes-reports-ai-facial-recognition-push/

Rowland, A. (2025) *Sex Worker Activism and the Regulatory Liminality of Rights.* University of California. PDF

Rowland, A. (2025). *Sex Workers, Work! Anticarceral Approaches to Decriminalisation*. Routledge. DOI: 10.4324/9781003401162-38

Roy, P. K. R. K. (2019). *The role of state in Prostitution: An anthropological exploration in a frontier city of Bangladesh. 2*(9), 14–28. DOI: 10.5281/ZENODO.3386549

Ryan, A. (2020) 'Sex Work, Justice and Decriminalisation: Beyond a Politics of Recognition in Promoting a Social Justice Response to Women at the Margins', in *Women, Peace and Welfare*. Emerald Publishing. PDF DOI: 10.1108/978-1-83982-882-920200015

S. Khushboo v. Kanniammal, (2010) 5 SCC 600 (India).

S.S. Rana & Co. (2025, April 27). *Facial recognition technology - A growing challenge for privacy.* https://ssrana.in/articles/facial-recognition-technology-a-growing-challenge-for-privacy/

Sabates-Wheeler, R., & Sumberg, J. (2022). Breaking out of the policy enclave approach to child labour in sub-Saharan African agriculture. *Global Social Policy, 22*(1), 46–66. DOI: 10.1177/1468018121991813

Sadhan Haldar v. State of NCT of Delhi, (2018) Delhi HC (India).

Saeed, S., & Qureshi, M. B. (2024). Health Issues Faced by Home Based Women Bangle Workers of Hyderabad Sindh, Pakistan. *Research Mosaic, 4*(1), 37–52. DOI: 10.64428/rm/v4.i1.5

Safdar, R., & Kataria, J. R. (2024). Exploring the Causes of Child Labor and its Implications on their Mental Well-Being. *Pakistan Social Sciences Review, 8*(2), 707–721. DOI: 10.35484/pssr.2024(8-II-S)62

Sales, R. (2002). The deserving and the undeserving? Refugees, asylum seekers and welfare in Britain. *Critical Social Policy, 22*(3), 456–478. DOI: 10.1177/026101830202200305

Samaddar, R. (1999). The marginal nation: Transborder migration from Bangladesh to West Bengal. *Sage (Atlanta, Ga.).*

Sanger, W. W. (2022). *The history of prostitution: Its extent, causes, and effects throughout the world.* DigiCat. https://books.google.com/books?hl=en&lr=&id=9AxzEAAAQBAJ&oi=fnd&pg=PT10&dq=history+of+prostitution+&ots=ejVinmiQqu&sig=hEb4PTZZNLdJMA8LsFfCLDkBAIk

Sangram. (2012). *Trafficking, sex work and law reform in India.* Sangram Policy Report.

Santos, B. de S. (2007). *Cognitive Justice in a Global World: Prudent Knowledges for a Decent Life*. Lexington Books. DOI: 10.5771/9780739153130

Sarin, M. (2020). Customary Practices and Women's Property Rights in India: A Regional Perspective. *Indiana Law Review*, *4*(2), 145–168. DOI: 10.1080/24730580.2020.1715749

Sasmal, J., & Guillen, J. (2015). Poverty, educational failure and the child-labour trap: The Indian experience. *Global Business Review*, *16*(2), 270–280. DOI: 10.1177/0972150914564419

Satish, A. H., Rao, K. A., Bhushan, B., Chouhan, H., & Shah, J. H, L. J., Mohapatra, M., & G.D, N. (2021). *Gender, human rights and law* (S. E. Thomas, Ed.; Vol. 9). Centre for Women and the Law, National Law School of India University. https://www.nls.ac.in/wp-content/uploads/2021/10/GHRL-Vol-9-11-10-2021.pdf

SCOT-PEP. (2020) *Response to the Equally Safe Consultation*. Available at: https://www.scot-pep.org.uk/resources/response-to-the-equally-safe-consultation/ (Accessed: 18 August 2025).

Scott, G. R. (2014). *A history of prostitution: From antiquity to the present day*. Routledge. https://www.taylorfrancis.com/books/mono/10.4324/9781315828091/history-prostitution-george-ryley-scott

Scottish Government. (2018). *Equally Safe: Scotland's Strategy to Prevent and Eradicate Violence Against Women and Girls*. Available at: https://www.gov.scot/publications/equally-safe/ (Accessed: 18 August 2025).

Scott, N. B., & Pocock, N. S. (2021). The health impacts of hazardous chemical exposures among child labourers in low-and middle-income countries. *International Journal of Environmental Research and Public Health*, *18*(10), 5496. DOI: 10.3390/ijerph18105496

Scoular, J. (2004). The 'subject' of prostitution: Interpreting the discursive, symbolic and material position of sex/work in feminist theory. *Feminist Theory*, *5*(3), 343–355. DOI: 10.1177/1464700104046983

Scoular, J. (2010). What's Law Got To Do With it? How and Why Law Matters in the Regulation of Sex Work. *Journal of Law and Society*, *37*(1), 12–39. DOI: 10.1111/j.1467-6478.2010.00493.x

Scoular, J. (2015). *The Subject of Prostitution: Sex Work, Law and Social Theory*. Routledge. DOI: 10.4324/9781315778433

Secretary of State for the Home Department. (2014). *The government response to the report from the Joint Committee on the Draft Modern Slavery Bill*. Home Office.

Security Industry Association. (2020, June 25). *Security Industry Association strongly opposes the Facial Recognition and Biometric Technology Moratorium Act*. https://www.securityindustry.org/2020/06/26/security-industry-association-strongly-opposes-the-facial-recognition-and-biometric-technology-moratorium-act-citing-immeasurable-benefits-of-the-proven-technology/

Selkova, A. (2022). Would online legal services guarantee the availability of justice and legal aid? *SHS Web of Conferences, 134*, 00035. https://doi.org/10.1051/shsconf/202213400035

Sequeira, M. (2022) *Decriminalisation of Sex Work in England and Wales: A Step Towards Normalising Sex Work*. Available at: https://www.researchgate.net/publication/363383341_Decriminalisation_of_sex_work_in_England_and_Wales_A_step_towards_normalising_sex_work

Serughetti, G. (2013). Prostitution: A difficult choice. Between consent, coercion and recognition. *Revista de Bioetica y Derecho*, (29), 37–47. https://e-revistas.uc3m.es/index.php/EUNOM/article/view/1913

Sex Worker as the Juridical Subject: Interrogating the Violence of Legal Interpretation. (n.d.). *Journal of Indian Law and Society*.

Shachar, A. (2001). *Multicultural jurisdictions: Cultural differences and women's rights*. Cambridge University Press. DOI: 10.1017/CBO9780511490330

Shah, S. P. (2007). Distinguishing poverty and trafficking: Lessons from field research in Mumbai. *Georgetown Journal on Poverty Law & Policy, 14*(3), 441–454.

Shamir, H. (2012). A labor paradigm for human trafficking. *UCLA Law Review. University of California, Los Angeles. School of Law, 60*(1), 76–136. https://papers.ssrn.com/sol3/papers.cfm?abstract_id=2047432

Shankar, S., & Ganesan, P. (2021). *The devadasis, dance community of South India: A legal and social outlook. International Journal on Minority and Group Rights*. https://www.researchgate.net/publication/354164302_The_Devadasis_Dance_Community_of_South_India_A_Legal_and_Social_Outlook

Shannon, K., Strathdee, S. A., Goldenberg, S. M., Duff, P., Mwangi, P., Rusakova, M., Reza-Paul, S., Lau, J., Deering, K., Pickles, M. R., & Boily, M. C. (2015). Global epidemiology of HIV among female sex workers: Influence of structural determinants. *Lancet, 385*(9962), 55–71. DOI: 10.1016/S0140-6736(14)60931-4 PMID: 25059947

Sharma, K. (2018). PESA and women's participation gaps. Vishnu IAS Academy analysis.

Sharma, S. (2009). Trends, Causes and Consequences of Child Labour in India. *The Indian Journal of Public Administration, 55*(2), 220–236. DOI: 10.1177/0019556120090205

Shayara Bano v. Union of India, (2017) 9 SCC 1 (SC)

Shendell, D. G., Noomnual, S., Chishti, S., Sorensen Allacci, M., & Madrigano, J. (2016). Exposures resulting in safety and health concerns for child laborers in less developed countries. *Journal of Environmental and Public Health, 2016*(1), 3985498. DOI: 10.1155/2016/3985498

Shore, C., Però, D., & Wright, S. (2011). Policy worlds: Anthropology and the analysis of contemporary power.

Shousha, N. M., & Taha, D. M. (2025). Sacred Bonds, Silent Pain: Understanding Women's Perceptions and Experiences of Marital Rape in Egypt. *Journal of Family Violence*. Advance online publication. DOI: 10.1007/s10896-025-00902-4

Shrage, L. (2004). Feminist perspectives on sex markets.

Shukla, S., & Bhat, A. (2022). Legal awareness and utilization of empowerment services among rural women: A study from Dharwad district. *International Journal of Food and Agricultural Nutrition Sciences, 5*(2), 45–55. https://ijfans.org/uploads/paper/5646f9187d3fba14c24e15834e01dcf5.pdf

Sidhu Kundal, N. (2023). Land rights of tribal women in India. *International Journal for Multidisciplinary Research, 5*(6), 1–15. https://www.ijfmr.com/papers/2023/6/9351.pdf

Singh, R. (2025). Customary law vs state law in tribal jurisprudence – Harmony or conflict. International Journal of Law and Legal Research. https://www.ijllr.com/post/customary-law-vs-state-law-in-tribal-jurisprudence-harmony-or-conflict

Singh, D. (2024). Challenges women face in accessing justice in India. *International Journal of Research Publication and Reviews, 5*(11), 6032–6037.

Singh, M., & Upadhyay, S. N. (2024). Digitization Of Legal Aid Services And Criminal Justice To The Detainees In India. *Law and World, 10*(1), 37–49. https://doi.org/10.36475/10.1.4DOI: 10.36475/10.1.4

Smith, E.J. (2015) *"Violence Can Mean a Lot of Things, Can't It?" An Exploration of Responses to Harm Associated with Indoor Sex Work in Scotland*. University of Stirling. PDF

Smith, J. (2024). Bending Reality to Match Ideology: A Critique of "Criminalising the Sex Buyer". *Review of Studies in State Policy, 51*(2), 233–251. DOI: 10.1093/restud/rdx065

Smyth, S. M. (2019). *Biometrics, surveillance and the law: Societies of restricted access, discipline and control.* Routledge. DOI: 10.4324/9780429022326

Sohel, M. S., Alam, S., Rahman, M. M., Obaidullah, M., Anam, A. S. M. T., Hossain, B., & Hossain, M. A. (2024). Exploring the multifaceted vulnerabilities of female street child labor in the capital city of Bangladesh. *Heliyon, 10*(18), e37302. https://www.cell.com/heliyon/fulltext/S2405-8440(24)13333-6. DOI: 10.1016/j.heliyon.2024.e37302

Spivak, G. C. (1988). Can the Subaltern Speak? In Nelson, C., & Grossberg, L. (Eds.), *Marxism and the Interpretation of Culture* (pp. 271–313). Macmillan.

Spyra, J. Z. (2025). Jewish Prostitution in the Archives: Reflections on Stigma, Access, and Anonymization. *Journal of Jewish Identities, 18*(2), 307–332. DOI: 10.1353/jji.2025.a966367

Srivastava, R. N. (2019). Children at work, child labor and modern slavery in India: An overview. *Indian Pediatrics, 56*(8), 633–638. DOI: 10.1007/s13312-019-1584-5

Stahlberg, S. G. (2022). From prison gangs to transnational mafia: The expansion of organized crime in Brazil. *Trends in Organized Crime, 25*(4), 443–465. DOI: 10.1007/s12117-022-09453-2

State of Maharashtra v. Madhukar Narayan Mardikar, (1991) 1 SCC 57 (India).

Steinert, J. I., Valli, E., Chan, J. K., & Brahmbhatt, H. (2023). Evidence from focus group discussions on economic abuse against women in India. *BMJ Global Health, 8*(10), e012576. https://gh.bmj.com/content/8/10/e012576. DOI: 10.1136/bmjgh-2023-012576 PMID: 37798047

Stella, F., Gawlewicz, A. and Flynn, M. (2016) *Intimate Migrations: Lesbian, Gay, Bisexual and Transgender Migrants in Scotland.* University of Glasgow. PDF

Stella, F., & Binnie, J. (2025). Homing Desires: Transnational Queer Migrants Negotiating Homes and Homelands in Scotland. *Sociological Review, 73*(1), 81–103. DOI: 10.1177/00380261241244654

Stephenson, S., Ramjit, L., Ristenpart, T., & Dell, N. (2025). Digital technologies and human trafficking: Combating coercive control and navigating digital autonomy. *Proceedings of the 2025 CHI Conference on Human Factors in Computing Systems*, 1–21. https://doi.org/10.1145/3706598.3713544 DOI: 10.1145/3706598.3713544

Stopping people trafficking. (n.d.). Immigration New Zealand. https://www.immigration.govt.nz/about-us/our-strategies-and-programmes/stopping-fraud-and-exploitation/stopping-people-trafficking/

Stumpf, J. (2010). The justice of crimmigration law and the security of home. In Hudson, B., & Ugelvik, S. (Eds.), *Justice and security in the 21st century* (pp. 43–63). Routledge.

Supreme Court of India. (1993). *Unni Krishnan, J.P. v. State of Andhra Pradesh*, AIR 1993 SC 2178.

Supreme Court of India. (1997). *D.K. Basu v. State of West Bengal*, (1997) 1 SCC 416.

Supreme Court of India. (2006). Lata Singh v. State of Uttar Pradesh, (2006) 5 SCC 475.

Supreme Court of India. (2022). *B.N. Srikrishna Committee report*. https://www.sci.gov.in/

SWARM. (2021). *Sex Work During COVID-19: Impacts and Responses*. Sex Worker Advocacy and Resistance Movement. Available at: https://www.swarmcollective.org

Tandon, N., Basu, P., Krishnan, O., & RV, B. (2022). *Emerging work trends in Urban India: COVID-19 and beyond*. Routledge India.

Tandon, B., & Nayak, P. (2025). Reconsidering criminalisation of prostitution: A comparative critical study of the models in vogue in India, Sweden and the Netherlands. *International Journal of Public Law and Policy*, *11*(2), 210–231. DOI: 10.1504/IJPLAP.2025.145307

Tarlow, P. E., & Spencer, A. (2025). From Slavery to Prostitution: Entrance to Human and Sex Trafficking. In *Human Trafficking and the Tourism Industry* (pp. 83–111). Emerald Publishing Limited. https://www.emerald.com/insight/content/doi/10.1108/978-1-83797-929-520251004/full/html

Taylor, C. (2025). Women in the ancient Greek world: History and historiography. *The Journal of Hellenic Studies*, *145*, 1–13. DOI: 10.1017/S0075426925100414

TechGDPR. (2025, May 25). *Comparing the UK and EU framework on facial recognition technology*. https://techgdpr.com/blog/comparing-the-uk-and-eu-framework-on-facial-recognition-technology/

Teixeira, P. N. (2024). Between ethics and science: Economic and political arguments against child labor in the progressive period. *Review of Political Economy*, *36*(1), 76–96. DOI: 10.1080/09538259.2023.2181063

Thapa, R., & Sarkar, K. K. (2019). Universal elementary education in India: Barriers and persistent challenges. *Social Change*, *49*(2), 257–275. DOI: 10.1177/0049085719844105

The Better India. (2015, June 12). The Bedia Community Prostitutes its girls. An NGO, Samvedna, is changing that. Retrieved from https://www.thebetterindia.com/

The Melammu Project. (n.d.). Retrieved October 24, 2025, from http://www.melammu-project.eu/database/gen_html/a0000237.html

The New Indian Express. (2017, August 29). Madhya Pradesh woman fights to protect daughters from forced prostitution. Retrieved from https://www.newindianexpress.com/

Thévenon, O., & Edmonds, E. (2019). Child labour: Causes, consequences and policies to tackle it. *OECD Social, Employment, and Migration Working Papers*, (235), 4-82.

Tiefenbrun, S. (2002). The saga of Susannah-A US remedy for sex trafficking in women: The Victims of Trafficking and Violence Protection Act of 2000. *Utah L. Rev.*, 107.

Times of India. (2024).

Times of India. (2025, August 28). *Cops unleash AI arsenal to crush human trafficking, prostitution rackets*. https://timesofindia.indiatimes.com/city/nagpur/cops-unleash-ai-arsenal-to-crush-human-trafficking-prostitution-rackets/articleshow/123551729.cms

Tony, H. (2025, April 16). Grubesic, Edward Helderop, Jorge A. Sefair & Dominique Roe- Sepowitz (16 Apr 2025): Human Trafficking: A Scientometric Review of the Knowledge Domain. *Journal of Human Trafficking*, 1–22. Advance online publication. DOI: 10.1080/23322705.2025.2483115

Trauma and Prostitution. (2018). *The German Model: 17 years after the legalization of prostitution.*

Tschalaer, M. (2009). Women entering the legal landscape: Negotiating legal gender reforms in a 'tribal' women's forum. Commission on Legal Pluralism. https://clp.thebestwebshop.org/system/commission-on-legal-pluralism/volumes/60/tschalaer-art.pdf

Tweed, E.J. (2022) *Understanding the Health of People Experiencing Homelessness, Justice Involvement, Substance Use, Sex Work, and Severe Mental Illness.* University of Glasgow. PDF

Two Birds. (2025, April 22). *European Union Artificial Intelligence Act: A guide.* https://www.twobirds.com/-/media/new-website-content/pdfs/capabilities/artificial-intelligence/european-union-artificial-intelligence-act-guide.pdf

Tyagi, K. (2024). Gender bias in the criminal justice system: Analyzing the treatment of female offenders in India. *International Journal of Finance and Management Research*, *6*(6), 1–12. https://www.ijfmr.com/papers/2024/6/31306.pdf

Tyler, M. (2021). All roads lead to abolition? Debates about prostitution and sex work through the lens of unacceptable work. *Labour & Industry: A Journal of the Social and Economic Relations of Work, 31*(1), 66–86. DOI: 10.1080/10301763.2020.1847806

U.S. Congress. (2018). *Allow States and Victims to Fight Online Sex Trafficking Act of 2017* and *Stop Enabling Sex Traffickers Act* (FOSTA-SESTA), Pub. L. No. 115-164, 132 Stat. 1253 (2018).

U.S. Department of Justice. (2025). *Attorney General's annual report to Congress on U.S. government human trafficking projects*. https://www.justice.gov/

U.S. Department of State. (2025). *Trafficking in persons report*. https://www.state.gov/

U.S. Department of Transportation. (2024). *Preventing and addressing human trafficking*. https://www.transportation.gov/

Udoh, E. (2024). The Effect of Gender Inequality and Early Marriage on Girl-Child Education in Ikot Ekpene Senatorial District. *AKSU Annals of Sustainable Development*, 29-39. DOI: 10.60787/AASD-1-1-6

Umbrella Lane. (2022). *Hardship and Health: A Community Response to the Pandemic*.

Umejiaku, N. (2024). Multidimensional Child Poverty and Its Implication on Juvenile Justice System. *Journal of Commercial and Property Law, 11*(4), 177–186.

UNAIDS. (2012). *UNAIDS guidance note on HIV and sex work*. Joint United Nations Programme on HIV/AIDS.

UNAIDS. (2024). *HIV and sex work—Human rights fact sheet series 2024*.

UNDP. (1994). *Human development report 1994: Human security*.

UNDP. (2009). *Human development report 2009: Human mobility and development*.

UNDP. (2022). *Human development report 2021/2022: Uncertain times, unsettled lives*.

UNFPA. (2010). Violence against women in India. Retrieved from https://india.unfpa.org/sites/default/files/pub-pdf/435.pdf

UNHCR & IOM. (2020). *Framework on developing standard operating procedures to facilitate the protection of trafficked persons*. https://www.refworld.org/policy/opguidance/unhcr/2020/en/123233

UNICEF. (2017, March 7). *Syrian children forced to quit school and marry early to survive*. https://www.unicef.org/stories/syrian-children-forced-quit-school-marry-early-survive

United Nations Children's Fund. (2021). *Technical note on the implementation of the United Nations protocol on the provision of assistance to victims of sexual exploitation and abuse*. UNICEF.

United Nations Entity for Gender Equality and the Empowerment of Women (UN Women). (2024, January 19). *Gender alert: The gendered impact of the crisis in Gaza*. https://www.unwomen.org/en/digital-library/publications/2024/01/gender-alert-the-gendered-impact-of-the-crisis-in-gaza

United Nations General Assembly. (1995). *Beijing Declaration and Platform for Action* (A/CONF.177/20/Rev.1). United Nations.

United Nations General Assembly. (2000). Protocol to prevent, suppress and punish trafficking in persons, especially women and children, supplementing the United Nations Convention against Transnational Organized Crime (Resolution 55/25). United Nations Office of the High Commissioner for Human Rights. https://www.ohchr.org/en/instruments-mechanisms/instruments/protocol-prevent-suppress-and-punish-trafficking-persons

United Nations General Assembly. (2005). Basic principles and guidelines on the right to a remedy and reparation for victims of gross violations of international human rights law and serious violations of international humanitarian law (Vol. A). United Nations., RES/60/147.

United Nations High Commissioner for Human Rights. (2002). *Recommended principles and guidelines on human rights and human trafficking*. Office of the High Commissioner for Human Rights.

United Nations High Commissioner for Refugees (UNHCR). (2024, September 30). *New study on vulnerability to trafficking in persons in the context of the war in Ukraine*. https://www.unhcr.org/europe/news/announcements/new-study-vulnerability-trafficking-persons-context-war-ukraine

United Nations Office on Drugs and Crime (UNODC). (2010, September). *United Nations launches global plan of action against human trafficking*. https://www.unodc.org/unodc/en/frontpage/2010/September/un-launches-global-plan-of-action-against-human-trafficking.html

United Nations Office on Drugs and Crime (UNODC). (2022). *Global report on trafficking in persons 2022*. https://www.unodc.org/documents/data-and-analysis/glotip/2022/GLOTiP_2022_web.pdf

United Nations Office on Drugs and Crime (UNODC). (2022). *Trafficking data harmonization in South Asia: Gaps and challenges*. UNODC Regional Office for South Asia.

United Nations Office on Drugs and Crime (UNODC). (2023, January). Press release: Global report on trafficking in persons 2022 — crises shift trafficking patterns. https://www.unodc.org/unodc/press/releases/2023/January/global-report-on-trafficking-in-persons-2022.html

United Nations Office on Drugs and Crime (UNODC). (n.d.). *A/CONF.222/11: Global and national data on trafficking victims* (para. 18). United Nations. https://www.unodc.org/documents/congress/Documentation/A-CONF.222-11/ACONF222_11_e_V1500612.pdf

United Nations Office on Drugs and Crime. (2008). *Ethical and safety recommendations for interviewing trafficked persons*.

United Nations Office on Drugs and Crime. (2018). *Assessment of trafficking routes in South Asia*.

United Nations Office on Drugs and Crime. (2020). *Global report on trafficking in persons*.

United Nations Office on Drugs and Crime. (2022). *Global report on trafficking in persons 2022*. UNODC.

United Nations Office on Drugs and Crime. (2022). *Global report on trafficking in persons*.

United Nations Office on Drugs and Crime. (2024). *Global report on trafficking in persons 2024*. United Nations.

United Nations Office on Drugs and Crime. (2024). *Global report on trafficking in persons*. https://www.unodc.org/documents/data-and-analysis/glotip/2024/GLOTIP2024_BOOK.pdf

United Nations Office on Drugs and Crime. (2025). *Action against human trafficking and migrant smuggling*. https://www.unodc.org

United Nations Office on Drugs and Crime. (2025). *Inflection Point: Global Implications of Scam Centre Expansion.*

United Nations Population Fund (UNFPA). (2024). *Voices from Syria 2024: Gender-based violence and protection assessment*. https://arabstates.unfpa.org/en/publications/voices-syria-2024

United Nations Population Fund (UNFPA). (2025, April). *Gender-based violence snapshot: Gaza*. https://palestine.unfpa.org/sites/default/files/pub-pdf/2025-04/GBV-Snapshot-2025-Final.pdf

United Nations Population Fund. (2024). *State of world population 2024: Interwoven lives, threads of hope*. UNFPA.

United Nations Relief and Works Agency for Palestine Refugees in the Near East (UNRWA). (2025, July 4). *UNRWA situation report #178 on the humanitarian crisis in the Gaza Strip and the West Bank, including East Jerusalem*. https://www.unrwa.org/resources/reports/unrwa-situation-report-178-situation-gaza-strip-and-west-bank-including-east-jerusalem

United Nations. (1949). *Convention for the suppression of the traffic in persons and of the exploitation of the prostitution of others,* Dec. 2, 1949, 96 U.N.T.S. 271.

United Nations. (1966). International Covenant on Civil and Political Rights. Treaty Series, 999 U.N.T.S. 171.

United Nations. (1979). Convention on the Elimination of all forms of Discrimination Against Women. Treaty Series, 1249 U.N.T.S. 13.

United Nations. (2000). *Protocol to prevent, suppress and punish trafficking in persons, especially women and children (Palermo Protocol)*. United Nations.

United Nations. (2000). *Protocol to prevent, suppress and punish trafficking in persons, especially women and children, supplementing the United Nations Convention against Transnational Organized Crime*. https://www.ohchr.org/en/instruments-mechanisms/instruments/protocol-prevent-suppress-and-punish-trafficking-persons

United Nations. (2000). Protocol to prevent, suppress and punish trafficking in persons, especially women and children, supplementing the United Nations convention against transnational organized crime. In Vienna: United Nations Office on Drugs and Crime, United Nations Convention against Transnational Organized Crime and the Protocols Thereto.

United Nations. (2000). *Protocol to prevent, suppress and punish trafficking in persons, especially women and children*. Palermo Protocol.

United Nations. (2010). *United Nations rules for the treatment of women prisoners and non-custodial measures for women offenders (the Bangkok Rules)*. United Nations.

United Nations. (2025). *Report of the Secretary-General on special measures for protection from sexual exploitation and abuse: A new approach* (A/79/789). https://conduct.unmissions.org/sites/default/files/report_of_the_secretary-general_on_special_measures_for_protection_from-sexual-exploitation-and-abuse_a79789.pdf

United States Department of State. (2025). *Trafficking in persons report 2025*. https://www.state.gov/reports/2025-trafficking-in-persons-report/

United States Department of State. (2025a). *Trafficking in persons report 2025: Afghanistan*. https://www.state.gov/reports/2025-trafficking-in-persons-report/afghanistan/

United States Department of State. (2025b). *Trafficking in persons report 2025: Syria*. https://www.state.gov/reports/2025-trafficking-in-persons-report/syria

United States Department of State. (2025c). *Trafficking in persons report 2025: Israel, West Bank, and Gaza*. https://www.state.gov/reports/2025-trafficking-in-persons-report/israel

United States Department of State. (2025d). *Trafficking in persons report 2025: Haiti*. https://www.state.gov/reports/2025-trafficking-in-persons-report/haiti

UNTC.(n.d.). https://treaties.un.org/pages/ViewDetails.aspx?src=TREATY&mtdsg_no=XVIII-12-a&chapter=18

Upadhyay, R. (2021). Decentralization without democratization in tribal governance. Drishti IAS. https://www.drishtiias.com/daily-news-analysis/panchayat-extension-to-scheduled-areas-pesa-act-1996

V.C.L. & A.N. v. United Kingdom. (2021). App. Nos. 77587/12 & 74603/12 (ECHR).

Vahedi, L., Stark, L., Ding, R., Masboungi, C., Erskine, D., Poulton, C., & Seff, I. (2024). A qualitative investigation of gender-based violence prevention and response using digital technologies in low resource settings and refugee populations. *European Journal of Psychotraumatology, 15*(1), 2347106. https://doi.org/10.1080/20008066.2024.2347106DOI: 10.1080/20008066.2024.2347106 PMID: 38722768

Vamvaka-Tatsi, O. (2024) *Examining the Strategic Response and Approach to Integration of Queer Forced Migrants in Wales*. Cardiff University. PDF

Van der Kolk, B. (2014). The body keeps the score: Brain, mind, and body in the healing of trauma. *New York, 3*, 14-211.

van Schendel, W. (2005). *The Bengal borderland: Beyond state and nation in South Asia*. Anthem Press.

Vashishth, K. (2024). Khap Panchayat system in India – A detailed analysis. *Indian Journal of Integrated Research in Law, IV*(III), 494–500. https://ijirl.com/wp-content/uploads/2024/05/KHAP-PANCHAYAT-SYSTEM-IN-INDIA-%E2%80%93-A-DETAILED-ANALYSIS.pdf

Veena, S. (2023). Automated facial recognition and the Indian criminal justice system: Promise and pitfalls. *Indiana Law Review, 7*(2), 145–168.

Verez, M. (2023). An Ever-Narrowing Divide: Morality and Decriminalizing Sex Work in North Carolina. *NCCRL Rev., 4*, 455.

Verma, A., & Bohra, S. (2023). The vague perception of commercial sex work and exploitation of women: The Indian legal framework. *International Journal of Human Rights and Constitutional Studies, 10*(2), 176. DOI: 10.1504/IJHRCS.2023.130016

Verma, A., & Bohra, S. (2024). The rights of commercial sex workers in India: A critical analysis of the legislative and judicial trends. *International Journal of Human Rights and Constitutional Studies, 11*(2), 169–185. DOI: 10.1504/IJHRCS.2024.137723

Victims of Trafficking and Violence Protection Act of 2000. (n.d.). U.S. Department of State. https://2009-2017.state.gov/j/tip/laws/61124.htm

Vidhi Centre for Legal Policy. (2024, March 12). *The landscape of facial recognition technologies in India*. TechPolicy Press. https://www.techpolicy.press/the-landscape-of-facial-recognition-technologies-in-india/

Vineeta Sharma v. Rakesh Sharma, (2020) 9 SCC 1 (SC)

Vishaka v. State of Rajasthan, (1997) 6 SCC 241 (SC).

Vollinger, A. (2020). Victimhood and Visibility: The State's Role in Constructing Sex Work Discourse. *Feminist Legal Studies, 28*(1), 67–89.

Vuolajärvi, N. (2022). Criminalising the sex buyer: experiences from the Nordic region.

Vuolajärvi, N. (2019). Governing in the name of caring—The Nordic model of prostitution and its punitive consequences for migrants who sell sex. *Sexuality Research & Social Policy, 16*(2), 151–165. DOI: 10.1007/s13178-018-0338-9

Wacquant, L. (1999). "Suitable enemies": Foreigners and immigrants in the prisons of Europe. *Punishment & Society*, *1*(2), 215–222. DOI: 10.1177/14624749922227784

Wacquant, L. (2009). *Punishing the poor: The neoliberal government of social insecurity*. Duke University Press.

Wagenaar, H., & Altink, S. (2012). Prostitution as morality politics or why it is exceedingly difficult to design and sustain effective prostitution policy. *Sexuality Research & Social Policy*, *9*(3), 279–292. DOI: 10.1007/s13178-012-0095-0

Wagenaar, H., Altink, S., & Amesberger, H. (2017). *Designing Prostitution Policy: Intention and Reality in Regulating the Sex Trade*. Policy Press.

Wahito, N. (2024). Mutuality and Power: An Analysis of Non-State Actors' Influence in Mitigating the Negative Consequences of State Response to COVID-19 on Adolescent Girls in Kenya. *Leadership and Developing Societies*, *9*(1), 49–65. DOI: 10.47697/lds.38380014

Walk Free Foundation. (2023). *Global slavery index 2023*. https://www.walkfree.org

Weatherall, A., & Priestley, A. (2001). A feminist discourse analysis of sexwork'. *Feminism & Psychology*, *11*(3), 323–340. DOI: 10.1177/0959353501011003005

Webbink, E., Smits, J., & De Jong, E. (2012). Hidden child labor: Determinants of housework and family business work of children in 16 developing countries. *World Development*, *40*(3), 631–642. DOI: 10.1016/j.worlddev.2011.07.005

Weitzer, R. (2007). The social construction of sex trafficking: Ideology and institutionalization of a moral crusade. *Politics & Society*, *35*(3), 447–475. DOI: 10.1177/0032329207304319

Weitzer, R. (2009). Sociology of sex work. *Annual Review of Sociology*, *35*(1), 213–234. DOI: 10.1146/annurev-soc-070308-120025

Weitzer, R. (2012). *Legalizing prostitution: From illicit vice to lawful business*. New York University Press.

White House Archives. (2024). *National action plan to combat human trafficking*. https://www.whitehouse.gov/

Whore Laws of Yore: How New South Wales Decriminalised Sex Work 1979-1995. (n.d.). Retrieved October 26, 2025, from https://www.tiki-toki.com/timeline/entry/754853/-Whore-Laws-of-Yore-How-New-South-Wales-Decriminalised-Sex-Work-1979-1995/

Wood, L. C. (2020). Child modern slavery, trafficking and health: A practical review of factors contributing to children's vulnerability and the potential impacts of severe exploitation on health. *BMJ Paediatrics Open*, *4*(1), e000327. DOI: 10.1136/bmjpo-2018-000327

Woolf, A. D. (2002). Health hazards for children at work. *Journal of Toxicology. Clinical Toxicology*, *40*(4), 477–482. DOI: 10.1081/CLT-120006750

World Bank. (2020). *Poverty and shared prosperity report*. World Bank.

World Health Organization (WHO). (n.d.). *Mental health & psychosocial support (MHPSS)*. https://wkc.who.int/our-work/health-emergencies/knowledge-hub/mental-health-psychosocial-support-%28mhpss%29

World Health Organization. (2013). *Prevention and treatment of HIV and other sexually transmitted infections for sex workers*. WHO.

World Vision International. (2020). *Stolen future: War and child marriage in Northwest Syria*. https://www.wvi.org/sites/default/files/2020-07/Stolen%20Future-War%20and%20Child%20Marriage%20in%20Northwest%20Syria-Online.pdf

XYZ v. State of Maharashtra, (2021) Bom HC (India).

Yadav, M. A. (2019). Implementation of Right to Education: A Constitutional overview. *International Journal of Research in Social Sciences*, *9*(3), 1.

Yale Global Health Justice Partnership. (2020). *Sex work vs. trafficking: How They are different and why it matters*. Yale Law School.

Yousaf, M. N., Khan, A., Hayat, U., & Ahmad, A. (2025). Socioeconomic Perspective and Analysis of the Linkage of Education and Child Labor in Pakistan: Challenges and Prospects. *Journal of Religion and Society*, *3*(02), 25–39.

Zaher, S., Khalil, H., & Rustom, A. (2025). Beyond borders and blockades: Human trafficking risks among vulnerable Palestinian populations under occupation. *BMC Public Health*, *25*(1), 3544. DOI: 10.1186/s12889-025-24893-5 PMID: 41120982

Zangger, C. (2016) *For Better or Worse?: Decriminalisation, Work Conditions, and Indoor Sex Work in Auckland, New Zealand/Aotearoa*. PhD thesis. Available at: https://www.sexworklaw.co.nz/pdfs/Zangger_(2016)_PhD_Thesis.pdf

Zarnowski, A. (2024, December 23). *INTERPOL identifies over 140 human traffickers in new initiative*. Infosecurity-Magazine. https://www.infosecurity-magazine.com/news/interpol-identifies-140-human/

Zheng, S. (2021). The application of facial recognition in China and India: Potential risks and regulation suggestions. *Journal of Politics and Law*, *18*(3), 125–140. https://www.davidpublisher.com/Public/uploads/Contribute/6123074d2bb20.pdf

Zimmerman, C., Hossain, M., & Watts, C. (2011). Human trafficking and health: A conceptual model to inform policy, intervention and research. *Social Science & Medicine*, *73*(2), 327–335. DOI: 10.1016/j.socscimed.2011.05.028 PMID: 21723653

Zimmerman, C., & Kiss, L. (2017). Human trafficking and exploitation: A global health concern. *PLoS Medicine*, *14*(11), e1002437. DOI: 10.1371/journal.pmed.1002437 PMID: 29166396

Zimmerman, Y. C. (2005). Situating the Ninety-Nine: A critique of the Trafficking Victims Protection Act. *Journal of Religion & Abuse*, *7*(3), 37–56. DOI: 10.1300/J154v07n03_03

About the Contributors

Aradhya Singh is a Ph.D. from the Faculty of Law, Banaras Hindu University. Her academic journey includes an LL.M. from National Law Institute University, Bhopal, and a B.A.LL.B. (Gold-Medalist) from Law College Dehradun, Hemwati Nandan Bahuguna Garhwal Central University, Dehradun. Dr. Aradhya is also UGC-NET (Law) qualified. Dr. Aradhya has made significant contributions to legal academic research through various published research articles and presentations at esteemed International & National conferences. Her research has been recognized with multiple Best Presenter Awards, highlighting her ability to effectively communicate complex legal ideas. Her work spans a range of legal topics, reflecting a deep engagement with contemporary issues and a commitment to advancing knowledge in the field of law.

Sara Balkh is an accomplished attorney, human rights expert, and educator with over a decade of experience. She serves as a Director and Human Rights Ambassador at the United Nations Association of Orange County (UNA-OC), advancing global human rights initiatives and the UN's Sustainable Development Goals (SDGs). Holding a Ph.D. in International Law from the University of Tehran, Sara has published 1 book, 3 book chapters, 1 booklet, and over 10 papers on human rights law, cultural heritage, and international organizations. She previously founded the Sara Balkh Law Firm in Iran, specializing in women's rights and domestic violence, and has taught international law at the university level.

Amit Anand is a scholar of International Human Rights Law with a particular focus on gender-based violence, caste-based discrimination, and the intersection of law, culture, and social exclusion. He holds a PhD in Law from Lancaster University, UK, where his doctoral research critically examined culturally entrenched and institutionally neglected forms of violence against women in India, including witch-hunting, honour killings, and the Devadasi system. Dr. Anand also holds an LL.M in Human Rights from the University of Reading, UK, and a B.A., LL.B. (Hons.) from the National Law School of India University, Bengaluru.

***

Arvind Bhanu is a legal professional with over three decades of experience as a teacher, researcher, and trainer in the field of law. Throughout his career, he has held various prestigious positions across multiple institutions, progressing from Lecturer and Assistant Professor to Principal and Head/Director. Notably, he served as a Professor of Law with a strong focus on legal research and as the Acting Director of the Amity Law School, Delhi (ALSD), which ranked among India's top five law schools. Currently, Dr. Bhanu is Adjunct Professor, Adelaide Law School, University of Adelaide, Australia, Professor of Law and Research, as well as the Additional Director/Joint Head of the Institution at Amity Law School, Noida, India. His commitment to legal education and research continues to influence the next generation of legal professionals. Dr. Bhanu is scholarly specializing in the Law of Crimes, Comparative Constitutional Law, Law and Religion, Human rights and Jurisprudence. He obtained his doctoral degree in this field from Aligarh Muslim University, Uttar Pradesh, India. In addition to his doctorate, he possesses a UGC (NET) qualification in law, a master's degree in economics, and a Postgraduate Diploma in Labor Law and Relations (PGDLLR). His extensive research portfolio includes more than 150 publications that span a wide range of legal topics. These works have been published in esteemed international and national journals, digital platforms, and books. Notably, Dr. Bhanu's research has been featured in flagship U.S. law reviews and recognized by prestigious publishers such as Edward Elgar (UK), Springer, and Routledge, Taylor and Francis etc. His contributions are indexed in reputable databases like SCOPUS and Web of Science and UGC Care listed journals, with many accessible through digital libraries at universities in the USA and Australia. Dr. Bhanu's academic reach extends to supervising numerous Master's and Doctoral dissertations, establishing him as a dedicated mentor in the field. He has served as an editor of a UGC-listed journal and participates as a co-editor and advisory board member for various reputed national legal journals. Additionally, he had contributed as a columnist for the national magazine 'LAWZ' for over a year. Dr. Bhanu has significantly contributed to the field of law through his extensive research and involvement in government-funded project/s that explore the legal implications of human rights. As advancements in technology, particularly in artificial intelligence (AI), reshape various sectors, including legal education, Dr. Bhanu has proactively developed research cursor and published legal issues digitally to enhance legal learning for students. In addition to his primary responsibilities in teaching, training, and research, Dr. Bhanu plays a vital role in university governance. He holds key positions on various university committees, councils, and commissions, including serving as a member of the Academic Council. His work not only addresses pressing legal challenges but also aims to equip future legal professionals with the necessary tools to navigate the evolving landscape of law influenced by technological advancements. Dr. Bhanu has actively participated in numerous national and international conferences, presenting his research work and organizing various academic events such as seminars, workshops, Faculty Development Programs (FDPs), Moot Courts, and Legal Debates. He has chaired multiple technical sessions at prestigious global conferences and delivered lectures at the national level. Additionally, Dr. Bhanu has been invited as a keynote speaker and resource person for conferences and refresher courses organized by UGC-HRDC (University Grants Commission-Human Resource Development Centre). His expertise is frequently sought by media outlets; he has appeared on Doordarshan, a national television channel, to share his insights on pressing legal issues. Dr. Bhanu also serves on the panel of examiners for doctoral research across various universities, as well as for Judicial Service Examinations and Public Service Commission assessments. In recognition of his contributions to legal education and research, Dr. Bhanu has been honoured with several awards, including the Commendable Performance Award (2013 and 2014), the Best Teacher Award (2017), NOVRA Sammaan (   ) (2023), the Academic Honour from the University of Adelaide, Australia, and the Distinguished Scholar Award (2025). His commitment to advancing legal scholarship and education continues to be evident through his active engagement in academic deliberations. Academic research referee on board is Professor Paul T. Babie, Bonython Chair in Law and Professor, Adelaide Law School, University of Adelaide, Australia.

Priyamvada Bhargava is a law professor at Sri Sathya Sai College for Women, Bhopal, specializing in criminology and legal research. She is a PhD scholar at Jagran Lakecity University and has a strong focus on gender justice, women's rights, and the intersection of law and social issues in India. Her academic work involves extensive research on the enforcement of statutory rights and the impact of customary practices on vulnerable groups, particularly women in rural Madhya Pradesh. As an active legal researcher and educator, she contributes to advancing legal scholarship and capacity-building in the areas of gender sensitivity and access to justice. Priyamvada is also engaged in community outreach and has organized workshops and seminars to bridge the gap between formal legal institutions and local customary practices, aiming to make legal protections more effective and accessible for marginalized women.

Tushar Bhatia, Research Scholar, pursuing PhD from Graphic Era University, India. I am pursuing research in India-ASEAN Bilateral Relations. As an IR scholar, beyond my research area. I am interested to write in other key fields related with International Politics and International foreign affairs like in South Asia, South-East Asia, West Asia, Maritime relations in Indo-pacific, climate change issue, Human rights problem, Blue Economy, AI and International diplomacy. Recently, three papers published as Review paper in maritime relations, India-Gulf relations and Oil diplomacy at global level. Despite this, I completed my graduation in Political Science and post-graduation in International relation discipline of Political Science subject from Gautam Buddha University.

Angelo Brown Received his master's at Arizona State University and his Ph.D. Criminal Justice and Criminology at Washington State University. His research and teaching in criminal justice and criminology are primarily on policy and policing from a comparative and intersectional perspective.

Jipson Joseph has a PhD in Ethics from DVK Bangalore. Currently, he is a Research Scholar in the School of Law at Christ University, Bangalore. His research interests encompass the fields of ethics, gender studies, constitutional law, human rights, human security, environmental justice, BRICS countries, development policies, and global poverty.

Swarlata Pandey is currently working as Assistant Professor at School of Law, VIT Chennai, Tamil Nadu where she has taught courses in Constitutional Law, Women and Law etc. She is currently pursuing her PhD in VIT Chennai on "Right to Maternal Health in India: A Critical Study in the Context of Sustainable Development" which explores the intersection of constitutional guarantees, social justice, and gendered vulnerabilities. She holds a Bachelors of Law (B.A. LL.B. Hons.) from National Law University, Patna and has previously worked as Legal Researcher at National Human Rights Commission (NHRC), New Delhi where she was indulged in research addressing human rights violation and access to justice. Her academic and research interests relate to constitutional law, human rights, and public health governance, with a focus on the lived realities of women in marginalized spaces.

Ravikumar R. Natarajan is an experienced academician with over 13+ years of teaching and research expertise across institutions in India, the UAE, and the Maldives. He currently serves as an Assistant Professor at Marwadi University, Rajkot, specializing in Machine Learning, Recommender Systems, and AI-driven applications in healthcare and security. He holds a Ph.D. in Machine Learning and Recommender Systems from Amity University, Jaipur, a Master of Engineering in

CSE from VMRF University, Salem, and a Bachelor of Engineering in CSE from Anna University. He also has a MiniMBA from the Swiss eLearning Institute. Dr. Ravikumar has authored more than 8+ multiple SCIE/Scopus-indexed journal articles, 25+ IEEE/Springer conference papers, and co-authored a book on Artificial Intelligence. He has also published 9 patents and contributed 85+ book chapters in emerging domains such as Federated Learning, Blockchain, and Digital Twins for IGI Global, Wiley and Springer publisher. He actively mentors students through initiatives like the Research Activities Club (RAC) and Student Research Internship Training (SRIT), promoting innovation and research culture.

B. Ravi Narayan Sarma is an Associate Professor at Chanakya National Law University (CNLU), Patna, with around 15 years of teaching experience in law. He completed his LL.B. and LL.M. from Berhampur University, Orissa, and earned his Doctorate in Law from Andhra University. Academic and Professional Profile Dr. Sarma specializes in the Law of Contracts, Property Laws, Procedural Laws, and Criminal Law, making significant contributions to legal education and research in these domains. His expertise is reflected in his teaching, research, and participation in national seminars and conferences, where he has presented papers on various aspects of law. Teaching and Research With a career spanning over a decade, Dr. Sarma has mentored numerous law students and contributed to the academic development of CNLU. His research interests include the practical application and theoretical foundations of contract law, property law, procedural law, and criminal law, areas in which he continues to publish and present at academic forums. Recognition and Contributions Dr. Sarma is recognized for his commitment to legal education and his active involvement in academic and professional legal circles. His work has helped shape the curriculum and pedagogy in law schools, particularly in the fields of contracts, property, and criminal law. Dr. B. Ravi Narayan Sarma stands out as a dedicated legal educator and scholar, whose expertise and experience have enriched the legal academic landscape in India

Bharvi Shahi Currently pursuing masters in Intellectual Property and Trade Law from School of Law, Christ University, Bengaluru.

Kavi Shankar is an Assistant Professor of Law at VIT School of Law, Chennai. He specialises in International Law, Labour Laws, Access To Justice and Constitutional History and Interpretation. He has done his BA LLB (International Law Honours) from National Law University, Ranchi and a LLM in Access to Justice from Tata Institute of Social Sciences, Mumbai. He has been to multiple universities to deliver special lectures as well as conduct Moot Court Orientation sessions and has adjudged advanced rounds of National-level moot court competitions in NLUs and other colleges.

Ankita Sharma is currently serving as an Assistant Professor at GLA University, Mathura. She is pursuing her Ph.D. from Banasthali Vidyapeeth and has completed her education from the University of Delhi. Her areas of interest include the rights and welfare of women and children.

Anuj Singh is presently Assistant Professor in GLA University, Mathura. He is holding Ph.D and has worked in elaborate manner dealing with rights relating to Person with Disability. He is also having special interest in human rights law.

Sushmita Singh is an Assistant Professor of Law at Chanakya National Law University Patna. She has keen interest in criminal laws, criminology, penology and victimology, contracts and consumer laws. Her research interest includes sentencing in capital offences, anti-trafficking laws, rescue and rehabilitation of trafficked victims.

Gargi Singla is a postgraduate law student currently pursuing her LL.M. in Tax Laws from Amity University Uttar Pradesh. She is an enrolled as an advocate, actively exploring the intersections of public policy and governance. This research marks one of her early academic contributions in the field, reflecting her growing interest in doctrinal and policy-oriented legal studies. With a keen focus on developing her research and analytical skills.

Anil Kumar Tiwari is a highly experienced academic leader currently serving as the Head of the Department of Economics at Tilka Manjhi Bhagalpur University. With a remarkable teaching career spanning approximately 32 years, Dr. Tiwari is recognized for his commitment to economics education, innovative research, and effective mentorship. Throughout his tenure at the university, he has played a key role in shaping the academic direction of the department, advancing the study and application of economics, and supporting the academic growth of both students and faculty

Rohit Tiwari is an accomplished legal scholar and educator who specializes in both corporate insolvency law and criminal law, with a robust record of academic achievements and contributions to legal research and teaching. Education PhD from Chanakya National Law University, Patna (enrolled 2021). LLM in Corporate Law from GGS Indraprastha University, Delhi. BBA.LLB from GGS Indraprastha University, Delhi. Specialized in seminar papers on Banking & Insurance Laws, Election Laws, and Socio-Economic Offenses, including study of criminal statutes like the Essential Commodities Act and the Central Vigilance Commission Act. Rohit has established his career as a law academic and researcher with key interests in corporate insolvency and criminal law. In his role as Assistant Professor of Law at Amity University, Kolkata (2022-2025), he taught courses including Insolvency and Bankruptcy Law, Banking Law, Hindu Personal Law, and Business Law, bringing a multidisciplinary approach that incorporates substantial elements of Indian criminal law. He actively integrates criminal law into his research and pedagogy, reflected in his presentations and publications on topics such as economic offenses, banking fraud, and fugitive economic offenders, in addition to his acclaimed work in corporate insolvency and competition law. His scholarly output appears in Scopus-indexed and peer-reviewed journals, and he has been a regular presenter at national and international conferences addressing both economic crimes and legal reforms. Rohit's leadership is evident in his work as faculty coordinator, resource person for legal workshops, and as a para-legal volunteer focused on access to justice. His career is distinguished by an integrative legal perspective that bridges business law, corporate governance, and the evolving field of criminal law within India's legal system. Through extensive research, committed teaching, and dynamic academic leadership, Rohit Tiwari continues to contribute to legal education and scholarship in both corporate and criminal law.

Kavya Tyagi is a Research Assistant to Prof. (Dr.) Arvind P. Bhanu at Amity Law School, Amity University, Uttar Pradesh, India.

Srinivasan Vasan is an Assistant Professor in the Department of Humanities and Social Sciences at Graphic Era (Deemed to be University), with 14 years of teaching and field expertise. He has served in the Ministry of Health and Family Welfare, as a Guest Faculty, and as a Mobilization Training Specialist with the State Government. Recently, he contributed to a tuberculosis project funded by GFATM and USAID. He has published 60 papers, with 20 more under peer review in UGC-CARE and SCOPUS journals.

Alisha Verma is a seasoned legal scholar and Assistant Professor of Law at Symbiosis Law School, Pune, which is a constituent of Symbiosis International (Deemed University). With over a decade of rich experience in teaching, research, and advocacy, Dr. Verma has established herself as a leading voice in the field of socio-legal studies and gender equality. Her work seamlessly integrates academic precision with a profound commitment to human rights and social justice. She is a dynamic writer who regularly contributes thought-provoking articles to newspapers, shedding light on critical legal and societal issues. Known for her engaging teaching style and dedication to mentoring, Dr. Verma remains deeply committed to advancing legal education and social justice.

Index

A

C

D

E

F

G

H

I

J

T

V

www.ingramcontent.com/pod-product-compliance
Lightning Source LLC
LaVergne TN
LVHW062340300926
849161LV00007B/1766
* 9 7 9 8 3 3 7 3 5 8 4 1 3 *